Partners with God

Theological and Critical Readings of the Bible in Honor of Marvin A. Sweeney

Partners with God

Theological and Critical Readings of the Bible in Honor of Marvin A. Sweeney

Shelley L. Birdsong
&
Serge Frolov
Editors

CLAREMONT STUDIES IN
HEBREW BIBLE AND SEPTUAGINT 2

Partners with God
Theological and Critical Readings of the Bible in Honor of Marvin A. Sweeney
©2017 Claremont Press
1325 N. College Ave
Claremont, CA 91711

ISBN 978-1-946230-13-3

Library of Congress Cataloging-in-Publication Data

Partners with God: Theological and Critical Readings of the Bible in
    Honor of Marvin A. Sweeney / edited by Shelley L. Birdsong
        & Serge Frolov
    xxi + 473 pp. 22 x 15 cm. –(Claremont Studies in Hebrew Bible
        and Septuagint 2)
    Includes bibliographical references and index.
    ISBN 978-1-946230-13-3
    1. Bible—Criticism, Narrative 2. Bible—Criticism, Form.
    BS 1192.5 .P37 2017

Cover: *The Prophet Jeremiah* by Barthélemy d'Eyck

Table of Contents

Abbreviations	ix
Preface	xv
Selected Bibliography of Marvin A. Sweeney's Writings	xvii
Introduction	1

Pentateuch

Is Form Criticism Compatible with Diachronic Exegesis?	13
Rethinking Genesis 1–2 after Knierim and Sweeney	
Serge Frolov	
Exploring Narrative Forms and Trajectories	27
Form Criticism and the Noahic Covenant	
Peter Benjamin Boeckel	
Natural Law Recorded in Divine Revelation	41
A Critical and Theological Reflection on Genesis 9:1-7	
Timothy D. Finlay	
The Holiness Redaction of the Abrahamic Covenant	51
(Genesis 17)	
Bill T. Arnold	

Former Prophets

Miscellaneous Observations on the Samson Saga	63
with an Excursus on Bees in Greek and Roman	
Buogonia Traditions	
John T. Fitzgerald	
The Sword of Solomon	73
The Subversive Underbelly of Solomon's Judgment	
of the Two Prostitutes	
Craig Evan Anderson	
Two Mothers and Two Sons	83
Reading 1 Kings 3:16–28 as a Parody on Solomon's	
Coup (1 Kings 1–2)	
Hyun Chul Paul Kim	

Heavenly Porkies   101
   Prophecy and Divine Deception in 1 Kings 13 and 22
   Lester L. Grabbe
"What Have I Done to You?" – 1 Kings 19:19–21   111
   A Study in Prophetic Ethics
   Jeremiah Unterman
Jezebel   123
A Phoenician Princess Gone Bad?
   Tammi J. Schneider
King Lists as a Structuring Principle in the Book of Kings   133
   John H. Hull, Jr.

Latter Prophets

A Form Critical Reappraisal of Isaiah 8:9–10   147
   H. G. M. Williamson
Who Says What to Whom
      Speakers, Hearers, and Overhearers in Second Isaiah   157
   Patricia K. Tull
Too Many Hands?   169
   Isaiah 65–66 and the Reading of the Book of Isaiah
   Reinhard Kratz
And the Word Became Words   189
   The Inscription of the Divine Word on Jeremiah
   the Prophet in Jeremiah the Book
   Else K. Holt
The Structure of MT Jeremiah, with Special Attention   201
   to Chapters 21–45
   Richard D. Weis
Literary Structure in Ezekiel 25   225
   Addressee, Formulas, and Genres
   Tyler D. Mayfield
Was Ezekiel a Messenger? A Manager? Or a Moving Sanctuary?   237
   A Beckettian Reading of the Book of Ezekiel
   in the Inquiry of the Divine Presence
   Soo J. Kim
The Encounter between Hosea's YHWH (Hosea 11)   251
   and Taiwanese Matzu
   A Cross-Religious Hermeneutics of the Two Divine Images
   Hye Kyung Park

The Psalm in Habakkuk 3	263
Steven S. Tuell	
"Have We Not All One Father? Has Not One God Created Us?"	275
Revisiting Malachi 2:10a	
Ehud Ben Zvi	

Miscellaneous

Pots, Pits, and Promises	297
Jeremiah as Allusion to Genesis	
Shelley L. Birdsong	
(Para)textual Composition on Both Sides of the Canonical Divide	311
William Yarchin	
Job 31:9–10	321
Erotic Euphemisms in the Bible and Ancient Near Eastern and Rabbinic Literature	
Shalom M. Paul	
Miscategorizing Chosenness	327
Jon D. Levenson	
From Deuteronomy to the Lost Gospel	345
An Intra-Jewish Controversy about Group Annihilation	
Dennis R. MacDonald	
List of Contributors	355
Bibliography	359
Indices	409

Abbreviations

AB	Anchor Bible
ABG	Arbeiten zur Bibel und ihrer Geschichte
AcJTS	Acta Jutlandica, Theological Series
AES	*Archives Européennes de Sociologie*
AHw	*Akkadisches Handwörterbuch*
AIL	Ancient Israel and Its Literature
AKL	Assyrian King List
AnBib	Analecta Biblica
ANETS	Ancient Near Eastern Texts and Studies
AOAT	Alter Orient und Altes Testament
AOS	American Oriental Series
AOTC	Abingdon Old Testament Commentaries
ARAB	*Ancient Records of Assyria and Babylonia*
ASR	*American Sociological Review*
ATA	Alttestamentliche Abhandlungen
ATANT	Abhandlungen zur Theologie des Alten und Neuen Testaments
BAR	*Biblical Archaeology Review*
BARIS	(British Archaeological Reports) International Series
BBB	Bonner biblische Beiträge
BETL	Bibliotheca Ephemeridum Theologicarum Lovaniensium
BEvT	Beiträge zur evangelischen Theologie
BHS	*Biblia Hebraica Stuttgartensia*
Bib	*Biblica*
BibInt	*Biblical Interpretation*
BibInt	Biblical Interpretation Series
BibSem	The Biblical Seminar
BJS	Brown Judaic Studies
BKAT	Biblischer Kommentar, Altes Testament
BLS	Bible and Literature Series
BM	*Beth Mikra*
BMus	Bibliothèque de Muséon

BOSHNP	Berit Olam: Studies in Hebrew Narrative and Poetry
BRS	The Biblical Resource Series
BSHT	Biblical Studies Historic Texts
BThSt	Biblisch-theologische Studien
BWA(N)T	Beiträge zur Wissenschaft vom Alten (und Neuen) Testament
BZABR	Beihefte zur Zeitschrift für altorientalische und biblische Rechtsgeschichte
BZAW	Beihefte zur Zeitschrift für die alttestamentliche Wissenschaft
CAD	*The Assyrian Dictionary of the Oriental Institute of the University of Chicago*
CB	The Century Bible
CBET	Contributions to Biblical Exegesis and Theology
CBQ	*Catholic Biblical Quarterly*
CBS	Core Biblical Studies
CBSC	Cambridge Bible for Schools and Colleges
CC	Continental Commentaries
CSHBS	Claremont Studies in Hebrew Bible and Septuagint
CurBS	*Currents in Research: Biblical Studies*
DBOT	De Boeken van het Oude Testament
DCH	*Dictionary of Classical Hebrew*
DDD	*Dictionary of Deities and Demons in the Bible*
DJD	Discoveries in the Judaean Desert
DSBLH	Dove Studies in Bible, Language, and History
EBib	*Etudes bibliques*
ECL	Early Christianity and Its Literature
ELLS	*English Language and Literature Studies*
FAT	Forschungen zum Alten Testament
FOTL	Forms of the Old Testament Literature
FRLANT	Forschungen zur Religion und Literatur des Alten und Neuen Testaments
FS	Foundations of Semiotics
GKC	*Gesenius' Hebrew Grammar*
HALOT	*The Hebrew and Aramaic Lexicon of the Old Testament*
HAT	Handbuch zum Alten Testament
HBM	Hebrew Bible Monographs
HBT	*Horizons in Biblical Theology*

Hen		*Henoch*
HKAT		Handkommentar zum Alten Testament
HS		*Hebrew Studies*
HSM		Harvard Semitic Monographs
HThKAT		Herders Theologischer Kommentar zum Alten Testament
HUCA		*Hebrew Union College Annual*
HUCM		Monographs of the Hebrew Union College
Int		*Interpretation*
IB		*Interpreter's Bible*
IBC		Interpretation: A Bible Commentary for Preaching and Teaching
IBT		Interpreting Biblical Texts Series
ICC		International Critical Commentary
ISBL		Indiana Studies in Biblical Literature
JBA		*Jewish Book Annual*
JAOS		*Journal of the American Oriental Society*
JBL		*Journal of Biblical Literature*
JHebS		*Journal of Hebrew Scriptures*
JIBS		*Journal of the Institute of Biblical Studies*
JNES		*Journal of Near Eastern Studies*
JNSL		*Journal of Northwest Semitic Languages*
JPOS		*Journal of the Palestine Oriental Society*
JPSEJ		JPS Essential Judaism
JPSTC		JPS Torah Commentary
JQR		*Jewish Quarterly Review*
JKOTS		*Journal of the Korean Old Testament Society*
JRitSt		*Journal of Ritual Studies*
JSJ		*Journal for the Study of Judaism*
JSJSup		Journal for the Study of Judaism in the Persian, Hellenistic, and Roman Periods Supplements
JSOT		*Journal for the Study of the Old Testament*
JSOTSup		Journal for the Study of the Old Testament Supplement Series
JSS		*Journal of Jewish Studies*
JTISup		Journal of Theological Interpretation, Supplements
JTS		*Journal of Theological Studies*
KAR		*Keilschrifturkunden aus Boghazköi*

KAT	Kommentar zum Alten Testament
KEHAT	Kurzgefasstes exegetisches Handbuch zum Alten Testament
KHC	Kurzer Hand-Commentar zume Alten Testament
KUSATU	*Kleine Untersuchungen zur Sprache des Alten Testaments und seiner Umwelt*
LAS	Leipziger altorientalistische Studien
LHBOTS	The Library of Hebrew Bible/Old Testament Studies
LJI	Library of Jewish Ideas
LJK	Library of Jewish Knowledge
LSTS	The Library of the Second Temple Series
MARIP	Middle American Research Institute Publications
MDAI	*Mitteilungen des Deutschen archäologischen Instituts*
MJ	*Modern Judaism*
MLBS	Mercer Library of Biblical Studies
MnemoSup	Mnemosyne Supplements
MSL	*Materialien zum sumerischen Lexikon*
NAC	New American Commentary
NCBC	New Century Bible Commentary
NIBC	New International Bible Commentary. Edited by Leander E. Keck. *The New Interpreter's Bible.* 12 vols. Nashville: Abingdon, 1994–2004.
NICOT	New International Commentary on the Old Testament
NIB	*New Interpreter's Bible*
NIDB	*New Interpreter's Dictionary of the Bible*. Ed. Katherine Doob Sakenfeld. *New Interpreter's Dictionary of the Bible.* 5 vols. Nashville: Abingdon, 2006–09.
NLH	*New Literary History*
OBC	Orientalia Biblica et Christiana
OBO	Orbis Biblicus et Orientalis
Or	*Orientalia*
OTL	Old Testament Library
OTM	Oxford Theological Monographs
OtSt	*Oudtestamentische Studiën*
OWC	Oxford World's Classics
PAB	Potsdamer altertumswissenschaftliche Beiträge
PFES	Publications of the Finnish Exegetical Society
RA	*Revue d'assyriologie et d'archéologie orientale*

RB	*Revue biblique*
RelSRev	*Religious Studies Review*
RevQ	*Revue de Qumran*
RlA	*Reallexikon der Assyriologie*
ROT	Reading the Old Testament
RIMA	Royal Inscriptions of Mesopotamia, Assyrian Periods
RINAP	Royal Inscriptions of the Neo-Assyrian Period
SemeiaSt	*Semeia Studies*
SANE	Sources from the Ancient Near East
SBS	Stuttgarter Bibelstudien
SBLDS	Society of Biblical Literature Dissertation Series
SBLMS	Society of Biblical Literature Monograph Series
SBLRBS	Society of Biblical Literature Resources for Biblical Study
SBLSP	Society of Biblical Literature Seminar Papers
SBT	Studies in Biblical Theology
SDSSRS	Studies in the Dead Sea Scrolls and Related Literature
SHBC	Smyth & Helwys Bible Commentary
SKGG	Schriften der Königsberger Gelehrten Gesellschaft
SMANE	Sources and Monographs on the Ancient Near East: Sources from the Ancient Near East
SOTI	Studies in Old Testament Interpretation
Spec	*Speculum*
SSLL	Studies in Semitic Languages and Linguistics
SSN	Studia Semitica Neerlandica
STDJ	Studies on the Texts of the Desert of Judah
STHB	Supplements to the Textual History of the Bible
SubBi	Subsidia Biblica
TB	Theologische Bücherei: Neudrucke und Berichte aus dem 20. Jahrhundert
TDOT	*Theological Dictionary of the New Testament*
ThSt	Theologische Studiën
TK	Texte und Kommentare
TQ	*Theologische Quartalschrift*
TSK	*Theologische Studien und Kritiken*
TynBul	*Tyndale Bulletin*
UF	*Ugarit-Forschungen*
VSPU	*Vestnik of Saint Petersburg University*

VT	*Vetus Testamentum*
VTSup	Supplements to Vetus Testamentum
WBC	Word Biblical Commentary
WMANT	Wissenschaftliche Monographien zum Alten und Neuen Testament
ZABR	*Zeitschrift für altorientalische und biblische Rechtgeschichte*
ZAW	*Zeitschrift für die alttestamentliche Wissenschaft*
ZBK	Zürcher Bibelkommentare
ZKT	*Zeitschrift für katholische Theologie*
ZTK	*Zeitschrift für Theologie and Kirche*

Preface

Normally, the series editor, Marv Sweeney, would approve any new volume in this series. However, given the immense respect and deep affection that Marv's friends and colleagues have toward him, we at Claremont School of Theology wanted to honor Marv with a festschrift. The festschrift, as set of studies in Hebrew Bible, clearly belonged in this series. Of course, it was equally clear that Marv could not be asked to review and approve his own festschrift. Therefore, as senior editor of the Press, I took it upon myself to approve this volume. I trust that the readers—including Marv—will find this volume a worthy addition to the series.

Typically a festschrift is presented at some key point in a scholar's career, at retirement or in celebration of a particularly significant birthday (perhaps 65, 70, or 80). In this case, however, the cause for our celebration is twofold: the approach of Marv's 65th birthday and his return to health. We write both in celebration of Marv's approaching the cultural significant milestone of three score and five years and also in celebration of his recent recovery from a season of less than optimal health. We write in anticipation of the many years of scholarship, teaching and service which lie ahead for Marv in the wake of his defeat of cancer! (No one who knows Marv's passion for both scholarship and teaching has any expectation that he will retire in the near future.)

As a personal note, I want to thank Marv for his exemplary service to Claremont School of Theology and his unwavering commitment to the highest scholarly standards in the field of Hebrew Bible. I am honored to have Marv as a colleague and friend.

Thomas E. Phillips

Selected Bibliography of Marvin A. Sweeney's Writings

Books and Monographs

Introduction to the Pentateuch: The Foundations of Israel's Identity. CBS. Nashville: Abingdon, 2017.

Isaiah 40–66. FOTL. Grand Rapids: Eerdmans, 2016.

The Cambridge Companion to the Old Testament/Hebrew Bible. (Co-edited with Stephen Chapman.) Cambridge: Cambridge University Press, 2016.

Reading Prophetic Books: Form, Intertextuality, and Reception in Prophetic and Post-biblical Literature. FAT 89. Tübingen: Mohr Siebeck, 2014.

Reading Ezekiel: A Literary and Theological Commentary. ROT. Macon: Smyth and Helwys, 2013.

The Cambridge History of Religions in the Ancient World: Volume 1: From the Bronze Age through the Hellenistic Age. Editor. M. Salzman, gen. ed. Cambridge: Cambridge University Press, 2013.

Tanak: A Theological and Critical Introduction to the Jewish Bible. Minneapolis: Fortress, 2012.

Form and Intertextuality in Prophetic and Apocalyptic Literature. FAT 45. Tübingen: Mohr Siebeck, 2005. Repr. Eugene, OR: Wipf & Stock, 2010.

"Mitarbeiter for Prophecy and Apocalyptic." *Encyclopedia of the Bible and its Reception.* Volumes 1–13. H.-J. Klauck et al., eds. Berlin: Walter de Gruyter, 2009–present.

Reading the Hebrew Bible after the Shoah: Engaging Holocaust Theology. Minneapolis: Fortress, 2008.

1 & 2 Kings: A Commentary. OTL. Louisville: Westminster John Knox, 2007.

The Prophetic Literature. IBT. Nashville: Abingdon, 2005. Korean translation by Koog Pyoung Hong. Seoul: The Christian Literature Society of Korea, 2015.

Zephaniah. Hermeneia. Minneapolis: Fortress, 2003.

The Changing Face of Form Criticism for the Twenty-First Century. (Co-Edited with Ehud Ben Zvi.) Grand Rapids: William Eerdmans, 2003.

King Josiah of Judah: The Lost Messiah of Israel. Oxford and New York: Oxford University Press, 2001.

The Twelve Prophets. BOSHNP. Collegeville, MN: Liturgical Press, 2000.

New Visions of Isaiah. (Co-edited with Roy F. Melugin.) JSOTSup 214. Sheffield: JSOT Press, 1996. Repr. Atlanta: Society of Biblical Literature, 2006.

Isaiah 1–39, with an Introduction to Prophetic Literature. FOTL 16. Grand Rapids: Eerdmans, 1996.

Isaiah 1–4 and the Post-Exilic Understanding of the Isaianic Tradition. BZAW 171. Berlin: de Gruyter, 1988.

Articles and Book Chapters

"The Shofar in War and Warship in the Bible." *Qol Tamid: The Shofar in Ritual, History, and Culture*, 31–55. Edited by Joel Gereboff and Jonathan Friedmann. CSHBS 1. Claremont: Claremont Press, 2017.

"Hosea's Reading of Pentateuchal Narratives: A Window for Foundational E Stratum." *The Formation of the Pentateuch*, 851–71. Edited by J. C. Gertz et al. FAT 111. Tübingen: Mohr Siebeck, 2016.

"Isaiah." *Encyclopedia of the Bible and its Reception*, 13:297–305. Edited by T. Römer et al. Berlin: Walter de Gruyter, 2016.

"Contemporary Jewish Readings of the Prophets." *Oxford Handbook of the Prophets*, 447–66. Edited by Carolyn Sharp. New York: Oxford University Press, 2016.

"Isaiah 1–39." *The Prophets: Fortress Commentary on the Bible Study Edition*, 673–97. Edited by Gale Yee et al. Minneapolis: Fortress, 2016.

"Jewish Biblical Theology: An Ongoing Dialogue." *Int* 70 (2016): 314–25.

"The Jacob Narratives: An E-Stratum Text?" *CBQ* 78 (2016): 236–55.

"Eschatology in the Book of Jeremiah." *Marbeh Hochma: Memorial Volume for Avigdor Victor Hurowitz*, 525–39. Edited by Shamir Yona et al. Winona Lake: Eisenbrauns, 2015.

"Form and Eschatology in the Book of the Twelve Prophets." *The Book of the Twelve And the New Form Criticism*, 137–61. Edited by Mark J. Boda et al. Atlanta: SBL Press, 2015.

"The Prophets and the Prophetic Books, Prophetic Circles and Traditions—New Trends, Including Religious-Psychological Aspects." *Hebrew Bible – Old Testament: The History of Its Interpretation. III/2: The Twentieth Century*, 500–30. Edited by Magne Saebo; Berlin: Walter de Gruyter, 2015.

"Myth and History in Ezekiel's Oracles concerning Tyre (Ezekiel 26-28)." *Myth and Scripture: Contemporary Perspectives on Religion, Language, and Imagination*, 129–47. Edited by D. Callendar. SBLRBS 78. Atlanta: Society of Biblical Literature Press, 2014.

"Eschatology in the Book of Isaiah." *The Book of Isaiah: Enduring Questions Answered Anew: Essays Honoring Joseph Blenkinsopp and His Contribution to the Study of Isaiah*, 179–95. Edited by Richard J. Bautch and J. Todd Hibbard: Grand Rapids: Eerdmans, 2014.

"Dimensions of the Shekhinah: The Meaning of the Shiur Qomah in Jewish Mysticism, Liturgy, and Rabbinic Thought." *HS* 54 (2013): 107–20.

"Prophets and Priests in the Deuteronomistic History." *Israelite Prophecy and the Deuteronomistic History*, 35–49. Edited by Mignon Jacobs and Raymond F. Person. AIL 14. Atlanta: Society of Biblical Literature, 2013.

"Unfinished Tasks in the Book of Isaiah." *JKOTS* 3 (2012): 206–40.

"Genesis in the Context of Jewish Thought." *The Book of Genesis: Composition, Reception, and Interpretation*, 657–82. Edited by Craig A. Evans et al. VTSup 152. Leiden: Brill, 2012.

"The Question of Theodicy in the Historical Books: Contrasting Views Concerning the Destruction of Jerusalem According to the DtrH and ChrH." *JBIS* 5 (2011): 7–37.

"The Portrayal of Assyria in the Books of Kings." *The Bible as a Witness to Divine Revelation*, 274–84. Edited by Randall Heskett and Brian Irwin. LHBOTS 469. London: T & T Clark, 2010.

"The Nash Papyrus." *BAR* (July/August 2010): 43–47, 77.

"Form Criticism and the Endangered Matriarch Narratives of Genesis." *Method Matters: Essays on the Interpretation of the Hebrew Bible in Honor of David L. Petersen*, 17–38. Edited by Joel M. LeMon and Kent H. Richards. SBLRBS 56. Atlanta: Society of Biblical Literature, 2009.

"Jeremiah, the Shoah, and the Restoration of Israel." *Maven in Blue Jeans: A Festschrift in Honor of Zev Garber*, 88–104. Edited by Steven L. Jacobs. West Lafayette, IN: Purdue University Press, 2008.

"Jewish Biblical Theology." *Reading the Bible in the Twenty-First Century*, 191–208. Edited by Frederick Greenspahn. New York: New York University Press, 2008.

"Dating Prophetic Texts." *HS* 48 (2007): 55–73.

"A Reassessment of the Masoretic and Septuagint Versions of the Jeroboam Narratives in 1 Kings/3 Kingdoms 11-14." *JSJ* 38 (2007): 165–95.

"On the Road to Duhm: Isaiah in Nineteenth Century Critical Scholarship." *As Those Who Are Taught: The Reception of Isaiah from the LXX to the SBL*, 243–61. Edited by Claire Matthews and Patricia Tull. Atlanta: Society of Biblical Literature, 2006.

"The Dystopianization of Utopian Prophetic Literature: The Case of Amos 9:11-15." *Utopia and Dystopia in Prophetic Literature*, 175–85. Edited by Ehud Ben Zvi. Göttingen: Vandenhoeck & Ruprecht, 2006.

"King Manasseh of Judah and the Problem of Theodicy in the Deuteronomistic History." *Good Kings and Bad Kings*, 264–78. LBS 393. Edited by Lester L. Grabbe. London: T & T Clark, 2005.

"Why Jews are Interested in Biblical Theology: A Retrospective on the Work of Jon D. Levenson." *Jewish Book Annual* 55/56 (2001): 134–68.

"The Religious World of Israel, to 586." *The Blackwell Reader in Judaism*, 19–30. Edited by Jacob Neusner. Oxford: Basil Blackwell, 2001.

"The Religious World of Israel, to 586." *The Companion to Judaism*, 20–36. Edited by Jacob Neusner. Oxford: Basil Blackwell, 2000.

"Isaiah and Theodicy after the Shoah." *Strange Fire: The Hebrew Scriptures after the Holocaust*, 208–19. Edited by Tod Linafelt. Sheffield: Sheffield Academic Press, 2000.

"Zephaniah: A Paradigm for the Study of the Prophetic Books." *CurBS* 6 (1999): 119–45.

"Form Criticism." *To Each Its Own Meaning: An Introduction to Biblical Criticisms and Their Application*, 58–89. Edited by Steven L. McKenzie and Stephen R. Haynes. Louisville: Westminster John Knox, 1999.

"Davidic Polemics in the Book of Judges." *VT* 47 (1997): 517–29.

"Tanak versus Old Testament: Concerning the Foundation for a Jewish Theology of the Bible." *Problems in Biblical Theology: Essays in Honor of Rolf Knierim*, 353–72. Edited by Henry T. C. Sun and Keith L. Eades, with J. M. Robinson and G. I. Moller. Grand Rapids: Eerdmans, 1997.

"The Critique of Solomon in the Josianic Edition of the Deuteronomistic History." *JBL* 114 (1995): 607–22.

"Prophetic Books as Literature?" *Prooftexts* 15 (1995): 195–208.

"Sargon's Threat Against Jerusalem in Isaiah 10,27–32." *Bib* 75 (1994): 457–70.

Introduction

Shelley L. Birdsong and Serge Frolov

Fortuitously rather than by any kind of conscious design, there are 26 articles in the present volume. This is the gematric value of the tetragrammaton, the explicit divine name of the Hebrew Bible. As such, it is a reminder of a groundwork principle of the honoree's theology, derived from the famous *tikkun olam* (mending of the world) concept of Lurianic Kabbalah—human partnership with the deity in making this world a better place.[1]

Throughout his life, Marvin Sweeney has been an exemplary partner of God—first and foremost, by being a *Mensch*. He is everyone's friend, and everyone is his friend. Teachers, students, and colleagues feel honored to have shared a classroom or a conference room with him or to have worked together on a project. In the academic world often wracked by petty squabble and intrigue, he rises above the conflict and often helps to resolve it. His writing exudes respect for fellow scholars even while disagreeing with them. This is not to say that he does not respond forcefully to incompetence or backstabbing (or that he is lenient to lazy students), but he does so with integrity, always mindful of the maxim, "love your neighbor as yourself."

While coming from a mixed family, Marvin is also a model Jew (when asked in the presence of one of these writers, "How is Sweeney a Jewish last name?" he responded, "Now it is"). His Judaism fully reflects his personality—it is intense yet unobtrusive, personal yet communal, proud yet inclusive. He follows the path of *tikkun olam* in both Reform and Orthodox senses of the concept, combining Jewish observance with social responsibility.

---

[1] Marvin A. Sweeney, *Reading the Hebrew Bible after the Shoah: Engaging Holocaust Theology* (Minneapolis: Fortress, 2008), 14.

It is in Marvin's scholarship, however, where the theme of partnership with the deity truly comes to the forefront. The meaning of a text always emerges in a cooperative effort of the author and the audience, and, assuming with the Jewish and Christian traditions, that the biblical texts go back in one way or another to God, the deity must rely on partnership with the readers, especially highly competent readers, to get its message across. In this respect, Marvin's contribution is matched by few in his generation. With 15 authored books, nine volumes of edited essays, more than 100 articles, and 550 reviews under his belt, Marvin's footprint in biblical scholarship is nothing short of gigantic. He has also been Editor of two professional journals, *Hebrew Studies* and *The Review of Biblical Literature*.

As noted in several contributions to the present *Festschrift*, Marvin has been particularly instrumental in bringing about, through theoretical reflection and especially in his exegetical practice, an epoch-making change to the second-oldest methodology of biblical studies — form criticism, transforming it from a rather stale diachronic approach into a vibrant, predominantly synchronic one. He is co-editor of the only series of form critical biblical commentaries, Forms of Old Testament Literature. Marvin's work has also been vital in developing Jewish and post-Shoah biblical theology, placing both firmly on the map of biblical theological studies.

Among the different corpora of biblical literature, Marvin has always been primarily interested (starting with his 1983 doctoral dissertation) in what Jewish tradition terms the Latter Prophets. At least nine of his books deal entirely or to a great extent with this corpus. However, he has also published extensively on the Pentateuch (especially Genesis), the Former Prophets (especially Kings), and apocalyptic literature. He is currently poised to make a major step beyond the biblical canon by completing a major study of the Jewish mystical tradition.

Marvin is also famous, and well-loved, as a teacher. After receiving his B.A. from the University of Illinois in Political Science and Religious Studies (with distinction) and his M.A. and Ph.D. from Claremont Graduate School, he taught for eleven years at the University of Miami before returning more than twenty years ago to Claremont as Professor of Religion. He has also held temporary or vising appointments at Chang Jung Christian University in Tainan, Taiwan; Yonsei University in Seoul, Korea; Academy for Jewish Religion in California; and the Hebrew Union College-Jewish Institute of Religion, Los Angeles. He has lectured throughout the United States and the world, including Argentina, Australia, Austria, Belgium, Canada, China, Finland, Germany, Ireland, Israel, Italy, Japan, Korea, the Netherlands, Norway, Slovenia, South Africa, the former Soviet Union, Switzerland, and Taiwan. Regardless of the venue, Marvin has always worked diligently and creatively to shape new generations of partners with God in rendering the Hebrew Bible meaningful—be that for the purposes of ministry or in an academic setting. His three-hour doctoral seminars, taught on Friday mornings, have been legendary not only for their meticulous attention to "every jot, every tittle" in the studied text but also for ending, reluctantly, at least an hour and a half past the allotted time.

Despite his towering stature in the profession, there is not a hint of hauteur in Marvin. In fact, he is well-known for his gregariousness. At conferences and meetings, there is always a posse of friends around him—which usually ends up in the evening at a cozy pub, preferably one serving authentic Irish Guinness. So, on this celebratory occasion, it appears to us that the most appropriate thing to say would be: Cheers, Marv! *Ad meah ve-esrim*!

Now, a few words about the present volume. In another bout of fortuity (*Festschriften* are eclectic by nature), most articles here are reflective of the main foci of the honoree's scholarship noted above and, even more importantly, of the overlaps between them.

Several contributions offer form critical treatments of biblical texts, either in their own right or as test cases in theoretical discussions concerning various aspects of this methodology. **Peter Benjamin Boeckel** traces the evolution of form criticism from Gunkel to Sweeney, paying special attention to the shifting concepts of genre. He then applies the form critical procedure developed by Sweeney and his *Doktorvater* Rolf Knierim to Gen 9:8-18 where the idea of covenant makes its first-ever appearance in the Hebrew Bible. After examining the structure, genre, and setting of the piece, he describes it as a report that plays an important role in the larger context of Genesis by changing the narrative trajectory from the creation – un-creation – re-creation loop to an arrow pointing to Abraham and thus establishes covenant's centrality in the Enneateuch as a whole.

Timothy D. Finlay also deals with the concluding part of the flood narrative in Gen 9, but he is primarily interested in the divine instructions for human beings in vv. 1-7. The article analyzes the structure of this pronouncement, the various categories of speech acts (in essence, micro-genres of speech) that are utilized in it, and its multiple intertextual connections to Gen 1-2. On the basis of this analysis, Finlay concludes that although the appropriate term does not occur until the next divine discourse (studied by Boeckel), rabbinic tradition was correct in viewing Gen 9:1-7, complete with its prohibition of murder and associated requirement of capital punishment for it, as part and parcel of what it terms Noahide covenant.

The purpose of **Serge Frolov**'s piece is to position form criticism in its different incarnations vis-à-vis the synchronic/diachronic divide that currently bedevils biblical scholarship. He emphasizes that although Gunkel conceived his method as an extension of (archetypically diachronic) source criticism, for Knierim and Sweeney diachronic (mainly redaction critical) analysis is but an extension of essentially synchronic form critical investigation. Moreover, as Frolov tries to demonstrate by his brief but comprehensive form critical study of creation compositions in Gen 1 and 2, even this extension is redundant. Consistently synchronic form critical inquiry is eminently capable of resolving the problems that have long been diachronic showcases, and even where it might seem to fail, the diachronic approach would not fare any better.

In contrast to Frolov, **H. G. M. Williamson** does believe that form critical analysis may have diachronic corollaries. In a sustained conversation with Sweeney's exegesis of Isa 8:9-10, Williamson argues that semantics of key verbs in this passage preclude its characterization as a (probably ironic) call for battle. Rather, it is an "address before battle of one army commander to his opponents"—a genre attested in the Hebrew Bible as well as in Greek and ancient Near Eastern literatures. Accordingly, the two verses present themselves as a redactional insertion, adding a positive note to what is otherwise a predominantly grim prophecy.

Williamson's contribution brings a form critical approach to bear on what has been Marvin's earliest passion and what remains his primary area of expertise—the study of the Latter Prophets. The same is true of **Tyler D. Mayfield**, who seeks to unravel the complicated literary structure of Ezek 25 by treating it, in accordance with the basics of Knierim-Sweeney form criticism, synchronically (at least in the first instance) and favoring literary form over content. Based on various formulae and genres identified in the text, Mayfield describes the bulk of the chapter as an oracle addressed to Ammon and falling into five proof sayings, two concerning Ammon and one each concerning Moab, Edom, and Philistia. He also suggests that in the diachronic perspective this structure points to four-stage composition, in which an oracle concerning Ammon alone was gradually expanded and supplemented by discourses on other nations.

Unsurprisingly, articles on the Latter Prophets constitute the largest group in the present *Festschrift*, covering all three "major" prophetic books and several of the Twelve. **Reinhard Kratz** works with the two concluding chapters of Isaiah in a predominantly redaction critical rather than form critical mode but he begins, in accordance with the main premise of Knierim-Sweeney form criticism, with the final form of the biblical text and converses with Sweeney's two monographs covering Isaiah 65–66. Based on the readings of Isaiah in Daniel, Ben Sira, and 4Q176, the chapters' structuring in 1QIsa[a], and intertextual links between different parts of Isaiah, Kratz argues that Isaiah 65–66 is not a unity. Rather, it received its current shape through successive supplementations (*Fortschreibungen*). In his opinion, seeing "too many hands" behind the text does not invalidate this hypothesis because the "flow of tradition" must involve multiple scribes.

Unlike Kratz, **Patricia K. Tull** approaches Isaiah synchronically. Her interest lies in delineating the implied audiences and speakers in chs. 40–55 (the so-called Second Isaiah). The former, in her analysis, include primarily a feminine singular figure called Jerusalem, Zion, or Daughter Zion, a masculine singular figure identified as Israel/Jacob and the Servant, and a masculine plural audience related to both. Predominating among the latter are the prophet (particularly in ch. 40) and the divine voice (chs. 41–55). Second Isaiah also makes liberal use of a double-voicing technique, in which one speaker quotes another, explicitly or implicitly embedding somebody else's discourse into his or her own.

The objective of **Richard D. Weis** is to reconstruct the structure of Jeremiah in its canonical Masoretic formulation. Guided by reader-response criticism, Weis postulates that even "disorderly" features (such as repetitions or shifts of genre and narrative voice), often treated as signs of redactional development, are interpretable as authorial means of encouraging the audience to discover the composition's orderliness. Starting from these premises, Weis sees three main parts in Jeremiah, chs. 1-20, 21-45, and 46-51, with the central section also being tripartite (21:1-38:28; 39:1-14; 39:15-45:15), and its first segment, central in the book, falling into seven units. He maintains that this structure must have arisen in the Persian I period, 538-450 BCE.

Jeremiah's allusions to Genesis are traced by **Shelley L. Birdsong**. Bringing together materials from different parts of the prophetic book, she finds, to begin with, consistent use of vocabulary and tropes associated with the creation account in Gen 2:4-4:1, especially of the metaphor of YHWH as a potter. Further, there are persistent references to the divine promise to Abraham in Jer 1:4-10 and chs. 30-33 of the book. Finally, Jeremiah's story in chs. 38-43 displays multiple parallels to Joseph's story in Gen 37-50, especially with regard to both characters being confined to a pit. The purpose of these allusions, argues Birdsong, is to inject hope (associated with Abraham) into the bitterness of exile (despite which Eve and Adam as well as Joseph's family manage to survive and succeed).

Else K. Holt uses the book of Jeremiah to reflect on the conceptuality underlying the process of nonmaterial divine word becoming a material object, a book. She describes two main stages of this metamorphosis. First, the literary figure of the prophet becomes a metaphorical embodiment of the divine discourse, as seen in Jer 8:18-22, where God's voice is indistinguishable from Jeremiah's. Second, the prophet's words are written down (a process uniquely emphasized in the book of Jeremiah), in part for preservation, but mainly to render the text a metonymy for the deity, replacing or supplementing the temple as such. Such a replacement was typical for the religious transformation characterizing the "axial age" — the second half of the first millennium BCE.

A similar conclusion is reached by **Soo J. Kim** who reads the book of Ezekiel together with Samuel Beckett's *Waiting for Godot*. She notes that in Ezekiel (unlike Isaiah and Jeremiah) communication between God and the people of Israel is scant: divine messages to the prophet rarely seem to reach his contemporaries. As a result, Israelite exiles are left in a situation that makes them counterparts of Beckett's characters: confused, passive, and hopelessly waiting for clarity from someone who keeps promising, through an intermediary, to arrive the next day but never does. For Kim, that means that Ezekiel does not play the traditional role of a preacher; rather, he becomes a walking sanctuary that embodies the divine word without immediately imparting it.

The article of **Hye Kyung Park** draws cross-cultural parallels between the images of YHWH in Hosea 11 and sea goddess Matzu in Taiwanese folk religion. Park argues that Hosea 11 represents YHWH as a motherly deity, merciful, compassionate, and inseparable from her beloved son Israel even in exile just as a pregnant woman is inseparable from her unborn child. Likewise, Matzu is described as accompanying seafarers, especially migrants who cross the sea, on their journeys and offering them motherly protection; she is also a patron of women, particularly in pregnancy. These similarities suggest that even monotheism, where the deity is predominantly male, contains substantial elements of the feminine divine because certain aspects associated with it are indispensable to any religion.

Taking a new look at a one-of-a-kind piece of the Book of the Twelve—the prayer in Habakkuk 3—**Steven Tuell** highlights the contrast between the bulk of the chapter (vv. 3–15), where the might of YHWH as a divine warrior is on full theophanic display, and the framing fragments (vv. 2–3, 16–19), where the deity seems to be absent. On this basis, Tuell posits that the chapter emerged when an old theophanic hymn was extended to become a prayer for help. Since the plaintive mood of the extensions matches that predominating in the rest of Habakkuk, the article ascribes ch. 3 to the prophet himself rather than to the book's more optimistic redactors.

Reception of Mal 2:10a is the topic of **Ehud Ben Zvi**. He begins by documenting the fragment's uses by such variegated groups as church fathers, traditional Jewish commentators, Enlightenment thinkers, abolitionists, suffragists, Unitarians, and liberal Reform rabbis. Ben Zvi then asks how the text in question might have been understood by the group that produced it—late-Persian period literati of Judah/Yehud. He demonstrates that their construal would depend on multiple interlocking factors—for example, whether the following verses come into consideration (which seem to contradict the piece's supposedly universalist message by denouncing marriage to a "daughter of foreign god") or whether the "one father" of Mal 2:10a is construed as God, Adam, Abraham, or Aaron—that generate an intricate web of meanings.

Another major group of contributions to the present volume deals with the book of Kings, on which Marvin has published a commentary in the venerable Old Testament Library series and which is central to his classic *King Josiah of Judah*. Two articles challenge, each in its own way, the conventional interpretation of the famous "Solomon's judgment" scene in the book's third chapter as nothing but laudatory as far as the king is concerned. Building upon Roger Whybray's observation that wisdom plays a major role in the so-called Succession Narrative (2 Samuel 9-20; 1 Kings 1-2), **Craig Evan Anderson** points out, first, that in these chapters the advice offered by the characters identified as wise is usually immoral and foolish. Second, "wisdom" and "counsel" are inextricably linked here to violence, with "sword" functioning as a *Leitwort*. Solomon's characterization as the wisest of all people, followed by an immediate demonstration that his wisdom entails readiness to put a sword to a newborn baby (which was not even necessary to resolve the case), thus subverts the monarchic ideal exemplified by Solomon (and David) rather than buttressing it.

A different intertextual approach to "Solomon's judgment" is pursued by **Hyun Chul Paul Kim** who draws parallels with the king's accession to the throne in 1 Kings 1-2. Kim contends that the dispute between two prostitute mothers, one of whom has lost a son, mirrors the implicit conflict between Solomon's mother Bathsheba and Adonijah's mother Haggith who ends up losing her son. The king's order to kill a baby then reminds the reader about his order to execute his half-brother and, more broadly, about the violent and ethically dubious means whereby Solomon came to power. The judgment scene consequently functions as a parable-style parody on the preceding part of the narrative and foreshadows Solomon's eventual failure as king.

Cross-cultural analogues to the instances of divine deception in Kings (chs. 13 and 22) are explored by **Lester L. Grabbe**. These analogues include Mesopotamian flood stories (almost all of which have gods swear not to warn humans about the impending disaster), gods' determination not to honor an agreement with a builder in the *Poetic Edda*, their decision to deprive humans of the extraordinary far-sightedness they initially possessed in Mayan mythology, and misleading prophecies of the ancient Greek tradition related by Herodotus. In all these instances, as well as in 1 Kgs 13 and 22, the divine purpose is justifiable but the means to achieve it are dubious.

Jeremiah Unterman aims to unravel the cryptic pronouncement of Mal 3:24 about Elijah reuniting parents and children and thus preventing a cosmic catastrophe. The article connects this pronouncement to the prophet's first encounter with his future disciple Elisha in 1 Kgs 19:19–21. According to Unterman, when Elisha requests to say good-bye to his parents before following Elijah and the latter responds, "Go, return, for what have I done to you?" the implication is that even a divinely ordained mission does not obviate normal ethical behavior exemplified by an act of filial respect. Building on this episode, Malachi emphasizes that the world cannot be saved if reconciliation between parents and their children does not take place.

Addressing Kings from a feminist standpoint, **Tammi J. Schneider** rethinks one of the book's greatest villains—Jezebel. Reviewing the ways in which the biblical narrators refer to the queen, Schneider notes that her Sidonian origin is often stressed and argues that Jezebel mostly does what would be expected of her as a Phoenician princess married to a foreign ruler. She worships Baal (both she and her father Ethbaal bear theophoric Baal names), works to enlarge the royal estate in accordance with her husband's wishes, and dresses formally in public even when facing death (2 Kgs 9:30). Jezebel's extremely negative portrayal is thus a function not of her "going bad," but rather of biblical authors having drastically different expectations.

The organization of Kings as a whole is the subject of *John H. Hull, Jr.*'s contribution. His observations reveal multiple interlocking patterns in the way the book lists post-Solomonic rulers of both Israel and Judah with regard to their names and reported acts. For example, apart from Jehu, there are nine rulers with a יהו element in their names listed for both monarchies and falling into groups of three or six depending on whether this element is a prefix or a suffix. Moreover, several of these patterns match the Assyrian King List (AKL), even in seemingly irrelevant numerical details (while AKL has two groups of 38 kings, in Kings Israel and Judah each have 19 rulers after Solomon), suggesting literary dependence.

Although many articles in the present volume have explicit or implicit theological implications, only one, by **Jon D. Levenson**, is fully devoted to yet another major passion of the honoree — Jewish biblical theology. Levenson calls for a proper understanding of the biblical idea of Israel's chosenness, which offends the sensibilities of many today because of its particularistism. Over against growing calls to discard the concept or at least to interpret it in instrumental terms, the article stresses that the Hebrew Bible consistently presents chosenness as unmerited and often presents it more specifically as the result of divine love — a relationship that is exclusive by nature, does not have a purpose, and cannot be couched in terms of justice because it does not require or presuppose any merit on the recipient's part. Neither does it involve rejection of the non-chosen or justify violence against them.

Broad as are Marvin's interests and contributions to biblical studies, the field is just too diverse today for a single person to leave his imprint everywhere. Reflecting this diversity, several contributions to this *Festschrift* go where the honoree has not gone — at least not yet.

Bill T. Arnold offers a redaction critical analysis of Gen 17. Whereas previous scholarship has tended to see here a Priestly account of the Abrahamic covenant, Arnold argues that both the chapter's terminology and the concepts underlying it point to a more complex trajectory of its formation. In his opinion, the text received its canonical form at the hands of Holiness scribes who had both J and P sources available to them. They conflated the two while rewriting, revising, and expanding P with a view to shifting its agenda so that cultic concerns are supplemented by ethical ones. A similar strategy is traceable, according to Arnold, in the flood narrative (Gen 6–9).

The article of **John T. Fitzgerald** sheds light on two insufficiently understood details of the Samson narratives in Judg 13-16. First, he demonstrates that Samson's violation of prohibitions associated with his lifelong Nazirite consecration in ch. 13 can be seen not only in his famously losing his hair in ch. 16 but also in his willing participation in a "drinking feast" in ch. 14. The audience's expectation that Samson would live a life of piety is thus dashed from the outset. Second, Fitzgerald explains, citing multiple sources, that the picture of bees living in the carcass of a lion (Judg 14:8) would not be bizarre for ancient Greeks who believed that these insects are born out of dead mammals.

The role of paratextual elements in bridging production, transmission, and reception of the Hebrew Bible is the focus of **William Yarchin**'s attention. He contends that a manuscript is much more than just a receptacle for the text; through various means, such as page layout, marginalia, and spacing, it always reads the text in a certain way. Therefore, on the one hand, scholars never have access to the text as such — only to its receptions in the extant manuscripts. On the other, in a certain sense, composition of the biblical books has never ceased — it continues even today, in modern publications of the Bible as well as in scholarly commentaries, including those by the present volume's honoree.

Philological analysis of Job 31:9-10 is pursued by **Shalom Paul**. Based on inner-biblical evidence, as well as on numerous Sumerian, Akkadian, Egyptian, and rabbinic sources, he establishes that the noun "door" in the passage is a euphemism for the *pudendum muliebre* while the verbs "to grind" and "to kneel" allude to sexual intercourse. Job's discourse thus proceeds in a talionic fashion: if he has ever committed adultery, may his wife do the same.

Last but by no means the least, **Dennis R. MacDonald** bridges the Hebrew Bible and the New Testament by tracing the transformations of Deuteronomic texts in his reconstruction of a lost gospel, which he dubs the *Logoi of Jesus* or Q+. MacDonald shows that *Logoi* consistently, if implicitly, critiques Moses's commands to destroy entire populations. For example, the echo of the blessing to Israel in Deut 33:29 omits the reference to the people trampling upon their enemies. Such adjustments were in line with concerns found in the writings of Hellenized Jews, such as Philo and Josephus, and they are also at home in the pluralistic strand of modern Judaism, prominently represented by Marvin Sweeney.

Is Form Criticism Compatible with Diachronic Exegesis? Rethinking Genesis 1-2 after Knierim and Sweeney

Serge Frolov

In one of our very first conversations—when an early-onset midlife crisis brought me to Claremont, where Marvin was already Professor of Hebrew Bible, as an eager but methodologically innocent doctoral student—he referred to himself as "a form critical scholar." It was not long before I learned that this was a display of Marvin's well-known humility. Rather than being just a rank-and-file practitioner of the approach, he turned out to be one of its leading theoreticians, especially in his generation, and a major figure, alongside his *Doktorvater* Rolf Knierim and several other scholars, in the profound transformation that the paradigm underwent in the late 20th and early 21st centuries. In memory of that bygone conversation, the purpose of the present article is to honor Marvin as *the* form critical scholar, and to express my deep appreciation of him as a teacher, colleague, and friend, by exploring some largely overlooked ramifications of the paradigm shift in which he has been so instrumental.

Methodological Preliminaries

In the last few decades, the dichotomy of the synchronic and the diachronic has established itself—to the great chagrin of many—as pivotal in modern biblical exegesis. At the seventeenth century inception of biblical criticism, Isaac La Peyrère, Thomas Hobbes, and Baruch-Benedict de Spinoza argued that the Hebrew Bible as we know it is an amorphous and poorly preserved (Spinoza's favorite term was *truncatum*—"incomplete") assemblage of unrelated texts, created by different hands, at different times, and for different (often poorly compatible and even mutually exclusive) purposes.[1] Over the next

---

[1] See Steven Nadler, *A Book Forged in Hell: Spinoza's Scandalous Tractate and the Birth of the Secular Age* (Princeton: Princeton University Press, 2011), 104-42.

three hundred years, and especially since 1800, critical studies were mostly focused on two closely related questions: what processes brought the received books and corpora into being and what did their building blocks originally look like?[1] Specific methods of analysis varied but the basic paradigm—often termed historical-critical but better called diachronic—remained firmly in place.[2] The basic, if largely unspoken, presuppositions underlying it—that the biblical compositions presenting themselves as integral are anything but and that tracing the trajectories of their formation over time is both feasible and exegetically advantageous—went largely unchallenged. Only in the 1970s, and especially the 1980s, did what was initially a small minority of scholars venture to try an entirely different, synchronic (or literary-critical) tack, denying or ignoring the text's previous incarnations and dealing exclusively with its received formulation.

The new development split biblical criticism into two irreconcilable camps, for the simple reason that diachronic and synchronic approaches are not readily compatible. If a given text is indeed not of a piece, it cannot be studied as though it were; and if synchronic analysis can plausibly and profitably account for the text's received shape, it is redundant to postulate diachronic development. With that in mind, it is no wonder that the advent of synchronic scholarship had little impact on two out of three major diachronic approaches that remained viable—source criticism and redaction criticism.[3] Their proponents largely ignored all things synchronic and in their turn were ignored by synchronically minded scholars, aside from an occasional barb.[4]

---

[1] The Talmud (b. B. Bat. 14b–15a) recognizes that biblical books were created over time but not that there may be traces of diachronic development within them, except for Joshua possibly writing about Moses' death in Deut 34.

[2] On "diachronic" as the best available term, see Serge Frolov, "Synchronic Readings of Joshua-Kings," *The Oxford Handbook on the Historical Books of the Hebrew Bible* (eds. Brad E. Kelle and Brent A. Strawn; Oxford: Oxford University Press, forthcoming).

[3] Tradition criticism was almost dead by this time, subsumed in part into redaction criticism, in part into form criticism (indeed, it is not even clear if it ever truly existed as a methodology in its own right). Currently, source criticism seems to be also fading, with all diachronic research becoming redaction criticism.

[4] E.g., Jan P. Fokkelman, *Narrative Art and Poetry in the Books of Samuel: A Full Interpretation Based on Stylistic and Structural Analyses* (SSN 20; Assen: Van Gorcum, 1981), 1:419 and Barry G. Webb, *The Book of Judges* (NICOT; Grand Rapids: Eerdmans, 2012), xvi.

Form criticism took a different path. It emerged at the turn of the twentieth century as an unambiguously diachronic procedure. Its founder, Hermann Gunkel, was dissatisfied with source criticism, which reigned supreme in his day, because its practitioners saw resolving the alleged problems in the biblical text by isolating originally independent strands within it as their only task and hardly ever asked about the origins of the materials contained in these strands. In other words, Gunkel wanted to broaden the scope of diachronic analysis, by no means to challenge its overall validity; as made clear in a letter written very late in his career, he was committed to studying *Literaturgeschichte*—"*history* of literature."[1] It is precisely for this purpose that Gunkel made his most notable and lasting methodological contribution to biblical studies, introducing the concepts of *Gattung* ("genre") and its *Sitz im Leben* ("setting in life"). His hope was that classifying (*ordnen*) relatively small units recognized as belonging to a single source (say, J or P) by their genres would make it possible to trace their ultimate provenance to the real-life context (such as folk storytelling or temple service) with which these genres are typically associated. Gunkel's form criticism was a supplement to source criticism, whose findings it presupposed. Even when his followers pushed the limits of the approach far enough for it to become more of an alternative (Gerhard von Rad's "The Form-Critical Problem of the Hexateuch" stands out in this respect), the methodology's overall diachronic character remained unchanged.[2]

Yet, from the outset there was also a significant synchronic aspect to it. The categories of *Gattung* and *Sitz im Leben* are applicable only to a specific formulation of the text, whether actually existing (such as the Masoretic canon) or hypothetical (such as P in source criticism). Even if temporal evolution is assumed, in order to be classified according to genre and associated with a real-life situation a piece has to be frozen in time. Since source and redaction critics usually have precious little to say about precanonical strands or layers *qua*

---

[1] Hans Rollmann, "Zwei Briefe Hermann Gunkels an Adolf Jülicher zur religionsgeschichtlichen und formgeschichtlichen Methode," *ZTK* 78 (1981): 276–88, here 284.

[2] Gerhard von Rad, "The Form-Critical Problem of the Hexateuch," *The Problem of the Hexateuch and Other Essays* (tr. E. W. Trueman Dicken; New York: McGraw-Hill, 1966), 1–78.

literature (apart from ascribing to them certain religious or political views), these methodologies have never been anything but fully diachronic. By contrast, although the form criticism of Gunkel and his immediate followers built upon source criticism and often even added a diachronic dimension of its own — by dismissing as secondary the features that did not fit the genre assigned to the piece — its unique and defining procedure was always essentially synchronic.

With that in mind, only one step was needed to redefine form criticism as *predominantly* synchronic, namely, a recognition that attested formulations of the biblical text hold indisputable primacy over hypothetical ones — first, because the former are scholarship's only anchor in reality (and thus its only means of control against idle speculations), and second, because understanding the received Bible is the ultimate purpose of all exegesis. This step was made by Knierim already in the early 1970s — importantly, and by no means accidentally, before actual synchronic studies of the Hebrew Bible began to appear. He asserted that form critical analysis should eschew all diachronic assumptions and start with analyzing the formal and contextual features of biblical literary artifacts as we know them. Only when this analysis is complete, and only based upon it, does it become legitimate to ask questions about the prehistory of the examined piece.[1] Later, starting in the 1980s, Sweeney powerfully affirmed Knierim's conclusions in his theoretical publications and especially in his exegetical practice.[2] He argued, moreover, that "the form critic must be prepared to consider multiple forms, genres, settings, and intentions in

---

[1] Rolf Knierim, "Old Testament Form Criticism Reconsidered," *Int* 27 (1973): 435–68; cf. also Rolf Knierim, "Criticism of Literary Features, Form, Tradition, and Redaction," *The Hebrew Bible and Its Modern Interpreters* (eds. Douglas A. Knight and Gene M. Tucker; Chico, CA: Scholars Press, 1985), 123–65. Knierim (and later Sweeney) only discuss the relationship between form criticism and redaction criticism, but their reasoning is easily applicable to all diachronic approaches.

[2] Marvin A. Sweeney, "Form Criticism: The Question of the Endangered Matriarchs in Genesis," *Method Matters: Essays on the Interpretation of the Hebrew Bible in Honor of David L. Petersen* (eds. Joel LeMon and Kent Harold Richards; Atlanta: SBL, 2009), 17–38; Marvin A. Sweeney, "Form Criticism," *Dictionary of the Old Testament: Wisdom, Poetry and Writings* (eds. Tremper Longman and Peter Enns; Downers Grove, IL: IVP Academic, 2008), 227–41; and Marvin A. Sweeney, "Form Criticism," *To Each Its Own Meaning: An Introduction to Biblical Criticisms and Their Application* (eds. Steven L. McKenzie and Stephen R. Haynes; Louisville: Westminster John Knox, 1999), 58–89.

the interpretation of the biblical text throughout its literary history."[1] In other words, even in the diachronic mode of exegesis, each postulated stage of the Bible's development over time must be explored in its synchronic horizon.

With that, form criticism was repositioned a full 180 degrees vis-à-vis the diachronic-synchronic divide. Whereas for Gunkel the essentially synchronic investigation of the text's genre and real-life setting was dependent upon diachronic analysis and served as a means of furthering it, for Knierim and especially for Sweeney diachronic analysis is dependent upon such investigation and serves as a dispensable means of furthering it. But what if this about-face can be taken even further? Before Gunkel, diachronic exegesis was considered fully self-sufficient; perhaps, the time has come to claim that form criticism is not only the alpha of biblical scholarship but also its omega? In what follows, I will try to answer these questions by applying the insights of Knierim and Sweeney to one of the best known *cruces interpretum* in the Hebrew Bible—the two creation compositions in Gen 1-2. I will proceed under the standard rubrics of the FOTL biblical commentary series (founded by Knierim and Gene Tucker and currently edited by Knierim and Sweeney), discussing the text's structure, genre, setting, and intention, and then address the diachronic ramifications of this discussion.

Structure

As is well known, source critics more or less unanimously ascribe Gen 1:1-2:3 to P and Gen 2:4-3:24 to J. For Gunkel, this was the point of departure; in his Genesis commentary, the two pieces are discussed in different chapters, dozens of pages apart.[2] However, from the viewpoint of Knierim and Sweeney this is not how a form critical investigation is to proceed: the text in its final form is to be analyzed first, no matter how strong the case for seeing different strands or redactional layers behind it may seem to be.

In this respect, we should start by noting that the entire text of Gen 1-2 is a part of a much larger composition—Genesis-Kings, or the

---

[1] Sweeney, "Form Criticism" (1999), 68.
[2] Hermann Gunkel, *Genesis* (tr. Mark E. Biddle; MLBS; Macon, GA: Mercer University Press, 1997), 4-40, 103-33.

Enneateuch.[1] Generically, it is dominated by narrative, to which other forms are for the most part subordinated (e.g., commandments, paraenesis, and poetry are always introduced as characters' quoted speech) or assimilated (e.g., ancestral genealogies in Gen 5 and 11); self-standing non-narrative pieces introduced by אלה or ואלה are relatively rare (one example is the Table of Nations in Gen 10). Accordingly, the (mega)-unit is held together by the string of clauses governed by *wayyiqtol* verbs—the main narrative form of Standard Biblical Hebrew—that represents its syntactic master sequence. This sequence is frequently broken and therefore structured by intrusions of other syntactic forms—such as *qatal, weqatal,* and *yiqtol* verbs, infinitives, participles, and nominal clauses.

In Gen 1-2, three such intrusions are prominent: the combination of two clauses governed by *qatal* verbs, a nominal clause, and a participial clause in 1:1-2; the cluster of *yiqtol* verbs in 2:5-6a preceded by a nominal clause in 2:4 and followed by a *weqatal* clause in 2:6b; and a block of mostly nominal clauses in 2:10-14. The text consequently falls into three main narrative strings: 1:3-2:3 with an introductory digression in 1:1-2; 2:7-9 with an introductory digression in 2:4-6 and a concluding digression in 2:10-14; and 2:15-25, cut short by the *qatal* clause in 3:1a.[2]

Yet there is another major structural observation to be made here. Genesis 1:3-31 is formulaic throughout, arguably more so than any other biblical texts: recurring expressions, such as "And God said, let there be X," "And God saw that it is good," or "And there was evening, and there was morning, day N," constitute almost 50% of its volume, by word count. An additional formula, "and these are תולדת of heaven and earth," is found in 2:4a, but it is a part of a very different pattern. While the clichés of Gen 1 never show up elsewhere, that of 2:4a appears only once in that chapter but recurs in Gen 5:1; 6:9; 10:1; 11:10, 27; 25:12, 19; 36:1, 9; 37:2; Num 3:1. In other words, Gen 2:4a

---

[1] On this composition as a form critical (mega)-unit, see Serge Frolov, *Judges* (FOTL 6b; Grand Rapids: Eerdmans, 2013), 333-46; and Serge Frolov, "Structure, Genre, and Rhetoric of the Enneateuch," *Vestnik of Saint Petersburg University Philosophy and Conflict Studies* 33.3 (2017): 254-63.

[2] The use of *qatal* in 1:27aβ-b is probably motivated by rhetorical considerations and therefore has no structural value: the author started the two clauses with complements in order to emphasize that both sexes are created in the deity's image.

opens a substantial segment of the Enneateuch characterized by the תולדות formula, 2:4–14 and 2:15–25 being but two out of this segment's many constituent elements. By the same token, Gen 1:1–2:3 presents itself as the segment's structural counterpart.[1] An important corollary is that the creation composition in Gen 2:4–25 belongs together with Gen 3–4 (the תולדות formula in 5:1 ushers in a new unit) as well as, more remotely, with the ancestral sequence that occupies most of Genesis and perhaps even with the opening chapters of Exodus.[2] The creation composition in Gen 1:1–2:3 does not.

Narrative Presentation of Events from the Creation of the World to the Elevation of Jehoiachin (Gen 1:1–2 Kgs 25:30)

1. Creation segment	Gen 1:1–2:3
1.1. Opening digression	Gen 1:1–2
1.2. Creation proper	Gen 1:3–2:3
2. Ancestral segment	Gen 2:4–50:26 (Exod 11:10?)
2.1. תולדות of heaven and earth	Gen 2:4–4:26
2.1.1. Creation of Adam	Gen 2:4–14
2.1.1.1. Opening digression	Gen 2:4–6
2.1.1.2. Creation proper	Gen 2:7–9
2.1.1.3. Closing digression	Gen 2:10–14
2.1.2. Creation of Eve	Gen 2:15–25 (Etc., etc.)

Genre

Gunkel, in his Genesis commentary, describes both creation compositions of the Hebrew Bible as "legends;" indeed, according to him the entire book is nothing else.[3] He characterizes legend as a

---

[1] Other formulaically defined segments of the Enneateuch include Exod 12:1–Deut 34:12 (date formulae), with a possible extension in Josh 1:1–Judg 1:26; Judg 1:27–1 Sam 12:25 (cycle formulae); and 1 Sam 13:1–2 Kgs 25:30 (regnal formulae and summaries).

[2] It is not immediately clear where exactly the תולדות segment ends. The תלדות יעקב headlined in Gen 37:2 can be reasonably seen as extending at least through the character's death at the end of the book, and a new pattern, that of precise date formulae, begins to establish itself in Exod 12:1 (תולדות in Num 3:1 notwithstanding). Exod 1:1–11:10 thus can be seen as an extension of the תולדות segment or a transitional zone between it and the date-formula segment. Since the issue is irrelevant for the purposes of the present article, it will be left open.

[3] Gunkel, *Genesis*, vii–xi.

"popular, long-transmitted, poetic account dealing with past persons or events."[1] The first element of this description is patently unverifiable (how do we assess a text's popularity in the distant past?). The second smacks of circular reasoning (since per Gunkel reconstructing the transmission history of a given piece is the primary task of form criticism, it cannot start with the assumption that this history is long). The third, as understood by Gunkel ("poetic tone… that seeks to gladden, elevate, inspire, touch"), is vague and subjective (in strictly technical terms, neither Gen 1:1–2:3 nor Gen 2:4–25 is poetry).[2] Finally, the fourth is applicable to the entire Enneateuch as well as many other artifacts of biblical literature.

At the same time, Gunkel seems to overlook arguably the most basic property shared by most if not all works of literature ever dubbed legends: they are usually stories, namely, more or less extended narratives "controlled by plot, moving from exposition and the initial introduction of characters through forms of complication to resolution and conclusion."[3] Of course, not every story is a legend, but just about every legend is a story.[4]

In this respect, there is a fundamental difference between Gen 1:1–2:3 and Gen 2:4–25 despite their being more or less uniformly dominated by *wayyiqtol* verbs. The latter qualifies as a story. The creation of Adam and his placement in an environment that is full of plants but devoid of other humans or animals (2:4–9) serves as an exposition, his resultant loneliness (v. 18) as a complication, creation of animals and Eve (vv. 19–23) as a slightly suspenseful resolution, and the emergence of sexuality, complete with the issue of nakedness (vv. 24–25), as a denouement. At the same time, the piece serves as an exposition for Gen 3, by introducing the tree of knowledge and the

---

[1] Gunkel, *Genesis*, viii.
[2] Gunkel, *Genesis*, xi.
[3] Antony F. Campbell, *1 Samuel* (FOTL 7; Grand Rapids: Eerdmans, 2004), 348.
[4] It is doubtful, of course, whether legend is even a genre in its own right. Gunkel, *Genesis*, vii–xi, starts his Genesis commentary by outlining differences between legend and historiography, but almost all of them concern circulation (oral vs. written), content (private vs. public), and verisimilitude (history needs to be credible whereas legend "frequently reports extraordinary things incredible to us"). There is no mention of literary form; even when juxtaposing (supposedly) prosaic historiography with (supposedly) poetic legend, Gunkel references, as mentioned above, the composition's tone rather than its formal features.

prohibition to eat its fruit (vv. 9, 16-17), and together with it as an exposition for the entire Enneateuch, by explaining why despite being God's creations humans are so far removed from the divine realm and divine perfection.

Not so in Gen 1:1-2:3. As perspicaciously noted by George Coats, "it develops no plot; there is no arc of tension, no resolution of crisis," just an accumulation of order-fulfilment sequences that are nearly identical except with regard to the level of detail (which seems gradually to increase).[1] Everything is "good" (טוב) from the outset: even the initial chaotic state of the earth is reported matter-of-factly, without any indication of its being a problem of any kind. Everything ordained by the deity comes into being exactly as ordained (ויהי־כן), with no resistance and no failures (unlike ch. 2 where the initial attempt to resolve the issue of Adam's loneliness by creating animals comes to naught). All entities, starting with light and darkness and ending with animals, behave according to specified parameters, confining themselves to their assigned niches and never mixing or transforming into each other. Significantly for our further discussion, such a perfect picture leaves no place for further developments: once the world is completed, there is nothing left for God to do but rest. The fragment is then best described as an account—a narrative that is relatively long and complex but that describes the events of the past "without any need for plot, raising tension and reaching resolution."[1] Moreover, it has some makings of a list, most of it being in essence an enumeration of the world's most obvious components—ranked from the most basic to the most complex—under the common rubric "Existing in exact accordance with God's uncontested decree." Although nominal clauses are more typical in lists, clauses governed by *wayyiqtol* verbs feature prominently in some of them, 1 Chr 1-9 being a major example.

In sum, Gunkel erred in assigning Gen 1:1-2:3 and Gen 2:4-25 to the same generic category (despite noticing how different they are). The two texts not only differ in their presentation of the creation process and belong to different segments of the Enneateuch, but they

---

[1] George W. Coats, *Genesis, with an Introduction to Narrative Literature* (FOTL 1; Grand Rapids: Eerdmans, 1983), 47.

are also written in different genres. The import of this conclusion will become apparent in "Intention" section of the present article.

Setting

For Gunkel and his immediate followers, it was self-evident that texts assigned to different *Sitzen im Leben* must come from different hands. And since each genre has its own *Sitz im Leben*, pieces that are dissimilar in this respect cannot possibly be interpreted as components of the same literary design—in full agreement with the source-critical practice of associating narratives with (mostly) J and E, paraenesis with D, and lists (among other things) with P. A major vulnerability of this reasoning is that, apart from a few very short inscriptions, the Hebrew Bible is the only ancient Israelite text available today; accordingly, we simply have no data about the forms that this society's communications would assume under given circumstances. As a result, in classical form criticism everything pertaining to *Sitz im Leben* was either heavily speculative (for example, Sigmund Mowinckel's conjectures about otherwise unattested festivals and rites as settings for many psalms) or based exclusively on biblical reports and descriptions, leading to *circulus in probando* (for example, Gerhard von Rad's identification of the Sukkot festival in Shechem and Shavuot festival in Gilgal as the backgrounds of the Hexateuch).[2] The possibility, nay likelihood, of the biblical author(s) appropriating generic patterns associated with a given communicative situation for their own rhetorical purposes likewise never came into consideration.

Sweeney makes an important distinction between three types of settings—literary (*Sitz in der Literatur*), social, and historical.[3] The first appears to be adequately covered under "structure" on the one hand (with regard to the text's positioning vis-à-vis other literary entities) and "intention" (see "Intention" section below) on the other

---

[1] Campbell, *1 Samuel*, 341; see also Frolov, *Judges*, 363. Coats, *Genesis*, uses the term "report" (47), which is roughly synonymous, as a generic definition, with "account" (both translate into German as Bericht).

[2] Sigmund Mowinckel, *Psalmenstudien I–II* (repr.; Amsterdam: P. Schippers, 1961) and von Rad, "Hexateuch," 33–48.

[3] Sweeney, "Form Criticism" (1999), 79–82; cf. Knierim, "Old Testament Form Criticism Reconsidered," 445–49, 463–66. The term *Sitz in der Literatur* was introduced by Wolfgang Richter, *Exegese als Literaturwissenschaft. Entwurf einen alttestamentlichen Literaturtheorie und Methodologie* (Göttingen: Vandenhoeck & Ruprecht, 1971).

(as far as the objectives of this positioning are concerned). As to the last two, they can become diachronic Trojan horses of sorts: exploring the social and/or historical setting of a unit that is a part of a larger literary entity is tantamount to prejudging the relationship between the two as diachronic before the synchronic investigation of the text as we know it is complete. Since, as pointed out previously, in the received Hebrew Bible both creation compositions are components of the Enneateuch, all that can be said at this point is that they share its *Sitz im Leben*. Indeed, despite their dissimilarity, it would be hard to come up with a separate setting for each of them.

Intention

For an ancient Israelite author, finding a suitable opening for the Enneateuch would not have been an easy task. On the one hand, demonstrating the uncontested power and supreme benevolence of the composition's only true God was indispensable to its primary goal—convincing the audience that Israel should abide by the covenant with this deity by observing the commandments it promulgated.[1] This called for the world created by this deity to be perfect. On the other hand, such an outcome of the creation would leave no place for further developments, not to mention that it would fly in the face of the world's empirically observable, rather sorry state.

Genesis 1-2 resolves the problem by tapping into ancient Near Eastern scribal tradition, according to which it is permissible, and even desirable, for compositions in different genres to recount the same events in different ways.[2] Closer to home, the device of parallelism in Hebrew poetry could provide an inspiration.[3] Creation of the perfect world is fashioned as an entirely self-contained account (Gen 1:1-2:3), allowing for no sequel. Placed side by side with it is an open-ended

---

[1] See Frolov, *Judges*, 342-46 and Frolov, "Structure, Genre, and Rhetoric of the Enneateuch."

[2] K. Lawson Younger, "Heads! Tails! Or the Whole Coin?! Contextual Method and Intertextual Analysis: Judges 4 and 5," *The Biblical Canon in Comparative Perspective: Scripture in Context IV* (eds. K. Lawson Younger, William W. Hallo, and Bernard F. Batto; ANETS 11; Lewiston, NY: Edwin Mellen, 1991), 109-46.

[3] See, e.g., James L. Kugel, *The Idea of Biblical Poetry: Parallelism and Its History* (New Haven: Yale University Press, 1981); Stephen A. Geller, *Parallelism in Early Biblical Poetry* (HSM 20; Missoula, MT: Scholars Press, 1979); and Adele Berlin, *The Dynamics of Biblical Parallelism* (rev. ed.; BRS; Grand Rapids: Eerdmans, 2008).

story (Gen 2:4-25) that not only presents the first-ever problem (Adam's loneliness) but also uses it to prepare for Gen 3-4 (where an unsuitable helpmate for Adam seduces the suitable one) and through it, the rest of the Enneateuch.

Pivotal to this arrangement is the תולדות formula in 2:4a. First, as already mentioned, it implicitly isolates 1:1-2:3 as a major segment of the Enneateuch in its own right, structurally equivalent not to 2:4-25 but to the rest of Genesis at the very least (see "Structure" section above). Second, it resets the narrative's clock. Every time the formula is used, it signifies a step back in time.[1] In this particular case, the mention of heaven and earth takes the audience back to the very beginning—namely, to the point marked by Gen 1:1. On both counts, Gen 2:4-25 presents itself as an alternative, or correction, to Gen 1:1-2:3, not its sequel.

A form critical study of Gen 1-2 undertaken without diachronic presuppositions thus reveals that the current shape of the biblical text can be adequately accounted for by an integral overarching design. That, in turn, renders all source-critical or redaction critical reconstructions redundant: the rule of parsimony (Ockham's razor) forbids conjuring hypothetical entities, such as multiple authors or redactors, without need. Despite technically applying to a very narrow fragment of the Hebrew Bible, this conclusion has broad epistemic implications.

Synchronic and Diachronic (in Lieu of Conclusion)

In both religious tradition and modern critical scholarship, Gen 1-2 is no ordinary text. Specifically, in the latter, it has long served as a showcase of inconsistencies in the Hebrew Bible warranting diachronic investigation and of diachronic methodology (mostly of the source-critical variety) being utile in resolving them. Yet, when subjected to

---

[1] In Gen 6:9, the shift is from the deity's decision to destroy creation to the corruption that preceded it; in 10:1, to the birth of Canaan and other grandchildren of Noah presupposed by 9:20-27; in 11:10, to the time right after the flood; in 11:27, to the births of Abram and his brothers reported in the previous verse; in 25:12, to the birth of Ishmael's children that presumably preceded Abraham's death in 25:8; in 25:19, to Isaac's birth; in 36:1, to Esau's marriages reported in 26:34; in 36:9, to the birth of Esau's sons reported in 36:4; in 37:2, to Esau's lifetime (after multiple generations of his descendants listed in ch. 36); and in Num 3:1, to the birth of Aaron's sons and the death of two of them reported in Lev 10:1-2.

form critical analysis as per Knierim and Sweeney — most importantly, without diachronic presuppositions leading the study — the text in question turns out to be an integral, if sophisticated, composition generated by a single design, which obviates any need for diachronic examination. Do we deal here with an outlier or a predictable, even unavoidable outcome?

In order to determine this, let us conduct a mental experiment. Suppose, after faithfully following Knierim-Sweeney guidelines, a form critic concludes that a diachronic investigation of Gen 1–2 is in order. To begin with, this would be tantamount to saying that despite its being a continuous text within a larger composition (the Enneateuch) no plausible authorial design can be detected behind it. But can a synchronic examination that ends in such a way be considered successfully completed, and does not the switch to the diachronic mode become, to all intents and purposes, a function of the exegete throwing in the towel?

Further, and much more important, if the diachronic cavalry is called in to make sense of the received text, it has to, well, make sense of it. No matter how many sources, traditions, or redactional layers are postulated, it must inevitably come to the individual who brought the piece to its observed condition, if only by combining preexisting fragments, and his or her intention has to be explained because otherwise the whole diachronic enterprise would be for naught. Yet, any design ascribable to the final redactor or compiler can also be ascribed to an author, thereby making diachronic analysis redundant.[1] Indeed, this outcome is unavoidable even when exegesis starts in the diachronic mode: whether synchronic form criticism is initially the alpha or the omega of biblical interpretation, ultimately it ends up as both.

That, in turn, raises another question: if this incarnation of form criticism is entirely self-sufficient and cannot legitimately serve as a launching pad for diachronic approaches, how is it different from what has been referred to in recent decades as literary criticism?[2] The

---

[1] Even if the redactor is implicitly or explicitly judged inept, the author may be inept as well (of course, exegetical yield in both cases would be zero).

[2] Erhard Blum, "Formgeschichte — A Misleading Category? Some Critical Remarks," *The Changing Face of Form Criticism for the Twenty-First Century* (eds. Marvin A.

answer lies in recognizing, first, that although the latter can be reasonably expected to deal with the issues that are indispensable in form criticism—the text's structure and its genre—it rarely addresses the former and hardly ever the latter.[1] Second, the matters that literary criticism as it is actually practiced is primarily interested in—plot development, suspense, characterization, differing viewpoints, the role of the narrator, and the like—are organically subsumable under the form critical rubrics of structure, genre, and intention. With that in mind, the form criticism of Knierim and Sweeney presents itself as greater literary criticism. Indeed, with diachronic criticism epistemically suspect, it may even be coterminous with text-oriented biblical criticism as a whole.[2]

Sweeney and Ehud Ben Zvi; Grand Rapids: Eerdmans, 2003), 32–45, here 43–44, seems to express a similar concern. Historically, source criticism was known as literary criticism, but lately the term has been exclusively reserved for synchronic readings of the Hebrew Bible.

[1] With regard to structure, the publications of Jan P. Fokkelman (e.g., his four-volume *Narrative Art and Poetry in the Books of Samuel*) are a major exception, but while highly attentive to the small literary units in the text, he mostly neglects the larger ones; in particular, the Enneateuchal context of Samuel—and its literary boundaries within this context—never come up in his studies.

[2] Reader-oriented criticism (feminist, queer, postcolonial, ecological, etc.) has at best marginal interest in these matters. Indeed, it appears that for many of its practitioners the Bible is but a pretext to talk about what really matters to them.

Exploring Narrative Forms and Trajectories
Form Criticism and the Noahic Covenant

Peter Benjamin Boeckel

After becoming a staple of historical-critical exegesis, form criticism eventually fell into disfavor when it failed to satiate appetites for literary analysis in the late twentieth century. Some have even suggested the method remains woefully misguided and that only by burying its decaying heritage concerned with the text's historical setting can it revive.[1] Such evaluations fail to recognize a Copernican-like revolution within form criticism during the past fifty years. Therefore, the present chapter offers a historical review of the methodology's development so as to better understand how it is practiced today. Following that review, we will demonstrate the method on Gen 9:8-19.

The Origination of Form Criticism

Despite his dissatisfaction with the terms *Formgeschichte* and "form criticism," Hermann Gunkel became the methodology's progenitor.[2] Although he remained a diachronic scholar in many ways, Gunkel was eminently concerned with synchronic analysis.[3] Thus, although he assumed and proffered theses about the text's history, he primarily focused on its form.

---

* It is my honor to dedicate this piece to Dr. Marvin Sweeney whose work on form criticism has been very formative in my own approach to the Hebrew Scriptures.

[1] Antony F. Campbell, "Form Criticism's Future," *The Changing Face of Form Criticism for The Twenty-First Century* (eds. Marvin A. Sweeney and Ehud Ben Zvi; Grand Rapids: Eerdmans 2003), 15-31, here 31.

[2] Gunkel himself preferred the term "literary history" since he was not concerned with a text's form alone. See Hans Rollmann, "Zwei Briefe Hermann Gunkels an Adolf Jülicher zur religionsgeschichtlichen und formgeschichtlichen Methode," *ZTK* 78 (1981): 276-88, here 283-84.

[3] Martin Buss, *The Changing Shape of Form Criticism: A Relational Approach* (HBM 18; Sheffield: Sheffield Phoenix, 2010), 17-18.

Gunkel's methodology accomplished two tasks.[1] First, it studied the literary types employed in the Old Testament, which entailed three steps.[2] Step one grouped texts based on literary type (genre) rather than their canonical arrangement.[3] Step two studied each genre to ascertain the "materials with which it deals and the forms which it necessarily assumes."[4] Lastly, step three considered each genre in light of its historical development, which often entailed tracing a tradition's growth from a prewritten stage of development.[5]

These facets of Gunkel's generic analysis represent only the first task of form criticism. Its second task researched "the mentality and the work" of the writers who employed the genres for their own purposes.[6] Gunkel recognized the ancient writer's ability to adapt and mix genres in ways that may or may not cohere with their normal usage.

Thus, form criticism's father avoided—in theory, if not in practice—what his successors became accused of: obsessing over a composition's oral stages while failing to explain the meaning of the text. Although he assigned paramount importance to studying ancient Hebrew writers, Gunkel recognized that the best way to do this was though examining their writings.[7] Consequently, he believed scholars should begin their research by studying literary types.[1]

Of course, Gunkel also conducted historical analysis. But the nature of his analysis differed from that of his followers. Gunkel's discussion of *Sitz im Leben* was often non-specific, focusing on the types

---

[1] Gunkel never wrote systematically regarding the application of his method. The following discussion is based on a synthetic reading of several of his works, especially Hermann Gunkel, "Fundamental Problems of Hebrew Literary History," *What Remains of the Old Testament and Other Essays* (tr. A. K. Dallas; New York: Macmillan, 1928), 57–68 and Hermann Gunkel and Joachim Begrich, *Introduction to the Psalms: The Genres of the Religious Lyric of Israel* (tr. James Nogalski; Macon: Mercer University Press, 1998).

[2] Gunkel once stated that the first step of his approach was the determination of the genres employed in the text ("Fundamental Problems," 59). Nevertheless, in practice, relatively little of his discussion addressed this issue. Consequently, "a study of the literary types" used in the Bible represents the first major component of Gunkel's method.

[3] Gunkel, "Fundamental Problems," 59.
[4] Gunkel, "Fundamental Problems," 60.
[5] Gunkel, "Fundamental Problems," 61–64.
[6] Gunkel, "Fundamental Problems," 63–64.
[7] Gunkel, "Fundamental Problems," 65.

of settings (plural) in which a text could be used.[2] This vagueness afforded him more time for tasks like tracing motifs throughout a narrative cycle. Thus, although Gunkel spent ample time in *Legends of Genesis* articulating the literary characteristics and themes of the *Sagen*, he was primarily concerned with the text's form and content. Only after thoroughly exploring this topic did he address the issue of textual growth and show how the originally small compositions developed into cycles and, eventually, into Genesis.

Post-Gunkel Developments

Three methodological developments grew out of the trajectory Gunkel set for form criticism. The first development was a focus on very small textual units. This trend began with Gunkel, who advocated studying the smallest unit—the "original" source or legend—first.[3]

This is not a major problem if such units cohere with the text's structure. However, many form critics defined their base units for interpretation by presupposing redaction- and source-critical proposals, which resulted in atomizing the text at the expense of its formal coherence. Rolf Knierim argued rightly that historical critics should revisit this method of beginning one's analysis with the earliest editorial layer rather than interpreting the text in its final redacted form, a task for which form criticism is well suited.[4]

Form criticism's second development was its sustained reflection on generic analysis. This theme is a hallmark of form critical studies: form critics are concerned with studying literary types (genre). Klaus Koch advanced this interest in significant ways by postulating the existence of component and complex genres (*Gleidgattungen* and *Rahmengattungen*).[5] The former category describes stand alone compositions. When several such texts combine, the genre of the larger

---

[1] Gunkel, "Fundamental Problems," 65.

[2] Buss, *The Changing Shape of Form Criticism*, 26.

[3] Hermann Gunkel, *The Legends of Genesis* (tr. William Herbert Carruth; New York: Schocken Books, 1964), 42–44.

[4] Rolf Knierim, "Criticism of Literary Features, Form, Tradition, and Redaction," *The Hebrew Bible and Its Modern Interpreters* (eds. Douglas Knight and Gene Tucker; Chico, CA: Scholars Press, 1985), 117.

[5] Klaus Koch, *The Growth of the Biblical Tradition: The Form critical Method* (tr. S. Cupitt; New York: Scribner, 1969), 23.

unit exhibits Koch's complex genre.[1] Such categories assist the analysis of a text's literary setting, which is a major interest among recent form critics.

Despite progress in generic studies, a problem emerged as form critics assumed generic realism, which "posits that texts are uniquely and intrinsically related" to their genre.[2] In other words, form critics treated genre in a semi-Platonic fashion that assumed, for instance, an ontological category of communal laments into which any biblical texts warranting that label must fall.[3] The problem with this approach is the refusal of most texts to cohere with the proposed ideal form of any given category. Such difficulties led later form critics to adopt different understandings of genre.

Form criticism's third post-Gunkel development was a shift in focus to history. For many form critics, historical investigation became the method's primary objective and earned them the reputation of being scholars obsessed with studying *Sitz im Leben*. Albrecht Alt exemplifies the early shift toward historical analysis. For Alt, the delimitation of legal genres was a means to the end of investigating the Israel's historical origins. Thus, although he paid careful attention to textual syntax and structure, his theorizing about the life-settings of the text outstripped what his literary work could support.[4]

Of course, Alt was not alone. Gerhard von Rad used form and redaction criticism to understand the evolution of the Hexateuch.[5] Koch believed each genre could be tied to a particular setting in life, while other scholars postulated increasingly specific genres and sub-

---

[1] Koch offers an example by observing how sermons represent a standalone genre in themselves, but when they are combined with other literary types (prayer, songs, etc.) they form a liturgy (*Growth of Biblical Tradition*, 111).

[2] Kenton Sparks, *Ancient Texts for the Study of the Hebrew Bible: A Guide to the Background Literature* (Peabody: Hendrickson, 2005), 6.

[3] Gunkel apparently adopts this position when he mentions "pure and unmixed forms" ("Fundamental Problems," 65).

[4] See Albrecht Alt, "The Origins of Israelite Law," *Essays on the Old Testament and Religion* (tr. Robert Wilson; Sheffield: JSOT Press, 1989), 107-71. Interestingly, Alt usually posited a religious setting regardless of the genre; see Alt, "Origins," 125-28 and Alt, "The God of the Fathers," *Essays on Old Testament History and Religion* (tr. Robert Wilson; Sheffield: JSOT Press, 1989), 10-86, here 49.

[5] Gerhard von Rad, "The Form critical Problem of the Hexateuch," *The Problem of the Hexateuch and Other Essays* (tr. E. W. Trueman Dicken; New York: McGraw-Hill, 1966), 1-78, esp. 33-48.

genres.[1] As these tendencies progressed, Gunkel's caution against the speedy invention of genres and his focus on textual content faded into the background.

Turning the Tide

In 1969, James Muilenburg's published address to the Society of Biblical Literature inaugurated rhetorical criticism to supplement form critical analysis.[2] A chief concern of Muilenburg was form criticism's overemphasis on a given text's typical characteristics at the expense of seeing its uniqueness.[3] This problem's development is understandable: as form critics categorized texts according to genre, they acquired a tunnel vision that focused on commonalities between different compositions.

Without questioning the usefulness of form criticism, Muilenburg felt that rhetorical criticism could accomplish two tasks that fell outside its scope. First, it could define a pericope's literary boundaries.[4] Form critical scholarship was sorely lacking in this regard; determining where a text began and ended received little attention.[5] Rhetorical criticism's second task was to analyze the composition's structure "and to discern the configuration of its component parts" so as to identify rhetorical devices marking the "sequence and movement of the pericope" as well as the development of the writer's thought.[6] Muilenburg maintained that rhetorical criticism could achieve these tasks through paying close attention to literary phenomena such as inclusios, key words and word repetitions, and the breakdown of poetic strophes.

---

[1] Koch, *Growth of Biblical Tradition*, 27. On the proliferation of genres, Simon DeVries is a prime offender: he proposes eleven subgenres of "prophetic legends," which likely signals excessive attentiveness to minor differences between compositions. Cf. Simon DeVries, *Prophet against Prophet: The Role of the Micaiah Narrative (1 Kings 22) in the Development of Early Prophetic Tradition* (Grand Rapids: Eerdmans, 1979), 53–56.

[2] James Muilenburg, "Form Criticism and Beyond," *JBL* 88 (1969): 1–18.

[3] Muilenburg, "Form Criticism," 5.

[4] Muilenburg, "Form Criticism," 9.

[5] For example, von Rad recognized a continuous story running throughout the Hexateuch, but he did not consider what formal criteria marked Josh 24 as that story's conclusion. Had he asked this question, he may have seen what Martin Noth later identified as the large uninterrupted story that spans Genesis–Kings (*Überlieferungsgeschichtliche Studien: Die sammelnden und bearbeitenden Geschichtswerke im Alten Testament* [Darmstadt: Wissenschaftliche Buchgesellschaft, 1963], 212).

[6] Muilenburg, "Form Criticism," 10.

One way to illuminate the difference between Muilenburg and his interlocutors is to consider their hermeneutical programs. One might ask whether Muilenburg truly went *beyond* form criticism, or simply pointed it in a new direction. Whereas Alt used form criticism for historical analysis, Muilenburg exhibited an interest in aesthetic features and styles. As such, he asked different questions and arguably used form criticism as the means to a different end.

The fact that later form critics internalized Muilenburg's critiques supports this supposition. Rolf Knierim's work is a case in point.[1] He felt that form criticism had the capacity to study the unique features of a given text through structural analysis. Therefore, he advocated that form critics incorporate such an analysis as the initial step of their method.[2]

This change prioritized the synchronic element of form criticism before permitting questions about redaction and oral development. While not denying the existence of such diachronic processes, Knierim pointed out that scholars are presented with a written text and before studying its oral stages they must "take seriously the problems of structure, genre, setting, and function/intention of the written texts as literature in their own right."[3] It is precisely these topics that became the pillars of new form criticism, which is best exemplified in Marvin Sweeney's work.

Marvin Sweeney and New Form Criticism

Sweeney has been one of the most prolific form critical writers over the past quarter century.[4] Sweeney's brand of form criticism — like Knierim's — operates synchronically before treating the text's

---

[1] Knierim, "Criticism," 123-65.
[2] Knierim, "Criticism," 138.
[3] Knierim, "Criticism," 145.
[4] Marvin A. Sweeney, "Form Criticism: The Question of the Endangered Matriarchs in Genesis," *Method Matters: Essays on the Interpretation of the Hebrew Bible in Honor of David L. Petersen* (eds. Joel LeMon and Kent Harold Richards; Atlanta: SBL, 2009), 17-38; Marvin A. Sweeney, "Form Criticism," *Dictionary of the Old Testament: Wisdom, Poetry and Writings* (eds. Tremper Longman and Peter Enns; Downers Grove, IL: IVP Academic, 2008), 227-41; and Marvin A. Sweeney, "Form Criticism," *To Each Its Own Meaning: An Introduction to Biblical Criticisms and Their Application* (eds. Steven McKenzie and Stephen R. Haynes; Louisville: Westminster John Knox, 1999), 58-89. Cf. Marvin A. Sweeney, *Isaiah 1-39: With an Introduction to Prophetic Literature* (FOTL 16; Grand Rapids: Eerdmans, 1996).

composition history. With this in mind, it is appropriate for us to consider the methodology as Sweeney outlines it.

Form criticism's initial step involves formal analysis of the text's literary features. This includes taking one's lead from Muilenburg and Knierim to devote careful attention to demarcating a unit's literary boundaries and after that to provide a structural analysis based on the unit's literary and syntactic formulation.

Step two engages in generic analysis. At this point, many form critics fall victim to what Kenton Sparks designates "generic realism" (see above). Sweeney, however, adopts a different approach to genre that is akin to Sparks's "generic nominalism."[1] Generic nominalism understands genres as taxonomic categories that may overlap. Thus, one animal can be simultaneously called vertebrate, cold-blooded, and webbed-footed. Similarly, Sweeney observes that genres are "typical conventions of expression or language that appear within a text."[2] Significant here is that Sweeney does not equate genre with the text's form. Genre exists within form. Furthermore—and in line with generic nominalism—Sweeney contends that one text can simultaneously display various genres, which allows one to avoid either/or scenarios.[3] Thus, without contradiction, Sweeney concludes that Gen 15 contains elements of multiple prophetic genres, inheritance-type language, and oath language.[4]

Sweeney's third step investigates the setting of the text. Whereas previous scholars focused on the social setting (*Sitz im Leben*), Sweeney identifies additional settings that require the form critic's attention: the historical setting in which the text was written (i.e., the historical period) and the literary setting.[5] Even though new form criticism does retain a diachronic component that prods to describe the historical and social settings of the text, the literary setting is most important.[6] The reason is that scholars can only make educated guesses

---

[1] Sparks, *Ancient Texts*, 6.
[2] Sweeney, "Form Criticism" (2008), 227.
[3] Sweeney, "Form Criticism" (1999), 75–78.
[4] Sweeney, "Form Criticism" (1999), 75–78.
[5] Sweeney, "Form Criticism" (2009), 21.
[6] Although one should note that Serge Frolov's contribution to this volume argues that form criticism ought to shed its diachronic components.

about the other two settings. By contrast, the literary setting is available for examination as it recolors any fragments of the text's other settings.

The final step of the form critical process assesses the text's intention or function. By "intention," Sweeney "refers to the meanings conveyed by a text on the basis of its unique literary form, the generic language that constitutes that form, and the settings from which the text derives and in which it functions."[1] Although he recognizes the subjectivity of attempting to uncover a composition's intention since scholars can never be certain about their conclusions, his point is well made that making the attempt is "simply a necessary aspect of textual interpretation."[2]

With this, our survey of form criticism draws to a close. While continuing Gunkel's original concern with literary features, such as the text's structure and genre, form criticism has evolved in important ways. It no longer focuses solely on small texts and now operates much more synchronically as it enjoys the benefits gained from over a century of reflection on the nature of genre. With these pieces in place, it is time to put our theoretical discussion into practice.

Form Criticism and the Noahic Covenant

Form critical studies of covenantal texts are nothing new, but most such analyses represent the old-guard form critical methodology.[3] Therefore, the first biblical text in which the idea of covenant appears, Gen 9:8-18, offers an ideal place to conduct our analysis. These verses appear within a unit that continues a *wayyiqtol* chain from Gen 8. The Flood Narrative's concluding unit begins with a digression sandwiched between two date formulas (Gen 8:13-14) and stretches to a concluding digression about Noah's sons spreading over the land (9:19). Within these boundaries, the unit's structure is as follows:

---

[1] Sweeney, "Form Criticism" (1999), 82.
[2] Sweeney, "Form Criticism" (1999), 83.
[3] Into this category, the present writer would place most of the comparative studies of covenant, including those by scholars who would not necessarily describe themselves as form critics. Cf. George Mendenhall, *Law and Covenant in Israel and the Ancient Near East* (Pittsburgh: Biblical Colloquium, 1955); Klaus Baltzer, *The Covenant Formulary in Old Testament, Jewish, and Early Christian Writings* (tr. David Green; Philadelphia: Fortress, 1971); and Dennis McCarthy, *Treaty and Covenant: A Study in Form in the Ancient Oriental Documents and in the Old Testament* (2nd ed.; AnBib 21A; Rome: Biblical Institute Press, 1981).

Events after the Flood	Gen 8:13-9:19
Opening Digression	Gen 8:13-14
1. Date when the waters dried up	Gen 8:13a
2. Noah uncovered the ark	Gen 8:13bα
3. Noah looked	Gen 8:13bβ
4. Narrator's statement of what he saw	Gen 8:13bγ
5. Date when the land was dry	Gen 8:14
Events after the Flood	Gen 8:15-9:18
6. Deity's first speech act	Gen 8:15-17
7. Humans leave the ark	Gen 8:18
8. Animals leave the ark	Gen 8:19
9. Noah builds an altar	Gen 8:20a
10. Noah takes animals to sacrifice	Gen 8:20bα
11. Noah offers a sacrifice	Gen 8:20bβ
12. Deity smells the offering	Gen 8:21aα
13. Deity's second speech act	Gen 8:21aβ-22
14. Deity blesses Noah and his sons	Gen 9:1a
15. Deity's third speech act	Gen 9:1b-7
16. Deity's fourth speech act	Gen 9:8-11
17. Deity's fifth speech act	Gen 9:12-16
18. Deity's sixth speech act	Gen 9:17
19. List of Noah's sons	Gen 9:18
Concluding Digression	Gen 9:19
20. The land is filled by Noah's sons	Gen 9:19

The deity's six speeches constitute the text's main content and drive the narrative. Respectively, speeches one through three instruct Noah to leave the ark, report YHWH's internal dialogue about never again destroying all life, and reinvoke the initial creation mandate to be fruitful and multiply. The final three speeches relate to the covenant by establishing it (speech four), instituting a sign for it (speech five), and stating that the sign of the covenant had been established (speech six).

A key structural question in the pericope is the relationship between the third and fourth speeches: is the creation mandate part of the covenant? Steven Mason argues that it is and that it provides the covenantal stipulations laid upon humans whereas the ensuing speeches report the deity's obligations.[1] As evidence, he observes that ואתם ("and you") followed by a volitional idea in 9:7 and ואני הנני ("and I,

---

[1] Steven Mason, *"Eternal Covenant" in the Pentateuch: The Contours of an Elusive Phrase* (New York: T & T Clark, 2008), 69-87.

behold") in 9:9 reflect formulaic introductions to covenant stipulations, such as those in Gen 17:4, 9.

There are problems with these parallels. Mason's "volitional idea" is too vague to function as a formal criterion for introducing covenant stipulations. Such vagueness conceals the different verbal roots and forms predicating the ואתה/ואתם in Gen 9:7 and 17:9-10. Furthermore, the two texts are structured differently. In 9:7, ואתם immediately precedes an imperative, but in 17:9-10 the pronoun is very much removed from the infinitive absolute that governs it. Given these differences, can Mason's parallels warrant the conclusion that Gen 9:1-7 is a covenantal text?

This is especially questionable in light of James Barr's observation that Gen 9:1-7 says nothing about a covenant whereas the ensuing speeches repetitiously employ the word ברית seven times.[1] Barr insists that a redactor could have easily clarified things by using the word in Gen 9:1-7, "but this is what the text did not do. Why should this not have importance too?"[2] Without an answer to this critique, we follow Barr's lead in concluding that the text's discussion of Noah's covenant is limited to the final three speeches in Gen 9:8-17.

It is now appropriate to consider the generic formulation of this covenant sub-unit. On one level, the text's explanation of the rainbow's origin appears etiological (vv. 13-16). On a different level, the larger context of the story that fashions Noah as protagonist of the Flood Narrative raises the saga or legend as generic possibilities. The latter is well-suited to Gen 9 given the religious character Gunkel identified in *Legenden*.[3] This would cohere with Noah's offering in 8:20 and the binding of God to creation in the covenant reported in 9:8-11.

Another possibility would be to contend that Gen 9:8-19 exemplifies Moshe Weinfeld's covenant of grant, but this conclusion requires overcoming the devastating critique of Gary Knoppers, who demonstrated that ancient Near Eastern texts exhibit no consistent

---

[1] James Barr, "Reflections on the Covenant with Noah," *Covenant as Context: Essays in Honour of E. W. Nicholson* (eds. Andrew Hastings Mayes and Robert B. Salters; Oxford: Oxford University Press, 2003), 22.

[2] Barr, "Reflections," 22.

[3] Hermann Gunkel, *The Folktale in the Old Testament* (tr. Michael Rutter; Sheffield: Almond, 1987), 26.

structure that can be associated with Weinfeld's grant genre.[1] Even if the grant genre were well established, the fact remains that Gen 9:8–19 is not a grant document.

Rather, it reports the creation of a covenant. This is an important generic distinction. Covenant documents do not employ third-person narration and do not offer theological commentary. By contrast, reports appear within a narrative framework and allow for commentary, whether it is spoken by the narrator or a character in the story. It is this generic descriptor that fits Gen 9:8–19 best.

The historical and social settings of the Flood Narrative as a whole, let alone its conclusion, are notoriously difficult to pin down with certainty. Scholars routinely associate Noahic covenant text with a post-exilic Priestly source, but the present writer sees little reason for requiring a date later than the exile. The unit's emphasis on the deity's irrevocable and unconditional covenant with Noah and his seed after him (Gen 9:9) would serve well the rhetorical needs of exiled Judean scribes reeling from the fall of Jerusalem and tasked with answering questions about Israel's future. Whether the scribes reworked an earlier Hebrew source, or wrote a new one, they incorporated the material into a larger composition that advanced their rhetorical goals. Thus, Frolov's mantra proves helpful: the text's "*Sitz im Leben* is defined by its *Sitz in der Literatur*."[2]

The literary setting of Gen 9:8–19 within the Flood Narrative's conclusion highlights intertextual links to several other pericopes. The conclusion echoes Gen 1:22, 28:

(Gen 1:22) פְּרוּ וּרְבוּ וּמִלְאוּ אֶת־הַמַּיִם בַּיַּמִּים וְהָעוֹף יִרֶב בָּאָרֶץ

(Gen 1:28) פְּרוּ וּרְבוּ וּמִלְאוּ אֶת־הָאָרֶץ

(Gen 8:17) וְשָׁרְצוּ בָאָרֶץ וּפָרוּ וְרָבוּ עַל־הָאָרֶץ

(Gen 9:1) פְּרוּ וּרְבוּ וּמִלְאוּ אֶת־הָאָרֶץ

(Gen 9:7) פְּרוּ וּרְבוּ שִׁרְצוּ בָאָרֶץ וּרְבוּ־בָהּ

For such reasons, Joseph Blenkinsopp identifies a cycle of creation, un-creation, and re-creation in Gen 1–9.[3] At the end of the

---

[1] Moshe Weinfeld, "The Covenant of Grant in the Old Testament and in the Ancient Near East," *JAOS* 90 (1970): 184-203 and Gary N. Knoppers, "Ancient Near Eastern Royal Grants and the Davidic Covenant: A Parallel?" *JAOS* 116 (1996): 670-97.

[2] Serge Frolov, *Judges* (FOTL 6b; Grand Rapids: Eerdmans, 2013), 8.

[3] Joseph Blenkinsopp, *Creation, Un-Creation, Re-Creation: A Discursive Commentary on Genesis 1–11* (London: T & T Clark, 2011).

Flood Narrative, the ark's occupants emerge into a remade creation as the deity repeats the mandate from Gen 1, which completes a narrative loop and raises the question of whether anything is different in the postdiluvian world. Blenkinsopp observes that humanity's relationship to animals changes after the flood (Gen 9:1–5), but the text's sustained focus on the covenant in 9:8–19 suggests it is the primary difference.[1]

The covenant changes the looping narrative trajectory by preventing a repetition of Gen 1–9. The literary context makes clear that the flood did not solve the problem of humanity's corruption (Gen 8:21; 9:20–28). Consequently, there was nothing to prevent a second deluge. The covenant precludes this and leads into humanity's dispersal (9:19; 10:1–32), the eventual focus on Shem's lineage (11:10–26), and the Abraham cycle (11:27–25:11) where covenant will again play a pivotal role.

Significantly, Gen 9:8–19 contains lexical similarities to the next unit in which the noun ברית ("covenant") makes repeated appearances: Gen 17. One example of this is the link between Gen 9:9 and 17:7 where different forms of the verb "establish" (hi. קום) predicate ברית. Likewise, both texts report that the covenant is presented to the addressees and their seed after them.[2] Although it is speculation, one might wonder whether Judean exiles reading about an eternal Noahic covenant could find traction for contemplating their own identity as co-recipients of Abraham's eternal covenant.

Given the above discussion, we must now surmise the intention of the passage. Within the plot, the literary setting of the unit shows its function to be a prevention of a repetition of Blenkinsopp's creation—un-creation—re-creation cycle. The flood did not resolve the problem of evil in humanity's heart, nor would additional inundations. Genesis 9:8–19 departs from the narrative's looping trajectory and initiates one that points to Abraham.

Rhetorically, the unit teaches that God's covenant with creation endures in spite of humanity's sin. Unlike most biblical covenants, the one in Gen 9 was unconditional. For readers who understood the fall of

---

[1] Blenkinsopp, *Creation*, 145.
[2] The difference between plural pronominal suffixes in Gen 9:9 and singular ones in 17:7 is inconsequential; it is required by the fact that Noah's sons are addressed along with him in 9:9.

Judah through the lens of Deut 29 and/or Lev 26, an affirmation of the deity's covenant fidelity in spite of human sin could bolster hope for a restoration (or re-creation) of Israel's life in the land (Deut 30:1-3). This is especially possible given the connections to Abraham's covenant in Gen 17, which, while conditional, is similarly called an eternal covenant.

Conclusion

This study has traced the development of form criticism from its inception to modern application. Although the method has evolved over the years, elements remain consistent. Form criticism continues to investigate literary types and the settings of scripture. It endeavors to explore the shape and content of the biblical text so as to understand better its argument. In the case of Gen 9, we saw the usefulness of form criticism in understanding a covenant report and in ascertaining its role within the larger argument of Genesis while also raising tentative speculations about a historical context in which this argument would resonate. Granted, there is more to say about this unit, but our discussion has achieved its goal of demonstrating the enduring vitality and utility of a method that is far from being defunct.

Natural Law Recorded in Divine Revelation
A Critical and Theological Reflection on Genesis 9:1-7

Timothy D. Finlay

In Gen 9:1-17, G-d gives a series of speeches to Noah and his sons that together constitute what has come to be known as the Noahic covenant. The first mention of the word "covenant" (בְּרִית) in scripture occurs here (Gen 9:9) in the context of G-d giving instructions to the survivors of the flood and, by implication, to their descendants who would make up the seventy nations of the world. In Jewish tradition, the laws in this covenant are incumbent upon all human beings, not just Israelites. Nachmanides comments, "The literal reading of scripture [states that] these are rational commandments and every individual who recognizes his creator must be careful about them, as it is written of Abraham [who commanded his children] to keep the way of God, to do righteousness and justice [Gen 18:19] even though [there was no more defined command]."[1]

The Tosefta contains an early enumeration of the laws involved in the Noahic covenant:

> The descendants of Noah were commanded [to keep] seven commandments, [those] concerning [the establishment of a set of] laws and [forbidding] idolatry and cursing with the name [of G-d] and forbidden unions and murder and theft and eating a limb from a living animal" (t. 'Abod. Zar. 8:4).

The law against forbidden sexual unions includes numerous taboos specified in more detail in Leviticus, and the same is true of several other laws, so that over one hundred laws in the Torah would count as being obligatory on all people. The corresponding category in Christian thought is that of natural law,[2] that part of the eternal law which

---

[1] Moshe ben Nachman, "תורת השם תמימה," כתבי רבנו משה בן נחמן (ed. Chayim Dov Chevel; Jerusalem: Mossad Harav Kook, 1984), 163-64.

[2] The concept of natural law is thus clearly attested in Judaism, even though the particular term is not as frequently used, with David Novak being a notable exception. Novak writes, "(1) We cannot cogently assert that humans without the Torah

humans can know (and to which they are obligated) because of their rationality even without the special revelation in scripture.

Genesis 9:1-17 thus represents an important intersection of biblical theology (critical and theological reflection upon biblical passages) and natural law (philosophical reflection upon what ethical responsibilities are incumbent upon all humankind). The prohibition of murder and violence is central to all such discussions. In his pioneering work of Jewish biblical theology, *Tanak: A Theological and Critical Introduction to the Jewish Bible*, our honoree Marvin A. Sweeney comments, "After renewing the command to 'be fruitful and multiply' (Gen 9:1; cf. 1:28), G-d strikes a *bĕrît 'ôlām*, 'eternal covenant,' with Noah and humankind that is designed to deal with the problem of human violence."[1] In this article, I offer the honoree a theological and critical reflection upon the first of G-d's speeches to Noah and humankind (Gen 9:1-7) that concentrates on the instruction concerning human violence.

In homage to Sweeney, I begin with a structural outline of the passage.[2]

    I. Speech Introduction (1a-bα)
        A. Divine blessing on Noah and his descendants (1a)
        B. Speech Introduction proper (1bα)
    II. Speech: Instructions for all human beings (1bβ-7)
        A. Introductory commands to be fertile (1bβ)

---

have no moral insight; (2) humans bring an intelligence to revelation before they receive governance from revelation; (3) revelation gives to the Jews more than we could ever devise on our own; (4) revelation is G-d's unique speech that can only be partially apprehended, never comprehended" (*Natural Law in Judaism* [Cambridge: Cambridge University Press, 1998], 28). See also Steven Wilf, *The Law Before the Law* (Lanham: Lexington, 2008), who argues that G-d's initial commands to humans "contained three expectations—for obedience to norms; the requirement to transmit legal rules to others; and, lastly, the mastery of the art of statutory interpretation. These expectations relied upon the rational faculty" (39).

[1] Marvin A. Sweeney, *Tanak: A Theological and Critical Introduction to the Jewish Bible* (Minneapolis: Fortress, 2012), 62. It is a great pleasure and privilege to offer this article to my friend and doctoral advisor, Marvin Sweeney. Marv, in addition to what we learned from you regarding form criticism and historical criticism, you helped us to integrate form critical and historical-critical insights into our respective theological traditions.

[2] Any student wanting to perform structural outlines should consult the marvelously detailed outlines in Marvin A. Sweeney, *Isaiah 1-39, with an Introduction to Prophetic Literature* (FOTL 16; Grand Rapids: Eerdmans, 1996) and Sweeney, *Isaiah 40-66* (FOTL 19; Grand Rapids, Eerdmans, 2016).

    1. Compound command to be fertile and increase (1bβ¹⁻²)
    2. Command to fill the earth (1bβ³⁻⁴)
  B. Instruction concerning animals and human blood (2-6)
    1. Instruction concerning animals (2-4)
      a. Granting of human dominion over animals (2)
        1) Assertion: animals will fear humans (2a)
        2) Exercitive: human dominion over animals (2b)
      b. Restricted permission to eat animals (3-4)
        1) The permission section (3)
          a) Jussive-clause permission to eat animals (3a)
          b) Divine first-person granting of permission (3b)
        2) Restriction: prohibition against eating blood (4)
    2. Instruction concerning shedding human blood (5-6)
      a. Threat to require a reckoning for human blood (5)
        1) Basic threat (5aα)
        2) Specifically addressed threats (5aβ–b)
          a) Animals that shed human blood (5aβ)
          b) Humans that shed human blood (5b)
      b. Punishment for shedding human blood (6)
        1) Chiastic parallelism prescription (6a)
        2) Reason: Humans are created in G-d's image (6b)
  C. Concluding commands to be fertile (7)
    1. Command to be fertile and increase (7a)
    2. Command to abound and increase on the earth (7b)

The passage begins with two third-person past tense assertives:[1] G-d blessed Noah and his sons, and G-d said to them. It is an interesting feature of biblical narrative that every clause by the narrator (not including the embedded speeches by the characters) is an

---

[1] Assertives are the first of five categories of speech acts catalogued by John Searle and William Alston that cover all forms of human communication. Assertives are speech acts that make a claim about some aspect (whether past, present, or future) of the way things are. They are the sort of speech act that can be true or false. The other categories of speech act, three of which we shall see in this short passage, are directive, commissive, expressive, and exercitive (so named by Alston, but called a declaration by Searle). See John Searle, *Speech Acts* (Cambridge: Cambridge University Press, 1969) and William P. Alston, *Illocutionary Acts and Sentence Meaning* (Ithaca: Cornell University Press, 2000). Both Searle and Alston build on the foundational work done in James L. Austin, *How to Do Things with Words* (Cambridge: Harvard University Press, 1962). For an analysis of the genres in the Hebrew Bible that consistently invokes speech act theory, see Timothy Finlay, *A Handbook of Genres and Formulae in the Hebrew Bible* (Atlanta: SBL Press, 2017).

assertive.[1] G-d's blessing of Noah and his sons in v. 1 recalls G-d's blessing of "them" (humankind) in Gen 1:28. Moreover, both verses begin the speech proper with the directive[2] פְּרוּ וּרְבוּ וּמִלְאוּ אֶת־הָאָרֶץ "Be fruitful and multiply and fill the earth." In Gen 1, the addressee (literally "them") is presumably the male and female that make up הָאָדָם, humankind. So, although the addressee throughout G-d's speeches in Gen 9 is exclusively male,[3] the larger intended audience of the narrator would include women. After all, the wives of Noah's sons would be actively involved in the commands to be fruitful and multiply, the instructions given in Gen 9:1-7 pertain not just to the immediate family but to all future generations, and men and women are equally permitted to eat animals and equally forbidden to shed the blood of הָאָדָם (a term which itself includes both male and female). We shall discuss further the theological significance of the connections between Gen 9:1-7 and Gen 1:26-31 later in this essay.

The speech itself begins and ends with positive authoritative directives (commands) from G-d (Gen 9:1bβ, 7). Authoritative[4] directives may obligate the other party to perform a particular action (command), they may permit but not obligate the other party to perform an action (permission), or they may forbid a particular action (prohibition).[5] In this short passage, all three of these modes are

---

[1] For example, there are no directives to the reader not to worry about the fate of a certain character that one occasionally finds in Anthony Trollope's *Chronicles of Barsetshire* series. Nor are there any expressives by the narrator interjecting something like "O how wonderful is G-d's providence!" When the biblical narrator does use an aside to the audience, it is an informative assertive.

[2] Directives are another category of speech acts catalogued by John Searle and William Alston (see p. 43, n. 1 above). Basically, in directives the speaker urges/requests/orders another party to do something or not to do something. They can be obeyed or disobeyed. Related to directives are commissives, such as promises and threats, where the speaker commits to a future action. Commissives are the sort of speech acts that can be kept or carried out (or not). In contrast to assertives (which attempt to fit the words to the way the world is), directives and commissives strive to change the world according to the commandment or promise given.

[3] Hermann Gunkel, *Genesis* (tr. Mark E. Biddle; MLBS. Macon: Mercer University Press, 1997), 148. Gunkel also makes a stronger case that Gen 9:1-7 may be an addition to an earlier flood narrative.

[4] Non-authoritative directives include such genres/speech-acts as requests, pleas, exhortations, and admonitions.

[5] These authoritative commands and prohibitions can be further categorized according to the nature of the authority: divine, parental, royal, judicial, etc. They can also be categorized according to the syntactical form of the particular directive, the type

present. The commands to be fruitful in v. 1b are complemented by another set of commands to be fertile in v. 7, and these form an envelope around the main body of instruction in vv. 2–6. In v. 1bβ$^{1\text{-}2}$ (and in v. 7a), the imperatives "be fruitful" and "multiply"[1] are intransitive and are synonyms for the same action so that one basic command is uttered via two imperative verbs. In v. 1bβ$^{3\text{-}4}$, there is a single command conveyed by the transitive imperative verb "fill" with "the earth" as its direct object. Likewise, v. 7b offers a compound command consisting of two synonymous verbs, "abound" and "multiply," each followed by an indirect object whose referent is the earth. The connections between v. 1bβ and v. 7 are very strong indeed, supporting the structural outline above.

The main instruction[2] in vv. 2–6 is divided into two parts with an important theological connection. The first part (vv. 2–4) contains a restricted permission to eat animals, and the second part (vv. 5–6) concerns the prohibition against shedding human blood. Nahum Sarna comments:

> The slaughter of animals, now sanctioned, might easily become a dehumanizing experience. Also, the mass annihilation of human beings in the Flood might have tended to cheapen life in the eyes of the survivors. According, the reaffirmation of the sanctity of human life and the inviolability of the human person is singularly appropriate here.[3]

The granting of human dominion over animals begins a future assertive: animals will fear humans (Gen 9:2a). This is followed by what seems to be an exercitive[4] granting to humans dominion over the

---

of behavior that is being addressed, or the presence/absence of a penalty for disobedience and its severity.

[1] While Gen 9:1-17 does not contain any direct prohibitions of sexually immoral acts, its command of sexually appropriate ones may imply them.

[2] Instruction is a complicated genre that has elements of the directive and assertive speech acts. As an assertive, it imparts information (often on how to do something) but it also directs others to certain actions.

[3] Nahum Sarna, *Genesis* (JPSTC; Philadelphia: Jewish Publication Society, 1989).

[4] Exercitives are the final category of speech acts discussed by Searle and by Alston. An exercitive is an authoritative declaration, which in the very act of being spoken brings about a new situation in the world. Examples include "I pronounce you man and wife" when uttered by someone with the appropriate authority, or "strike" or "out," spoken by an umpire. There are remarkably few exercitives in biblical narratives. Narratives of ceremonies that would have included exercitives—coronations, ordinations

animals. Its parallel is in Gen 1:28b, where the divine command for the man and woman to rule over the animals presupposes that they have been given some form of dominion. The following verse does contain an exercitive, in which G-d grants to the man and the woman ("you" plural) the plants for food (Gen 1:29), something which is also granted to animals (Gen 1:30). The divine permission to eat animals in v. 3 does not have a counterpart in Gen 1. This liberty is then restricted to prohibit eating meat with the life-blood in it.[1]

There is a divine permission involving eating in Gen 2, however, and this also is followed by a restriction. G-d permits the man to eat from every tree in the garden (Gen 2:16), but restricts him from eating from the tree of knowledge of good and bad (v. 17). And it is from a theological exegesis of each word or phrase in Gen 2:16 that the Rabbis derived the biblical basis for all seven principles of the Noahic covenant (b. Sanh. 56b).[2] While the details of that exegesis are beyond the scope of this paper, the basic assertion that natural law, or the terms of the Noahic covenant, applied from the garden onwards is surely valid. Philosophically, if these laws are rationally discernible by all human beings and obligatory for them, then they must have applied before the flood. Exegetically, there are numerous pointers that Gen 9:1-17 is a reaffirmation (and slight modification) of G-d's creation purpose for humankind in Gen 1 and 2.

This connection to Gen 1 continues in the instruction concerning the shedding of human blood. Verse 5 is a divine threat[3] to require a reckoning for any human bloodshed. Just as the plants were granted for food to both humans and animals (Gen 1:29-30), so this threat is directed against both humans and animals that shed human blood. Then comes a prescription[4] of punishment followed by the reason, a

---

of priests, etc.—are typically described by the narrator using only assertives and the speeches by the officials who would have pronounced these exercitives are omitted.

[1] The Noahic principle forbidding eating a limb from a living animal derives from here.

[2] For example, the second word was the Tetragrammaton and this signaled the law against blasphemy, the third word, "G-d," signaled the law against other gods, etc.

[3] A threat is a commissive in which the action committed to by the speaker would have a negative impact upon the addressee. Its positive counterpart is promise.

[4] In casuistic law, the standard pattern is a *case* in an if-clause or protasis followed by a *prescription* in a then-clause or apodosis. Here the subject of the prescription, "the one who sheds the blood of a human," includes within itself the content matter normally conveyed in a case.

reason—that humans are made in the divine image—taken directly from Gen 1:27.

The prescription itself is a magnificent chiastically arranged couplet.[1] It has two lines of three words each, with the lexeme "shed" in the first and sixth positions, the lexeme "blood" in the second and fifth positions, and the lexeme "human" in the third and fourth positions. It roughly translates as "The one who sheds the blood of a human, by humankind shall that one's blood be shed" (Gen 9:6a).[2] This is literally poetic justice![3]

The prescription works on several levels. The activity being prohibited is not limited to murder but includes other violence resulting in human bloodshed and, by extension, other violence resulting in physical damage to another human being. But it clearly prohibits murder, and murder is usually regarded as the most obvious of the natural laws.[4] The prohibition against murder was not new. Cain knew he had done wrong by killing his brother; he just believed that the divine punishment was too great (Gen 4:8-14).

As a prescription against murder, Gen 9:6 likely limits the exercise of blood vengeance so that only the murderer and not his family die.[5] Even as it limits punishment to the murderer, however, its prescription of capital punishment is severe.[6] Moreover, the ב in the

---

[1] For a more detailed exposition of the poetry in this verse, see Timothy Finlay and Jim Herst, *Exploring the Word of God: The Old Testament* (San Bernardino: Grace Communion International, 2013), 17-19.

[2] Although masculine singular forms of the verb "to shed" are used here, this verse has always been understood in Judaism and Christianity to include men and women as both potential perpetrators and victims of the crime. In actuality, the perpetrators are overwhelmingly male and there are biological facts (testosterone, etc.) rooted in male nature as to why this is so. This is not to deny that the same biological facts (testosterone, etc.) yield benefits in certain other fields of activity.

[3] Sarna, *Genesis*, notes that the principle of *lex talionis* is expressed in poetry where the second line of the couplet reverses the order of the first line (61).

[4] John Barton comments, "The prohibition of murder is not seen by the writer as a potentially arbitrary commandment—as perhaps are the cultic laws—but as simply an explicit statement of what is held to be evident in any case from the existence of humans as made in God's image, namely their essential sacrosanctity" (*Understanding Old Testament Ethics: Approaches and Explorations* [Louisville: Westminster John Knox, 2003], 34).

[5] Gerhard von Rad, *Genesis: A Commentary* (tr. John H. Marks. rev. ed; OTL; Philadelphia: Westminster, 1972), 132.

[6] The prescription of capital punishment is not explicit in this verse, but the principle of proportionality, which is implied in it, has the logical corollary that capital punishment would be the prescription for murder. It has also been traditionally

Hebrew word בָּאָדָם is traditionally understood as one of agency, i.e. "by a human" or "by humankind," so that "human beings are also being ordered to punish murder themselves, that is, to set up some sort of court system to determine guilt and mete out the required punishment. Thus this law also contains a hidden requirement for all human beings to establish courts of law."[1] Hence, the first of the rabbinic principles of Noahic law, the establishment of law courts, can be derived from the implications of straightforward exegesis of Gen 9:6. Targum Onkelos makes clear this understanding in its translation of Gen 9:6. According to the Targum, whoever sheds the blood of a human "before witnesses," that person's blood will be shed "by sentence of judges," with the implication that only a murderer convicted on the evidence of witnesses by an established court could properly be executed. Much rabbinic and Catholic tradition strives to limit the application of the death penalty to as few cases as possible, but that is a different issue than the basic justice of capital punishment for murderers.

Another way used by Jewish interpreters to read the ב in בָּאָדָם is that of its most common usage of "in." In this reading, the "human in a human" is the unborn baby in the womb of a woman, so that Rabbi Ishmael proclaimed, "A Noahide is liable for capital punishment even in the case of feticide." David Novak comments, "For Jews, feticide is not regarded by the Tannaitic sources as a capital offense, although it is prohibited in situations where the mother's life is not threatened by the fetus within her."[1] Abortion has traditionally also been considered a crime in Christian circles, by evangelicals and Catholics alike, and the view that this is part of natural law gains strength from the fact that the

---

understood that way by Jews and Christians alike. As Novak notes, "In Jewish law one could not be explicitly opposed to capital punishment in principle inasmuch as it was positively ordained by Torah in numerous places" (David Novak, *The Image of the Non-Jew in Judaism* [ed. Matthew Lagrone; 2nd ed.; Oxford: Littman Library of Jewish Civilization, 2011], 100). For a fully developed natural law argument for the validity of capital punishment based on the principle of proportionality, see Edward Feser and Joseph M. Bessette, *By Man Shall His Blood be Shed: A Catholic Defense of the Death Penalty* (San Francisco: Ignatius Press, forthcoming 2017). This work, which also answers objections that the New Testament has done away with capital punishment, is a great resource for Catholic pronouncements on the topic and defends the traditional Catholic view against a variety of arguments recently put forward by American bishops in their campaign to abolish the death penalty.

[1] James L. Kugel, *Traditions of the Bible: A Guide to the Bible as It Was at the Start of the Common Era* (Cambridge: Harvard University Press, 1998), 225.

prohibition of abortion was part of the Hippocratic oath taken by Greek doctors as early as the 5th century BCE.

The reason clause "for in the image of G-d, he made humankind" (Gen 9:6b) likewise contains multiple layers of significance. The basic layer is that "murder is wrong and is fittingly punished, because to kill a human is to kill someone made in the image of God."[2] In this layer, it is the principle of the sanctity of human life that is derived from humans being made in the image of G-d.[3] As Gerhard von Rad observes, this verse thus holds two fundamental principles in strange tension: the sanctity of human life (murder deserves capital punishment) and the human responsibility to carry out the capital punishment (killing a human is permissible in the case of executing a murderer).[4]

Hence, the human responsibility to carry out punishment has also been grounded in the fact that humans are created in G-d's image. Wilf, drawing on Rambam's *Guide to the Perplexed*, comments, "God was first imitated through Adam's identification as a law giver rather than (as in the case with reproduction) a biological creator."[5] Being made in the image of G-d carries with it in Gen 1 "the capacity to exercise authority for the sake of a higher principle,"[6] and now in Gen 9:1-7 we see that this divinely given authority to punish murder is grounded in the human ability as the image of G-d.

In summary, even before we get to the speeches that specifically mention "covenant" (Gen 9:8-17), a critical exegesis of Gen 9:1-7 supports many aspects of the theological conclusions of the Rabbis concerning the Noahic covenant, especially with regard to the prohibition of murder and human violence, and its connection back to

---

[1] Novak, *Image*, 110.

[2] Rusty R. Reno, *Genesis* (Grand Rapids: Brazos Press, 2010), 125.

[3] Christopher J. H. Wright comments, "The sanctity of human life is one of the earliest explicit moral values in the Old Testament, based, as it is, on the creation of man in God's image" (*An Eye for an Eye: The Place of Old Testament Ethics Today* [Downers Grove: InterVarsity Press, 1983], 163-64).

[4] Von Rad, *Genesis*, 132-33.

[5] Wilf, *The Law Before the Law*, 45. For a Reformed Protestant perspective, see David VanDrunen's comment: "The Image of God carried along with it a natural law, a law inherent to human nature and directing human beings to fulfill their royal commission to rule over creation in righteousness and holiness," *A Biblical Case for Natural Law* (Grand Rapids: Acton Institute, 2008), 14.

[6] Reno, *Genesis*, 125.

G-d's original instructions to humankind in Gen 1 and 2. Further, there is a considerable overlap between Jewish discussion of the Noahic covenant and the Christian natural law tradition, which critical and theological exegesis of Gen 9:1–17 can help strengthen.

The Holiness Redaction
of the Abrahamic Covenant (Genesis 17)

Bill T. Arnold

The familiar criteria used by source critics to identify and isolate the sources of the Pentateuch—divine names, doublets, contradictions, and differences of style, vocabulary, and theology— have been substantially supplemented, or even supplanted, by newer approaches. The convergence of other lines of evidence essentially confirms the older source and redaction critical conclusions, and in the view of some, moves the Documentary "Hypothesis" into the category of "theory" and beyond, confirming it as "fact."[1] These lines of evidence include (1) the historical stages of development of the Hebrew language along lines that seem to confirm the source documents, (2) the evidence of literary continuity within the original sources, and (3) the empirical evidence related to scribal practices and the manner of text composition in the ancient Near East. Most compelling in this newer convergence of evidence is our growing appreciation for the scribal culture of the ancient world, which has a direct bearing on our reconstructions of ancient Israel's history, and in particular, of the way Israel produced literary compositions.[2] Periodically, we need to revise

---

* Among the accomplishments of Professor Sweeney's distinguished career, he has advanced our understanding of the Tanak, and more specifically, he has refined and renewed form criticism for the twenty-first century. I am pleased to present here a modest proposal on a related methodological approach. Many thanks to my students, Wesley Crouser, Dustin Mills, and Paavo Tucker, for their invaluable assistance with this paper.

[1] See Richard Elliott Friedman, "Foreword," *Empirical Models for Biblical Criticism* (repr.; ed. Jeffrey H. Tigay; DSBLH; Eugene, OR: Wipf and Stock, 2005), where he asserts that the Documentary Hypothesis ought now to be accepted as "fact" and also discusses the three lines of evidence listed in this paragraph.

[2] In what is perhaps a watershed volume in the history of this discussion, Jeffrey H. Tigay concluded that our empirical models from the ancient Near East inform our "recognition of redaction as a literarily significant undertaking" ("Summary and Conclusions," *Empirical Models*, 239-41, here 241). And since then, we have learned much more; see David M. Carr, *Writing on the Tablet of the Heart: Origins of Scripture and Literature*, (New York: Oxford University Press, 2005); William M. Schniedewind, *How the*

our models and theories of composition in light of new lines of evidence, and especially, in light of refinements of our critical methodologies.[1] In this brief tribute to Professor Sweeney, I offer such a reconsideration of one text that I believe has been incorrectly assigned, given the blunt critical tools of an earlier era, in the hopes that sharper instruments are now available.

The text under consideration here is the most important articulation of what is routinely taken as P's covenant between God and Abraham. After a survey of the main exegetical features of Gen 17:1–22, I offer here a different interpretation in light of recent developments in the study of the Pentateuch's priestly materials. Instead of P's version of a patriarchal covenant, I will argue here that Gen 17 is a unified composition of Holiness scribes, who revised, rewrote, and expanded an older P in order to move the old priestly agenda beyond the purely cultic interests of P in a more ethical and moral direction. These Holiness authors and editors contributed far more to Genesis than we have previously identified and perhaps served as the final redactors of the Pentateuch.

The main features of Gen 17:1–22 are straightforward. The passage bears structural resemblance to the two paragraphs of Gen 15 (15:1–6 and 15:7–21), both of which also relate encounters between God and Abram. The two declarations of Gen 15 confirm the promises of "seed" and "land" respectively, and appear intentionally to modify and complement each other. Each of those episodes is initiated by God in self-revelatory disclosure and continues in dialogue between God and Abram. Like those two passages, Gen 17 opens the self-disclosure with a predicate nominative of identification: "I am God Almighty" (*'ănî-'ēl šadday*) compared with "I am your shield" (15:1) and "I am YHWH" (15:7).[2] The declaration in 17:1 appears to be deliberately

---

Bible Became a Book: The Textualization of Ancient Israel, (New York: Cambridge University Press, 2004); and Karel van der Toorn, *Scribal Culture and the Making of the Hebrew Bible*, (Cambridge, MA: Harvard University Press, 2007). Specific to the topic of redaction criticism, see H. G. M. Williamson, "Reflections on Redaction," *The Centre and the Periphery: A European Tribute to Walter Brueggemann* (eds. Jill Anne Middlemas, David J. A. Clines, and Else Kragelund Holt; Sheffield: Sheffield Phoenix Press, 2010), 79–91.

[1] Luis Alonso Schökel, "Of Methods and Models," *Congress Volume Salamanca, 1983* (ed. J. A. Emerton; VTSup 36; Leiden: Brill, 1985), 3–13.

[2] Bill T. Arnold and John H. Choi, *A Guide to Biblical Hebrew Syntax* (Cambridge: Cambridge University Press, 2003), 6–7, here 166. On "I am YHWH" as a

modeled on those, which assumes also that Gen 15 is older than Gen 17. While the promises of "seed" and "land" are in view in Gen 15, here the initiating and opening divine disclosure introduces the covenant between God and Abram/Abraham. Another difference is that Abram speaks hardly at all but instead hears five divine speeches.[1]

The opening verses of Gen 17 present a general speech of God (vv. 1-2), followed in vv. 3-22 by an extended further divine speech, which is divided grammatically into four sub-speeches.[2] The patriarch's age-formula opens the chapter with the characteristically priestly concern for the age of Abram, which we know from P's account of the flood (7:6) and from the typical genealogical details continued from Gen 5:32.[3] Thus, the priestly concern going back to the primeval history continues in P's account of Abram, marking its narrative with his age at key points of transition: at 75 years of age (Gen 12:4b), 86 years of age (Gen 16:16a), 99 years of age (Gen 17:1a, 24a), and 100 years of age (Gen 21:5a). Abram's age at 99 is the only one noted twice in the text (17:1a and 24a), and at least this raises a question of redactional activity. In light of other features I will comment upon here, it is possible that the genealogical detail of v. 1a takes up the voice and line of thought of the old priestly text in order to introduce the "appearance" of YHWH to Abram and the revelation of El Shadday (v.

---

rhetorical device characteristic of H's theology of reciprocal sanctification, see Reinhard Müller, "The Sanctifying Divine Voice: Observations on the אני יהוה-formula in the Holiness Code," *Text, Time, and Temple: Literary, Historical and Ritual Studies in Leviticus* (eds. Francis Landy, Leigh M. Trevaskis, and Bryan Bibb; HBM 64; Sheffield: Sheffield Phoenix, 2015), 70-84.

[1] For details, see Bill T. Arnold, *Genesis* (New Cambridge Bible Commentary; Cambridge: Cambridge University Press, 2009), 167-74.

[2] I agree with Claus Westermann that the relationship of vv. 1-3a to vv. 3b-21 "is that of text to interpretation," although I draw different conclusions from this observation [Claus Westermann, *Genesis 12-36: A Commentary* (tr. John J. Scullion; Minneapolis: Augsburg, 1985)], 257. While my approach here necessarily takes up diachronic questions, I will also assume a considerably more synchronic and holistic view than in the recent reconstruction of Joseph Blenkinsopp: a Neo-Babylonian P narrative (vv. 1-8), expanded by an early Achaemenid priestly addition (vv. 15-22), was followed finally by a late Achaemenid priestly focus on circumcision (vv. 9-14 and 23-37). See Joseph Blenkinsopp, "The 'Covenant of Circumcision' (Gen 17) in the Context of the Abraham Cycle (Gen 11:27-25:11): Preliminary Considerations," *The Post-Priestly Pentateuch: New Perspectives on its Redactional Development and Theological Profiles* (eds. Federico Giuntoli and Konrad Schmid; FAT 101; Tübingen: Mohr Siebeck, 2015), 145-56.

[3] Characterizing not only Gen 5 but also the genealogy of Shem (Gen 11:10-26).

1b).[1] The identification of the deity as El Shadday is famously unclear, although the name occurs seven times in the Hebrew Bible,[2] and numerous more times abbreviated as "Almighty" (*šadday*) in the book of Job.[3] I share the opinion that the priestly narration envisions a progression of revelation from (a) general revelation to humanity as Elohim in the primeval account, (b) to a more particular revelation as El Shadday to the patriarchs as a separate and independent epoch, and finally, (c) to the specific revelation of YHWH to Israel, as explained in detail in Exod 6:2-8, exhibiting a theological structure behind the priestly account in Genesis, Exodus, and beyond.[4] However, for reasons that will become clearer below, I am less convinced this careful schema can be attributed to an original, unified P source.

Although routinely taken as characteristic phraseology of P, I have argued elsewhere that the concept of "walking with/before" YHWH (hithpael, *hlk*) may have originated in an old P source, but has been taken up and developed by Holiness redactors in the description of Noah at Gen 6:9.[5] The evidence suggests that Holiness authors/redactors developed an old priestly theme while anticipating and preparing for the Yahwistic epic, which was also before them as a venerated source. Such redaction strategies develop and tie together previous P themes with Yahwistic texts that were simply enveloped into the new composition because they were considered too sacred to alter. In this way, the Holiness authors were inspired by P's terminology and committed to continuing its ideological agenda, indebted as they were to the older P document as their "guiding spiritual source."[6] Similarly, the priestly configuration of this command

---

[1] On the causative-reflexive niphal "appeared" (*r'h*, "see") for revelatory communiqués to Israel's ancestors, see Arnold, *Genesis*, 135-36, 168.

[2] Gen 17:1; 28:3; 35:11; 43:14; 48:3; Exod 6:3; Ezek 10:5.

[3] A deity Shadday is known elsewhere in the ancient Near East, although we are still without uncontested etymology for the name. See Ernst Axel Knauf, "Shadday," *DDD* (2nd ed.), 749-53.

[4] Westermann, *Genesis 12-36*, 257-58.

[5] Bill T. Arnold, "The Holiness Redaction of the Flood Narrative (Genesis 6:9-9:29)," *Windows to the Ancient World of the Hebrew Bible: Essays in Honor of Samuel Greengus* (eds. Bill T. Arnold, Nancy L. Erickson, and John H. Walton; Winona Lake, IN: Eisenbrauns, 2014), 13-40, here 19-20.

[6] Israel Knohl, *The Sanctuary of Silence: The Priestly Torah and the Holiness School* (Minneapolis: Fortress, 1995), 102. Knohl identifies H's mission as an attempt to move the

to "walk before" YHWH introduced by an anthropomorphic "appearance" of the deity in v. 1 sits uncomfortably with our understanding of the P document but is more at home among the Holiness authors/redactors of the narrative. Here again, the Holiness redactors have taken up the central themes of P but moved them forward with an ethical and moral agenda unknown to P. Moreover, the use of the first-person independent personal pronoun to mark divine speech (*'ănî*, in "I am God Almighty") may be considered characteristic of H's phraseology, especially, of course, in the formula, "I am YHWH."[1] Tellingly, *'ănî* never appears in divine speech in P materials in Exodus–Numbers, and only five times in Genesis: 6:17; 9:9, 12; 17:1, 4. Some have argued these are exceptional anthropomorphic uses in P, which is required by the hypothesis that these covenant-focused texts are all part of the original P source.[2] This investigation will pose a different explanation. The walking metaphor relates to conduct, and here it is linked causally with cultic purity ("walk before me, in order to be blameless") stressing positive behavior as well as negative attributes to avoid. In this way, the Holiness redactors have relied on priestly cultic imagery (blamelessness), while moving beyond it to articulate a moral vision of a higher ethical quality preparing for the covenant introduced in v. 2.

While the parallel accounts of Gen 15 introduced divine assurances of "seed" and "land" promises, here the divine speech introduces in a general way the patriarchal covenant (v. 2), which is then particularized in the four divine speeches of the chapter (the term "covenant," *bərît*, occurs thirteen times in vv. 1–22). In this case, the covenant as binding assurance that God gives (*ntn*) is established "between me and you" in what is most frequently taken as priestly terminology. The covenantal formula using the preposition "between" carries special significance describing the relationship between the

---

priestly agenda beyond the purely cultic interests of the priestly elites to a more ethical vision.

[1] Knohl, *Sanctuary of Silence*, 1–2 n3; Walther Zimmerli, *Gottes Offenbarung: Gesammelte Aufsätze zum Alten Testament* (TB 19; München: Kaiser Verlag, 1963), 11–40; Jan Joosten, *People and Land in the Holiness Code: An Exegetical Study of the Ideational Framework of the Law in Leviticus 17–26* (VTSup 67; Leiden: Brill, 1996), 94; and Müller, "Sanctifying Divine Voice," 72–75.

[2] Knohl, *Sanctuary of Silence*, 86 n78, 125–28.

parties of the agreement, while also highlighting that the initiation of the agreement rests solely on one side. This "between" formula is used here in first- and second-person intimacy, while clearly also linked intertextually to five occurrences of a similar use of the preposition to unpack the covenant between God, Noah, and all living creatures of the earth (Gen 9:12-17).[1] Indeed, this is the Bible's priestly theologian, defining *bərît* as a binding commitment between God and Abram (and Noah before him) — a commitment corresponding to an oath or pledge and containing promises.

But here is a problem that has occupied scholars for years. Interpreters have long puzzled over the centrality of *bərît* theology for both Noah and Abraham in P, while the Priestly Code itself has no such *bərît* attributed to Moses at Sinai. Rather, P's preferred nomenclature is *'ēdût*, "testimony, witness; legal provisions."[2] Other sources of the Pentateuch, including Deuteronomy, associate the concept of "covenant" especially with the exodus, while P highlights only the covenants of Noah and Abraham. The most widely accepted solution is to assume P removed any traces of a Sinai *bərît* in order to eliminate the idea that the relationship between YHWH and Israel was conditioned upon obedience to the law.[3] Rather than a *tôrâ*-bound type of covenant, P envisions a grace-bound covenant of promises to Abraham, for which Sinai's law is only a fulfillment. In this explanation, P's patriarchal covenant in Gen 17 is "a covenant of grace" in which *bərît* is a unilateral obligation on the part of God. By contrast, P's relationship between YHWH and Israel at Sinai is an *'ēdût*, thought to be defined by the proclamation of laws buttressed by blessings and

---

[1] Claus Westermann, *Genesis 1-11: A Commentary* (tr. John J. Scullion; Minneapolis: Augsburg, 1984), 473. For argument that Gen 9:8-17 is H's post-flood covenant, corresponding to this version of the patriarchal covenant, see Arnold, "Flood Narrative," 30-35.

[2] *DCH* 6:279-80 and *HALOT* 790-91. Typically, the *'ēdût* denotes the content of the ark of the covenant according to the priestly tradition: *TLOT* 2:844-45 and *TDOT* 10:495-515, here 512-13.

[3] Walther Zimmerli, "Sinaibund und Abrahambund: Ein Beitrag zum Verständnis der Priesterschrift," *Gottes Offenbarung: Gesammelte Aufsätze zum Alten Testament* (TB 19; München: Kaiser, 1963), 205-16. For recent developments of this interpretation, see Jakob Wöhrle, "Abraham amidst the Nations: The Priestly Concept of Covenant and the Persian Imperial Ideology," *Covenant in the Persian Period: From Genesis to Chronicles* (eds. Richard J. Bautch and Gary N. Knoppers; Winona Lake, IN:

curses. Therefore, the foundation of Israel's existence and its relationship to YHWH is not rigid obedience to the law but acceptance of God's eternal grace.

This theory has much explanatory power, but it fails on several points. The assumption that the Abrahamic covenant was thought of as unconditional needs critiquing in light of the imperative to "walk with" God and practice circumcision (17:9–14).[1] It is more likely that we have here different theological perceptions and emphases. The old priestly understanding focused on the numinous presence of YHWH at Sinai as the motivation for obedience to the law, while the later Holiness redactors developed a more nuanced ethical and moral foundation for *tôrâ*-obedience.[2] For P, the law was little focused on creating a social order *per se*, on the principles of righteousness and justice, but was narrowly committed to the ritual-cultic sphere and to the numinous presence of God at the tabernacle/temple represented by the name of YHWH there.[3] The impersonal and non-anthropomorphic diction of P is everywhere elevating the majesty of the holy, whereas other portions of the Pentateuch, most especially the Holiness Legislation, turn more to a construction of holistic moral and social consciousness. Israel Knohl locates P's transition from one theological ideology in Genesis to another in Exodus–Numbers in a Copernican revolution — the revelation of the name "YHWH" to Moses — in which the essence of divine nature moves from the general revelation of God to humanity, regulated by principles of justice and righteousness, to the specific revelation of YHWH to Israel, regulated by the *'ēdût*-pact centered around the presence of YHWH.

The idea of theological differences before and after the revelation of the name "YHWH" is helpful as far as it goes, but it fails ultimately to explain why P has no covenantal ceremony or mention of the term *barît* in the revelation at Sinai. It is possible we have been

---

Eisenbrauns, 2015), 23–39 and Andreas Schüle, "The 'Eternal Covenant' in the Priestly Pentateuch and the Major Prophets," *Covenant in the Persian Period*, 41–58.

[1] On the conditionality of the patriarchal covenant, see Arnold, *Genesis*, 101–02, 169–70.

[2] The laws of P confront Israel with the numinous presence of YHWH, and therefore the rationale of those laws and the reason for observance is not "morality, but awe of the holy" (Joosten, *People and Land*, 112).

[3] Knohl, *Sanctuary of Silence*, 137–48.

limited by our long tradition of a model of composition for P that perceives an expansive narrative prelude leading to the *'ēdût* legislation. If P indeed predates H, as I have come to believe, and has been substantially redacted and updated by H, then our redactional models for Gen 17 and other texts previously taken as P should be reconsidered.[1] How likely is it that P objected to a *bərît*-type relationship in the Sinai revelation but attributed just such a covenant to Israel's ancestors in Genesis? Or to put it another way, is the Copernican revolution that no doubt occurred more likely to have been a theological innovation of the older Priestly source, or later Holiness authors/redactors? Perhaps a simpler solution is to reject the assumption that Gen 6:11-22, 9:8-17, and 17:1-22, narrating *bərît*-covenants with Noah and Abraham, are of the same narrative cloth as the P texts of Exodus that have no covenant. Genesis may, in fact, contain more H material than previously thought, in which case original P was a continuous text, although greatly attenuated.[2]

The rest of the unit before us, Gen 17:3-22, exhibits a tightly structured literary arrangement organizing the remaining four sub-speeches by literary focus markers, achieved through topicalization by preposing (either formal *casus pendens* or simple fronting), to emphasize the role of each party related to the covenant: first God, then Abraham, followed by Sarah, and Ishmael.[3]

vv. 4-8, God's covenant obligations: "As for me, …"

vv. 9-14, Abraham's covenant obligations: "As for you, …"

vv. 15-16, Sarah's blessing: "As for Sarai, …"

vv. 19-21, Ishmael's blessing: "As for Ishmael, …"

Thus, the speeches are elegantly arranged around four topicalized expressions: one topicalizing the subject by dislocation (*casus pendens*; v. 4), one topicalizing the subject by fronting (v. 9), and

---

[1] For the variety of redactional models and compositional types that I believe useful for this reconsideration, see Stephen A. Kaufman, "The Temple Scroll and Higher Criticism," *HUCA* 53 (1982): 29-43, here 34-43.

[2] Bill T. Arnold, "Genesis 1 as Holiness Preamble," *Let Us Go up to Zion: Essays in Honour of H. G. M. Williamson on the Occasion of his Sixty-Fifth Birthday* (eds. Iain Provan and Mark J. Boda; VTSup 153; Leiden: Brill, 2012), 331-43 and Arnold, "Flood Narrative," 37-40. For this discussion, I will use the siglum "H" for the chapters identified as the so-called "Holiness Code" (Lev 17-26), as well as for the work of authors and redactors belonging to the Holiness school of the priestly legislation.

[3] For this analysis, see Arnold, *Genesis*, 168-69.

one marking the possessor of the direct object, again by dislocation (v. 15).[1] The final topicalization is complex because it also uses a *lamed* of specification to mark the accusative (v. 20).[2] While most of these grammatical details are beyond the scope of the present investigation, one observation merits further comment. In both Gen 6:17 and 9:9, passages we have already seen are linked lexically and theologically with 17:1-22, we find the same syntactical use of dislocation in divine diction, again using the first-person pronoun *'ănî*, raising the question of whether H's characteristic style may prefer such uses of *casus pendens*.[3]

The speech of vv. 9-14 introduces a "sign" (*'ôt*) of the covenant, circumcision, for Abraham's seed, as did Noah's rainbow for all humanity (Gen 9:12-17). Repetition is the hallmark of the speech, stressing that everyone in Abraham's household must be circumcised, whether house-born or purchased slave (vv. 12-13). Circumcision is both the sign of the covenant and the covenant itself ("this is my covenant," v. 10).[4] If this is a holiness composition, the authors/editors were clarifying an older text that highlighted the practice (vv. 23-27; 21:4) but believed those references needed further explanation. The

---

[1] Arnold and Choi, *Guide*, 7; Paul Joüon and Takamitsu Muraoka, *A Grammar of Biblical Hebrew* (2nd ed.; SubBi 27; Roma: Pontificio Istituto Biblico, 2006), 551-54; and Bruce K. Waltke and Michael Patrick O'Connor, *An Introduction to Biblical Hebrew Syntax* (Winona Lake, IN: Eisenbrauns, 1990), 76-77. For definitions and examples of fronting and dislocation, see Robert D. Holmstedt, "Critical at the Margins: Edge Constituents in Biblical Hebrew," *KUSATU* 17 (2014): 109-56.

[2] Arnold and Choi, *Guide*, 113. The use of fronting to highlight the object of a statement is unusual, but it has been recently confirmed as a regular feature of standard Akkadian: Leonid Kogan, "Accusative as *Casus Pendens*? A Hitherto Unrecognized Emphatic Construction in Early Akkadian Royal Inscriptions," *RA* 102 (2008): 17-26.

[3] A possibility I raised already at Arnold, "Flood Narrative," 22 n31.

[4] Rather than being of exilic or postexilic origin, it is likely that the practice of circumcision appeared first in Upper Syria in the early third millennium BCE and moved from there to the south. It was practiced by most of Israel's neighbors except the Babylonians, Greeks, and most notably, of course, the Philistines. The third divine speech (17:9-14) transformed the practice for Israel from a magical prenuptial rite, probably with apotropaic significance, to a much earlier mnemonic and cognitive aid ("eight days old," v. 12) in order to remind Abraham's descendants to keep the covenant. See Arnold, *Genesis*, 172. Blenkinsopp's speculation that this paragraph reflects a context only decades before or just after the conquests of Alexander (Blenkinsopp, "Covenant of Circumcision," 149-53) fails to consider, in my view, the extent to which ancient societies were characterized by ritual autoplasty, which perhaps relates to this chapter's focus not only on circumcision, but also name change and covenant (Mary Douglas, *Purity and Danger: An Analysis of the Concepts of Pollution and Taboo* [London: Routledge, 2005], 141-59).

holiness author, as conjunctive theologian, has nuanced and prepared the reader for P's routine but unexplained, and therefore perceived as inadequate, references to circumcision. Similarly, the changes of Abram's and Sarai's names have two older sources in view, the Yahwistic epic and the original P source, and bring them together, now tied to the covenant by this discourse.

These and other features of Gen 17:1-22 may be explained just as easily, and perhaps more economically, as the result of redactional activity in the process of conflating two sources. As is typical of holiness authors/redactors, the Yahwistic epic is surrounded and supplemented but not altered, while the P source has been modified substantially, at times extending, paraphrasing, and at times composing whole cloth new compositions in the spirit of P.[1] Elsewhere, I have argued that Gen 1 is a new Holiness composition, while the flood narrative in Gen 6:9-9:29 illustrates the H scribes' ability to redact, conflate, and expand original sources.[2] Genesis 17, then, is another example of H's new composition, providing a central text for the rest of the priestly agenda with linkages to key passages such as Exod 6:2-8, 29:45-46, and 31:12-17. This raises, therefore, questions about these texts as well, as further H redactions, providing structure to the whole priestly narrative of Exodus.[3] And of course, a separate study would be needed to explore the way Gen 17 is written to anticipate, supplement, and prepare for H's covenant in Lev 26, just as Gen 1 was composed whole cloth to anticipate and prepare for Sabbath observance (Exod 31:12-17 and 35:2-3), dietary law (Lev 11), and religious festivals (Lev 23) in other Holiness texts.[4] If Israel Knohl is correct, as I believe he is, that authors and editors of the Holiness School produced more than a single pentateuchal source (Lev 17-26), also serving as the final redactors of the Pentateuch, then perhaps they

---

[1] On the compositional types, such as "original composition," varieties of "conflation," and "modified" and "extended" quotation, see Kaufman, "Temple Scroll," 34-43.

[2] Arnold, "Genesis 1" and Arnold, "Flood Narrative."

[3] Suggesting these texts are also part of the same H layer as Lev 17-26 (Jan Joosten, "Covenant Theology in the Holiness Code," ZABR 4 [1998]: 145-64, here 147).

[4] Arnold, "Genesis 1," 342.

also contributed far more to Genesis than we have previously identified.[1]

Indeed, I believe it likely that the Holiness scribes revised, rewrote, and expanded upon P as "innovators of the basic platform of the Priestly code," which served as a "guiding spiritual source" far more than Knohl allows.[2] They were conjunctive theologians, accepting the old Yahwistic epic and tying it together with their venerated P material as well as borrowing terminology from both. But especially in Gen 1 and Gen 17, new compositions have moved the old priestly agenda beyond the purely cultic interests of P in a more ethical and moral direction. The Holiness scribes exhibit a moralizing tone lacking in P and most evident here in the editorial layers added as new compositions.

---

[1] Knohl, *Sanctuary of Silence*, 100-03. Knohl credits H for much of the books of Exodus and Numbers, but allows much less H activity in Genesis, attributing only vv. 7-8 of the patriarchal covenant to H (102).

[2] Knohl, *Sanctuary of Silence*, 102.

Miscellaneous Observations on the Samson Saga with an Excursus on Bees in Greek and Roman Buogonia Traditions

John T. Fitzgerald

The Samson saga (Judg 13:1-16:31), which is arguably the most famous part of the Book of Judges, has often elicited comment from a variety of readers, with entire monographs devoted to it[1] as well as numerous articles and sections of books.[2] The book of Judges itself, of course, belongs to the Prophets (Nevi'im) of the Tanak in terms of canon, and to the Deuteronomistic History in terms of literary history. Scholars interpret this material quite differently, with some adopting a synchronic-literary approach that emphasizes reading the text in terms of its final canonical form and others adopting a diachronic-historical approach that takes into account the literary and redactional history of the biblical narrative.[3] Inasmuch as the two methods offer valuable but different insights into the text, an approach that incorporates aspects of both is often the most fruitful to employ and is the method adopted here.

It is relatively certain that the text of Judges, like certain other books of the Tanak, evolved over time, with the surviving portions of Judges found among the Dead Sea Scrolls providing persuasive

---

* This study is dedicated to Marvin A. Sweeney, my friend and former colleague at the University of Miami, whose broad interests include the book of Judges. See especially Marvin A. Sweeney, "Davidic Polemics in the Book of Judges," *VT* 47 (1997): 517-29 and, also, Marvin A. Sweeney, Review of *The Book of Judges* by Marc Zvi Brettler, *Int* 57 (2003): 78.

[1] See, e.g., James L. Crenshaw, *Samson: A Secret Betrayed, a Vow Ignored* (Atlanta: John Knox, 1978). Jewish and Christian interest in Samson begins already in antiquity; see, for instance, Hel. Syn. Pr. 6:7 and Heb 11:32.

[2] See, e.g., Barry G. Webb, *The Book of Judges: An Integrated Reading* (JSOTSup 46; Sheffield: Sheffield Academic Press, 1987), 162-74 and Jacobus Marais, *Representation in Old Testament Narrative Texts* (BibInt 36; Leiden: Brill, 1998), 122-32.

[3] For different perspectives on this debate, see Johannes C. de Moor, ed., *Synchronic or Diachronic? A Debate on Method in Old Testament Exegesis* (OtSt 34; Leiden: Brill, 1995).

evidence of this development.[1] Unfortunately, none of the Dead Sea Scroll texts of Judges contains any portions of the Samson saga,[2] yet most scholars agree that it comprises stories from multiple sources that have been collected and edited. Three such sources are typically identified: the annunciation and birth of Samson (Judg 13:2-24), Samson and the woman from Timnah (14:1-15:19), and Delilah and the death of Samson (16:4-31).[3] When these separate stories were brought together is debated. Some view the Samson saga as preDeuteronomistic,[4] others as the result of Deuteronomistic editing,[5] and still others as post-Deuteronomistic additions.[6]

---

[1] The clearest evidence for an earlier literary form of at least portions of Judges (but not necessarily of an earlier edition of the book) is provided by 4Q49 (4QJudg^a), which lacks Judg 6:7-10 of the MT; see especially J. Trebolle Barrera, "Textual Variants in 4QJudg^a and the Textual and Editorial History of the Book of Judges," *RevQ* 14/54 (1989): 229-45; Eugene C. Ulrich, "Deuteronomistically Inspired Scribal Insertions into the Developing Biblical Texts: 4QJudg^a and 4QJer^a," *Houses Full of All Good Things: Essays in Memory of Timo Veijola* (eds. Juha Pakkala and Martti Nissinen; PFES 95; Helsinki: Finnish Exegetical Society, 2008), 489-506, esp. 490-94; Eugene C. Ulrich, *The Dead Sea Scrolls and the Developmental Composition of the Bible* (VTSup 169; Leiden: Brill, 2015), 67-70; and Robert Rezetko, "The Qumran Scrolls of the Book of Judges: Literary Formation, Textual Criticism, and Historical Linguistics," *JHebS* 13:2 (2013): 1-68, esp. 10-31.

[2] For a recent discussion of the Judges material, see Esther Eshel, Hanan Eshel, and Årstein Justnes, "XJudg with MS 2861 (Judges 4.5-6)," *Gleanings from the Caves: Dead Sea Scrolls and Artefacts from The Schøyen Collection* (eds. Torleif Elgvin with Kipp Davis and Michael Langlois; LSTS 71; London: Bloomsbury, 2016), 193-201.

[3] The story of the Gaza prostitute (Judg 16:1-3) may either have formed a separate source or have been an original part of the Delilah narrative. In either case, it is interesting that Pseudo-Philo conflates the two women, which has the effect of turning Delilah into a harlot who becomes Samson's second wife (LAB 43:5).

[4] Susan Niditch, *Judges: A Commentary* (OTL; Louisville: Westminster John Knox, 2008): "Stories of Samson may well be as old as Israel's origins" (154).

[5] See especially Wolfgang Richter, *Die Bearbeitung des "Retterbuches" in der deuteronomischen Epoche* (BBB 21; Bonn: Hanstein, 1964), 128-29, 134. See also Ernst Sellin and Georg Fohrer, *Introduction to the Old Testament* (tr. David E. Green; Nashville: Abingdon, 1968), 210-14, who identify three literary stages: a preDeuteronomistic book of Judges, a Deuteronomistic book of Judges, and later additions. They believe that the Samson materials—"a series of self-sufficient narratives and anecdotes" (213)—belong to the Deuteronomistic book but were added in two distinct temporal stages. The first stage consisted of the incorporation into Judges of the various stories found in 13:2-15:19, and it ended with the Deuteronomistic concluding formula found in 15:20. At the second stage, the stories found in 16:1-31a were appended to those of the first stage and marked by a new concluding formula (16:31b).

[6] See especially Martin Noth, *Überlieferungsgeschichtliche Studien. I. Die sammelnden und bearbeitenden Gesichtswerke im Alten Testament* (SKGG 18/2; Halle: Max Niemeyer, 1943), 103. See also Hartmut Gese, "Die ältere Simsonüberlieferung (Richter c. 14-15)," *ZTK* 82 (1985): 261-80, esp. 261-62 and Mark A. O'Brien, *The Deuteronomistic History Hypothesis: A Reassessment* (OBO 92; Freiburg: Universitätsverlag, 1989), 94-96,

For the purposes of this brief study, it is sufficient to argue that the joining of the annunciation narrative to those involving the woman from Timnah and Delilah dramatically affects the way in which Samson is portrayed. The annunciation narrative introduces the idea that Samson is to be a nazirite, consecrated and dedicated to God, from birth (13:5, 7). This appellation creates the expectation that Samson will be a religious individual, and, in addition to having no razor touch his head (13:5; 16:17), particular emphasis is placed on strict abstinence from wine and strong drink. This abstinence begins with his mother during her pregnancy (13:5, 7, 14) and is to continue until the day of Samson's death (13:7). That is, from womb (16:17) to tomb (16:31), Samson is to be a holy man, dedicated to God. Samson's nazirite status is thus not a temporary vow (as in Num 6:1-21), but a way of life.

Inasmuch as individuals' manner of living was commonly viewed in antiquity as a reflection of the kind of goal that they were pursuing,[1] the annunciation narrative thus raises readers' expectations that Samson's life will be pursued with a religious goal in mind and be exemplary for its holiness. Yet those hopes are shattered by the following narratives. Instead of giving a series of episodes in which Samson is depicted as living a consecrated way of life, the narrator shows him systematically defiling his status as a holy man.[2] He thus stands in vivid contrast to Samuel, a nazirite who lives in accordance with the vow made on his behalf by his mother Hannah (1 Sam 1:11 LXX; 4QSam[a] 1:11, 22).[3] In short, because of the annunciation narrative, readers inevitably view Samson's actions more negatively than they

---

287, who views the Samson saga as pre-exilic in origin but added to the Deuteronomistic History by a late post-Deuteronomistic editor.

[1] See, e.g., Aristotle, *Eth. nic.* 1.5.2 (1095b17-18), who distinguishes three kinds of life and John T. Fitzgerald, "Greco-Roman Philosophical Schools," *The World of the New Testament: Cultural, Social, and Historical Contexts* (eds. Joel B. Green and Lee Martin McDonald; Grand Rapids: Baker Academic, 2013), 135-48, esp. 135-38.

[2] Contrast the attempt to depict Samson's youth as lived in accordance with nazirite practices: "It was plain from the frugality of his diet and his loosely flowing locks that he was to be a prophet" (Josephus, *Ant.* 5.285).

[3] The Septuagint and 4QSam[a] do not invent the contrast but simply make it more explicit than does the MT. For a recent treatment of certain comparisons and contrasts between the two judges, see Paola Mollo, "Did It Please God to Kill Them? Literary Comparison between the Birth Accounts of Samson and Samuel," *Hen* 36 (2014): 86-106.

would if he had not been introduced as a nazirite, and the converse is true of Samuel.

In chs. 14–16 Samson will break both of the central facets of his nazirite status that are emphasized in the annunciation. The injunction that no razor is to touch his head is famously and explicitly violated in the narrative about Delilah (16:19), the femme fatale who is his final lover. That Samson violated the injunction regarding abstinence from wine occurs in the story about his first lover, the Philistine woman who lived at Timnah (14:1–15:8).

The first hint that Samson will drink wine appears in Judg 14:5, when he approaches the vineyards of Timnah. The second hint comes during the wedding feast that Samson hosts once he arrives in Timnah (14:10, 12, 17). Wedding feasts, both ancient and modern, are occasions that are typically conspicuous for the consumption of wine (John 2:1–11), and Samson's feast is no exception. It is a *mishteh*, a "drinking feast," with the noun derived from the verb *shatah*, "to drink."[1] Wine was naturally served at these feasts (Isa 5:12; 25:6; Esth 1:7; 5:6; 7:2; Dan 1:16), and if too much wine was consumed on these occasions (Esth 1:8), one could become drunk (1 Sam 25:36; Jer 51:39).[2] The translators of the Septuagint (Judg 14:10 LXX, both A and B) clearly understood the meaning of the Hebrew term and rendered it as a *potos*, a "drinking-bout," a "drinking party," with the noun derived from the Greek verb *pinō* ("to drink"). In the Greek-speaking world, such drinking parties were intimately associated with drunkenness (*oinophlygia*) and sexual misbehavior (1 Pet 4:3), and the same was true for the social world of the Samson saga.[3] It is precisely such a social context—seven days of heavy drinking—that narratively makes possible Samson's sexually charged accusation that the companions have "plowed" with his heifer (Judg 14:18). That Samson does not simply attend but also hosts such a drinking party makes it abundantly clear that he does not abstain from consuming any alcohol. In contrast

---

[1] That the emphasis falls upon drinking is also seen in those texts where *mishteh* simply means "drink" in contrast to food (Ezra 3:7; Dan 1:10).

[2] On drunkenness in antiquity, see John T. Fitzgerald, "Paul, Wine in the Ancient Mediterranean World, and the Problem of Intoxication," *Paul's Graeco-Roman Context* (ed. C. Breytenbach; BETL 277; Leuven: Peeters, 2015), 331–56.

[3] According to Josephus, Samson proposed his riddle "when the drinking was far gone" (*Ant.* 5.289).

to the crucial role played by Delilah in regard to the shaving of his locks of hair (16:19), Samson is here the agent of his violation of the injunction regarding wine and strong drink, which was a serious breach of his nazirite way of life (Amos 2:12).

Prior to the story of the drinking party (Judg 14:10-18), the narrator provides stories of three trips that Samson makes to Timnah. The first is when he sees the woman (14:1), the second is when the marriage is arranged (14:5-8), and the third is for the wedding (14:8). On the second trip, a young lion roars at Samson (14:5), and, empowered by YHWH's spirit, he kills the lion, tearing it apart with his bare hands (14:6).[1] On the third trip, Samson turns aside to see the carcass of the dead lion and discovers that a swarm of bees are inside the lion's body, along with honey (14:8). After scraping the honey into his hand, he eats some of it himself and gives some of it to his parents (14:9). Later at the wedding feast, Samson composes a riddle based on the dead lion and the honey inside its carcass: "Out of the eater came something to eat. Out of the strong came something sweet" (14:13). Samson ultimately discloses the meaning of this riddle to his bride, who in turn reveals it to the people of Timnah (14:17). They solve the riddle when they say, "What is sweeter than honey? What is stronger than a lion?" (14:18).

Three aspects of the anecdote about the bees and the honey in the lion's carcass merit attention. First, there are differences in the textual tradition. In the Hebrew text, the bees and the honey are in the lion's carcass or fallen body (*mappelet*). But in the Septuagint, whereas Samson turns aside to the lion's fallen body or carcass (*ptōma*: 14:8 LXX [A and B]), he finds the bees and the honey in the lion's mouth (*stoma*: 14:8 LXX [A and B]; 14:10 LXX [A]).[2] Similarly, the Vulgate has Samson see the lion's carcass (*cadaver*), but he finds the bees and a comb of

---

[1] Already in antiquity Samson's great strength prompted some to identify him with Hercules (see Augustine, *Civ.* 18.19).

[2] According to Alfred Rahlfs's "A Text" of the Septuagint of Judges, Samson takes the honey from the mouth of the lion (14:8) and places it in his own mouth (14:9), not in his hands (*Septuaginta, id est Vetus Testamentum graece iuxta LXX interpretes* [9th ed.; Stuttgart: Deutsche Bibelstiftung, 1935], 1:464). He apparently eats some of the honey and, despite having placed the honey in his mouth, gives some to his parents to eat. In 14:9, he does not tell his parents that he had taken the honey from the *hexis* of the lion. The word *hexis* here perhaps reflects the use of the term in medical circles to refer to the body's "system" (see, e.g., Athenaeus, *Deipn.* 2.45e, 59b) or now "fixed condition."

honey in the lion's mouth (*ore*). The mouth, of course, is part of the body, and in 14:9 Samson does not disclose to his parents that the honey had come from the lion's body (*corpore*). Josephus, by contrast, places the bees in the dead lion's chest (*stēthos*), and instead of having Samson take the honey into his hand and eat it, he has him take three honeycombs and give them to his Timnah bride as part of his wedding gifts to her (*Ant.* 5.288).

Second, the deviations from and additions to the Hebrew text represented by the Septuagint, the Vulgate, and Josephus are picked up in various ways in early Christian interpretation, with some new ideas added. The poet Prudentius, for example, devotes two quatrains of his *Dittochaeon* (17 and 18) to Samson, and in the first of these he says, "A lion tries to rend Samson, whose hair makes him invincible. He slays the wild beast, but from the lion's mouth flow streams of honey" (*Ditt.* 17). Further, Ambrose of Milan in his works gives slightly different depictions of what happens. In his treatise on the Holy Spirit, he says that Samson found the bees in the lion's body but the honey in its mouth, and that he gave the honey to his parents to eat (*Spir.* 2, Introduction 6). In *Epistulae* 19 (CSEL), by contrast, Samson finds a honeycomb in the lion's belly and gives it as a gift to his parents and the maiden, which Ambrose deemed fully appropriate, since "such gifts befit a bride" (*Ep.* 19.14).

Caesarius of Arles goes much further in two sermons that he preached on Samson. He seeks to acknowledge the shortcomings of Samson, yet to see in him aspects of a Christ figure. In Sermon 118, he argues, "Inasmuch as Samson performed virtues and miracles, he prefigured Christ, the head of the Church. When he acted prudently, he was an image of those who live justly in the Church, but when he was overtaken and acted carelessly, he represented those who are sinners in the Church" (*Serm.* 118.3). In Sermon 119, he takes the same Christianizing approach to the lion and the honey:

> Many of the fathers have spoken a great deal about this lion, beloved brethren, and all of them have said what is fitting and in accord with the facts. Some have said that the lion prefigured Christ our Lord. Truly, this is very appropriate, for to us Christ is a lion in whose mouth we found the food of honey after His death. What is sweeter than the word of God? Or what is stronger than His right hand? In whose mouth after death is

there food and bees, except His in whose word is the good of our salvation and the congregation of Gentiles? The lion can further be understood as the Gentiles who believed. First, it was a body of vanity, but is now the body of Christ in which the apostles like bees stored the honey of wisdom gathered from the dew of heaven and the flowers of divine grace. Thus, food came out of the mouth of the one who died; because nations which were as fierce as lions at first, accepted with a devout heart the word of God which they received, and produced the fruit of salvation (*Serm.* 119.1).

Third, the story of bees and honey associated with the carcass of a dead animal has certain similarities to Greco-Roman buogonia traditions, and a brief excursus on the traditions will serve to conclude this essay. The word "buogonia" or "bugonia" is derived from the Greek word *bougonēs*, which means "born of an ox" and was especially associated with the idea that bees were generated from the carcass of a cow. The origin of this theory is old, possibly Egyptian (Vergil, *Georg.* 4.287) or African in origin,[1] and in ancient Greece linked ultimately to the figure of Aristaus and thus to the cult of Apollo.[2] According to Eusebius (*Chron.* 1254), the eighth century epic poet Eumelus of Corinth wrote a work titled *Buogonia*, which, unfortunately, does not survive. According to Columella, the preSocratic philosopher Democritus of Abdera (born 460-457 BCE) was among those who "have recorded that bees can be generated at this same time of the year from a slain bullock" (*Rust.* 9.6). Columella attributes the same belief to Mago of Carthage (flourished 550-520 BCE), adding that Mago also "asserts that the same thing may be done from the bellies of oxen" (*Rust.* 9.6).

Despite this early origin, references to buogonia only become widespread during the Hellenistic and Roman periods, when the generation of bees was regarded as a well-recognized scientific aporia. Indeed, Aristotle begins his discussion of the generation of bees (*Gen. an.* 3.10, 759a9-761a2) with the declaration that this issue was a great

---

[1] Floris Overduin, *Nicander of Colophon's Theriaca: A Literary Commentary* (MnemoSup 374; Leiden: Brill, 2015), 460.

[2] See especially Vergil, *Georg.* 4.281, 315-17 and Haralampos V. Harissis and Anastasios V. Harissis, *Apiculture in the Prehistoric Aegean: Minoan and Mycenaean Symbols Revisited* (BARIS 1958; Oxford: John and Erica Hedges, 2009), 73-81.

puzzle (*Gen. an.* 3.10, 759a9), for which there were various explanations. He mentions the possibilities that bees were generated either spontaneously or by other animals (*Gen. an.* 3.10, 759a14), but he dismisses these solutions as impossible (*Gen. an.* 3.10, 759a25). In short, Aristotle has apparently heard about the theory of buogonia, but he does not mention it explicitly, not wanting "to include unobserved, and therefore unreliable, material."[1] He was wise to do so, since buogonia "is fictitious and belongs to the realm of folklore and paradoxography."[2]

The earliest literary reference to the buogonia tradition appears to be that of Philetas (Philitas) of Cos (late fourth–early third century BCE), who in a line from an uncertain work refers to bees as "born of bulls" (*bougeneas*).[3] Another early reference is by Theocritus of Syracuse (early third century BCE), who refers to bees as "sprung from a bull" (*Syrinx* 3: *tauropatōr*). A third early reference to oxen as the source for bees is the *Theriaca* of Nicander of Colophon, who flourished about 130 BCE. In line 741 of this didactic poem on poisonous animals and insects, he says, "For horses (are) the origin of wasps, but bulls of bees." He probably treated this theory more fully in his *Melissurgica*, which was devoted to bee-keeping and almost certainly served as a major source for Book 4 of Vergil's *Georgics*. A fourth early reference to buogonia is provided by Meleager of Gadara, who says, "The bees that the bull's carcass generates bethink them of their artful labors, and seated on the hive they build the fresh white loveliness of their many-celled comb" (*Anthologia palatina* 9.363,13–15).[4] A fifth reference is provided by Varro (116–27 BCE), who indicates how widespread the buogonia tradition was in the Greek-speaking world when he says, "It is from the putrefied body of this animal [the ox] that there spring the

---

[1] Overduin, *Nicander*, 406.
[2] Overduin, *Nicander*, 406.
[3] "Frag. 22," *Collectanea Alexandria* (ed. J. U. Powell; Oxford: Clarendon, 1925). The same Greek word is used by Bianor of Bithynia (first century BCE–first century CE) in an epigram preserved in *Anth. pal.* 9.548.
[4] Callimachus, "frag. 383.4," *Callimachus* (ed. Rudolf Pfeiffer; Oxford: Clarendon, 1949), 1:308 = "frag. 254.4" *Supplementum Hellenisticum* (Hugh Lloyd-Jones and Peter Parsons; TK 11; Berlin: Walter de Gruyter, 1983), 101], uses the word *bougenēs* of Danaus, regarding Io as the cow who gave him birth. On this text, see Susan Stephens, "Whose Rituals in Ink?" *Rituals in Ink: A Conference on Religion and Literary Production in Ancient Rome* (eds. Alesandro Barchiesi, Jörg Rüpke, and Susan Stephens; PAB 10; Munich: Steiner, 2004), 157–60, esp. 159–60.

sweetest bees, those honey-mothers from which the Greeks therefore call bees 'the ox-sprung' (*bougeneis*)" (*Rust.* 2.5.5; see also 3.16.4).

It was Vergil (70–19 BCE) who, in Book 4 of his *Georgics* (4.281–314), gives buogonia its fullest early literary treatment:

> First is chosen a place, small and straitened for this very purpose. This they confine with a narrow roof of tiles and close walls, and towards the four winds add four windows with slanting light. Then a bullock is sought, one just arching his horns on a brow of two summer's growth. Struggle as he will, both his nostrils are stopped up, and the breath of his mouth; then he is beaten to death, and his flesh is pounded to a pulp through the unbroken hide. As thus he lies, they leave him in his prison, and strew beneath his sides broken boughs, thyme, and fresh cassia. This is done when the zephyrs begin to stir the waves, before ever the meadows blush with their fresh hues, before the chattering swallow hangs her nest from the rafters. Meantime the moisture, warming in the softened bones, ferments, and creatures of wondrous wise to view, footless at first, soon with buzzing wings as well, swarm together, and more and more essay the light air, until, like a shower pouring from summer clouds, they burst forth, or like arrows from the string's rebound, when the light-armed Parthians enter on the opening battle. (*Georg.* 4.295–314)[1]

After Vergil, and thanks partly to his influence, references to bougonia become increasingly common. What this widespread Greco-Roman tradition shares with the Samson saga is the belief that bees are generated from the carcass of a dead animal. It differs dramatically in the animal connected with the generation of bees — in the Samson saga, it is a dead lion, not a dead ox, which produces the swarm of bees that Samson finds. There is, to my knowledge, no Greek or Roman text that links bees to dead lions.

---

[1] For the bougonia tradition prior to Vergil, see especially Kenneth F. Kitchell, "The Origins of Vergil's Myth of the Bugonia," *Daidalikon: Studies in Memory of Raymond V. Schoder, S.J.* (ed. Robert F. Sutton; Wauconda: Bolchazy-Carducci, 1989), 193–206.

The Sword of Solomon

The Subversive Underbelly of Solomon's Judgment of the Two Prostitutes

Craig Evan Anderson

The book of Kings provides a textured portrayal of Solomon, intermixing positive and negative material about him.[1] Although scholars universally accept the damning nature of the conclusion of Solomon's reign (1 Kgs 11), there is wide disagreement regarding how scholars assess the portrayal of Solomon in the *Thronfolge* (1 Kgs 1-2) and Solomon's reign proper (1 Kgs 3-10).[2]

---

[1] See, e.g., Gary N. Knoppers, *Two Nations under God: The Deuteronomistic History of Solomon and the Dual Monarchies, Volume 1: The Reign of Solomon and the Rise of Jeroboam* (HSM 52; Atlanta: Scholars, 1993), 4-5, 8.

[2] Throughout the twentieth century most scholars interpreted the negative material about David and Solomon as vestiges of tenth century BCE court reporting that scribes later overlaid with propagandistic material in order to whitewash the story of the founding of the Davidic-Solomonic dynasty following the theories of Leonhard Rost, *The Succession to the Throne of David* (BSHT 1; Sheffield: Almond, 1982); tr. of *Die Überlieferung von der Thronnachfolge Davids* (BWA(N)T 42; Stuttgart: W. Kohlhammer, 1926). For an earlier and much briefer expression of the *Thronfolge* theory, see Julius Wellhausen, *Die Composition des Hexateuchs und der historischen Bücher des Alten Testaments* (Berlin: de Gruyter, 1876; repr., Saarbrücken: Südwestdeutscher Verlag für Hochschulschriften, 2009), 255-59; see also Gerhard von Rad, "The Beginning of Historical Writing in Ancient Israel," *The Problem of the Hexateuch and other Essays*, (tr. E. W. Trueman Dicken; New York: McGraw-Hill, 1966), 205-21; Roger N. Whybray, *The Succession Narrative: A Study of II Samuel 9-20; I Kings 1 and 2* (SBT 2/9; London: SCM, 1968), 11-16; and Gene M. Tucker, *Form Criticism of the Old Testament* (Philadelphia: Fortress, 1971), 36. However, in recent years, the theory of a *Thronfolge* document underlying much of 2 Sam 9-20; 1 Kgs 1-2 has come under serious attack; see esp. Serge Frolov, "Succession Narrative: A 'Document' or a Phantom?" *JBL* 121 (2002): 81-104; for negative readings of Solomon, see Lienhard Delekat, "Tendenz und Theologie der David-Salomo-Erzahlung," *Das ferne und nahe Wort* (ed. Fritz Maass; BZAW 105; Berlin: Töpelmann, 1967), 26-36; Marvin A. Sweeney, "The Critique of Solomon in the Josianic Edition of the Deuteronomistic History," *JBL* 114 (1995): 607-22; Marvin A. Sweeney, *King Josiah of Judah: The Lost Messiah of Israel* (New York: Oxford University Press, 2001); and Sweeney, *I & II Kings: A Commentary* (OTL; Louisville: Westminster John Knox, 2007). See also François Langlamet, "Pour ou contre Salomon? Le rédaction prosalomonienne de 1 Rois I-II," *RB* 83 (1976): 321-79, 481-528; J. Daniel Hays, "Has the Narrator Come to Praise Solomon or to Bury Him? Narrative Subtlety in 1 Kings 1-11," *JSOT* 28 (2003): 149-74; Eric A. Seibert, "Solomon's Execution Orders (1 Kgs 2:13-46): Political Propaganda or Scribal Subversion?" *Proceedings Eastern*

Despite the variety of views concerning whether the book of Kings portrays Solomon positively or negatively, Solomon's famous judgment of the two prostitutes (1 Kgs 3:16-28) stands as one of the episodes most resilient to critique. Most scholars regard this story as absolutely laudatory toward Solomon as the king solves a seemingly unsolvable case[1] and, consequently, it serves as an exemplar of wisdom.[2] However, there are still some who detect a subversive undercurrent within this story.[3]

The challenge that Solomon faces with the two prostitutes is the interchangeability of the women. It is exceedingly difficult to find any external factors indicating which of the two women is the true mother of the living baby. The narrative highlights the challenge of this judicial quandary through its use of chiasmus in 1 Kgs 3:22, following the initial presentation of the problem.[4] The rhetorical effect of this chiastic structure is to balance their testimony, demonstrating the evenness of their claims. Notably, King Solomon responds to the women by quoting the claims of the women, replicating its chiastic structure (1 Kgs 3:23). By replying in this way, Solomon acknowledges the balance of their claims, demonstrating the difficulty of the case.[5] As such, the text invites the reader into the narrative as if the reader were a court attendant, an onlooker amidst a crowd puzzling over a solution

---

Great Lakes and Midwest Biblical Societies 24 (2004): 141-52; and Seibert, *Subversive Scribes and the Solomonic Narrative: A Rereading of 1 Kings 1-11* (LHBOTS 436; New York: T & T Clark, 2006).

[1] See, e.g., Simon J. DeVries, *1 Kings* (WBC 12; Waco, TX: Word Books, 1985), 58 and Richard D. Nelson, *First and Second Kings* (IBC; Atlanta: John Knox, 1987) 38-39.

[2] The אז particle followed by the imperfect verb that introduces this unit (1 Kgs 3:16-28) indicates that it serves to illuminate the previous unit in which Solomon receives divine wisdom (1 Kgs 3:4-15). For an analogue, see, e.g., the Song of the Sea (Exod 15:1). Isaac Rabinowitz, "'Āz followed by Imperfect Verb-Form in Preterite Contexts: A Redactional Device in Biblical Hebrew," *VT* 34 (1984): 53-62; DeVries, *1 Kings*, 57; and Sweeney, *I & II Kings*, 81.

[3] See, e.g., Sweeney, who notes that the fact that women are prostitutes "trivializes Solomon as a monarchy who spends his time resolving quarrels between prostitutes" (*I & II Kings*, 82). Moreover, Sweeney states, "from the perspective of Deuteronomy and the DtrH, Solomon's assumption of judicial power is illegal."

[4] Burke O. Long, *1 Kings, with an Introduction to Historical Literature* (FOTL 9; Grand Rapids: William B. Eerdmans, 1984), 69 and Nelson, *First and Second Kings*, 38.

[5] Nelson claims that "the repetitious dialogue has the effect of tiring and bemusing the reader" (*First and Second Kings*, 38). Although I cannot agree with Nelson's assertion that the repetition is "tiring," I think that it is intentionally dizzying in order to immerse the reader into the seemingly unsolvable quandary.

to a seemingly impossible problem and anxiously waiting to see how Solomon will solve the dilemma.

In an important article on this episode, Gary Rendsburg has convincingly demonstrated that, if read very carefully, one can see that the narrative provides subtle clues indicating that the plaintiff is in fact the liar.[1] First, Rendsburg notes that the story faithfully refers to the plaintiff (Woman A) first as האשה האחת ("the one woman") and thereafter as זאת ("this" one) whereas it refers to the defendant (Woman B) as האשה האחרת ("the other woman"), culminating at the point in v. 26 in which "this" (זאת) woman agrees to divide the child.[2] Second, Rendsburg notes that the voices of the two women consistently alternate forming a chiastic structure, regardless of whether they themselves are speaking directly or Solomon is quoting them, so that the last woman to speak (v. 26b), the woman agreeing to divide the child, is also the first woman to speak (vv. 17-21), i.e. the plaintiff.

In addition to Rendsburg's two arguments, there is yet a third means by which the story indicates that the plaintiff is the liar: her argument before Solomon is riddled with illogicalities and

---

[1] Gary A. Rendsburg, "The Guilty Party in 1 Kings III 16-28," *VT* 48 (1998): 534-41. As Rendsburg notes, this conclusion runs opposite of the assumptions of most readers (539). See, e.g., Nelson, *First and Second Kings*, 38. Moshe Garsiel, in his article, "Revealing and Concealing as a Narrative Strategy in Solomon's Judgment (1 Kings 3:16-28)," argues for the opposite conclusion of Rendsburg; i.e., Garsiel contends that the plaintiff is the true mother (*CBQ* 64 [2002]: 229-47). His argument essentially rests on two points: First, Garsiel notes that the extended speech that the plaintiff offers casts the plaintiff in a positive light; second, Garsiel detects commonalities in speech patterns linking the plaintiff to the true mother and the defendant to the liar. Neither of these arguments is persuasive. Concerning Garsiel's first argument, there is no question that the plaintiff paints herself positively and the defendant negatively. And, Garsiel correctly recognizes that typically biblical narratives utilize a character's speech in order to enlist the reader's sympathy toward that character. However, the rhetorical skill of the plaintiff does not validate her claim. On the contrary, this is precisely one of the key elements that makes Solomon's display of wisdom impressive in this case—he is able to see through the plaintiff's farce. Contra Garsiel, what we find in 1 Kgs 3:16-28 is that the woman in the greatest need is the more submissive and impassioned in her plea (at first, the liar; later, the true mother). In the opening argument, the lying plaintiff is distressed at the recent loss of her baby, leading her to plead submissively (addressing the king with בִּי אֲדֹנִי in 3:17) for the king's intervention, whereas the true mother is less in need (content with her baby) and speaks tersely. Upon the king's judgment, the situation is reversed: The true mother is then in distress at the prospect of losing her baby and, consequently, she becomes more desperate and submissive (addressing the king with בִּי אֲדֹנִי in 3:26) of the two, whereas the lying plaintiff now speaks tersely, satisfied by the king's decision to split the child in half.

[2] Rendsburg, "The Guilty Party," 536-37.

inconsistencies.[1] For example, many have asked, how could the plaintiff know what the other woman was doing while the plaintiff remained soundly asleep?[2] Although Rendsburg cites this third argument, he rejects it, claiming that "it places the reader in the peculiar position of out-Solomoning Solomon, that is, by utilizing the same information that the wise king and judge had at his disposal to solve the case, and that certainly cannot be the author's intent. Quite the contrary, the story's intent is to show the singularity of Solomon's wisdom."[3] Furthermore, Rendsburg states that the notion that the reader would detect the problems within the plaintiff's story "removes all the punch from Solomon's famous words קחו לי חרב, 'bring me a sword' (v. 24) and גזרו את הילד, 'cut the child' (v. 25), and this too cannot have been the author's intent."[4] Rendsburg's analysis prompts the question, what does the verbal use of "Solomon" connote? For Rendsburg, it seems to express Solomon's capacity "to solve the case." However, I think that assumption is unfounded. Although Rendsburg is correct in that this "story's intent is to show the singularity of Solomon's wisdom," he misunderstands Solomon's wisdom, confusing it with Solomon's ability to determine the guilty party in the case of these two women. In the context of the books of Samuel and Kings, Solomon's wisdom carries other connotations, central to this story that Rendsburg overlooks. In this work, I intend to demonstrate that "the singularity of Solomon's wisdom" rests not in Solomon's *ability* to solve the case, but rather the *manner* in which he does it.

In his 1968 monograph, *The Succession Narrative*, Roger N. Whybray showcased the centrality of wisdom within 2 Sam 9-20 and 1 Kgs 1-2.[5] In fact, Whybray contended that there is such a great

---

[1] E. and G. Leibowitz, "Solomon's Judgment," *BM* 35 (1989-90): 242-44; Ellen van Wolde, "Who Guides Whom? Embeddedness and Perspective in Biblical Hebrew and in 1 Kings 3:16-28," *JBL* 114 (1995): 623-42; and Rendsburg, "The Guilty Party," 535.

[2] Van Wolde, "Who Guides Whom?" 629-30; Rendsburg, "The Guilty Party," 535; and Mordechai Cogan, *I Kings: A New Translation with Introduction and Commentary* (AB 10; New York: Doubleday, 2001), 194-95.

[3] Rendsburg, "The Guilty Party," 535.

[4] Rendsburg, "The Guilty Party," 535.

[5] Whybray, *The Succession Narrative*, 56-95. For other works highlighting the importance of wisdom in this material see Rolf A. Carlson, *David, the Chosen King: A Traditio-Historical Approach to the Second Book of Samuel* (tr. Eric J. Sharpe and Stanley Rudman; Stockholm: Almqvist & Wiksell, 1964); Joseph Blenkinsopp, "Theme and Motif in the Succession History (2 Sam xi 2ff) and the Yahwist Corpus," *Volume Du Congrès:*

correlation between the Succession Narrative and the Book of Proverbs that we should conclude that the author of the Succession Narrative "was himself a wisdom teacher in the sense that he set out deliberately to illustrate specific proverbial teaching" throughout the narrative of 2 Sam 9-20 and 1 Kgs 1-2.[1]

In accordance with Whybray's observation that wisdom constitutes a dominant theme throughout 2 Sam 9-20 and 1 Kgs 1-2, it seems proper for us to read 1 Kgs 3, which almost exclusively focuses upon Solomon's wisdom, in the light of the wisdom-saturated material that contextually precedes it (i.e. 2 Sam 9-1 Kgs 2).[2] Whybray presents a compelling set of data demonstrating thematic and conceptual connections between the (so-called) Succession Narrative and the Book of Proverbs. However, he does not seem to fully recognize that the two texts operate from differing perspectives regarding the nature of "wisdom" (חכמה). Although the Book of Proverbs offers a glowing presentation of "wisdom" (חכמה), the same cannot be said for the David-Solomon narratives.

First, the counsel given by the wise throughout the books of Samuel and Kings tends to be questionable at best; it is immoral and foolish at worst. There are three characters that the narrator explicitly labels "wise" (חכם) or offer "wisdom" (חכמה) in the Book of Samuel: Jonadab (2 Sam 13:3), the Woman of Tekoa (2 Sam 14:2), and the Woman of Abel of Beth-maacah (2 Sam 20:22). There are two characters that offer "counsel" (עצה) in the Book of Samuel: Ahithophel and Hushai.[3] In most of these cases, the so-called "wisdom" can be difficult to detect: Jonadab facilitates Amnon's rape of his sister, which leads to Amnon's death;[4] the Woman of Tekoa is merely an actress, parroting

---

Genève, 1965 (VTSup 15; Leiden: Brill, 1966), 44-57; David M. Gunn, *The Story of King David: Genre and Interpretation* (JSOTSup 6; Sheffield: University of Sheffield Press, 1978); and Carole Fontaine, "The Bearing of Wisdom on the Shape of 2 Samuel 11-12 and 1 Kings 3," *JSOT* 34 (1986): 61-77. See also Moshe Weinfeld, *Deuteronomy and the Deuteronomic School* (Winona Lake, IN: Eisenbrauns, 1992), 244-81.

[1] Whybray, *The Succession Narrative*, 95.

[2] Note Fontaine's article, "The Bearing of Wisdom," which juxtaposes David's folly in 2 Sam 11-12 with Solomon's wisdom in 1 Kgs 3.

[3] See Whybray, *The Succession Narrative*, 57-58, for the close connection between "wisdom" (חכמה) and "counsel" (עצה).

[4] See esp. Baruch Halpern, *David's Secret Demons: Messiah, Murderer, Traitor, King* (Grand Rapids: William B. Eerdmans, 2001), 87-88. In *1, 2 Samuel* (NAC; Nashville: Broadman & Holman, 1996), Robert D. Bergen notes that חָכָם is "the term normally

the words that Joab places in her mouth, yielding essentially no original thought of her own;[1] Ahithophel advises Absalom to commit public incest;[2] and Hushai knowingly feeds Absalom bad advice.

It is only the wisdom of the Woman of Abel of Beth-maacah that seems to be truly moral and prudent; she saves lives, nullifying another potential civil war, by plotting the execution of a dissident.[3] However, this leads to the second characteristic of "wisdom" and "counsel" in Second Samuel: it is violent. Once again, "wise" Jonadab orchestrates the rape of Tamar (2 Sam 13:1-6); the Wise Woman of Tekoa plays a central role in retrieving Absalom back into Israel (2 Sam 14), which (in the very next chapter) leads to a civil war; the dueling counselors, Hushai and Ahithophel, offer conflicting warfare stratagems (2 Sam 17:1-14); the rejection of Ahithophel's counsel leads to his suicide (2 Sam 17:23); finally, as was mentioned, the Woman of Abel of Beth-macaah devises the wise plan to decapitate a man and throw his severed head over a city wall (2 Sam 20).

Based upon this background, it then becomes no surprise that David predicates his dying instructions for Solomon to execute two

---

rendered in the positive sense as 'wise.' Yet, as events would soon demonstrate, Jonadab's wisdom was, 'earthly, unspiritual, of the devil' (Jas 3:15; cf. also Jer 4:22; I Cor 2:6)" (380). Whybray cites Jonadab in 2 Sam 13:3-5 in order to show "that 'wisdom' is a purely intellectual and morally neutral quality" (*The Succession Narrative*, 58).

[1] Whybray claims that "the story in II Sam 14 of Joab's use of the woman of Tekoa is really a story of Joab's wisdom rather than that of the woman: Joab applied his wisdom 'in order to change the course of affairs' (v. 20)" (*The Succession Narrative*, 59). However, Whybray's claim runs against the grain of the biblical text. The story of Joab and the Woman of Tekoa plainly labels the woman אִשָּׁה חֲכָמָה, "a wise woman" (2 Sam 14:2); it does not label Joab as wise. Consequently, Whybray denies the overt claims of the biblical text based upon his assumption that he must harmonize the application of חָכְמָה, "wisdom," in the David-Solomon story with its usage in the Book of Proverbs.

[2] Ahithophel's recommendation that Absalom should commandeer David's harem clearly is politically expedient (Gunn, *The Story of King David*, 116). Nevertheless, it certainly raises moralistic concerns in tension with Deuteronomic instruction (Ernst Würthwein, *Die Erzählung von der Thronfolge Davids — theologische oder politische Geschichtsschreibung?* [ThSt 115; Zürich: Theologischer Verlag, 1974]).

[3] P. Kyle McCarter, Jr. (*II Samuel: A New Translation with Introduction and Commentary* [AB 9; New York: Doubleday, 1984], 431) building upon the observations of Charles Conroy (*Absalom Absalom!* [AnBib 81; 1978; repr., Rome: Editrice Pontificio Istituto Biblico, 2006], 142), demonstrates a series of inverted parallels between the wise woman of Tekoa in 2 Sam 14 and the wise woman of Abel of Maacah in 2 Sam 20: whereas the wise woman of Tekoa follows the plan of Joab to ultimately cultivate a rebellion for the sake of one man, Joab follows the plan of the wise woman of Abel of Maacah to sacrifice one man for the sake of quelling a rebellion.

men, Joab and Shimei (for highly questionable reasons),[1] upon the premise that Solomon should "act according to your wisdom," וְעָשִׂיתָ כְחָכְמָתֶךָ (1 Kgs 2:6) and kill these men "for you are a wise man," כִּי אִישׁ חָכָם אָתָּה (1 Kgs 2:9). We then witness the manifestation of this "wisdom" in the bloodbath that follows throughout the remainder of 1 Kgs 2 as Adonijah, Joab, and Shimei are all butchered according to the execution orders of "wise" Solomon.

Given the disturbingly violent definition of "wisdom" (חכמה) that 2 Sam 13-1 Kgs 2 has crafted, it then becomes somewhat troubling for the reader to learn in 1 Kgs 3:4-15 that Solomon will now be the "wisest" of people.[2] We see an application of Solomon's wisdom in the judgment of the two prostitutes (1 Kgs 3:16-28), which immediately follows his divine acquisition of superlative wisdom (1 Kgs 3:4-15). Once again, contra Rendsburg, the notion that the case of the two prostitutes may be solvable *in no way* "removes all the punch from Solomon's famous words קחו לי חרב, 'bring me a sword' (v. 24)."[3] The punch for his call for a sword lies in shock and horror of the question (in the light of the massacre of the previous chapter) of whether Solomon's violent wisdom now extends to a readiness to chop babies in half.

Notably, all of the violence that we see throughout 2 Sam 13-1 Kgs 2 is framed by "the sword." Upon learning from Joab's messenger that some Israelite soldiers died while executing David's plan to have Uriah killed in the context of the Ammonite war, David returns an encouraging message back to Joab, "Do not let this matter trouble you for the sword devours now one and now another," אַל־יֵרַע בְּעֵינֶיךָ אֶת־הַדָּבָר הַזֶּה כִּי־כָזֹה וְכָזֶה תֹּאכַל הֶחָרֶב (2 Sam 11:25). In the next chapter, David learns from Nathan that he will pay a price for his blasé attitude toward the devouring sword as Nathan delivers a prophetic judgment from YHWH stating, because David "struck down Uriah the Hittite with the sword," אֵת אוּרִיָּה הַחִתִּי הִכִּיתָ בַחֶרֶב, killing him with "the sword of the Ammonites," בְּחֶרֶב בְּנֵי עַמּוֹן (2 Sam 12:9), "the sword shall never depart

---

[1] Sweeney, *I & II Kings*, 60.
[2] Although it is hard to deny that 1 Kgs 3:4-15 portrays Solomon positively when read in isolation, scholars have noted that negative elements emerge when we read it within its greater literary context; see Sweeney, *I & II Kings*, 79-81 and Seibert, *Subversive Scribes*, 164-66.
[3] Rendsburg, "The Guilty Party," 535.

from your house," לֹא־תָסוּר חֶרֶב מִבֵּיתְךָ עַד־עוֹלָם (2 Sam 12:10). This pronouncement drives the narrative, establishing a trajectory of violence that features the murders of David's sons, Amnon and Absalom, and ultimately culminates in Solomon's slaughter of Adonijah, David's son, and Joab, David's nephew and commander (1 Kgs 2). Thus, in addition to the shock of the mere violence of it, the "punch" of Solomon's call to "bring me a sword," קְחוּ לִי־חָרֶב (1 Kgs 3:24) also rests in his echoing of the curse lingering over the House of David.

Finally, Solomon's judgment to "divide the living child into two," (גְּזְרוּ אֶת־הַיֶּלֶד הַחַי לִשְׁנָיִם 1 Kgs 3:25) seems hauntingly reminiscent of David's sloppy justice in the land dispute between Mephibosheth and Ziba, in which, without carefully weighing the facts, David lazily decides: "I have spoken: You and Ziba will divide the field," אָמַרְתִּי אַתָּה וְצִיבָא תַּחְלְקוּ אֶת־הַשָּׂדֶה (2 Sam 19:30 [=Eng 2 Sam 19:29]).[1] David's casual proposal to "divide the field" without serious concern for rightful ownership is ironic given that it is contextually situated between Absalom's civil war (2 Sam 15-18) and Sheba ben Bichri's abortive attempt at a secession (2 Sam 20), i.e. two disputes over governance of land. David's crude handing of justice is especially significant given the fact that Absalom predicated his rebellion upon David's ineptitude for rendering justice (2 Sam 15:1-6). Similarly, it would be reasonable to consider that Sheba's grievances reflect the concerns of a disaffected portion of his fellow Benjaminite tribesmen who, in the case of Shimei ben Gera, have charged David with unjustly attaining the throne by the shedding of Saulide blood, or in the case of Mephibosheth, have received an unsatisfying judicial rendering.[2]

As scholars have long observed, Sheba's rebel cry, "We have no portion in David, no share in the son of Jesse! Everyone to your tents, O Israel!" אֵין־לָנוּ חֵלֶק בְּדָוִד וְלֹא נַחֲלָה־לָנוּ בְּבֶן־יִשַׁי אִישׁ לְאֹהָלָיו יִשְׂרָאֵל (2 Sam 20:1) matches nearly verbatim Jeroboam's call for secession, "What

---

[1] For an argument that Mephibosheth is the righteous party and Ziba is the unrighteous party in their dispute, see Jan P. Fokkelman, *Narrative Art and Poetry in the Books of Samuel: A Full Interpretation Based on Stylistic and Structural Analyses* (SSN 20; Assen: Van Gorcum, 1981), 1:23-40.

[2] The deferential behavior of both Shimei and Mephibosheth as they welcome King David back into the land (2 Sam 19) following his decisive victory over Absalom's forces does not tarnish the validity of Benjaminite grievances. We could safely question their humble posturing as tokens of mere expediency.

share do we have in David? We have no inheritance in the son of Jesse. To your tents, O Israel!" מַה־לָּנוּ חֵלֶק בְּדָוִד וְלֹא נַחֲלָה בְּבֶן־יִשַׁי לְאֹהָלֶיךָ יִשְׂרָאֵל (1 Kgs 12:16).[1] Thus, David's inability to provide justice, exemplified by his decision simply to "divide the field," seems to aggravate the political fissures that will eventually cleave the nation into two (1 Kgs 12). Along those lines, many commentators have noticed Solomon's proposal to split the baby as foreshadowing of the eventual splitting of the nation.[2]

Collectively these observations suggest that Solomon's call for a sword is much more than a dramatic device that he implements to solve a difficult judicial case. Indeed, as we have seen, the sword is not even necessary for determining the guilty party. Although the sword provides a theatrical flourish that leaves Solomon's audience stunned by his witty solution to the problem, it also serves as a signal for the reader to appraise carefully the manner of Solomon's response in the light of themes laced throughout the greater narrative context.[3] As such, the sword of Solomon serves as a chilling reminder that, even amidst the most impressive displays, the Davidic-Solomonic monarchy was founded upon injustice and blood.

---

[1] See, e.g., Hans W. Hertzberg, *I & II Samuel* (OTL; Philadelphia: Westminster, 1964), 371; McCarter, *II Samuel*, 423; Nelson, *First and Second Kings*, 79; and Sweeney, *I & II Kings*, 171.

[2] Knoppers, *Two Nations*, 136-37, notes a series of parallels between 1 Kgs 3 and 1 Kgs 11, in which items initially introduced positively reappear later negatively: e.g., Solomon's love for YHWH (3:3) coupled with his love for women (11:1-6), Solomon's sacrifices to YHWH (3:3) coupled with his sacrifices to foreign gods (11:8), YHWH appearance to Solomon (3:4-14) coupled with a reference of YHWH's appearance to Solomon (11:9). Thus Solomon's clever proposal to cut the baby into two (3:25) coupled with YHWH's decision to split the land of Israel into two (11:9-13) seems to participate within this series of parallels.

[3] One might be tempted to argue that Solomon's actions in 1 Kgs 3:16-28 redeem the past. This is essentially the argument that Fontaine, "The Bearing of Wisdom," 68-69, makes for the correlation between 2 Sam 11-12 and 1 Kgs 3. Nevertheless, what would be the outcome of such redemption in the light of the failure Solomon's reign within the Book of Kings? For analyses of Solomon's failure and its significance for the book of Kings, see esp. Sweeney, "The Critique of Solomon;" Sweeney, *King Josiah of Judah*; and Sweeney, *I & II Kings*; cf. Seibert, "Solomon's Execution Orders" and Seibert, *Subversive Scribes*.

Two Mothers and Two Sons
Reading 1 Kings 3:16-28 as a Parody on Solomon's Coup (1 Kings 1-2)

Hyun Chul Paul Kim

Though Martin Noth profoundly championed the role of the Deuteronomistic historian as the interpretive redactor rather than mechanical compiler, many scholars agree that the Deuteronomistic History (DtrH) is a compendium of complex redactional strata.[1] Hence, it is no surprise that we find pro-monarchy and anti-monarchy layers side-by-side (1 Sam 8-12).[2] Likewise, the Elijah and Elisha cycles stand out as counternarratives to the inherent monarchical system.[3] Similarly, the golden age of Solomon's regime contains both positive and negative accounts. The present form of the Solomon narrative (1 Kgs 1-11) is thus commonly seen to portray the transition of King Solomon's extraordinary wisdom and governance, culminating in his construction of the temple (1 Kgs 3:4-8:66) but then gradually decaying into his wealth, intermarriages, and idolatry (1 Kgs 9:1-11:43).[4]

---

* A Claremont legend goes like this: An M.Div. student and a Ph.D. student were bragging. The former said, "Sweeney treats me like I am the only advisee he has." Then the latter replied, "I thought I was the only one he has." Rabbi Alum concluded, "It is neither legend nor folktale, but an ongoing historical fact." It is a great honor to contribute to a Festschrift for Professor Sweeney, an internationally renowned scholar and down-to-earth caring human being. *Todah rabbah* for teaching me by showing what mentorship and leadership should be like with your genuine care, integrity, and encouragement!

[1] Martin Noth, *The Deuteronomistic History* (2nd ed.; JSOTSup 15; Sheffield: JSOT Press, 1981).

[2] Thomas C. Römer, *The So-Called Deuteronomistic History: A Sociological, Historical and Literary Introduction* (London: T & T Clark, 2005): "The present arrangement of 1 Sam. 8-12 reveals an ambiguous attitude to the institution of monarchy" (143).

[3] Cameron B. R. Howard, "1 and 2 Kings," *Women's Bible Commentary* (eds. C. A. Newsom, S. H. Ringe, and J. E. Lapsley; 3rd ed.; Louisville: Westminster John Knox, 2012), 164-79: "At the same time, the prophetic legends provide an effective counternarrative to monarchic profligacy" (172).

[4] Whereas the prevalent view has been to consider 1 Kgs 1-10 as favorable to Solomon and 1 Kgs 11 as negative, recent scholars propose different distinctions. For example, on 1 Kgs 3-8 as positive and 1 Kgs 9:10-11:43 as negative, see Thomas C.

The present study proposes to read the episode of Solomon's wise jurisdiction (1 Kgs 3:16-28) as a parable-like critique of Solomon's bloody coup (1 Kgs 1-2).[1] The subtle yet interrelated clues between the two episodes compare and contrast the two queen/prostitute mothers and two royal/baby sons (1 Kgs 1-2). Beneath the surface depictions of a model king, the story, from the very beginning, contains subversive voices that criticize the dangers of power in a monarchy, where royals easily wield the sword, while a prostitute possesses genuine heart and wisdom.[2]

Comparison between 1 Kings 1-2 and 1 Kgs 3:16-28

Beyond the adjacent placement, 1 Kgs 3:16-28 contains subtle yet notable linguistic and thematic allusions to 1 Kgs 1-2. First of all, there are *two mothers* as key characters in our text. Although they are depicted as prostitutes, they are also mothers. The rivalry between these two prostitute mothers mirrors the implicit rivalry between the two queen mothers — Haggith (1 Kgs 1:5; cf. 2 Sam 3:4) and Bathsheba (1 Kgs 1:11; cf. 2 Sam 11:3; 12:24). Admittedly, in 1 Kgs 1-2, Haggith the mother of Adonijah does not play a major part, whereas Bathsheba the mother of Solomon plays a significant role in securing Solomon's heirship.[3] In the end, Solomon gets rid of Adonijah (1 Kgs 2:25) and takes the kingdom in his hand (1 Kgs 2:46). The tension between the two queens results in a son dying while the other rises to the throne. Likewise, the two prostitutes claim to "live in the same house" (1 Kgs

---

Römer, "The Case of the Book of Kings," *Deuteronomy-Kings as Emerging Authoritative Books: A Conversation* (ed. Diana V. Edelman; Atlanta: SBL Press, 2014), 187-201, here 193; on 1 Kgs 3:3-9:23 as positive and 1 Kgs 9:26-11:40 as negative, see Marc Zvi Brettler, "The Structure of 1 Kings 1-11," *JSOT* 49 (1991): 87-97.

[1] First Kings 1-2, in the final form, functions as a hinge, dovetailing the Succession Narrative (2 Samuel 9-1 Kgs 2) and the Solomon narrative (1 Kgs 1-11). Redactionally, our text (1 Kgs 3:16-28) may have originally circulated as a popular folktale. See Jerome T. Walsh, *1 Kings* (BOSHNP; Collegeville, MN: Liturgical Press, 1996), 78; Choon-Leong Seow, "The First and Second Books of Kings," *The New Interpreter's Bible* (eds. L. E. Keck et al.; Nashville: Abingdon, 1999), 3:42-43; and Volkmar Fritz, *1 & 2 Kings* (tr. Anselm Hagedorn; CC; Minneapolis: Fortress, 2003), 42-43.

[2] For pertinent proposals, see Lyle Eslinger, *Into the Hands of the Living God* (JSOTSup 84; Sheffield: Almond, 1989), 123-76.

[3] Consider the conjecture of Beverly W. Cushman ("The Politics of the Royal Harem and the Case of Bat-Sheba," *JSOT* 30 [2006]: 327-43, here 337-38, that even Haggith assumed the role of the Great Lady for Adonijah in their palace at En-Rogel (1 Kgs 1:9).

3:17). The two queens may have lived at one point, or at least figuratively, in the same royal harem. Just as Queen Bathsheba "went to the king in his room" (1 Kgs 1:15; cf. 1 Kgs 2:19), so the "two women who were prostitutes came to the king" (1 Kgs 3:16).

Here, readers may detect an element of secrecy. In the case of heirship to David's throne, there appear to be many witnesses involved. However, the text makes it possible to retain suspicions as to whether King David actually designated a successor. In fact, when Bathsheba reminds David of his alleged prior appointment of a successor, Nathan's promise to reassert her claim makes its validity puzzling (1 Kgs 1:14, 22–27).[1] Readers are left wondering whose words are true: Adonijah's, Nathan's, or David's. Similarly, the anonymous prostitute's report reveals ambivalence and hiddenness. As to the tragic death of one child, the reporting prostitute states, "there was no stranger with us, only the two of us were in the house" (1 Kgs 3:18). No eyewitness is available. In fact, the text is unclear as to which woman is speaking in the conversations: "one woman" (1 Kgs 3:17), "this woman" (1 Kgs 3:18), "the other woman" (1 Kgs 3:22), or "this (first) woman" (1 Kgs 3:22).[2] Moreover, readers may wonder how the woman who makes the initial report to the king (1 Kgs 3:17-21) knows the entire incident, whether because she recognizes her living son or because she is the one who committed the crime in secret.

Second, both texts depict life-and-death dealings with the *two sons* of (rival) mothers. In both texts, one son is dead, while the other becomes the target of conflict. In 1 Kgs 1-2, the sons are named— Adonijah the "very handsome man" (1 Kgs 1:6; cf. Absalom in 2 Sam 14:25) and Solomon. Adonijah, with whom Joab and Abiathar side (1 Kgs 1:7), claims to be the heir. In opposition, Solomon, with whom

---

[1] See Joyce Willis, Andrew Pleffer, and Stephen Llewelyn, "Conversation in the Succession Narrative of Solomon," *VT* 61 (2011): 133-47: "The fabricated premise of the whole ploy is further indicated by Nathan's rehearsal entry after Bathsheba to confirm the alleged promise that Solomon would succeed as king" (137) and Timo Veijola, "Solomon: Bathsheba's Firstborn," *Reconsidering Israel and Judah: Recent Studies on the Deuteronomistic History* (eds. G. N. Knoppers and J. G. McConville; Winona Lake, IN: Eisenbrauns, 2000), 340-57: "With a masterly trick, Nathan and Bathsheba dupe the age-enfeebled David … by persuading him to fulfill a vow he is said to have made" (357).

[2] Adele Reinhartz, "Anonymous Women and the Collapse of the Monarchy: A Study in Narrative Technique," *A Feminist Companion to Samuel and Kings* (ed. Athalya Brenner; Sheffield: Sheffield Academic Press, 1994), 43-65, here 53.

Zadok, Benaiah, Nathan, and Shimei side (1 Kgs 1:8), succeeds in usurping the throne and executes Adonijah. Comparatively, in 1 Kgs 3, one of the two unnamed sons dies. Two mothers then come to the royal court. If the strife between the mothers/queens led to the death of one son in 1 Kgs 1-2, in 1 Kgs 3 the death of one son leads to the strife between the mothers/prostitutes. Whereas the target of strife in 1 Kgs 1-2 is the throne, the target in 1 Kgs 3 is the life of the son. The goal in the former episode may be the ownership of the kingdom, but the goal in the latter episode is the ownership of the son.

There is another parallel between the two episodes, but with twists. In 1 Kgs 1-2, Bathsheba the mother is the one who conveys Adonijah's lethal request for Abishag the Shunammite (1 Kgs 2:19-21). This enables Solomon's legitimate excuse, "Ask for [Adonijah] the kingdom as well!" (1 Kgs 2:22), for the resultant killing of Adonijah, Haggith's son. In 1 Kgs 3, it is the king (Solomon!) who intends to "divide" — kill — the living boy (1 Kgs 3:24), while the mother of the living son interferes and pleads to save the son: "Please, my lord, give her the living child; certainly do not kill him!" (1 Kgs 3:26). On the one hand, Bathsheba's act contributes to the killing of the other son while the prostitute's giving up of her own son saves him. On the other hand, whereas in 1 Kgs 1-2 one son (Solomon) kills the other son (Adonijah), in 1 Kgs 3 the king (Solomon) orders the only surviving son (Solomon himself, if read as a parody) killed, which was thwarted by the prostitute mother.

Hidden Transcripts: Split the Child or the Kingdom?

At the outset, the surface plot illustrates the marvelous wisdom of Solomon.[1] In his dream by night at Gibeon, when God appears to him, Solomon requests "a discerning heart" (1 Kgs 3:9) instead of longevity, wealth, or glory. In return, he is endowed with an extraordinary wisdom, which is showcased by an impressive judgment (1 Kgs 3:28).

However, some scholars question whether the depiction of Solomon's succession to the throne in 1 Kgs 1-2 is favorable. Beneath

---

[1] For a reading of the didactic element of wisdom tradition, see Carole Fontaine, "The Bearing of Wisdom on the Shape of 2 Samuel 11-12 and 1 Kings 3," *JSOT* 34 (1986): 61-77.

the layers of royal propaganda, numerous literary gaps and clues at the subsurface level reveal negative portrayals of Solomon's coup.[1] Focusing on our text (1 Kgs 3:16-28), we thus similarly ask whether there is a parody of hidden transcripts underlying concepts beneath the surface plot. Let us look for clues from the close relationship between 1 Kgs 1-2 and 1 Kgs 3:16-28, as though the two episodes eclipse each other, the latter offering midrashim on the meaning of the former.

Also, we note a literary continuity between the two accounts. It can be compared to the continuity between 2 Sam 11 (David's rape of Bathsheba and murder of Uriah) and 2 Sam 12-13 (Nathan's parable revealing David's sin and its tragic consequences). In both cases, there is the event (2 Sam 11; 1 Kgs 1-2) and the parable (2 Sam 12; 1 Kgs 3:16-28).[2] Reading comparatively, in Nathan's parable, the rich man is King David, the poor man is Uriah, and the "one little ewe lamb" (2 Sam 12:3) is Bathsheba. In our text, the two prostitutes are the two queen mothers. The slain son is Adonijah, and the living son Solomon. Among these implied correlations, we now take a closer look at the two thematic threads — *two mothers* and *two sons*.[3]

---

[1] See Jerome T. Walsh, "The Characterization of Solomon in First Kings 1-5," *CBQ* 57 (1995), 471-93: "It is difficult to escape the impression that the more covert pattern of characterization is likely to be closer to the opinion of the author. . . . For the author of this text, the bottom line was disapproval of Solomon" (493); Jerome T. Walsh, *1 Kings*, 84-85; Bruce A. Power, "'All the King's Horses...': Narrative Subversion in the Story of Solomon's Golden Age," *From Babel to Babylon: Essays on Biblical History and Literature in Honor of Brian Peckham* (eds. J. R. Wood, J. E. Harvey, and M. Leuchter; LHBOTS 455; London: Bloomsbury T & T Clark, 2006), 111-23; and Eric A. Seibert, *Subversive Scribes and the Solomonic Narrative: A Rereading of 1 Kings 1-11* (LHBOTS 436; New York: T & T Clark, 2006), 111-57.

[2] For a redactional analysis of the "Solomon narratives" (or "Solomonic Apology") in 2 Samuel 11-12 and 1 Kgs 1-2 (which together frame the "Absalom cycle" in 2 Samuel 13-20), see Reinhard G. Kratz, *The Composition of the Narrative Books of the Old Testament* (tr. John Bowden; London: T & T Clark, 2005), 174-86 and Jeremy M. Hutton, *The Transjordanian Palimpsest: The Overwritten Texts of Personal Exile and Transformation in the Deuteronomistic History* (BZAW 396; Berlin: Walter de Gruyter, 2009), 192-96. Joseph Blenkinsopp ("Another Contribution to the Succession Narrative Debate [2 Samuel 11-20; 1 Kings 1-2]," *JSOT* 38 [2013]: 35-58) elucidates that the fratricide, "that of Amnon by Absalom" (2 Samuel 13), is mirrored in "story within the story" parodied by the woman of Tekoa (2 Sam 14:1-17; especially note "two sons" in v. 6 (57).

[3] John A. Davies, "Heptadic Verbal Patterns in the Solomon Narrative of 1 Kings 1-11," *TynBul* 63 (2012): 21-35: "The word 'woman' occurs seven times (1 Kings 3:16, 17 [2x], 18, 19, 22, 26) while the root ילד [to 'give birth' (verb) or "child" (noun)] also occurs seven times [3:17, 18, 21, 25, 26, 27] in various forms" (28). See also Matthew Michael, "The Two Prostitutes or the Two Kingdoms? A Critical Reading of King Solomon's Wise Ruling (1 Kgs 3:16-28)," *HBT* 37 (2015): 69-88, here 86.

First, concerning the pair of *two mothers*, whereas the queen mothers have to fight to protect their own sons, the prostitute whose son survived yields him to her rival "because her compassion for her son burned within her" (1 Kgs 3:26). The lowly yet compassionate woman stands in a sharp contrast with Bathsheba the queen who contributed to the killing of Adonijah. Admittedly, parables are difficult to decipher exactly, as many clues are elusive.[1] Yet, it is precisely because of such complexity and subtlety that our parable seems to expose Solomon's massacre. In 1 Kgs 3, the "bad" prostitute kills her own son, but in 1 Kgs 1-2, Bathsheba is involved in the killing of another woman's son. In 1 Kgs 2:19-21, Bathsheba asks Solomon that Abishag the (young) virgin (cf. 1 Kgs 1:3-4) "be given to your brother Adonijah as wife."[2] Similarly, in 1 Kgs 3:26, the "good" prostitute implores the king to "give [the other prostitute] the living child" (1 Kgs 3:26). Whereas Bathsheba's request to the king to "give" Abishag leads to the death of Adonijah, the prostitute's plea to the king to "give" her own son away leads to the preservation of the son's life.

Ellen van Wolde remarks: "The linguistic markers show that the turning point in the story is brought about by the [prostitute] woman [rather than the royal king]."[3] The prostitute's motherly compassion, her willingness to give up her own son, creates a climactic contrast with the queen involved in politically motivated killing. Readers may hear a didactic message in the thematic contrast between the upper-class queen mother and the lower-class prostitute mother. Prostitutes are easily considered outsiders, the opposite of queens, the supreme insiders in the monarchy. Whether Bathsheba is merely

---

[1] For example, in Nathan's parable, presumably the poor man is Uriah and the ewe lamb is Bathsheba. In the parable, it is the ewe lamb Bathsheba who is slaughtered, metaphorically implying her violation by the rich man David. But in the actual event, it is the poor man Uriah who is murdered.

[2] See Cushman, "The Politics of the Royal Harem," 340: "She also points out the implicit threat contained in the request by reminding Solomon that Adonijah is his brother."

[3] Ellen van Wolde, "Who Guides Whom? Embeddedness and Perspective in Biblical Hebrew and in 1 Kings 3:16-28," *JBL* 114 (1995): 423-642, here 641. Note also Willem A. M. Beuken, "No Wise King without a Wise Woman (1 Kings III 16-28)," *The New Avenues in the Study of the Old Testament* (ed. A. S. van der Woude; Leiden: Brill, 1989), 1-10: "What the woman to whom the living child belongs experiences when she is informed about the bogus solution of the king for the legal impasse, forms a climax in the narrative structure" (4).

manipulated by the prophet Nathan or she assumes the role of the Great Lady as the queen mother,[1] our text, like a mirror, reflects the murder of a son in 1 Kgs 2. In this mirror image, the prostitute mother's outcry not to kill her son may echo the outcry of Adonijah's mother, Haggith. The hidden transcript in the parable-like episode conveys the theme of protest against the powers-that-be, the queen in this case.

Furthermore, if these thematic correlations between 1 Kgs 1–2 and 1 Kgs 3 stand, then the latter text may carry another theme: subversion. Just as the two sons may allude to two heirs, Adonijah and Solomon, so the two prostitute mothers suggest the two queen mothers. If the lowly prostitute symbolizes the lofty queen, then Bathsheba is *de facto* made equal to a prostitute. The queen may exercise immense power "to kill" but such an abuse of power reduces her to the status of a prostitute. On the contrary, the prostitute with genuine compassion "to give" becomes a model wise woman.

Second, concerning the pair of *two sons*, they too are tangled up in the fierce power game. It is a trickster's game, reminiscent of the sibling rivalry between two sons—Esau and Jacob—in Genesis.[2] Yet there is a plot twist in the intertextuality of trickery by the younger sons. Whereas Jacob the younger son greatly "feared" Esau (Gen 32:6-7), it is Adonijah the older son who "fears" Solomon (1 Kgs 1:50-51).[3] Whereas Esau vows to "kill" his younger brother (Gen 27:41-42), it is Solomon who threatens to kill his older brother (1 Kgs 1:52). In contrast to the reconciliation between Jacob and Esau (Gen 33:4-11; cf. 35:29; 45:14-15; 50:19-21), Solomon gets rid of his older brother (cf. Gen 4:8).

---

[1] Claudia V. Camp, *Wise, Strange and Holy: The Strange Woman and the Making of the Bible* (JSOTSup 320; Sheffield: Sheffield Academic Press, 2000), 164: "The characterization of Bathsheba has shifted, then, from that of a woman constituted by male desire to a woman constituted by words, an analog to her change in status from lover/wife to queen mother." See also Cushman, "The Politics of the Royal Harem," 327-43.

[2] Isaac became old (Gen 27:1-2) and the younger son Jacob, under the guidance of Rebekah, stole the inheritance from the older son Esau; likewise, King David becomes old (1 Kgs 1:1-2) and through Bathsheba's suggestion (going back to Nathan; cf. 1 Kgs 1:11-14), the younger son Solomon usurps the throne from the older son Adonijah. Just as the birthright once belonged to Esau (Gen 25:32; 27:36), Adonijah recollects, "the kingship was mine" (1 Kgs 2:15).

[3] Concerning the thematic connections of the asylum for the fugitives between Exod 21:12-14 and 1 Kgs 1:50-53 (Adonijah) and 2:28-34 (Joab), see Jonathan Burnside, "Flight of the Fugitives: Rethinking the Relationship between Biblical Law (Exod 21:12-14) and the Davidic Succession Narrative (1 Kings 1-2)," *JBL* 129 (2010): 418-31.

Finally, echoing Jacob's reconciliation with his older brother Esau after the wrestling "by night" (Gen 32:24-31 [MT 32:25-32]), Solomon acquires divine wisdom in a dream "by night" (1 Kgs 3:5) which results in his sage judgment (1 Kgs 3:16-28). Yet, amid that sage judgment, readers also hear a tone of haunting outcry (cf. Gen 4:10).

First Kings 3:16-28 thus offers critique of the life-or-death court games. The cruel strife causes the mother to cry out, "he was not my son I had borne" (1 Kgs 3:21; cf. Gen 27:22). In the crucial exchange between the mothers, we find chiasm, centering on the dead son:

> My son is the living one,
> > your son is the dead one …
> > your son is the dead one,
> my son is the living one. (1 Kgs 3:22)

This chiastic alternation recurs in the king's reply (1 Kgs 3:23). The parable of the incident "by night" (1 Kgs 3:19-20) unequivocally relays the death of a son. As though shouting to King David, "You are the man [the criminal]" (2 Sam 12:7), the legal case is brought by the female prostitutes (in the setting of a royal court drama), crying out that one son, recalling Adonijah, is already dead. If so, the living son is Solomon—and eventually the kingdom—against whom the king himself pronounces a death sentence (1 Kgs 3:24-25; cf. 2 Sam 12:5).

However, the king's verdict to kill is canceled by the rebuttal of the prostitute mother, which forms another chiasm: "to cut, to give—to give, not to kill" (1 Kgs 3:25-26).[1] Contrary to the king, whose naked cruelty has been exposed, "the whore who follows the dictates of her motherly feelings becomes wise as a result of it."[2] The prostitute is wise, but the king is foolish, insofar as the child to be sliced embodies the king himself. Alas, though foolish, the king is still powerful. The unnamed king remains remote (in the royal court), emotionless (in the office of a judge), and authoritarian (in terms of the unmatched power to exert).[3] The king who is aloof may neither fathom nor empathize with the mundane struggles of the commoners, let alone the lowly

---

[1] Beuken, "No Wise King without a Woman," 8.
[2] Beuken, "No Wise King without a Woman," 7.
[3] Moshe Garsiel, "Revealing and Concealing as a Narrative Strategy in Solomon's Judgment (1 Kings 3:16-28)," *CBQ* 64 (2002): 229-47: "In the previous story, which relates Solomon's request at Gibeon for wisdom, he is always referred to as 'Solomon.'

prostitutes. Thus, while the command to cut the baby may be alarming to the commoners, to the lofty king, the prostitutes' children are mere commodities, easily disposable.

Nevertheless, the text's hidden transcripts not only objectify the anonymous king but also poke fun at his unreachability.[1] Concerning the male king's association with the female prostitutes, scholars ponder whether this incident glorifies Solomon for marvelously making justice accessible to the society's lowest class (even today many people cannot seek redress in a court of law because hiring an attorney is beyond their means), or rather condemns the king who is too busy mingling with outsiders, such as the Pharaoh's daughter (1 Kgs 3:1) and many foreign women (1 Kgs 11:1, 8).[2] Be that as it may, the subversive contrast between the noble king and the shunned prostitutes may imply mockery of the dubious socio-ethnic status of Solomon, who was "born of an illicit union" between David and Bathsheba, a woman already married to the "Hittite" outsider (cf. Deut 7:1; 20:17; 23:2-3).[3] Additionally, the king who commands to "divide [גזרו] the living child into two" (1 Kgs 3:25) is likened to the "bad" prostitute who echoes the order, "divide it" [גזרו] (1 Kgs 3:26). Who is noble or base? Who is truly powerful—the queen or the prostitute? Who is really wise—the king or the whore?

However, in our story he is referred to only by his title 'the king,' for he functions as the royal dispenser of justice" (235).

[1] Seow, "The First and Second Books of Kings," 45: "Josephus... says... 'all the people secretly made fun of the king as of a boy' [Josephus, *Antiquities of the Jews* VIII.2.32]."

[2] Simon J. DeVries, *1 Kings* (2nd ed.; WBC 12; Nashville: Thomas Nelson, 2003): "It shows how the wise king would act on behalf of the very lowest of his subjects" (61) and Marvin A. Sweeney, *I & II Kings: A Commentary* (OTL; Louisville: Westminster John Knox, 2007): "The narrative passes no moral judgment on the women, but their designation as prostitutes trivializes Solomon as a monarch who spends his time resolving quarrels between prostitutes" (82).

[3] Power, "All the King's Horses," 116. For a proposal that Solomon (whose name connotes not only "peace" but also "replacement" of Bathsheba's deceased husband Uriah) was actually the son of Bathsheba and Uriah, see Veijola, "Solomon: Bathsheba's Firstborn," 345. We also wonder whether there is an implied connection between the queen Bath-*Sheba* (שבע), Solomon's mother, in 1 Kgs 1-2 and the foreign queen of *Sheba* (שבא) in 1 Kgs 10.

Peace versus Sword: A Wise Judge or a Fearful Tyrant?

Solomon's name denotes peace (שלמה). However, as the hidden transcripts of the parable in 1 Kgs 3 signify, careful readers may wonder whether Solomon's reign exemplifies honor, virtue, and peace as opposed to coup, connivance, and sword. In 1 Kgs 2:5, David condemns Joab for shedding blood during "peace" (שלם; cf. 1 Kgs 2:32) and advises Solomon to follow "wisdom," which is ironically defined as making sure Joab's "gray hair" does not "go down in Sheol in peace" (1 Kgs 2:5-6). As Joab seeks asylum inside the tent of YHWH, Solomon still orders him killed to preserve the "peace" of his own throne, at the expense of defiling the sanctuary (1 Kgs 2:29-30, 33).[1] Solomon also shrewdly entraps and executes Shimei, whom David earlier swore not to kill by the "sword" (1 Kgs 2:8, 46). The irony recurs in David's request to Solomon: "You are a wise man ... bring his gray hair down to Sheol in blood" (1 Kgs 2:9; cf. v 6).[2] Thus, Adonijah rightfully fears Solomon's "sword" (1 Kgs 1:51), despite Solomon's dubious promise that "not one of [Adonijah's] hairs will fall to the ground" (1 Kgs 1:52; cf. on Absalom in 2 Sam 14:11; 18:11). When Adonijah approaches Queen Bathsheba, the conversation is loaded with puns: "Do you come for peace [or 'Solomon']" ... "Yes, for peace [or 'Solomon']" (1 Kgs 2:13). Against his wish for "peace," Adonijah meets the fate of death by his brother Solomon (1 Kgs 2:24-25).

Similarly, 1 Kgs 3 both mentions Solomon's "peace offerings" (1 Kgs 3:15) and cites his ruling, "Get me a sword" (1 Kgs 3:24). Peace meets sword: In sword we trust. We note the king's wise decision, yet, as Walter Bruggemann demurs, "This is a strange wisdom that governs by violence."[3] Just as King Solomon ruthlessly annihilates his rival brother Adonijah (1 Kgs 2:25), the king commands the prostitute's

---

[1] For an interpretation that Joab's death was planned by Bathsheba to avenge "herself on the murderer of her first husband," see J. W. Wesselius, "Joab's Death and the Central Theme of the Succession Narrative (2 Samuel IX-1 Kings II)," *VT* 40 (1990): 336-51, here 348.

[2] Marvin A. Sweeney, *King Josiah of Judah: The Lost Messiah of Israel* (Oxford: Oxford University Press, 2001): "Whereas each of the previous figures [e.g., Moses, Joshua, and Samuel] counsels his listeners to follow Deuteronomic commandments, David advises Solomon to kill or banish his opponents, which hardly presents either David or Solomon as an ideal leader in the perspective of the DtrH" (107).

[3] Walter Brueggemann, *1 & 2 Kings* (SHBC 8; Macon, GA: Smyth & Helwys, 2000), 54.

living son to be killed (1 Kgs 3:24). The monarch's wisdom and power boil down to brandishing a sword over a vulnerable baby. The move may sound like a smart idea to resolve a stalemate (1 Kgs 3:28b). But what if the real mother did not intervene to save the boy?[1] What if the guards executed the king's order, disregarding the mother's plea? What if the king could come up with a solution other than such a deadly option?[2] That there was a chance of the sword actually "dividing" the boy, the king could not care less. Moreover, perhaps the proposal to split the child foreshadows Solomon's eventual contribution to the splitting of his own kingdom (cf. 1 Kgs 11:11, 31)?[3] The didactic message is evident: for the king, the "sword" is the solution, an easy one that comes in handy.[4]

In a broader intertextual perspective, 1 Kgs 3:16-28 eerily echoes the Akedah passage in Gen 22—the binding and near slaying of Isaac. In this correlation, the king requests the "sword" (1 Kgs 3:24) and threatens to use against the boy, just as Abraham fetched and lifted the "knife" against his son (Gen 22:6, 10). Here, our text makes a thematic twist. Who plays the role of God or the angel of YHWH? It is not Solomon but the prostitute mother who intervenes at the unthinkable moment of slaughter (1 Kgs 3:26), just as the angel of YHWH from heaven stopped Abraham (Gen 22:11).[5] On the contrary, Solomon's

---

[1] Mordechai Cogan, *1 Kings* (AB 10; New York: Doubleday, 2001): "Had one of the women not acted upon her motherly feelings and saved the king from carrying out his threat, a wholly other conclusion might be imagined" (197).

[2] "Solomon could have cross-examined the women, looked for other unknown witnesses, character witnesses, or he could have looked for physical evidence such as the babies' navels. If the babies were born several days apart, the degree of healing where the umbilical cord was severed would indicate relative age" (Avaren E. Ipsen, "Solomon and the Two Prostitutes," *The Bible and Critical Theory* 3.1 [2007]: 1-12, 7-8). See also Seow, "The First and Second Books of Kings," 3:44-45.

[3] For a study of the two prostitutes as the Deuteronomist's symbolic clues for the two kingdoms (northern Israel and southern Judah), see Michael, "The Two Prostitutes or the Two Kingdoms?" He states, "In this symbolic personification at the opening of the book of Kings, for the Dtr, the kingdoms of Israel and Judah had become like the two prostitutes at the beginning of Solomon's rule" (88).

[4] Gina Hens-Piazza, *1-2 Kings* (AOTC; Nashville: Abingdon, 2006): "Solomon's summons for a sword conjures up an ambiguous meaning. The image, which connotes authority to judge as well as potential to do violence, reminds us of the two paradigms of kingship weighing upon this king" (44).

[5] Garsiel, "Revealing and Concealing as a Narrative Strategy:" "Indeed, this is an extremely rare case in the Bible where a person of lower social status gives a command in the presence of the king to his servants to carry out his decision" (245). For a

brutal resolve to "cut" the child is more comparable to Jephthah (Judg 11:39) or the Levite who cut his concubine into twelve pieces (Judg 19:29).[1]

In Genesis, the angel declares, speaking for God: "Now I know that you fear [ירא] God; you have not withheld your only son from me" (Gen 22:12). Similarly, after the dramatic resolution of the case, the people marvel at the wisdom of the king: "All Israel heard of the judgment that the king had judged; and they feared [וייראו] the king" (1 Kgs 3:28a). The wisdom is apparently said to come from God: "for they saw that the wisdom of God was in him to do justice" (1 Kgs 3:28b). Still the expression signals that instead of fearing God, as was the case for Abraham, now the people are said to fear Solomon the king. Can the sentence be translated as follows: "for they feared that the divine wisdom was in him to execute judgment" (1 Kgs 3:28b; cf. Gen 3:5, 7)? If so, Jerome T. Walsh's remark is apt: "It is striking, too, that popular reaction to Solomon's judgment is not rejoicing, or praise of [YHWH], or the like; it is 'fear.'"[2] No cheers but silence. No applause but consternation.

In the larger Solomon narrative (1 Kgs 1–11), scholars debate where the negative account starts, as well as what redactional layers are retrievable. In his dream by night, Solomon requests "a discerning [literally, 'hearing'] heart" (1 Kgs 3:9). This is the quintessential theme of the Deuteronomic law: "Hear, O Israel… You shall love your YHWH with all your heart" (Deut 6:4–5). However, following the divine test of Solomon's laudable request (1 Kgs 3:1-15) we learn of the human test of the king's purported wise decision (1 Kgs 3:16-28). Like Dr. Jekyll and Mr. Hyde, Solomon plays a model king (1 Kgs 3:1-15) but then shows a faulty, monstrous human side (1 Kgs 3:16-28). The (imperfectly) symmetrical structure of the Solomon narrative reveals

---

comparison with Gen 22 in which Abraham parallels the true mother, see Seow, "The First and Second Books of Kings," 47.

[1] Ken Stone, "Animal Difference, Sexual Difference, and the Daughter of Jephthah," *BibInt* 24 (2016): 1–16.

[2] Walsh, "The Characterization of Solomon in First Kings 1–5," 489. See also Hens-Piazza, *1–2 Kings*: "We must decide whether this first appropriation of Solomon's gift conjures awe or evokes fear on the part of those he would govern in the years to come" (45).

negative signs both at the start and at the close, enveloping somewhat positive descriptions in the middle:[1]
a Solomon's coup initiated by the prophet Nathan (1 Kgs 1-2)
  b Pharaoh's daughter (3:1)
    c First dream account (3:2-15)
      d Women (prostitutes) and wisdom (3:16-28)
        e Administrative wisdom (4:1-34 [MT 4:1-5:14])
          f Hiram and forced labor (5:1-18 [MT 5:15-32])
            g Temple (6:1-38)
              h Palace (7:1-12)
            g' Temple (7:13-8:66)
          f' Hiram and forced labor (9:10-28)
        e' Wealth and wisdom (10:14-29)
      d' Woman (Queen of Sheba) and wisdom (*10:1-13*)
    c' Second dream account (*9:1-9*)
  b' Many foreign women (11:1-13)
a' Jeroboam's coup initiated by the prophet Ahijah (11:14-43)

So,[2] where is the heart of Solomon? Already in 1 Kgs 3:1-2, we learn that "Solomon became the son-in-law of Pharaoh, the king of Egypt, when he married the daughter of Pharaoh" (1 Kgs 3:1). Echoing the Exodus motif, scholars note here that Solomon is already like the fearful Pharaoh (cf. Neh 13:26).[3] Solomon "loved YHWH" (cf. Deut 6:5), except he also loved the high places (1 Kgs 3:3; cf. Deut 12:2-3). Solomon "loved" many foreign women, along with Pharaoh's daughter, turning his "heart" after other gods and being "not wholly

---

[1] Sweeney, *King Josiah of Judah*: "The critique of Solomon appears to be placed primarily at the beginning and end of the narrative [1 Kings 1-11]" (99). Note also J. Daniel Hays, "Has the Narrator Come to Praise Solomon or to Bury Him? Narrative Subtlety in 1 Kings 1-11," *JSOT* 28 (2003): 149-74: "The Narrator in 1 Kings 1-11 is not praising Solomon or his kingdom at all, even in the first ten chapters, but instead, is presenting a scathing critique" (149).

[2] This chiastic structure is adapted and modified from the proposals by Kim Ian Parker, "Repetition as a Structuring Device in 1 Kings 1-11," *JSOT* 42 (1988): 19-27, here 24, and John W. Olley, "Pharaoh's Daughter, Solomon's Palace, and the Temple: Another Look at the Structure of 1 Kings 1-11," *JSOT* 27 (2003): 355-69, here 364. As far as the framing bookends (a-a') are concerned, Solomon manages to kill Adonijah (1 Kgs 2:24-25) but not Jeroboam (1 Kgs 11:40).

[3] Consider Yong Ho Jeon, "The Retroactive Re-evaluation Technique with Pharaoh's Daughter and the Nature of Solomon's Corruption in 1 Kings 1-12," *TynBul* 62 (2011): 15-40: "They have been living in an 'Egypt' under Solomon's reign" (32) and Power, "All the King's Horses," 118: "Egypt is now at the heart of David's capital."

(שלם) true to YHWH" (1 Kgs 11:4).[1] Solomon conscripted forced laborers (particularly from the northern tribes) and imposed heavy taxes (1 Kgs 5:13-16 [MT 5:27-30]; 9:15-23) to build not only the temple but especially his own palace, which ended up taking 13 years to finish, as compared to seven years for the temple (1 Kgs 6:38-7:1), and was twice the size of the temple (1 Kgs 6:2; 7:2). All the lavish riches and chariotry (1 Kgs 4:22-28 [MT 5:2-8]; 10:14-29) are explicitly unfit for an ideal king as per Deut 17:16-17.

Redactionally, the competing theories as to how positively or negatively Solomon's regime is portrayed in 1 Kgs 1-11 are in a way comparable to the dilemma concerning the Succession Narrative (2 Sam 9-20 and 1 Kgs 1-2).[2] Was the original negative record of David (as well as Solomon) subsequently supplemented by positive idealistic portrayals in the DtrH? Or was the originally apologetic pro-Davidic/Solomonic material later reformulated into anti-Davidic/Solomonic critiques?[3] Whichever compositional routes we take, synchronically, readers find both "good" Solomon and "bad" Solomon in the present form. We should note that the DtrH displays marked differences with the Chronicler's History (ChrH). Read together, the negative descriptions of Solomon in the DtrH that are missing in the ChrH (2 Chr 1-9) mirror the bad Solomon disguised

---

[1] Römer, "The Case of the Book of Kings," 148. "Even if the story of the Queen of Sheba was originally written to enhance Solomon's glory, the context in which it now stands transforms the narrative into an example of Solomon's mingling with foreign women"(193). Note also Camp, *Wise, Strange and Holy*: "These two episodes [two harlots and the queen of Sheba], one near the beginning of the Solomon narrative and the other near its end, subtly link one sort of strangeness (that of the foreigner) to another (that of the sexual outsider)."

[2] For a recent debate on the Succession Narrative, see Serge Frolov, "Succession Narrative: A 'Document or a Phantom?" *JBL* 121 (2002): 81-104; John Barton, "Dating the 'Succession Narrative,'" *In Search of Pre-Exilic Israel: Proceedings of the Oxford Old Testament Seminar* (ed. John Day; London: T & T Clark, 2004), 99-100; Hutton, *The Transjordanian Palimpsest*, 176-227, 364-71; and Joseph Blenkinsopp, "Another Contribution to the Succession Narrative Debate (2 Samuel 11-20; 1 Kings 1-2)," *JSOT* 38 (2013): 35-58.

[3] Sweeney, *I & II Kings*, 73, 96. "The narrative framework of the DtrH deliberately undermines the positive portrayal of Solomon that underlies 1 Kgs 2:46b-4:20.... When viewed in relation to the entire DtrH, it is clear that the critique of Solomon functions in relation to exilic and Josianic editions of the DtrH." See also Römer, *The So-Called Deuteronomistic History*, 97-106, 115-23, 139-49 and Allison L. Joseph, *Portrait of the Kings: The Davidic Prototype in Deuteronomistic Poetics* (Minneapolis: Fortress, 2015), 58-76.

under the good Solomon.[1] The propaganda of the ideal king of peace and wise heart cannot completely conceal the realities of heartless violence wrought by the king's sword detectable amid the hidden transcripts of subversive voices.[2]

When Solomon awakes from the theophany in 1 Kgs 3:1-15, the text clarifies that "it was a dream" (1 Kgs 3:15). Could the depiction of an obedient king be a mere *dream*?[3] However we take the dream to be, the *reality* in the subsequent episode (1 Kgs 3:16-28) is fraught with sword and fear, not so much peace or wisdom of a discerning heart. If we take the entire Solomon narrative as a detective story, careful readers may thus find clues of a wise-king-gone-terrifying already hidden in 1 Kgs 3, not to mention 1 Kgs 1-2.

Conclusion

"Long live King Solomon," they proclaimed (1 Kgs 1:39). But, in their sorrows and tears under the king's rampant power abuse, the common people (*minjung* in Korean) may have feared and resented such power. As a parable-like parody on the preceding episode (1 Kgs 1-2), the underlying concept of Solomon's showcase of the discerning heart (1 Kgs 3:1-15) does not portray him positively but rather negatively, especially in light of the intersections of two queen/prostitute mothers and two royal/baby sons (1 Kgs 3:16-28).

At the end of the coups, betrayal, and murder in the so-called Succession Narrative, we finally learn that "the kingdom was consolidated by the hand of Solomon" (1 Kgs 2:46; cf. 1 Kgs 2:12). But how was it secured? Not by wisdom but by trickery. Not by peace but by sword. Just as Absalom (meaning "my father is peace") killed his older brother Amnon (2 Sam 13:28), so Solomon (meaning "peace") killed his older brother Adonijah. The kingdom may appear to enjoy

---

[1] Interestingly, even in the LXX, 1 Kgs 3:1 (Solomon's marriage to Pharaoh's daughter) is missing. See Percy S. F. van Keulen, *Two Versions of the Solomon Narrative: An Inquiry into the Relationship between MT 1Kgs. 2-11 and LXX 3 Reg. 2-11* (VTSup 104; Leiden: Brill, 2005), 55-61.

[2] Consider Seibert's remark on the "subversive scribe(s)" who, "in the process of completing that assignment, took the liberty to inscribe his/their own subtle critique of the king" (*Subversive Scribes and the Solomonic Narrative*, 157).

[3] Hugh S. Pyper, "Judging the Wisdom of Solomon: The Two-Way Effect of Intertextuality," *JSOT* 59 (1993): 25-36: "It may, however, be significant that this high praise of Solomon is represented as a dream" (30).

tranquility and security after Solomon took over the throne. Yet the quiet moment of peace is interrupted not by natural disaster or invading armies, but rather by two unnamed prostitutes. Their outcry chastises Solomon for the brutal murder of his brother. The lowly prostitute's plea not to wield the sword criticizes the prevalent power abuse of the queen and the king while demonstrating the compassionate and obedient heart the king disregards outright.

In light of this reading, we may still wonder how to interpret the seeming discrepancy of many biblical episodes and characters, let alone the seemingly alternating presence and absence of God. Such conflicting records are quite common in the Hebrew Bible.[1] Despite the ambiguity, it is more likely that the biblical narratives depict Bathsheba as a victim of King David's rape through abuse of power (2 Sam 11-12; cf. Gen 12:12; 20:11; 26:7, 9; 1 Sam 25:39-42).[2] If so, the same Bathsheba has now changed in her position of a queen, albeit via the likely manipulation of Nathan (1 Kgs 1-2).[3] Our text (1 Kgs 3:16-28) is therefore not only a defiant outcry against the power abuse of the queen and the king but also a sorrowful lament about the monarchical system replete with flaws and dangers.[4] Whoever becomes the ruler, it is all too common for them to eschew compassion and wield the sword. The story of two prostitutes then may be an exposure of the ugliness and shortcomings of the monarchy, both Israel's and that of its imperial nemeses. The piece further accentuates the ideals of the kingdom of God when "nations shall not lift up a sword against nation" (Isa 2:4). At the same time, the dream account of divine approval of the murderous king (1 Kgs 3:10-13, 28) may signify the commoners' outcry

---

[1] For example, faithful Abraham versus mischievous Abraham, oppressed Sarah versus oppressive Sarah, benevolent Joseph versus tyrannical Joseph, evil Manasseh (2 Kgs 21:1-8) versus repentant Manasseh (2 Chr 33:10-17), obedient Josiah versus proud Josiah (2 Kgs 23:25 vs. 2 Chr 35:20-27; cf. 2 Chr 32:24-25), and so on.

[2] Hyun Chul Paul Kim and M. Fulgence Nyengele, "Murder S/He Wrote? A Cultural and Psychological Reading of 2 Samuel 11-12," *SemeiaSt* 44 (2003): 95-116.

[3] Similarly, on tension between the ideal Solomon and the real Solomon, note DeVries, *1 Kings*, 55: "Perhaps the two were not irreconcilably divorced, for elements of the real and the ideal are present in every person."

[4] Concerning a key theme of Kings as a whole, see Römer, "The Case of the Book of Kings," 191: "The book [of Kings] begins with a weak and dying David and ends with the last Davidic king living comfortably in Babylonian exile.... [this] creates an ambiguous depiction of the Davidic dynasty."

against the divine absence in human history. Marvin Sweeney's biblical theology offers a profound insight:

> In the aftermath of the Shoah, we human beings... suffered as a result of divine absence, and we must now make choices for the future even though we do not possess full knowledge of our situation.... Will we continue to uphold the ideals learned from G-d of power, righteousness, fidelity, and engagement in our own lives? Or will we abandon those ideals because we perceive G-d to have abandoned us? Do we recognize that perhaps G-d needs us just as much as we need G-d? We are, after all, created as partners with G-d, and our task is to assist G-d in the completion and sanctification of the world of creation.[1]

Readers of 1 Kgs 3:16–28 are presented with two choices—the king's and the prostitute's.

---

[1] Marvin A. Sweeney, *Reading the Hebrew Bible after the Shoah: Engaging Holocaust Theology* (Minneapolis: Fortress, 2008), 240–41.

Heavenly Porkies
Prophecy and Divine Deception in 1 Kings 13 and 22

Lester L. Grabbe

One of the interesting aspects of British colloquial speech is rhyming slang. It does not seem to be so productive anymore, but there are many fossilized examples still widely used, especially in the London area. One frequent expression is to "to take a butcher's," meaning "take a look" ("look" rhyming with "butcher's hook"). The convention is to drop the final part of the rhyme ("hook" in this case) but keep the first part ("butcher's"). I shall not give further examples (such as "blow a raspberry") except for the one used in this article: "tell a porky," meaning "tell a lie" (rhyming with "porky pie").

In 1 Kings, we have at least two examples in which lying or deception have a place in a prophetic context, and in both cases the deity seems to be involved: 1 Kgs 13 and 1 Kgs 22. Since YHWH as a deceiver is not usually the first image that springs to mind, a number of questions arise. Is this a unique event? What is the significance of such a divine deception in the history of prophecy? In order to get a handle on these fascinating incidents, I propose to look not only at the two accounts but also at cross-cultural parallels that might assist us. I shall look at the parallels first, and then bring their contents to bear in helping to elucidate the biblical passages when we analyze them.

Cross-Cultural Examples of Divine Deception

A number of the examples involve a divine council or assembly of the gods. Perhaps the best picture of such a council is found in the Ugaritic texts.[1] In the extant Ugaritic texts, however, I am not aware of deception as such on the part of any of the gods, though there is plenty of conflict.

---

* It is with pleasure that I dedicate this essay to Professor Marvin Sweeney. His personal welcome and solicitous attention when Claremont Graduate University kindly hosted the William Brownlee Lecture, which I gave in 2008, was warm and memorable.

[1] See especially E. Theodore Mullen, *The Divine Council in Canaanite and Early Hebrew Literature* (HSM 24; Chico, CA: Scholars Press, 1980).

The Mesopotamian Flood Story

The flood story occurs in a number of Mesopotamian texts, both Sumerian and Akkadian.[1] Although they differ in many details — not the least because of the preservation of tablets — they all give a fairly uniform outline of events (see table below), and even in the stories which have gaps in the plot (because of text not preserved in some cases) the element in question was probably there in the original story. In any case, a number of the stories describe the consultation among the gods, in which a decision is made to send a flood to wipe out humanity but to keep silent about it. They then go on to record that the god of wisdom, Ea in Sumerian and Enki in Akkadian, got around this oath by talking to the wall of the house in which Ziusudra or Atra-ḫasis or Utnapishtim lived, so that this Mesopotamian "Noah" would hear and prepare to save himself and his family from the coming flood.

Genesis 6-9	**Gilgamesh 11**	**Berossus**	**Atra-ḫasis**	**Sumerian Account**
Humans are wicked	Humans rebellious			[Humans rebellious]
	Gods swear to keep planned flood secret		Enlil makes gods swear to bring flood	Gods take an oath
God warns Noah	Ea warns Utnapishtim	Cronus warns Xisouthros	Enki warns Atra-ḫasis	Enki warns Ziusudra
Noah builds ark	Utnapishtim builds boat		Atra-ḫasis builds boat	[Ziusudra builds boat]
Ark 300 x 50 x 30 cubits	Boat equals (a cube?), 120 x 120 cubits	Boat 5 x 2 stades		

---

[1] For a discussion of these, see Irving Finkel, *The Ark before Noah: Decoding the Story of the Flood* (London: Hodder and Stoughton, 2014); Andrew R. George, ed. and tr., *The Epic of Gilgamesh: The Babylonian Epic Poem and Other Texts in Akkadian and Sumerian* (Penguin Classics; London: Penguin Books, 1999); and W. G. Lambert and A. R. Millard, *Atra-Ḥasīs: The Babylonian Story of the Flood* (Oxford: Clarendon Press, 1969). For the Greek account in Berossus, see Stanley Mayer Burstein, *The Babyloniaca of Berossus* (SMANE 1.5; Malibu, CA: Undena, 1978).

Genesis 6-9	Gilgamesh 11	Berossus	Atra-ḫasis	Sumerian Account
Takes 2 of every kind plus family	Takes all living creatures, kin, crafts workers	Takes winged and four-footed creatures, kin, closest friends	Takes various creatures and family	
Food and drink loaded	Bread and wheat	Food and drink loaded	Provisions provided	
40 days and nights of rain	7 days of rain		7 days and nights of rain	7 days and nights of rain
	Creator goddess repents of human death		Nintu and other gods repent of their decision	
Raven sent out, does not return	Dove sent, returns			
Dove sent, returns	Swallow sent, returns	Birds sent, return		
Dove sent, returns with olive leaf		Birds sent, do not return		
Ark lands in mountains of Ararat		Ark lands in Armenia		Ark lands
Offers sacrifices	Offers sacrifices		Offers sacrifices	Offers sacrifices
	Enlil angry that humans survived		Enlil angry that humans survived	

103

The full nature of the divine deception is indicated in Gilgamesh and Atra-ḥasis, in which Enlil becomes angry that some humans survived and would repopulate the earth. It may be that the original Sumerian version also had this episode but does not show it because of incomplete preservation. As for Berossus, it may not have suited his purpose to include it, but we should keep in mind that the account may be only partially preserved in the extant sources. Overall, we can say that the Mesopotamian flood story (in contrast to the biblical account) had a divine deception at its heart.

Divine Deception in Norse Mythology[1]

The Old Norse mythology is known primarily from two medieval sources. There is the "Poetic Edda," which is found in the Codex Regius from about the 13th century.[2] This is thought to be the older version on the whole, but it obviously omits some of the stories about the gods that were in circulation in medieval and earlier times. Another source is the *Edda of Snorri Sturluson*.[3] Snorri was an Icelandic poet, as well as a politician, who lived from about 1179 to 1241. He wrote a version of the Norse mythology of his own time. It generally follows the "Poetic Edda" but seems to represent his own formulation, at least at times. There has been debate as to how much Snorri's version has been influenced ("contaminated") by his Christian outlook, but the immediate impression is that he is presenting an Old Norse picture, not a Christian one.

The *Edda of Snorri Sturluson* seems to allude to a story (in the *Gylfaginning* 41–43), which is not found as such anywhere in the "Poetic Edda." However, Snorri includes a full version of what seems to be a traditional tale. The background is the world ash tree (*Yggdrasil*), which is in the place of the gods called *Asgard*. Here, the gods congregated in council each day to decide all matters. This was toward the beginning of things, with the gods having established

---

[1] I wish to thank Professor Hans Barstad with whom I discussed certain aspects of Norse mythology, which I take up in this section. I also want to thank Professor Martti Nissinen and Dr. Risto Pulkkinen for confirming that there seems to be no example in Finnish mythology to use for comparison here. Dr. Pulkkinen recently published a book on ancient Finnish popular beliefs, unfortunately, only in Finnish.

[2] For a recent translation, see Carolyne Larrington, tr. and ed., *The Poetic Edda* (OWC; Oxford: Oxford University Press, 1996).

[3] See Anthony Faulkes, tr. and ed., *Snorri Sturluson: Edda* (Everyman Library; London: J. M. Dent, 1987).

Midgard (the rampart around the world of humans) and Val-hall, the palace of Odin. A certain builder came and offered to build secure fortifications that would protect the gods from the mountain-giants and frost-giants. The gods were often opposed by the giants, and there was a fear that the giants might come over Midgard and attack them. So the gods made a deal with the builder that if he built the fortifications in three seasons (autumn, winter, and spring), they would pay his asking price: the sun, the moon, and the goddess Freyia for a wife. However, they stipulated that he could have no helper, but he asked that he might use his stallion Svadilfæri in his work. The gods agreed, as urged by the god Loki.

Although it is not so stated, the implication is that the gods did not intend to pay the builder, because of their stipulation that he have no helper. They assumed that without an assistant, he would not finish in time, and they could go back on their agreement. However, it turned out that Svadilfæri was a big help in hauling great stones and greatly assisted the progress of the work. The time was getting close to the beginning of the summer but the work was nearly finished. The gods met to decide what to do and turned on Loki who had convinced them to accept the builder's bargain. In Norse mythology, Loki is an ambiguous figure. He is often compared with the trickster figures in North American myths. He is the offspring of a god and a giant. He sides with the gods in the present, but at the end time he will fight on the side of the giants, against the gods.

Loki swore that he would sort the matter out. He changed himself into a mare and attracted the attention of Svadilfæri. The two horses disappeared for a night, and work was held up by a day and a night. When the builder realized he could not complete the task in time, he flew into a rage, revealing himself as a mountain-giant. The gods had sworn an oath to provide safety for him, but now they reneged on this, and Thor slaughtered him with his hammer. However, Loki retained his mare form until s/he bore an eight-legged foal who became the famous Sleipnir, Odin's horse.

The plan of the gods to deceive the builder and break their oath is not stated explicitly, but it seems clear from the progress of the story. They could not have promised the builder the sun, the moon, and Freyia with the full intention of paying up, since that would have been an unacceptable price. Hence, their stipulation of no assistant for the builder. Allowing Thor to slay the builder also appears to be another deception, in the form of a broken promise.

Divine Deception in Mayan Mythology

In Mayan myths that have been preserved (even though much was destroyed by the Spanish missionaries), there is a story of the creation of human beings. This is contained primarily in the *Popol Vuh*.[1] According to it, the gods went through a series of stages (one might even say "experiments") before the first real human beings emerged. First, the gods made various animals, but these could not speak; they could only make various cries. They then took clay and fashioned humans but these could not speak, quickly deformed, and fell apart as they dried. Next, they made doll-like creatures from wood and other materials. These creatures could speak, but they were destructive and did not recognize or worship their creators.

Finally, they made human-like creatures from the kernels of white and yellow corn. These were intelligent creatures who could speak and worship the gods. But they were also able to see great distances without moving from their place. This far-sightedness was a concern for the gods, since it enabled great knowledge and perfect understanding, and they were afraid the creatures would become as great as the gods. So they took away some of their sight and made them the ordinary humans of today.

The gods clearly took some time and experimentation before coming up with an appropriate human being. But the endowment with distant sight of the final corn people was a mistake. It was not a deception, perhaps, but there is an uncanny parallel with the tree of knowledge of good and evil (and also the tree of life) in Gen 2–3. Yet, it was a lie or at least a deception of sorts because the humans created at this stage were given something which they then had taken away. Once again, the gods do not seem to have played completely fair in their dealings.

---

[1] For the Mayan text and initial English translation, see Munro S. Edmondson, *The Book of Counsel: The Popol Vuh of the Quiche Maya of Guatemala* (MARIP 35; New Orleans: Tulane University Press, 1971). Another English translation benefitting from

Misleading Prophecies in Herodotus

The Greek world had its prophets in the form of people who gave oracles. The most famous was the Pythian oracle. Herodotus relates several such prophecies in which national leaders consulted this oracle. One was the ruler of Phrygia, Croesus. Herodotus tells the story that he asked the oracle about fighting Cyrus the Persian. The reply came back, "If you fight Cyrus, you will destroy a great empire" (*Hist.* 1.53). Another oracle was that the Persians would overcome Croesus when a mule ruled "the Medes" (1.55). Croesus interpreted both of these oracles as favourable and went to battle. When Cyrus defeated him, Croesus was placed on a pyre to be burnt alive. As he awaited his fate, he commented on the faithlessness of the oracle. Cyrus heard this and asked him to relate his story. When he did so, Cyrus lifted the death sentence and kept him as a companion (1.86-87). Croesus sent a message to Delphi, charging the oracle with being false. But back came the "correct" interpretations of the oracle: there had been no falsehood because Croesus *had* destroyed a great empire—his own! Also, as the son of a Persian man and a Median princess, Cyrus qualified as the "mule" of the prophecy, so the oracle had been right (*Hist.* 1.90-91).

Another example is that of the Greeks sending messengers to Delphi when being attacked by Xerxes in 480 BCE; the oracles pronounced that the Greeks would be saved by their wooden wall (*Hist.* 7.140-43). Some argued that this was a wooden wall that had once protected the Acropolis but had fallen into disrepair through neglect: it should be rebuilt. But others argued that the oracle meant their navy, their wooden ships. A few diehards did indeed defend the Acropolis quite bravely but were eventually overcome and killed (8.51-53). Most depended on their ships, however, and the Greeks did indeed defeat the Persian fleet and save Greece (8.78-96), even though Athens was burnt to the ground.

In these two cases, it was not so much a lie from the divinity as a misleading oracle. This often seemed to be the case with such oracles: they were capable of being interpreted in more than one way and thus could seldom be shown to be wrong—not too different from horoscopes or Chinese fortune cookies. But in a number of examples

---

more recent study is that of Dennis Tedlock, tr. and ed., *Popol Vuh: The Mayan Book of the Dawn of Life* (rev. ed.; New York: Simon & Schuster, 1996).

quoted in our ancient sources, the people receiving the oracle misinterpreted it and could be said to be deceived by the divinity.

Divine Deception in 1 Kings

First Kings 13 is the story of the "man of God" who prophesies against Jeroboam. He is told not to eat or drink while in Jeroboam's territory but deliver his prophecy and leave. Yet, an "old prophet" tells him that he has received a revelation from YHWH and invites the man of God back to his house for food and drink (13:14-19). He then pronounces the death sentence because the man of God disobeyed the order (13:20-22). This is a very intriguing story. Some have immediately labelled the "old prophet" a false prophet, but this is not at all the case in the story. He is not called a false prophet; on the contrary, he receives messages from YHWH. The implication is that his lie to the "man of God" is also a divine revelation (13:18), while his revelation that the "man of God" will die is clearly from YHWH (13:20).

First Kings 22:5-23 contains the prophecy of Micaiah, who reveals the vision of the divine council that he had seen. In his vision, we have a very interesting image of YHWH sanctioning a heavenly spirit to be a lying spirit in the mouths of Ahab's prophets and to deceive Ahab (22:20-23). Why YHWH sends forth this lying spirit is not explained, but the implication is that the spirit makes the prophets predict Ahab's success to lure him into battle where he might be killed. It should be noted that Ahab's prophets are prophets of YHWH; therefore, the lying spirit inspires prophets of YHWH to give a false prophecy.

It is natural that researchers may consciously or unconsciously give precedent to their own tradition. Thus, the examples of deception in the Hebrew Bible might be justified or considered less egregious than those in "pagan" writings. Yet if we simply look at the various examples neutrally, we can note two things. First, these are not the only examples in the Hebrew Bible, another being 1 Sam 16:1-3 in which Samuel is told by YHWH to deceive Saul about his mission to anoint David. Second, all these provide a range of instances of divine deception in one form or another. The cross-cultural examples help us to interrogate the biblical examples and ask questions that might not occur if we considered only the biblical material.

From our contemporary situation, our view of morality may differ from that of past readers of the Hebrew Bible. We are not always prepared to accept or condone actions in the Bible if we think they offend against this view. Whereas past readers might have justified the divine deceptions noted here, it is not clear that they are so different from those in the cross-cultural examples. In every case the divine act of deception is justified (directly or by implication) in context. The Mesopotamian gods had their reasons for destroying humans by a flood, just as YHWH does in the Noah story. The Norse gods are concerned to protect their own home but also the world of human habitation when they make promises they do not intend to keep, an action that can be supported by a moral argument. The Mayan gods, who take away human far-sightedness, act in a way very parallel to the deity in the Adam and Eve story, where humans gain certain divine knowledge and as a result are denied immortality. In both cases, humans gain a divine characteristic but are prevented from gaining equality with divinity.

It is interesting that in every case, one can see a transcendent goal in the divine deception. In 1 Kgs 13, the prophet is given a divine message, but he must follow his divine instructions, and he is tested to see whether he will do so. In 1 Kgs 22, YHWH evidently wants to put Ahab in mortal peril or at least make him choose whether to go to war or not. So Ahab is placed in the position that the choice is entirely his; he does not have to go to war, but there is nothing to prevent him because of the prophetic message. Yet, the same applies to the Mesopotamian flood or the building of fortifications for the Norse gods, or the creation of humans by the Mayan divinities. The Pythian oracles may seem to be misleading, but in each case they allow the people involved to make a free decision. Croesus did not have to go against Cyrus. The Athenians had a choice in how to defend themselves. The examples may vary in moral seriousness, but we cannot set the biblical examples against the "pagan" ones; they have an unsettling similarity in a number of cases.

What all the examples bring to our attention is the making of decisions. In a number of cases, the decision involves making a choice among several less-than-ideal possibilities. The decisions are not black and white but a series of grays. This seems to me to be one of the main lessons to be drawn from most of these examples.

Conclusion

Many readers of the Bible will be surprised to be confronted with blatant cases of divine deception. Although the examples from 1 Kings given here are well known to biblical scholars, it is not often that one is confronted directly with such instances; they are generally addressed as part of the complex characterization of God in the Hebrew Bible. One might expect to find such examples in a "pagan" context since the doings of the gods in a polytheistic environment are not always admirable. But what comes to the fore in both the biblical and the cross-cultural examples considered here is that God/the gods have a positive aim in each case, although we might have a difference of opinion as to whether the aim is justified in the light of modern views of contemporary morality. The Norse gods wanted to protect their world and that of humans from the predations of the giants. YHWH wanted to lure Ahab into a battle where he might lose his life. Some modern religious people might find difficulties with both forms of justification, but both give us pause and make us think about deciding between a series of choices, all of which are less than perfectly righteous.

"What Have I Done to You?" — 1 Kings 19:19-21
A Study in Prophetic Ethics

Jeremiah Unterman

The last three verses of the Jewish Bible's prophetic literature are Mal 3:22-24:[1]

> 22 Be mindful of the Torah of My servant Moses, whom I charged at Horeb with laws and rules for all Israel. 23 Lo, I will send the prophet Elijah to you before the coming of the awesome, fearful day of the LORD. 24 He shall turn back the hearts of the parents to the children and the hearts of the children to the parents, lest I come and strike the earth with utter destruction.[2]

The most common rabbinic interpretation of v. 24 was to see Elijah's role as convincing parents and children together to repent to

---

* It is a pleasure for me to dedicate this article in honor of my dear friend, Professor Marvin A. Sweeney. It has not been published before (aside from a summary in a Yeshiva University student newspaper in 2004), but the material it covers lies at the basis of Jeremiah Unterman, *Justice for All: How the Jewish Bible Revolutionized Ethics* (JPSEJ; Philadelphia: Jewish Publication Society; Lincoln, NE: University of Nebraska Press, 2017), 250 n. 112. Prof. Sweeney was kind enough to carefully read and comment on an advanced draft of that book, for which he is gratefully acknowledged there.

When I was a beginning graduate student at the Hebrew University of Jerusalem forty-eight years ago, I took a course on medieval rabbinic exegesis of the Book of the Twelve (the "Minor Prophets") with Prof. Ezra Zion Melamed, z"l – a lovely person and a great scholar who was also a practicing Orthodox rabbi. At the end of the course, I went up to him and, with all the chutzpah of my youth, said to him something like, "Well, the prophets talk a good game — they're constantly demanding ethical behavior, but do they practice what they preach? Where is the evidence that they themselves behaved ethically?" Prof. Melamed looked at me with sad eyes and said softly, "Study, study. You'll see, you'll see." I pray that this article is a testimony to his wisdom.

It should be noted that the first presentation of this material, with its conclusions, occurred in 1979.

[1] Many scholars have claimed that these three verses are a later ending to the book, or the Book of the Twelve, or the prophetic collection as a whole. For a summary of their arguments, see Jacob Liver, "מלאכי," אנציקלופדיה מקראית (Jerusalem: Bialik, 1962), 4:1031-32.

[2] All translations are based upon NJPS (*JPS Hebrew-English Tanakh* [Philadelphia: JPS, 1999]), with my adjustments.

God.[1] However, the critical Hebrew phrase of the verse is *hŝyb* [hiphil of *ŝûb*] *lb* x *ᶜl* y, "will return (or, turn back) the heart(s) of parents (or, fathers) to children (or, sons)." *hŝyb* *ᶜl* (with or without a direct object in between) always means "to return to" or "turn upon, against," never "to return with;" see 2 Sam 16:8 (in the sense of "payback"); Isa 1:25; 46:8 ("take to heart"); Ezek 38:12; Amos 1:8; Hab 2:1. The exact meaning of the phrase receives further clarification in comparison with another nearly identical phrase in Ezra 6:22: "for the LORD made them happy and turned the heart of the king of Assyria to them, to strengthen their hands...." The phrase "turned the heart of x to y" here is the Hebrew *hsb* (Hiphil of *sbb*) *lb* x *ᶜl* y, where *hsb* in Ezra and *hŝyb* in Malachi, along with the whole phrases, are synonymous. It further should be noted that both texts posit a fifth century BCE date. Thus, Mal 3:24 is *not* referring to repentance, but rather to reconciliation between parents and children.

If v. 24, then, refers to some kind of reuniting of parents and children, to what specifically does it refer? Scholars, in their zeal to find the appropriate *Sitz im Leben*, have opined that it reflects the situation under Hellenism. "Apparently," states John Merlin Powis Smith, "the younger generation has taken up with some new philosophy or cult or political course and irreconcilable conflict has arisen between them and their elders. This condition best accords with the situation in Israel after the incoming of Greek thought and influence."[2] More recently, David Petersen has taken a different approach. He argues against those who would see ethical content in v. 24:

> The themes of the sons and the fathers is probably... a typical manner of speaking in certain eschatological texts, the resolution of opposites (Joel 3:1)... this theme functions less as an ethical imperative than as a way of describing the period just prior to the arrival of Yahweh in the eschatological age.[3]

Why ethics and eschatology cannot mix is a question upon which Petersen does not reflect. In any case, it should be noted that this is the

---

[1] For example, *Pirke de Rabbi Eliezer* (tr. Gerald Friedlander; London: Kegan Paul, Trench, Trubner, 1916), 344. See also Rashi, Ibn Ezra, and Radak—followed, consciously or not, by many moderns.

[2] John Merlin Powis Smith, "Malachi," *Haggai, Zechariah, Malachi and Jonah* (ICC; Edinburgh: T & T Clark, 1912), 2:1–88.

[3] David L. Petersen, *Late Israelite Prophecy: Studies in Deutero-Prophetic Literature and in Chronicles* (SBLMS 23; Missoula, MT: Scholars Press, 1977), 44.

first text that ascribes a redemptive role for Elijah, and all future references to Elijah in a messianic context hearken back to these verses.

With this brief background, several questions arise: Why does the author, Malachi or otherwise, find this act of parent-child reconciliation so meaningful? Why is Elijah's future act attached to remembrance of the *mitzvot* (commandments) of the Torah of Moses? And why, without this reconciliation, will complete destruction of the world result?

In attempting to respond to these questions, it seems obvious that v. 23 implies knowledge of Elijah's ascension to heaven in 2 Kgs 2:11. Are the answers to the above questions, then, to be found in the Book of Kings? In 1 Kgs 17:17-24, Elijah miraculously revives a child and returns him to his mother, but this type of physical resurrection does not appear to be reflected in Malachi's words concerning heart-turning. The meeting of Elijah and Elisha in 1 Kgs 19:19-21, though, appears to be most instructive:

> [19] He set out from there and came upon Elisha son of Shaphat as he was plowing with twelve yoke of oxen ahead of him, and he was with the twelfth. Elijah passed by him and threw his mantle over him. [20] He left the oxen and ran after Elijah, and said, "Let me kiss my father and mother (good-bye), and (then) I will follow you." And he said to him, "Go return, for what have I done to you?" [21] He turned back from him and took the yoke of oxen and slaughtered them; and with the gear of the oxen, he boiled their meat and gave it to the people, and they ate. Then he arose and followed Elijah and served him.

The "there" of v. 19 points back to Elijah's journey to Horeb (1 Kgs 19:8-18), in which we have the only unquestionable connection before Malachi to the relationship of Elijah to Moses: "With the strength of that meal, he walked forty days and forty nights to the mountain of God, Horeb" (v. 8) — a clear reference to Moses's forty days and nights with God on Sinai (another name for Horeb) without food or drink (Exod 34:28). Further, Elijah goes on Horeb into "*the* cave" (v. 9; often mistranslated as "a cave"), itself an allusion to the "cleft in the rock" in which Moses received a revelation from the LORD (Exod 33:22).[1]

The primary subject of vv. 19–21 is Elijah's fulfillment of the divine command in v. 16 to "anoint" Elisha as his successor.[2] "Anoint" is used here symbolically, but Elijah's mantle-throwing is no less powerful an image.[3] In v. 20, Elisha's response indicates that he at least understands that Elijah wishes to draw him into his service. However, Elisha begs him for permission to first return home to kiss his parents good-bye, that is, to perform a proper leave-taking. The comment of Ralbag (Gersonides) is notable here:

> This is a matter of ethical behavior, to convey that it is not worthy of a person that he will part from the house of his father and mother without informing them, so that he will not cause their heart to ache when they don't know where he is. Therefore, you find that even though Elisha greatly desires to follow Elijah, he still galvanized himself to go to his father and mother to kiss them in order to inform them of his parting from them.[4]

---

[1] Still the best literary analysis of Elijah on Horeb is that of Yair Zakovitch, "קול דממה דקה: צורה ותוכן במל״א יט,'" *Tarbiz* 51 (1982): 329–46. Zakovitch also offers here a detailed discussion of the similarities between God's revelation to Moses in connection with the Golden Calf and Elijah on Carmel (344–46). He notes that the midrash already recognized that "the cave" was the "cleft in the rock" (335); see Rashi, b. Pesaḥ 54a; b. Meg. 19b.

[2] In this deed, a number of scholars have found a tie-in to Moses's appointment of Joshua as his successor. A good discussion may be found in Marsha C. White, *The Elijah Legends and Jehu's Coup* (BJS; Atlanta: Scholars Press, 1997), 8–9; see also her elaborate examination of the Elijah–Moses connection (3–7). Both Joshua and Elisha start off as personal attendants, but their future as the people's leaders is never in doubt.

[3] Uriel Simon, *Reading Prophetic Narratives* (tr. Lenn J. Schramm; Bloomington: Indiana University Press, 1997), 219–20, convincingly points out that, "In Scripture, one's garment is viewed as part of one's being; to a certain extent, one's clothing is like one's body... Elijah's cloak, like Samuel's (1 Sam. 15:27 and 28:14), is the badge or uniform of the prophetic office (1 Kgs 19:13; 2 Kgs 2:13–14; Zech 13:4) as well as his distinctive mark of identity (2 Kgs 1:8). When he throws his mantle over Elisha it clearly signifies that Elijah is calling him to assume the mantle of prophecy 'in his stead.'"

[4] In "value" (or "moral lesson") #31, at the end of his commentary on 1 Kings. Similarly, see Leah Jacobsen, (מלכים א יט 20 א) "למשמעות דברי אלישע 'אשקה־נא לאבי ולאמי ואלכה אחריך," *Shnaton* 24 (2016): 57–75, here 40 n. 1, 72–74. According to the article's English abstract (Jacobsen, "למשמעות דברי אלישע," viii), "Elisha's words reflect the legal duty to honor his father and mother. As an obedient son, Elisha must obtain his parents' consent to follow Elijah, his new patron. He does not ask Elijah but informs him of his intention 'to kiss' his parents. In order to fulfill his desire to join Elijah without overlooking his legal obligation towards his parents, and without provoking the prophet's wrath, Elisha phrases his words with ingenuity and diplomacy, emphasizing his personal and emotional needs as

Elijah's reply, *lk šûb ky mh ᶜśyty lk*, "Go, return, for what have I done to you?" has been the subject of much commentary. Among the medieval rabbinic exegetes, Rashi, Radak, Ralbag, and Abravanel all understand that Elijah gave Elisha permission to say good-bye to his parents.[1] Rashi, however, understands the word "return" to mean "return home,"[2] while Ralbag and Abravanel understand it to mean "and then follow me," as if it were written *wšûb*, that is, "Go (back), *and* return (to me)." Radak explains that Elijah gives Elisha his consent in order to test him, to see if he was speaking truthfully and would indeed come back to Elijah.[3]

Concerning the phrase, "for what have I done to you?" the rabbinic interpretations are as follows: Rashi: "that you should follow me;" Radak: "if I have thrown my mantle upon you, then you must run after me;"[4] Ralbag: "I have already done this to awaken you that you will come to shelter under my wings;" and Abravanel: "after I have done a great thing to you, it's not worthy that you should throw it behind your back." The positive understanding of Elijah's comment by Radak, Ralbag, and Abravanel — "I have done a great thing to you" — is followed by Sweeney: "The question is a rhetorical statement that Elijah has indeed done something momentous to Elisha and that he [Elisha] should return to do as he [Elisha] proposed."[5]

Nonetheless, many modern scholars find Elijah's question mysterious. For example, James Montgomery states, "Elijah's response,

---

motives for the farewell from his parents, and thus making it difficult for Elijah to refuse."

[1] Already stated by Josephus, *Ant.* 8.13.7.

[2] Among the moderns, Simon, *Reading Prophetic Narratives*, 220; Simon J. DeVries, *1 Kings* (WBC; Waco, TX: Word Books, 1985), 239; Wesley J. Bergen, *Elisha and the End of Prophetism* (JSOTSup 286; Sheffield: Sheffield Academic Press, 1999), 51; and Yael Shemesh, "(21־19 מלכים א יט) מהליכה אחר הבקר להליכה אחר אליהו: מינוי אלישע למשרתו של אליהו", עיוני מקרא ופרשנות (eds. Moshe Garsiel et al.; Ramat Gan: Bar-Ilan University Press, 2000), 5:85–86; all claim that although Elijah gave Elisha permission to return home, Elijah was trying to make it clear that Elisha's following Elijah would be totally Elisha's decision, and that Elijah had no authority to tell him otherwise.

[3] Explicitly followed by Mordechai Cogan, *I Kings: A New Translation and Commentary* (AB 10; New York: Doubleday, 2001), 455.

[4] Inexplicably, מקראות גדולות הקתר־ מלכים (ed. Menachem Cohen; Ramat-Gan: Bar-Ilan University, 1995), 137, takes Radak's last words here as a question, "then you must run after me?"

[5] Marvin A. Sweeney, *I & II Kings: A Commentary* (OTL; Louisville: Westminster John Knox, 2007), 233. Others share this perspective, e.g., Norman Snaith in *IB*, 3:165 and Georg Fohrer, *Elia* (Zurich: Zwingli, 1957), 22.

Go back (again)..., for what have done to thee?, has puzzled comm[entators].... But the inquiry is simplest taken as an expression of mystery, exposition of which is reserved for the future."[1] Burke Long remarks, "Elisha... demurs, provoking an enigmatic response from Elijah."[2] Richard Nelson notes, "Elijah's response is enigmatic;"[3] and Gina Hens-Piazza concludes, "Whether Elijah was checking to see if Elisha understood what had just taken place or was retreating from having made any gesture of invitation to Elisha remains unclear. In either case, Elijah's cryptic response hardly qualifies as an encouraging reception of Elisha's willingness to follow."[4]

Is Elijah's question truly so obscure that it cannot be understood? Another line of interpretation denies any ambiguity — by reference to the words of Jesus in the New Testament. For example, John Gray points out, "the emphasis is on the uncompromising nature of the call. The interpretation is supported by the hyperbolic demand of Jesus in similar circumstances (Matt 8:21ff.; Luke 9:61);"[5] and Simon DeVries claims, "The best commentary on the Elisha call-story is Jesus's word recorded in Luke 9:61-62."[6] It behooves us then to look at Luke 9:61-62 (Matt 8:21-22 is a more concise version):

> [61] Another said, 'I will follow you, Lord; but let me first say farewell to those at my home.' [62] Jesus said to him, 'No one who puts a hand to the plow and looks back is fit for the kingdom of God.' (NRSV)

These verses seem to reflect Elisha's request, as well as his plowing with the oxen. If Jesus's remarks are an understanding of Elijah's response, then Jesus would be interpreting Elijah's reply as a negative, "Don't go back, for you cannot come into my service unless you follow me immediately."

---

[1] James A. Montgomery, *A Critical and Exegetical Commentary on the Books of Kings* (ed. Henry Snyder Gehman; ICC; Edinburgh: T & T Clark, 1951), 316.

[2] Burke O. Long, *1 Kings, with an Introduction to Historical Literature* (FOTL 9; Grand Rapids: Eerdmans, 1984), 205.

[3] Richard D. Nelson, *First and Second Kings* (IBC; Louisville: John Knox, 1987), 127.

[4] Gina Hens-Piazza, *1-2 Kings* (AOTC; Nashville: Abingdon, 2006), 193.

[5] John Gray, *I & II Kings: A Commentary* (OTL; London: SCM, 1970), 413.

[6] DeVries, *1 Kings*, 239. Nelson, *First and Second Kings*, 127, cites the connection to the NT as a question, "Is it a rebuke in the spirit of Jesus's sayings in Matt 8:21-22 and Luke 9:62?"

Nonetheless, the attempt to understand the meeting of Elijah and Elisha in 1 Kgs 19 through citations in the Gospels is methodologically unsound. To interpret a verse in one literature through verses in another, where the first text was composed more than half a millennium before the second—in a different language and under different social and religious conditions—is illogical, particularly when the verse in question has not been properly investigated within its own literary context. Medieval rabbinic commentaries, and others of their like, are also faulty for not having appropriately examined the language of the verse, although the rabbis can hardly be considered to be objective scholars in the modern academic mode. That circumstance does not, obviously, excuse modern commentators.

Let us agree on the meaning of *lk šûb ky mh ᶜśyty lk* within its immediate context. Elisha's response to Elijah's statement reveals that he comprehends that Elijah has given him permission to go home, to take a proper leave of his parents—even to the extent of having an elaborate farewell dinner with the local folk—and then come back to serve Elijah, for that is what he does. That much may be partially implied by Elijah's words, "Go, return," *lk šûb* (the only other exact occurrences of this word pair are in the same chapter, v. 15, and in Exod 4:19).[1]

But what of *ky mh ᶜśyty lk*? The *ky* seems to indicate "for" or "because;" that is, the following words, "what have I done to you," apparently provide the reason for the permission given to Elisha to return home and fulfill his wish. To what, then, could *mh ᶜśyty lk* possibly refer? In order to understand this clause, one needs to examine its occurrences elsewhere in the Tanak. The results of that investigation are that there are thirty-six other instances of the interrogative *mh* followed by the verb *ᶜśh* in the Qal perfect,[2] in only two of which is the verb in the first person followed by the preposition *l* with the second-person masculine suffix—*lk*, "to you" (see below). In

---

[1] Verse 20 almost certainly points back to v. 15, but does v. 15 purposely allude to Exod 4:19? In the latter case, both addresses—God to Moses and God to Elijah—are saying, "You have a job to do for me which will save the people."

[2] Gen 3:13; 4:10; 12:18; 20:9; 26:10; 29:25; 31:26; 42:28; 44:15; Exod 14:5, 11; 32:21; Num 22:28; 23:11; Josh 7:19; Judg 2:2; 8:1, 2; 15:11; 1 Sam 13:11; 14:43; 17:29; 20:1, 32; 26:18; 29:8; 2 Sam 3:24; 12:21; 24:17; Jer 2:23; 8:6; Jonah 1:10; Mic 6:3; Esth 9:12; 1 Chr 21:17; 2 Chr 32:13.

every single one of these thirty-six instances, the reference is *always* to a negative action, to something bad, to some harm that had occurred, *real or imagined*. To cite a few examples:

Gen 3:13 - God to the woman in the Garden: *mh z't ᶜśyt*, "What is this that you have done?" As we know, she passes the buck on to the snake.

Exod 14:11 - When the Israelites see the Egyptian army approaching, they turn on Moses, "Is it because there are no graves in Egypt that you have taken us to die in the desert, *mh z't ᶜśyt lnû*, what is this that you have done to us to bring us out of Egypt?"

Num 23:11 - After Balaam blesses Israel, Balak says to him, *mh ᶜśyt ly*, "What have you done to me? Here I brought you to damn my enemies, and instead you have blessed them!"

Josh 7:19 - When Achan takes of the banned items, Joshua says to him, "Tell me, *mh ᶜśyt*, what you have done; do not hold anything back from me." And in the next verse, Achan responds, "It is true, I have sinned against the LORD, the God of Israel. This is what I did, *ᶜśyty*."

Jer 8:6 - In God's accusation of the people, the prophet declares, "No one regrets his wickedness and says, '*mh ᶜśyty*, What have I done!'"

1 Sam 20:1 - In response to Saul's attempt to kill him, David asks Jonathan, *mh ᶜśyty*, "What have I done? What is my crime and guilt against your father, that he seeks my life?" — a protestation of innocence.

That statement of David is very similar to the only two other occurrences, outside of 1 Kgs 19:20, of "What have I done to you?"

Num 22:28 - After Balaam strikes his ass for the third time, the animal speaks up and says, *mh ᶜśyty lk*, "What have I done to you that you have beaten me these three times?" Balaam follows with his unwarranted complaint.

Mic 6:3 - In a suit against Israel for disobedience and immorality, God says, "My people, *mh ᶜśyty lk*, what have I done to you? What hardship have I caused you? Testify against me!" The next verse continues, "For I brought you up from the land of Egypt."

In both these instances, the speakers are protesting their innocence. They have done no wrong, therefore they are being treated unjustly.

In returning to 1 Kgs 19, the evidence forces us to realize that when Elijah asks, "what have I done to you?" he cannot be saying, "look at what good thing I have done to you." Rather, he must be saying, "Go, return home, for what bad thing have I done to you?" Indeed, what bad thing does Elijah think that Elisha thinks that Elijah had done, for that is what Elijah's question implies. We can only infer from the context. Whenever someone in the Hebrew Bible says, "What have I done to you," it is always in response to somebody else's action. What did Elisha do to evoke Elijah's response? It must be within Elisha's request that the answer is to be found. Elisha wants Elijah's permission to kiss his parents good-bye. The request seeks a "yes" or "no" answer, and therefore suggests that Elijah could actually say "No!" However, Elijah's response indicates that to deny Elisha's request is the furthest thing from his mind! Elijah reacts as though the answer is so obvious that the question need not have been asked and that to say "no" would be indeed a crime, a sin. Truly, Elijah turns Elisha's request into his own command, "Of course, go home, and enjoy a proper farewell, for what wrong have I done to you that you should suspect that I would not allow a son to fulfill the commandment to honor one's parents!" Elijah's exclamation is an instruction to Elisha to pay his filial respects (Elisha's farewell, naturally, would also enable his parents to reciprocate).[1] How could a prophet of God act otherwise!

What makes this little episode so fascinating is the context in which it appears. There is some agreement among scholars that vv. 19-21 were not originally connected to the previous parts of ch. 19.[2] Nevertheless, it must be noted that, at the very least, an editor placed vv. 19-21 here because he saw it as the beginning of the fulfillment of God's directives to Elijah in vv. 15-18. To put it in the appropriate

---

[1] Similarly, Mendel Hirsch, *The Haphtoroth* (tr. Isaac Levy; London: Isaac Levy, 1966): "There is almost a reproach in the form in which the permission was given. What then have I done to thee that thou couldst believe it would be my wish that thou shouldst follow me without first embracing thy Father and Mother?" (357)

[2] For convincing arguments that *do* see vv. 19-21 as an organic end to the chapter, see White, *The Elijah Legends*, 9 and Simon, *Reading Prophetic Narratives*, 220.

framework, Elijah had gone to Horeb in the darkest despair. His words in vv. 10 and 14 testify to his belief that the great experiment is over; the Israelites have abandoned the covenant with its attendant demands for obedience to God. There is no hope—the worship of God in Israel has died out. It is at this moment of profound depression that Elijah is shown God's plan to destroy the wicked idolaters and to be merciful to the faithful of Israel. The trend of history will be reversed and it is Elijah who will be the catalyst. God lifts Elijah up and sends him on this momentous mission to change the course of Israel's history. And the first person Elijah meets is the last person of whom God spoke— Elisha—and Elisha innocently asks Elijah's permission to kiss his parents good-bye. Does Elijah rebuke him and tell him that the divinely ordained task to change the course of history cannot be delayed? No, it *is* delayed, and delayed for the performance of a simple, mundane ethical act of filial respect. Taken in this context, Elijah's reply to Elisha acquires sublime ethical significance. The mission of God shall not be carried out while turning a blind eye toward moral behavior. Elijah fully comprehends that obedience to God on one level does not eliminate the need for obedience to God in moral action.

It is the contention here that 1 Kgs 19 in its entirety comes into the view of Malachi (or an editor) in the last verses of his book.[1] We noted above the connection in 1 Kgs 19 between Moses and Elijah, as in Mal 3:22-23. Why does the author of Mal 3:24 find the act of parent-child reconciliation so important? Why is Elijah's future act attached to remembrance of the *mitzvot* of Moses's Torah? And why, without this reconciliation, would complete destruction of the world result? In 1 Kgs 19:20, Elijah's command to Elisha to return to his parents with fitting behavior—based upon God's commandments—delays the divine mission to transform Israel's history for the better, to save the faithful ones (19:18), and destroy the wicked (19:17-18). Malachi 3:24, though, goes one better than 1 Kgs 19:20. If in 1 Kgs 19:20 the mission of God must be delayed for the simple ethical commandment of honoring one's parents, in Mal 3:24 the mission of God cannot be accomplished without the reconciliation of children and their parents. For are not these relationships at the heart of God's relationship to

---

[1] See Liver's arguments for the authenticity of Mal 3:22-24 ("מלאכי," 4:1032). Further, v. 23 ("the coming of the day") looks back on v. 19 ("the day that is coming").

Israel? See Mal 1:6, "A son should honor his father.... Now if I am a father, where is the honor due me?" and Mal 3:17, "I will be tender toward them as a man is tender toward his son who ministers to him."

In the end, the meeting of Elijah and Elisha is another illustration that the Hebrew Bible is a didactic book—and one which focuses on the importance of ethical behavior.

Jezebel
A Phoenician Princess Gone Bad?

Tammi J. Schneider

Jezebel does not fare well in the Hebrew Bible, New Testament, or just about any scholarly discussion of those texts. According to Athalya Brenner, Jezebel "is characterized as totally evil in the biblical text and beyond it: in the NT her name is a generic catchword for a whoring non-believing female adversary... she is evil incarnate."[1] The point of this article is not to turn Jezebel into a saint but to prove that the title, "Jezebel: A Phoenician Princess Gone Bad," minus the question mark at the end, is a biased view constructed through reading Jezebel's story only through the lens of the author of 1 and 2 Kings, which is further reinforced by modern scholarship.

The reality is that Jezebel, as a Sidonian princess, may have behaved perfectly fine for the Sidonians, but the authors of the biblical text had other expectations. Jezebel carried out the demands of her office of being married to a ruler of a foreign country,[2] but it is her role in the foreign land and the place from which we have the bulk of our data, the Bible, that depict her as a problem for the theological necessities of that text. Jezebel provides a perfect means for the authors of the books of Kings to justify aspects of Ahab by suggesting the bulk of the most heinous crimes of his reign were perpetrated by or because of her.

In order to make my point, I will examine closely the main data source for Jezebel, the Hebrew Bible, specifically the books of 1 and 2 Kings. For matters of space I will examine primarily her descriptions. I will then turn briefly to where she appears as the subject of a verb,

---

[1] Athalya Brenner, "Jezebel 1," *Women in Scripture: A Dictionary of Named and Unnamed Women in the Hebrew Bible, the Apocryphal/Deuteroncanonical Books, and the New Testament* (ed. Carol Meyers; Grand Rapids: Eerdmans, 2000), 101.

[2] Note that anywhere else Jezebel, because of her relationship to Ahab, would be labeled a "queen" but the Hebrew Bible never names her so. Brenner, "Jezebel 1," 101.

where she is an object, and what we can say about her relationships. Extrabiblical texts will be used when relevant.

Jezebel is described in a number of ways and not labeled with some traditional terms for women. Jezebel is characterized as follows: once as the daughter of Ethbaal, king of the Sidonians, twice the wife of Ahab; once hinted she is a mother; and once categorically as the mother of Johoram. Ironically, in the same verse where she is a mother she is also labeled a whore. Finally, she is described as wearing make-up.

When we first meet Jezebel she is described as the daughter of Ethbaal, who is labeled the King of the Sidonians (1 Kgs 16:31). This reference is important both for what it says about Jezebel and why it is included. First Kings 16:29 is the beginning of a new pericope and focuses on the reign of Ahab. In the verse prior to Jezebel's introduction, we learn that Ahab "did what was displeasing to the LORD, more than all who preceded him" (1 Kgs 16:30). According to some scholars, Jezebel is the trope proving v. 30 to be true: Ahab is even worse than those who preceded him.[1]

Jezebel's introduction begins with her name. A number of scholars suggest her name means something like "*zebul* exists" and *zebul* is understood as an epithet for Baal.[2] This is not shocking in light of the fact that her father's name is Ethbaal, clearly a Baal name and the first appearance of the name Baalin the book of Kings. It should not surprise anyone when Jezebel, named after Baal and daughter of someone with a Baal name, is an adherent of Baal. I would suggest that both names were known to Ahab prior to their marriage. Thus, the issue is not one Ahab has with Jezebel but foreshadows an issue the authors of Kings have with Ahab's choice.

Jezebel is named the "daughter of Ethbaal" a common designation of women prior to their marriage in the Hebrew Bible, except it is unusual in the book of Kings. As Solvang notes, "The rhetoric of the books of Kings directs the reader to take note of the

---

[1] Jerome T. Walsh, *I Kings* (BOSHNP; Collegeville, MN: Liturgical Press, 1996), 218-19 and Mordechai Cogan, *I Kings: A New Translation with Introduction and Commentary*, (AB 10; New York: Doubleday, 2000), 422, and we cannot forget, the reason for this Festschrift, Marvin A. Sweeney, *I & II Kings: A Commentary* (OTL; Louisville: Westminster John Knox, 2007), 206.

[2] Cogan, *I Kings*, 420-21.

mothers of the kings of Judah in each generation,"[1] and she has shown that "the inclusion of the mother's name in Judah is an innovation in the pattern of royal reporting in the ancient Near East. Neither the regnal reports of the Northern Kingdom which are synchronized with those of Judah, nor the King Lists and Chronicles of Judah's neighbors mention the names of the mothers."[2] Solvang claims the inclusion of the mother's name in the accession prior to the regnal report suggests the mother's significance is not limited to her connection to the previous reign, but rather it suggests she was visible, influential, and active during her son's reign, at least as long as she lived.[3] The problem with Jezebel is that we are in the book of Kings, and Jezebel is only obliquely referred to as a mother (see below) and is labeled a daughter. Note that in the book of 1 Kings some mothers are the daughters of a person or a place but only Jezebel is both (in 2 Kings it becomes more common, especially after the destruction of northern Israel).

The implication of Jezebel's father and place are relevant, probably explaining their inclusion. Her father is Ethbaal. There is limited extrabiblical evidence for him, including a king of Byblos with the same name and a reference by Josephus who, much later than the time period of the events, claims Ethbaalwas a priest of Astarte.[4] Modern scholarship variously labels him the king of the Phoenicians or the King of Tyre even though the text in the Hebrew Bible clearly states he is "king of the Sidonians."[5] Reasons modern scholars correct this "mistake" suggest that the title "king of the Sidonians" reflects the expansion and supremacy of Tyre over its northern neighbors.[6] The use of these differing titles by modern scholars suggests the ancient biblical writers did not understand what they were writing and that the Levantine coastal cities were some kind of unified group politically, socially, culturally, or some combination thereof. At issue is what kind of unity and/or homogeneity did exist. Archaeologically there is a case

---

[1] Elna Solvang, *A Woman's Place is in the House: Royal Women of Judah and their Involvement in the House of David* (JSOTSup 349; New York: Sheffield Academic, 2003), 79.

[2] Solvang, *Woman's Place*, 79.

[3] Solvang, *Woman's Place*, 84.

[4] Josephus cites Menander of Ephesus in *Ag. Ap.* i.18.

[5] Sweeney, *I & II Kings*, 206.

[6] Cogan, *I Kings*, 421. Note this "correction" of the biblical text is taken to such an extreme that the 1985 Jewish Publication Society translation of the text reads "Phoenicians" rather than "Sidonians."

for classifying a set of material remains as "Phoenician" though the organization of the cities and their relationship to each other is not defined.[1]

Textually, the unity of the northern Levantine coastal cities is a harder case to make. The Assyrians referred to this region more than any other ancient source. The Assyrians also categorized the areas in the Levant, including cities regularly labeled as "Phoenician" by modern scholars, though the different Assyrian kings were not consistent in their references. The term "Amurru" is used periodically, and in the eighth century Sennacherib lists who he means by that: Sidon, Arwad, Byblos, Ashdod, Bit-Ammon, Moab, and Edom.[2] Another list including similar cities or groups but not exactly the same is the list of the 12 kings of the seacoast. In the ninth century, Shalmaneser III, in his Kurkh Monolith Inscription, names these 12: Damascus, Hama, Israel, Byblos, Egypt, Irqanatu, Arvad, Usanata, Shianu, Arabs, Bit Ruhubi, and Ammon.[3] Later, in the seventh century, Esarhaddon uses the designation, 12 kings of the Hattiland to refer to a very similar list, but this time includes Tyre, Judah, Edom, Moab, Gaza, Ashkelon, Ekron, Byblos, Arvad, Samsimurruna, Bit-Ammon, and Ashdod.[4] Esahraddon does list 12 kings from the shore of the sea but that list includes Idalion, Kitrusi, Salamis, Paphos, Soloi, Curium, Tamassos, Qarti-hadasti, Kidir, and Nuria — 10 kings of Idana (Cyprus) in the midst of the sea.[5] While it is true that much changed politically in the few hundred years between Shalmaneser III and Esarhaddon, the point is that the similar terminology is used to reference a similar but not identical group. Possibly, more importantly, is the fact that the term "Phoenician" is never used by the biblical authors or any other ancient

---

[1] Maria Eugenia Aubet, "Phoenicia during the Iron Age II Period," *The Oxford Handbook of the Archaeology of the Levant c. 8000-332 BCE* (eds. Margreet L. Steiner and Ann E. Killebrew; Oxford: Oxford University Press, 2014), 706-16. Note that the focus of this chapter also highlights how the city of Tyre, not Sidon, is the mover and shaker of the notion of "Phoenicia."

[2] A. Kirk Grayson and Jamie Novotny, *The Royal Inscriptions of Sennacherib, King of Assyria (704-681 BC), Part 1* (RINAP 3/1; Toronto: University of Toronto Press, 2012), 114.

[3] A. Kirk Grayson, *Assyrian Rulers of the Early First Millennium BC II (858-745 BC)* (RIMA 3; Toronto: University of Toronto Press, 1996), 23.

[4] Erle Leichty, *The Royal Inscriptions of Esarhaddon, King of Assyria (680-669 BC)*, (RINAP 4; Toronto: University of Toronto Press, 2011), 23 and 46.

[5] Leichty, *Royal Inscriptions*, 23.

Near Eastern entity. Thus, for modern scholars to impose terminology on the text not used by the text or anyone else in the ancient Near East and to assume a political configuration proved by that terminology ignores the language that the Hebrew Bible actually employs. In fact, here the argument is the authors of the Hebrew Bible intentionally use the term Sidon.

The implication behind modern scholars changing the name of Jezebel's hometown is that the biblical writers did not understand the political situation and modern scholars will make it "easier" for modern readers to understand. Yet might the biblical text be trying to make a point? Earlier in this very text of Kings, the biblical text spends approximately three chapters explaining the building of Solomon's Temple in Jerusalem all through the help of Hiram of Tyre (1 Kgs 5:15-7:51). While a taxation problem ensued, nowhere does the book of Kings blame Hiram or complain about his "Phoenicianness," his adherence to Baal, or any other means of pulling the Israelites away from adherence to their deity. Such is clearly not the case with Jezebel and her father. Modern scholarship aside, the way the biblical text describes the situation is that a king of one place (Tyre) helps them (unified Israel and Judah) build the temple (for a steep price), and then the daughter of a king from a totally different place (Sidon) leads northern Israel astray. If, as archaeology suggests, there is a similar material culture and a group self-identifying as Phoencians, the text could have grouped them together. Instead, to the biblical authors, there are no Phoenicians, there are just cities, rulers, and people from Tyre and others from Sidon.

It is also not the case that the biblical authors were incapable of grouping peoples into categories to make theological or ideological points. The Assyrians do not group the various cities that the Bible categorizes as "Philistine" together.[1] Again, from archaeology, we know that there are well over five cities that have what we modern scholars label "Philistine" material, but it is clear that the concept of the Philistines as a trope serves a number of theological purposes for the

---

[1] David Ben-Shlomo, "Philistia during the Iron Age II Period," *The Oxford Handbook of the Archaeology of the Levant c. 8000–332 BCE* (eds. Margreet L. Steiner and Ann E. Killebrew; Oxford: Oxford University Press, 2014), 717–18.

biblical authors.[1] It is therefore as important to note that here they do not group the northern coastal Levantine cities in such a way. It does not mean that there are no possible connections, but, in the case of the Philistines, the Assyrians chose not to group them in the same way as the Hebrew Bible. Moreover, neither the Hebrew Bible nor the ancient Assyrians chose to group the norther Levantine coastal cities under some ethnic-type term. I suggest the authors of Kings want distance from Tyre. If the Baal-adhering Jezebel and her father, who are happy to destroy Israelite prophets, had a hand in building the temple, there could be serious theological issues surrounding the temple.

Twice Jezebel is labeled a wife of Ahab. In both of these contexts she is acting wifely. In 1 Kgs 21:1, Jezebel goes to Ahab because he is not eating and asks him why this is so. Six verses later, she tells him to act as the king of Israel, and his heart will be good, and she will give him the vineyards of Naboth, precisely the cause of his distress. There is considerable scholarly discussion about whether Ahab was playing her or not. Did he get her to do his dirty work, or was he really a wimp, and she wore the pants in the family? The bottom line is that she saw her husband, who was king, upset, and she carried out actions that alleviated his distress.[2] One aspect of her job as queen may have been to do what she thought best for the royal family.

It is also possible she is carrying out her job as the daughter of a foreign ruler. When examining the roles of ancient Near Eastern women in royal settings, Solvang notes that royal daughters in diplomatic marriages were expected to be seen and heard from in their new courts.[3] Royal daughters had their own access to royal scribes and messengers, at least at Mari.[4] Royal daughters communicated with their parents directly and without interference.[5] Thus, commanding the respect of the inhabitants of Israel and expanding the palace in

---

[1] Ben-Shlomo, "Philistia," 717–29.
[2] Cogan raises the issue of the tone of Jezebel's remark and how others have treated it. The point is that rarely is someone's "tone" of voice raised as an issue (*I Kings*, 478). Cogan goes so far as to question why Jezebel does not come in for more criticism than that already leveled at her given her central role in the drama (484).
[3] Solvang, *Woman's Place*, 24.
[4] Solvang, *Woman's Place*, 25.
[5] Solvang, *Woman's Place*, 25.

accordance with her husband's wishes might be well in line with her royal duties as defined by ancient Near Eastern expectations.

Second Kings 3:1 suggests Jezebel is the mother of Johoram, but the text does not state this categorically. It is only in 2 Kgs 9:22 that she is labeled the mother of Joram, and not by the narrator but by Jehu. He says it in response to Joram's question as to how he is. Jehu responds, "How can all be well as long as your mother, Jezebel, carries on her countless harlotries and sorceries?" This reference is particularly interesting in light of what and how women are mentioned in Kings. While the role of women in each biblical book is different depending on the book (and in each book they tend to serve as a different type of trope), for the rest of Kings, they are pretty much mothers.[1] Nowhere does the text suggest that Ahab "takes" her or that she becomes pregnant, bears, or names a child. As Solvang has shown, the women mentioned from Judah are mentioned in connection to their son's reigns, not their spouses.[2] The same is true of Bathsheba; her importance to the text is only relevant because of who her son is. As a result, for the narrator to never name Jezebel a mother, and the only person to do so is Jehu when he is also calling her a whore, is striking. Clearly Jezebel's role as a mother is far less important than her role as a ruling queen and wife of Ahab.

To call out Jezebel for her harlotries is also telling for her role in the story. By associating it with sorceries and raising it only in this context, the suggestion of the term is not so much that she slept around but rather went after foreign deities, a notion often used in Judges and Kings. Indeed, a major theme of both the books of Judges and Kings is that the Israelites betray their deity by going after other deities. So by using the same "whoring" language, the thrust both in Jehu's language and Jezebel's previous actions is that she is trying to lure everyone to Baalism by destroying the Israelite prophets. Thus, her label as whore is not actually sexual but religious.

Lastly, 2 Kgs 9:30 references Jezebel putting kohl on her eyes and making her head pretty. One suggestion is that she is dressing up

---

[1] For the difference between the role of women in Genesis, see Tammi J. Schneider, *Judges* (BOSHNP; Collegeville, MN: Liturgical Press, 2000) versus Schneider, *Mothers of Promise: Women in the Book of Genesis* (Grand Rapids: Baker Academic, 2004).

[2] Solvang, *Woman's Place*, 84–5.

because she is royalty, and this is an official reception.[1] If this is true, and I agree, then once again, Jezebel is acting as a true foreign princess ruling in a foreign land.

A review of a number of Jezebel's actions suggests why she is so hated by the biblical text and modern scholarship. Jezebel cuts down the prophets (i.e., killed; 1 Kgs 18:4), sends messengers (1 Kgs 19:2); says and comes (1 Kgs 21:5-7); writes and seals (1 Kgs 21:8); hears and instigates (1 Kgs 21:13-16); and puts kohl on her eyes and pretties herself (2 Kgs 9:30). A number of these verbs are standard for many characters such as saying, hearing, and coming. For a woman, it is fairly unique to send messengers, which she does numerous times; to seal letters, especially with her husband's seal; and to instigate. Again, Jezebel's introduction suggests she is no normal woman. Jezebel is a royal woman, and it is not unusual for royal women to carry out these actions; in fact, it is often expected. What is unusual is for women to cut down prophets of the deity who is the main deity of the land her husband rules. Cogan suggests,

> The portrayal of Jezebel as a zealot of Baal who undertook to exterminate the prophets of [J] is a caricature.... The intolerance that it implies is inconsistent with pagan thought.... Jezebel's behavior becomes understandable when viewed as a political response to the opposition raised by the loyal servants of [J] to the foreign cults that had been introduced into Israel's capital upon her arrival.[2]

Of course, at issue is how well entrenched worship of that deity was at that time and where that worship took place, which was precisely on the border of ancient Israel and "Phoenicia:" Mount Carmel.

Finally, when Jezebel is an object, she is usually still shown as in charge. First, Ahab "takes" her as a wife (1 Kgs 16:31). This is common Hebrew marriage construction and simply suggests that men decide who they marry and women do not. Ahab tells Jezebel all sorts of things (1 Kgs 19:1, 21:6) and the messengers send responses to Jezebel, even though she writes the letters in Ahab's name and uses his seal (1 Kgs 21:4). This suggests they too know who is behind the various

---

[1] Sweeney, *I & II Kings*, 335.
[2] Cogan, *I Kings*, 447.

schemes. Even the Israelite deity speaks of Jezebel saying dogs will eat her (1 Kgs 21:23); something that later comes true (2 Kgs 9:33). Finally, 1 Kgs 22:53 suggests Jezebel is the mother of Ahaziah without naming her, similar to the situation in 2 Kgs 3:13. It claims, "He (Ahaziah) did the bad thing in the eyes of J and he went the way of his father and the path of his mother."

In this short review of Jezebel, it becomes clear that the biblical material concerning Jezebel reveals a highly theological and ideological depiction of a woman about whom we know little. Furthermore, many of the characters referenced in regard to Jehu and Omri are known from extrabiblical material, namely the Assyrian texts of Shalmaneser III, and many of these characters are treated as more historically grounded than other characters by modern scholars. While this is legitimate, what is noteworthy is that the data we have from the Hebrew Bible is not always in line with what the Assyrians present. For example, elsewhere I have argued that Jehu actually is a descendant of Omri in line with the Assyrian material.[1] So too, the way women function in the ancient Near East suggests that some of the actions placed upon Jezebel in the ancient Near Eastern context may be read differently. In any case, on whichever side of the Carmel one dwells, one must agree that Jezebel is a strong queen who fights for her husband and carries out her duties as foreign royalty ruling in Israel. Clearly the biblical writers were not advocates of her policies, but within the Sidonian and ancient Near Eastern expectations of a royal spouse, she carries out her functions of wife and queen.

---

[1] Tammi J. Schneider, "Rethinking Jehu," *Bib* 77 (1996): 100–07.

King Lists as a Structuring Principle in the Book of Kings

John H. Hull, Jr.

This examination of Kings focuses on the book's king lists. The Assyrian King List has long been regarded as providing a model for king lists that may have stood behind the book of Kings. Whether or not documentary king lists existed for Israel and Judah, it is useful to examine Kings with an eye toward the structural principles of the Assyrian King List.

The post-Solomonic kings of Israel and Judah will first be viewed separately. Then the combined list of all kings from Saul to Zedekiah will be analyzed. Parallel themes emerge from the two kingdoms while examination of the combined list reveals principles that apply to the entire institution of monarchy in Israel and Judah.

Assyrian King Lists

The Assyrian King List (AKL) exists in three versions that differ in only a few details.[1] The lists end with different kings, suggesting expansion by later reigns. While historians have used them principally for constructing a chronology, numerical schematism is present in the lists.[2] The number, order, and lengths of reign are related in patterns.[3] The total length of reign for groups of identically named kings is frequently a multiple of 11 (Shalmaneser I-III; Aššur-nirari I-V; Šamši-Adad I-III; Tukulti-ninurta I-II; Ashurnasirpal I-II) or 29

---

* For Marvin Sweeney—friend, colleague, mentor, שומר שבת.

[1] For the text and bibliography, see A. Kirk Grayson, "Königlisten und Chroniken B. Akkadisch," *RlA* (1980–83): 6:86–135; for an English translation, see *ANET*, 564–66.

[2] J. A. Brinkman's chronology in A. Leo Oppenheim, *Ancient Mesopotamia: Portrait of a Dead Civilization* (rev. ed.; completed by Erica Reiner; Chicago: University of Chicago Press, 1977), 343–48, is largely based on these lists, although he has urged caution in using AKL for historical reconstruction; see J. A. Brinkman, "Comments on the Nassouhi Kinglist and the Assyrian Kinglist Tradition," *Or* 42 (1973): 306–19.

[3] For schematism in the Sumerian King List, see Dwight A. Young, "A Mathematical Approach to Certain Dynastic Spans in the Sumerian King List," *JNES* 47 (1988): 123–29.

(Shalmaneser I–IV; Aššur-dan I–III; Eriba-Adad I–II). The Adad-nirari kings involve square numbers: 49 (7^2) (II–III) and 81 (9^2) (I–III).

The lists are arranged in three main groups: A, B, and C. The first two groups contain 38 kings each, with 6 usurpers in each list. The number of kings in Group C varies in the three extant lists. Jens Høyrup has pointed to a particular interest in the numbers 7, 11, 19, 29, 31, 37, and 41, as well as squares and cubes in Mesopotamian literary texts. While the original interest in these "remarkable numbers" arose in mathematics, they eventually became part of the literary code.[1] Hence, in AKL the first two groups of 38 kings are twice 19.

Nineteen Kings

The post-Solomonic kingdoms of Israel and Judah were ruled by 19 kings in each kingdom. Each kingdom also has a usurper among its rulers. Athaliah (2 Kgs 11) and Tibni (1 Kgs 16:21–22) are designated as illegitimate by the lack of standard regnal formulas. This feature is analogous to AKL with its two groups of 38 (2x19) kings, six of whom are usurpers. The number 19 shows up in another feature of the Israelite "king lists." The combined kings of Israel and Judah include 19 with the theophoric element יהו.[2]

Table 1: The King Lists of Judah and Israel

1	Rehoboam	1	Jeroboam
2	Abijam	2	Nadab
3	Asa	3	Baasha
4	Jehosaphat	4	Elah
5	Jehoram	5	**Zimri**
6	**Ahaziah**	6	Omri
7	Jehoash	7	Ahab
8	Amaziah	8	Ahaziah
9	Azariah	9	Jehoram
10	JOTHAM	10	**JEHU**
11	**Ahaz**	11	Jehoahaz
12	Hezekiah	12	Jehoash

---

[1] Jens Høyrup, "Mathematics, Algebra, and Geometry," *ABD* 4:602–612 and Jens Høyrup, "'Remarkable Numbers' in Old Babylonian Mathematical Texts: A Note on the Psychology of Numbers," *JNES* 52 (1993): 281–86.

[2] AKL has 27 (3^3) kings whose names contain the name of the god Aššur.

13	Manasseh	13	Jeroboam
14	Amon	14	Zechariah
15	Josiah	**15**	**Shallum**
16	**Jehoahaz**	16	Menahem
17	Jehoikim	17	Pekahiah
18	Jehoichin	18	Pekah
19	Zedekiah	19	Hoshea

יהו *Kings in Israel and Judah*

Setting aside Jehu (יהוא) for a moment, the 18 יהו kings of Israel and Judah include the following:

יהו prefix (9 kings)

Israel (3): Jehoram, Jehoahaz, Jehoash

Judah (6): Jehoshaphat, Jehoram, Jehoash, Jehoahaz, Jehoiakim, Jehoiachin.

יהו suffix (9 kings)

Israel (3): Ahaziah, Zechariah, Pekahiah

Judah (6): Ahaziah, Amaziah, Azariah (Uzziah), Hezekiah, Josiah, Zedekiah

In addition to the 18 prefix and suffix kings, the anomalous Jehu (יהוא) gives Israel 7 יהו kings and Judah 12.[1] The distribution of the 18 יהו names is precise. Six prefix forms are Judean and three Israelite. The same two-to-one ratio holds for the suffix forms. Twice as many יהו kings are ascribed to Judah compared with Israel. This pattern corresponds with the general view expressed by the narrator of Kings that Judah maintains a higher standard of YHWHism than Israel. Even the Judean usurper Athaliah, עתליהו (2 Kgs 11:2), bears a יהו name, though it is usually written in truncated form עתליה (2 Kgs 11:1). The יהו king names appear in full form at the beginning of their respective regnal resumés.

Two other names are worth noting. The name Jotham is almost certainly derived from YHWH, but it is not a יהו name in Kings. Nevertheless, Jotham stands in the center of the post-Solomonic Judean kings (10th of 19). This position signals a connection between the

---

[1] Whatever the etymological origin of the name יהוא, it is a יהו name in Kings: Philip R. Davies, *In Search of "Ancient Israel"* (JSOTSup 148; Sheffield: JSOT Press, 1992), 72.

meaning of the name, "YHWH completes," and events during Jotham's reign.

Jotham's son, Ahaz, characterized as one of Judah's most evil kings, is likely based on an historical יהו king. The inscriptions of Tiglath-pileser III refer to a Jehoahaz (*Iauḫazi*) of Judah.[1] We should understand the narrative choice to strip Ahaz of יהו king status as significant. The Rezin-Pekah coalition marks the beginning of Israel's end. Kings locates the origin of the threat in Jotham's reign (2 Kgs 15:37) and the culmination in Ahaz's time (2 Kgs 16:5). Ahaz turns not to YHWH but to Tiglath-pileser (16:7) while also introducing foreign practices to the Jerusalem temple (16:10–18). No wonder the narrator never refers to Ahaz as "Jehoahaz."

Four of the five Ahaz kings, four of the five Ahab dynasty kings and four of five Jehu dynasty kings are יהו kings.[2] The exceptions are Ahaz, Ahab, and Jeroboam II. The worst rulers in Kings are Ahaz, Ahab, Jeroboam I, and Manasseh. All these names lack the יהו component. Jeroboam II, one of the better kings in Israel, restores the borders in trans-Jordan that Jeroboam I inherited.

In Kings, the first יהו king is Jehoshaphat in Judah,[3] followed immediately by the first Israelite יהו kings, Ahaziah and Jehoram.[4] It is only when YHWHism is in danger of being supplanted by the Baalism of Ahab and Jezebel that the Kings narrator introduces יהו royal names in both kingdoms. All of the first 13 kings (Saul through Ahab) in the complete list of 41 kings, as well as five of the 12 Israelite kings after Ahab, have non-יהו names. But among the 16 Judean kings from Jehoshaphat to Zedekiah, only Ahaz, Manasseh, and Amon are non-

---

[1] *ANET*, 282 and Mordecai Cogan and Haim Tadmor, *II Kings: A New Translation with Introduction and Commentary* (AB 11; Garden City, NY: Doubleday, 1988), 336 text 4.D.

[2] "Ahaz kings": Jehoahaz and Ahaziah in both Israel and Judah; "Ahab kings": Ahaziah and Jehoram in both kingdoms; Jehu dynasty kings: Jehu, Jehoahaz, Jehoash, and Zechariah. Each group is dominated by "Ahaz kings."

[3] The 14th of the 41 kings from Saul to Zedekiah. Aside from the fact that the numbers 14 and 41 form an "inverse" pair, 14 frequently stands as a positive symbol in Kings.

[4] Davies, *In Search of "Ancient Israel,"* is simply wrong in claiming, "Yahwistic names are given to all the Judaean kings (after the perhaps unhistorical David, Solomon and Rehoboam period)" (72).

YHWHistic names.[1] Once יהו royal names begin in Judah, only the most evil are not יהו kings.

The Beginning of יהו Leadership

From the beginning of biblical leadership lists, Jehoshaphat is only the second of Israel's national rulers who bears a יהו name. Joshua, יהושע/יהושוע (Josh 1:1; Judg 2:7), is the other. Potential יהו leaders, Jonathan יהונתן (1 Sam 14:6) and Adonijah אדניהו (1 Kgs 1:8), fail to succeed their fathers Saul and David. The introduction of יהו leadership comes at key points in the story. Joshua is YHWH's chosen leader when Israel is brought into and given possession of the promised land. Firm control is finally achieved only with David (who completes the mission of Joshua). But once again יהו leaders fail to take charge until the time of the "war between YHWH and Baal," when the house of Ahab threatens the house of David. Note, however, that יהו names do show up among Israel's prophets who announce the failure of the royal leadership: Ahijah אחיהו (1 Kgs 14:5), Jehu יהוא (16:1), and Elijah אליהו (17:1). When Elijah passes his mantle to Elisha אלישע, יהו names have already taken hold of the thrones of Israel and Judah. But the real story is that YHWH and his chosen leaders (the house of David) are being supplanted by Baal and the house of Ahab. Precisely at this point Elisha assists in the transition to Jehu יהוא. The false יהו kings of the house of Ahab are replaced by Jehu, a true יהו king and the only ruler since Solomon to be directly addressed by YHWH (2 Kgs 10:30).[2] Thus, יהו leadership is transferred to the king, though the kings eventually fail the test. YHWH appears as an "on-stage" character who speaks directly in the Kings narrative before the fall of Samaria only to Solomon, Elijah (1 Kgs 19:15), and Jehu. Following the transition to Jehu, YHWH does not speak to prophets or kings in Israel again.[3] Aside from Shemaiah's שמעיה brief word warning Rehoboam against attacking Israel (1 Kgs

---

[1] Jotham is a special case in that we may understand it as a YHWHistic name but not a יהו name.

[2] In contrast to the Ahab kings, Jehoshaphat (the first יהו king) has a positive a positive attitude toward the prophets Micaiah (1 Kings 22) and Elisha (2 Kings 3).

[3] The word of YHWH to Jonah ben Amittai is referenced in a narrative flashback (2 Kgs 14:25), but is neither quoted nor introduced into the main level of story time.

12:22-23), the first prophetic address to the king in Judah occurs when Hezekiah sends word to Isaiah ישעיהו (2 Kgs 19:2-7).

King List of Israel
Center of the list: Jehu

In the separate list of Israel's 19 kings (see Table 1), Jehu stands in the center (number 10) of Israel's 19 kings. Jehu removed the apostate Ahab dynasty, destroyed the house of Baal, and founded the only positively assessed dynasty in Israel. He even received a word of approval ("you have done well") and dynastic promise from YHWH (2 Kgs 10:30).[1] His position at the center of the Israelite "king list" denotes his significance in Kings.

Conspiracy

The conspirators Zimri and Shallum mark the other key turning points in the list. Assassination and throne conspiracy are very common in the story world of the Israelite kingdom. The assassinations by Baasha, Menahem, Pekah, and Hoshea all result in successful reigns but not in dynasties. However, Zimri and Shallum cannot even establish their own reign, let alone a dynasty.[2] Jehu, the middle king in our trio, represents the complete opposite of Zimri and Shallum. His act of קשר is the only one that results in a successful dynasty.[3] The magnitude of his act is enhanced by virtue of the fact that he is the only character to conspire against an "established" dynasty (the house of Ahab). Jehu's קשר does not prepare the stage for someone else (unlike Zimri and Shallum). Rather, Jehu himself takes control. Nevertheless, he is labeled a "Zimri" (2 Kgs 9:31). Thus, it is not surprising that Zimri, Jehu, and Shallum occupy position numbers 5, 10, and 15 in the list, bracketing a group of 11 kings that encompasses the Ahab and

---

[1] E. Theodore Mullen, "The Royal Dynastic Grant to Jehu and the Structure of the Book of Kings," *JBL* 107 (1988): 193-206.

[2] Zimri and Shallum are the only kings whose citation formulas are expanded by reference to their conspiracies, their only "heroic deeds" (1 Kgs 16:20; 2 Kgs 15:15). Their successors, Omri and Menahem, are not called conspirators because it is not קשר to overthrow failures like Zimri and Shallum.

[3] Only the houses of Omri/Ahab and Jehu were established as dynasties. All other sons who succeeded their fathers on the throne of Israel ruled for two years (Nadab, Elah, and Pekahiah), signaling their failure to establish dynastic rule. Compare

Jehu dynasties. They represent key turning points in the story of the kingdom. Out of the chaos surrounding Zimri's violent actions, Omri founds the first "successful" dynasty. The violence of Jehu's coup, even more disruptive of the status quo, leads to another successful dynasty. Finally, with his assassination of Zechariah of the Jehu dynasty, Shallum once again plunges the kingdom into turmoil from which it never recovers. It leads to Israel's incorporation into the Assyrian empire. Hence, these equally spaced reigns point to both plot and structure in the "king list," which undergirds the Israelite story world.

King List of Judah
Center of the List: Jotham

A different set of patterns emerges among Judah's 19 kings. Jotham stands at the center of the list. In contrast to Jehu's prominence, Jotham is a relatively minor figure. The presentation of his reign takes only 7 verses (2 Kgs 15:32-38). But like other minor figures, he plays an important transitional role. He stands at the close of the four kings who do right (but not like David),[1] a period that the narrator portrays in essentially positive terms after the violent elimination of the house of Ahab by Jehu and Jehoiada. Two key narrative statements mark Jotham's reign. First, Jotham built the upper gate of the house of YHWH (15:35b). Though this note does not appear particularly significant, Jotham's addition is one of only two positive acts of new temple construction following Solomon.[1] As such, Jotham's acts mark a transition to the period in which the illicit building projects of Ahaz and Manasseh must be countered by the reforms of Hezekiah and Josiah. The second important event in Jotham's reign is presented in an overt narrative comment: "In those days YHWH began to send Rezin, king of Aram, and Pekah, son of Remaliah, against Judah" (15:37). An analogous notice appears for Jehu's reign: "In those days YHWH began to cut off parts of Israel. And Hazael attacked them in all the borders of

---

the two-year reign of Ishbosheth as Saul's successor in Israel (2 Sam 2:10) and the MT's two-year reign for Saul (1 Sam 13:1).

[1] Jehoash, Amaziah, Azariah, and Jotham. The comparison to David is explicit for Amaziah. The others form a chain of kings following in their fathers' paths (2 Kgs 14:3; 15:3, 34).

Israel" (2 Kgs 10:32). These two comments represent the only occurrences of the phrase בימים ההם החל יהוה in Kings and they are particularly informative with regard to the narrator's evaluation of the foreign affairs of Israel and Judah. Both statements view Aramean attacks as YHWH's punishment. These attacks (against Ahaz and the Jehu kings) are not the climax since Aram is a penultimate enemy. These wars represent a preliminary stage in the development of the story of Kings—conflict on the regional scene of Syro-Palestine. The ultimate conflict involves a larger perspective covering the entire ancient Near East—the empires headed by Assyria and Babylon. Nevertheless, the narrator's commentary at the mid-point of these "king lists" clearly marks the path ahead. The reigns of Jehu and Jotham mark a turn away from uncertainty and toward the final drama. Despite reversals of the plot in Israel (Jeroboam II) and Judah (Hezekiah and Josiah), YHWH's judgment of the monarchic period begins in earnest with Jehu and Jotham who stand at the center of the two king lists.

Ahaz Kings

Following these central transitional points, both king lists continue with an "Ahaz king" in the 11th position. Jehu and Jotham are succeeded by their sons, Jehoahaz and Ahaz. These names bring up an interesting point about the Judean king list. Two names—Jehoahaz and Ahaziah—are formed by the combination of אחז and יהו. Both Israel and Judah have one of each. The three Judean Ahaz kings (Ahaziah, Ahaz, and Jehoahaz) are evenly spaced in the list (numbers 6, 11, and 16). Zimri, Jehu, and Shallum are also spaced five kings apart in the Israelite king list (numbers 5, 10, and 15).

The Judean Ahaz kings appear at important transition points in the list. Ahaziah, belonging to both the house of David and the house of Ahab, marks the end of the first period of kingship in Judah. His death in battle at the hands of Jehu is followed by the purge of the Judean royal house by Jehu and Athaliah. The reestablishment of the house of David by Jehoash marks a new beginning. The house of Baal

---

[1] Hezekiah's gold plating is revealed in a narrative retrospective at the time he strips away the same gold to pay Sennacherib (2 Kgs 18:16). Jehoash and Josiah repair (חזק) the temple (2 Kgs 12:5-17; 22:3-10).

is demolished, its priests slain (2 Kgs 11:18), and the house of YHWH repaired (2 Kgs 12:5-17). This period of restoration ends with Jotham. Ahaz marks the beginning of a new period of kingship in Judah. His alliance with Assyria and his cultic failures represent a low point in Judah's leadership, exceeded only by Manasseh. The final post-Josianic period of kingship begins with the Judean Jehoahaz. His brief reign opens a time in which three of the four kings are taken into exile.[1]

Thus, the Ahaz kings mark important turning points in the story of the Judean kingdom. Their positions in the king list point to a careful structuring. In fact, the two "יהו-Ahaz" kings help call attention to a type of mirror image in the Judean list (see Table 2). The cult reformers Jehoash and Josiah come immediately after and before the first and last Ahaz kings, respectively Ahaziah and Jehoahaz. Jehoash and Josiah destroy Baal worship and repair the house of YHWH. Israelite cult reform occurs with Jehu at the center of the list. Judean reform comes not in the center but rather at the outside edges of the Ahaz king structure. Ahaz himself stands in the central position of the Ahaz structure, singled out as the one king who "did not do right." He is responsible for a "counter-reformation" in the house of YHWH (2 Kgs 16:10-18).

Comparison of the Lists

Thus, the 11-king core structures in the Judean and Israelite "king lists" display contrasting synchronization when it comes to cult reform. Even though the reforms of Jehu and Jehoiada/Jehoash take place in immediate succession in the synchronized presentation of the 41 kings of Israel and Judah (2 Kgs 10-11), in terms of the separate "king list structures" of the individual kingdoms, they stand at different points.

---

[1]The chronology of Kings also supports periodization. From Ahaziah's death (with Athaliah threatening the continued existence of the house of David) through Jotham is 144 (12^2) years. From Ahaz to the exile of Jehoiachin is also 144 years. Jehoahaz foreshadows this exile.

Table 2: 11-King Core Structures: Reform and Counter-Reform

	King(s)	Disposition
Israel	Zimri	*Unable to rule* (קשׁר)
	Omri Dynasty (4 kings)	Baal introduced
	JEHU	**Reform** (Baal eliminated)
	Jehu Dynasty (4 kings)	YHWH saves from Arameans
	Shallum	*Unable to rule* (קשׁר)
Judah	Ahaziah	*Unable to rule* (death in battle)
	Jehoash	**Reform** (Baal removed; temple repaired)
Amaziah-Azariah		no new cultic deeds
	Jotham	temple gate built
	AHAZ	Counter-reform (altar)
	Hezekiah	**Reform** — YHWH saves from Assyrians
	Manasseh-Amon	Counter-reform
	Josiah	**Reform** (Baal eliminated)
	Jehoahaz	*Unable to rule* (exiled)

The longevity of the Davidic dynasty contrasts with Israel's constant revolutions. However, threats to the Davidic dynasty roughly parallel the dynastic changes in Israel. Continual reform keeps the Davidic house in power. When Athaliah's slaughter of David's royal house threatens to replace the dynasty with the house of Ahab, Jehoash begins the restoration of the house of David, though it must still survive the assassinations of Jehoash and his son Amaziah.[1] The reestablishment of the dynasty following the illegitimate Athaliah corresponds to the establishment of the Omri-Ahab dynasty following the illegitimate Tibni. Both "core structures" establish the kingdom in response to usurpers.

The kingdoms also correspond following the midpoints of Jehu and Ahaz. In Israel, Jehu's dynasty and Israel's existence are threatened by Hazael of Aram. But Jehoahaz entreats YHWH (את-פני יהוה) who hears him (שמע) and gives Israel a savior (מושיע), preventing their extermination (2 Kgs 13:4–5). The narrator says the rescue was on

---

[1] Kings declares the kingdom established (כון) under Solomon and Amaziah, the sons of the dynastic founder (David) and re-founder (Jehoash) (1 Kgs 2:12; 2:46; 2 Kgs 14:5).

account of God's covenant with Abraham, Isaac, and Jacob (13:23). A comparable deliverance of the Davidic dynasty and Judah occurs after the midpoint of Judah's core structure. In response to the Assyrian threat, Hezekiah prays before YHWH (לפני יהוה, 19:15). Isaiah announces that YHWH has heard (שמע 19:20), promising to "defend this city to save it on my account and on account of David my servant" (19:34). Salvation (ישע) is granted to Jehoahaz and Hezekiah by YHWH who hears (שמע) them and intervenes on account of (למען) a promise made to past ancestors.[1] However, a limitation is announced to Hezekiah (20:12-19), suggesting that David's house, like Jehu's, will not last forever. The structural similarities between the Judean and Israelite "king lists" and their core structures are striking. Following the last king in both core structures (Shallum and Jehoahaz), the next king is invaded by "the empire." Menahem (2 Kgs 15:19) and Jehoahaz (24:1) face invasion by Assyria and Babylon. Assimilation into the empire has been foreshadowed under Jehoahaz and Hezekiah.

The Combined King List

It is now time to view the whole king list structure of Israelite and Judean kingship, as it is presented in Kings. Even if there are separate patterns for the kingdoms, we do not have separate books. A listing of all official kings from Saul to Zedekiah includes a total of 41 individuals. Given that order in the overall list is intimately connected to structural patterns of transition and climax in the lists of the separate kingdoms, the question must be asked whether the same principle holds true for the combined list.

Table 3: The 41 Kings of Israel and Judah

1	Saul	15	**Ahaziah**	29	Pekahiah
2	David	16	*Jehoram*	30	Pekah
3	Solomon	17	*Jehoram*	31	*JOTHAM*
4	Jeroboam	18	**Ahaziah**	32	*Ahaz*
5	*Rehoboam*	19	**JEHU**	33	Hoshea
6	*Abjiam*	20	*Jehoash*	34	Hezekiah

---

[1] YHWH's forgiveness of Jehoahaz and Hezekiah contrasts with events under Ahab (Israel) and Ahaz (Judah). The house of Ahab is eliminated for refusing to turn to YHWH: Ahab (1 Kgs 22), Ahaziah (2 Kgs 1), and Jehoram (2 Kgs 9) all die for rejecting YHWH and YHWH's prophets. Likewise, Ahaz turns to the king of Assyria (2 Kgs 16:5-9) rather than YHWH when threatened by Rezin and Pekah.

7	Asa	21	*Jehoahaz*	35	*Manasseh*
8	Nadab	22	Jehoash	36	*Amon*
9	Baasha	23	*Amaziah*	37	*Josiah*
10	Elah	24	Jeroboam	38	*Jehoahaz*
11	Zimri	25	*Azariah*	39	Jehoiakim
12	Omri	26	Zechariah	40	Jehoiachin
13	Ahab	27	Shallum	41	Zedekiah
14	*Jehoshaphat*	28	Menahem		

Ahaz King brackets: 15-21, 32-38

While numerous patterns are woven together in this complete "king list," for our purposes it is necessary to highlight only a few. First, it is worth noting that Jehu and Jotham, the middle kings (number 10) in the 19-king separate lists are numbers 19 and 31 in the combined list, two of Høyrup's "remarkable numbers." Second, the first two kings who "do right," Asa and Jehoshaphat, are numbers 7 and 14, surrounding the rise of the house of Omri and Ahab (number 13). Third, the middle king of this list, Jehoahaz (number 21), is an "Ahaz king." As a member of the Jehu dynasty he is also the best of the "Ahaz kings."

The Ahaz kings bracket two groups of seven kings: First Ahaziah (15), Ahaziah (18), Jehoahaz (21) and second Ahaz (32), Jehoahaz (38). The first group has an Ahaz king at the beginning, middle, and end. Manasseh stands in the center (35) of the second group. Because his actions are comparable to Ahaz's (building altars, "passing a son through the fire"), Manasseh's middle position marks him as an honorary Ahaz king. The first group concludes with Jehoahaz (position 21) at the very center of the 41-king list. This group introduces the climactic period of foreign affairs for Israel as Jehoash and Jeroboam guide the nation to a revival period before the kings that follow begin incorporation into the Assyrian empire. The second Ahaz group itself encompasses the climactic culmination of the Assyrian crisis. Ahaz turns to the king of Assyria when threatened by Rezin and Pekah. This, in turn, leads to the "seizing" (אחז) of Israel in the reign of Hoshea. The narrator links the two nations by repeating a summary of the capture of Samaria (18:9-12) in the account of Hezekiah's reign. Hezekiah himself confesses to the king of Assyria before turning to YHWH for aid. Even though Manasseh was a chief sinner on the cultic front, Hezekiah's trust (בטח) in YHWH had steered Judah into a period free from foreign intervention.[1]

At this point, a final comparison between the "king lists" of Kings and the king lists of Assyria is necessary. Some of the basic principles of the Assyrian tradition have been followed in the structure of Kings. Whereas groups A and B of the AKL have 38 kings, the double lists of Israel and Judah consist of half that number with 19 kings in each kingdom—38 altogether. The more expansive "illegitimate" king concept of AKL is more limited, but still present in Tibni and Athaliah. The 82 Assyrian kings of the Synchronistic King List are also reflected in 41 kings of Israel and Judah, again half of the Assyrian number. Finally, the numerical patterns of Assyrian kings with similar names are also present in the structure of Kings. The three Tiglath-pilesers of AKL are numbers 11, 21, and 32 in group C of AKL. The Ahaz rulers of Kings reflect a similar pattern. Jehoahaz and Ahaz are numbers 21 and 32 among the 41 kings, but both kings are number 11 in the individual Israelite and Judean lists. Thus, the 11-21-32 pattern of AKL and the Tiglath-pilesers is reflected in Kings and the Ahaz kings.[2]

A further point reinforces the possibility of a relationship between the Assyrian tradition and Kings. It is to Tiglath-pileser III that Ahaz turns for help, sending a bribe (שחד) and proclaiming, "Your servant and your son am I. Come up (עלה) and save me from the hand of the king of Aram and from the hand of the king of Israel!" (2 Kgs 16:7-8). When his plea results in rescue, Ahaz meets Tiglath-pileser in Damascus. Ahaz then becomes a cultic anti-reformer, introducing a foreign-inspired altar in the house of YHWH. Here the Kings narrative overlaps the Assyrian narrative where *Iauḫazi* (Jehoahaz) of Judah pays tribute to Tiglath-pileser. Ahaz, the thirty-second biblical king, is connected to Tiglath-pileser, the thirty-second king of Group C in the Assyrian King List. The book of Kings employs structural principles of order that bear striking resemblance to the king list tradition in

---

[1] The historical Manasseh was a vassal of Esarhaddon and Assurbanipal (*ARAB* 2:265-66, 340-41). The biblical Manasseh occasioned announcement of future disaster but no invasion or tribute is mentioned.

[2] Tiglath-pileser I is number 87 (3x29) and Tiglath-pileser III is number 108 ($2^2 \times 3^3$) in the complete AKL.

Assyria. The Tiglath-pileser schematism is paralleled by the Ahaz kings.

Finally, the complex narrative portrait of Hezekiah reveals partial parallels to Ahaz. After Hezekiah's positive relationship to YHWH results in initial foreign policy success—even to the point of rebelling against Assyria (2 Kgs 18:7-8)—Hezekiah loses his nerve and pays tribute to Sennacherib (2 Kgs 18:14). However, Sennacherib invades, demanding fealty and surrender. Only then does Hezekiah recognize his true sin and turn to his true lord, YHWH. At that point, Hezekiah's foreign policy reform matches his cultic reform.

Our examination of king list principles in the book of Kings has shown that the principles evident in the Assyrian King List bear a striking similarity to order in Kings.

A Form Critical Reappraisal of Isaiah 8:9–10

H. G. M. Williamson

No scholar has done more than Marvin Sweeney to advance a form critical appraisal of the book of Isaiah. His two volumes in the FOTL series have set a scholarly benchmark in this regard that is so comprehensive and rigorous that it is unlikely soon to be matched.[1] It might therefore seem impertinent to propose a modest reappraisal of one element in this great edifice, but all who know him through personal conversation as well as more formal levels of exchange will be aware of his openness to discussion in the pursuit of scholarly excellence. This proposal is therefore advanced as a token of appreciation for all his past work and in anticipation of many more years of fruitful dialogue.

In Sweeney's analysis, Isa 8:9–10 are joined with vv. 11–15 following as part of the wider "account concerning YHWH's judgment against Judah" in 7:1–8:15. This lengthy section is divided into two shorter parts, our two verses coming in the second part, 8:1–15. In general terms, this makes obvious sense. Isaiah 8:1–4 speaks of encouragement for Judah by way of predicted doom for the Syro-Ephraimite coalition. Verses 5–8a then speak of doom for Judah because of their "refusal" of the waters of Shiloah, and vv. 11–15 draw these two together in terms of the unparalleled designation "the two houses of Israel" (8:14) that are set to stumble and fall. The whole is then committed to writing at the start of the next section (8:16–17).

A large majority of commentators finds vv. 9–10 intrusive within this tidy structure. They seem to speak of an unconditional promise of deliverance for "us" who claim that "God is with us" כי עמנו אל and of doom for a universal array of peoples who are coming against

---

[1] Marvin A. Sweeney, *Isaiah 1–39, with an Introduction to Prophetic Literature* (FOTL 16; Grand Rapids: Eerdmans, 1996) and Marvin A. Sweeney, *Isaiah 40–66* (FOTL 19; Grand Rapids: Eerdmans, 2016). These, of course, build on and amplify his pioneering earlier monograph, Marvin A. Sweeney, *Isaiah 1–4 and the Post-Exilic Understanding of the Isaianic Tradition* (BZAW 171; Berlin: Walter de Gruyter, 1988).

"us" but whose plans will be frustrated. Sweeney circumvents this standard analysis by finding in vv. 9-15 as a whole a disputation whose purpose is to confirm the preceding judgment speech. In line with that form critical designation, he finds in vv. 9-10 a modified form of the standard "summons to war,"[1] and then finds in 11-15 the refutation. He concludes that our two verses are "a sort of rhetorical straw dog insofar as the prophet's purpose is to refute it in the following verses." When later he comes to discuss the passage's setting, he finds its purpose in the present context telling overwhelmingly in favor of it being part of the original composition; it represents an expression of the people's popular belief in God's protection of them, which belief it is Isaiah's precise purpose to overthrow by way of his disputation. He wants to prepare them, rather, for the alternative view that God in fact stands behind the threat posed by Assyria.[2]

In advancing this interpretation of the passage as a whole, Sweeney acknowledges his indebtedness to an article by Saebø, even though he modifies it in some respects.[3] In addition, we need, in my opinion, to be sensitive to the fact that the passage is heavily ironic in nature and thus strictly speaking cannot be identified with any regular form as such. Nevertheless it may be assumed that the irony would be most effective if the passage were based on some familiar form, the subversion of which would be readily appreciated by the reader.

A large part of Saebø's article is devoted to a discussion of the first word in the passage, רֹעוּ – long a bone of contention. He has a fresh suggestion here (or, more strictly, he revives an older and generally neglected suggestion; see below), and although his form critical analysis is not wholly dependent upon his proposal, it inevitably has a bearing on the matter. It may therefore be most conveniently dealt with here first.

---

[1] Sweeney cites in support Judg 3:28; 4:6-7, 14; 7:9. The trouble here is that these are all addressed by the commander to his own troops, not to the enemy, as in our present passage.

[2] Sweeney's analysis is included within *Isaiah 1-39*, 165-75, esp. 168, 169, 171, and 173.

[3] Magne Saebø, "Zur Traditionsgeschichte von Jesaia 8,9-10: Klärungsversuch einer alten *crux interpretum*," *ZAW* 76 (1964): 132-44; repr. Magne Saebø, *Ordene og Orde: Gammeltestamentlige Studier* (Oslo: Universitetsforlaget, 1979), 71-83; ET: Magne Saebø, *On the Way to Canon: Creative Tradition History in the Old Testament* (JSOTSup 191; Sheffield: Sheffield Academic Press, 1998), 108-21.

The vocalization suggests that the Masoretes considered this to be from the root רעע. This might then be the denominative verb "be evil," which some have taken to have the extended meaning of "rage."[1] This has no ancient support, however, and it does not seem to be paralleled anywhere else or be otherwise justified. Most recently, Barthel has adopted this solution with the suggestion that it echoes the use of רעה ... יעץ in 7:5; hence "erbost euch."[2] While possible, this does not fit with what seems to be the form of the verse as an ironical reversal of the summons to war or similar (see further below), which requires that this first verb be of positive import, like its parallel התאזרו. Alternatively, there are a few examples where this form seems to be an Aramaic loanword equivalent to the more usual Hebrew רצץ, "break" (Kimhi and Ibn Ezra both compare תרעם in Ps 2:9). This would not be impossible, but a transitive sense of the verb ("break") would be awkward without an object and the usual appeal to the intransitive sense of "being broken" (so RSV) is not securely attested elsewhere. In addition, while it would make a good parallel with וחתו, it would be most curious for both verbs in the first line to indicate failure, while in the second line we find the combination of a positive verb התאזרו followed again by וחתו. It would be far preferable if the verb here were equally "positive."[3]

Several of the versions apparently linked the verb with the second root רעה as listed in BDB, "associate with" (cf. the familiar noun רע) and so rendered "assemble yourselves" or the like, which would be appropriate in a military context: Symmachus συναθροίσθητε,[4] Vulgate

---

[1] E.g., Conrad von Orelli, *Der Prophet Jesaja* (3rd ed.; Munich: Beck, 1904), 42 (ET: Conrad von Orelli, *The Prophecies of Isaiah* [tr. J. S. Banks; Edinburgh: T & T Clark, 1889], 61); Franz Delitzsch, *Commentar über das Buch Jesaia* (4th ed.; Leipzig: Dörffling & Franke, 1889), 156 (ET: Franz Delitzsch, *Biblical Commentary on the Prophecies of Isaiah* [tr. James Kennedy, William Hastie, and Thomas A. Bickerton; Edinburgh: T.& T Clark, 1894], 226); Bernhard L. Duhm, *Das Buch Jesaia* (HKAT 3/1; Göttingen: Vandenhoeck & Ruprecht, 1892), 81; John Skinner, *The Book of the Prophet Isaiah, Chapters i–xxxix* (CBSC; Cambridge: Cambridge University Press, 1897): "Be exasperated" (68); and A. L. H. M. van Wieringen, *The Implied Reader in Isaiah 6–12* (BibInt 34; Leiden: Brill, 1998), 91.

[2] Jörg Barthel, *Prophetenwort und Geschichte: die Jesajaüberlieferung in Jes 6–8 und 28–31* (FAT 19; Tübingen: Mohr Siebeck, 1997), 194–96; see also August Dillmann, *Der Prophet Jesaia* (5th ed.; KEHAT; Leipzig: Hirzel, 1890), 82.

[3] Cf. J. Blake Couey, *Reading the Poetry of First Isaiah: The Most Perfect Model of the Prophetic Poetry* (Oxford: Oxford University Press, 2015), 34–35.

[4] The edition of Joseph Ziegler, *Isaias* (5th ed.; Göttingen: Vandenhoeck & Ruprecht, 1983), 151, registers this as the reading also in Aquila and Theodotion, but

congregamini, and Targum אתחברו. This has been followed by many,[1] and it makes excellent sense in the context.[2] However, given that this could hardly be a Pu'al imperative (neither Pi'el nor Pu'al of this root are attested),[3] one would have expected a Hithpa'el for the reflexive (cf. Prov 22:24, though even there the sense is "associate with" rather than reflexive, and perhaps Prov 18:24). It could be that the vocalization was intended as an unusual form of the Qal (in place of the expected רְעוּ) in order to introduce assonance with וחתו, though the use of the Hithpa'el in the following line (התאזרו) may tell against this; nor is there any evidence that the Qal could have reflexive as opposed to the usual transitive sense.

Saebø himself proposed that the verb in question is רוע.[4] This verb is elsewhere usually Hiph'il and never Qal. It can have the meaning "shout a war-cry" (see, for instance, Josh 6:5, 10, 16, 20; 1 Sam 17:20, 52; Hos 5:8; 2 Chr 13:15),[5] which would be very suitable here, and Saebø simply conjectures that this is an otherwise unattested example

---

there is doubt about this; Lütkemann and Rahlfs argued, rather, that the reading in ms 710, σαθρουσθε, should be ascribed to them, leaving Symmachus alone with συναθροίσθητε; cf. Leonhard Lütkemann and Alfred Rahlfs, *Hexaplarische Randnoten zu Is 1–16* (Berlin: Weidmann, 1915), 68.

[1] Including Rashi, Calvin, ASV ("associate yourselves"), and Jimmy J. M. Roberts, *First Isaiah: A Commentary* (Hermeneia; Minneapolis: Fortress, 2015), 133 ("unite yourselves").

[2] So Hans Wildberger, *Jesaja 1: Jesaja 1–12* (2nd ed.; BKAT 10/1; Neukirchen-Vluyn: Neukirchener Verlag, 1980), 329. Part of its English translation, Hans Wildberger, *Isaiah 1–12* (tr. Thomas H. Trapp; CC; Minneapolis: Fortress, 1991), 350, is misleading.

[3] Some have claimed that רעה in Judg 14:20 might be a Pi'el of this root, but even if it is, it is of questionable relevance for our present purpose: it is probably a denominative from the nominal form מרע just preceding, and though it is possible that this derives etymologically from רעה, it has developed a specialized meaning ("companion, best man"), so that it would not have been perceived in antiquity as related to the usage we are concerned with in the present verse.

[4] On this, as he indicates, Saebø was anticipated by Hans Schmidt, "Jesaja 8, 9 und 10," *Stromata: Festgabe des Akademisch-Theologischen Vereins zu Giessen* (ed. Georg Bertram; Leipzig: Hinrichs, 1930), 3–10 (not available to me); even earlier, Gesenius entertained the possibility but rejected it because the verb never occurs in the Qal; see Wilhelm Gesenius, *Philologisch-kritischer und historischer Commentar über den Jesaia* (Leipzig: Vogel, 1821), 1:337. RV then rendered "make an uproar," and Gray explained this as being based on רוע; see G. Buchanan Gray, *A Critical and Exegetical Commentary on the Book of Isaiah I–XXVII* (ICC; Edinburgh: T & T Clark, 1912), 150.

[5] Cf. Gerhard von Rad, *Der heilige Krieg im alten Israel* (ATANT 20; Zürich: Zwingli, 1951), 11 (ET: Gerhard von Rad, *Holy War in Ancient Israel* [tr. Marva J. Dawn; Grand Rapids: Eerdmans, 1991], 48 and Robert Bach, *Die Aufforderungen zur Flucht und zum Kampf im alttestamentlichen Prophetenspruch* (WMANT 9; Neukirchen: Neukirchener Verlag, 1962), 64.

of the Qal. Although the vocalization seems to be that of a "double-ע" verb, he correctly notes that occasionally the vocalization of ע-waw verbs is assimilated to that of double-ע verbs.[1] This attractive proposal has been adopted by quite a number of commentators since,[2] though the problem of appealing to an otherwise unattested Qal remains (an objection that might be softened slightly by a possible example from the Dead Sea Scrolls).[3]

With its translation γνῶτε, LXX seems to have read דעו, and this too has been favored by a number of commentators.[4] It is thought to provide a good parallel with והאזינו in the following clause, and its absolute use is said to be comparable with Ps 46:11. These arguments are not strong, however. Psalm 46:11 does not use דעו absolutely, as it would be here, because it is followed by כי ("Be still, and *know that* I am

---

[1] Hans Bauer and Pontus Leander, *Historische Grammatik der hebräischen Sprache* (Halle: Max Niemeyer, 1922), 398–400, 402–05 and *GKC* §72*dd*.

[2] See, for instance, Gilbert Brunet, *Essai sur l'Isaïe de l'histoire: étude de quelques textes notamment dans Isa. vii, viii & xxii* (Paris: Picard, 1975), 31; Hanns-Martin Lutz, *Jahwe, Jerusalem und die Völker: zur Vorgeschichte von Sach. 12, 1–8 und 14, 1–5* (WMANT 27; Neukirchen-Vluyn: Neukirchener Verlag, 1968), 41–42; Antoon Schoors, *Jesaja* (DBOT 9A; Roermond: Romen & Zonen, 1972), 77–78; Georg Fohrer, *Das Buch Jesaja* (2nd ed.; ZBK; Zurich: Zwingli, 1966), 1:128; Hermann Barth, *Die Jesaja-Worte in der Josiazeit: Israel und Assur als Thema einer produktiven Neuinterpretation der Jesajaüberlieferung* (WMANT 48; Neukirchen-Vluyn: Neukirchener Verlag, 1977), 178; Hans-Peter Müller, "Glauben und Bleiben: zur Denkschrift Jesajas Kapitel vi 1–viii 18," *Studies on Prophecy: A Collection of Twelve Papers* (eds. George W. Anderson et al.; VTSup 26; Leiden: Brill, 1974), 25–54, here 47; and Francolino J. Gonçalves, *L'Expédition de Sennachérib en Palestine dans la littérature hébraïque ancienne* (EBib n.s. 7; Paris: Lecoffre, 1986), 309.

[3] Cf. *DCH* 7:451.

[4] E.g., Robert Lowth, *Isaiah: A New Translation; with a Preliminary Dissertation, and Notes* (London: Tegg, 1778), 2:93–94; Karl Marti, *Das Buch Jesaja* (KHC 10; Tübingen: Mohr [Siebeck], 1900), 85; Albert Condamin, *Le livre d'Isaïe* (EBib; Paris: Librairie Victor Lecoffre, 1905), 53; Gray, *Isaiah I–XXVII*, 149; Otto Procksch, *Jesaia I* (KAT 9/1; Leipzig: Deichert, 1930), 134–35; Godfrey R. Driver, "Isaiah i–xxxix: Textual and Linguistic Problems," *JSS* 13 (1968): 36–57, here 40; Edward J. Kissane, *The Book of Isaiah, Translated from a Critically Revised Hebrew Text with Commentary, 1: i–xxxix* (Dublin: Browne and Nolan, 1941), 102; Herbert Donner, *Israel unter den Völkern* (VTSup 11; Leiden: Brill, 1964), 25; Otto Kaiser, *Das Buch des Propheten Jesaja, Kapitel 1–12* (5th ed.; ATD 17; Göttingen: Vandenhoeck & Ruprecht, 1981), 182 (ET: Otto Kaiser, *Isaiah 1–12: A Commentary* [tr. John Bowden; OTL; London: SCM, 1983], 187); Joseph Blenkinsopp, *Isaiah 1–39: A New Translation with Introduction and Commentary* (AB 19; New York: Doubleday, 2000), 239–40; Kay Weißflog, *"Zeichen und Sinnbilder": Die Kinder der Propheten Jesaja und Hosea* (ABG 36; Leipzig: Evangelische Verlagsanstalt, 2011), 60–61; John Day, *The Recovery of the Ancient Hebrew Language: The Lexicographical Writings of D. Winton Thomas* (HBM 20; Sheffield: Sheffield Phoenix, 2013), 82; and Alexander V. Prokhorov, *The Isaianic Denkschrift and a Socio-Cultural Crisis in Yehud: A Rereading of Isaiah 6:1–9:6[7]* (FRLANT 261; Göttingen: Vandenhoeck & Ruprecht, 2015), 117; cf. NEB "take note."

God"); the proposed reading would thus in fact introduce an unparalleled use of the verb. In addition, as noted above, within the present verse the significant parallel word is התאזרו, not והאזינו.[1] Telling strongly against the proposed reading is the otherwise unanimous textual support for an initial ר rather than ד,[2] though whether Saebø is right to argue in addition that the rendering in the remainder of the verse raises suspicion may be doubted, since it does not seem any more independent of the known Hebrew text than usual. The likelihood of a misreading here either in the LXX's Vorlage or by the translator himself is strengthened by the observation that at 44:28 רעי is rendered φρονεῖν.[3]

It is clear in the light of this discussion that no solution is free of difficulty.[4] Given the context in which parallelism with התאזרו is perhaps the most significant single factor, the renderings "assemble yourselves" (from רעה) and "shout a war cry" (from רוע) seem most

---

[1] This also tells against Houbigant's conjecture ראו: Charles F. Houbigant, *Notæ criticæ in universos Veteris Testamenti libros cum Hebraice, tum Græce scriptos, cum integris ejusdem Prolegomenis* (Frankfurt am Main: Varrentrapp, 1777), 2: 354.

[2] This includes 1QIsa^a, 4QIsa^e, and 4QIsa^f, on none of which do the editors express any doubt. Dominique Barthélemy, *Critique textuelle de l'Ancien Testament, 2: Isaïe, Jérémie, Lamentations* (OBO 50/2; Freiburg: Éditions universitaires, 1986), 52, expresses some doubt about the last two on the basis of the photographs to which he had access, but this may be considered overridden by the subsequent DJD edition.

[3] On this, see Joseph Ziegler, *Untersuchungen zur Septuaginta des Buches Isaias* (ATA 12/3; Münster: Aschendorff, 1934), 157. The textually strong support for the Masoretic form of the consonantal text would also be sufficient to cast doubt on the alternative suggestion of Thomas to relate דע with his case for a second Hebrew root ידע, "to become still, quiet, at rest," for which he postulated an extended meaning here and elsewhere on the basis of the causative, leading to his translation "be ye reduced to submission" (David Winton Thomas, "The Root ידע in Hebrew, II," *JTS* 36 [1935]: 409–12, here 410). Thomas's appeal to Pesh's rendering *zw'w*, "tremble," does not add to the strength of his argument, as Pesh renders התרעה רעה at 24:19 with the same verb as here; it can more naturally be understood as an exegetically based rendering of the MT (cf. Barthélemy, *Critique textuelle*, 52). This theory, never certain in the present instance in any case (John A. Emerton, "A Consideration of Some Alleged Meanings of ידע in Hebrew," *JSS* 15 [1970]: 145–80, here 171), has now been seriously undermined, at least so far as the extended meaning is concerned, by more recent study of the meaning of the Arabic cognate, so that it should not be further entertained here (William Johnstone, "*yd'* II, 'be humbled, humiliated'?" *VT* 41 [1991]: 49–62 and John A. Emerton, "A Further Consideration of D. W. Thomas's Theories about *yāda'*," *VT* 41 [1991]: 145–63).

[4] Walter Dietrich, *Jesaja und die Politik* ([BEvT 74; Munich: Kaiser, 1976], 134) proposed conjecturally emending to שמעו on the ground of parallelism with והאזינו, but we have already noted that this is not the word with which parallelism should be sought. He might also have cited the evidence for such variant Greek renderings as ἀκούσετε (see the

plausible, though in neither case is the Qal the expected verbal theme. Since "girding" implies a relatively early stage in preparation for battle, I am inclined to think that, with our verb preceding it and so perhaps implying an even earlier stage of preparation, "assemble yourselves" is the more likely of the two; it is also better supported in antiquity. On the basis of the curious form להתרעע in Prov 18:24, Rosenmüller suggested that there might have been a verb רעע as a by-form of רעה.[1] That would help explain the vocalization, but would still leave the Qal as an unexplained verbal theme; was it considered contextually appropriate to furnish the tersest form of command that could be managed?

I return now to a broader consideration of the passage's form. Following a careful discussion of the principal items of vocabulary Saebø concluded that underlying the passage was a prophetic imitation of the ancient call to battle ("Gattung der Aufforderung zum Kampf/genre of invitation to battle"). Saebø based his work firmly on the previous study of this form by Bach, although Bach had not included the present passage in his corpus.[2] Significant examples of the form cited by Saebø are Jer 46:3-6, 9-10 and Joel 4:9-13. His proposal has overtaken older suggestions, such as that this is a fragment of a psalm or a brief song of triumph.

In my opinion, Saebø's proposal faces an unexplained difficulty, namely that not only is this supposed call to battle addressed to the peoples of the world in its widest extent but also that they are called to "give ear." In Bach's prophetic forms of the call to battle, there are certainly commands to make others hear and so on (e.g., Jer 50:29; 51:27) but never to listen. Saebø seeks to avoid this problem by suggesting that it is the war cry which he finds in the first word of the verse that they should hear, but even if we accepted his understanding of the word in question it would still leave unexplained the fact that in the tight parallelism of the passage those who live in "the distant places of the world" are the same as, and not a completely separate group

---

apparatus in Ziegler's edition), but he does not in fact do so. His proposal has not found any support.

[1] Ernst F. K. Rosenmüller, *Scholia in Vetus Testamentum, III/1: Jesajae Vaticinia Complectentis* (2nd ed.; Leipzig: Joh. Ambros. Barth, 1810), 1: 326.

[2] Bach, *Aufforderungen*.

from, the "peoples." It is far more natural to suppose that those in the second half of the first line are being told to listen to what the prophet is saying.

In view of this, I propose instead that what underlies the passage is the less frequently attested convention of the address before battle of one army commander to his opponents. Whether this was historical or is merely a literary convention is immaterial for our consideration, of course. While this form is familiar in Greek and various ancient Near Eastern forms of historiography,[1] there are also biblical examples (surely literary), such as 2 Chr 13:4-12, which starts with "hear me" and moves towards its conclusion with "behold God is with us at our head" (other examples, albeit in a slightly different setting, include 2 Kgs 18:19-25, 28-35; there may also be an allusion at 1 Kgs 20:10-11). Another strong example is Ps 2. This psalm issues a challenge to the rebellious nations and their kings in vv. 1-2 warning them not to proceed with their plans (see vv. 10-11). As part of this, the Davidic king reminds them of the promises made to him by God at his coronation (vv. 6-9), rather than this being in fact a coronation oracle, as is often implied. God is thus "with him" to assure him of victory, as in Isa 8:10 and 2 Chr 13:12, making opposition futile. Naturally, it may be assumed that the prophet has driven the convention further than would be normal in terms of egging the opposition on and then declaring that they would fail, but the basic pattern is the same and would be recognizable.[2]

If this brief analysis is correct, then it seems to me more difficult to follow Sweeney's proposal that vv. 11-15 following are the refutation of these verses as part of a more extended disputation. The arguments for vv. 9-10 being a later positive intrusion into what is otherwise a very dark presentation of the fate of both Israel and Judah in Isaiah's day remain strong, not the least because the verses include a

---

[1] For examples, see David G. Deboys, "History and Theology in the Chronicler's Portrayal of Abijah," *Bib* 71 (1990): 48-62, here 53-56, and John T. Willis, "A Cry of Defiance—Psalm 2," *JSOT* 47 (1990): 33-50 (with further bibliography). Somewhat related is also L. B. Kutler, "Features of the Battle Challenge in Biblical Hebrew, Akkadian, and Ugaritic," *UF* 19 (1987): 95-99.

[2] The same confident theology is also reflected in such Pss as 46, 48, and 76, as pointed out by, among others, Kaiser, *Jesaja, Kapitel 1-12*, 183 (ET: Kaiser, *Isaiah 1-12*, 188-89), but of course those Psalms do not use it in the same form as the one we are analysing here.

patchwork of citations and allusions to other material in both 7:1-17 and 14:24-27 that do not, perhaps, need to be presented in full detail here. I have argued elsewhere that ch. 7 cannot be an original part of Isaiah's own first-person account in the bulk of chs. 6 and 8, but that it is closely associated with chs. 20 and 36-39 and therefore must have been written considerably later than the events which it purports to relate.[1] Given Sweeney's brilliant presentation of the "universalizing" tendencies of Isa 24-27 (another passage in the book which makes extensive use of modified citations),[2] I wonder whether he might be prepared to consider that our two verses share much with those chapters. If so, a modest revision of his form critical proposal in one work may lead him to join that revision with the results of his research as presented in another.

---

[1] See H. G. M. Williamson, *Variations on a Theme: King, Messiah and Servant in the Book of Isaiah* (Carlisle: Paternoster, 1998), 73-100.

[2] Marvin A. Sweeney, "Textual Citations in Isaiah 24-27: Toward an Understanding of the Redactional Function of Chapters 24-27 in the Book of Isaiah," *JBL* 107 (1988): 39-52.

Who Says What to Whom
Speakers, Hearers, and Overhearers in Second Isaiah

Patricia K. Tull

Spoken words — or, more precisely, written words presented as audible speech — dominate the poetry of Isa 40–55, from its opening directive to a plural audience, calling them to comfort Jerusalem, to its memorable closing, describing the power of divine words. The chapters display exquisite creativity. Yet their positioning of both speakers and addressees is quite unusual among prophetic writings. One might think, for instance, that a work so overtly attuned to communication would clearly delineate its human speaker, giving the prophet a name and a biography, or at least indicating where this poet lived and whom in particular the prophecy was meant to address. But the prophet whose poetry was appended to that of Isaiah the son of Amoz of Jerusalem remains elusive, and the geographical and social location(s) of the audience can only be guessed from the prophecies themselves.

What dominates most of the text is not the prophet's own voice but God's — or rather, the prophet's presentation of God's voice, employing the divine first person with very little intervention. One researcher, Katie Heffelfinger, has estimated that 60% of the sixteen chapters' 333 verses consists of addresses presented as divine speech, while the prophet's voice occupies less than half of this, 25%.[1]

While my own statistics display a number of individual divergences, they are generally close to Heffelfinger's. I count 211 verses that can be attributed in all or part to God (63%). Omitting brief

---

[*] Many thanks for the invitation to contribute to this volume. Marv has been both pathfinder and cheerleader throughout my own career. I am deeply grateful for his fertile imagination, encyclopedic mind, and generous, gentle spirit.

[1] Katie Heffelfinger, *I Am Large, I Contain Multitudes: Lyric Cohesion and Conflict in Second Isaiah* (Leiden: Brill, 2011), 287-89, adding recognition that the voices often blend so much that rigid distinctions are impossible.

markers such as "says the LORD," I count 80 verses (24%) attributable either to the prophet or to an unidentified but non-divine voice the prophet quotes with full approval. Nearly one-third of this 24% is found in the opening chapter, Isa 40. Twenty-eight verses lack semantic or contextual clues for discerning whether the prophet is speaking directly or attributing speech to God (9.6%). A few sections remain unidentified (40:3-6; 53:1-10) or are attributed to servant Israel (49:1-6, 50:4-9). Where a speaker is quoted within another's speech, such as Jacob in 40:27, Daughter Babylon in 47:8 and 10, God in 49:3 and 6, Zion in 48:14, or the herald in 52:7, I credited the primary speaker, as discussed below. Since many speeches can reasonably be construed as either divine or prophetic, and many human speeches can be attributed to the prophet or to another human voice, precision is indeed impossible.

Muddying the waters further, unlike Samuel, Nathan, Elijah, Isaiah of Jerusalem, Jeremiah, Ezekiel, Amos, and Habakkuk, who all stand in dialogical relationship with God, inquiring, conversing, and even objecting, Second Isaiah's prophetic persona shows no perspective standing distinct from that of the deity. Some have claimed that the prophet raises an objection in 40:6, but this depends on choosing the LXX reading of the pronoun as "I" rather than the MT "he," and on reading the resulting question, "What shall I cry?" as an objection.[1] In addition, unlike First Isaiah, Jeremiah, Ezekiel, Amos, Hosea, and the many prophets who occupy narrative texts, Second Isaiah lacks all biographical accounting. Even if, as some claim, a prophetic call were to be discerned in Isa 40's opening verses, it would still yield no information about the poet's life and times. In fact, the designations "prophet" (*nābî*) and "seer" (*rō'eh*) fail entirely to appear in these chapters.

The presenter's self-effacement and the dominance of other voices have led some to understand Second Isaiah as a festal, liturgical, eschatological, or theological drama, or even the libretto of an actual performance, the plotline carrying the audience from the first

---

[1] The Masoretic text reads *wǝ'āmar*, "and he said," cf. Tanakh and KJV. Most modern translations follow 1QIsaᵃ, LXX, and Vulgate, which read "and I said."

announcement of divine comfort to the return of Judeans to Jerusalem.[1] But I agree with Heffelfinger that, like the book of Lamentations, which it frequently echoes, Second Isaiah more clearly reflects characteristics of lyric poetry than drama. Though too much tension and ambiguity exists among its poems to offer a continuous dramatic whole, the linkages created by repetitions of words, motifs, and themes and, even more, the continuity of the divine voice throughout create a lyric sequence that is capable of embodying and engaging the theological ambivalences probable in the Judean community during Babylonian rule. Heffelfinger calls Second Isaiah "a collection of lyric poems arranged into a meaningful whole" — with emphasis upon the whole, which takes precedence — composed to be presented orally to an exilic period audience.[2] "Second Isaiah's strongest cohesive device," she says, "is not a thematic or discursive claim like homecoming or comfort but the overwhelming presence of the speaking deity."[3] Indeed, much of Second Isaiah transcends the pragmatic goal of returning to Jerusalem, but it all attends to healing ruptured divine-human ties.

If Second Isaiah stresses the divine voice and other speaking voices, and systematically effaces the prophetic figure orchestrating these, and if it is best construed as poetry tailored for oral presentation, not displaying the clear-cut narrative arc that drama or epic would possess, but imaginatively traveling forward through related poems, caressing and smoothing ambiguities left by the Babylonian rupture, as Heffelfinger has demonstrated, it makes sense to pay close attention to the entities the poet configures as speakers and hearers. This is what I propose to do.

---

[1] For discussion of this movement, see Annemarieke van der Woude, "'Hearing Voices While Reading': Isaiah 40–55 as a Drama," *One Text, a Thousand Methods* (eds. Patrick Chatelion Counet and Ulrich Berges; Boston: Brill, 2005), 149–73 and Annemarieke van der Woude, "What Is New in Isaiah 41:14–20? On the Drama Theories of Klaus Baltzer and Henk Leene," *The New Things: Eschatology in Old Testament Prophecy* (eds. F. Postma et al.; Maastricht: Uitgeverij Shaker, 2002), 261–67.

[2] Heffelfinger, *I Am Large*, 29. For more on lyric poetry, see Brent A. Strawn, "Lyric Poetry," *Dictionary of the Old Testament: Wisdom, Poetry, and Writings* (eds. Tremper Longman III and Peter Enns; Downers Grove: InterVarsity Press, 2008).

[3] Heffelfinger, *I Am Large*, 34.

Audiences — Imagined and Actual

Before examining speakers, I will overview the poetry's implied audiences, which sometimes appear to coincide with Second Isaiah's evident intended hearers and sometimes do not. This slippage is clear when symbolic figures are addressed, such as the female figure Daughter Babylon in ch. 47, God's arm in ch. 51, and Jerusalem in chs. 51 and 52, for instance, as well as beings whose actuality is contested, such as other gods; nonhuman participants like mountains, trees, and Jerusalem's ruins; and historic and present personages who either can no longer hear (such as Jacob) or are unlikely to hear (such as Cyrus). These entities appear *as if* being spoken to, for the benefit of an audience positioned as overhearers, privileged with access to these speeches.

Beyond the many incidental imagined audiences, Second Isaiah consistently speaks to, and of, three entities, distinguished by the pronouns used of them, but all representing Judeans in one guise or another: a feminine singular figure called Jerusalem, Zion, or Daughter Zion, appearing primarily in chs. 40, 49, 51-52, and 54; a masculine singular figure identified as Israel/Jacob and the Servant, appearing primarily in chs. 40-48, 49, 50, and 53; and a masculine plural audience, found throughout, in relation to both Jerusalem and Servant Israel.[1]

This audience's relationship to the two singular entities differs markedly. Alternation between masculine singular and plural addressees in the book's first half is sometimes fluid, such as in 43:10, where they are called both "my witnesses" (plural) and "my servant" (singular). But they remain distinct from Zion, envisioned as her children, beckoned to return to her from afar (Isa 49:20-25; 52:11-12; 43:1, 13; 55:12). Among all the audiences in Second Isaiah's poetry, this one seems to correspond most closely to the prophet's actual audience, positioned sometimes as direct addressees and other times as overhearers of messages addressed to others, most often their symbolic ancestor Jacob/Israel and their mother city Jerusalem/Zion.

This audience appears as objects of comfort and encouragement, as debate partners, as Jerusalem's children, as Israel's offspring, and occasionally as sinners in the hands of an angry God.

---

[1] Patricia Tull Willey, *Remember the Former Things: The Recollection of Previous Texts in Second Isaiah* (SBLDS 161; Atlanta: Scholars Press, 1997), 175-81.

They are so fused with Israel that on occasion the pronouns trip over one another and become confused. They are less closely identified with mother Zion, but in the end, in 54:17, they are envisioned as God's servants (plural) in Jerusalem, and then beckoned in ch. 55 to "come, buy, and eat... without price," to call other nations to themselves, to seek mercy from the incomprehensible God and, finally, to set out joyfully for Jerusalem.

Speakers in Second Isaiah
The Prophetic Voice, Particularly in Isaiah 40

Who addresses all these audiences, and, through them, the Judeans of the late sixth century? The prophetic voice speaks out most clearly in ch. 40. Thereafter, outside of isolated introductions to divine speech (which can be protracted, as in 42:5; 42:16-17; 44:6; 45:18; 49:7; and 51:22), this voice reappears sporadically and often ambiguously. The following list encompasses all evident and possible* speeches attributable to the prophetic spokesperson after ch. 40:

42:10-13	praise chorus* and description of God going forth like a soldier
42:20-25	description of Israel's sins and rupture with God
44:23-24	praise chorus,* followed by lengthy introduction to divine speech
45:15-18	observation about God's self-hiding*; discussion of makers of idols going into disgrace, followed by lengthy introduction to divine speech
47:4	note of praise, interrupting divine speech*
48:20-21	exhortation to leave Babylon and reflection on the wilderness story
49:13	praise chorus*
50:10	reflection on servant's speech
51:3	reflection on God's comfort with themes of praise
51:9-10	summons to God's arm*
51:17-22	summons to Jerusalem*
52:1-2	summons to Jerusalem*
52:7-12	proclamation and celebration of God's approach to Jerusalem
53:1-10	surprised description of the servant*

55:5-7   prediction and exhortation
55:12-13   conclusion

  Much of what is clearly prophetic speech bears an omniscient explanatory tenor. The prophetic figure seems to take the role of resident theologian (or rather, since most of Second Isaiah's theology is developed in divine speeches, assistant theologian). The asterisks above indicate human speeches that could be understood as prophetic but need not necessarily be so. They could be others' words, often conveying not authority but discovery and wonder. For instance, each of the praise passages, reflective of psalmic speech, can be seen as the prophet's calling others to praise or as the praise itself, spoken by responsive witnesses. The implied source or sources of the "awake, awake" invocations in chs. 51 and 52, though evidently not divine, are likewise ambiguous, as is that of the first-person plural speech of ch. 53. Thus the prophet seems to take the role not of a dramatic player like Jeremiah or Ezekiel, but rather of producer or perhaps emcee, organizing the whole and offering introductions, conclusions, sotto voce interpretations, and transitions.[1] Yet the stage on which the lyric poems are performed is the audience's imagination, where the poetry's visual vividness can soar.

  Nearly all of scripture's prophetic books begin, following superscriptions, with prophetic introductions. These may be as lengthy as Ezekiel's, deferring God's voice to ch. 2, or as brief as Jeremiah's: "Now the word of the LORD came to me, saying..." (1:4). Precious few prophetic books—Joel, Zephaniah, and Malachi—launch directly into divine speech following the superscription. Isaiah 40:1 alone dispenses entirely with preamble: "'Comfort, comfort my people,' says your God." This opening is rendered all the more abrupt because it follows directly after King Hezekiah's final musing in 39:8: "There will be peace and security in my days." God's immediate announcement of comfort emphasizes the lacuna: even if there was peace and security in Hezekiah's days, those days ceased long ago. Suffering dominates Jerusalem's recent past. During the missing years, the city and its people evidently paid the high cost that Isaiah had just predicted, a

---

[1] Richtsje Abma ("Travelling from Babylon to Zion: Location and Its Function in Isaiah 49-55," *JSOT* [1997]: 3-28) viewed the prophet as director, organizing various voices.

cost rendered all the more gripping by the chasm between Hezekiah's words and God's. This abrupt beginning, "fraught with background," sets the stage for poetry in which God's voice is both badly needed and extravagantly offered.[1]

The opening voice is clearly marked by "says your God." But neither the plural audience nor the voices that follow are identified. Especially since ch. 39 clearly marked its speakers, the lack of orientation as ch. 40 launches is unsettling. Given the ease with which the prophet can identify speakers, these gaps seem deliberate. Who is announcing what God is saying, and to what audience is this command to "comfort" addressed? Is v. 2 a continuation of the divine imperative? If so, why does it refer to God's hand in the third person? Or alternatively, is whoever said "says your God" commencing with v. 2 to flesh out God's three-word speech?

Such ambiguities suffuse the prologue. Whose voice is being announced in v. 3 as crying out, and who is announcing this voice? Is the plural audience who is told to "prepare the way" the one addressed in vv. 1–2? Is the voice in v. 6, which directs someone else to call out, the same voice as in v. 3? And who responds with the question, "What shall I cry?" In what continues through v. 8, where does one speech end and another begin? Who speaks in v. 9, and to whom? Is a female messenger being asked to speak *to* Zion, or is Zion herself being commissioned as messenger? And is the message only, "Here is your God," or does it continue through v. 11?

These eleven verses offer a cascade of speakers and a crowd of hearers. An unidentified voice says that God speaks to some listeners, telling them to speak to Jerusalem, who, in the end, becomes either speaker or hearer. All this is auditioned in no particular space. The only visible landscape is the highway upon which God is seen returning, carrying out the passage's only clearly discernible action, approaching with a flock of sheep, treating them tenderly, mothers and young, demonstrating the comfort called forth in v. 1. The message of comfort travels from voice to voice throughout, but its sources are as difficult to distinguish as singers echoing in a stone cathedral.

---

[1] Erich Auerbach, *Mimesis: The Representation of Reality in Western Literature* (Princeton: Princeton University Press, 1953), 12.

Verses 12-31 of ch. 40, distinct from the prologue in form and substance, commence the next several chapters' arguments. A single voice speaks, clearly prophetic, declining to yield the floor even when attributing sound bites to God and Jacob in vv. 25 and 27. The divine voice that interjects in v. 25 repeats the prophet's claims in v. 18. The only other speech, that of Israel/Jacob in v. 27, is both enclosed as a quote and interrogated. Here Second Isaiah offers one of many of the poetry's double-voiced speeches, its words conveying one intention and their context quite another. Jacob may have meant to accuse God — and in fact does echo plaintive questions from Lamentations. But, quoted with objection and following lengthy assurances, his words indict himself.

Two addressees are evident in vv. 12-31. Verses 18, 25, and 26 — and presumably the rest of vv. 12-26 — instruct a masculine plural audience whose implicit identity is the prophet's Judean audience, whether situated in Babylon, Judah, or elsewhere. Beginning in v. 27, a masculine singular addressee is identified by the names "Israel" and "Jacob," just as Jerusalem is also called Zion.

Having established various entities — God, Zion/Jerusalem, Israel/Jacob, an array of unidentified voices, a plural audience, and a prophetic master of ceremonies — ch. 40 concludes with a divine promise. From here on the prophet speaks only to underscore God's words. Having established sympathy with the divine viewpoint, authority to describe the incomparable God, and confidence to address the audience with uncomfortable rhetorical questions, the poet yields the floor, without even a "says the LORD," to the figure the poetry has created, the deity not formed by hands — who is, ironically, being formed in human poetry and imagination. Not even the briefest of prophetic interjections appear again until 41:14.

Divine Speaker in Chapters 41-55

Once the divine voice takes over in Isa 41:1, it gives way infrequently, at first only to echoing, seconding, celebrating human voices. The poetry powerfully "persuades, not through argument but through encounter."[1] We are told often that God is speaking. But since

---
[1] Heffelfinger, *I Am Large*, 73.

contesting prophetic voices and depictions of the divine that may have existed in Second Isaiah's context have been silenced by time, mortality, and the loss of written witnesses, access to what else might have been offered as divine speech at the end of Babylonian dominance is unavailable to us. On this, the original audience differed from ourselves, having been necessarily more aware of the contested field of divine portraits. Steeped in traditions conferring on Second Isaiah divine authority, we must remind ourselves that what we encounter here is not God as such but as depicted by one prophet in a particular time and circumstance.

Heffelfinger pointed out three major tonalities, or attitudes toward the subject and the audience, found in divine addresses in these chapters. Shifts in these tonalities create flow from one lyric poem to the next that skillfully moves the message forward through discrete but interconnected sections. She identifies these tonalities as compassionate comfort ("fear not" exhortations, promises of provision, passionate appeals, comfort language, and familial metaphors); righteous indignation with accusation and disputation (disputation images such as lawsuits, violence, and war; rhetorical questions; accusations and invitations to argue; and sarcasm); and majestically supreme confidence (participial chains offering self-predications, magnanimous promises, and descriptions of past actions of creation and deliverance).[1] Identification of these three tones, which are revisited in theme and variation particularly in Isa 41–48, helps us attend to both the variety and the repetitive force of these speeches as they seek to bridge tensions between love and wrath; transcendence and immanence; past and present; tradition and innovation. The divine voice does heavy lifting, but takes its time throughout to weave imagery into claims that, if Second Isaiah's history of reception in Judaism and Christianity is any indication, have proven compelling.

Other Human Speakers

Much has rightly been made of the continuity between discussion of servant Israel in Bernhard Duhm's so-called "Servant Songs" and surrounding passages that highlight the servant,

---

[1] Heffelfinger, *I Am Large*, 177–89.

particularly in chs. 41-48, so much so that "a farewell to the servant songs"—to invoke Tryggve Mettinger's title—has become standard. Disputes against identifying God's servant as Israel/Jacob generally resort to dubious text-critical claims (as in the case of 49:3) or concern themselves with reconstructing earlier redactions. But there is one feature shared by Duhm's four "servant songs" that both unites and divides them: their implied speakers.

The servant first appears in the divine speech of Isa 41:8-9: "But you, Israel, my servant, Jacob, whom I have chosen... saying to you, 'You are my servant....'" Most of the divine speeches concerning the servant aim their words directly toward him, as in 42:6-7; 43:10; and 44:1-3, 21-22. One exception occurs in 45:4. This speech addresses Cyrus and envisions the Persian emperor as taking his marching orders from the Judeans' God; as such, it invites Judean hearers to overhear an intimate one-way conversation posed as occurring between their own divine king and the earthly ruler.

The other exception to the norm of God's speaking to rather than about the servant occurs in Duhm's first servant song, Isa 42:1-4. To whom does the deity speak? The previous unit, 41:21-29, addressed other gods, challenging them to demonstrate their foreknowledge, in order to claim that Judah's God alone roused Cyrus to save captive peoples. Beginning in 42:1, the audience is no longer marked. Yet this passage's speaking *of* rather than *to* the servant distinguishes it from surrounding servant passages.

The other three of Duhm's servant songs comprise virtually all of the passages offered in unmediated voices distinguishable from those of the deity and the prophet. Through ch. 48, the only unmediated voice discernible in the poetry is the prophet's own. Even God has been mediated by prophetic interjections such as "says the LORD." But suddenly in 49:1 a new figure appears, calling attention to himself. He is distinguished from the prophet by a proliferation of first person pronouns, eight in v. 4 alone. Within the space of six verses, twenty-five pronominal references to the speaker occur (including four second-person instances in quoted divine speeches). Unlike the prophet, this speaker is front and center, even enhancing his status by quoting God as identifying him with "you are my servant, Israel."

After six verses this speaker goes silent. The divine voice resumes for most of the chapter's remainder, three times offering enclosed speeches of others: Zion (vv. 14 and 21) and her children (v. 20). But the same unmediated human voice returns in ch. 50, in Duhm's third "servant song" for six more verses (vv. 4-9) encompassing twenty-three first-person references (one plural), discussing not only the deity and himself, as before, but also potential opponents. But even though the mood shifts from reflection to defiance, the audience easily discerns continuity with 49:1-6, the only other self-referencing human speech found in Second Isaiah.

These unmarked shifts prepare the audience for another encounter in ch. 53. The plural voice found here is new. Like 49:1-6 and 50:4-9, Isa 53's first six verses are characterized by abundant self-referencing pronouns. Seventeen plural first-person pronoun markers can be discerned in 53:1-6 — as well as twenty-three third-person masculine pronouns referring to the servant — continuing into some thirty-five more in vv. 7-12, focusing attention once again most personally on the servant.

This passage is contextualized by a divine reintroduction of the servant in 52:13, and in vv. 14-15 of "many," "many nations," and even "kings" who are astonished by him. Just as Israel himself was portrayed traveling in Second Isaiah's first half from complaints against God in 40:27 to acceptance of his role in chs. 49 and 50, now the nations, who were first introduced as "a drop from a bucket, dust on the scales" in 40:15, delivered along with their kings into Cyrus's hands in 41:2, are here likewise portrayed enjoying their moment of metanoia. Like Israel in ch. 49, they too reflect on what they used to think (53:3-4) and marvel at their own transformed perceptions of the figure who underwent a parallel change himself. In this way, Second Isaiah's one unmarked collective speech frames itself as the first fruit of Servant Israel's enlarged vocation as "light to the nations," which God announced (42:6) and the servant himself acknowledged (49:6). Fittingly, in 53:11-12 the capstone word about the servant belongs to God.

Double-Voicing

Much more could be said about the double-voiced speeches that proliferate in Second Isaiah, speeches within speeches that communicate one intention on the part of the enclosed speaker and another by the one quoting. Entities presented in this way include Israel/Jacob himself (40:27), makers and worshipers of idols (41:6, 7; 42:17; 44:16-20; 48:5, 7), clay (45:9), foreigners (45:14, 24-25), Daughter Babylon (47:7-10), Zion (49:14, 21) and her children (49:20), and enemies (51:23). Such vivid presentation of direct speech creates a perception of dialogism that is finally deceptive, since opinion-holders both foreign and domestic are held captive within others' speeches. Yet these represent, and seek to enact, the conquest of views presumably found in the audience's own world.

A subtler use of double-voicing occurs without attribution in the echoing of known Israelite speech. There is likely more of this than moderns can discern, since speech to which we lack independent witness cannot be identified. But the proliferation of discernible allusions to Lamentations, Jeremiah, and certain psalms and pentateuchal texts puts us on alert that the poet is both deeply embedded in Israelite traditions and bent on shifting them.[1]

Employing the illusion of many voices, most prominently the prevailing divine voice characterized by confidence, command, and compassion, Second Isaiah projects a world of divine promise and activity on Israel's behalf and populates it with incompetent rivals, heroic champions, and nonhuman cheerleaders, arranged to surround Judeans with a compelling vision of reconciliation with their God and their disrupted past. While the prophet positioned an actual audience as hearers and overhearers of this cascade of voices, subsequent readers from ancient times to now have become unintended overhearers of the text as well, reading it with a variety of aims and life contexts in mind. Independence in intent and response is the privilege of every audience. Hearing more than the ancient composer may have intended enriches our own understanding. Yet our competent interpretations begin by sorting out the prophet's distinctive rhetorical ploys.

---

[1] See discussion throughout Tull Willey, *Remember the Former Things*.

Too Many Hands?
Isaiah 65–66 and the Reading of the Book of Isaiah

Reinhard Kratz

According to a legend about Felix Mendelssohn Bartholdy—in another version it is Wolfgang Amadeus Mozart—the musicians of the time were unable to play the composer's latest work and so refused to perform it. Their argument: "Too many notes!" The same argument is often raised against literary analyses of biblical books, and it runs along the same lines: "too many hands" or "too many layers!" I am not sure what this argument is trying to say, but some scholars obviously take it to mean that literary and redactional criticism are irrelevant. But as little as the music of Mendelssohn Bartholdy or Mozart is irrelevant merely because it contains too many notes, so little are literary-historical hypotheses irrelevant because they take into account "many hands" or "many layers." The argument is too simplistic, and has no place in a serious academic discussion. Likewise, the argument often associated with it, i.e. of the "uncertainty" of literary-historical analyses, should also be dismissed. The hypothesis of text or author unity is no less "uncertain" than dividing the text on several hands. What counts is the accuracy of text reading and the plausibility of arguments.[1]

In the following, I would like to discuss this question, using the example of chs. 65–66 of Isaiah, which play a central role in the discussion on the formation of the book of Isaiah. On the basis of the final form, I will begin by considering different readings of these two chapters, which are external to the book. In this way I will approach the question of whether, in Isa 65–66, we are dealing with one or more readings of Isaiah and, consequently, with only one hand or with more than one. I am very pleased to dedicate this contribution to Marvin

---

[1] For the methodological principles, see Reinhard G. Kratz, "The Analysis of the Pentateuch: An Attempt to Overcome Barriers of Thinking," *ZAW* 128 (2016): 529–61.

Sweeney who — with his ground-breaking dissertation[1] and many further contributions — had such a great impact on the discussion of the formation of the book of Isaiah and my own work on Isaiah from the very beginning.

The Present Text and Its Versions

From Odil Hannes Steck, my academic teacher, I learned to begin with the given final text. Ever since the works of Cheyne,[2] Zillessen,[3] Abramowski,[4] Elliger,[5] Odeberg,[6] and Zimmeli,[7] it has been well known that the text of Trito-Isaiah, and in particular Isa 65-66, exhibits close literary connections to what is known as Deutero-Isaiah (Isa 40-55), which it regularly quotes and interprets. Less well-known but equally obvious is the relationship to Proto-Isaiah (Isa 1-39). This has been pointed out in particular by Liebreich,[8] Becker,[9] Lack,[10] Ackroyd,[11] Vermeylen,[12] Clements,[13] Rendtorff,[14] and Beuken.[1] The

---

[1] Marvin A. Sweeney, *Isaiah 1-4 and the Post-Exilic Understanding of the Isaianic Tradition* (BZAW 171; Berlin: Walter de Gruyter, 1988) and Marvin A. Sweeney, *Isaiah 1-39, with an Introduction to Prophetic Literature* (FOTL 16; Grand Rapids: Eerdmans, 1996).

[2] Thomas K. Cheyne, *Introduction to the Book of Isaiah* (London: Adam & Charles Black, 1895).

[3] Alfred Zillessen, "'Tritojesaja' und Deuterojesaja," *ZAW* 26 (1906): 231-76.

[4] Rudolf Abramowski, "Zum literarischen Problem des Tritojesaja," *TSK* 96-97 (1925): 90-143.

[5] Karl Elliger, *Die Einheit des Tritojesaja* (BWANT 45; Stuttgart: Kohlhammer, 1928); Karl Elliger, "Der Prophet Tritojesaja," *ZAW* 39 (1931): 112-41; and Karl Elliger, *Deuterojesaja in seinem Verhältnis zu Tritojesaja* (BWANT 63; Stuttgart: Kohlhammer, 1933).

[6] Hugo Odeberg, *Trito-Isaiah (Isaiah 55-66): A Literary and Linguistic Analysis* (Uppsala: Lundequistiska, 1931).

[7] Walther Zimmerli, "Zur Sprache Tritojesajas," *Gottes Offenbarung: Gesammelte Aufsätze* (2nd ed.; TB 19; München: Chr. Kaiser, 1969), 217-33.

[8] Leon J. Liebreich, "The Compilation of the Book of Isaiah," *JQR* 46 (1955-56): 259-77; 47 (1956/7): 114-38.

[9] Jürgen Becker, *Isaias: Der Prophet und sein Buch* (SBS 30; Stuttgart: Katholisches Bibelwerk, 1968).

[10] Rémi Lack, *La symbolique du livre d'Isaïe* (AnBib 59; Rome: Biblical Institute, 1973).

[11] Peter R. Ackroyd, "Isaiah I-XII: Presentation of a Prophet," *Congress Volume Göttingen 1977* (VTSup 29; Leiden: Brill, 1978), 16-48.

[12] Jacques Vermeylen, *Du prophète Isaïe á l'apocalyptique* (Paris: J. Gabalda, 1977-78).

[13] Ronald E. Clements, "The Prophecies of Isaiah and the Fall of Jerusalem in 587 B.C.," *VT* 30 (1980): 421-36; Ronald E. Clements, "The Unity of the Book of Isaiah," *Int* 36 (1982): 117-29; and Ronald E. Clements, "Beyond Tradition-History: Deutero-Isaianic Development of First Isaiah's Themes," *JSOT* 31 (1985): 95-113.

[14] Rolf Rendtorff, "Zur Komposition des Buches Jesaja," *VT* 34 (1984): 295-320.

issue was reviewed extensively in Steck's seminal studies on Trito-Isaiah[2] and received impressive corroboration in recent studies by Koenen,[3] Lau,[4] Sommer,[5] Ruszkowski,[6] Goldenstein,[7] Gärtner,[8] and, most recently, Stromberg.[9]

Although it is not possible for me to present the references in detail here, I would just like to give one example: Leon Liebreich's observations on inclusion between chs. 1 and 55-65, which he presented in his 1955/6 article, "The Compilation of the Book of Isaiah."[10] Liebreich highlights two connections in particular: first, the (plural) salutation שִׁמְעוּ דְבַר־יְהוָה, which is found in Isa 1:10 and 66:5, and

---

[1] Willem A. M. Beuken, "Isa. 56:9–57:13: An Example of Isaianic Legacy of Trito-Isaiah," *Tradition and Reinterpretation in Jewish and Early Christian Literature: Essays in Honour of Jürgen C. H. Lebram* (eds. Jan Willem van Henten et al.; Leiden: Brill, 1986), 48–66 and Willem A. M. Beuken, "Isaiah Chapters lxv–lxvi: Trito-Isaiah and the Closure of the Book of Isaiah," *Congress Volume Leuven 1989* (VTSup 43; Leiden: Brill, 1991), 204–21. See also his commentary on Isaiah: Willem A. M. Beuken, *Jesaja 1–12* (tr. Ulrich Berges; HThKAT; Freiburg: Herder, 2003); Willem A. M. Beuken, *Jesaja 13–27* (tr. Ulrich Berges and Andrea Spans; HThKAT; Freiburg: Herder, 2007); and Willem A.M. Beuken, *Jesaja 28–39* (tr. Andrea Spans; HThKAT; Freiburg: Herder, 2010); and continued by Ulrich Berges, *Jesaja 40–48* (HThKAT; Freiburg: Herder, 2008).

[2] Odil Hannes Steck, *Studien zu Tritojesaja* (BZAW 203; Berlin: Walter de Gruyter, 1991).

[3] Klaus Koenen, *Ethik und Eschatologie im Tritojesajabuch: Eine literarkritische und redaktionsgeschichtliche Studie* (WMANT 62; Neukirchen-Vluyn: Neukirchener Verlag, 1990).

[4] Wolfgang Lau, *Schriftgelehrte Prophetie in Jes 56–66: Eine Untersuchung zu den literarischen Bezügen in den letzten elf Kapiteln des Jesajabuches* (BZAW 225; Berlin: Walter de Gruyter, 1994).

[5] Benjamin D. Sommer, *A Prophet Reads Scripture: Allusion in Isaiah 40–66* (Stanford: Stanford University Press, 1998); see also Benjamin D. Sommer, "Allusions and Illusions: The Unity of the Book of Isaiah in the Light of Deutero-Isaiah's Use of Prophetic Tradition," *New Visions of Isaiah* (eds. Roy F. Melugin and Marvin A. Sweeney; JSOTSup 214; Sheffield: Sheffield Academic Press, 1996), 156–86; and Benjamin D. Sommer, "The Scroll of Isaiah as Jewish Scripture. Or, Why Jews Don't Read Books," SBLSP 35 (1996): 225–42.

[6] Leszek Ruszkowski, *Volk und Gemeinde im Wandel: Eine Untersuchung zu Jesaja 56–66* (FRLANT 191; Göttingen: Vandenhoeck & Ruprecht, 2000).

[7] Johannes Goldenstein, *Das Gebet der Gottesknechte: Jes 63,7–64,11 im Jesajabuch* (WMANT 92; Neukirchen-Vluyn: Neukirchener Verlag, 2001).

[8] Judith Gärtner, *Jesaja 66 und Sacharja 14 als Summe der Prophetie: Eine traditions- und redaktionsgeschichtliche Untersuchung zum Abschluss des Jesaja- und des Zwölfprophetenbuches* (WMANT 114; Neukirchen-Vluyn: Neukirchener Verlag, 2006).

[9] Jacob Stromberg, *Isaiah after Exile: The Author of Third Isaiah as Reader and Redactor of the Book* (OTM; Oxford: Oxford University Press, 2011).

[10] Liebreich, "Compilation," *JQR* 46, 276–77, *JQR* 47, 126–27; cf. also Beuken, "Isaiah Chapters lxv–lxvi."

also in Isa 39:5 (in the singular) at the end of the first part of the book;[1] and second, the concept of fiery judgement, which is mentioned in Isa 1:31 (וּבָעֲרוּ שְׁנֵיהֶם יַחְדָּו וְאֵין מְכַבֶּה) and also in Isa 66:24 (וְאִשָּׁם לֹא תִכְבֶּה).[2] The latter is indeed a very interesting observation because it may possibly explain the curious final verse of the book of Isaiah, Isa 66:24:

וְיָצְאוּ וְרָאוּ בְּפִגְרֵי הָאֲנָשִׁים הַפֹּשְׁעִים בִּי כִּי תוֹלַעְתָּם לֹא תָמוּת וְאִשָּׁם לֹא תִכְבֶּה
וְהָיוּ דֵרָאוֹן לְכָל־בָּשָׂר

And they will go out and look on the dead bodies of those who rebelled against me; the worms that eat them will not die, the fire that burns them will not be quenched, and they will be loathsome to all humankind.

As Liebreich correctly comments, this verse is a kind of "anti-climax" to the "happy ending" of the people's pilgrimage in the section of Isa 66:18-23 that immediately precedes it; in some manuscripts, this has led to v. 23 being repeated after v. 24 in order that the book draws to a conciliatory close:

וְהָיָה מִדֵּי־חֹדֶשׁ בְּחָדְשׁוֹ וּמִדֵּי שַׁבָּת בְּשַׁבַּתּוֹ יָבוֹא כָל־בָּשָׂר לְהִשְׁתַּחֲוֹת לְפָנַי אָמַר יְהוָה

From one New Moon to another and from one Sabbath to another, all mankind will come and bow down before me, says the LORD. (Note the inclusion with 1:13f).

Liebreich believes that it is especially this inclusion with 1:31 that shows that the "anti-climax" at the end of the book is intentional. Here, and in other keyword links, he discerns the techniques and principles of authors and editors, who have given the book its "final form," and believes that the "juxtaposition and association of ideas" also plays a decisive role.[3] From the clustering and inclusion of such links he arrives at a structuring of the book into main sections and subsections, even taking into account the changes between poetry and prose:[4]

Division IA Isa 1-5; Transition Isa 6; Division IB Isa 7-12
Division IIA Isa 13-19; Transition Isa 20; Division IIB Isa 21-27
Division III Isa 28-35
Division IV Isa 36-39
Unit Isa 40-66, three divisions: chs. 40-49; 50-55; 56-66.

---

[1] Isa 28:14 is ignored.
[2] Liebreich, "Compilation," *JQR* 46, 277.
[3] Liebreich, "Compilation," *JQR* 46, 259-60.
[4] See Liebreich, "Compilation," *JQR* 46, 263.

Marvin Sweeney, in his two monographs on the book of Isaiah,[1] followed this approach but proposed two different versions of structuring the book. In 1988, he finds a thematic thread and divides the book in three major units:

Isa 1	"Prologue: Exhortation: YHWH's Offer of Redemption to the People"
2-66	"Elaboration: Exhortation to People to Participate in YHWH's Plan for New World Order"
2-35	"A. Announcement of YHWH's Plan for New World Order Centered in Zion"
36-39	"B. Transition: Narrative Explanation for Delay in Implementation of Plan"
40-66	"C. Exhortation to Participate in YHWH's Renewed Covenant"

In his second contribution from 1996, Sweeney corrects himself and—following William H. Brownlee and the evidence of 1QIsa^a—divides the book into two parts, Isa 1-33 and 34-66. Here, too, he finds an overall thematic topic:

Isa 1-33, divided into ch. 1 and chs. 2-33: "Concerning YHWH's plan for worldwide sovereignty at Zion."

Isa 34-66, divided into chs. 34-54 and chs. 55-66: "Concerning realization of YHWH's plan for worldwide sovereignty at Zion"[2]

What do we gain from such observations on the surface of the available text? What do they teach us? Is the keyword link in Isa 1 and 66 the work of a single author or a redactor, who was responsible for editing the book of Isaiah?[3] Is this hand responsible for Isa 1 or for Isa 66 or for both? Or are we dealing in Isa 1 or Isa 66 or in both places with "small units" or "sources," originating from one or several prophets and then being collected secondarily?[4] Or are we dealing in Isa 66 with scribal *Tradentenliteratur*, which, although dependent on the

---

[1] See p. 170, n1 above.

[2] For further suggestions about the overall structure of the book, see John D. W. Watts, *Isaiah 1-33* (WBC 24; Waco, TX: Word Books, 1985); John D. W. Watts, *Isaiah 34-66* (WBC 25; Waco, TX: Word Books, 1987), different in the revised edition: for the discussion, see John D. W. Watts, *Isaiah 1-33* (rev. ed.; Edmonds: Nelson, 2005), lxxi-lxxiii; and Peter Höffken, *Jesaja: Der Stand der theologischen Diskussion* (Darmstadt: Wissenschaftliche Buchgesellschaft, 2004), 44–46.

[3] Thus Liebreich, "Compilation," and most recently Stromberg, *Isaiah*.

[4] Thus Elliger, *Einheit*, and Koenen, *Ethik*.

context of the book, nevertheless originated outside the book and was inserted later?[1] Or is Isa 66 or the strange verse in 66:24 one of several amendments, which do not constitute the prophetic book but take it for granted and (successively) supplement it?[2]

We can gather little information on these issues from the literary connections as such. This is not just because the cross-references are too uncertain. Despite Benjamin Sommer's justified warning against overdoing it and seeing a virtual Helen in every woman,[3] keyword links and inclusions such as that of Isa 1 and 66 are, indeed, a good indicator for discovering literary dependencies and explaining relative text relationships.[4] However, it is an open question whether the literary connections lie on one level and to what extent they are suitable for deciphering the genesis of the composition. The literary connections help in controlling the reading of the book, regardless of whether they originate from one or many hands, are primary or secondary, or are intentional or not.

The way the reading is controlled by keywords and literary links we can observe in the book of Ben Sira. Here the word "comfort" (נחם), which plays a central role as a keyword in the book of Isaiah,[5] appears to be recognized as such. Thus, in the *laus patrum* when characterising the prophet Isaiah, Ben Sira summarizes his ministry on the one hand with a reference to the miracle in Isa 38 (the sun turning back) and on the other hand with an expression from Isa 61:2-3: וינחם אבלי ציון (Sir 48:23-25). Perhaps we can also include a text such as 4Q176 here, which captions its quotations from the book of Isaiah with "comforts": ומן ספר ישעיה תנחומים. In this way, the keyword connections in the book of Isaiah do indeed provide information about what directed a reading of the prophetic book in antiquity.

This should also be valid for larger structures of the composition. It could be that Ben Sira is the first witness of the literary inclusion of Isa 1 and 65–66. The vision of Isaiah, which begins in Isa 1,

---

[1] Thus Lau, *Prophetie*.
[2] Thus Steck, *Studien*, and Goldenstein, *Gebet*.
[3] See p. 171, n1 above.
[4] For keyword links and cross-references within the book of Isaiah, see especially the work of Beuken (see p. 173, n 1).
[5] See Rolf Rendtorff, *Das Alte Testament: Eine Einführung* (3rd ed.; Neukirchen-Vluyn: Neukirchener Verlag, 1988), 201-03 and Rendtorff, "Komposition."

with the invocation of heaven and earth and ends in Isa 65–55, with the announcement of a new heaven and a new earth, is denoted as a vision of the end by Ben Sira (ברוח גבורה חזה אחרית), in which the prophet "proclaimed what is to come until eternity" (הגיד נהיות עד עולם) and — borrowing from Isa 42:9 and other passages — "(revealed) the hidden things before they occur" (ונסתרות לפני בואן). A possible candidate for the reception of the book's framing may also be the book of Daniel, which in Dan 12:2 provides the only parallel to the eternal "abhorrence" (דראון), which in Isa 66:24 denotes the never-ending agony of apostates due to worm and fire, both keywords that according to Liebreich refer back to Isa 1.

Ben Sira and Daniel thus represent two different ways of reading the book Isaiah 1–66 and both draw on the inclusion of Isa 1 and 66, which Liebreich had introduced into the discussion. Nevertheless, Ben Sira and Daniel are not the editors of the book of Isaiah, but take it for granted and represent two possible readings. Other readings are documented in the textual tradition. Thus, the Septuagint supplements in Isa 66:23 that the nations will bow down to YHWH "in Jerusalem" (neither on Mount Gerizim nor on the Temple Mount, see v. 20) and translates the "abhorrence" (דראון) in v. 24 as "perception" (εις ορασιν), probably because the root ראה was found in the word דראון. It has already been mentioned that in the Hebrew tradition v. 23 was repeated after v. 24 in order to provide the book with a "happy ending." Editorial activity is evident in both versions, Hebrew and Greek. But this activity is neither based on separate sources nor is it an argument for a single author or editor of the whole book, but rather for selective, individual additions. It stands to reason that this process of "re-lecture" can be applied to the genesis of the book itself.

The Manuscript 1QIsa[a]

Another variant of the ancient reading of the book of Isaiah is encountered in the manuscript 1QIsa[a]. This is also a version of the given text, but it provides additional hints on its reading; here, I am primarily referring to the manuscript's graphics, about which Steck has produced a short monograph.[1]

1QIsa[a] presents the text of the book of Isaiah in a structured form using line breaks, paragraphing (*alinea*), and spacing (*spatium*) in the middle of a line, by which means the main sections and subsections are marked. The function of *alinea* and *spatium* in relation to the line break, however, is controversial. I think that Steck is correct in restricting the main sections to the line break and interpreting *alinea* and *spatium* as markers of subsections.[2] The blank lines at the transition from col. 27 to col. 28 mark a greater caesura, dividing the book into two parts: Isa 1–33 and Isa 34–66. However, it is not clear whether the reasons for this are technical or have to do with the content.

In addition to the graphics, the manuscript has scribal marks at the edge of the right or left columns. The most common is the *paragraphos*, a stroke under the line or a bar with circle on top (like an *omega*), which perhaps stands for a *peh*, meaning פרש or פרשה, as suggested by Annette Steudel on the basis of 4Q426.[3] In addition to the *paragraphos*, we occasionally find a cross, a paleo-Hebrew *waw*, and other characters, which, like the *paragraphos*, can also be found in numerous other manuscripts. There has been much speculation about the form, origin, and above all the function of these scribal marks, but a complete explanation has not been possible so far.

Nevertheless, after the works of Martin, Oesch, Olley, Tov, and Steck,[4] this much seems to be clear to me concerning 1QIsa[a]. Firstly, the

---

[1] Odil Hannes Steck, *Die erste Jesajarolle von Qumran (1QIs[a]): Schreibweise als Leseanleitung für ein Prophetenbuch* (SBS 173/1-2; Stuttgart: Katholisches Bibelwerk, 1998). Meanwhile the new edition of the scroll appeared: Eugene C. Ulrich and Peter W. Flint with a contribution by Martin G. Abegg, eds., *Qumran Cave 1/II. The Isaiah Scrolls, Part 1: Plates and Transcriptions; Part 2: Introductions, Commentary, and Textual Variants* (DJD 32; Oxford: Clarendon Press, 2010).

[2] Steck, *Jesajarolle*, 28-33.

[3] Annette Steudel, "426: 4Q Sapiential-Hymnic Work A," *Qumran Cave 4 XV: Sapiential Texts, Part 1* (eds. Torleif Elgvin et al.; DJD 20; Oxford, Clarendon Press, 1997), 211-24, here 215.

[4] For the discussion, see Steck, *Jesajarolle*, 11-13. Furthermore, see Malachi Martin, *The Scribal Character of the Dead Sea Scrolls* (BMus 44-45; Louvain: Publications universitaires, 1958); Josef M. Oesch, "Textgliederung im Alten Testament und in den Qumranhandschriften," *Hen* 5 (1983): 289-321; John W. Olley, "'Hear the Word of Yhwh': The Structure of the Book of Isaiah in 1QIsa[a]," *VT* 43 (1983): 19-49; Emanuel Tov, "Scribal Markings in the Texts from the Judean Desert," *Current Research and Technological Developments on the Dead Sea Scrolls* (eds. Donald W. Parry and Stephen D. Ricks; STDJ 20;

marks in the margin are secondary to the text graphic, to which they refer in part but not consistently.[1] Secondly, it appears that at least the two forms of the *paragraphos* (stroke and the bar with a circle above or *peh*) function to structure the text.[2] As with the graphics, we need to distinguish between main and subsections: the bar with a circle above or *peh,* which is only found in the second part of the manuscript, Isa 34–66, seem to mark the main or major sections; the stroke marks the subsections.[3]

Even with all possible caution that is necessary when interpreting these scribal marks, there is much evidence that their function is to mark units of meaning in order to guide the reading of the book. This is more or less consensual in the case of the text graphic. The case for the *paragraphos* as a distinctive, secondary structuring system has, in my opinion, been convincingly proven by Steck, even though his interpretation, which is very strongly oriented on the content, should be defined more precisely in many places and probably needs clarification or correction.

All this means that in the external presentation of the text in 1QIsa[a] we have a very early form of reading the book of Isaiah: more correctly, two versions, if we evaluate the graphics and the scribal marks as being two different systems. We can see this clearly in Isa 65–66. The graphical text-structuring using line breaks and *alinea* or *spatium* in Isa 65–66 appears essentially (with two exceptions, 65:17-18 and 66:10-11) to be oriented on the formulae denoting the divine word, which introduce or channel out a section:

65:1-7:	v. 7 אָמַר יְהוָה
65:8-12:	v. 8 כֹּה אָמַר יְהוָה
65:13-16:	v. 13 לָכֵן כֹּה־אָמַר אֲדֹנָי יְהוִה
65:17-18a:	v. 17 כִּי־הִנְנִי בוֹרֵא שָׁמַיִם חֲדָשִׁים וָאָרֶץ חֲדָשָׁה
65:18b-25:	v. 18b כִּי הִנְנִי בוֹרֵא אֶת־יְרוּשָׁלַםִ גִּילָה וְעַמָּהּ מָשׂוֹשׂ,
	v. 25 אָמַר יְהוָה

Leiden: Brill, 1996), 41–77; Emanuel Tov, *Scribal Practices and Approaches Reflected in the Texts Found in the Judean Desert* (STDJ 54; Leiden: Brill 2004); and Emanuel Tov, *Textual Criticism of the Hebrew Bible* (3rd rev. ed.; Minneapolis: Fortress, 2012).

[1] Steck, *Jesajarolle,* 27.

[2] Steck, *Jesajarolle,* 30–32.

[3] Accordingly, the book is divided into the following main sections: Isa 1–35 or—taking the main division of the manuscript into two parts into account—Isa 1–33 and 34–35; 36–39; 40:1–42:12; 42:13–44:28; 45:1–52:6; 52:7–59:21; 60–66.

66:1–4:	v. 1 כֹּה אָמַר יְהוָה
66:5:	v. 5 שִׁמְעוּ דְּבַר־יְהוָה הַחֲרֵדִים אֶל־דְּבָרוֹ
66:6–9:	קוֹל v. 6 three times, v. 9 אָמַר אֱלֹהָיִךְ
66:10–11:	(v. 10 שִׂמְחוּ אֶת־יְרוּשָׁלַם)
66:12–20a:	v. 12 אָמַר יְהוָה, v. 20a כִּי־כֹה אָמַר יְהוָה
66:20b–21:	v. 21 אָמַר יְהוָה
66:22–24:	v. 22 נְאֻם־יְהוָה

With regard to content, this arrangement goes hand in hand with the narrative of the fate of the pious (servants) and the impious; in 65:8–12 (with v. 11) first the impious are addressed directly, and from 66:5 the pious. The fate of the two groups is sometimes depicted in the same section and sometimes in different ones.

The arrangement using *paragraphos* within the last major section of Isa 60–66 follows the graphical segmentation up to and including 62:9 and, like the text graphics in 64:11, provides a caesura after the closure of the prayer in Isa 63–64.[1] After this caesura the two systems go their separate ways. The arrangement using *paragraphos* bundles the graphically marked sections into larger units but does not keep consistently to the formulae denoting the divine word and, in two places, splits the text differently. Guided by keyword links and inclusions, the sections are split according to the fate of the two groups, the pious and the impious. In the following, I list the sections according to *paragraphos* in comparison with the graphical segmentation:

I 65:1–10 (graphical segmentation: 65:1–7, 8–12)

1 נִדְרַשְׁתִּי לְלוֹא שָׁאָלוּ נִמְצֵאתִי לְלֹא בִקְשֻׁנִי אָמַרְתִּי הִנֵּנִי הִנֵּנִי אֶל־גּוֹי לֹא־קֹרָא בִשְׁמִי
I revealed myself to those who did not ask for me; I was found by those who did not seek me. To a nation that did not call on my name, I said, "Here am I, here I am."

10 וְהָיָה הַשָּׁרוֹן לִנְוֵה־צֹאן וְעֵמֶק עָכוֹר לְרֵבֶץ בָּקָר לְעַמִּי אֲשֶׁר דְּרָשׁוּנִי
Sharon will become a pasture for flocks, and the Valley of Achor a resting place for herds, or my people who seek me.

---

[1] There is, however, a difference at the transition to the prayer. According to the *paragraphos*, the text is divided into Isa 62:10–63:6 and 63:7–9 (the beginning of the prayer!) instead of Isa 62:10–12 and 63:1–64:11 according to the graphical segmentation.

II 65:11–66:4 (graphical segmentation: 65:8-12, 13-16 etc.; 66:1-4)

¹¹ וְאַתֶּם עֹזְבֵי יְהוָה ...

¹² וּמָנִיתִי אֶתְכֶם לַחֶרֶב וְכֻלְּכֶם לַטֶּבַח תִּכְרָעוּ יַעַן קָרָאתִי וְלֹא עֲנִיתֶם דִּבַּרְתִּי וְלֹא שְׁמַעְתֶּם וַתַּעֲשׂוּ הָרַע בְּעֵינַי וּבַאֲשֶׁר לֹא־חָפַצְתִּי בְּחַרְתֶּם

But as for you who forsake the LORD and forget my holy mountain, who spread a table for Fortune and fill bowls of mixed wine for Destiny, I will destine you for the sword, and all of you will fall in the slaughter; for I called but you did not answer, I spoke but you did not listen. You did evil in my sight and chose what displeases me.

66:4 גַּם־אֲנִי אֶבְחַר בְּתַעֲלֻלֵיהֶם וּמְגוּרֹתָם אָבִיא לָהֶם יַעַן קָרָאתִי וְאֵין עוֹנֶה דִּבַּרְתִּי וְלֹא שָׁמֵעוּ וַיַּעֲשׂוּ הָרַע בְּעֵינַי וּבַאֲשֶׁר לֹא־חָפַצְתִּי בָּחָרוּ

So I also will choose harsh treatment for them and will bring on them what they dread. For when I called, no one answered, when I spoke, no one listened. They did evil in my sight and chose what displeases me.

III 66:5–14 (graphical segmentation: 66:5, 6-9, 10-11, 12-20a)

⁵ שִׁמְעוּ דְּבַר־יְהוָה הַחֲרֵדִים אֶל־דְּבָרוֹ אָמְרוּ אֲחֵיכֶם שֹׂנְאֵיכֶם מְנַדֵּיכֶם לְמַעַן שְׁמִי יִכְבַּד יְהוָה וְנִרְאֶה בְשִׂמְחַתְכֶם וְהֵם יֵבֹשׁוּ ⁶ קוֹל שָׁאוֹן מֵעִיר קוֹל מֵהֵיכָל קוֹל יְהוָה מְשַׁלֵּם גְּמוּל לְאֹיְבָיו

Hear the word of the LORD, you who tremble at his word: "Your own people who hate you, and exclude you because of my name, have said, 'Let the LORD be glorified, that we may see your joy!' Yet they will be put to shame. Hear that uproar from the city hear that noise from the temple! It is the sound of the LORD repaying his enemies all they deserve.

¹⁴ וּרְאִיתֶם וְשָׂשׂ לִבְּכֶם וְעַצְמוֹתֵיכֶם כַּדֶּשֶׁא תִפְרַחְנָה וְנוֹדְעָה יַד־יְהוָה אֶת־עֲבָדָיו וְזָעַם אֶת־אֹיְבָיו

When you see this, your heart will rejoice and you will flourish like grass; the hand of the LORD will be made known to his servants, but his fury will be shown to his foes.

IV 66:15–24 (graphical segmentation: 66:12-20a, 20b-21, 23-24)

¹⁵ כִּי־הִנֵּה יְהוָה בָּאֵשׁ יָבוֹא וְכַסּוּפָה מַרְכְּבֹתָיו לְהָשִׁיב בְּחֵמָה אַפּוֹ וְגַעֲרָתוֹ בְּלַהֲבֵי־אֵשׁ ¹⁶ כִּי בָאֵשׁ יְהוָה נִשְׁפָּט וּבְחַרְבּוֹ אֶת־כָּל־בָּשָׂר וְרַבּוּ חַלְלֵי יְהוָה

See, the LORD is coming with fire, and his chariots are like a whirlwind; he will bring down his anger with fury, and his rebuke with flames of fire. For with fire and with his sword the LORD will execute judgment on all people, and many will be those slain by the LORD.

²³ וְהָיָה מִדֵּי־חֹדֶשׁ בְּחָדְשׁוֹ וּמִדֵּי שַׁבָּת בְּשַׁבַּתּוֹ יָבוֹא כָל־בָּשָׂר לְהִשְׁתַּחֲוֹת לְפָנַי אָמַר יְהוָה

24 וְיָצְאוּ וְרָאוּ בְּפִגְרֵי הָאֲנָשִׁים הַפֹּשְׁעִים בִּי כִּי תוֹלַעְתָּם לֹא תָמוּת וְאִשָּׁם לֹא תִכְבֶּה וְהָיוּ דֵרָאוֹן לְכָל־בָּשָׂר

From one New Moon to another and from one Sabbath to another, all humankind will come and bow down before me, says the LORD. And they will go out and look on the dead bodies of those who rebelled against me; the worms that eat them will not die, the fire that burns them will not be quenched, and they will be loathsome to all mankind.

The first section, Isa 65:1-10, is oriented on the keyword "to search" (דרש) and focuses mainly on the fate of the pious, whereas the division of the people into servants and impious persons introduced from 65:8 onwards is also presupposed in 65:1-7: "the people (גוי or עם), who call on me / ask after me" (vv. 1-3 and v. 10).

The second section, Isa 65:11-66:4, clearly focuses on the address to the impious, as well as on the inclusion of 65:12/66:4: the impious did not respond when God called.

Accordingly, the third section begins in Isa 66:5 with an imperative to listen, which is directed at all those who tremble at YHWH's word, i.e. those who ask after YHWH and respond (cf. 66:2 וְחָרֵד עַל־דְּבָרִי).[1] According to the *paragraphos*, the section extends up to 66:14, included by the keywords ראה "to see" (what the enemies in v. 5 want to see, is seen in v. 14 by the servants) and איב "enemies" (vv. 6, 14), and seems on the whole to refer to the fate of the servants, in other words, the pious.

This is followed by the fourth and final section, Isa 66:15-24, which begins with "see" (כִּי־הִנֵּה) and ends in v. 24 with "and they will go out and look" (וְיָצְאוּ וְרָאוּ); the section is held together by the fiery judgement (אש) on or before "all flesh" (כָל־בָּשָׂר) in vv. 15-16, 24, which is obviously referring entirely to the fate of the impious.

It seems that in both text-structuring systems (text graphics and *paragraphos*) the decisive perspective of reception has been the division of the people into pious and impious, which is mentioned in the text itself in some passages. This perspective is noticeably expressed even more clearly and more comprehensively in the second, more recent system of marginal marks than in the text graphics.

The Greek version of Isa 66:5, however, is different. Instead of "your brothers who hate you have said" (אָמְרוּ אֲחֵיכֶם שֹׂנְאֵיכֶם), in the

---

[1] For the expression, see Ezra 9:4; 10:3.

Septuagint we read: "Say it, our brothers, to those who hate us and detest us" (εἴπατε, ἀδελφοὶ ἡμῶν, τοῖς μισοῦσιν ἡμᾶς καὶ βδελυσσομένοις). The variant reading sets aside an internal Jewish conflict and turns it instead into a conflict between brothers among the people and enemies among the nations. Accordingly, the participation of the nations in the salvation of Zion in Isa 66:12, 20 is qualified. Both readings take hold of certain aspects of the text and highlight them over other aspects. This occurs not only in the Septuagint, but also in 1QIsa[a], Ben Sira, 4Q176, and in the book of Daniel. As a consequence, the ancient readings of the book of Isaiah, which are based on Isa 65-66, perceive different perspectives in these chapters, act selectively, and read the whole text in the light of the individual. It stands to reason that this method of reading the book of Isaiah is also to be expected in the text of Isa 65-66 itself.

Readings in Isaiah 65-66

And so I turn again to Isa 65-66. So far we have looked at readings of the book of Isaiah that draw upon the available final text. Chapters 65-66 of Isaiah play an important role in these readings; however, they are read and received quite differently. In the following, I would like to show that these differences are created in Isa 65-66 itself, since we can also find several readings of the book of Isaiah itself here.

It is generally recognised that Isa 65-66 give a divine response to the prayer in Isa 63-64. The prayer starts with God's acts of salvation and the people's apostasy in the past. It then changes into a plea for rescue, pointing to the people's present situation. The people speak in the first person plural ("we"): they implore God, as the father of Israel (63:16; 64:7), to turn again to God's people and God's temple in Zion-Jerusalem, now lying in ruins. The prayer concerns all the people (63:8, 11, 14; 64:8), who are also known as "sons" (63: 8, following Isa 1:2 and other passages), "servants," and "tribes" (63:17) and have their cultic centre in Zion-Jerusalem (63:18; 64:9f). But the deity has turned away; it is not appealed to (64:6), and it keeps silent (64:11).

In scholarship, this prayer is considered to be a traditional piece from the so-called exilic period, the time after 587 BCE, which has found a secondary use. This is opposed by a number of literary connections to First and Second Isaiah, observed by Steck and investigated in detail by Goldenstein.[1] They suggest that the prayer in Isa 63-64, like everything else in Trito-Isaiah, is a literary supplement (*Fortschreibung*). The literary connections in the book of Isaiah are not explained by assuming an external source, and such an assumption introduces an additional, extremely tenuous redactional-historical hypothesis.

It is obvious that the response in Isa 65-66 refers to the prayer in Isa 63-64 as well as to the wider context of the book of Isaiah (namely the First and Second Isaiah). The response is extremely complex and in actual fact comprises not just one response but several.

A first response is addressed to all the people who, in the prayer, use the "we" form and say of themselves that they have neither asked for God nor called upon God's name (Isa 64:6). In Isa 65:1-7, it is affirmed that the people did not ask for God but went their own sinful way, and, as a consequence, will be punished. Their plight is therefore explained in the speech of God as righteous judgment. Somewhat later in the text, in Isa 65:16b-25, it is these same people, who, drawing upon Isa 1 (and Gen 1) as well as Isa 11, are presented with the prospect of creation of a new world, in which (following the example of Deutero-Isaiah) former troubles will be forgotten and, for Jerusalem and God's people, paradisiacal conditions (as described in Isaiah 11) will prevail.

Between the speech to the people who did not ask for God and the promise of a new world made for the same people, a second response is inserted in Isa 65:8-16a. This is also addressed to the people of God, but it differentiates between two groups of people: those asking for God (v. 10) and those not responding when God called (v. 12). Drawing on how the people refer to themselves in the prayer (Isa 63:17), one group is labelled "servants" and "chosen ones," while the other is addressed in the second person plural ("you") and condemned. This second group receives the blame for all the offenses of which – in the prayer in Isa 63-64 and in Isa 65:1-7 – all the people were accused. Only the chosen "servants" will participate in the salvation; the others are excluded. The promise of a new world in Isa 65:16b-25 thus only applies to the "servants" and no longer to all the people. The internal

---

[1] Steck, *Studien* and Goldenstein, *Gebet*.

Jewish conflict emerges again in Isa 66:5-6 and 66:14 (indicated by the *paragraphos* structuring in 1QIsa[a]). In connection with this, accusations are encountered again, which in Isa 66:8-16a are aimed at the enemies of the "servants," so that in addition to 65:8-16a the items that follow seem to refer only to the impious and enemies amongst their own people and not to all people (66:1-6, 14b-17).

Both responses react to the prayer in Isa 63-64 and its portrayal of a sinful people of God, but they do so in different ways. Whereas the first response, like the prayer, addresses the people as a whole (they being surrounded by external enemies and crushed down), the second response itself introduces a separation of God's people into "servants" and their enemies. In Isa 66:7-14a, a third group is addressed as God's people: the "children of Zion." Clues given in the prayer are the expressions "not heard of" and "not seen yet" (64:3), as well as the focus on the lament on Zion-Jerusalem in Isa 64:9-10. Even the prophecy of a new heaven and a new earth in Isa 65:16b-26 applies to Jerusalem and the God's people (following the example of Isa 40:1-2). However, in Isa 66:7-14a (following the example in Isa 49-54 and 60-62), Zion and her children are placed at the center; they are to be comforted, and the wealth of nations should flow to them. In the context of Isa 66:1-6 and 66:14b-17, we should understand "Zion's children" as a reference to the "servants," to whom the prophecies of salvation apply, in contrast to the "brothers who hate you" (66:5).

Finally, in Isa 66:18-24, the response addresses a fourth group of people, again inspired by the expressions "not heard" and "not seen." But this time the expression is not applying to God (Isa 64:3) and divine work of salvation (Isa 66:8), but to those nations that have never before heard of or seen God (66:19). Following Isa 40:5, they too should see and hear the glory of God. If the nations in the prayer of Isa 63-64 only seem to be enemies (64:1), from now on the trial and the separation of the pious and the impious cuts through the middle of "all flesh," as stated in the reception of the terminology of Isa 40:5 and 49:26 (60:16, 23, 24). Instead of the "brothers who hate you," in their procession to Jerusalem, the people bring the "brothers of all nations" as offering, so that under the new heaven and the new earth in Isa 65:17 "all flesh" from God's people and the nations worship God, unless they are counted among the apostates who are abandoned to worm and fire for all eternity.

This is the evidence within the final form of the given text. But how is it to be explained? The easiest and seemingly most certain explanation assumes that Isa 65–66 come from a single source. But, on closer consideration, this explanation is neither the easiest nor the most certain; on the contrary, it is the most difficult and most uncertain explanation of all. The readings in Ben Sira, 4Q149, Daniel, and the textual tradition, which we have already discussed above, have shown that this text provides clues for different readings and only a selective reading can understand it to be a literary unit. This means that we are dependent on highly subjective criteria, on a concept imported from outside, or on personal taste, in order to reduce the complexity of the text and discover the hand of a single author. The reduction of complexity does not solve the problems in the text but obscures them and does not take them seriously.

In addition, the whole hypothesis of the unity of Trito-Isaiah is highly inconsistent. Usually scholars accept the literary division introduced by Bernhard Duhm of Proto-, Deutero- and Trito-Isaiah, as well as a few additions here and there, such as Deutero-Isaianic glosses in Proto-Isaiah, or Proto-Isaianic allusions in Deutero- and Trito-Isaiah. They even sometimes count on some "sources" like the prayer in Isa 63–64, which came out of nowhere into the hands of the authors. But then the blinkers come up and without being quite clear why, many scholars abandon their work half done.

In my opinion, decisive for an explanation of the text are two phenomena: first, the continuous literary dependence of Isa 65–66 on Proto-, Deutero- and the rest of Trito-Isaiah (Isa 56–64); and second, the internal literary cross-references in Isa 65–66, which, in repeated new attempts, respond to the prayer in Isa 63–64, thereby setting different accents in their relation to the prayer, as well as in the interrelationship between the responses proper. The most obvious is the difference between those responses that affect all of God's people and those that introduce a separation within the people into "servants" and "brothers who hate you." Added to this is the focus on the "children of Zion" and the entire world of nations, "all flesh." Only if we take these different perspectives seriously and put them in proportion do we step onto safe ground and become able to explain the complexity of the different responses in Isa 65–66.

Should we decide not to follow the hypothesis of unity leaving everything in suspense, these findings are explainable in a number of different ways. Scholarly discussions revolve around "small units" of the prophets,[1] "source fragments" from nowhere,[2] individual pieces from scribes working within various traditional circles,[3] or successive supplementations, i.e. *Fortschreibungen*.[4] Needless to say, it seems obvious to me that of all these possibilities the last is the most likely.[5] The assumption of "small units" or individual "source fragments" is again burdened with great uncertainty; it does not explain the high density of literary dependencies, and it requires a number of additional assumptions, which cannot be proven from the text. In contrast, the supplementary hypothesis offers a means of establishing a relative chronology in the text itself, which allows both differences and similarities alike to be evaluated and the process of interpretation to be accurately classified, not just selectively, but for every detail in the text. Of course, this is only a hypothesis, but without a hypothesis we have no explanation, not even the hypothesis of unity, which is burdened with much greater uncertainty.

Moreover, the findings in the whole book of Isaiah speak in favour of the supplementary hypothesis. Isaiah 65–66 is not the only area in which a new text is created out of literary borrowings from the whole of the book of Isaiah and a new reading is inscribed in the book. There is now consensus that this is the case for Trito-Isaiah (i.e., Isa 56–66), but it is also true for large parts of Deutero-Isaiah, in particular for Isa 49–55[6] and for a number of texts in Proto-Isaiah (e.g., Isa 11–12 or

---

[1] Thus Elliger, *Tritojesaja*; Elliger, *Verhältnis*; and Koenen, *Ethik*.

[2] Thus Sommer, *Prophet*.

[3] Thus Lau, *Prophetie*.

[4] Thus Steck, *Studien* and Goldenstein, *Gebet*.

[5] See Reinhard G. Kratz, "Tritojesaja," *Prophetenstudien: Kleine Schriften II* (FAT 74; Tübingen: Mohr Siebeck, 2011), 233–42.

[6] See especially Odil Hannes Steck, *Bereitete Heimkehr: Jesaja 35 als redaktionelle Brücke zwischen dem Ersten und dem Zweiten Jesaja* (SBS 121; Stuttgart: Katholisches Bibelwerk, 1985); Odil Hannes Steck, *Gottesknecht und Zion: Gesammelte Aufsätze zu Deuterojesaja* (FAT 4; Tübingen: Mohr [Siebeck], 1992); Odil Hannes Steck, *Der Abschluß der Prophetie im Alten Testament: Ein Versuch zur Frage der Vorgeschichte des Kanons* (BThSt 17; Neukirchen-Vluyn: Neukirchener Verlag, 1991); and Odil Hannes Steck, *Studien*. Furthermore, especially on Second Isaiah, see Klaus Kiesow, *Exodustexte im Jesajabuch:*

Isa 35).[1] The literary cross-references exclude the hypothesis of "small units" or "fragmentary sources;" the differences between the numerous additional pieces rule out the hypothesis of unity. We only have to think of the reformulation and interpretation of prophecies concerning Zion taken from Isa 49-54 and found in 60-62, the spiritualisation of "light" and "road" metaphors from Isa 60-62 in Isa 56-59, the questioning of Isa 60-62 by means of the prayer in Isa 63-64, and the various divine responses in Isa 65-66, which in turn outbid Isa (1-39 and) 40-62. If we do not attempt to establish a relative chronology of these pieces on the basis of the obvious literary connections, we would lose the ground under our feet and drown in the material. Isa 65-66 clearly belong to the latest phases of the formation of the book.[2]

Finally, I would like to call attention again to the various readings outside the book of Isaiah, in the textual tradition (Septuagint, Qumran), Ben Sira, 4Q176 or Daniel. They are a clear proof that there have been different readings of the book in ancient Judaism on the basis of the final form of the book and even just on that basis. They suggest that the process of reception and interpretation of the book of Isaiah, which has resulted in a variety of readings, began in the book itself, and internal as well as external readings can be traced back not to one hand, but to many. The various readings inside and outside the book of Isaiah are evidence of a flow of tradition, which begins in the book itself and continues in the textual tradition (such as 1QIsa[a]), the versions (above all the Septuagint), the summaries (Ben Sira, 4Q176), the allusions (Daniel), and the commentaries (such as the pesharim).[3]

Literarkritische und motivgeschichtliche Analysen (OBO 24; Göttingen: Vandenhoeck & Ruprecht, 1979); Reinhard G. Kratz, *Kyros im Deuterojesaja-Buch: Redaktionsgeschichtliche Untersuchungen zu Entstehung und Theologie von Jes 40-55* (FAT 1; Tübingen: Mohr [Siebeck], 1991); and Jürgen van Oorschot, *Von Babel zum Zion: Eine literarkritische und redaktionsgeschichtliche Untersuchung zu Jesaja 40-55* (BZAW 206; Berlin: Walter de Gruyter, 1993).

[1] See H. G. M. Williamson, *The Book Called Isaiah: Deutero-Isaiah's Role in Composition and Redaction* (Oxford: Clarendon Press, 1994).

[2] Steck, *Abschluß*; and Steck, *Studien*, 217-19. Steck's hypothesis was taken up and confirmed by Gärtner, *Summe*, and developed by Lau, *Prophetie*, and Goldenstein, *Gebet*. Stromberg, *Isaiah*, takes a step backward and again suggests a single author of Trito-Isaiah as reader and redactor of the book of Isaiah.

[3] On this, see Reinhard G. Kratz, "Innerbiblische Exegese und Redaktionsgeschichte im Lichte der empirischen Evidenz," *Das Judentum im Zeitalter des Zweiten Tempels: Kleine Schriften I* (2nd ed.; FAT 42; Tübingen: Mohr Siebeck, 2013), 126-56; see also

Many hands are involved in this flow of tradition, not only outside the book, but also inside it. And so my *ceterum censeo*: not "too many hands" but "too many sources" and "too much unity" stand in the way of a historical explanation; they do not guarantee more "certainty" in explanation but, on the contrary, create greater "uncertainty."

---

case studies in Kratz, *Prophetenstudien*, esp. 99-145 (on the book and pesher of Nahum), 147-271 (on the book of Isaiah).

And the Word Became Words
The Inscription of the Divine Word on Jeremiah the Prophet in Jeremiah the Book

Else K. Holt

When our youngest son, Morten, was about five years old, the family visited Louisiana—the Danish museum of modern art in Humlebæk, north of Copenhagen. In the garden with a beautiful view of the beaches and the sound between Denmark and Sweden, we stopped at one of the English sculptor Henry Spencer Moore's large bronze sculptures, and the boy asked his father to read him the name plaque. The title was *Human Concretion on Oval Bowl*, and Morten frowned and asked, "What does 'oval' mean?" This was not a stupid question for a five year old, and neither for his proud parents. He could, though, have asked another: "What does 'concretion' mean?"

This is more or less my exegetical and theological question in what follows. How does the concept of a nonmaterial divine word become a material concretion in the book of Jeremiah? And what is the meaning of this concretion?

My thoughts are based on three preconditions:
1. The figure of Jeremiah is not a representation of a historical person, but of a literary *persona*, Jeremiah the prophet.[1]
2. This literary *persona* serves as a representation of the divine word.
3. The inscription of the divine word as *persona* in a book (or books) serves to preserve and authorize the word for subsequent generations of readers.

The first two assertions, which I have argued for earlier,[2] are exegetical-methodological. They do not deny the historicity of the

---

[1] Cf. Timothy Polk, *The Prophetic Persona: Jeremiah and the Language of the Self* (JSOTSup 32; Sheffield: JSOT Press, 1984).

[2] Else K. Holt, "The Prophet as Persona," *The Oxford Handbook of Prophecy* (ed. Carolyn J. Sharp; Oxford: Oxford University Press, 2016), 299-318; Else K. Holt,

person named Jeremiah *per se*; rather, they serve as a hermeneutical signpost, indicating that I take as my point of departure a synchronic-literary reading of the book of Jeremiah. The third hermeneutical claim might seem trivial at the outset, but I contend that there is more to say about it than "writing is preservation." Talking about authorization of the prophetic word—or other biblical material—inevitably leads to matters of theology: Why do important existential messages need embodiment and inscription to survive? Could not we just as well stick to the oral tradition of plain, informative discourse for the education of humankind? What is the use of personifications, metaphors, narratives, and parables when it comes to theological matters? And matters of theology are—we should remember—what we are talking about in biblical studies. Theology matters.

Religious, or theological, communication to the lay and the learned was and is the ultimate ambition of the Hebrew Bible. We do, of course, find messages for specialists in Leviticus, Numbers, and parts of Ecclesiastes, to cite a few obvious examples, but the bulk of communication gives the impression of being aimed at a broader audience. So, taking the book of Jeremiah as an example *instar omnium*, what are the communicative strategies in the Hebrew Bible, and what is their cognitive background?

Of Metaphor, Embodiment, and God

All communication about God is and must be metaphorical. The divine is transcendent *per se*, transcendence being defined as transgression of the material and mundane. The divine, then, cannot be discussed on the basis of material, immanent experience; what we need for theological communication about the divine is a discursive vehicle, a mode of linking the nonmaterial to material, experience-based speech.

"Communication of Authority: The 'Prophet' in the Book of Jeremiah," *The Discursive Fight over Religious Texts in Antiquity: Religion and Normativity*, (ed. Anders-Christian Jacobsen; Aarhus: Aarhus University Press, 2009), 110–18; and Else K. Holt, "Narrative Normativity in Diasporic Jeremiah—and Today," *Jeremiah (Dis)placed: New Directions in Writing/Reading Jeremiah* (eds. A. R. Pete Diamond and Louis Stulman; LHBOTS 529; New York: T & T Clark 2011), 125–35.

According to George Lakoff and Mark Johnson's scholarly evergreen, *Metaphors We Live By*,[1] this is in fact what we do most of the time. Our speech about the world around us is by and large structured by metaphor. We talk and structure everyday life in orientational or spatialized metaphors,[2] up/down, in/out, front/back, and so on, thus: more is up, less is down; happy is up, sad is down; good is up, bad is down. And I add: light is up, darkness is down; God is up, human is down, since God is in heaven, human beings are on earth, or even worse: human beings are *below* or *in* the earth, in the darkness of Sheol.

Already here, however, we recognize the second type of metaphor identified by Lakoff and Johnson, the ontological metaphor, that is, metaphors that help us comprehend experiences "in terms of objects and substances." In the words of Lakoff and Johnson,

> Once we can identify our experiences as entities or substances, we can refer to them, categorize them, group them, and quantify them—and, by this means, reason about them.... [O]ur own experiences with physical objects (especially our own bodies) provide the basis for an extraordinarily wide variety of ontological metaphors, that is, ways of viewing events, activities, emotions, ideas, etc., as entities and substances.[3]

They conclude:

> Perhaps the most obvious ontological metaphors are those where the physical object is further specified as being a person. This allows us to comprehend a wide variety of experiences with nonhuman entities in terms of human motivations, characteristics, and activities.[4]

In my opinion, the divine and the divine word is such an experience, which is in need of metaphorization in order to be comprehended. Later, Lakoff and Mark Turner state that metaphor

---

[1] George Lakoff and Mark Johnson, *Metaphors We Live By* (Chicago: University of Chicago Press, 1980).

[2] Lakoff and Johnson, *Metaphors We Live By*, 14.

[3] Lakoff and Johnson, *Metaphors We Live By*, 25.

[4] Lakoff and Johnson, *Metaphors We Live By*, 33. "The physical object" here covers what cognitive metaphor theory later would label "source domain"; cf., e.g., George Lakoff and Mark Turner, *More than Cool Reason: A Field Guide to Poetic Metaphor* (Chicago: University of Chicago Press, 1989) and Job Y. Jindo, *Biblical Metaphor Reconsidered: A Cognitive Approach to Poetic Prophecy in Jeremiah 1-24* (HSM 64; Winona Lake: Eisenbrauns, 2010).

allows us to understand our selves and our world in a way that no other modes of thought can. Far from being merely a matter of words, metaphor is a matter of thought—all kinds of thought.... It is indispensable not only to our imagination but also to our reason.[1]

Only a few of us experience the divine word as something concrete, and so we need metaphors to talk about the divine being, to make theology. Put differently, the inconcrete, transcendently experienced needs concretization to be comprehended and communicated, and in considering this process the theory of cognitive metaphor is helpful.

In the book of Jeremiah, the implied audience obtains the divine word through the material vehicle of a book about a physical, although literary, persona, and this helps them incorporate the nonmaterial, although experienced, religious message in their consciousness. In what follow, I will label this materialization *embodiment*.[2]

Metaphor and Embodiment—A Case Study

For the sake of clarification and documentation, let us have a closer look at an example of the process of God's embodiment in writing. My example is the well-known lament in Jer 8:18-22:[3]

[18] There is no healing (גֵּהָה),[4] grief (יָגוֹן) comes over me,
my heart is faint (דַּוָּי)
[19] Hear, the sound of the cry of my poor people
from the length and breadth of the land:
"Is YHWH not on Zion?
Is there no king with her?"
Why have they made me grieve with their graven images (פְּסִלֵיהֶם)
with foreign no-goods (הַבְלֵי נֵכָר)?
[20] "Harvest is over, summer has ended

---

[1] Lakoff and Turner, *More than Cool Reason*, xi.
[2] I do not use the term within the methodological framework of cognitive philosophy, but merely as a word for making a transcendent "object" obtainable in a material form. On embodiment and cognitive philosophy, see Robert A. Wilson and Lucia Foglia, "Embodied Cognition," *The Stanford Encyclopedia of Philosophy* (ed. Edward N. Zalta; 2016): https://plato.stanford.edu/archives/win2016/entries/embodied-cognition (accessed 01/17/17).
[3] Translation mine. I place the subdivision in the larger pericope, 8:18-9:9, between 8:22 and 8:23 due to the imagery of tears.
[4] Cf. *BHS*, reading with Targum and some manuscripts but without following the editorial proposal of moving the words to 8:17.

But we have not been saved."
²¹ Because of the wound (שֶׁבֶר) of my poor people I am wounded (הָשְׁבָּרְתִּי), I mourn, overwhelmed by desolation (שַׁמָּה)).
²² Is there no balm (צֳרִי) in Gilead, is no healer (רֹפֵא) there?
So, why has new skin not grown over my poor people's wound?[1]

One of the questions discussed at length in recent scholarship is whether the speaker of Jer 8:18-22 is God or the prophet. Twentieth century commentators often claimed that the speaker must be Jeremiah, since, to quote Wilhelm Rudolph, this short lament does not talk about human sinfulness as the reason for the suffering, but rather expresses compassion, a token of human invention, not of revelation.[2] Later, Terence Fretheim interpreted Jer 8:18-23 (NRSV 8:18-9:1) as the prophet mirroring the mourning of God: "The people not only hear the prophet as spokesman of God but they also see the lamentation of God embodied in the person of the prophet."[3]

Earlier I have argued, similarly, for example, to Kathleen O'Connor, that it is impossible to distinguish between the two voices in Jer 8:18-22.[4] The divine compassion is embodied in the words of the prophet, conveyed to us through the physical medium of a written — and later printed — book, challenging our imagination to co-operation. Thus, Jer 8:18-22 makes a fine example of the incorporation of God and prophet in one oracle.

---

[1] For this translation, see Robert P. Carroll, *Jeremiah: A Commentary* (OTL; Philadelphia: Westminster, 1986), 235.

[2] Wilhelm Rudolph, *Jeremia* (3rd ed.; HAT 1/12; Tübingen: Mohr [Siebeck], 1968), 65.

[3] Terence E. Fretheim, *The Suffering of God: An Old Testament Perspective* (Philadelphia: Fortress Press, 1984), 135.

[4] Kathleen M. O'Connor, "The Tears of God and Divine Character in Jeremiah 2-9," *Troubling Jeremiah* (eds. Pete A.R. Diamond, Kathleen M. O'Connor, and Louis Stulman; JSOTSup 260; Sheffield: Sheffield Academic Press, 1999), 387–401 and Else K. Holt, "The Helpless Potentate," *The Centre and Periphery: A European Tribute to Walter Brueggemann* (eds. Jill Middlemas, David J. A. Clines, and Else K. Holt; HBM 27; Sheffield: Sheffield Phoenix, 2010), 179–90.

The divine compassion[1] is communicated through the very corporeal imagery of illness that surrounds and delimits the pericope. There is no healing (גֵּהָה), and God's heart is faint, (דַּוָּי, 8:18); the injury (שֶׁבֶר) of the people injures God as well (הָשְׁבַּרְתִּי) (8:21); the request for balm (צֳרִי) and a healer (רֹפֵא) is in vain, new skin has not grown over the wound (8:22). These bodily images, in and of themselves metaphors for suffering and grief, unite the human and divine domains in the words of Jeremiah, the prophetic book. As indicated in the text, the wounds are metaphorical, not physical: in 8:18, the two terms for being injured, גֵּהָה and דַּוָּי, surround the central concept of יָגוֹן, grief, and in 8:21, God mourns — literally, God wears dark clothes[2] — and is overwhelmed by horror and desolation (שַׁמָּה). Nonetheless, the metaphorical wounds point to embodiment. The choice of a metaphor is rarely random, and the choice of the wound as the governing metaphor in this section places the grief directly on the divine body. Furthermore, the wounded, suffering speaker is made concrete through the incorporation or incarnation in the literary persona, Jeremiah *the prophet* who pronounces the divine words, and from there on incorporated or incarnated in Jeremiah *the book*.

In the central part of the pericope, vv. 19–20, the language of wounds disappears, and it is substituted by nonmetaphorical complaints, partly from the people, partly from the divine speaker.

> [19] Hear, the sound of the cry of my poor people
> from the length and breadth of the land:
> "Is YHWH not on Zion?
> Is there no king with her?"
> "Why have they made me grieve with their graven images (פְּסִלֵיהֶם) with foreign no-goods (הַבְלֵי נֵכָר)?"
> [20] "Harvest is over, summer has ended
> But we have not been saved."

The divine question in 8:19c obviously breaks off the voice of the people, and some commentators follow the editorial proposal in *Biblia Hebraica* and consider the questions about the foreign gods a mere Deuteronomistic gloss, added from 7:18-19.[3] That might well be

---

[1] The word "compassion" is itself a metaphorical concept, from the Latin *compassionem*, "suffering with," or in German *Mit-leiden*.
[2] *DCH* 7:189.
[3] Carroll, *Jeremiah*, 235.

the case from a diachronic point of view, but a synchronic reading of the text allows for a new, more complex meaning. The two questions, the people's—"Is YHWH not on Zion? Is there no king with her?"— and God's—"Why have they made me grieve with their graven images with foreign no-goods?"—serve as recriminations. God, the people lament, does not take the responsibility for them, something that could be expected of a deity; the people, God claims, fail on their part to fulfill their obligation of serving God and God alone. God's question serves as a counter-allegation to the people's complaint, but in the end, the people have the last say: "Harvest is over, summer has ended but we have not been saved,"—as it would be expected from a decent and powerful god.

This exchange of denunciations, the discussion between God and the people as to who is to blame for the current situation, ends with the people's ascertainment that God is to blame—and the resumption of the divine lament directly follows this declaration. What is the function of this embedded discussion? From the perspective of embodiment, the dispute between God and people appears as a fragment of repeated debates, internalized in God's memory and serving to explain the current sickness. It is God who is wounded most severely: "Because of the wound of my poor people I am wounded, I mourn, overwhelmed by desolation" (8:21). The calamity overwhelms God more than it does the people and sets God apart from them, in desolation (שַׁמָּה).

The closing request for balm and healer in Gilead (Jer 8:22) is rhetorical. Yes, there is balm and healer in Gilead, but this wound is too severe to be healed, even by God. Hence his tears in the following section; hence the call for wailing women later, in Jer 9.[1]

Writing and the Axial Age

In Jer 8:18-22, the audience, the messenger, the speaker, and the book converge, and this leads us to our consideration of writing as embodiment. What makes writing so important for the understanding of theological communication in the book of Jeremiah? First of all, writing is one of the hallmarks of the so-called "axial age"—the second

---

[1] On Jer 9, see Holt, "The Helpless Potentate."

half of the first millennium BCE, in other words, of the period when the Hebrew Bible was formed, and the book of Jeremiah found its final shape. In all the high cultures of the world, from China to Greece, and certainly in ancient Israel this period is characterized by growth of philosophical and critical thinking. The idea of an axial age goes back to Continental philosophy in the beginning of the twentieth century,[1] but in 1964, the American sociologist Robert N. Bellah applied it in his concept of religious evolution as proceeding in five stages, primitive/tribal, archaic, historic/axial, early modern, and modern.[2] In tribal religion, ritual involves most of the group's members, while "ritual in archaic societies focuses above all on one person, the divine or semi-divine king, and only a few people, priests or members of the royal lineage, participate."[3] The book of Jeremiah belongs to the following phase,[4] the axial age, which Bellah in his earliest article describes as "transcendental." Axial-age religiosity is characterized by dualism between "this world" and the life after death, demythologization, [5] and first and foremost critical thinking and theoretic culture, which Bellah in his later work relates to the development of writing.[6]

---

[1] For an overview of the development of the concept of axial age through the intellectual history of the twentieth century, see Robert N. Bellah, "What is Axial about the Axial Age?" *AES* 46.1 (2005): 69–89, here 72–77.

[2] Robert N. Bellah, "Religious Evolution," *ASR* 29 (1964): 358–74; cf. Bellah, "What is Axial about the Axial Age?" The concept of religious evolution has been discussed by and has influenced biblical scholars like Erhard Gerstenberger, *Theologies in the Old Testament* (Minneapolis: Fortress, 2002) and Bernhard Lang, "Der religiöse Mensch," *Homo religiosus* (Paderborn: Wilhelm Fink, 2014), 11–117.

[3] Bellah, "What is Axial about the Axial Age?" 69. In Israelite religion, the tribal stage would *grosso modo* be abundant in the patriarchal narratives while features of archaic religion are to be found, for example, in the Priestly writings, Zion theology, and royal theology.

[4] A central principle in Bellah's work on religious evolution, though, is that "nothing is ever lost," meaning that the stages are not totally separated; concepts and rituals continue from stage to stage, and theoretic culture is added to mythic and mimetic cultures, which, however "remain in their respective spheres indispensable." See Bellah, "What is Axial about the Axial Age?" 72, 83.

[5] Bellah, "Religious Evolution," 267. In the book of Jeremiah, demythologization and intellectualization are present in the book's deuteronomistic and post-deuteronomistic critique of the temple cult and sacrifice and the emphasis on ethics and mono-Yahwism.

[6] Of course, the invention of writing precedes the axial age by millennia, but following the Canadian cognitive psychologist Merlin Donald, Bellah argues that "the unwieldy early writing systems and the limited number of people who could use them meant that they were precursors to, rather than full realizations of, the possibility of

This is not the place to go deeper into the characteristics of the axial age. My interest here is the importance of writing in understanding the development of the book of Jeremiah. Another aspect of the axial age must be mentioned before we return to the text, though. In her recent Aarhus thesis, Line Søgaard Christensen shows how archaic religion and ritual are characterized by heavy (immovable) architecture and monuments, that is, artifacts like altars, arks, houses, and temples, while axial-age ritual prefers the light, the weightless, sometimes immaterial, like spoken and written words, which are easy to change and transport and often laden with complex messages.[1] Complexity, of course, is also a quality of the critical thinking, as mentioned before, and it depends on what Merlin Donald calls the "external memory" of writing.[2]

Embodiment and Jeremiah the Book

It is no secret that writing is of special interest in the book of Jeremiah. Jeremiah never writes himself, but his scribe, Baruch ben Neriah, is constantly depicted as writing down the words of the prophet, words that ultimately are God's. This, of course is the theme of ch. 36, where Baruch writes down the words of God at Jeremiah's dictation and even replaces and enlarges the collection—*die Urrolle*—when the original is destroyed by the wicked king. The narrative points to the role of the scribe as a tradent, a preserver of a message, threatened by opposition or neglect, as epitomized by the king in ch. 36.[1] This special role is confirmed by the special blessing for Baruch the scribe in ch. 45, once the closing of the book of Jeremiah. It also points to the renewability of the written word, when the spoken words, in danger of ridicule and oblivion, become something material. Divine discourse, the least touchable in the world, is turning into an artifact, a written scroll and later a book, printed and reprinted in an endless number of copies.

---

theoretic culture" (Bellah, "What is Axial about the Axial Age?" 78, with reference to Merlin Donald, *Origins of the Modern Mind: Three Stages in the Evolution of Culture and Cognition* (Cambridge: Harvard University Press 1991), 272.

[1] Line Søgaard Christensen, "Instructing the Israelites: Axiality, Teaching, and Rituals in the Hebrew Bible" (PhD diss., Aarhus University, 2016), 148.

[2] Cf. Bellah, "What is Axial about the Axial Age?" 78.

This is quite a metamorphosis. What was heard or seen or experienced by the prophet from the beginning turns into an object, but a movable one as opposed to the heavy, immovable—and, alas, destroyed—temple in Jerusalem. One might almost say, with the gospel of John, that the Word became flesh (1:14). But not quite, for after becoming flesh in the shape of the prophet the word continues its journey of embodiment and becomes a book.

What is the use of scrolls and books? They serve as media of conservation, but also of discussion (see. above). Once the word of Jeremiah was written down, there were innumerable additions inscribed in the margins and between the lines, additions that were part of the discussion of the meaning of the divine word. Moreover, there were oral and written comments—the oral comments also being preserved for the future through writing in the Mishnah, the Talmud, and the works of the Church Fathers. The comments added prolonged actuality to the writings, while the writings infused the comments with authority: "Thus says the LORD."

A parallel example to the book of Jeremiah is the Torah. It has a prehistory of oral narrative, religious, educational, and entertaining, but at one point it turns into writing, embodied in the tablets in the ark of the covenant (which, by the way, God Godself rewrote in Exodus 34 like Baruch rewriting Jeremiah's scroll), in the scroll the high priest Hilkiah found in the temple in Jerusalem (2 Kgs 22), and in the book that Ezra the scribe *and* priest read aloud for the Jewish inhabitants of the new Jerusalem (Neh 8).

It is no mere coincidence that these narratives belong to the time of the so-called axial age, the time of empires and elaborate administrative structures, the time of the beginning of philosophy and second-order thinking. The textual development of the biblical books[2] is dependent on writing; if trained, an individual can learn enormous quantities of fixed text by heart, but the additions, emendations, and omissions need to be fixed in writing before they can be memorized. And additions, emendations, and omissions are the results of critical thinking, typical for the axial age.

---

[1] Also of note is the importance of the Shafan scribal family as supporters of Jeremiah and his message, e.g., Jer 26:24; 36:10–12; 40:5–6.

[2] As identified by redaction criticism over the past, say, 50 years.

However, traits of archaic religion remain within axiality, namely, in the need for materiality.[1] The writing down of oral communication not only serves as a basis for critical augmentation and discussion, it embodies the divine word in materiality, turning the intangible and incorporeal into an artifact. Moreover, the embodiment or manifestation in writing of God's communication to humans would serve as a replacement for the lost access to the temple(s). Marianne Schleicher maintains that, "When the temple was destroyed in 70 CE, Jews no longer had access to the sacred place... where contact with God could be mediated.... [T]he Torah replaced the temple as the centre of cultic activity."[2] I believe that this observation holds true already for the temple-less time after the destruction of the first temple. The main point of orientation in the synagogue is the Torah scroll in its vestments and its house behind the curtains. In my — admittedly desultory — observation, the care for the scrolls in today's synagogue mirrors that afforded the most important member of the family, and its vestments are, so to speak, those of the high priest. As stated by Marianne Schleicher, "The architecture of the synagogue points to and stresses the holy status of the Torah, leaving the congregants and this analyst with the impression that the Torah is a metonymy of God."[3] Moreover, the awe and reverence inspired by the scrolls mirrors the awe and reverence toward God Godself, so that at least in the body language of the congregation, the embodiment of the divine word is manifest.[4] This reverence is also apparent in the ceremonial treatment of the Bible in some Christian denominations, with the carrying in procession and adoration of the book of gospels in the Episcopal liturgy before the gospel reading being the most illustrative example.

The book of Jeremiah is not part of the Torah, and my remarks above might take the argument a little too far. Nevertheless, the

---

[1] Cf. p. 197, n.

[2] Marianne Schleicher, "The Many Faces of the Torah: Reception and Transformation of the Torah in Jewish Communities," *Religion and Normativity 2: Receptions and Transformations of the Bible* (ed. Kirsten Nielsen; AcJTS; Aarhus: Aarhus University Press, 2009), 141–58, here 143.

[3] Schleicher, "The Many Faces of the Torah," 144; cf. p. 147.

[4] Likewise instructive is the Jewish tradition of storing discarded objects carrying the divine name, such as Torah books, Bibles, scrolls, *benchers, tefillin, talitot, mezuzot,* Torah mantles/sashes (and any items that have been in direct contact with a Torah scroll) in *genizot* and ultimately burying them in cemeteries.

importance of writing in Jeremiah and the parallelization of the figures of Moses, Jeremiah, and Baruch, so often emphasized in scholarship, confirm the impression that the focus on embodiment through writing of the divine word in the book of Jeremiah in the temple-less and second-temple periods marks a step towards the Jewish and Christian veneration of their written, but living, authoritative word of God in the Bible.[1]

---

[1] Cf. Schleicher, "The Many Faces of the Torah."

The Structure of MT Jeremiah, with Special Attention to Chapters 21-45

Richard D. Weis

At the beginning of the twentieth century, Bernhard Duhm and Sigmund Mowinckel, in two highly influential studies, argued that the book of Jeremiah could not be regarded as a coherent composition in synchronic terms.[1] Following their work, for nearly three quarters of the century, most scholars regarded the study of the structure and coherence of the book of Jeremiah as an exercise in futility.[2] In the last quarter of the twentieth century, scholars reopened the question of the coherence of the book in synchronic terms and elucidated significant aspects of the book's literary coherence in its final form (i.e., the text attested in the MT). [3] A number of these studies work within a frame

---

* I am delighted to offer this study in honor of my friend and colleague Marvin Sweeney, who has done so much to advance the study of the prophetic books of the Hebrew Bible.

[1] Bernhard L. Duhm, *Das Buch Jeremia* (HKAT 11; Tübingen: Mohr [Siebeck], 1901), xx-xxi and Sigmund Mowinckel, *Zur Komposition des Buches Jeremia* (Kristiania: Jacob Dybwad, 1914), 5.

[2] See, e.g., J. P. Hyatt, "The Book of Jeremiah: Introduction and Exegesis," *IB* 5:787; John Bright, *Jeremiah* (AB 21; Garden City: Doubleday, 1965), lvi; John A. Thompson, *The Book of Jeremiah* (NICOT; Grand Rapids: Eerdmans, 1980), 30; Robert P. Carroll, *Jeremiah: A Commentary* (OTL; Philadelphia: Westminster, 1986), 38; William McKane, *A Critical and Exegetical Commentary on Jeremiah* (ICC; Edinburgh: T & T Clark, 1996), 1:xlix-l; and Jack R. Lundbom, "Jeremiah, Book of," *ABD* 3: 684-98, here 711.

[3] Jack R. Lundbom, *Jeremiah: A Study in Ancient Hebrew Rhetoric* (SBLDS 18; Missoula, MT: Scholars Press, 1975), 28-30; William L. Holladay, *The Architecture of Jeremiah 1-20* (Lewisburg, PA: Bucknell University Press, 1976); A. R. Pete Diamond, *The Confessions of Jeremiah in Context* (JSOTSup 45; Sheffield: JSOT Press, 1987), 177-88; Ronald E. Clements, *Jeremiah* (IBC; Atlanta: John Knox, 1988), ix-xi; Kathleen M. O'Connor, *The Confessions of Jeremiah: Their Interpretation and Role in Chapters 1-25* (SBLDS 94; Atlanta: Scholars Press, 1988), 115-48; Alexander Rofé, *The Prophetical Stories: The Narratives about the Prophets in the Hebew Bible* (Jerusalem: Magnes, 1988), 111-14; Alexander Rofé, "The Arrangement of the Book of Jeremiah," *ZAW* 101 (1989): 390-98; Christopher R. Seitz, "The Crisis of Interpretation Over the Meaning and Purpose of the Exile," *VT* 35 (1985): 78-97; Christopher R. Seitz, *Theology in Conflict: Reactions to the Exile in the Book of Jeremiah* (BZAW 176; Berlin: Walter de Gruyter, 1989), 222-35; Christopher R. Seitz, "The Prophet Moses and the Canonical Shape of Jeremiah," *ZAW* 101 (1989): 3-27; Mark S. Smith, *The Laments of Jeremiah and Their Contexts: A Literary and Redactional*

suggested by earlier diachronic studies of the book, and assume a major boundary in the book associated with ch. 25. However, other studies no longer accept this assumed boundary.[1] The diversity of patterns proposed for the structure of the book is considerable enough for Martin Kessler to observe that, "regarding Jeremiah, we are far from achieving a consensus or even a majority view on the structure of the book except in very rough outlines."[2]

The importance of analyzing the synchronic structure of the book of Jeremiah has only been heightened by the realization, now supported by a majority of scholars, that in antiquity the book existed in two different text forms with different structures.[3] James Watts, Hermann-Josef Stipp, and Marvin Sweeney, the honoree of this volume, have begun the comparative study of the respective structures of the text forms.[4] Sweeney has made two valuable initial studies of

---

Study of Jeremiah 11–20 (SBLMS 42; Atlanta: Scholars Press, 1990); Mark E. Biddle, *Polyphony and Symphony in Prophetic Literature: Rereading Jeremiah 7–20* (SOTI 2; Macon: Mercer University Press, 1996); Louis Stulman, *Order Amid Chaos: Jeremiah as Symbolic Tapestry* (BibSem 57; Sheffield: Sheffield Academic Press, 1998); Martin Kessler, "The Function of Chapters 25 and 50-51 in the Book of Jeremiah," *Troubling Jeremiah* (eds. A. R. Pete Diamond, Kathleen M. O'Connor, and Louis Stulman; JSOTSup 260; Sheffield: Sheffield Academic Press, 1999), 64–72; Martin Kessler, "The Scaffolding of the Book of Jeremiah," *Reading the Book of Jeremiah: A Search for Coherence* (ed. Martin Kessler; Winona Lake, IN: Eisenbrauns, 2004), 57–66; Georg Fischer, *Jeremia 1–25* (HThKAT; Freiburg: Herder, 2005), 75–94; Joseph M. Henderson, "Jeremiah 2–10 as a Unified Literary Composition: Evidence of Dramatic Portrayal and Narrative Progression," *Uprooting and Planting: Essays on Jeremiah for Leslie Allen* (ed. John Goldingay; LHBOTS 459; New York: T & T Clark, 2007), 116–52; and Leslie C. Allen, *Jeremiah* (OTL; Louisville: Westminster John Knox, 2008), 12–13.

[1] See A. J. O. van der Wal, "Toward a Synchronic Analysis of the Masoretic Text of the Book of Jeremiah," *Reading the Book of Jeremiah: A Search for Coherence* (ed. Martin Kessler; Winona Lake, IN: Eisenbrauns, 2004), 13–23, for a review of some major options, to which more have been added since.

[2] Kessler, "Scaffolding," 57–66.

[3] For a review of the conversation and issues see Richard D. Weis, "Textual History of Jeremiah," *Textual History of the Bible* (eds. Armin Lange and Emanuel Tov; Leiden: Brill, 2016), 1B:495–513 and Armin Lange, "Jeremia," *Handbuch der Textfunde vom Toten Meer* (Tübingen: Mohr Siebeck, 2009), 1:297–319.

[4] James W. Watts, "Text and Redaction in Jeremiah's Oracles against the Nations," *CBQ* 54 (1992): 42–47; Hermann-Josef Stipp, "Eschatologisches Schema im alexandrinischen Jeremiabuch? Strukturprobleme eines komplexen Prophetenbuches," *JNSL* 23 (1997): 153–79; Hermann-Josef Stipp, "Legenden der Jeremia-Exegese (I): Das eschatologische Schema im alexandrinischen Jeremiabuch," *VT* 64 (2014): 484–501; and Marvin A. Sweeney, "The Masoretic and Septuagint Versions of the Book of Jeremiah in Synchronic and Diachronic Perspective," *Form and Intertextuality in Prophetic and Apocalyptic Literature* (FAT 45; Tübingen: Mohr Siebeck, 2005), 65–77.

them.[1] In one of these studies, he evaluates previous examinations of the book's structure, and notes the considerable number of analyses that

> presuppose that [chs. 1-25] represent the first major unit within the literary structure of the book [overlook] the role of the most fundamental markers of literary structure within both versions of the book, i.e., the superscriptions that appear throughout the book to introduce and characterize the individual blocks of material that comprise both versions of the book of Jeremiah.[2]

The present study continues this exploration of the synchronic coherence of the final form of Jeremiah. It corroborates the view that the book is arranged in an orderly fashion, and it will offer an interpretation of that order for chs. 21-45. The article focuses on the version of the book preserved in the MT. The investigation of the structure of LXX Jeremiah and the Hebrew version attested by it require a separate study. Following a presentation of the approach to be taken, the structure of the book as a whole will be considered in broad terms in order to set the stage for closer consideration of the organization of chs. 21-45, and within them, chs. 21-38. The concluding section draws implications for the further examination of Jeremiah.

The Approach Taken in This Study

This study begins from a position derived from reader-response criticism, namely, the view that the coherence of a text is always the construction of a reader. At the same time, the text itself provokes, contributes to, and guides the reader's construction of that coherence.[3] Thus, in speaking of the coherence of texts, we must take

---

[1] Sweeney, "The Masoretic and Septuagint Versions" and Marvin A. Sweeney, "Differing Perspectives in the LXX and MT Versions of Jeremiah 1-10," *Reading Prophetic Books* (FAT 89; Tübingen: Mohr Siebeck, 2014), 135-53. An important step toward a comprehensive understanding of the structure of both versions is represented by the analysis of communications structures in Karin Finsterbusch and Norbert Jacoby, *MT-Jeremia und LXX-Jeremia 1-24: Synoptische Übersetzung und Analyse der Kommunikationsstruktur* (WMANT 145; Neukirchen-Vluyn: Neukirchener Theologie, 2016) and Karin Finsterbusch and Norbert Jacoby, *MT-Jeremia und LXX-Jeremia 25-52: Synoptische Übersetzung und Analyse der Kommunikationsstruktur* (WMANT 146; Neukirchen-Vluyn: Neukirchener Theologie, 2017).

[2] Sweeney, "Masoretic and Septuagint Versions," 69.

[3] Wolfgang Iser, *The Implied Reader* (Baltimore: Johns Hopkins University Press, 1978), 274-94; Wolfgang Iser, *Prospecting: From Reader Response to Literary Anthropology* (Baltimore: Johns Hopkins University Press, 1989), 31-41; Wolfgang Iser, "Indeterminacy

care to avoid the twin extremes of assuming that a text would cohere in one way only, or that an unlimited number of expressions of coherence may be ascribed to it. Moreover, reader-response theory, as formulated by Wolfgang Iser, points out that it is precisely at the points where the text is indeterminate (e.g., at "gaps," conflicts, inconsistencies, tensions) that the reader is forced to construct the text's coherence. Thus, my investigation will not assume that textual coherence takes the form of a unified or homogeneous text, a text without variation or contradiction, because such expectations leave no room for the phenomena of the reading process. Instead, I assume the necessity of surface diversity within a text since this results from the marking of boundaries for the reader. At the same time, I assume that the text will find ways to signal connections within that diversity so that a reader is able to construct the text's diversity into a meaningfully related whole or set of wholes.

Since the coherence of a text is a product of the reading process, instead of seeking a particular conceptual expression of coherence as many attempts to discern the structure of Jeremiah do, I aim to explore the ways specific textual elements obstruct or inhibit, permit, or encourage or support a particular ordering or integration by the reader. This means attending to concrete surface-level textual phenomena that incite and guide the reader, rather than to the conceptual construction(s) I imagine that the reader would build around them. Moreover, since texts are read in sequence, we must evaluate these clues as a reader would encounter them — in sequence.[1] When reading

---

and the Reader's Response in Prose Fiction," *Aspects of Narrative* (ed. J. Hillis Miller; New York: Columbia University Press, 1971), 1–45; and Meir Sternberg, *Poetics of Biblical Narrative* (Bloomington: Indiana University Press, 1985), 186–89. For examples of the application of reader-oriented approaches to questions of coherence in Jeremiah see Biddle, *Polyphony and Symphony*; Mary C. Callaway, "Exegesis as Banquet: Reading Jeremiah with the Rabbis," *A Gift of God in Due Season: Essays in Scripture and Community in Honor of James A. Sanders* (eds. Richard D. Weis and David M. Carr; JSOTSup 225; Sheffield: Sheffield Academic Press, 1996), 219–30; and A. R. Pete Diamond, "Portraying Prophecy: Of Doublets, Variants and Analogies in the Narrative Representation of Jeremiah's Oracles — Reconstructing the Hermeneutics of Prophecy," *JSOT* 57 (1993): 99–119.

[1] Iser, *Implied Reader*, 277–282. Such a modern assumption about the reading process is reasonably applied also to reading in antiquity for a variety of reasons. Sentences still unfold linearly, that is, in sequence. Even parallel poetic lines, by the progression built across such parallels, have a measure of linearity (sequence) about them. The mechanics of reading from a scroll would tend to promote reading in sequence to a greater degree than reading from a codex, wherein skipping around is far easier (see

in sequence, particular textual phenomena seem most likely to call on the reader to construct an orderly pattern: surface level change (e.g., in form [superscriptions, prose/poetry, genre], overall content, and chronological sequence), inclusio, and repetition. Change in the textual surface seems likely to mark the beginning of a new unit. Inclusio seems likely to mark the end of a unit. Repetition seems likely to signal connections between units.[1]

Paradoxically, when seen in this way, some of the apparent disorder and repetitiousness observed at the surface level of the book of Jeremiah may actually be the means by which the book encourages and supports the reader in creating the book's orderliness. For example, marked changes of genre, narrative voice, and chronology create boundaries for the reader to negotiate. Such boundaries may represent the beginning of something new. They may also function as a form of heightening or highlighting.[2] The instances of repetition (i.e., so-called doublets) often noted in the book of Jeremiah also belong to those phenomena of synchronic "disorder" that are actually ordering elements. From a readerly point of view, a repetition returns the audience to an earlier point, suggesting a connection, a new beginning, or an ending. Indeed, this structuring device is used in both Hebrew narrative[3] and poetry (parallelism) to highlight difference and development across the repetition.[4]

Susan Niditch, *Oral World and Written Word: Ancient Israelite Literature* [Louisville: Westminster John Knox. 1996], 76). The sequential structure of the Qumran *pesharim* (e.g., 1QpHab) certainly implies reading as a sequential process. As far as the book of Jeremiah is concerned, the reference from Jer 51:64b, עַד־הֵנָּה דִּבְרֵי יִרְמְיָהוּ, back to Jer 1:1, דִּבְרֵי יִרְמְיָהוּ, by marking the end of something whose beginning was also clearly marked, seems to assume a linear process of encounter with the book.

[1] Sweeney ("Masoretic and Septuagint Versions," 69), in calling attention to the superscriptions, and Lundbom (*Jeremiah: A Study*, 23–60), in calling attention much earlier to the use of inclusio, have already pursued related approaches.

[2] An example of such a heightening/highlighting effect is found in the shift from prose to poetry in Hebrew narrative to which Robert Alter has called attention (*The Art of Biblical Narrative* [New York: Basic Books, 1981], 4). Similarly, Shimon Bar-Efrat points out the highlighting effect of the use of poetry-like parallelism in prose narrative (*Narrative Art in the Bible* [JSOTSup 70; Sheffield: Almond, 1989], 218).

[3] Alter, *Art of Biblical Narrative*, 88–113; Bar-Efrat, *Narrative Art*, 219; Sternberg, *Poetics*, 365–440.

[4] Robert Alter, *The Art of Biblical Poetry* (New York: Basic Books, 1985), 3–26; Robert Alter, *The World of Biblical Literature* (New York: Basic Books, 1991), 178–86; and Adele Berlin, *The Dynamics of Biblical Parallelism* (Bloomington: Indiana University Press, 1985), 140–41.

The Book as a Whole

The first words a reader encounters on opening the book of Jeremiah are דִּבְרֵי יִרְמְיָהוּ בֶּן־חִלְקִיָּהוּ. These opening words invite the reader to understand what follows as a collection of separate speeches delivered by a particular person, whose life followed a particular trajectory in a particular time and place, and thus to find the orderliness of the text in the patterns of Jeremiah's career as a prophet. Explanations of the book's coherence in terms of the prophet's personal history follow the path pointed out by these opening words.[1] One can argue, however, that such a reading is *obstructed*, beginning in ch. 2, by the presentation of speeches strung together without chronological marker or distinguishing frame.

Another option for reading emerges from the fact that those opening words, indeed the entire first three verses of the book, are not in Jeremiah's voice, but in the voice of an anonymous narrator. Thus, at the same time we are introduced to Jeremiah and his speeches, we are introduced to an anonymous "reporter." This narratorial voice returns with increasing frequency as a reader moves through the book, becoming especially prominent in chs. 21–45. For fifty-one chapters, this third-person narrator frames our reception of the words of Jeremiah (who appears as first-person narrator and as orator) and of YHWH. Then, in 51:64b the narratorial voice recalls its entrance in 1:1 with these words, עַד־הֵנָּה דִּבְרֵי יִרְמְיָהוּ.[2] The last chapter contains not so much as a word from Jeremiah or YHWH. It does not even mention Jeremiah's name. The speeches of Jeremiah come to an end, but the narrator's book of Jeremiah goes on.

Thus, the highest-level structure of the book of Jeremiah shows a binary pattern that sets the speeches of Jeremiah in chs. 1–51

---

[1] See especially J. Bright, *Jeremiah*, who, in presenting the dated passages of the book in his commentary, rearranges them in chronological order. See also William L. Holladay, *Jeremiah 1: A Commentary on the Book of the Prophet Jeremiah, Chapters 1–25* (Hermeneia; Philadelphia: Fortress, 1986) and William L. Holladay, *Jeremiah 2: A Commentary on the Book of the Prophet Jeremiah, Chapters 26–52* (Hermeneia; Minneapolis: Fortress, 1989).

[2] Lundbom, *Jeremiah: A Study*, 23, and Karin Finsterbusch, "Different Beginnings, Different Book Profiles: Exegetical Perspectives on the Hebrew *Vorlage* of LXX-Jer 1 and MT-Jer 1," *Texts and Contexts of Jeremiah: The Exegesis of Jeremiah 1 and 10 in the Light of Text and Reception History* (eds. Karin Finsterbusch and Armin Lange; CBET 82; Leuven: Peeters, 2016), 51–65, here 59, also note the inclusio.

alongside a narrative of the fall of Jerusalem in ch. 52. There is a sense in which the superscript in Jer 1:1 and the postscript in Jer 51:64b, by framing chs. 1-51, mark for the reader a kind of parallelism between chs. 1-51 on the one hand, and ch. 52 on the other.[1] The topic of the parallel is the destruction of Jerusalem and collaterally the destruction of Judah. The narrator's frame that identifies chs. 1-51 as the "speeches of Jeremiah" directs the reader to a contrast within the parallelism. Chs. 1-51, when read as the speeches of Jeremiah, announce the destruction of Jerusalem (also of Judah and the nations, as well as the restoration of Jerusalem and Judah) as future possibility, whereas ch. 52 reports that destruction as past event. Such a juxtaposition invites the reader to construct a coherent and meaningful relation between the two parts of the book. Given the book's well-known attention to the issue of who correctly reports YHWH's message, and as well the theme of the reliability of YHWH (Jeremiah's complaints and ch. 44), it seems reasonable to conclude that the reader is guided to a construction of a relation between chs. 1-51 and ch. 52 in which ch. 52 documents the accuracy of Jeremiah's transmission of some of YHWH's announcements contained in chs. 1-51. This undergirds the validity and reliability of the remaining announcements whose accomplishment is not reported.[2] We now turn to consider whether and how chs. 1-51 themselves may cohere.

From the point of view of the approach taken in this study, the coherence of 46:1-51:64a is easily confirmed. The initial boundary of the unit is marked by a clear introductory expression, 46:1.[3] This introduction signals a change from Judah and Jerusalem to the nations that continued reading confirms. There is also a shift from prose to poetry, as well as a shift from heavily narrated text to minimally narrated text. Moreover, most of the individual units in chs. 46-51 are not marked chronologically in the manner of the preceding chapters. Finally, as Georg Fischer has pointed out, there is a shift from texts in

---

[1] Finsterbusch ("Different Beginnings," 59) has noted the same demarcation of Jeremiah's speeches.

[2] Moreover, the differing fates reported for Zedekiah and Jehoiachin in ch. 52 can also be constructed as a specific and partial documentation of the announcement in ch. 24.

[3] It also uses the relatively rare formula אֲשֶׁר הָיָה דְבַר־יְהוָה אֶל־ (seen only at 1:2; 14:1; 46:1; 47:1; 49:34).

which report genres are a prominent feature to texts where the category of genres on greatest display is announcement.[1] These surface characteristics that appear at the beginning of chs. 46-51 predominate throughout the unit, and the speeches within these chapters show a coherent organization that would be sensible to a reader. Rofé has argued that by beginning with speeches about Egypt and concluding with speeches about Babylon the section is structured by an inclusio of oracles against the great powers of the day.[2] Although Rofé is skeptical of the idea, it also appears that the arrangement of the speeches within the inclusio is geographic, following in approximate fashion the Fertile Crescent from Egypt to Babylon.

The long-standing, but now by no means universal, view that 25:15 or 26:1 marks the boundary between the first section of the book and what follows is, as Sweeney has observed, grounded in assumptions derived from Mowinckel's diachronic analysis.[3] When the text is read in sequence there is no significant shift either from poetry to prose, or from speeches without chronological marker to chronologically marked speeches, or in the presence of the third person narrator, and so on. There is no marking of a significant boundary. In the last analysis, it seems that this has been understood as a textual boundary because in the LXX the speeches concerning foreign nations are found between what in the MT are 25:14 and 15. That marks a clear boundary in the text of the LXX of Jeremiah. It seems that previous research has assumed that this would remain a boundary once the speeches against the foreign nations had been moved to their location in the MT. It has then developed conceptual schemata of the book's structure based on that assumption. Such an assumption cannot be sustained.

---

[1] Georg Fischer, "Jer 25 und die Fremdvölkersprüche: Unterschiede zwischen hebräischem und griechischem Text," *Bib* 72 (1991): 474-99 (although I would not agree with the redaction-historical conclusions that Fischer draws from this observation).

[2] Rofé, "Arrangement," 392. See also Georg Fischer, *Jeremia 26-52* (HThKAT; Freiburg: Herder, 2005), 463 and Martin Kessler, *The Battle of the Gods: The God of Israel versus Marduk of Babylon* (SSN 42; Assen: Van Gorcum, 2003), 163-68.

[3] Sweeney, "Masoretic and Septuagint Versions," 69.

I propose that the substantive textual boundary is between ch. 20 and ch. 21.[1] This boundary is marked in a variety of ways. First of all, the third-person narrator assumes a much more significant role beginning with ch. 21. Prior to ch. 21, the narrator appears only in 7:1, 11:1, 14:1, 18:1, 19:14 and 20:1-3a. In the first five instances, this intervention takes the form only of a formulaic introduction to Jeremiah's own narration of the speeches he received. In 20:1-3a, a narrative context for the ensuing speeches is provided, but it is rather minimal, and undated. In ch. 21, the third-person narrator provides a substantive narrative context for the speech, and this narrative context dates the speech by its reference to Zedekiah and the Babylonian siege of Jerusalem.[2] From ch. 21 through ch. 45, every speech except those in 30-31 will be given a date, either expressed in terms of a king's reign, or in terms of the sieges of Jerusalem and ensuing events.[3] Thus, ch. 21 begins a cohesive narration of speeches in relation to national events, a narration that is sustained through to the end of ch. 45. In addition, ch. 21 seems to mark a shift from poetry to prose. This is blurred somewhat by the presence of substantial amounts of prose in chs. 16-20 and of substantial amounts of poetry in chs. 21-23. However, I would argue that the balance between which style is fundamental and which is exceptional shifts at ch. 21.[4]

---

[1] So also Seitz, "Crisis of Interpretation," 82 ("Ch. xxi breaks with what precedes, and suddenly the reader is in a much later historical period..."); Clements, *Jeremiah*, 125; and Allen, *Jeremiah*, 237-39.

[2] Terence E. Fretheim, *Jeremiah* (SHBC; Macon, GA: Smyth & Helwys, 2002), 303 and Fischer (*Jeremia 1-25*, 628) also note the contrast between earlier chapters that are undated and the dated chapters beginning with 21.

[3] Lundbom has made a similar observation (Jack R. Lundbom, "Baruch, Seraiah, and Expanded Colophons in the Book of Jeremiah," *JSOT* 36 [1986]: 89-114, here 96). In this understanding of chs. 21-45, the narrative framework introducing speeches is taken seriously at the level of the final form of the book. Thus, because that voice does not reappear in 21:4-24:10 (although Jeremiah appears as narrator, as well as orator) those verses are to be regarded as a single speech at the level of the final form, regardless of their possible origin as a composite of once separate speeches (so also Winfried Thiel, *Die deuteronomistische Redaktion von Jeremia 1-25* [WMANT 41; Neukirchen-Vluyn: Neukirchener Verlag, 1973], 230). In addition, Pohlmann noted a number of strong connections between 21:1-10 and ch. 24 (Karl-Friedrich Pohlmann, *Studien zum Jeremiabuch* [FRLANT 118; Göttingen: Vandenhoeck & Ruprecht, 1978], 19-47).

[4] Allen (*Jeremiah*, 237) notes that the oracles of the block chs. 21-24 are given a substantial prose frame in the form of 21:1-10 and 24:1-10.

Another commonly held view sees a significant boundary between chs. 36 and 37.[1] However, from the point of view of the reader there is no major boundary marked at 37:1. Chapter 36 is prose; so is ch. 37. Both are third-person narratives, but have short speeches of Jeremiah embedded in them as part of the narrative flow. Both are dated, albeit with varying degrees of precision since 36:1 gives a regnal year date and 37:1 does not. Moreover, the chronological sequence is not disturbed since ch. 36 dates to the fourth year of Jehoiakim and ch. 37 to the reign of Zedekiah.[2]

The coherence of chs. 21-45 as a unit—and, correspondingly, of chs. 1-20 rather than 1-25—is also marked by a series of repetitions, which on examination appear to arise from the use of inclusio to signal the reader that a section is closing. The first is the now well-known inclusio, demonstrated by Lundbom, that connects the first verse of poetry in 1:4-20:18 (1:5) with the last (20:18), signaling the closure of the section begun in 1:4-10.[3] This understanding of the inclusio is corroborated by subsequent demonstrations, especially by Holladay, Lundbom, and Plant, that Jer 1:4-20:18 represents a coherent unit within the book.[4] Two other instances of inclusio are relevant to the overall definition of these units as well. One links chs. 21 and 45; the other links chs. 1 and 45. In both cases, the language in question is

---

[1] T. R. Hobbs, "Some Remarks on the Composition and Structure of the Book of Jeremiah," *A Prophet to the Nations* (eds. Leo G. Perdue and Brian W. Kovacs; Winona Lake, IN: Eisenbrauns, 1984), 175-91, here 185; Carroll, *Jeremiah*, 87, 669-70; Rofé, *Prophetical Stories*, 112; Rofé, "Arrangement," 392-93; Seitz, *Theology in Conflict*, 231-34; Holladay, *Jeremiah 2*, 282-86; Else K. Holt, "The Potent Word of God: Remarks on the Composition of Jeremiah 37-44," *Troubling Jeremiah* (eds. A. R. Pete Diamond, Kathleen M. O'Connor, and Louis Stulman; JSOTSup 260; Sheffield: Sheffield Academic Press, 1999), 161-70, here 162-63; Robin J. R. Plant, *Good Figs, Bad Figs: Judicial Differentiation in the Book of Jeremiah* (LHBOTS 481; New York: T & T Clark, 2008), 134-37; and Jack R. Lundbom, *Jeremiah 37-52* (AB 21C; New York: Doubleday, 2004), 50-51.

[2] Indeed, the weakness of the traditional position can be illustrated by Rofé's description of chs. 25-36 as "speeches of Jeremiah and stories about him, all dated." ("Arrangement," 395). This description applies as well to chs. 37-45 (and, for that matter, chs. 21-24). The tendency to see a structural boundary between chs. 36 and 37 is certainly related to Mowinckel's assignment of chs. 26-36 (excepting 30-31) to the C-source and chs. 37-45 to the B-source.

[3] Lundbom, *Jeremiah: A Study*, 28-30; Jack R. Lundbom, *Jeremiah 1-20* (AB 21A; New York: Doubleday, 1999), 93.

[4] Holladay, *Architecture*; Lundbom, *Jeremiah 1-20*, 93-95; and Plant, *Good Figs*, 47-48. The arguments of Biddle (*Polyphony and Symphony*) for the coherence of chs. 7-20 as a literary unit and of Diamond (*Confessions*, 177-88) for the coherence of chs. 11-20 as a literary unit complement this view.

repeated elsewhere, but for varying reasons seems nevertheless to serve as an organizational signal to the reader.

The inclusio between chs. 21 and 45 depends on the repetition of an important expression for individual survival in the catastrophe that befalls Jerusalem: וְהָיְתָה־לּוֹ נַפְשׁוֹ לְשָׁלָל (21:9) and וְנָתַתִּי לְךָ אֶת־נַפְשְׁךָ לְשָׁלָל (45:5). This expression occurs in only two other locations in the entire book: 38:2 in a speech of Jeremiah's that results in his imprisonment, and 39:18 in a speech addressed to Ebed-Melech who rescues him.[1] In these locations, too, it contributes to the definition of a connection and boundary within the book, in this case within chs. 21-45, as will be discussed below. In 45:5, because 46:1 obviously introduces a new section, the repetition seems to close off the section begun in ch. 21. Indeed, since ch. 21 begins with the account of Zedekiah's embassy to Jeremiah to request YHWH's intervention to allow Jerusalem and its inhabitants to survive, this inclusio seems to signal the scope of the response to that question.

Chapter 45 also repeats significant expressions from the beginning of the book. The beginning of YHWH's reply to Baruch's lament (45:4) is an expression of YHWH's immediate purpose with Jerusalem, אֲשֶׁר־בָּנִיתִי אֲנִי הֹרֵס וְאֵת אֲשֶׁר־נָטַעְתִּי אֲנִי נֹתֵשׁ. This explicitly repeats the language YHWH used in 1:10 to describe the purpose for which YHWH appointed Jeremiah, לִנְתוֹשׁ וְלִנְתוֹץ וּלְהַאֲבִיד וְלַהֲרוֹס לִבְנוֹת וְלִנְטוֹעַ.[2] The particular quartet of verbs reprised in 45:4 appears also in 24:6, 31:28, and 42:10. However, in each of these cases the repetition of a version of the formula in 1:10 is used to express YHWH's intention to *restore* Jerusalem and Judah. Only in 45:4 is the quartet repeated to describe

---

[1] Winfried Thiel, *Die deuteronomistische Redaktion von Jeremia 26-45* (WMANT 52; Neukirchen-Vluyn: Neukirchener Verlag, 1981), 86; McKane, *Jeremiah*, 1:504; Carroll, *Jeremiah*, 406, 744-45; Thompson, *Jeremiah*, 469, 684; Holladay, *Jeremiah 1*, 574; Holladay, *Jeremiah 2*, 310; Gerald L. Keown, Pamela J. Scalise, and Thomas G. Smothers, *Jeremiah 26-52* (WBC 27; Dallas: Word Books, 1995), 273; Fretheim, *Jeremiah*, 308, 573; and Fischer, *Jeremia 26-52*, 459, all note these correspondences, but do not always develop their structural significance.

[2] Seitz ("Prophet Moses and the Canonical Shape," 21-22) interprets this repetition in 45:4 as a kind of reapplication of this language specifically to YHWH's actions with the nations announced in chs. 46-51, as part of an overall interpretation of ch. 45 as the introduction to chs. 46-51. Gosse has persuasively rebutted this view (Bernard Gosse, "Jérémie xlv et la place du recueil d'oracles contre les nations dans le livre de Jérémie," *VT* 40 [1990]: 145-51).

YHWH's intention to *destroy* Jerusalem.[1] The repetition seems again to signal to the reader a kind of closure, this time of a section, begun in ch. 1, of reflections on the destruction (as well as restoration) of Jerusalem.

Thus, within the report of the speeches of Jeremiah (chs. 1-51) there are significant clues for a tripartite structure: 1:4-20:18, 21:1-45:5, and 46:1-51:64a. This tripartite structure appears to use chs. 21-45 as a kind of hinge. In both a literal and a substantive sense they are the center of the book. On the opposite sides of this hinge, chs. 1-20 and chs. 46-51 represent a kind of synonymous parallelism writ large. These two sections are predominantly poetry and predominantly speeches announcing impending catastrophe. By contrast, in chs. 21-45 prose predominates, and the speeches are embedded in extensive narration. The content of this middle section embraces restoration as well as catastrophe, and seems especially focused on the questions of who survives the catastrophe and on what terms they survive.

Since the catastrophe befalls a different group in chs. 46-51 from that in chs. 1-20, one may also see a linear development across or through the paralleling of these sections. In spite of the occasional hint at restoration, chs. 1-20 focus on the destruction of Israel, Judah, and finally, Jerusalem. At the very end of the section it names Babylon as the agent of destruction (20:4-6). On the other hand, chs. 46-51 lay out the overturning of the entire political order from Egypt, around the Fertile Crescent, ending with and—by virtue of end stress and the amount of text devoted to it (110 verses out of 231 verses for the oracles against the nations)—focusing on Babylon.[2] Throughout the speeches about Babylon, a reader meets asides that announce YHWH's action to restore Judah and Jerusalem, and indeed interpret YHWH's action against Babylon as undertaken on behalf of Judah and Jerusalem, and that call on the book's readers to come out of Babylon.[3] Chapters 21-45 bridge these differences by giving significant scope to the possibility of the restoration of Jerusalem and Judah after their destruction, by their elaboration of the role and limitations of Babylon in YHWH's plan and

---

[1] There is a repetition of a different selection of verbs from 1:10 in ch. 18 that serves as another structural boundary but within chs. 1-20.

[2] John Hill, *Friend or Foe? The Figure of Babylon in the Book of Jeremiah MT* (BibInt 40; Leiden: Brill, 1999), 161-64.

[3] Jer 50:4-10, 17-20, 33-34; 51:6-10, 34-44, 45-53. There is one such aside in an oracle against Egypt as well, 46:27-28.

by their repeated linking of Jerusalem and Babylon. The result is a structure that appears to move the reader toward reflection on a moment which is not yet *described* as a historical event in the book, the destruction of Babylon/restoration of Jerusalem.

Chapters 21–45

We now focus on the internal coherence of chs. 21–45. We begin by returning to the repetition of the expression from 21:9 (הָיְתָה־לּוֹ נַפְשׁוֹ לְשָׁלָל) in 38:2, 39:18, and 45:5, noted previously. The repetition in 38:2 is actually more extensive than in 39:18 and 45:5. Verse 38:2 is a nearly verbatim repetition of 21:9.[1] Thus, the core of Jeremiah's answer to Zedekiah's request for intercession so that Jerusalem might survive (21:2) is repeated as the essence of his message that in ch. 38 is understood as treason. Moreover, the two members of the embassy from Zedekiah who hear this message in ch. 21 reappear in chs. 37 and 38. One, the priest Zephaniah son of Maaseiah, reappears in 37:3 as a member of a delegation delivering a request from Zedekiah that is much like the one delivered in ch. 21. The other, Pashhur son of Malchiah, reappears in 38:1 as one of those who hear the answer repeated from 21:9.[2] Additionally, the time frame of ch. 21 and chs. 37–38 are the same, the final Babylonian siege of Jerusalem in 587/6 BCE.

Thus, chs. 37 and 38 recapitulate significant aspects of 21:1–10. Indeed, they almost literally return the reader to the beginning of the section. In the intervening chapters, the timeline will flash back years before the time of the final siege and come forward to that time. However, throughout chs. 21–38 it will never progress beyond a point in the midst of that final siege. Taken together, all of this suggests that the reader is intended to construct chs. 21–38 as a group of chapters that belong together within the larger block of chs. 21–45.

---

[1] Rudolph has noted this repetition, but he regards the occurrence in 38:2 as a gloss (Wilhelm Rudolph, *Jeremia* [HAT 12; Tübingen: Mohr (Siebeck), 1968], 240). In the absence of any supporting evidence in the textual tradition for such a conclusion, this view implies assumptions about the origin and function of repetition in a literary work that would now be regarded as untenable. Carroll (*Jeremiah*, 406) and Plant (*Good Figs*, 64) note the repetition, but do not develop its significance.

[2] Pohlmann (*Jeremiabuch*, 32) notes these repetitions as part of developing a larger picture of connections between 21:1–10 and ch. 37. McKane (*Jeremiah*, 1:496) and Thompson (*Jeremiah*, 631) both note the reappearance of these members of the delegation in ch. 21, but do not develop its significance.

The expression of an individual retaining their life as a prize of war is also repeated in 39:18 and 45:5. In each instance, 21:9 is not repeated fully, but approximately the same portion of the verse is reprised. Moreover, in both cases the verse is addressed to an individual who in some way has kept faith with YHWH or YHWH's servant, Jeremiah, in the midst of the catastrophe, and in response is given their life as a "prize of war." Each of these two short speeches begins by announcing YHWH's intention to bring catastrophe upon the city but concludes by granting personal safety to the individual addressed. This repetition, by linking 39:15-18 and 45:1-5, signals to the reader that the sequence of stories begun in 39:15 ends in 45:5.[1] That these stories are bound together thematically around the question of individual survival in the context of communal catastrophe, rather than chronologically, is signaled by the disruption of the timeline created by the dating of the speech to Baruch to Jehoiakim's reign. Otherwise, the speeches unfold in chronological sequence following the report of the destruction of Jerusalem in 39:1-14.

The shortening of the repeated expression in 39:18 and 45:5 is appropriate to their narrative contexts. The portion of the expression that is missing described the fate of those who stayed in the city. Before 39:1-14, this fate was not yet reported in the narrative and so required continued announcement and description. Following 39:1-14, that fate has befallen those who stayed in the city; the only question is whether anyone else will survive. So chs. 21-38 and 39:15-45:5 constitute another synonymous parallelism arrayed around a distinguishing center, 39:1-14. Both sides of the parallelism are about the way to survive that Zedekiah sought in his entreaty in 21:2. Chapters 21-38 focus on the survival of Jerusalem and the community in and around it. Jeremiah 39:15-45:5 focuses on the survival of the remnant of the community left in Judah following the destruction of Jerusalem. So these sections belong together even as their difference creates a kind of development and distinguishes 39:1-14 as a focal point.

This structural detail in chs. 21-45 may be displayed schematically as follows:

---

[1] Carroll (*Jeremiah*, 748-49) notes the connections between 39:15-18 and 45:1-5 and develops their thematic implications, but not their structural significance.

Narratized Argumentation Concerning Survival in the Face Of Crisis
I. Argument for trusting YHWH's promises to restore Israel and Judah
21:1-38:28
II. Report of the destruction of Jerusalem 39:1-14
III. Promises and stories of survival in Judah after the destruction 39:15-45:5
   A. Introduction: promise of individual survival 39:15-18
   B. Stories of survival after the destruction 40:1-44:30
   C. Conclusion: promise of individual survival 45:1-5

Chapters 21-38

Within chs. 21-38, another focal point for this section emerges, chs. 30-31. We have noted previously that these two chapters are distinguished from their surroundings by lacking a chronological marker and by being poetry in a section that is predominantly prose. They are also predominantly speeches of hope and restoration following chapters which mostly emphasize disaster. Commentators often treat them as distinct from their surroundings.[1]

Moreover, these two chapters are situated at the center of a concentric pattern that shapes all of chs. 21-38. This pattern is signaled first of all by the chronological markers attached to the other passages in the section. These markers show that the passages in these chapters are not arranged in chronological sequence.[2] Instead, they mark the concentric arrangement of chs. 21-29 and 32-38 around chs. 30-31. The arrangement is as follows:[3]

   chs. 21-24   dated to the reign of Zedekiah[4]
   chs. 25-26   dated to the reign of Jehoiakim

---

[1] See, e.g., Sweeney, "Masoretic and Septuagint Versions," 71 and Allen, *Jeremiah*, 333.

[2] As noted by Fretheim, *Jeremiah*, 17 and Jack R. Lundbom, *Jeremiah 21-36* (AB 21B; New York: Doubleday, 2004), 253.

[3] Rofé proposes a similar arrangement for chs. 25-36, but he regards the concentric order as unfolding chapter by chapter, i.e., ch. 25 ∥ 36; ch. 26 ∥ 35; etc. (*Prophetical Stories*, 113). However, the dates do not correspond exactly on a chapter-by-chapter basis. Indeed, in supporting his position Rofé does not cite the specific dates given in each text, but simply the king to whose reign it is dated (e.g., ch. 25, Jehoiakim's reign; ch. 26, Jehoiakim's reign; ch. 27, Zedekiah's reign; etc.). See Stulman, *Order amid Chaos*, 86-88, for a similar proposal for chs. 26-36 albeit not based on the superscriptions.

[4] Rudolph, *Jeremia*, 1; Thiel, *Jeremia 1-25*, 230; Konrad Schmid, *Buchgestalten des Jeremiabuches* (WMANT 72; Neukirchen-Vluyn: Neukirchener Verlag, 1996), 261; Fischer, *Jeremia 1-25*, 86, 628; Sweeney, "Masoretic and Septuagint Versions," 71; Plant, *Good Figs*, 55-58; and Allen, *Jeremiah*, 237-39 also regard chs. 21-24 as a structural unit.

chs. 27-29	dated to the reign of Zedekiah[1]
chs. 30-31	undated
chs. 32-34	dated to the reign of Zedekiah
chs. 35-36	dated to the reign of Jehoiakim[2]
chs. 37-38	dated to the reign of Zedekiah[3]

Although the reader is alerted to this pattern by the chronological markers, there are more substantive parallels of theme and imagery, and repetitions of motifs and language that build the connections between the corresponding sections.

Some of the connections between chs. 21-24 and 37-38 have already been noted above: a narrative setting in Zedekiah's reign during the Babylonian siege, stories that begin with Zedekiah sending an embassy to Jeremiah asking him to intercede with God on behalf of the city, a repetition in chs. 37-38 of the names of the two participants in the embassy in ch. 21, and a nearly verbatim repetition of Jeremiah's response about the terms of survival (21:9, 38:2).[4] In addition, there is a repetition of technical language for inquiring of YHWH (דרש 21:1, 37:7). At 21:4, 9 and 37:5, we encounter the only occurrences in the entire book of the phrase הַכַּשְׂדִּים הַצָּרִים עַל-. The language Jeremiah uses in 21:9 to

---

[1] Reading with the Syriac in 27:1 צִדְקִיָּהוּ for יְהוֹיָקִם. So Keown, Scalise, and Smothers, *Jeremiah 26-52*, 41; McKane, *Jeremiah*, 2:685; and Lundbom, *Jeremiah 21-36*, 307-08; but *pace* Adrian Schenker, "Nebuchadnezzars Metamorphose vom Unterjocher zum Gottesknecht," *RB* 89 (1982): 510-13 and Dominique Barthélemy, *Critique textuelle de l'Ancien Testament, 2: Isaïe, Jérémie, Lamentations* (OBO 50/2; Fribourg: Editions Universitaires, 1986), 665-66. The proto-Masoretic Syriac stands alone against the other proto-Masoretic witnesses, MT, Aquila, and Vulgate. Their reading is explicable as an assimilation to 26:1. Since that verse precedes 27:1 and both verses begin in the same striking way, that explanation seems more likely than that Syriac harmonizes. Thiel (*Jeremia 26-45*, 5), Rudolf (*Jeremia*, 172), Thompson (*Jeremiah*, 128), Keown, Scalise, and Smothers (*Jeremiah 26-52*, 35-36), Holladay (*Jeremiah 2*, 114-16), and Plant (*Good Figs*, 96-98) all regard chs. 27-29 as a structural unit.

[2] Carroll describes these two chapters as "two stories set in the reign of king Jehoiakim, thus forming a closure with 26" (*Jeremiah*, 653). Fischer (*Jeremia 26-52*, 285) also notes the tight connections between chs. 35 and 36.

[3] See Seitz, "Crisis of Interpretation," "The text of these two chapters [i.e., 37 and 38] as we now have them is certainly meant to be read as an organic whole, as a continuous narrative" (86). So also Carroll, *Jeremiah*, 672 and Callaway, "Exegesis as Banquet," 223-26.

[4] Carroll, *Jeremiah*, 409, 672-74; Thiel, *Jeremia 1-25*, 231-34; Holladay, *Jeremiah 1*, 569-70; McKane, *Jeremiah*, 1:496-97, 502; Peter C. Craigie, Page H. Kelley, and Joel F. Drinkard, *Jeremiah 1-25* (WBC 26; Dallas, Word, 1991), 284-85; Allen, *Jeremiah*, 239-40; Fretheim, *Jeremiah*, 303; Lundbom, *Jeremiah 21-36*, 95, 98, 105; Fischer, *Jeremia 1-25*, 631-33; and Fischer, *Jeremia 26-52*, 313, 331 all note varying combinations of the many strong connections between 21:1-10 and chs. 37-38.

describe surrender to the Chaldeans (נָפַל עַל־הַכַּשְׂדִּים) returns in 37:13 and 14 in Irijah's accusation of Jeremiah and Jeremiah's denial. The name כָּנְיָהוּ appears in 37:1 in what appears to be an otherwise unnecessary reference. However, the other two occurrences of the name in that spelling are in 22:24, 28.[1] Within chs. 21-38, the only occurrences of the phrase הַנִּשְׁאָרִים בָּעִיר הַזֹּאת are found at 21:7 and 38:4.[2] Within the whole book of Jeremiah, the triadic reference to the king, his servants and the (or his) people appears only in 21:7; 22:2, 4, on the one hand, and in 37:2, 18, on the other.[3]

In addition to the verbal echoes of 21-24 in 37-38, there are thematic consonances between the two sections as well. In both sections, the theme of not listening to the words of YHWH and Jeremiah is prominent, and the issue is specifically articulated in 22:5, 37:2, and 38:15. The repetition in the declaration at 37:2 of the conditional language of 22:5 is particularly significant since it appears to have no immediate function in the narrative context of ch. 37. Together with the repetition of the name כָּנְיָהוּ, this appears to be a deliberate connection back to 21-24. Finally, both 21-24 and 37-38 are significantly concerned with the behavior that leads to survival and the question of who will survive in the face of the Babylonian threat.[4]

Similarly, there are strong connections between chs. 25-26 and chs. 35-36 in the form of repeated language and motifs, as well as common themes.[5] In 25:13 and 36:2, we find reference to a book in which Jeremiah's prophecies are written.[6] Otherwise, this motif is encountered only in 30:2 and 45:1.[7] In 36:10, the reference to the דִּבְרֵי

---

[1] As Thompson (*Jeremiah*, 484), Carroll (*Jeremiah*, 437), and Holladay (*Jeremiah 1*, 605) also note.

[2] In truth, they are the only occurrences of that precise phrase in the book, but הַנִּשְׁאָרִים בָּעִיר is found in 39:9 and 52:15. Note also the occurrence of הַנִּשְׁאָרִים בָּאָרֶץ הַזֹּאת in 24:8.

[3] Thiel notes the occurrences in 21:7; 22:2, 4; 37:18, but not in 37:2 (*Jeremia 26-45*, 52).

[4] Pohlmann, although he regards chs. 21-24 as the conclusion to chs. 1-20, has noted a variety of strong links between 21:1-10 and ch. 37 (*Jeremiabuch*, 19-47).

[5] Fischer (*Jeremia 26-52*, 285) notes the strong connection between chs. 35-36 and chs. 25-26. Holladay (*Jeremiah 2*, 22-23) notes a strong series of connections between chs. 26 and 36.

[6] See also Craigie, Kelley, and Drinkard, *Jeremiah 1-25*, 368.

[7] In 51:60, the reference is to prophecies about Babylon only, not all of Jeremiah's prophecies. סֵפֶר in ch. 32 refers to a property deed.

יִרְמְיָהוּ in 26:20 is repeated. Apart from these two verses, the expression occurs only in 1:1 and 51:64. Elnathan son of Achbor is a participant in the action in ch. 26 and ch. 36, and appears nowhere else in the book.[1] YHWH's declaration in 25:4-5 of having sent the prophets to warn the people to change their ways is repeated in substantially the same language in 35:15.[2] YHWH's expression of the possibility that people might listen in 26:3 is repeated in 36:3, 7.[3] Both ch. 25 and ch. 35 contain commands to Jeremiah to make a group drink from a cup of wine (25:15 and 35:2, 5),[4] and both chapters refer to the possible or actual refusal to drink by those to whom it is offered (25:28 and 35:6). The scene for part or all of the action in ch. 26 on the one hand, and chs. 35 and 36 on the other, is the בית יהוה. Throughout both pairs of chapters (25-26 and 35-36), there is a strong focus on the opportunity to listen to YHWH, especially to listen to YHWH's message through Jeremiah, and an equal focus on the refusal to do so, especially on the part of Judah's leaders. The related theme of the threat to Jeremiah's life and his protection by court officials and/or YHWH is prominent in both sections as well.[5]

Finally, a number of verbal repetitions and thematic correspondences also link chs. 27-29 and 32-34 for the reader, in addition to the temporal location of both sets of narratives in Zedekiah's reign. Jeremiah 27:5 contains YHWH's declaration,

אָנֹכִי עָשִׂיתִי אֶת־הָאָרֶץ אֶת־הָאָדָם וְאֶת־הַבְּהֵמָה אֲשֶׁר עַל־פְּנֵי הָאָרֶץ בְּכֹחִי הַגָּדוֹל וּבִזְרוֹעִי הַנְּטוּיָה

which Jeremiah repeats back to YHWH in 32:17,

אַתָּה עָשִׂיתָ אֶת־הַשָּׁמַיִם וְאֶת־הָאָרֶץ בְּכֹחֲךָ הַגָּדוֹל וּבִזְרֹעֲךָ הַנְּטוּיָה.[6]

---

[1] Thompson, *Jeremiah*, 527; Holladay, *Jeremiah 2*, 109; Fretheim, *Jeremiah*, 375; Lundbom, *Jeremiah 21-36*, 297; and Fischer, *Jeremia 26-52*, 39.

[2] Rudolph (*Jeremia*, 226), Thiel (*Jeremia 1-25*, 265-67), Carroll (*Jeremiah*, 490), and Keown, Scalise, and Smothers (*Jeremiah 26-52*, 13-14) note this repetition. Only Carroll attributes structural significance to it within a broader picture of connection between chs. 26 and 36.

[3] Although neither 36:3 nor 36:7 by itself repeats all of 26:3, all the key expressions in that verse are found in one of the two verses in ch. 36. See also Keown, Scalise, and Smothers, *Jeremiah 26-52*, 13.

[4] As Fischer (*Jeremia 1-25*, 746-47) also notes, along with a careful accounting of the differences in the offered cups.

[5] Carroll argues particularly for a variety of correspondences and resonances between chs. 26 and 36 (*Jeremiah*, 513-14, 662-63).

[6] See also Keown, Scalise, and Smothers, *Jeremiah 26-52*, 49 and Fischer, *Jeremia 26-52*, 201.

These are the only places in the book where YHWH is so described. YHWH's declaration to the exiles in Babylon in 29:14, שְׁבָתִי אֶת־שְׁבִיתְכֶם, is repeated in 32:44 as well as in 33:7, 11, and 26.[1] The expression, when applied to Judahite exiles, is found otherwise only at 30:3, the introduction to the prophecies of restoration that form the center of this concentric structure in 21-38.[2] In 29:14, we find that the deity declares that it will gather (קבץ) the exiles from the nations and places where it has scattered (נדח) them and will bring them back (שוב) to the place (מקום) from which they were exiled. In 32:37, this declaration is repeated using much the same language. Finally, in 29:10 YHWH declares to the exiles, הֲקִמֹתִי עֲלֵיכֶם אֶת־דְּבָרִי הַטּוֹב. In 32:42, that declaration is echoed in another one, אָנֹכִי מֵבִיא עֲלֵיהֶם אֵת כָּל־הַטּוֹבָה אֲשֶׁר אָנֹכִי דֹּבֵר עֲלֵיהֶם.

Not surprisingly, given the substantive contents of these repeated expressions, chs. 27-29 and 32-34 are linked by common themes. Both ch. 29 and ch. 32 are concerned with providing for an orderly continuation of communal life across the generations until YHWH's salvific purpose is realized.[3] Both ch. 28, in its conflicting prophetic articulations of the future, and ch. 32, in Jeremiah's protest that the sense of the future implied in carefully recording a land sale conflicts with YHWH's declared and visible purpose, deal with conflicts among interpretations of human reality and YHWH's purpose. Both sections aim to articulate that YHWH's ultimate plan for the exiles is their restoration, and the restoration of Jerusalem (29:11-14; 32:26-33:26). Finally, I would argue that Jeremiah's announcement to Zedekiah in 34:3-5, that he will die in peace amid people who will properly mourn him, presupposes the existence of the intact community that 29:4-7 calls on the exiles to establish.

Even when one grants that a certain number of the repetitions and thematic similarities connecting these sections have occurrences outside the paired sections, the proposed result remains. Other indicated repetitions and thematic similarities are unique to these pairings, and some of those found elsewhere are found within chs. 21-38 only in these pairings. Moreover, these repetitions and similarities

---

[1] Allen (*Jeremiah*, 371) notes the repetition of the language of 29:14 in 32:44.
[2] There are also two similar occurrences in the oracles against nations (49:6 of the Ammonites and 49:39 of Elam), which do not bear on our argument here.
[3] Carroll also points to the similarity between 29:5 and 32:15 (*Jeremiah*, 556).

are not the means of marking the concentric structure; they reinforce it. The chronological marking of a nonchronological sequence (i.e., the fact that narrated sequence does not match story sequence) signals the structure for the reader. The repetitions and similarities demonstrate that this signaling is not incidental.

When these repetitions and similarities are taken into account, the concentric pattern around chs. 30-31 takes on the appearance of an elaborate, large-scale synonymous parallelism. Moreover, as one would expect from the behavior of synonymous parallelism at the level of poetic lines, there is a linear development or movement across the similarity as well. The second half of each element in the pattern (after the prophecies of hope in chs. 30-31) repeats the first, but with a change. Thus, chs. 21-24 offer an initial answer to Zedekiah's question of communal survival in the face of the destructive power of Babylon. Chapters 37-38 resume the theme, but with a particular focus on the survival of individuals, the theme continued in 39:15-45:5. Chapters 25-26 lay out the choices that YHWH places before the nations and before Judah and Jerusalem, and are concerned with the possibility that YHWH's people might listen and avoid their impending fate. The themes of the choices YHWH offers and of listening to YHWH return in chs. 35-36, but with the focus on how human beings' responses to those choices (listening or not) determine their fate. Chapters 27-29 present the view that the reign of YHWH in the world is for the time being expressed in the reign of the kings of Babylon, and outline the steps needed to ensure communal survival under that regime. They also focus on a conflict between an accepted understanding of YHWH's intention as the preservation of Jerusalem and an advocated understanding of YHWH's intention as destruction. Chapters 32-34 return to these themes, but now with an inversion of what is the accepted understanding of YHWH's intention and the understanding advocated by the text, as well as an exploration of the link between the destructiveness of Babylon and YHWH's ultimate purpose of restoration. In so doing, they elaborate the purpose for seeking to survive under the Babylonian regime.

These patterns in chs. 21-38 may be displayed schematically as follows:

Argument for Trusting YHWH's Promises to Restore Israel and Judah
I. Speeches from the end of Zedekiah's reign: The question of communal survival in the face of Babylonian power 21:1-24:10
II. Speeches from Jehoiakim's reign: The choices YHWH places before the nations and Jerusalem/Judah 25:1-26:24
III. Speeches from the beginning of Zedekiah's reign: YHWH's reign is expressed in the reign of Babylon 27:1-29:32
IV. Speeches concerning the restoration of Israel and Judah 30:1-31:40
   A. Narrative introduction 30:1-4
   B. The speeches 30:5-31:40
V. Speeches from the end of Zedekiah's reign: The link between Babylon's destruction of Jerusalem and YHWH's purpose of restoration 32:1-34:22
VI. Speeches from Jehoiakim's reign: response to YHWH determines the survival of future generations 35:1-36:32
VII. Speeches from the end of Zedekiah's reign: How individuals survive in the face of Babylonian power 37:1-38:28

Conclusions and Implications

The orderly arrangements of the book of Jeremiah discussed above are marked for the reader of the book by shifts, "gaps," and repetitions of concrete textual phenomena. They also arrange the material in the book in a way that brings certain elements in focus and presents certain relationships to the reader.

The juxtaposition of chs. 1-51, marked as "the speeches of Jeremiah," with ch. 52, a narrative of the destruction of Jerusalem and the exile of its leading citizens, poses the question for the reader of the relation between Jeremiah's speeches and the facts of Jerusalem's destruction and the leadership's exile. Within chs. 1-51, the paralleling of chs. 1-20 and 46-51 creates a kind of opposition, which is mediated by chs. 21-45. In chs. 1-20, the reader meets announcements of the destruction of Judah and Jerusalem, and Babylon is introduced as their destroyer. In chs. 46-51, these relations are inverted. The destruction of Babylon is announced, whereas that of Judah and Jerusalem has already happened. Their restoration and renewal is announced. Moreover, their people are urged on account of the twin announcements (destruction for Babylon, restoration for Judah and Jerusalem) to leave Babylon. Implicit in this is the paradox that Babylon, which in chs. 1-20 has the role of the destroyer of YHWH's people, has also played the role of preserver of YHWH's people in the period between destruction and restoration.

Chapters 21–45, in their twin foci of announcements of restoration for Israel and Judah in chs. 30–31 and the report of Jerusalem's destruction in 39:1-14, contain their own opposition, between promised restoration and renewal and actual destruction and exile as the expression of YHWH's ultimate purpose for Israel, Judah, and Jerusalem. The sections arrayed around these focal points of chs. 21–45 serve to mediate the various oppositions and juxtapositions within the larger structure. Among other matters, these sections reflect on who is a reliable interpreter of YHWH's intentions, the relation of destruction and restoration in YHWH's purposes, the terms of survival in the interim between destruction and restoration, and the nature and limits of Babylon's role in the achievement of YHWH's purposes. Thus, the reader is encouraged to resolve the juxtapositions and oppositions in favor of reading the destruction of Jerusalem as the documentation of the reliability of Jeremiah and YHWH, undergirding the reliability of the counterposed promises to restore Jerusalem. The reader is also encouraged to read Babylonian victory and hegemony as instrumental and limited within YHWH's larger design, and thus not to be resisted or evaded but also not to be embraced past the point where the realization of the promises of restoration becomes possible.[1]

Finally, we may identify three implications of this study for further research. Two are methodological in nature; the third is substantive. First, the tendency of previous research in the redaction history of the book of Jeremiah to assume that breaks, boundaries, "gaps," and repetitions in the text of the book have significance *only* as clues to redactional layers needs to be corrected to recognize the possibility of their contributing to the synchronic coherence of the book. Second, the literary coherence of the book as a whole in the MT form suggests that models of the compositional process that allow for a small number of book-wide redactional interventions will be more useful in explaining the evidence. This does not exclude the possibility

---

[1] For another perspective on this dynamic, see Richard D. Weis, "A Conflicted Book for a Marginal People: Thematic Oppositions in MT Jeremiah," *Reading the Hebrew Bible for a New Millennium* (Wonil Kim, ed.; Harrisburg, PA: Trinity Press International, 2000), 2:297-308.

of a series of redactional interventions of smaller scope, but it seems less probable that the large-scale coherence proposed here would arise from a process that consisted exclusively, or even primarily, of such small-scale interventions.[1] Third, although the character of the large-scale coherence found in this study does not permit us to speak precisely of the historical context within which that coherence was shaped, it does permit us to set some parameters based on what the text presumes about its audience. It presumes an audience that needs encouragement to maintain belief in YHWH's promises of restoration concerning Israel, Judah, and Jerusalem. It assumes an audience that needs encouragement to leave Babylon. The destruction of Jerusalem is in the past as far as the book is concerned. Its rebuilding, however, is still in the future as far as the book is concerned. Of course, this immediately suggests either a context in the exilic period proper or in the first decades of the return from exile (i.e., the sixth century BCE) when the slowness of the rebuilding process and the reluctance of many to return from Babylon loomed large as issues. Since the longer text-form of the book found in the MT is based on the shorter text-form, we necessarily must allow time for that development, making it unlikely that the longer text form existed before the Persian period.[2]

---

[1] I have in mind McKane's concept of a "rolling corpus" (McKane, *Jeremiah*, 1:l), a term also accepted by Hermann-Josef Stipp, "The Prophetic Messenger Formulas in Jeremiah according to the Masoretic and Alexandrian Texts," *Text* 18 (1995): 63-85, here 84-85, although it is not a full description of how he sees the process (see Hermann-Josef Stipp, *Das masoretische und alexandrinische Sondergut des Jeremiabuches* [OBO 136; Freiburg Schweiz: Universitätsverlag; Göttingen: Vandehoeck & Ruprecht, 1994], 137-44). See, further, Richard D. Weis, "Jeremiah amid Actual and Virtual Editions: Textual Plurality and the Editing of the Book of Jeremiah," *The Text of the Hebrew Bible and Its Editions: Studies in Celebration of the Fifth Centennial of the Complutensian Polyglot* (eds. Andrés Piquer Otero and Pablo Torijano Morales; STHB 1; Leiden: Brill, 2016), 370-99, here 374-76.

[2] Similar dates have been proposed by Yohanan Goldman, *Prophétie et royauté au retour de l'exil: les origins littéraires de la forme massorétique de livre de Jérémie* (OBO 118; Göttingen: Vandenhoeck & Ruprecht, 1992), 143-44, 225-35; Bernard Gosse, "La Malédiction contre Babylone de Jérémie 51,59-64 et les redactions du livre de Jérémie," *ZAW* 98 (1986): 383-99; Godefroid Bambi Kilunga, *Prééminence de YHWH ou autonomie du prophète: Etude comparative et critique des confessions de Jérémie dans le texte hébreu massorétique et la «Septante»* (OBO 254; Fribourg: Academic Press, 2011), 195-97; and Roy D. Wells, "Indications of Late Reinterpretation of the Jeremianic Tradition from the LXX of Jer 21:1-23:8," *ZAW* 96 (1984): 405-20. See also Richard D. Weis, "The Textual Situation in the Book of Jeremiah," *Sôfer Mahîr: Essays in Honour of Adrian Schenker Offered by the Editors of* Biblia Hebraica Quinta (eds. Yohanan A. P. Goldman, Arie van der Kooij, and Richard D. Weis; VTSup 110; Leiden: Brill, 2006), 269-93, here 278; Richard D. Weis,

Thus, it seems most likely that this arrangement of the book was shaped between the first return from Babylon and the completion of the rebuilding of Jerusalem and the stabilization of the community there, that is, the Persian I Period, 538–450 BCE.[1]

"Actual and Virtual Editions," 376; and John Hill, "The Book of Jeremiah (MT) and Its Early Second Temple Background," *Uprooting and Planting*, 153-71. Aaron D. Hornkohl (*Ancient Hebrew Periodization and the Language of the Book of Jeremiah: The Case for a Sixth-Century Date of Composition* [SSLL 74; Leiden: Brill, 2014], 366-69), proposes an even earlier date in the sixth century. For a review of the range of opinion on the date of the longer text form see Weis, "Textual History," 501-03.

[1] Charles E. Carter, *The Emergence of Yehud in the Persian Period* (JSOTSup 294; Sheffield: Sheffield Academic Press, 1999).

Literary Structure in Ezekiel 25
Addressee, Formulas, and Genres

Tyler D. Mayfield

To honor Marvin's scholarly work and demonstrate my gratitude for his instruction and friendship, I offer here a thoroughly form critical reading of a prophetic passage. I engage the exegetical topics of literary addressee, formulas, and genre as ways to discern literary structure but also as key elements of a form critical reading. Marvin taught me the importance of these topics in his classroom and through his commentaries, and I am still learning.

This essay argues for a particular surface structure of Ezek 25: a methodologically rigorous type of literary structure that accounts for the surface textual features, not the content or thematic material. To arrive at this structure, I take first a methodical and methodological route through the various literary issues that need clarifying in order to create such a structure. I argue that literary addressee, formulas, and genre are crucial factors for establishing the structure of Ezek 25. Examining these textual features results in a surface structure that provides a compelling literary reading of the oracle as a divine address to the son of man figure, an address which includes a command to prophesy to Ammon alone concerning the punishment of Ammon, Moab, Edom, and Philistia. This reading is in considerable disagreement with most scholars, who agree on the literary division of Ezek 25 into vv. 1-7, 8-11, 12-14, and 15-17 based on the single criterion of content.[1]

This essay begins with a separate section introducing the problems of literary addressee, formulas, and genres in Ezek 25. In order to create a literary structure, we need to attend to these

---

[1] For the most detailed structure that includes these basic divisions, see Ronald M. Hals, *Ezekiel* (FOTL 19; Grand Rapids: Eerdmans, 1989), 180-82. See also Steven Tuell, *Ezekiel* (NIBC; Peabody, MA: Hendrickson, 2009), 169-74 and Daniel I. Block, *The Book of Ezekiel: Chapters 25-48* (NICOT; Grand Rapids: Eerdmans, 1998), 13-28.

interpretive matters. Then, the essay introduces a new literary structure for Ezek 25 and demonstrates how this structure addresses the aforementioned literary problems.

Literary Addressee

Ezek 25 presents a challenge with regard to literary addressee, including the mixture of second and third person speech regarding the nations of Ammon, Moab, Edom, and Philistia—as well as the use of first person speech in the chapter's opening verse. One textual curiosity within Ezek 25 concerns the inclusion of both second and third person speech insofar as Ezek 25:3-7 contains a direct, second person address to the people of Ammon, while Ezek 25:8-17 uses third person speech in relation to Moab, Edom, and Philistia. For example, the phrases "because *you* said" and "because *you* have clapped *your* hands" in vv. 3 and 6 respectively can be compared to "because *Moab* said" and "because *Edom* acted" in vv. 8 and 12. When read with a focus on addressee, Ezek 25 presents an obvious, but often overlooked, question: to whom precisely is the overall oracle addressed? The people of Ammon only? All four nations in turn? The prophet?

Furthermore, most literary readings of Ezek 25 do not adequately deal with the literary presentation of the introductory verses, Ezek 25:1-3a[3], as a divine address to Ezekiel. These verses are neither concerned with, nor addressed to, Ammon. It is difficult then to include them with vv. 4-7, although that is the typical interpretive move.

These concerns, in turn, raise the larger, literary concern of how one reads the various sections of Ezek 25. Two options exist. First, Ezek 25 in its current form can be read as a single oracle with one or more addressees such that a reader can observe the chapter as a unit. Second, the chapter can be read as the result of disorganized, textual additions accrued without literary consequence such that Ezek 25 does not constitute a literary whole but a disjointed series of oracles arranged loosely.

Recent commentators dutifully note the literary oddity of the change in person despite their general lack of an explanation; for them, the switch from second person to third person speech has little interpretive effect on a literary reading.[1] According to the standard reading, the text is addressing all four nations sequentially. Greenberg attempts to elucidate briefly the switch in address as follows: "We miss a specific command to address the remaining three nations, a token of the relative perfunctoriness with which they are treated."[2] So, for Greenberg, the nations of Moab, Edom, and Philistia are treated hastily and therefore do not receive the correct second person speech form of direct address. Yet, these three nations each receive a separate, developed treatment within Ezek 25 that does not seem particularly hurried. The three nations may not receive the same amount of textual verses as Tyre and Egypt in Ezekiel, but their literary presentation is certainly comparable in length to Ammon's within this same chapter. Ultimately, Greenberg recognizes the issue of addressee within Ezek 25 but fails to link this unique literary form to any significant textual meaning.

However, the switch of address remains embedded in the chapter's presentation of judgment toward the four nations. The oracle's overall literary presentation of the three nations of Moab, Edom, and Philistia remains fundamentally different from its relationship to Ammon, the sole addressee. If one takes seriously the literary form of the chapter, then one needs to understand the text's depiction of, and relationship to, Ammon differently.

Thus, at least two interrelated questions linger in the discussion of Ezek 25. First, is it possible to interpret the switch from second person to third person speech in a meaningful way? Second, how does one read Ezek 25 as a literary whole, i.e., a single oracle, given its complex literary presentation? The combined questions seek to understand the chapter not as a loose assemblage of texts but as a piece of literature.[3] In what follows, I suggest a literary structure of the chapter that pays close attention to the explicit features at the surface of

---

[1] Paul M. Joyce, *Ezekiel: A Commentary* (LHBOTS 482; New York: T & T Clark, 2007), 172; Margaret S. Odell, *Ezekiel* (SHBC; Macon, GA: Smyth & Helwys, 2005), 326; John W. Wevers, *Ezekiel* (NCBC; Grand Rapids: Eerdmans, 1969), 144; Leslie C. Allen, *Ezekiel 20–48* (WBC 29; Dallas: Word, 1990), 66; and Walther Eichrodt, *Ezekiel* (OTL; Philadelphia: Westminster Press 1970), 356–64.

[2] Moshe Greenberg, *Ezekiel 21–37* (AB 22A; New York: Doubleday, 1997), 522.

[3] Contra Eichrodt, who states concerning Ezek 25: "the oracles which follow are arranged in a very loose order, and we find a similar looseness in their shape and material" (*Ezekiel*, 360).

the text.[1] These features combine to present a coherent oracle within the chapter with a distinctive and clear literary structure.

Formulas

The typical scholarly structure of Ezek 25 (vv. 1–7, 8–11, 12–14, and 15–17) is based primarily on content, insofar as each subunit deals with a separate people group, and secondarily on some of the formulas present in the chapter. For example, the messenger formulas in vv. 8, 12, and 15 are often used to establish the new subunits. However, this standard structure suffers from methodological weaknesses, including foremost a lack of awareness concerning the additional messenger formulas in vv. 3b and 6a as well as various other formulas such as the prophetic word formula and the recognition formula within the chapter.

Let me briefly introduce these formulas and their interpretive weight within our passage. It is well-established that the book of Ezekiel is a book of formulas; in total, there are over three hundred formulaic occurrences in the book's forty-eight chapters. Ezekiel 25, our focal passage, includes three distinct formulas, which occur eleven times total in the chapter.

Chapter 25 opens with a prophetic word formula ("And the word of YHWH was to me saying"), signifying the beginning of a new oracle. This formula occurs forty-eight times in the book of Ezekiel, seven of which are in conjunction with a chronological formula. The formula serves as a secondary, macrostructural marker by dividing the thirteen largest literary units of the book into smaller subunits consisting of oracles.[2] As a "secondary macrostructural marker," the prophetic word formula does not divide Ezekiel at its highest level; the book uses chronological formulas to mark its primary macrostructure. The prophetic word formula then introduces each individual oracle within the larger literary unit, with each oracle continuing until the

---

[1] For a fuller discussion of the methodological issues of this approach, see Tyler D. Mayfield, *Literary Structure and Setting in Ezekiel* (FAT 2/43; Tübingen: Mohr Siebeck, 2010), 36–65.

[2] For example, Ezek 1–7, the first major section of the book, contains a prophetic word formula in Ezek 3:16, 6:1, and 7:1, thereby creating four subunits: 1:1–3:15, 3:16–5:17, 6:1–14, and 7:1–27. For more analysis of prophetic word formulas in

next occurrence of the formula unless it concludes the larger unit. For Ezek 25, I anticipate then that the prophetic word formula both introduces the single oracle in this chapter and points to the chapter's placement within a larger literary unit, a unit that begins with a chronological formula.

The messenger formula ("Thus says the Lord YHWH") occurs five times in Ezek 25 and approximately 126 times in the whole book of Ezekiel.[1] Its usage in the book of Ezekiel is not as fixed as the usage of the chronological formulas and the prophetic word formulas. The formula is generally viewed as introducing divine speech, which makes sense of the formula's actual meaning; however, this common understanding does not accurately reflect all the occurrences of the formula in Ezekiel.[2] The formula does not always introduce divine speech; it can function to begin, end, or simply resume divine speech. In Ezek 34, I have noted that the formula highlights the subtle shift in addressee. I anticipate then that the formula in Ezek 25 will introduce, or be connected to, divine speech and might note a shift in addressee.

The recognition formula is an expansion of the self-introduction formula ("I am YHWH"), in which the verb "to know" is added.[3] In the third person ("And they will know that I am YHWH"), it occurs fifty-four times; in the second person ("And you will know that I am YHWH"), there are eighteen occurrences. Its common occurrence in numerous literary contexts limits its use as a structuring device. Because of the formula's meaning, it seems to play more of a theological purpose than a literary one in Ezekiel. Yet, in Ezek 25 the formula does seem to participate as a final element of a particular genre.

Ezekiel, see Tyler D. Mayfield, "A Re-examination of Ezekiel's Prophetic Word Formulas," *HS* LVII (2016): 139–55.

[1] The total count for the messenger formula in Ezekiel includes the three times when an occurrence lacks both divine names (Ezek 11:5, 21:8, 30:6).

[2] See Tyler D. Mayfield, "Literary Structure and Formulas in Ezekiel 34–37," *Ezekiel: Current Debates and Future Directions* (eds. William A. Tooman and Penelope Barter; FAT 1/112; Tübingen: Mohr Siebeck, 2017), 235–44, for an assessment of the messenger formula in selected chapters.

[3] For the definitive treatment of the self-introduction formula, see Walther Zimmerli, "I Am Yahweh," and "Knowledge of God According to the Book of Ezekiel," *I am Yahweh* (trans. D. W. Scott; Atlanta: John Knox, 1982): 1–98.

Genres

In addition to literary addressee and formulas, the standard structure of Ezek 25, which I am attempting to problematize here, does not take into account the ways in which various genres (e.g., proof sayings, oracles, divine commands) and their textual elements shape the chapter.

The first genre to mention briefly is the oracle. I use this genre designation for the material that follows a prophetic word formula. Scholars who wish to be more specific may apply the label "oracle against the nations" because of the content contained in the oracle. Sweeney notes that the genre does not have a particular structure or form; it can involve a variety of other genres as well.[1] No matter whether we use the term *oracle* or *oracles against the nations*, the designation does create a certain sense of literary unity for the passage.

Another genre designation at play in Ezek 25 is prophetic proof sayings.[2] This genre occurs frequently throughout the book of Ezekiel. The genre can consist of several different elements — as few as two basic parts — but in Ezek 25 the genre is fairly uniform. All five prophecy proof sayings in Ezek 25 have an introductory messenger formula, a statement of the reason for the punishment, the statement of the punishment, and finally a recognition formula. Therefore, the strict, internal structure of this genre, as displayed in our focal passage, can help with the overall structure of the whole chapter.

Literary Structure of Ezekiel 25

Now that I have introduced the primary interpretive problems for Ezek 25, I propose a new surface structure of Ezek 25, a structure which attends to the challenging topics noted above. Before I get to the Ezekiel passage, though, it may be helpful to introduce briefly my understanding of literary structure.

---

[1] Marvin A. Sweeney, *Isaiah 1-39, with an Introduction to Prophetic Literature* (FOTL; Grand Rapids: Eerdmans, 1996), 528.

[2] See Walther Zimmerli, "The Word of Divine Self-Manifestation (Proof-Saying): A Prophetic Genre," *I am Yahweh* (Atlanta: John Knox, 1982), 99-110. Zimmerli defines the genre as a "very rigid schema" consisting of three parts. Sweeney, *Isaiah 1-39*, 535, finds two main parts: "the prophetic announcement of punishment" and "the recognition formula." However, he does note that often a reason for the punishment is provided with a transition to the announcement of punishment.

Many ways of structuring prophetic passages exist; yet few scholars have reflected deliberately on the methodology of structuring literarily so as to create clear criteria for the process.[1] Scholars tend to assert a structure or set of divisions for a textual unit without arguing for those divisions. Nevertheless, it remains an important exegetical exercise to offer structures of passages and to note how one arrived at such divisions. To structure a biblical passage from a synchronic perspective requires careful attention to the unique, important literary features of the text on the surface level. I have previously proposed a new way of defining a surface structure:

> First, surface structure is a specific subcategory of literary structure, which as a category contributes together with other categories such as content, semantics, and style to the overall form of an individual text or genre.... Second, surface structure is an organizing principle that draws together, and provides clear demarcation to, a unit of text. In other words, a surface structure delineates, setting borders around units of text so that a text is read within and among particular textual boundaries.... Third, a surface structure uses linguistic markers to delineate these units, not content. These linguistic markers serve as the disjunctive and conjunctive syntactical features of the text.... Fourth, a surface structure does not mix criteria so that any level of structure uses two different criteria. An obvious example is synchronic and diachronic criteria, but other subtle mixtures are sometimes used such as two different formulas. To summarize: a surface structure, as a subcategory of structure, organizes a unit of text using linguistic markers in a consistent way at each level of the structure.[2]

By examining the surface structure of Ezek 25, I attempt to construct a more methodologically rigorous type of structure for the chapter; this structure depends on clearly identifiable words or phrases

---

[1] It is helpful to mention here Marvin Sweeney's own doctoral teacher, Rolf Knierim, who in his teaching emphasized structural analysis. Antony F. Campbell, "Structure Analysis and the Art of Exegesis (1 Samuel 16:14–18:30)," *Problems in Biblical Theology: Essays in Honor of Rolf Knierim* (eds. Henry T. C. Sun and Keith L. Eades; Grand Rapids: Eerdmans, 1997), 76–103, here 77, notes "one of the tools that Knierim uses most powerfully to introduce students to a text, to involve them in it and enthrall them with it, is what he calls 'structure analysis.'" See Rolf P. Knierim, *Text and Concept in Leviticus 1:1–9: A Case in Exegetical Method* (FAT 2; Tübingen: J. C. B. Mohr [Paul Siebeck], 1992), for a masterful example of self-conscious exegesis rooted in reflective methodology.

[2] Mayfield, *Literary Structure*, 53–55.

as opposed to the more hypothetical notions of theme and content. The following structure accounts for both the surface features of the text (e.g., numerous formulas within the chapter, literary presentation of divine address, genres) and the switch in addressee in the middle of the chapter. Below I present a detailed surface structure of Ezek 25:1-17 and a discussion of this proposed structure that resolves the major interpretive issues previously introduced.

Surface Structure of Ezekiel 25
Oracle concerning Ammon, Moab, Edom, and Philistia 25:1-17
A. Prophetic Word Formula: "And the Word of YHWH Was to
     Me Saying" 25:1
B. Divine Address to Son of Man concerning Four Nations 25:2-17
   1. Title: "Son of Man" 25:2a$^{1-2}$
   2. Command #1: "Set Your Face toward the Sons of Ammon" 25:2a$^{3-6}$
   3. Command #2: "Prophesy against Them" 25:2b
   4. Command #3: "Say to the Sons of Ammon" 25:3-17
      a. Command Proper: 25:3a$^{1-3}$
      b. Divine Speech 25:3a^4-17
         1) Exhortation to Hear 25:3a$^{4-6}$
         2) Two Proof Sayings concerning Ammon 25:3b-7
            a) First Proof Saying (2nd pers. fem.) 25:3b-5
               i) Messenger Formula 25:3b$^{1-3}$
               ii) Reason for Punishment (y'n) 25:3b$^{4-17}$
               iii) Announcement of Punishment 25:4-5a
               iv) Recognition Formula 25:5b
            b) Second Proof Saying (2nd pers. masc.) 25:6-7
               i) Messenger Formula 25:6a$^{1-5}$
               ii) Reason for Punishment (y'n) 25:6a^6-b
               iii) Announcement of Punishment 25:7a-b^1
               iv) Recognition Formula 25:7b$^{2-4}$
         3) Proof Saying concerning Moab (3rd pers.) 25:8-11
            a) Messenger Formula 25:8a
            b) Reason for Punishment (y'n) 25:8b
            c) Announcement of Punishment 25:9-11a
            d) Recognition Formula 25:11b

4) Proof Saying concerning Edom (3rd pers.) 25:12–14
   a) Messenger Formula 25:12a$^{1-4}$
   b) Reason for Punishment ($y'n$) 25:12a^5–b
   c) Announcement of Punishment 25:13–14a
   d) Expanded Recognition Formula 25:14b

5) Proof Saying concerning (3rd pers.) 25:15–17
   a) Messenger Formula 25:15a$^{1-4}$
   b) Reason for Punishment ($y'n$) 25:15a^5–b
   c) Announcement of Punishment 25:16–17a
   d) Expanded Recognition Formula 25:17b

As noted above in the section of formulas, Ezek 25 commences with a prophetic word formula, which signifies the beginning of a new oracle: "And the word of YHWH was to me saying." Hals and Sweeney correctly distinguish the formula in v. 1 from vv. 2–17, although most scholars simply gather the introductory verse together with vv. 2–7.[1] The latter division would seem warranted only if v. 8 contains yet another prophetic word formula. Instead, the formula in v. 1 introduces literarily the whole chapter and should be placed apart from the divine address it introduces.

Ezekiel 25:2–17 constitutes a divine address to Ezekiel in which the prophet is first called "son of man" (2a$^{1-2}$) then given a series of three short commands (2a$^{3-6}$; 2b; 3a$^{1-3}$). Thus, the chapter presents itself, literarily, foremost as an address to the son of man figure regarding the four nations. This important aspect is often ignored in traditional, content-focused structures, which skip intuitively to the message to Ammon, resulting in a reading that prioritizes content over literary form. Of course, these types of readings are possible and worthwhile even as they ignore the literary presentation of the oracle. In fact, the oversight of the unique oracle's form by modern scholars is quite common in discussions of oracular material within the prophetic literature in that the literary introduction of the oracle receives less attention than the theme or content of the oracle. Yet, the literary presentation here emphasizes the role of the "son of man" figure in Ezekiel as the recipient of the divine address.

---

[1] Hals, *Ezekiel*, 180 and Marvin A. Sweeney, *Reading Ezekiel* (Macon: Smyth & Helwys, 2013), 125.

Due to the emphasis within Ezekiel studies on the history behind the text (e.g., the historical relationship between Judah and other nations), the literary presentation of this text as a series of divine commands has been overlooked. Thus, it becomes important to note that, within the world of the text, these oracles are not actually delivered to the nations. They are—from a literary perspective—divine words concerning the nations that are given to the prophet. Their historical delivery to the nations is of little consequence.

Next, the chapter clarifies precisely in 25:2a^3–3a^3 the addressee of the son of man's prophecy. The son of man figure is commanded to set his face toward, and prophesy to, Ammon alone. Note how two of the three short commands (2a$^{3-6}$ and 3a$^{1-3}$) explicitly mention Ammon only. This nation is the sole recipient of the prophetic message in Ezek 25, given that the chapter does not elsewhere instruct Ezekiel to prophesy to another nation. Thus, the switch from second person address to third person speech later within the chapter remains consistent with the literary presentation of Ezek 25. Three of the nations are spoken about, not spoken to. Moab, Edom, and Philistia are used as examples of the judgment that will occur, but within the chapter they are not told directly about their fate. Only Ammon should receive the speech. Further evidence for this literary presentation occurs in Ezek 25:10 when Ammon is mentioned in the middle of the Moab section.

The divine speech (25:3a^4–17) to Ammon contains five prophetic proof sayings concerning Ammon, Moab, Edom, and Philistia.[1] These proof sayings provide the structure for the speech insofar as they all include four distinct features. First, a messenger formula begins each of the proof sayings (3b$^{1-3}$; 6a$^{1-5}$; 8a; 12a$^{1-4}$; 15a$^{1-4}$). Whereas several scholars use some of the messenger formulas to furnish a structure, my proposed structure accounts for all of their appearances within the chapter, not just a few. Thus, the messenger formula serves as a way to introduce each proof saying. Second, a reason for punishment is stated in each of the proof sayings; this reason begins with $y'n$ in every instance (3b^4; 6a^6; 8b^1; 12a^5; 15a^5). Third, the formal announcement of punishment is the next feature of the proof

---

[1] For a discussion of the prophetic proof saying, see Hals, *Ezekiel*, 353–54 and Zimmerli, "The Word of Divine Self-Manifestation," 99–110.

saying; it also begins with a formulaic *lkn* in each case (4a[1]; 7a[1]; 9a[1]; 13a[1]; 16a[1]). Finally, a recognition formula concludes each of the proof sayings (5b; 7b[2-4]; 11b; 14b; 17b). Thus, Ezek 25:3a[4]-17 constitutes a highly structured and formulaic speech. Each of the four parts of the prophetic proof sayings begin with a formulaic element that allows for a clear demarcation and understanding of the text.

In summary, the surface structure proposed here provides a coherent, synchronic reading of Ezek 25 as a divine address to the son of man, which includes a command to prophesy to Ammon alone concerning the punishment of Ammon, Moab, Edom, and Philistia.

Excursus
Ezekiel 25 in Diachronic Development

After examining the chapter's surface structure and noting its coherence as an oracle, I turn briefly to the literary development of the oracle. By reading synchronically first, certain literary tensions within the chapter are made prominent. These tensions point to diachronic developments within Ezek 25 insofar as each textual insertion contains its own surface structure, even if that structure is subsumed into a large structure or attempts to mimic the existing structure. I suggest that Ezek 25 developed in four general stages as the oracles concerning Ammon, Moab, Edom, and Philistia were grouped eventually together to create one large oracle addressed solely to Ammon. The redactional scheme below updates the earlier work of Eichrodt and Zimmerli by including more support for their general proposal.[1]

The first stage of the oracle consisted of a single proof saying (25:3b-5). The proof saying concerns Ammon who is addressed in the second person feminine. The second stage includes Ezek 25:6-7, a second proof-saying that still concerns Ammon but uses a different gender (masculine) to speak of it. Zimmerli notes correctly that this section does not reintroduce the recipient and therefore probably did not stand independently from the earlier material.[2] Indeed, the material does appear linked to 25:1-5 by the *ky* particle. In addition, vv. 6-7 as

---

[1] Eichrodt, *Ezekiel*, 356-64 and Walther Zimmerli, *Ezekiel 2* (Hermeneia; Philadelphia: Fortress, 1983), 10-20.
[2] Zimmerli, *Ezekiel 2*, 11.1.

an addition is generally recognized.[1] The third stage, Ezek 25:8-11 expands on the Ammon oracle with another proof saying concerning Moab. This saying uses third person speech because the oracle is addressed in Ezek 25:2 to Ammon alone. Ezekiel 25:10 refers to Ammon in the third person to tie this section to the first Ammon oracle. The last stage, Ezek 25:12-17, which includes the two prophetic proof sayings concerning Edom and Philistia, were added later together. Both of these sayings have expanded recognition formulas unlike the standard recognition formulas used in the previous three proof sayings.

---

[1] Gustav Hölscher, *Hesekiel: Der Dichter und das Buch* (BZAW 39; Giessen: A. Töpelmann, 1924), 133.

Was Ezekiel a Messenger? A Manager? Or a Moving Sanctuary?
A Beckettian Reading of the Book of Ezekiel in the Inquiry of the Divine Presence

Soo J. Kim

Have you been waiting for someone to arrive or for something to happen in your life? For how long? A week? Five years? Ten years? How about for forty years? What if that "someone" was supposed to come very soon, but continually sent a messenger to repeat the message, 'It will happen tomorrow'? And what if that "something" was delayed and delayed until your life ended?

For me, the exilic priest-prophet Ezekiel personifies this ordeal as he is often commanded to give incomprehensible performances.[1] In this essay, I will take Samuel Beckett's postmodern play, *Waiting for Godot*,[2] and read it with the book of Ezekiel in order to understand the communication issue between YHWH, Ezekiel, and the people.

The Book of Ezekiel
Its Uniqueness in Terms of Communication
Lack of Performances: Unfulfilled? Or Unreported?

In the book of Ezekiel, the titular character appears disobedient in delivering the divine commands. Although he does not resist YHWH like Jonah or Jeremiah, strangely enough, the divine commands

---

* I am greatly honored to write an article for a *Festschrift* in honor of Prof. Marvin A. Sweeney. I appreciate his unreserved support during my Ph.D. study and related research, his encouragement, and his immense knowledge. It is he who called me to study at Claremont School of Theology; it is he who never gave up on his student as she was finishing her work; and now it is he who has shown me the genuine meaning of "teacher" and "scholar." Professor Sweeney's contributions include theological study on the interactive relationship between God and human beings, text-oriented form critical analysis, and dynamic intertextual reading. Hopefully, my work can also contribute following his footsteps. This article is an extended version of my presentation for the Theological Perspectives of the Book of Ezekiel session at the 2015 SBL National Meeting.

[1] For psychological analysis on this topic, see David J. Halperin, *Seeking Ezekiel: Text and Psychology* (University Park, PA: Pennsylvania State University Press, 1993).

[2] Samuel Beckett, *Waiting for Godot* (New York: Grove Press, 1954).

more often than not come to naught. Out of more than 40 divine commissions[1] in the book of Ezekiel, only three are reported as fulfilled;[2] the status of 90% of them is unknown: either they remain unfulfilled or their fulfilment is not reported. Even when the book reports the appearance of specific audiences before Ezekiel,[3] the communications are but one-way dialogues of question or answer.[4] Although God warns Ezekiel that all the curses of the message would fall upon the unfaithful messenger,[5] neither Ezekiel nor the book of Ezekiel is eager to show those vivid performance scenes. Several incomprehensible actions of God also suggest that the "unfaithful" behavior of Ezekiel must have been originally included in God's plan.

First, as shown in 3:24-27, Ezekiel was commanded not only to proclaim but also to shut himself inside his house. To my knowledge, no performer proclaims the divine message in his or her chamber. Moreover, what about Ezekiel becoming mute until God's designated time?[6] All these conditions surrounding Ezekiel prove that the primary purpose of the divine oracles might not be their successful deliverance. The oracles in the book of Ezekiel often include a call to repent. Unfortunately, however, the book seldom shows the executionary scenes or reactions from the audience, and we start doubting the

---

[1] For the definitions and examples of prophetic commission, see Marvin A. Sweeney, *Isaiah 40-66* (FOTL 19; Grand Rapids, Eerdmans: 2016), 389.

[2] Those three cases are 11:25, 12:7, and 24:18. Very interestingly, all three reports of the divine commands are related to the fall of Jerusalem rather than to the call to repent. In the first case (11:25), Ezekiel recounts the first temple vision of chs. 8-11, which displays the complete scenario of accusation, judgment, and execution. The immediate execution of the destruction of Jerusalem and the defilement of the temple strongly shows that repentance is not an option anymore. In the second case (12:7), Ezekiel symbolically performs the exiles' forced relocation as commanded. It is harder to view this as a call to repent rather than to give up any hope for Jerusalem. The third case (24:18-24) shows the most interaction with the audience regarding the symbolic meaning of the death of Ezekiel's wife. Obviously this is the final announcement of the death sentence on the Jerusalem temple. As we will see, the people who came to Ezekiel interacted only as the interlocutor(s), not as the discussion partners of Ezekiel/YHWH.

[3] For example, in 8:1, 14:1, and 20:1, elders sat before Ezekiel in order to make an oracular inquiry. But because their action and reaction are very passive, this does not go beyond a literary demarcation of the beginning of the new scene.

[4] For example, as explained earlier, on the day that Ezekiel's wife died in Ezek 24 this one-way communication pattern continues. People came to Ezekiel and asked him to explain the sign of his wife's death. Ezekiel answered as commanded, but the text stops without showing further interactions between the prophet and the exiles.

[5] As shown in Ezek 3:16-21; 33:1-11.

[6] Cf. 3:27; 24:27; 33:22.

accessibility of YHWH's message to the audience. According to Thomas Renz, the scene of swallowing the scroll constitutes the climax of this concealing trend of God's message.[1] This unique phenomenon suggests that the book of Ezekiel is reader-oriented prophetic literature[2] rather than a collection of performed oracles.[3] Moreover, the weight of the book of Ezekiel does not lie in persuading its audience to deter the divine wrath by divorcing themselves from their sins.[4] The book instead shows the determination of the divine judgment, that is, no negotiation or deference is possible.[5]

As additional evidence of the nondelivering tendency of the book, I would point out that YHWH only talks with Ezekiel and never reveals YHWH's self to people. Furthermore, Ezekiel embodies and personifies YHWH's message by digesting the scroll rather than actually proclaiming its words.[6] So what messages did the contemporaries of Ezekiel receive from the prophet? To answer this question, we need to distinguish the reader of the book from the audience of the prophet Ezekiel,[7] because the implied readers, including us as modern readers, receive all the information within the book, while its literary audience might not hear anything from the

---

[1] Thomas Renz, *The Rhetorical Function of the Book of Ezekiel* (VTSup 76; Leiden: Brill, 2002), 18.

[2] Cf. Steven Tuell, "Divine Presence and Absence in Ezekiel's Prophecy," *The Book of Ezekiel: Theological and Anthropological Perspectives* (eds. Margaret S. Odell and John T. Strong; Atlanta: SBL, 2000), 109-14.

[3] For a review of the model study on the book of Ezekiel, see Yoo Hong Min, *Die Grundschrift des Ezechielbuches und ihre Botschaft* (FAT 2/81; Tübingen: Mohr Siebeck, 2015), 18-34. For the typical transition from the prophetic speech to the prophetic book, see Daniel I. Block, *The Book of Ezekiel: Chapters 25-48* (Grand Rapids: Eerdmans, 1997), 18.

[4] This is a typical pattern of the Deuteronomic idea of restoration as shown in Deut 30:1-10.

[5] Andrew Mein, *Ezekiel and the Ethics of Exile* (OTM; New York: Oxford University Press, 2001), esp. 40-75, 216-56 and Paul M. Joyce, *Divine Initiative and Human Response in Ezekiel* (JSOTSup 51; Sheffield: Sheffield Academic Press, 1989).

[6] Edgar Conrad, *Reading the Latter Prophets: Toward A New Canonical Criticism* (JSOTSup 376; London: T & T Clark, 2004), 2-15.

[7] Among others, Nicholas Wolterstorff, Meir Sternberg, Ellen Davis, and Shimon Bar-Efrat insist on distinguishing these two agents. See Nicholas Wolterstorff, *Divine Discourse: Philosophical Reflections on the Claim that God Speaks* (Cambridge: Cambridge University Press, 1995); Meir Sternberg, *The Poetics of Biblical Narrative: Ideological Literature and the Drama of Reading* (repr.; ISBL; Bloomington, IN: Indiana University Press, 1987); Ellen F. Davis, *Swallowing the Scroll: Textuality and the Dynamics of Discourse in Ezekiel's Prophecy* (JSOTSup 78; BLS 213; Sheffield: Almond Press, 1989); and Shimon Bar-Efrat, *Narrative Art in the Bible* (JSOTSup 70; Sheffield: Almond, 1989).

prophet Ezekiel himself.[1]

With regard to evaluating the lack of prophetic performances, I conclude that it is wise to open both possibilities: either the lack of Ezekiel's performances in reality or the lack of the book's report of them.[2] YHWH's one-way commands are dominant throughout the book, not only in the series of oracles but also in the later visions, including chs. 37 and 40–48. However, the book shows other situations, too. YHWH's confirming questions upon Ezekiel's performances suggest that there must be unreported prophetic speeches.[3]

A nondynamic interaction between the speaker and the audience in the literary representation adds a meaning by itself. This unique compositional strategy emphasizes two points: the hatred towards the accused audience[4] and the reality of the destruction of Jerusalem. The book of Ezekiel evinces a strong desire to blame Jerusalem's tragedy on the stubborn Israelites and to portray the Babylonian invasion as YHWH's solemn verdict stemming from the unquenched divine wrath. Ezekiel's audience is utterly rebellious and would never listen to the prophet's message. Because of their stubbornness, from the beginning, the author has already determined the destiny of the house of Israel. Strategically speaking, then, the reproduction of all steps from commission to deliverance is not necessary, even for the reasons of pure economy. Also, the unfathomable period of exile[5] necessitates the scenery of the

---

[1] "Literary audience" means the addressee(s) shown in the text. Because they appear in the text, they are also characters. "Implied reader" presupposes the existence of the oracle's written form. As a tangible text, it can be either read either aloud in public settings or privately, the way we do today. Cf. Stanley Fish, *Is There a Text in This Class? The Authority of Interpretive Communities* (Cambridge: Harvard University Press, 1980).

[2] Mein (*Ezekiel*, 59–73) emphasizes the probability of public space for discussion and interaction between the prophet and the exiles based on the elders visiting Ezekiel.

[3] References in the book of Ezekiel include 2:2; 3:8 (anticipating possible encounters with the audience); 3:17–21; 33:2–20 (warnings to the watchman); 12:7–9 (review question); and 33:24; 33:30–31 (quotation from the implied audience's argument).

[4] The book of Ezekiel has various audience groups: "exiles" (3:11; 3:15; 33:32); "rebellious house" which includes both the remaining Israelites and the exiles (2:3); "Israel's mountains" (6:2); "the land of Israel" (7:2; 36:1–22); "false prophets in Israel" (13:2); specific "Israelites in the land" (12:22); specific exiles, especially "elders of Israel in Babylon with Ezekiel" (14:1; 20:1); "Jerusalem" (ch. 16); "king of Israel" (21:25). For the relationship between Ezekiel and elders, see also Halperin, *Seeking Ezekiel*, 58–79 and Daniel I. Block, *Ezekiel 1–24* (NICOT; Grand Rapids: Eerdmans, 1997), 34.

[5] For recent discussion of the compositional and edited dates, see Mein, *Ezekiel*, 45–50.

unintelligible echoes of divine commands and dry-bone-like audience as the major portion of the book. On that desolated ground, stands a weird messenger alone.

In sum, the uniqueness of the book of Ezekiel in terms of communication can be summarized as follows: 1) the book does not assign any space for 90% of the divine commissions to be unpacked; thus, they may be interpreted as either unfulfilled or unreported; 2) this "unfaithful" behavior of Ezekiel might be originally included in God's plan; 3) all three reported performances are never reproduced as the performed version but simply reported as "I told" or "I did as I was commanded." When the author uses the direct quotation of YHWH's speeches to Ezekiel, its vividness is felt only by the readers, while the audience often plays the role of interlocutors to bring about more divine tirades.

Compared with the Books of Isaiah and Jeremiah

As we have observed, the fact that the book of Ezekiel avoids reproducing the performance scenes is a significant point in our understanding of the book's theology. Before moving forward, however, I invite my readers to check whether this phenomenon is really unique to Ezekiel.

The books of both Isaiah and Jeremiah contain prophets' interactions and confrontations with people.[1] The former opens with the titular character standing on the podium and performing the internalized divine message; the typical framework of prophetic commission is missing. Let us read Isa 1:2, the direct speech of the prophet Isaiah. After the superscription, "the vision of Isaiah," in 1:1, verse 2 continues: "*Hear, O heavens, and give ear, O earth*; for *the LORD has spoken*: 'Children have *I* reared and brought up, but they have rebelled against *me*.'"[2]

Isaiah delivers YHWH's words, but the requisite procedure of the divine command delivered to the messenger and the messenger's internalizing process are missing. Without any preliminaries, we watch

---

[1] For comparison with the book of Jeremiah, see also Min, *Die Grundschrift des Ezechielbuches*, 44–48.

[2] For the English translation, ESV is used here and throughout. Emphasis is mine.

the messenger in the process of delivering the message to his unspecified audience, which is broad enough to include the heaven and the earth.

Let us now read Ezek 20:1-4:

¹ In the seventh year, in the fifth month, on the tenth day of the month, certain elders of Israel came to consult the LORD, and sat down before *me*.

² And the word of the LORD came to *me*:

³ "Mortal, speak to the elders of Israel, and say to *them*:
Thus says the Lord GOD:
'Why are *you* coming? To consult *me*? As I live, says the Lord GOD, I will not be consulted by *you*.'

⁴ Will *you* judge *them*, mortal, will *you* judge *them*?
Then let *them* know the abominations of *their* ancestors[.]

In my reconstruction of the structure of Ezek 20:3-4, the indented lines reflect the levels of discourse, from the left: narrative line; YHWH's speech line; YHWH's speech formula line for the direct quotation; and direct quotation of YHWH's message. The narrative framework (vv. 1-2) shows that Ezek 20 is a first-person narrative with three characters: YHWH, Ezekiel, and the elders. In the framed speech, the speaker is YHWH and the listener is Ezekiel. The "elders of Israel" appear under the conventional rule of being unable to listen to this divine oracle, and YHWH never speaks to them directly. The deity never emerges from the invisible door but remains with/within Ezekiel.

Let us continue examining how this discourse ends. The divine speech that begins in v. 2 ends in v. 48 (Heb. 21:4), "All flesh shall see that *I the LORD* (אֲנִי יְהוָה) have kindled it." The divine speech begins with the first-person pronoun "I", and after almost 50 verses, the last verse reveals that that "I" was YHWH. Frustrating our expectation of delivery, v. 49 (Heb. 21:5) wraps up with the prophet's attempt to offer feeble resistance by quoting audience's former reaction. In brief, until the end of this section, the supposedly faithful messenger Ezekiel was not delivering YHWH's long and crucial message but only responding to it.

Jeremiah 28 makes a better comparative case regarding the communication matter since, similarly to Ezekiel, its narrative setting has the prophet and the third party in the same space. At first, when Jeremiah responds to Hananiah, the prophet uses his divine insight, not the divine command (vv. 6-9); but the next moment, the private commission from YHWH to the prophet (vv. 13-14) occurs that parallels the scene in Ezek 20. At this, the text shows Jeremiah's immediate delivery of the message (vv. 15-16) as well as its consequence (v. 17).[1]

The book of Jeremiah frequently reports execution of the divine prophetic commands, and sometimes the contents of the divine messages are not presented until the actual performance takes place.[2] In contrast, the book of Ezekiel demands us to distinguish between the perception of the readers and that of the audience. As readers, we experience what character Ezekiel experienced so that we cannot deny the powerful presence of God and his words. But we should admit that to his listeners as literary characters YHWH must be hidden or at best inaccessible.

Of course *qua* readers we might want to know the situation of the "people," the audience of YHWH/Ezekiel to see the other side of the story. Unfortunately, we can hardly face them directly because for the most part audience is doubly obscured by the narrator as well as the character YHWH. My intertextual reading of the book of Ezekiel with *Waiting for Godot* will provide a glimpse into the world of receiver by showing the other side of the mirror.

Waiting for Godot: Those Who Wait for No Arrival

The ambience of *Waiting for Godot* includes a nearly dead tree, abandoned boots, and repeated pauses produced by the ironic combination of the two characters, Estragon and Vladimir. Let us briefly review these characters, focusing on their flaws. What Estragon lacks is memory, which makes him a representative of the unending

---

[1] I am aware of Jeremiah's interpretive deliverance of the divine message and the text's dynamic presentations in delivering God's messages, but that is another interesting topic for the future study.

[2] For example, observe the strategy of unpacking the divine message in Jer 25. The chapter shows the prophet's own interpretation or introduction (vv. 3-4), which comes first before the delivery of YHWH's message (vv. 5-7, 8-14). See the comparison of the two prophetic books in Davis, *Swallowing the Scroll*, 81.

present.[1] Although he acts compulsively due to the lack of ability to recognize who he is, whom he waits for, and what is the cause of his sorrow, ironically he can endure this miserable situation for that same reason: he does not remember the past. Meanwhile, what Vladimir lacks is assurance that his extraordinary memory serves him well. He needs someone to instill in him confidence that this is the right time and right place and his is the right hope. Ironically again, Estragon's impatient request to leave the place helps Vladimir elaborate the reason of their remaining, while Vladimir's patient accounts of their history make Estragon return to the initial point.

Messenger Boy identifies himself as an emissary of Godot. He appears in each act to inform Vladimir and Estragon that Mr. Godot will not come that evening but will surely come the next day. In my reading, the truly shocking news from the boy lies not in the frustrating news of Godot's deferred coming but in his denial of recognition/memory of "yesterday," that is, in critical discontinuity. If the messenger does not know of himself and of the receiver, his very message about the sender should also be under suspicion from the outset. Unfortunately, Vladimir, who can recount the past, the present, and the future, and who encourages himself to try until the last moment, is surrounded by those who have lost or denied their memories.[2] The absence is therefore not only that of Godot but also of the ability to escape from Godot. Only futile speeches are floating until Messenger Boy arrives and releases the main characters from the place until the next evening.

Gilles Deleuze described this phenomenon as "false movement" because the characters neither abandon their wait nor cross the line to follow the Messenger Boy to confirm the message.[3] The play

---

[1] According to Estragon, he either forgets immediately or does not forget ever. Thus, sometimes the pattern of asking and reminding between Estragon and Vladimir is reversed.

[2] They are Estragon, Pozzo, and the Messenger Boy—those who explicitly exhibit their discontinuities on time. The only other character, Lucky, a potential witness of "history" ironically became a mute in Act 2.

[3] Gilles Deleuze, *Cinema 1: The Movement Image* (tr. Hugh Tomlinson and Barbara Habberjam; Minneapolis: University of Minnesota Press, 1986). This false movement and strong desire to keep the status quo sharply contrast the freer, more activist spirit of American novel by L. Frank Baum, *The Wonderful Wizard of Oz* (Chicago: Geo. M. Hill, 1900), in which the characters actually keep moving forward and ultimately discover the reality of the wizard.

ultimately shows that nothing is certain — time, place, the existence of Godot, and even the identity of Messenger Boy. All characters of the play are ruled by the ghost of forgetfulness or uncertainty.[1] Forgetfulness of the past soothes one's painful start-over. If this is the case, the characters indeed start over without extra emotions, such as disappointment, unease, shame, or anger. Meanwhile, uncertainty stemming from self-censored distrust is a real pain, making the person unable to move forward. Sadly enough, this uncertainty is indeed the product of chronic disappointment or, in biblical terms, continuing experiences of prophecy's failure to come to fulfilment. In this, the characters of Beckett resemble Ezekiel's listeners who identified themselves as piled-up "dried bones" that cannot comment on their past.

"Mr. Godot will come tomorrow." What does it mean? Is it hope? Or hopelessness? The worst case is neither A nor B, and that is the case here. The referential word "tomorrow" is strong enough to hold both hope and hopelessness. As Noorbakhsh Hooti points out, it is the "trap of waiting."[2] The secret to waiting forever lies in the forgetfulness of one's history of frustration and the uncertainty of the future. Waiting people are bound by the violating power of temporal indeterminacy. Unfortunately, I read the same tragedy and frustration in the book of Ezekiel.

---

[1] On the question of who would be the most tragic figure in this play, I would argue that it is none but us, the audience. We need to admit that it is us, not the characters, who remember their past and present and are concerned about the future. According to Jennifer Birkett, the audience is "the watchers who watch Vladimir watching the sleeping Estragon" and the ultimate driving force (*Undoing Time: The Life and Work of Samuel Beckett* [Sallins, Kildare: Irish Academic Press, 2015], 118). By showing the characters' own denial of their paths (or any history), the play constantly pushes out the audience whose desire is to stick to the characters; instead, Beckett makes us reflect on our history through various perspectives. This effort resembles the "estrangement effect" of the Russian Formalists and Bertolt Brecht. For Brecht's "estrangement effect" (*Verfremdungseffekt*), see Henry Glade, "Major Brecht Productions in the Soviet Union since 1957," *Bertolt Brecht: Political Theory and Literary Practice* (eds. Betty Nance Weber and Hubert Heinen; Athens: University of Georgia Press, 2010), 88–99. For Viktor Shklovsky's "defamiliarization," see Lee T. Lemon and Marion J. Reis, eds. and trs., *Russian Formalist Criticism* (2nd ed.; Lincoln: University of Nebraska Press, 2012) and Min Tian, *The Poetics of Difference and Displacement: Twentieth-Century Chinese-Western Intercultural Theatre* (Hong Kong: Hong Kong University Press, 2008).

[2] Noorbakhsh Hooti, "Samuel Beckett's *Waiting for Godot*: A Postmodernist Study," *ELLS* 1 (2011): 40–50, here 40.

A Messenger? A Manipulator? Or a Walking Sanctuary?
Waiting for Godot and the Book of Ezekiel as Each Other's Mirrors

"Nothing to be done" or "nothing to do" is the common echo of the two texts. Somewhat hilariously, desperate shouts of "nothing to do except waiting" in Beckett's play might become the gloomy experiential reality of captives in the book of Ezekiel. The deadline to repent had already expired before the audience's clear recognition of YHWH's wrath; the date of return is not yet given to even messenger Ezekiel. While *Waiting for Godot* shows Vladimir as the only person who can barely recognize the stream of time, the book of Ezekiel provides explicit chronological demarcations including the dates of Jerusalem's fall and the vision of the rebuilt temple.

In this intertextual reading, I see the parallels between the two works, especially with regard to the hierarchical accessibility of information to characters. The most powerful characters (YHWH and Godot) are the least accessible to the least influential characters (Vladimir and Estragon; the captives). Positioned in-between are manager-like messengers (Messenger Boy and Ezekiel) who are the actual plot-movers.

Based on this observation, we realize that the divine hiddenness in the book of Ezekiel is a matter of disconnection between the sender, the messenger, and the receiver, rather than YHWH's indifference to the people. Divine speeches are ubiquitous throughout the book, but they stop with Ezekiel the messenger. The ancient sacred book abounding in scenes of interaction between the sender and the messenger ironically resembles the postmodern play, which shows only the messenger/receiver side. What if we put the two works together side-by-side? The whole sender/messenger/receiver picture is revealed to us, showing that both the sender and the receiver are eager to communicate but hindered by some unknown factors.

Let us examine the role played by the peculiar prophet named Ezekiel. To begin with, he does not seem particularly apt as a messenger. In most cases, he does not seek to confront the people. Or, to be more precise, the book attempts to hide the action and reaction between the messenger and the receiver. I would rather abandon this option: at the very least, Ezekiel is not a traditional, faithful divine emissary.

How about another possibility, Ezekiel as a manipulator? This characterization comes from the unique presentation of YHWH in the book. Although it is common for deities to communicate mainly with their messengers/mediators, in Ezekiel this phenomenon is heavily emphasized. As we observed in the case of Ezek 20, YHWH often talks *about* the captives by quoting their thoughts and sayings but studiously avoids directly communicating with them. In the book of Exodus, for example, the deity also talks only with Moses and Aaron, and in the book of Jeremiah, only with the titular character. Nonetheless, it reveals its presence to the broader public by showing its glory or exercising its supernatural powers. More importantly, those books assign narrative space to receivers' reactions, even allowing their direct speeches. What does this difference encourage us to think? How shall we understand the languid king-like deity and its clever manager? The latter would resemble the Messenger Boy in *Waiting for Godot*. There, Mr. Godot exists only in the repeated echo of the boy's interpreted message and the interpreted memory of Vladimir.

However, the image of Ezekiel as a shrewd manager of the spiritless YHWH is theologically problematic. Images of a manipulating prophet and his confined deity are sharply incongruent with other prophetic traditions and biblical traditions in general. Therefore, this second option should be rejected.

This leaves us with only one choice, Ezekiel as a walking sanctuary. The first clear indication to that effect can be found in Ezekiel swallowing the scroll in Ezek 3:1-3. As Ellen Davis asserts, a transparent characteristic of Ezekiel comes from this embodiment of God/God's message.[1] Edgar Conrad also argues that Ezekiel is not volitional or emotional but rather very passive. With this presupposition, Conrad interprets the tying up of Ezekiel's body with cords as the tying up of the scroll with cords and the clinging of his tongue to the roof of his mouth as the sealing of the scroll by its writer. Just as the scroll in which the divine oracle is written would be sent to the people who are waiting for the oracle, Ezekiel was sent to the captives as a walking document.[2]

---

[1] Davis, *Swallowing the Scroll*, 29-38.
[2] Conrad, *Reading the Latter Prophets*, 165-78.

The second marker would be the small/temporary sanctuary of 11:16, where YHWH says, "I will *become* to them (וָאֱהִי לָהֶם) the small/temporary sanctuary" rather than "I will *allow* you the sanctuary," implying divine transformation into the sanctuary in a mysterious way.[1] Thus, when we are looking for the fulfillment of this prophecy, we need to regard the scroll-bearer Ezekiel as the first candidate.

This logic allows us to go further by surmising that holy YHWH set up YHWH's holy dwelling place (מִקְדָּשׁ) in the mind of Ezekiel in the polluted foreign land. Then, once Ezekiel moves, he becomes a walking sanctuary so that he always can be in a dialogue with the deity who dwells in him. Like the main character of *Avatar* and the control tower, Ezekiel and YHWH are in a very close connection indeed. This picture fits well the passive character like Ezekiel. Then, all the divine commands including 90% of unreported or unfulfilled commissions can be understood as written in Ezekiel's mind, waiting for the time when the scroll's seal is opened, in other words, when Ezekiel's tongue is set free.

When Deictic Language Is All That Is Left

The term "deictic language" refers to words like "here" and "there," "today" and "yesterday," "you" and "I," which cannot be fully understood without additional contextual information.[1] *Waiting for Godot* intentionally uses those terms in most cases; thus, the

---

[1] Regarding this transformation from the spirit to the material being and the relationship between the Torah and the Torah bearer, more substantial discussions are necessary, but for the sake of brevity, bibliographical information should suffice. According to Jacob Neusner, in the rabbinic tradition, the concept of the Torah has been broadened to include the notion that a Torah scroll and a man of Torah are interchangeable: Jacob Neusner, *Vanquished Nation, Broken Spirit: The Virtues of the Heart in Formative Judaism* (New York: Cambridge University Press, 1987), 152. For the exiled God and the perception of such a deity, especially the matter of silent/hidden God, see Andrea Fröchtling, *Exiled God and Exiled Peoples: Memoria Passionis and the Perception of God During and after Apartheid and Shoah* (Münster: LIT, 2002), 174. For the relationship between the exile of humans and that of the deity in Lurianic Kabbalah, especially with regard to the connection between *Ein Sof* and *Shekinah*, see the classical study by Gershom G. Scholem, *Kabbalah* (LJK; New York: Quadrangle/The New York Times Book Company, 1974), 166-67. For the negative view of the small sanctuary in Ezek 11:16 as a sign of deprivation, see Moshe Greenberg, *Ezekiel 1-20* (AB 22; Garden City, NY: Doubleday, 1983), 186.

demarcation of the specific time in the play produces a greater sense of despair. For example, to Estragon's question how long they have been together Vladimir answers, "Maybe fifty years" — a meaningful number for the Bible's readers mindful of the Jubilee commandments (Lev 25). Unfortunately, although the year of Jubilee has passed, the play closes the same night without answers.

By contrast, the book of Ezekiel is replete with explicit chronological remarks and uses those temporal indications to signal the beginning of each unit within it. This is significant in two respects. First, time for Ezekiel is progressive, or at least wishes to be progressive; this attitude can break the trap of waiting in circles. Moreover, awareness of the date and its recording in every unit suggest that character Ezekiel remembers the past events, that is, the causes of the present of the community. The time will surely come, although it is uncertain when exactly. The book also employs date references for the uncertain time of restoration.[2] Ubiquitous indeterminacy leads the author to use this deictic language when he talks about the hope for return. Once ejected from the homeland, the captives became rootless; everything is uncertain, from their identity to their faith in YHWH. The only certainty for them lies in what they see now is unreliable. Therefore, the audience/reader is neither catapulted into the world of restoration with strong hope nor left prostrate in a Sheol-like desperation. The mission of the book of Ezekiel is to keep people in a designated place, just as the wait of Estragon and Vladimir keeps them under the nearly dead tree. This place is a heterotopia, which Ezekiel and his God created together: it is designated as the center of the hope. It is also heterotopic for the people in terms of their lack of ability to comprehend or access God: now this is the pit of hopelessness.

The exiled prophet-priest, whose tongue was once paralyzed and released, whose hair was scattered in the air, whose body was tied up, assured the people that they had someone who was connected to the supernatural invisible power. One of the catchphrases of Ezekiel,

---

[1] Karl Bühler, *Theory of Language: The Representational Function of Language* (tr. Donald Fraser Goodwin; FS 25; Amsterdam: John Benjamins, 1990), esp. 93–166.

[2] בַּיּוֹם "on that day" (36:33) and מִיּוֹם "from that day" (48:35) are the typical manifestations of deictic language in the book of Ezekiel.

"People may know that there was a prophet among them" can be translated, "People may know that there was somebody who embodied the presence of God."

A Beckettian reading of the book of Ezekiel allows us to apply the pendulum-like oscillation between the hope to see the face of God and the continuing frustration of the pervasive indeterminacies in the exilic situation as a key concept in understanding Ezekiel who accepts YHWH as his inner self. As an intertextual reader, I imagine that the dream of Estragon, to which Vladimir consistently refuses to listen, might resemble the vision of Ezekiel, the inexpressible hope to see the glory of YHWH.

Using the Lurianic thematic concept of *tikkun olam* (repair of the world),[1] Marvin Sweeney, the honoree of this volume, interprets the hiddenness or absence of God as a call for humans to act as responsible partners with God.[2] Sweeney's theological understanding of the relationship between God and humans would be applicable in our case because Ezekiel stands as God's partner by becoming YHWH's walking sanctuary. The hope is cut off; everybody feels like dry bones, abandoned in the polluted and scary foreign land. In the situation where only deictic language is available, the book of Ezekiel shows one person who bears the presence of God by becoming a temporary sanctuary and thus the center of the universe in the midst of chaos, the land of the dead.[3] The best way of living in the time of exile is walking with God who creates the world, who continues to sanctify the world, and who will bring his people back to the promised land. However, this is, unfortunately, a very tall order because it means living with hope *and* without hope.

---

[1] Elliot N. Dorff, *The Way into Tikkun Olam: Repairing the World* (Woodstock, VT: Jewish Lights Publishing, 2005), esp. 226–49.

[2] See, among many relevant works, Marvin A. Sweeney, *Reading the Hebrew Bible after the Shoah: Engaging Holocaust Theology* (Minneapolis: Fortress, 2008) and Marvin A. Sweeney, "Absence of G-d and Human Responsibility in the Book of Esther," *Reading the Hebrew Bible for a New Millennium: Form, Concept, and Theological Perspective* (eds. Wonil Kim et al.; SAC; Harrisburg, PA: Trinity Press International, 2000), 2:264–75.

[3] Cf. Marvin A. Sweeney, "The Ezekiel that G-d Creates," *The God Ezekiel Creates* (eds. Paul M. Joyce and Dalit Rom-Shiloni; New York: Bloomsbury, 2015), 150–61, here 159.

The Encounter between Hosea's YHWH (Hosea 11) and Taiwanese Matzu

A Cross-Religious Hermeneutics of the Two Divine Images

Hye Kyung Park

Asian hermeneutics of the biblical world focuses its attention on the dialogue between the Bible and Asian societies. The biblical world's religious traditions have profoundly influenced ancient Near Eastern cultures. Similarly, the characteristics of Asian religions have exerted a tremendous influence on Asian societies, and consequently on the development of Asian hermeneutics. The process of Asian hermeneutics involves seeking the identity of Asianism. Archie Lee proposes that a cross-textual reading of Asian texts and the biblical texts could inform the interpretations of biblical texts in an Asian context.[1]

The comparison of two texts in a hermeneutic operation involves reconstruction and integration through the fusion of a biblical and an Asian perspective.[2] Intratextual hermeneutics in comparative religion compares divine images in the Bible and the Asian traditions. The present comparison between the divine images in the Bible and a Taiwanese religion is a potentially informative case study in Asian hermeneutics.

In this paper, I would like to propose a cross-religious hermeneutical comparison between Hosea's YHWH (Hos 11) and Taiwanese Matzu. When the prophet Hosea in the eighth century BCE prophesied of the return of the Israelites to YHWH, he used a metaphor of the motherly deity in ch. 11. When the Taiwanese people

---

[1] Archie C. Lee, "The Bible in Asia: Contesting and Contextualizing," *Mapping and Engaging the Bible in Asian Cultures: Congress of the Society of Asian Biblical Studies 2008 Seoul Conference* (eds. Yeong Mee Lee and Yoon Jong Yoo; Seoul: Christian Literature Society of Korea, 2009), 19–33.

[2] For the concept of fusion of horizons, see Hans-Georg Gadamer, *Truth and Method* (tr. Joel Weinsheimer and Donald G. Marshall; 2nd ed.; New York: Continuum, 2006).

worship the goddess Matzu, I suggest that they respond to three metaphorical characteristics of the goddess: motherhood, companionship, and compassion. These characteristics of Matzu correspond to the divine characteristics of the deity in Hos 11 as motherly YHWH, the companion of the Israelites in their diaspora, and compassionate YHWH.

Matzu, a sea goddess in China and other Asian nations, including Taiwan, was born in the Fujian Province of China around 960 CE, in the Song dynasty. People in broader southern China began to worship Matzu around 1200 CE.[1] When early immigrants to Taiwan crossed the Taiwan Straits in the late Ming dynasty (1368–1644 CE), they brought the image of Matzu with them. Over six million Taiwanese claim to be Matzu believers and practice Matzu worship,[2] making this the largest of the Taiwanese folk religions. An understanding of the concepts of the divine operative in Matzu worship offers insight into a Taiwanese religious phenomenon, which can serve as a platform for hermeneutic intersection between the Bible and an Asian religion.

Motherly Deity: Caring and Respectful

Hosea lived in a turbulent period of the history of both northern and southern Israelite monarchies. Six kings reigned in northern Israel after the death of Jeroboam II in 743 BCE, and four of them were assassinated by their successors. Moreover, there were three invasions from Assyria under Tiglath-pileser III and the Syro-Ephraimitic War in the time of King Pekah of Israel (734 BCE). The political turmoil in Hosea's time stimulated worship of YHWH by the Israelites. Hosea adopted an implied role as YHWH's oracle and used multiple metaphors in his pronouncements.

The book of Hosea expresses its concepts of the divine using metaphors of family: husband and wife (Hos 1–3), parent and child (4–11), and husband and wife with a rebellious son (Hos 12–14).[3] The

---

[1] Pamela J. Stewart and Andrew Strathern, "Growth of the Mazu Complex in Cross-Straits Contexts (Taiwan, and Fujian Province, China)," *JRitSt* 23 (2009): 67–72, here 67.

[2] Cheng-Tian Kuo, *Religion and Democracy in Taiwan* (Albany, NY: State University of New York Press, 2008), 79.

[3] Gale A. Yee, "The Book of Hosea," *NIB* 7:198.

metaphor of parent and child comes to its climax in Hos 11, proclaiming the everlasting love of YHWH as a reflection of the motherly metaphor of the deity. Verse 1 calls Israel a נַעַר (*na'ar*, "boy, youth") and the deity's beloved son, introducing the relationship between the two in terms of parental protection.[1] From here, Hosea develops the parental metaphor of YHWH and represents the deity as a mother figure in v. 3.

Verse 3 presents an exegetical problem though, since it is not clear how to translate תִרְגַּלְתִּי (*tirgaltî*), the verb describing YHWH's action. It is most often understood as "teaching to walk," but Helen Schüngel-Straumann argues that the root of *tirgaltî* is *rgl*, in Arabic "to suckle, to breastfeed."[2] Accordingly, she translates the verse as follows: "But it was I who nursed Ephraim, taking him in my arms. Yet they did not understand that it was I who took care of them."[3] It is reasonable to construe the verb in such a way, since in no other biblical texts does *tirgaltî* mean "to teach to walk." Moreover, breastfeeding by YHWH is further implied by "taking him in my arms" in the same verse. Schüngel-Straumann suggests a logical sequence in v. 3 by saying that "the infant is embraced and taken up in mother's arm to be nursed" in the metaphor of God's breastfeeding. The independent first-person pronoun אָנֹכִי (*ānōkî*) in front of *tirgaltî* emphasizes the role of YHWH as a nursing mother. The deity is conceptualized through the metaphor of a mother.

Matzu's case is less abstract, in that she started as a human being. Lin Yuan and his wife Wang prayed to the goddess Kuan Yin for a son, since their first son was physically weak. A daughter was born on the evening of the 23rd of the third month of the first year of the reign of the Emperor Tai-Zu (960 CE) in a red light from heaven. They named her as Mo-Niang (silent girl) since she did not cry for a month after her birth.[4] Matzu became a clever and mysterious girl, who grew

---

[1] Joy Philip Kakkanattu, *God's Enduring Love in the Book of Hosea* (Tübingen: Mohr Siebeck, 2006), 32–33.

[2] Helen Schüngel-Straumann, "Gott als Mutter in Hosea 11," *TQ* 166 (1986): 119–34, here 123–24.

[3] Helen Schüngel-Straumann, "God as Mother in Hosea 11," *A Feminist Companion to the Latter Prophets* (ed. Athalya Brenner; tr. L. M. Maloney; London: T & T Clark, 2004), 194–218, here 195.

[4] Gerald P. Kramer and George Wu, *An Introduction to Taiwanese Folk Religions* (Taipei, Taiwan: n.p., 1970), 24–25.

in stature and in favor with people. After receiving a bronze charm from a *xian* (immortal), she was able to get rid of demons, relieve disasters, and save ships at sea. The people called her "The Sagacious Divine Lady."[1]

There are two different theories about the origin of Matzu's divine nature. Either she was a real woman, who was deified after her death,[2] or she was originally conceived as a deity, and her mortal history was created later in the process of worship.[3] The representation of Matzu as a human being makes it easier for adherents to relate to her.

Even though the scholars of Matzu disagree regarding the origin of her divinity, they agree that one of the salient characteristics of Matzu is motherhood. Her name is spelled using two Chinese characters. Ma (媽) means "mother" and Tzu (祖), "ancestor." This is curious, since she never married and died at the young age of 27. In addition, her death resulted in her transformation into a divine being and ascension into heaven. The motherly image of Matzu was clearly not based on her real life but added by later generations whose respect and awe for the mother image was part of the deification process.

The worshippers of Matzu enter her temple showing the respect that "one shows toward a mother as toward an official."[4] When they worship Matzu and pray for their well-being, they regard her not as a bureaucratic god, but as a merciful goddess. The divine images of both YHWH and Matzu reflect the motherly divinity, which reinforces the strong relationship between a deity without male characteristics and her human worshippers.

---

[1] Hsun Chang, "Incense-Offering and Obtaining the Magical Power of Qi: The Mazu (Heavenly Mother) Pilgrimage in Taiwan" (PhD diss., University of California at Berkeley, 1993), 51.

[2] Morris I. Berkowitz and Frederick P. Brandauer, *Folk Religion in an Urban Setting: A Study of Hakka Villagers in Tradition* (Hong Kong: Christian Study Centre on Chinese Religion and Culture, 1969), 84.

[3] Chang, "Incense-Offering," 48–49.

[4] P. Steven Sangren, "American Anthropology and the Study of Mazu Worship," 媽祖信仰的發展與變遷:媽祖信仰與現代社會國際研討會論文集 (eds. Linmei Rong, Zhang Xun, and Caixian Hui; Běigǎng: Táiwān Zōngjiào Xuéhuì, 2003), 7–23, here 9.

Divine Companion of the Diaspora Community

The history of the Israelites as told by the Hebrew Bible prominently features the migration from Egypt to the promised land. Hosea 11:5 also prophesies a diasporic situation for the future of Israel: "He will not return to the land of Egypt but Assyria will be his king," since "they refused to return." However, Hosea emphasizes the everlasting relationship between YHWH and the Israelites by using a mother/fetus analogy in v. 4. Hosea enhances the image of the deity using the image of the powerful bonds between mother and baby.

Verse 4 is difficult to translate because of several uncertain Hebrew lexemes. I construe it as follows, "I drew them with the human being's umbilical cords (בְּחַבְלֵי אָדָם), in the interwoven love (בַּעֲבֹתוֹת אַהֲבָה). Also I was to them like those who lift a baby to their cheeks and I inclined to him and gave him to suck." *Bəḥablê 'ādām* could be translated "with cords of love"[1] or "with human cords."[2] Andrew Alexander Macintosh interprets it as a metaphorical phrase, "with bonds of friendship."[3] According to BDB, חבל (*ḥbl*) carries two different groups of meaning—"cord, territory, band, pain, mast" and "act corruptly and destructively."[4] With *bəḥablê 'ādām* translatable as "in cords of life," the rabbinic tradition pointed out that, "within the body of the pregnant woman are 'ropes' that hold the unborn infant. The undoing of their knots marks the onset of labor and birth."[5] Thus, *bəḥablê 'ādām* can be rendered as "the human being's umbilical cords." The umbilical cord is the fundamental tie between mother and baby. If the first vowel of חבלי is changed to *segol* in accordance with Hos 13:13, the word would mean "the pains of travail or birth-pangs."[6] Now the umbilical cord in 11:4 is metaphorically related to the mother's labor pains. Such a lovely and powerful image expresses "bonds of love and

---

[1] Francis I. Andersen and David Noel Freedman, *Hosea* (AB 24; New York: Doubleday, 1980), 574.

[2] James L. Mays, *Hosea: A Commentary* (Philadelphia: Westminster, 1969), 150 and Hans Walter Wolff, *Hosea* (tr. Gary Stansell; Philadelphia: Fortress, 1974), 191.

[3] Andrew Alexander Macintosh, *Hosea* (ICC; Edinburgh: T & T Clark, 1997), 445-46.

[4] BDB, 286-87.

[5] *TDOT*, 4:189.

[6] BDB, 286.

childbirth that tie mother and child together."[1] Hosea's use of a mother image reveals YHWH's act of love toward the Israelites, something that would be unpalatable to the male elites of Israel.[2] In the next line, Hosea emphasizes the mother-fetus relationship by mentioning *'ăḇōṯōṯ 'ahăbā(h)*. The root of *'ăḇōṯōṯ* is עבת (*'bt*), which means "wind, weave" in the verbal forms, and "cord, rope, cordage, interwoven foliage" in the nominal forms.[3] I translate *ba'ăḇōṯōṯ 'ahăbā(h)*, "with interwoven love." Through this expression, Hosea focuses on the cord of life connecting the mother and the fetus.

The relationship between YHWH and the Israelites is thus implicitly compared to the strong tie, the umbilical cord, between the mother and the unborn baby. The mother provides essential nutrition for her unborn baby through this nexus of love. It is impossible for a child to remember the life inside of their mother's womb, although it is their original home. As a mother is connected to her fetus with the umbilical cord, YHWH is with the Israelites during their migration. The umbilical cord symbolizes the emotional and powerful companionship between the deity and the deity's children. As a mother is always with a fetus, so is YHWH with the Israelites.

Likewise, Matzu moved from her birthplace to Taiwan with the people who crossed the Taiwan Strait. When the villagers around her home areas traveled or migrated overseas, they brought an image of Matzu to their destination. After landing, they built a temple of Matzu in gratitude for her providence.[4]

Many stories exist about the protection offered by Matzu at sea. I would like to share a few of them in this paper. According to one legend, one day she dreamed that her parents' boat was about capsized while they were engaged in earning their bread at sea. Matzu ran to the

---

[1] Marvin A. Sweeney, *The Twelve Prophets* (BOSHNP; Collegeville, MN: Liturgical Press, 2000), 1:114.

[2] Marvin Chaney insists that Gomer, the wife of Hosea, was metaphorically the male upper class of the eighth century BCE. According to him, "Hosea's 'wife of promiscuity' becomes a sarcastic trope for the male urban warrior elite of Israel and for the land whose agricultural priorities and techniques they increasingly dictated" (Marvin Chaney, "Agricultural Intensification as Promiscuity in the Book of Hosea," [paper presented at the Annual Meeting of the SBL, Washington D. C., 22 November, 1993], 1).

[3] BDB, 721.

[4] Kuo, *Religion and Democracy in Taiwan*, 79.

beach and saved the boat.[1] Ever since that happened, those sailing on a boat invoked Matzu to ask for her protection.

Furthermore, in 1122, Lu Yundi, the ambassador of Huizong in the Song Dynasty, crossed the East Sea to reach Koryo. He and his companions struggled against the wind and waves. The ship only survived the stormy sea thanks to Matzu, who appeared in a red garment and calmed the waves. Lu Yundi's mysterious experience is an example of the manifestation of Matzu in a stormy sea. According to Mircea Eliade, such manifestation (hierophany) can be of two kinds: theophany (an appearance of a god) and kratophany (a manifestation of power).[2] In this episode, Matzu displays both, which makes her a perfect companion deity to believers in crisis. In particular, Matzu's breath is a sign of divine presence.[3] Lu Yundi confessed, "Even though my parents gave me a birth and raised me in their love, they could not save my life from this heavy sea. It was Matzu who protected me with her breath."[4] His salvation thus made Matzu his surrogate parent, further underlining her role as a motherly deity.

An individual worshipper of Matzu does not necessarily have a personal acquaintance with other worshippers, nor is there any institutionally organized Matzu theology. Matzu temples are operated by ad-hoc local committees, which usually disband after each holiday.[5] How has Matzu come to play such an important "grassroots" role in local communities in Taiwan? The answer to this question lies in the devotion of female worshippers to family life and the Matzu religious community.[6]

The fact that many of Matzu's worshippers are of the same gender as the deity suggests that some of her popularity in Taiwan may be due to shared motherhood. According to Steven Sangren, it is impossible to find agnatic relationships in the portrayal of Matzu,

---

[1] Berkowite and Brandauer, *Folk Religion in an Urban Setting*, 84–85.
[2] Mircea Eliade and Lawrence Sullivan, "Hierophany," *Mircea Eliade: A Critical Reader* (ed. Bryan Rennie; London: Equinox, 2006), 86–93.
[3] Cf. Eliade and Sullivan, "Hierophany," 88.
[4] Hye-Ryun Koh, "동중국해의 마조 신앙: 천비현성록을 통해 본 마조 일화와 그 성격," *Tosuhmoonwha* 25 (2005): 161–99, here 179.
[5] Kuo, *Religion and Democracy in Taiwan*, 82.
[6] Sangren, "American Anthropology and the Study of Mazu Worship," 9–10.

which predominantly employs affinal and natal images.[1] These images offer comfort and help diaspora communities to remember their home, creating a more intimate relationship with the goddess. Since Matzu worship in Taiwan is based on displaced communities, the images of Matzu are often released to go on their own "pilgrimages."[2] The motherly image of YHWH in Hosea and Matzu are reminiscent of "Immanuel" (Isa 7:14): God is with us. When people migrate and cross the ocean or the desert, their deities accompany them.

Deity's Compassion and Deliverance

The most important feature of a companion deity is protection. According to Émile Durkheim, deities emerge in a protective psychological response to the immense forces that human beings cannot control.[3] People are awed by the infinity of time and space, and their admiration of the deity is a more concrete manifestation of this response to nature.

The Israelites in Hos 11 did not recognize YHWH as their God, but followed Baal. In vv. 8-9, Hosea proclaims the everlasting promise of YHWH who is unable "to give up the rebellious child Israel for punishment by the law concerning a rebellious son in Deut 21:18-21."[4] In v. 8, the deity proclaims, "How can I give you up, O Ephraim? How can I have over you, O Israel? How can I give you up like Admah? How can I treat you like Zeboiim? My heart recoils against me, my womb is utterly inflamed within me."[5] Although in the MT the last word of v. 8 is נִחוּמָי (niḥûmāy, "my remorse" or "my compassion"), יַחַד נִכְמְרוּ נִחוּמָי (yaḥad nikmĕrû nīḥûmāy) does not make much sense. The probable reading of the Peshitta and the Targum, raḥămāy ("my womb"), thus appears preferable.[6] This expression would amplify YHWH's maternal attitude to Ephraim, who will escape destruction thanks to it. The image of the womb encapsulates the infinite mercy

---

[1] P. Steven Sangren, "Female Gender in Chinese Religious Symbols: Kuan Yin, Ma Tsu, and the 'Eternal Mother,'" *Signs* 9.1 (1983): 4–25, here 9.

[2] Sangren, "American Anthropology and the Study of Mazu Worship," 18.

[3] Émile Durkheim, "The Elementary Forms of the Religious Life," *Reader in Comparative Religion: An Anthropological Approach* (ed. William A. Lessa; 4th ed.; New York: Harper & Row, 1979), 31.

[4] Sweeney, *Hosea*, 115.

[5] Schüngel-Straumann, "God as Mother," 196.

[6] *BHS*, 1005.

and passion of the mother. It is filled with creative energy, since a new life is conceived there.

Furthermore, it is important for YHWH not to be identified as a man (אִישׁ), but as a deity (אֵל) in v. 9b. Hosea does not use אָדָם ('ādām), but אִישׁ ('îš) in order to reveal the identity of YHWH. 'ādām can be translated as "humanity,"[1] while 'îš means "man" or "husband," the binary opposite of woman. Hosea is here ascribing male qualities to YHWH while maintaining a distinction between the deity and a man.[2] Hosea undermines the male metaphors for YHWH to criticize male upper classes.

The official titles of Matzu have been changed several times; they include Madam, Queen, Heavenly Queen, and Heavenly Empress.[3] In the Song dynasty (1156 CE), Matzu received the title of Madam Young Hea, and in the Yuan Dynasty (1281 CE) her status was elevated to Queen Young Hea. Finally, the Kangxi Emperor of the Qing Dynasty bestowed the title of Heavenly Empress upon Matzu. The fact that the process of official recognition was initiated by the authorities reflects the strong influence of Matzu on local people.

However, the worshippers prefer to call her Matzu instead of her official titles. The motherhood of Matzu creates an intimate relationship with the deity. As Hosea presents YHWH as a mother who has a warm womb, Tian-Shang Sheng-Mu-Jing (天上聖母經) describes Matzu as a mother who feels compassion for babies. Tian-Shang Sheng-Mu-Jing states, "With a motherly heart she sees all the sentient beings as her own infants. [She] shows her power and spirit continually and responds to whatever one prays,"[4] for Matzu's motherly heart watches after and takes care of her infants.

Furthermore, the emphasis on Matzu's emotional bonds with her children continued in her actions in defense of justice. When people committed injustice, she received the report from two generals named The Clairvoyant and The Clairaudient. They followed Matzu and assisted her to save the world from trouble:

---

[1] See v. 4.
[2] Schüngel-Straumann, "God as Mother," 212.
[3] Yoo Jin Lee, "마조신앙의 국가 공인화 과정과 그 의미," Chungkukehmoonhaknonzip 70 (2011): 466–67.
[4] Chang, "Incense-Offering," 57.

Whether [a woman] has hard delivery, or someone is troubled by a judicial officer, or has various anxieties and troubles, where people were weak or are seriously ill; if any one of you can call my name reverently with a focused mind, I will respond to make your wishes come true and dissolve your miseries and troubles.[1]

Matzu always travels throughout the world with a motherly disposition and exterminates the army of evil. Moreover, the fact that Matzu obtained a high degree of official recognition is "an eloquent testimony of an underlying need to legitimize the power and grace of the feminine principle."[2] Her image can be compared with YHWH, who saved the Israelites from the oppression in Egypt. Hosea's purpose is to reinforce the compassion of YHWH that comes from the enduring love of a mother.

Conclusion

Hosea proclaimed the oracle of YHWH to the Israelites who were called upon to return to the deity, but departed from it. Hosea depicts YHWH as mother. A mother lives together with a baby while she is pregnant. As she connects with her baby through the umbilical cords, so also YHWH maintains a connection with the Israelites. When they confront dangerous situations, YHWH saves them. Similarly, Matzu, a goddess, saves her worshippers because of her motherly heart. She travels everywhere with them in her compassion. If someone experiences the love of his or her mother, he or she recognizes this in the divine images of YHWH and Matzu. The divine image of a motherly deity in both Hos 11 and Matzu worship suggests a basic similarity between the Bible and an Asian religion.

The study of hermeneutics encourages us to define Asian identity and to set up cross-religious hermeneutics.[3] Asian hermeneutics invites us to compare two traditions: biblical texts and Asian religions. In this comparative paper, I present a cross-religious hermeneutics exploration of YHWH in Hos 11 and Matzu worship, showing commonalities that might inform Bible reading in Asia. The

---

[1] Chang, "Incense-Offering," 57–58.
[2] Lee Irwin, "Divinity and Salvation: The Great Goddesses of China," *Asian Folklore Studies* 49 (1990): 53–68, here 64.
[3] Tat-Siong Benny Liew, *What is Asian American Biblical Hermeneutics: Reading the New Testament* (Honolulu: University of Hawaii Press, 2008), ix–xiv.

motherly images of YHWH and Matzu break a new ground in cross-religious hermeneutics.

The Psalm in Habakkuk 3

Steven S. Tuell

Marvin Sweeney divides Habakkuk into two parts, each with its own heading: Hab 1-2, Habakkuk's pronouncement (משא), and Hab 3, Habakkuk's prayer (תפלה).[1] Readers of the prophetic book have long wondered about the relationship between those parts. In the Habakkuk *pesher* from Qumran (1QpHab),[2] Hab 3 is absent altogether! Conversely, the "Barberini version" from late first to early second century CE Alexandria is a distinctive Greek translation of Hab 3 alone.[3] Some ancient readers regarded Hab 3 as the report of Habakkuk's vision,[4] which he is commanded to write in 2:2-3.[5] The

---

* Marv Sweeney has been my friend for many years. We first met poring over the prophet Ezekiel, and as our scholarly paths have crossed and recrossed, I have learned much from him about the Hebrew Bible and about Jewish faith and life. It is my joy and privilege to be included in this project in his honor.

[1] Marvin A. Sweeney, *The Twelve Prophets* (BOSHNP; Collegeville, MN: Liturgical Press, 2000) 2:457-58. Cf. also Marvin A. Sweeney, "Structure, Genre, and Intent in the Book of Habakkuk," *VT* 41 (1991): 63-83.

[2] 1QpHab is one of seven scrolls from Cave One at Qumran, dating from the late first century BCE. The extensive quotes strewn through this pesher provide our oldest and best witness to the Hebrew text of Habakkuk. Cf. Florentino Garcia Martinez and Eibert J. C. Tigchelaar, eds., *The Dead Sea Scrolls Study Edition, vol. 1, 1Q1-4Q273* (Leiden: Brill, 1997), 11-21.

[3] Edwin M. Good, "The Barberini Greek Version of Habakkuk III," *VT* 9 (1959): 11-30. Sweeney describes Barberini as "an alternative to the Septuagint with affinities to the Palestinian Syriac text, the Peshitta, and Coptic and Latin versions from Africa" (Sweeney, *Twelve*, 2:479).

[4] Modern interpreters proposing this include Ernst Sellin, *Das Zwölfprophetenbuch überstetz und eklärt*, vol. 2, *Zweite Hälfte: Nahum-Maleachi*, 2nd and 3rd ed. (KAT 12; Leipzig: A. Deichersche, 1930), 405 and Jimmy J. M. Roberts, *Nahum, Habakkuk, and Zephaniah* (OTL; Louisville: Westminster John Knox, 1991), 148-49. David S. Vanderhooft ascribes this view to William Foxwell Albright ("The *tokakhat*, 'disputation,' of Habakkuk as a Contrarian Argument in the Book of the Twelve" [paper presented at the Annual Meeting of the SBL, Atlanta, GA, 2010]).

[5] Sweeney proposes, "The basic statement of the vision appears in verse 4.... In contrast to the Babylonian who will perish because of his arrogance, the righteous will live as a result of his reliance on YHWH" (Sweeney, *Twelve*, 2:471-72). While I agree that this is the point of the final form of Habakkuk, I am persuaded that Habakkuk's original vision concerned the end of *Judah*, not of Babylon, and is expressed already in 2:2; just as Amos saw summer fruit (כלוב קיץ) and learned that the end (הקץ) had come upon Israel

Talmud (*b. Meg.* 31a) assigns both Ezek 1 and Hab 3 for reading on Shavuot, suggesting that the sages understood these as related prophetic visions. Gregory of Nazianzus read 3:1-19 as Habakkuk's vision of the risen Christ.[1] But as we will see, the prophet refers to the theophany set forth in 3:3-15 not as a vision that he has seen but as a report that he has *heard* (3:2, 16). Sweeney rightly refers to 3:1-19 as "The Prayer/Petition by Habakkuk to YHWH."[2] This study will argue that Hab 3 is an old psalm depicting YHWH as the Divine Warrior,[3] expanded into a prayer for help. We will propose that, based on the theology and language of Hab 3, this revision was the work of Habakkuk, rather than the book's editors.

Habakkuk 3:3-15 as a Theophanic Hymn

J. J. M. Roberts observes that in Hab 3, "[t]he archaic features of the poetry are concentrated" in 3:3-15, which Sweeney calls a "theophany report."[4] Habakkuk 3:3-15 also features the term (סלה is left untranslated in NRSV, in 3:3, 9, and 13), which appears only here and in the Psalms (70 times). Both the meaning and the derivation of סלה are obscure.[5] However, in Hab 3:3-15 as in the Psalms, סלה marks the transition from one section to another, and so may reveal the structure of an original psalm, prior to its incorporation into this book: the opening in Hab 3:3a, the depiction of YHWH's warlike advance in 3:3b-9a, the storm theophany in 3:9b-13, and the announcement of YHWH's victory in 3:14-15. Rich in ancient themes and vocabulary, 3:3-15 could accurately be described as a theophanic hymn.[6]

(Amos 8:1-2), so Habakkuk sees (and writes) the word סלה: "the end" (cf. Steven Tuell, *Reading Nahum–Malachi,* [ROT; Macon, GA: Smith-Helwys, 2016], 77-80).

[1] Bogdan G. Bucur and Elijah N. Mueller, "Gregory Nazianzen's Reading of Habakkuk 3:2 and Its Reception: A Lesson from Byzantine Scripture Exegesis," *ProEccl* 20 (2011): 88-90, 97-98.

[2] Sweeney, *Twelve,* 2:478.

[3] Theodore Hiebert proposes that Hab 3:1-19 is a very old hymn of the Divine Warrior (*God of My Victory: The Ancient Hymn in Habakkuk 3* [HSM 38; Atlanta: Scholars, 1986], 119), comparable to such ancient songs as Exod 15:1-18 or Judg 5:1-31, and incorporated by Habakkuk's editors (137-39); Theodore Hiebert, "The Book of Habakkuk: Introduction, Commentary, and Reflections," *NIB,* 7:652-55.

[4] Roberts, *Habakkuk,* 148; Sweeney (*Twelve* 2: 482)

[5] סלה may indicate a change of pitch, a pause, an instrumental interlude, or a coda (*HALOT,* 756).

[6] Cf. James Luther Mays, *Psalms* (Interpretation; Louisville: John Knox, 1994), 26-27. While, as Mays observes, the typical pattern in the hymn is "summons plus

The psalmist declares, "God came from Teman, the Holy One from Mount Paran" (3:3);[1] he is manifest among the "the tents of Cushan" and in the "land of Midian" (3:7). The location of Teman is uncertain, though the name is consistently used in reference to Edom (e.g., Gen 36:11; Ezek 25:13; Amos 1:12; Job 2:11). Mount Paran[2] likely is a poetic reference to Sinai (cf. Deut 33:2, which also says that YHWH "dawned from Sier [i.e., Edom]"). Cushan is mentioned only here,[3] but the reference to tents and the parallel with the "land of Midian" (associated particularly with the Sinai; e.g., Exod 2:15-16) suggest that Cushan was probably an Arab tribe. As in other ancient songs of the Divine Warrior, YHWH marches out of the south (e.g., Deut 33:2-3; Judg 5:4-5).

Sweeney proposes, "Overall, these verses employ the imagery of the rising sun to depict YHWH's manifestation in the world"[4] (cf. NRSV and NIV of Hab 3:4). However, the reference to the קרנים (literally, "two horns") coming from G-d's hand in Hab 3:4 sounds as though the Divine is wielding a forked lightning bolt as a weapon.[5] Indeed, Gregory of Nazianzus wrote of this theophany, "behold a man riding on the clouds and he is very high, and his countenance is like the countenance of an angel, and his vesture is like the brightness of piercing lightning."[6] The poem describes not a sunrise but an approaching storm; the "brilliant light" (NJPS; Hebrew נגה כאור) of this divine manifestation is the lightning flash (cf. Job 36:30, 32; 37:11, 15).[7]

---

proclamation (invocation and praise). . . [t]here are hymns that do not follow the pattern. Some employ only the second part, the proclamatory body of praise" (Mays, *Psalms*, 27).

[1] The Divine is referred to אלוה ("G-d") in 3:3, and אלהי ישעי ("G-d of my salvation") in 3:18; the Name is used in 3:2 (twice), 8, 18, and 19 (יהוה אדני, rendered GOD, the Lord" in the NRSV).

[2] The LXX renders this as ορους κατασκιου δασεος ("dark, shady mountain"), although Barberini has φαραν; cf. Good, "Barberini," 12-13. Theodoret of Cyrus (Theodoret of Cyrus: Commentary on the Twelve Prophets, ed. Robert Charles Hill [Brookline: Holy Cross, 2006], 2000) and Irenaeus (Haer. 4.33.11) interpret Hab 3:3 as predicting Jesus' birth in Bethlehem, to the south of Zion, the "shady mountain."

[3] LXX has Αιθιοπων ("Ethiopia"), evidently reading "Cush" (e.g., Jer 46:9; Ezek 29:10), while *Targ. Neb.* assumes the reference is to Cushan-rishathaim ("Cushan the Doubly Wicked"), an enemy of Israel in Judg 3:7-11; *Targ. Neb.* reads כושן חייבא ("Cushan the Sinner") in both places.

[4] Sweeney, *Twelve*, 2:482.

[5] So Roberts, *Habakkuk*, 128; cf. Hab 3:6.

[6] *Orat.* 45:1, cited by Bucur and Mueller, "Gregory Nazianzen's Reading," 99.

[7] With Roberts, *Habakkuk*, 134.

The description in Hab 3:6 of the earth shaken, nations trembling, and mountains shattered at YHWH's advance is typical of the storm theophany (cf. Judg 5:4-5; Ps 18:7-15; Nah 1:5-6).[1] The emphasis upon antiquity in this verse ("eternal mountains," "ancient pathways," "everlasting hills") recalls the Divine Warrior's defeat of chaos and establishment of order at the dawn of time (cf. 3:8-11), but YHWH also acts before the psalmist's eyes:

> I saw the tents of Cushan under affliction;
> the tent-curtains of the land of Midian trembled (3:7).

Habakkuk 3:8 opens with a question: "Was your wrath against the rivers, O LORD?" The form נהרים ("rivers") is unusual; the expected plural is נהרות. This suggests that the Hebrew originally read נַהֲרַיִם: that is, "*two* rivers," a term used in Canaanite myth to describe the dwelling of the high god 'El "at the source of the twin rivers, by the pools of the double-deep,"[2] where the waters of chaos were vanquished. It is best then to capitalize "Rivers" and "Sea" (with the footnotes in NRSV) or to leave them untranslated (with NJPS), as the names of YHWH's mythic adversaries.[3]

YHWH rides into battle, leading the heavenly chariotry (Hab 3:8)[4] and wielding a bow against the enemy (3:9).[5] Sun and Moon (again, best regarded as personified heavenly powers; cf. footnotes in NRSV), together with the earth and the mountains, witness YHWH's victory—not, after all, against cosmic, mythic enemies, but against Israel's earthly oppressors:

---

[1] Cf. Tuell, *Reading Nahum-Malachi*, 24. Theodoret of Cyrus understood this as the earthquake associated with Jesus's crucifixion in Matt 27:51 (*Theodoret of Cyrus: Commentary on the Twelve Prophets*, [ed. Robert Charles Hill; Brookline: Holy Cross, 2006], 201).

[2] *CTA* 4.4.21-22. Cf. Steven Tuell, "The Rivers of Paradise: Ezek 47:1-12 and Gen 2:10-14," *God Who Creates: Essays in Honor of W. Sibley Towner* (eds. S. Dean McBride, Jr. and William Brown; Grand Rapids: Eerdmans, 2000), 171-89, here 180; Roberts, *Habakkuk*, 137-38; and Hiebert, *God of My Victory*, 23.

[3] Similarly, it is better to leave דבר and רשף untranslated in 3:5 and capitalize them as names: *Deber* and *Resheph*, Pestilence and Plague personified. Just as Marduk is flanked by fearsome warrior demons in the *Enuma 'elish*, so *Deber* and *Resheph* march alongside as YHWH goes into battle (Cf. Hiebert, *God of My Victory*, 4, 92-94; G. del Olmo Lete, "Deber," *DDD* 231-32; and P. Xella, "Resheph," *DDD* 700-03).

[4] 2 Kgs 2:11-12; 6:17; 7:6; 13:14; 23:11; Zech 6:1-8; Ps 68:18 [17]; cf. also the depictions of YHWH riding on the storm, e.g., Ps 18:9-12 [10-13], and the depiction of the wheeled chariot throne of YHWH in Ezek 1 and Dan 7.

[5] For God's bow and arrows, see also, e.g., Gen 9:12-17; Ps 18:14, and cf. *Enuma 'elish*, Tablet 4.100-04.

> In fury you trod the earth,
> > in anger you trampled nations.
> You came forth to save your people,
> > to save your anointed (3:12-13).

The juxtaposition of creation imagery with deliverance from historical oppressors is a very old idea. The Song of the Sea, likely the oldest text in scripture (Exod 15:1-18), relates YHWH's victory over the Sea directly to the defeat of Pharaoh (Exod 15:4). Similarly, in the ancient Song of Deborah (Judg 5:2-31), YHWH marches out of the south and manifests G-dself in the storm to defeat the forces of Sisera, and the poem that opens Nahum juxtaposes the exodus out of Egypt and YHWH's creative power to express (in its context) YHWH's triumph over Assyria (Nah 1:4; cf. also Isa 51:9-11). The Divine Warrior manifest in the storm comes to deliver!

Habakkuk 3:3-15 shows a clear thematic unity, and uses consistently archaic language and imagery. These distinctive features are best explained if this is an old psalm, selected and adapted for its context either by the prophet Habakkuk or by the book's editors. The nature and effect of the changes make it most likely that this selection and adaptation can be attributed to the prophet himself.

Habakkuk 3:1-19 as a Prayer for Help

In its current form, Hab 3 is doubly marked as a psalm. The chapter opens with a Psalm title: "A prayer of the prophet Habakkuk according to Shigionoth." Only two poems in scripture are designated as שגינות: Hab 3 and Ps 7, called in the NRSV "A Shiggaion of David." The pattern על ("according to") followed by an apparent song title occurs sixteen times in the titles of Psalms. The word תפלה ("prayer") appears 32 times in the Psalter (out of 77 times in MT); in the prophets, it appears only in Isa 1:15; 37:4//2 Kgs 19:4; 38:5//2 Kgs 20:5; 56:7; Jer 7:16; 11:14, Jonah 2:7; and Hab 3:1.

Curiously, Hab 3 also concludes with a Psalm-like dedication: "To the choirmaster: with stringed instruments" (3:19b). Apart from 3:19, the dedication למנצח (rendered "To the choirmaster" in the NRSV of 3:19 and "To the leader" in the Psalms) appears only in the Psalter (55 times; although the term מנצחים, "overseers," occurs in 2 Chr 2:1, 17; 34:13). The expression בנגינותי ("with stringed instruments") also appears only here and in the Psalms, always following למנצח (Pss 4; 6;

55; 67; 76). In every instance apart from Habakkuk, these expressions appear in the title at the opening of a psalm. However Haim M. I. Gevaryahu[1] and Bruce K. Waltke[2] have argued on differing grounds that this material was originally found at the end of a unit, as in 3:19. If this is so, then the postscript in 3:19 may provide further evidence for the antiquity of the original psalm.[3]

At first, Hab 3 seems to begin like the typical hymn,[4] with praise: "O LORD, I have heard of your renown, and I stand in awe, O LORD, of your work" (3:2). Yet, a contrast is immediately apparent between the speaker in this opening verse, who has only *heard* of the LORD's renown, and the poet in the source hymn, who says, "I *saw* the tents of Cushan under affliction; the tent-curtains of the land of Midian trembled" (3:7, emphasis mine). The remainder of this verse draws that distinction vividly:

> In our own time revive it;
> > in our own time make it known;
> > > in wrath may you remember mercy (3:2).

The expression rendered "in our own time" in the NRSV is בקרב שנים (that is, "in the midst of years"). Although this phrase appears twice in 3:2, it is found nowhere else.[5] But while unusual, the phrase is meaningful: בקרב שנים, rendered in the NJPS as "in these years," could be aptly paraphrased "right now." The prophet longs for YHWH to manifest YHWH's power clearly and unmistakably against oppression

---

[1] Haim M. I. Gevaryahu, "Biblical Colophons: A Source for the 'Biography' of Authors, Texts, and Books," *Congress Volume: Edinburgh 1974* (eds. G. W. Anderson et al.; VTSup 28; Leiden: E. J. Brill, 1975), 42–59.

[2] Bruce K. Waltke, "Superscripts, Postscripts, or Both," *JBL* 110 (1991): 594–95.

[3] So Hiebert, *God of My Victory*, 141–42.

[4] Mays, *Psalms*, 26–27.

[5] In its first occurrence, both the LXX and Barberini render this expression as "between the two living creatures," reading שנים ("years") as שתים ("two") and the verb חיהו ("revive") as the noun חיות ("living creatures"); cf. Good, "Barberini," 28–30 and Bucur and Mueller, "Gregory Nazianzen's Reading," 91–92, though Good holds that Barberini and the LXX are conflated in 3:1-2 (Good, "Barberini," 12). Significantly, the same Greek word, ζῳων, is used in the LXX of 3:2 and to translate the Hebrew חיה ("living creature") in Ezek 1:5, 13, 14, 19–20, 22; 3:13; 10:15, 20 (cf. Bucur and Mueller, 96–99), so it is likely that the translators had in mind Ezekiel's visions of the living creatures accompanying YHWH's Glory. Christian interpreters from Tertullian to the Venerable Bede found here Jesus's Transfiguration appearance with Moses and Elijah (Bucur and Mueller, "Gregory Nazianzen's Reading," 94–95). Theodoret of Cyrus found reference "to lives, the present and the future, between which the just Judge appears" (Theodoret, *Commentary on the Twelve*, 200).

in his own day, as in times past—as, indeed, in the days of the psalm he now cites—and prays, "in your wrath remember mercy" (3:2; cf. the prophet's vain plea for moderation in judgment in Hab 1:12-13). Rather than a hymn's call to praise, then, 3:2 opens this psalm with a plea for YHWH to show mercy—indeed, to show *up*. That is the pattern we expect to find in a quite different genre of psalm (e.g., Ps 13:1 [MT 13:2]; 22:1 [MT 22:2]; 130:1).[1] The ancient hymn has become Habakkuk's prayer for help.

The reference to hearing in Hab 3:2 parallels the statement in 3:16, "I hear, and I tremble within,"[2] bracketing the original hymn in 3:3-15 and also expressing neatly the theme of the prayer in its final form: I have *heard* of YHWH's mighty acts of salvation, but where is YHWH now? There is a clear grammatical shift in 3:16 from second-person descriptions of YHWH's activity (3:3-15) to a first person account of Habakkuk's experience (3:16-19). Habakkuk's response to the paean to divine power in 3:3-15 is sometimes understood positively: the prophet is overwhelmed by God's glory.[3] Yet elsewhere, the verb used for "trembling" (רגז) refers to panic at the approach of a foe (Deut 2:25; 2 Sam 18:33), to overwhelming grief (2 Sam 18:33), to shame (Prov 29:9), or to divine judgment (Isa 5:25; Jer 33:9; 50:34; Ezek 16:43); it is not used anywhere else for a faithful person's response to a theophany. Rottenness of the bones, similarly, refers elsewhere to overwhelming shame (Prov 12:4; 14:3). In short, the prophet's response to this ancient poem is not exaltation and awe but shame and terror. The power of YHWH described in the theophanic hymn elicits not confidence but bewildered disappointment. Why would such a G-d fail to act against Babylon? Habakkuk sees no evidence of YHWH's activity but must instead sigh and wait "for the day of calamity to come upon the people who attack us" (Hab 3:16).

Nevertheless, rather than succumbing to despair, Habakkuk chooses paradoxically to affirm G-d's presence in a world from which G-d appears to be absent:

---

[1] Mays, *Psalms*, 21-26.
[2] So Roberts, *Habakkuk*, 149.
[3] Sweeney, *Twelve* 2:487; cf., also, Elizabeth Achtemeier, *Nahum-Malachi* (IBC; Louisville: John Knox, 1986), 53-54 and Roberts, *Habakkuk*, 157.

> Though the fig tree does not blossom,
> and no fruit is on the vines;
> though the produce of the olive fails
> and the fields yield no food;
> though the flock is cut off from the fold
> and there is no herd in the stalls,
> yet I will rejoice in the LORD;
> I will exult in the God of my salvation (3:17-18).

This movement through anger and despair to praise is, again, typical of the prayer for help. In psalms in this genre, "[s]tatements of confidence in God, confessions of trust, are usually made," and "[a] promise of sacrifice and/or praise may round out the prayer" (e.g., Pss 13:5-6 [MT 13:6]; 22:29-31 [MT 22:30-32]; 130:7-8).[1] Through his prayer, Habakkuk experiences G-d's presence in the midst of his trouble — a theme in continuity with the prophet's struggles with G-d's justice but in tension with the theology of the *book* of Habakkuk, which in its final form emphasizes YHWH's victory over Babylon.

Theology of Habakkuk: the Prophet and the Book

In the theodicy dialogue in Hab 1:1-17, YHWH replies to Habakkuk's outcry against injustice and oppression in Judah by announcing the coming of Babylon (a common prophetic reading for foreign oppression; e.g., Jer 25:8-11; Ezek 24:1-14; Isa 40:1-2). But the Babylonian assault does not resolve Habakkuk's original complaint against the violence he sees in Judah, abetted by its corrupt or incompetent leaders. Indeed, Babylon brings more violence and oppression![2] Habakkuk responds in plea and protest,

> Are you not from of old,
> O LORD my God, my Holy One?
> We shall not die (1:12, my translation).

Here, I propose staying with the MT and LXX of Hab 1:12.[3] The NRSV, instead, follows the Jewish tradition identifying this passage as

---

[1] Mays, *Psalms*, 21.

[2] Donald E. Gowan, *The Triumph of Faith in Habakkuk* (Atlanta: John Knox, 1976), 35-36; Michael H. Floyd, *The Minor Prophets, Part 2* (FOTL 22; Grand Rapids: Eerdmans, 2000), 81; and Tuell, *Reading Nahum-Malachi*, 71-72.

[3] Cf. KJV and the old NIV. While Hab 1:12a is not quoted, 1QpHab 5:3 also assumes the MT, interpreting this verse to mean, "God will not destroy his people by the hand of the nations." Achtemeier also sees this passage as an expression of confident faithfulness: YHWH will preserve YHWH's own (*Nahum – Malachi*, 39-40). See also James

one of the *Tiqqune Sopherim*, scribal emendations to preserve divine honor,[1] and so reads "*You* [i.e., YHWH] shall not die."[2] But Habakkuk has never doubted G-d's eternity (YHWH is, after all, "from of old"), only G-d's justice. In the very next verse, the prophet asks, "Your eyes are too pure and you cannot look on wrongdoing; why do you look on the treacherous, and are silent when the wicked swallow those more righteous than they?" (Hab 1:13). A particularly interesting parallel is Hos 8:8: "Israel is swallowed up; now they are among the nations." Habakkuk fears that Judah is now about to suffer the same fate. "We shall not die" is a cry of hopeful desperation: surely, surely we will not die; surely the G-d whom Habakkuk addresses as "my Holy One," who is faithful "from of old," will not permit the destruction of Judah!

Habakkuk resolves to "stand at my watchpost" (Hab 2:1) until G-d responds to his complaint. YHWH answers with a vision:

It speaks of the end, and does not lie.
If it seems to tarry, wait for it;
it will surely come, it will not delay (2:3).

But what does this vision mean? Is it about Babylon whose inevitable end is declared, or is it Judah? Habakkuk 2:4-5b deals generally with wealth and arrogance in wisdom language (cf. Prov 30:15-16), and seems to address Jerusalem's leadership,[3] while 2:5c ("They gather nations for themselves, and collect all peoples as their own") certainly addresses Babylon. The five woes that follow (2:6-19)

D. Nogalski (*Redactional Processes in the Book of the Twelve*, BZAW 218 [Berlin: de Gruyter, 1993], 149), who assigns this statement to Habakkuk's redaction.

[1] Cf. Sweeney, *Twelve*, 2:467-68.

[2] E.g., NJPS, NIV 2011, and Gowan, *Triumph of Faith*, 30.

[3] *Contra* Sweeney, *Twelve*, 2:471-73. The MT of Hab 2:5 reads היין בוגד ("wine is treacherous," cf. KJV and NIV), which is also assumed by LXX and Targ. Neb., but 1QpHab 8.3 reads instead הון בוגד ("wealth will betray;" NRSV). Similarly, Hab 1:5 likely should read ראו מבוגדים ("Behold, traitors. . .") instead of ראו בגוים (NRSV "Look at the nations;" see also Targ. Neb., NIV, and NJPS). The LXX ἴδετε, οἱ καταφρονηταί ("Behold, despisers") assumes Hebrew בוגדים ("traitors, treacherous ones") rather than בגוים ("at/among the nations"), a reading that appears in one Hebrew manuscript and is presupposed by the Syriac. 1QpHab 2:1-2 says that this verse concerns הבוגדים אם איש הכזב: "the traitors with the Man of the Lie" (the chief adversary of the Teacher of Righteousness). We do best then to follow the LXX here, and emend בגוים to בוגדים. This explains why Hab 1:5-11 addresses a plural audience: the oracle is spoken by the prophet in the LORD's name to the traitors (בוגדים) identified in 1:2-4, who render Torah impotent and pervert justice. The emended text also provides a clear terminological connection between the leaders accused in 1:1-4 of perverting justice and the proud betrayed by their wealth in 2:4-5.

also do not yield a simple answer. Gowan proposes that this uncertainty is deliberate: the woes have "purposely been expressed in general terms which could apply again and again to tyranny in many forms."[1] However, these verses are characterized not so much by ambiguity as by tension, between isolated lines referring to Babylon and their context.[2] The woes give the overall impression that editors have reworked words originally addressed to Jerusalem to address Babylon. Their inserts confirm God's judgment upon Babylon, so that the word of Babylon's demise in Habakkuk prefigures the coming Day of the LORD, a central theme of the Book of the Twelve.[3]

Still, in the Twelve, the word קֵץ ("end") appears only in Hab 2:3 and in Amos 8:1-2, where that prophet's vision of קַיִץ ("summer fruit") is a punning reference to Israel's end (קֵץ). Hosea and Ezekiel, who like Habakkuk were metaphorical sentinels on the wall (Hab 2:1; Hos 9:8; Ezek 3:17; 33:2, 6-7), also declare to their audiences that the end has come. Habakkuk 2:4-5a vindicates YHWH's harsh judgment in response to the prophet's earlier complaint, but YHWH's grim answer to the prophet's implicit prayer for preservation ("We shall not die," Hab 1:12) is that Judah's end *will* come, and soon.

In contrast to the optimistic theology of Habakkuk's editors, evident most plainly in the final form of Habakkuk's woes, the psalm in Hab 3 expresses concern about God's seeming absence, although defiantly declaring God's faithfulness in the face of tragedy. This seems to be consistent with what we have identified as Habakkuk's own position.

---

[1] Gowan, *Triumph of Faith*, 57; cf. also John Goldingay and Pamela J. Scalise, *Minor Prophets II* (NIBCOT 18; Peabody MA: Hendrickson, 2009), 50.

[2] Cf. Tuell, *Reading Nahum–Malachi*, 75–95.

[3] Cf. James D. Nogalski, "Recurring Themes in the Book of the Twelve: Creating Points of Contact for a Theological Reading," *Int* 61 (2007): 125–27. This theme of Divine victory in the Twelve is well expressed in Sir 49:10: "May the bones of the Twelve Prophets send forth new life from where they lie, for they comforted the people of Jacob and delivered them with confident hope." Michael H. Floyd summarizes the message of Habakkuk in its final form succinctly: "Yahweh can be seen as responsible for Babylon's rise, as the oracle in 1:5-11 asserts, but not for the injustice that has accompanied the imposition of their rule. If one recognizes that Babylon is now destined to fall and trusts that YHWH will eventually bring about this destiny, faith in him as Lord of history can become compatible with a commitment to justice" (*The Minor Prophets*, 83).

Terminological Evidence: the Verb גזר

In Hab 3:17, the prophet resolves to praise YHWH "though the flock is cut off [Hebrew גזר] from the fold." The verb גזר is not common, appearing only twelve times in the Hebrew Bible. But we can identify characteristic shifts in the use of this term over time, which may help us to date the redaction of Hab 3.

The oldest meaning of the word seems to be "cut in two" (1 Kgs 3:25-26; see also Ps 136:13) or "cut down" (2 Kgs 6:4). But texts from the exilic period use גזר in the Niphal in an abstract sense, for the separation of death. So, in Ezek 37:11, the exiles say, "Our bones are dried up, and our hope is lost; we are cut off [נגזרנו] completely." In Lam 3:54, the poet, descending into the waters of the underworld, says נגזרתי ("I am lost"), and in the fourth Servant Song, the witnesses declare of the Servant, "he was cut off [נגזר] from the land of the living" (Isa 53:8; see also Ps 88:5). Unquestionably late texts seem to use גזר in contexts where earlier texts would use כרת ("cut"). So, 2 Chr 26:21 records that King Uzziah was "excluded [נגזר] from the house of the LORD" due to his leprosy; priestly law (e.g., Lev 7:20-21; 17:10-11; 18:29; 19:8; 20:5-6) uses כרת for expulsion from the worshipping congregation. Esther 2:1 and Job 22:28 both use גזר for issuing a decree, again reminiscent of כרת, often used for making a covenant (e.g., Deut 29:11; 1 Kgs 8:9; Hag 2:5, and compare the use of גזר for "decide" in Middle Hebrew).

Habakkuk's use of גזר for lost sheep missing from the fold is unlike those clearly postexilic instances, and so unlikely to derive from the Twelve's editors. It is closest to the exilic usage cited above. Indeed, the usage of גזר in Hab 3:17 for a flock lost, stolen, strayed or dead seems best understood as a transitional stage between the original, concrete sense of the term and its abstract usage in exilic contexts, supporting our proposal that the prophet himself reworked this psalm and included it as the conclusion of his prophecy in the late seventh or the early sixth century BCE.

Conclusion

In the Vulgate, Habakkuk's psalm is entitled *oratio Abacuc prophetae pro ignorationibus*: "a speech of the prophet Habakkuk on behalf of his errors," or perhaps, "his ignorances." Although this translation of the Hebrew שגינות is unlikely,[1] the Latin title is nonetheless evocative. To be sure, this poem *does* address our ignorance: what do we do when the Divine will and way are unclear, when indeed G-d seems absent from our world? Habakkuk is concerned with how we are to live in the midst of the struggle, and so his answer is existential, not theological.[2] Although G-d's justice will one day prevail, we ourselves may not see it. Therefore, in the meantime, people of faith must reject the counsel of despair, and with Habakkuk, resolve to say, despite our circumstances,

I will rejoice in the LORD;
I will exult in the God of my salvation (Hab 3:18).

---

[1] The Vulgate reads שגינות in Hab 3:1 as derived from Hebrew שגה ("stray, stagger, do wrong"): cf. *Targ. Neb.*, Aquila, Symmachus, and Theodotion. Significantly, in Jerome's translation from the Hebrew rather than the Greek, a similar reading is found in the title of Ps 7. Evidently assuming the same root but a different meaning, Sellin (*Das Zwölfprophetenbuch*, 406) renders שגיון as "an enthusiastic, rambling, or ecstatic song," and Mitchell Dahood (*Psalms I: 1–50* [AB 16; Garden City NY: Doubleday, 1965], 41), as "dithyramb:" a wild, ecstatic song (the term originally related to the worship of Dionysus). But the most probable derivation for שגיון is the Akkadian *shigu*, a term for penitential prayer (Marie-Joseph Seux, "Shiggayon=shigu?" *Mélanges bibliques et orietaux en l'honneur de M. Henri Cazelles* [ed. A. Caquot and M. Delcor; AOAT 12; Neukirchen-Vluyn: Butzton and Bercker Kevelaer, 1981], 438) — an interpretation strengthened in 3:1 by pairing שגינות with תפלה, often used in prayers for help in the Psalter (e.g., Ps 4:1 [MT 2]; 17:1; 54:2 [MT 4]; 55:1 [MT 2]; 61:1 [MT 2]). If this reading is correct, then Habakkuk himself may be responsible for designating this poem תפלה... לע שגינות.

[2] Gowan, *Triumph of Faith*, 10–11.

"Have We Not All One Father? Has Not One God Created Us?" Revisiting Malachi 2:10a

Ehud Ben Zvi

The main goal of this essay is to explore the two opening rhetorical questions of Mal 2:10a[1] and their ability to provide a safe and shared playground for exploring multiple issues and advance various positions among the Yehudite literati in the late Persian period. Such an exploration cannot but shed considerable light on some aspects of the social mindscape of these literati.

To be sure, these literati constitute just one among many communities of readers and "users" of these two questions. In fact, there is a very rich history of readings and social and rhetorical uses of these two questions. Although the focus of this contribution is on a particular time and a particular group, some basic observations about this lengthy history are also in order. This is so because "readings" of a text are "infinite but of limited diversity."[2] The main patterns that emerge from this history of readings and uses may thus have the potential to contribute, at the very least heuristically, to the present endeavor.

In the particular case addressed here, as it will be shown below, these patterns draw attention to some basic dynamics of

---

[*] Marvin Sweeney and I began our academic careers more or less at the same time. I remember with great affection our shared projects and our conversations about prophetic literature. It is with great pleasure and much appreciation that I dedicate this essay to him. This contribution deals with numerous matters that he will likely find of interest.

[1] The order of the questions is reversed in the LXX. The LXX order is usually considered secondary and may well be the result of a reading of the first question in the MT as referring to Abraham (rather than YHWH). See, e.g., Anthony Gelston, *The Twelve Prophets* (*BHQ* 13; Stuttgart: Deutsche Bibelgesellschaft, 2010), 150, and bibliography there. Although the order may well be considered secondary, it still attests to one significant, ancient reading of the text. These matters will be discussed below.

[2] Paraphrasing the title of the chapter in which this matter is discussed at length in Ehud Ben Zvi, *Signs of Jonah: Reading and Rereading in Ancient Yehud* (JSOTSup 367; Sheffield: Sheffield Academic Press, 2003), 129–54.

inclusion and exclusion that are associated with basic, semantic contents of these questions (i.e., in discourse analysis terms, their semantic macrostructures)[1] and particularly their implied narrative and rhetorically construed and recalled shared memory.

To be sure, each of these readings, uses, and memories of the text emerge in interaction with basic metanarratives and the general discourse of the particular community shaping the "read" text, and their contingent world, including the identities they assign to those asking these rhetorical questions and to those from whom the questions are asked.[2]

In addition, multiple textual markers suggest that when it comes to the community of literati in the late Persian period in which the book of Malachi emerged, the two questions were not read by themselves. To the contrary, readings of them were strongly influenced by their literary contexts, of which Mal 2:10-16 is particularly important.

Thus, a second background section in this essay is required to draw attention to some observations about Mal 2:10-16 that would allow us to move into the third section in which the discussion moves to the two opening rhetorical questions of Mal 2:10a as read by the said literati and to how and why these questions, in that particular literary (and historically contingent) setting, were likely to provide a safe and

---

[1] See, among others, Teun A. van Dijk and W. Kintsch, *Strategies of Discourse Comprehension* (New York: Academic Press, 1983); Teun A. van Dijk, *Macrostructures* (Hillsdale, NJ: Erlbaum, 1980); Jan Renkema, *Discourse Studies* (Amsterdam: John Benjamins, 1993), 56-60; and my own application of the concept to Jonah in Ben Zvi, *Signs of Jonah*, 129-54.

[2] I continue to argue for the working hypothesis I advanced and tested in Ben Zvi, *Signs of Jonah*, esp. 131-37, namely "that three factors play a substantial role, regulating, and to some extent delimiting, the range of potential interpretations and social uses of the book or portions thereof as a narrative. These three factors are (a) *the horizon of pertinence* claimed by the text, and as perceived by a most substantial number of interpretive communities in history; (b) *basic global, semantic contents* (or macrostructures) that can be attributed to either the narrative of the book or selected sections thereof, which include already clear limits on the number and nature of the characters and accordingly, on the possible permutations of their relationships; and (c) *the degree of perceived coherence or integration between the global content of a selected section of the narrative (or the book as a whole) and central meta-narratives* of the interpretative community" (131). Given that all the reading communities mentioned in this essay understood Mal 2:10a (and the entire book of Malachi) as authoritative and as communicating a godly message, points (b) and (c) carry most of the weight in terms of regulating the range of potential interpretations and social uses of Mal 2:10.

shared playground for exploring multiple issues and advance various positions in Yehud in the late Persian period.

There can be no doubt that the issues discussed in the two background sections each deserve a specialized monograph,[1] but given the genre constraints of a chapter in a Festschrift (and in any volume) matters will be developed only to the point necessary to provide a context out of which the main, third section emerges.

Some Relevant Observations about Readings and Uses of Mal 2:10a in a Variety of Social and Historical Contexts

The two rhetorical questions of Mal 2:10a have often been helpful to and used as persuasive tools by disempowered, "marginal," or oppressed groups and those who supported their struggles against discrimination and oppression. By evoking the memory of a father that the disempowered or marginalized group shares with the central, more powerful group at which these questions were asked, at least rhetorically, the questions themselves were meant to construe a sense of "brotherhood"[2] shared by the marginal and the central group, between the oppressed and the oppressors. Such "brotherhood" not only undermined rigid constructions of the other that provided the ground for the discrimination, but also communicated a sense of positive obligation upon the most powerful brother to help the socially

---

[1] Marv Sweeney is an obvious candidate to write both volumes, and this observation played a role in choosing this topic for his FS.

[2] I use here the language of "brother" and "brotherhood" purposefully. Given the hierarchical constructions of gender in most relevant societies, it is unlikely that they attempted to convince the powerful social group that they are all "sisters." Even suffragists used to refer to "the fatherhood of God and the brotherhood of man" (see Danny O. Crew, *Suffragist Sheet Music: An Illustrated Catalogue of Published Music Associated with the Women's Rights and Suffrage Movement in America, 1795–1921, with Complete Lyrics* (Jefferson, NC: McFarland, 2002), 48–49. Needless to say, Adolf von Harnack and may protestant theologians after him in the late nineteenth century spoke about "the universal fatherhood of God and the universal brotherhood of man," not the universal motherhood of God and the sisterhood of humankind. The cultural and social limitations of the concept of "universal" in European Protestant liberal traditions of the time and its counterparts in contemporaneous liberal Judaism in the same societies and cultures are well-known and need not be discussed here. Note also the particular importance of the related ideological construction of the opposition of "universal" vs "particular" that played a very substantial role in the social and ideological shaping of taxonomies and hierarchies of religions in European discourses of the time. On these issues, see Tomoko Masuzawa, *The Invention of World Religions* (Chicago: University of Chicago Press, 2005).

and politically weaker. Moreover, the reference to a shared creator reinforced the previous motif by suggesting that this "brotherhood" is rooted in divine action and thus implying that denying it is tantamount to resistance to a divine order.

To be sure, this "brotherhood" was not necessarily meant to completely erase boundaries between the groups, but to create a shared past constructed and characterized by shared images and memories of a paternal deity that apply to all. In sum, the questions were meant to recall (and construe) the existence of this shared realm so as to elicit a sense of shared identity and fraternity that in itself would make discrimination and oppression of the marginal group untenable.

Instances of this type of reading and use of these rhetorical questions or their implied logic are well attested. A few examples suffice: It was used by the suffragist movement,[1] by the anti-slavery movement,[2] and of course, it was used also in antiquity, as b. Ta'anit 18a clearly shows.

To be sure, these questions were not used necessarily or solely for instrumental purposes by relatively disempowered groups. These questions served to express the deep theological values of particular groups too. For instance, they became a relatively common site of memory to be recalled and activated within theological discourses that stressed a "universal fraternity."[3] Again, a few examples suffice to make the point. Philipp Jakob Spener (1635–1705) wrote, "therefore [our] neighbors are all human beings, every single one without exception and therefore those who are our brothers according to creation and in that sense have the same God as father as we do according to Malachi 2:10."[4] Later, in the 19th century, it is not

---

[1] Crew, *Suffragist Sheet Music*, 48–49.
[2] See, e.g., the image "Have We All Not One Father?" available from The New York Public Library Digital Collections at http://digitalcollections.nypl.org/items/510d47df-bb3b-a3d9-e040-e00a18064a99, which was published by the American Anti-Slavery Society in 1843.
[3] To be sure, "universal fraternity" in the way and within the constraints in which it was understood in the relevant, historically contingent communities.
[4] See Philipp Jakob Spener, *Christliche Verpflegung der Armen* (Hartmann: Frankfurt an der Oder, 1697), 20; available at http://digitale.bibliothek.uni-halle.de/vd17/content/ pageview/612471. The cited English translation is from Jens Zimmermann, *Recovering Theological Hermeneutics: An Incarnational-Trinitarian Theory of Interpretation* (Grand Rapids: Baker Academic, 2004), 121.

surprising that Unitarians[1] and liberal Reform rabbis (e.g., Isaac M. Wise)[2] tended to refer to this verse and that others who advanced similar positions referred to its implied narrative, even if they did not mention the verse.[3] This type of readings and use of Mal 2:10a

---

[1] See, e.g., "Sermon X," on Mal 2:10 in *Sermons by Rev. John Budd Pitkin, with a Memoir by Stephen Greenleaf Bulfinch* (Boston: David Reid, 1837), 223–45, available at https://books.google.ca/books/about/Sermons.html?id=dv-7B_DhMqgC&redir_esc=y.

[2] E.g., "…we rejoice and glorify in the great idea, that, however slowly, the time is nevertheless approaching, when all mankind is striving to verify the words of the last prophet 'Have we not all got one father, has not one God created us all, why should we become faithless one to another do defile the covenant of our forefathers?'" *The Israelite* 2.15 (Oct 19, 1855): 116; available at http://www.americanjewisharchives.org/collections/ wise/attachment/2798/TIS-1855-10-19-001.pdf. *The Israelite* was Wise's highly influential newspaper. Compare also, "Go into any enlightened society, and in general you will find the spirit ruling there to be a liberal one, a disposition of tolerance and reconciliation among the different sects, so that you must think 'At least they will forbear considering a man rejected by God, and contesting his claims to heaven, on account of his creed; at last our broad principle that the pious Gentiles will have their share in a future world, is gaining ground among these self-same gentiles! Have we not all one father, hath not one God created us? why should we become faithless one to another do defile the covenant of our forefathers?" *The Israelite* 16.44 (May 6, 1870): 9; available at http://www.americanjewisharchives.org/collections/wise/attachment/ 3568/TIS-1870-05-06-001.pdf. It is worth noting that Wise hoped that non-Jews would eventually reshape their religion into something that resembles his Judaism — for example, the first citation above continues with "Our motto is: Religion is a blessing of mankind; religions are the misfortune of the human race." The cited text ("Go into any enlightened society…") from May 6, 1870, proves that Wise's universalism converged with resistance to some underlying anti-Jewish/Judaism themes. The point is explicit in another text where Mal 2:10 is openly recalled, this time to fight claims of parochialism and discrimination raised against Judaism or Jews; see "Review of a portion of Professor Tayler Lewis D.D.'s 'Patriarchal and Jewish Servitude,'" *The Israelite* 7.48 (May 31, 1861): 380–381; available at http://collections.americanjewisharchives.org/wise/attachment/ 3094/TIS-1861-05-3101.pdf. For an example of the use of rhetorical questions of Mal 2:10 in the early 20th century, see the sermon by J. Leonard Levy, "A Time for War, and a Time for Peace," given in Pittsburgh on April 8, 1917, included in Marc Saperstein, *Jewish Preaching in Times of War 1800–2001* (Oxford: Littman Library of Jewish Civilization, 2008), 324–45, here 338. The date is particularly worth noting, since on April 6, 1917 the US Congress declared war on Germany.

[3] For example, Samuel David Luzzatto (a well-known Italian Orthodox rabbi, philosopher, and author, 1800–1865) wrote: "La misericordia dal Giudaismo raccomandata e universale. Si estende, come quella di Dio, a tutte le sue creature. Nessuna razza e fuori della Legge, poichè gli uomini tutti, secondo ch'il Giudaismo insegna, sono fratelli, sono figli d'uno stesso padre, e sono creati ad immagine di Dio" (S. D. Luzzatto, *Il giudaismo illustrato nella sua teorica, nella sua storia e nella sua letteratura* [Padua: Antonio Bianchi, 1848], 1:11). It is worth noting that this text was eventually "reshaped" by a twentieth century translator so as to make it state that all Jews (rather than all human beings) are brothers and children of one father, created in the image of the deity. See Marc Gopin, "An Orthodox Embrace of Gentiles? Interfaith Tolerance in the Thought of S. D. Luzzatto and E. Benamozegh," *MJ* 18 (1998): 173–95, esp. 175–77). On the general issue of "reshaping" of texts that carried authority in Orthodox Judaism,

continues during the entire 20th century and up to the present within relevant Christian, Jewish, or public discourses informed by Christian or Jewish traditions.[1]

This said, readings of Mal 2:10a as a text that evoke the mentioned implied narrative and the accompanying lesson to learn from it depend completely on one key process of identification. In fact, the pragmatic meaning of "Have We Not All One Father? Has Not One God Created Us?" can vary drastically depending on what is construed as "we" and "us."

The "we" may refer to "humanity" in general, as in the cases discussed above, but also to one particular group distinct from others. When the latter is the case, the rhetorical questions are tantamount to a call for in-group solidarity rooted in their shared origins and identity and dependent on a deity construed as legitimizing these.

In addition, the very same person may in one context recall Mal 2:10a in one sense and in a difference context in another. Thus, for instance, the already mentioned Rabbi Isaac Wise, who often read these questions as referring to an in-group that consists of all humanity, could on one occasion read them in reference to German and Polish Jews in Chicago of his days who split into two independent congregations, one of about 90 individuals and the other of about 50, and whom he preferred to be members of one single congregation. In this case, "we" means not "humanity in general," but "American (not German or Polish) Jews."[2]

But, of course, Mal 2:10a was often read and remembered not as a separate set of questions and an implied narrative, but as an

---

see Marc B. Shapiro, *Changing the Immutable: How Orthodox Judaism Rewrites Its History* (Oxford: Littman Library of Jewish Civilization, 2015), which also briefly discusses Mal 2:10, within a larger context. In any event, the change from "all human beings" to "the Jews" is worth noting in the context of the present study as it will become evident below.

[1] See, e.g., Sylvan D. Schwartzman and Jack D. Spiro, *The Living Bible* (New York: Union of American Hebrew Congregations, 1962), 39, 138, 267; Dov Peretz Elkins and Abigail Treu, *The Bible's Top 50 Ideas: The Essential Concepts Everyone Should Know* (New York: SPI, 2005), 38; also, see public speeches, such as those reported by the US Department of State at http://www.state.gov/secretary/remarks/2015/02/237715.htm; and by Rabbi Norman Patz at http://www.sholom.net/2016/01/a-historic-act-of-reconciliation-nostra-aetate-at-the-cathedral-of-old-san-juan/.

[2] Editorial Correspondence, letter 4, *The Israelite* 3.5 (August 8, 1856): 37; available at http://collections.americanjewisharchives.org/wise/attachment/2840/TIS-1856-08-08-01.pdf.

integral part of Mal 2:10-16 that draws its meaning from the larger unit. When the text was read in this manner, a very strongly attested tendency emerges across time and space, namely to understand "we" not in terms of humanity as a whole but as referring to Judah (/Israel), their priests, and among many Christian readers through time and space, the Church, which from their perspective stood for Israel.

Within these readings the two rhetorical questions did not imply a call for "inclusion" of an out-group/the Other into a comprehensive in-group, but to the contrary the exclusion and at times even the actual expulsion of an out-group from a perceived in-group. In these cases, whether the particular reading identified the father with Abraham (e.g., Calvin and Jerome), Jacob (e.g., Ibn Ezra and Radak) or YHWH (e.g., Athanasius and Irenaeus) becomes less relevant,[1] because the key issue was that the child was identified as Judah/Israel or the Church. Within the context of the unit as grasped by these readers, this identification led them to understand the two rhetorical questions as a key and integral part of what they perceived to be a formidable argument against marrying outside Israel/the Church and against men divorcing in-group wives while at the same time urging them to send away out-group wives.[2]

In sum, through time, Mal 2:10a was read, understood, and used to evoke very dissimilar attitudes and messages, depending on the context within which the text was read and the worldview and main meta-narratives of its readers. Communities of readers could and did approach Mal 2:10a as an excellent representative of both flexible and rigid social mindscapes depending on the case. Mal 2:10a could and did serve as a site of memory, backing those who wished to maintain social boundaries as impermeable as possible and thus

---

[1] To be sure, less relevant for the main issues discussed in this contribution. The question certainly has importance. See, e.g., John Calvin, *Commentaries on the Twelve Minor Prophets* [repr.; tr. John Owen; Grand Rapids: Baker Academic, 1989], 5:540-41.

[2] See, e.g., St. Cyril of Alexandria, *Commentary on the Twelve Prophets* (tr. Robert C. Hill; Washington, DC: Catholic University of America Press, 2012), 3:312-313 and Jerome on Mal 2:11, who uses the opportunity to teach "how utterly unlawful it is for a Christian woman to marry a Gentile..." (*Jov.* 1.10). See also Ibn Ezra and Radak on Mal 2:10.

support purges of "outsiders," but also for those who conceive these boundaries as porous and shifting.[1]

Which was the situation in ancient Yehud, among its literati? How did they likely read this text? To address these matters, a few observations on Mal 2:10-16 within the context of the intellectual world of the relevant literati are necessary, because, as mentioned above, their readings of Mal 2:10a were likely influenced by their reading of Mal 2:10-16.

A Few Observations on Mal 2:10-16

There is no lack of historical studies on Mal 2:10-16 (or Mal 2:10-12 and Mal 2:13-16).[2] The focus of much attention in this research

---

[1] See, e.g., Eviatar Zerubavel, *The Fine Line: Making Distinctions in Everyday Life* (Chicago: Chicago University Press, 1991).

[2] See, e.g., Stefan Schreiner, "Mischehen – Ehebruch – Ehescheidung: Betrachtungen zu Mal 2:10-16," *ZAW* 91 (1979): 207-28; Wilhelm Rudolph, "Zu Mal 2:10-16," *ZAW* 93 (1981): 85-90; Adam S. van der Woude, "Malachi's Struggle for a Pure Community: Reflections on Malachi 2:10-16," *Tradition and Re-interpretation in Jewish and Early Christian Literature* (eds. J. W. van Henten et al.; Leiden: Brill, 1986), 65-71; Beth Glazier McDonald, "Intermarriage, Divorce, and *bat-'ēl nēkār*: Insights into Mal 2:10-16," *JBL* 106 (1987): 603-11; Beth Glazier McDonald, *Malachi: The Divine Messenger* (SBLDS 98; Atlanta: Scholars Press, 1987), 81-120; Julia M. O'Brien, *Priest and Levite in Malachi* (SBLDS 121; Atlanta: Scholars Press, 1990), 66-73; Julia M. O'Brien, "Judah as Wife and Husband: Deconstructing Gender in Malachi," *JBL* 115 (1996): 241-50; David Clyde Jones, "A Note on the LXX of Malachi 2:16," *JBL* 109 (1990): 683-85; Russell Earl Fuller, "Text-Critical problems in Malachi 2:10-16," *JBL* 110 (1991): 47-57; Gordon P. Hugenberger, *Marriage as a Covenant: Biblical Law and Ethics as Developed from Malachi* (VTSup 52; Leiden: Brill, 1994), 85-94; Martin A. Shields, "Syncretism and Divorce in Malachi 2,10-16," *ZAW* 111 (1999): 68-86; Karl William Weyde, *Prophecy and Teaching: Prophetic Authority, Form Problems and the Use of Traditions in the Book of Malachi* (BZAW 288; Berlin: de Gruyter, 2000), 215-79; Markus Zehnder, "A Fresh Look at Malachi ii 13-16," *VT* 53 (2003): 224-59; Elie Assis, "Love, Hate and Self-Identity in Malachi: A New Perspective to Mal 1:1-5 and 2:10-16," *JNSL* 35 (2009): 109-20; Michael R. Fox, *A Message from the Great King: Reading Malachi in Light of Ancient Persian Royal Messenger Texts From the Time of Xerxes* (Siphrut 17; Winona Lake, IN: Eisenbrauns; 2015), 91-98, 124-25; and works cited in these publications. See also, e.g., Karl Marti, *Das Dodekapropheton* (KHC; Tübingen: Mohr [Siebeck], 1904), 457, 468-72; S. R. Driver, *The Minor Prophets: Nahum, Habakkuk, Zephaniah, Haggai, Zechariah, Malachi* (CB; New York: Henry Frowde, 1906), 312-17; Wilhelm Rudolph, *Haggai, Sacharja 1-8, Sacharja 9-14, Maleachi* (KAT 13/4; Gütersloh: Gütersloher Verlagshaus Mohn, 1976); Rex Mason, *The Books of Haggai, Zechariah and Malachi* (Cambridge: Cambridge University Press, 1977), 148-51; David L. Petersen, *Zechariah 9-14 and Malachi: A Commentary* (OTL; Louisville: Westminster John Knox, 1995), 193-206; Pieter A. Verhoef, *The Books of Haggai and Malachi* (NICOT; Grand Rapids: Eerdmans, 1987), 262-81; Andrew E. Hill, *Malachi* (2nd ed.; AB 26; New Haven: Yale University Press, 2008), 221-59; Marvin A. Sweeney, *The Twelve Prophets* (BOSHNP; Collegeville, MN: Liturgical Press, 2000), 2: 731-39; James D. Nogalski, *The Book of the*

has been the question of whether the text refers to matters of actual intermarriages—which were construed as improper by the community of readers and their implied author—and the impact of these marriages on the family, including divorces of previous wives (the so-called literal approach), or whether it is about worship construed as improper by the community of readers and their implied author, and thus cultic impurity (the so-called figurative approach), or both at the same time, or one more in one of these two (sub-)units and the other in the second. The reference to divorce in Mal 2:16 and its multiple textual versions have also drawn much scholarly attention. Some expressions in the pericope, besides the famous MT כִּי־שָׂנֵא שַׁלַּח in v. 16, (e.g., אֲשֶׁר אָהֵב in v. 11; עֵר וְעֹנֶה in v. 12; הָאֶחָד in v. 15) have also drawn substantial scholarly discussion.[1]

Although there is no doubt that readings of particular units in a text that were understood as at least potentially carrying a clear "global, semantic content," as is the case with Mal 2:10a, may be and were read as texts independent of their co-texts in their respective books (see, e.g., the case of Jonah 1–2; Jonah 1–3 and then also Jonah 1–4),[2] there are plenty of textually inscribed markers that suggest that the target readership of the book of Malachi in the late Persian period was asked to read Mal 2:10 as opening a literary unit, namely Mal 2:10–12, which in itself was likely read, though neither solely nor exclusively,[3] as a subunit of what I would call a prophetic reading (i.e., a reading about a prophet of old), namely Mal 2:10–16 that was meant to shape and evoke memories of such a prophet and of a particular instance of

---

Twelve, Micah-Malachi (Macon, GA: Smyth & Helwys, 2011), 1033-45; and the works cited in these commentaries.

[1] For the sake of space—this contribution has already been much longer than the originally allocated space—references to works supporting the various positions mentioned in this section are omitted. Readers may consult Hugenberger, *Marriage as a Covenant*; Shields, "Syncretism and Divorce;" and Weyde, *Prophecy and Teaching* for helpful summaries.

[2] See p. 275, n2.

[3] In addition to reading Mal 2:10–12 and Mal 2:13–16 as part of a higher-level unit (i.e., Mal 2:10–16), Mal 2:10–12 could be read in its own terms. The same holds true for Mal 2:13–16 (e.g., the former as a text dealing with improper marriages/idolatry and the latter with divorce). Probably all these readings informed each other, but these issues stand beyond the scope of this essay.

YHWH's word associated with this character, along with the other prophetic readings in the book.[1]

When Mal 2:10–12 was read in a way strongly informed by Mal 2:13–16,[2] as the readers are suggested to do by opening words of Mal 2:13–16, namely וְזֹאת שֵׁנִית תַּעֲשׂוּ "this second matter you also do,"[3] it is safe to assume that the text here could not but evoke the conceptual realm of human marriages and marital behavior construed to be unacceptable by YHWH and the images associated with that realm.

Within the context of the world of ideas and knowledge of the late Persian period, the activation of that realm served, *inter alia*, to socialize the readership of the text against such social practices. The text of Mal 2:11 is particularly significant in this respect, because when the text was read in this way, it explicitly construed and drew attention to the identity of a socially improper female partner of Judah, i.e., male Yehudites.

In addition, the choice of the term בַּת־אֵל נֵכָר to refer to these women conveyed an important taxonomic principle: it organized human beings in terms of "boxes" construed around their kinship with a deity.[4] This is consistent with an ideological discourse in which male Israelites/Yehudites were construed as adopted sons of YHWH and female Israelites as the deity's (adopted) daughters.[5] The choice is also

---

[1] The present form of Mal 2:10–16 may well represent the outcome of a substantial redactional history. Moreover, the link between Mal 2:10–12 and Mal 2:13–16 may well have been the result of redactional processes, which may have influenced the texts of both subunits. The present essay deals, however, with the present form of Mal 2:10–16, because the goal of this contribution is to explore the readings of these two rhetorical questions within a late Persian community that read and reread the book of Malachi, as already the description of them as Mal 2:10a suggests. For debates on the potential redactional history of Mal 2:10–16 see, e.g., van der Woude, "Malachi's Struggle;" Hugenberger, *Marriage as Covenant*, 85–94; and the works cited there.

[2] Fox, *Message from the Great King*, stands in the clear minority when he proposes that the unit is 2:10–17.

[3] Whether this is or is not a later addition is irrelevant to the discussion here; see above.

[4] Compare and contrast with בְּנֵי אֵל־חָי in Hos 2:1; see also Num 21:29, and its reference to the sons and daughters of Chemosh.

[5] E.g., Exod 4:23; Deut 32:5; Hos 2:1; 11:1; Isa 43:6 (note the explicit reference to the daughters); 45:11; 63:8. It is worth noting that references to Israel as the first-born (Exod 4:22; cf. Jer 31:9) are suggestive of constructions of other nations as "sons" of YHWH; but if the latter are not acknowledging and behaving as proper subordinates to their "father," YHWH, such a construction would lead to imagining them as rebellious against the deity (cf. Isa 30:1)

consistent with the continuous activation of the conceptual realm of family relationships in this pericope, including explicit references to roles and identities—such as father, wife, children—and familial issues, such as marriage, conjugal betrayal, and divorce.

But, of course, the fact that the activation and selection of this classification principle fit well and contributed to shaping and communicating a sense of textual and conceptual realm coherence to this prophetic reading does not mean that such a choice did not carry additional important meanings to the community. Quite the contrary, often a conveyed sense of "coherence" evoked by the text serves more effectively to communicate directly or indirectly ideological messages.

In the case of Mal 2:10–16, one may mention that the said classification and its emphasis on the adopted (divine) father rather than a human one and his "seed" construed and conveyed a principle of organization that is not essentially rooted in (human) genealogical descent, but in loyalty to a divine father. In practical terms, this choice allowed for the inclusion of women like, for instance, Ruth and Rahab among YHWH's daughters, in contrast to the paradigm of זרע הקדש (see Ezra 9:2) advanced in much of the text of Ezra, but not elsewhere.[1]

In any event, characterizing a woman as בַּת־אֵל נֵכָר within the context of Mal 2:10–16 meant characterizing her as belonging to a taxonomic category inadmissible for pairing with proper Judahite/Israelite/Yehudite men and thus meant portraying such pairings in terms of forbidden mixtures, which within this discourse (a) cannot but be a clear case of disloyalty to the hierarchically superordinate, divine father, YHWH, (b) are explicitly construed as an abomination (see Mal 2:11; cf., for instance, Deut 13:15), (c) are conceived as incapable of resulting in proper sons of YHWH/Elohim (see Mal 2:15),[2] and given the *Sitz im Diskurs* of the text and the fact that reading Mal 2:11–12 evoked the language of Lev 18:29 and Lev 19:8, a

---

[1] I discussed this issue elsewhere: see Ehud Ben Zvi, "Re-negotiating a Putative Utopia and the Stories of the Rejection of the Foreign Wives in Ezra-Nehemiah," *Worlds that Could Not Be: Utopia in Chronicles, Ezra and Nehemiah* (eds. Steven J. Schweitzer and Frauke Uhlenbruch; LHBOTS 620; London: Bloomsbury T & T Clark), 105–28 and cited bibliography.

[2] Cf. the case of the offspring of two taxonomically different groups (e.g., Gen 6:2–4).

statement concerning a punishment linked to the conceptual realm of being "cut off" from the community was expected (and see Mal 2:12).

One may argue that this language and the punishment might have evoked the possibility of an allusion to a different realm of marital infidelity, that between YHWH and Israel. But a far stronger argument is that the literati had no choice but to construe a sophisticated implied author who, in a seemingly "unexpected" way, decided to refer to and thus construe Judah as a feminine character (see בָּגְדָה in Mal 2:11) within a unit in which what might have been understood to be the "sole" narrative is about Judah as husband who is faithless to his wife of his youth, who marries the "daughter of a foreign god," and who is able to send away his wife.

In other words, the literati encountered here a clear textually inscribed marker (left by their implied author) that drew their attention away from any sense of security that there was only one narrative at work. In fact, such a marker served as call to notice (and therefore to "construe") a secondary narrative informing the first. The basic contours of this secondary narrative became easy to notice because the reference to Judah as a disloyal wife (2:11) could not but evoke the common motif of Judah as YHWH's disloyal wife within the discourse of the community. Further, the concentration of terms of marriage, disloyalty to YHWH, love, hate and divorce created between them an atmosphere conducive to reading the text in a way informed by this common motif. Of course, the moment that such a reading is advanced, other potential markers emerge: for instance, a potential hint at interplay between Mal 2:10–16 and Jer 3:8 in particular may be noticed.[1]

It is markedly significant in this regard that when the text was read in such a way, in which these two readings inform each other, not only Judah is both a male and a husband in relation to his women and a wife in relation to YHWH — which is the typical case of using gender

---

[1] In addition to the reference to the disloyalty of Judah (בגד), one may note the reference to divorce/sending away (שלח) and the pun created by two different words of the root כרת, which both communicate punishment and at least raise the question of how comparable are indeed the outcomes of these punishments, or to put in another way, that of the extent to which substantial semantic difference communicates comparable pragmatic meanings in this case.

as a proxy for hierarchy — but matters of rejection and divorce begin to play in more than way.

For instance, given a choice of two (hierarchically) inferior women, Judah is supposed to reject/hate and send away the "non-Israelite," just as YHWH rejected and sent away Esau and demonstrated his love for Jacob (the Israelite) by doing so (cf. Mal 1:2-3), except that the non-Israelite in Mal 2:10-16 is construed as the daughter of a foreign god and the Israelite as YHWH's son, which in turn draws attention to the additional signpost in Mal 1:6 (בֵּן יְכַבֵּד אָב) and its connection with 2:10, and to what all these connections may convey in terms of a potential reading in Mal 2:10a.[1]

But there is more: when the text is read in this mutually informing way, the motif of divorce, as a potential outcome, emerges as far more complex, because the matter is not only about Judah's potential divorce from "the wife of his youth," but also of YHWH's divorce from the wife of his youth (i.e., Israel). Reading the text in this way meant pondering about the meaning(s) conveyed by the interplay of identities concerning husbands and wives, both godly and ungodly, and concerning the godly seed (2:15) which, at least in one of several possible readings of this verse, is what YHWH wants as outcome of the union of Judah and the wife that YHWH explicitly made (2:15 in one of its possible meanings; see below).

This web of interlinked meanings of the text, all well supported by textually inscribed markers and references to common concepts well-known to the literati, is made even more complex by a significant textual choice at the beginning of v. 16 and its implications for the literati's construction of their implied author. The literati must have been aware that an author could have opened this crucial verse about "divorce" with a clear and univocal textual choice but the choice made left them with multiple options.

---

[1] Incidentally, this may raise the question of who was considered to be the daughter of a foreign god. If there is any level of background historicity, it is possible that they included or consisted mainly of the "sisters" of the daughters of Jerusalem and Judah, namely, Samarian women. Although the book of Malachi does not contain anything explicitly against the Samarians, the repeated emphasis on the temple in Jerusalem, proper offering to it, and the centrality of this temple for Jacob/Israel indicate that it falls well within a larger discourse in which the Samarians are often an or "the" implied "other."

The text may be read as a statement that (a) YHWH hates divorce (of proper wives, of course; the "foreigner" is implicitly, but clearly to be sent away), or (b) YHWH does not "hate" divorce, but censures men divorcing their wives on the grounds that they "hate" or possibly "dislike" them, or (c) YHWH explicitly allows divorce on these grounds and may or may not (again more than one reading is possible) censure them. It is particularly worth stressing that precisely a text in which a main narrative seems to suggest a very negative attitude towards a man who divorces his unloved wife includes one ending in which this is at the very least permissible.

This is not the place to address in detail these issues, nor several other instances of multiple potential readings within Mal 2:10–16, such as that v. 15 may be read as opening in the following ways: (a) "Did not the one God (i.e., YHWH) make her? Both flesh and spirit are his" (NRSV), or "Did not the One (i.e., YHWH) make all, so that all remaining life-breath is his?" (NJPSV); (b) "Did YHWH not make them one, with flesh and spirit?" (NAB); or even (c) "No one who has even a small portion of the spirit in him does this" (NET); or that the implied author was likely construed as playing with connoted double meanings, because of his chosen sound sequence at the conclusion of v. 11, namely אֲשֶׁר אָהֵב וּבָעַל בַּת־אֵל נֵכָר.

These considerations, however, suffice to the set the proper stage for addressing the social roles of reading these two questions within the context of Mal 2:10–16 by the late Persian period and within the discourse of the literati of the time. Phrases, sentences, and expressions carrying multiple levels of meanings, interwoven in complex ways are not a rare exception but a trait of Mal 2:10–16.

This trait, in turn, contributed much to the characterization of the implied author of the text by its readers and the shaping of their expectations from the text as readers. It also indicates the existence of an underlying, implied generative grammar governing the production and acceptance of texts in the community that allowed or even facilitated the production of texts such as Mal 2:10–16.[1]

---

[1] It is worth stressing that either univocal or far more univocal "versions" of the text were technically possible and easy to produce—the literati knew their Hebrew well. The fact that the text that emerged is so polyvocal represents the outcome of a social/communal process of selection and choice.

As for the social role of reading texts such as Mal 2:10-16, besides the obvious cognitive price to understanding them and the corresponding cultural capital that doing so generated among the literati, one should consider that they provided a kind of playground for exploring interrelations among multiple images and concepts that existed within the community, which could now be addressed through multiple, mutually informing potential readings of a single "text," which in its "singleness" embodied a sense of balancing complementarity, of a "whole" that is "whole" because it includes (existing) diversity, complementary tensions, and fuzziness.[1] Against this background, it is easier to address the potential meanings of Mal 2:10a.

Readings of Malachi 2:10a in Yehud

When the literati read Mal 20:10a and understood and voiced these words as spoken by the godly prophetic character, then the reference to Judah, Israel, and Jerusalem in v. 11 most likely led them to associate the "we" in v. 10 with a Judah that is conceptually identified as the Jerusalem-centered Israel that is so characteristic of the literati discourse of the Persian and early Hellenistic periods and so ubiquitous in their authoritative repertoire. This concept of Israel stands at the core of the ideological self-understanding of these literati, their construction of their past (see the Deuteronomistic historical collection as well as Chronicles) and future (see Jerusalem-centered utopian texts in prophetic literature), and may be understood, to some extent, in terms of literature and ideology of resistance *vis à vis* the more powerful Samaria and their claims about Israel. Significantly, within this general understanding of the "we" of v. 10, several possible identifications for the figure of the father in v. 10a are possible:

(a) YHWH as father of Israel—as suggested by the clear connections between this text and Deut 32:6, the characterization of the counterpart "Other" as "the daughter of a foreign god" this reading was consistent with the common characterization of YHWH as father

---

[1] Of course, this text is not alone in this respect. I discussed multiple other examples in various works. See, e.g., Ehud Ben Zvi, "Exploring the Memory of Moses 'The Prophet' in Late Persian/Early Hellenistic Yehud/Judah," *Remembering Biblical*

of Israel in the ideological discourse and written repertoire of the literati and their main metanarratives (see, e.g., Exod 4:22; Deut 32:18; Isa 63:16; 64:7; cf. Jer 31:9; Hos 11:1).[1]

(b) One of the "human" forefathers of Israel, in which case the reference to "father" in v. 10 evoked the memory of either Jacob or Abraham,[2] but far more likely, by refraining to mention either name explicitly—and thus implicitly communicating that knowledge about who precisely was the forefather mentioned was not so worthwhile from the perspective of the implied author and the intended readership—the verse shaped a conceptual realm that overlapped and thus linked the two characters, again in a way consistent with the general discourse of the period[3] and with the reference to בְּרִית אֲבֹתֵינוּ in v. 10.

(c) To a point, when Mal 2:10 was read as a kind of Janus text, thus informing and informed not only by the following text, but also the preceding text, the literati might have evoked the figure of Aaron, the father of the priests.

Each of these potential identities of the "father" of Mal 2:10a carries its own set of connotations and reading associations. For instance, thinking of YHWH as the father in v. 10 shaped a reading well interwoven with other prophetic readings in the book of Malachi (see 1:6), and drawing attention to the "adopted" character of Israel. This reading highlights obedience to the divine father as a primary duty of proper behavior, even if it does not reject the role of solidarity among the "brothers and sisters." In other words, it would stress the vertical rather than the horizontal axis.

Figures in the Late Persian and Early Hellenistic Periods: Social Memory and Imagination (eds. Diana V. Edelman and Ehud Ben Zvi; Oxford: Oxford University Press, 2013), 335–64.

[1] E.g., van der Woude, "Malachi's Struggle," and Verhoef, *The Books of Haggai and Malachi*, 265.

[2] Given that when the literati read Mal 2:10, they were informed by their knowledge of the book of Malachi, one may assume that the memory of Jacob was likely activated when they read Mal 2:10a (see explicit references to Jacob in Mal 1:2; 2:12; 3:6). At the same time, given that they were informed by the general discourse and memory world of the literati (see, e.g., Isa 51:2; 2 Chr 20:7), the memory of Abraham was also likely activated (cf. also Mic 7:20, which brings together and intertwines memories of both). Memories of Isaac enjoyed far smaller mindshare among the literati who were socialized by and socialized themselves by reading this corpus of authoritative texts.

[3] Cf. the conceptual messages connoted (in a different way) by, e.g., Isa 41:8; Ps 105:6.

Thinking of Jacob or Abraham as the father in v. 10 shaped a reading that was well interwoven with other prophetic readings in the book of Malachi. As it did so, it stressed the issue of the covenant with the ancestors and the rejection of brother Esau when the reference was to Jacob, and connoted a strong lionization of the male ancestor by associating him with the structural slot of being associated with YHWH in the second half of Mal 2:10a. Needless to say, this reading or set of readings was consistent with the discourse and textual repertoire of the literati and their main metanarratives.

When the figure of Aaron and priesthood was evoked, then the text recalled, informed, and was informed by all the other references to the priests in Malachi and by the general discourse about the more stringent marriage regulations that apply to Aaron and his sons.[1]

In all the preceding cases, the text was read as shaping strong boundaries between the sons and daughters of YHWH (namely Israel, i.e., the Jerusalem-centered Israel of the literati's discourse) and the daughters and sons of other deities (those who are not part of that Israel) and as leading to demands for a purge of "outsiders" from the inner group (see Mal 2:1-16).

There was, however, another set of possible readings. The rhetorical questions of 2:10a could as easily be read as spoken by the godly prophetic character as by the "sinful" Judahites.[2] The preceding readings all emerged out of the first option, but what about the readings that emerged from the second option, namely, that the speakers are "sinful" Judahites or perhaps even the priests of the putative time of the personages of memory evoked through the reading of the book?

Read from this second perspective, the "we" of *"Have we not one Father? Did not one God create us?"* would most likely point to humanity in general and serve the purpose of providing an ideological explanation for the behavior of the speakers. Within this reading, the

---

[1] It is worth noting that in Chronicles, which is the prime example of a book shaping and encoding multiple examples of successful "intermarriages" and (often) the divine blessing that followed, there are no such examples for priests. If this is true of Chronicles, then could it not also be the case elsewhere?

[2] E.g., Sweeney, *Twelve Prophets*, 735; Mordechai Zer-Kavod, "ספר מלאכי," תרי עשר (Da'at Mikra; Jerusalem: Mossad Harav Kook, 1970), 2:9; and Assis, "Love, Hate and Self-Identity."

turning point in the text is thus encapsulated in the sharp, memorable contrast between the words of these supposed "sinners," who say מַדּוּעַ נִבְגָּד, and the prophetic voice immediately responding בָּגְדָה יְהוּדָה (that is, between their "why would/how can we be 'faithless'" and the prophetic thundering voice: "Judah is faithless").

The attention drawn to the exchange reinforces the point that the supposed sinners do not think that they are, and of course, that the prophetic character is not one of them. Moreover, when the words of the sinner were read in a way informed by the preceding text and thus with at least in one potential reading as set in the mouth of priests, the prophet's response, בָּגְדָה יְהוּדָה, clearly expands the matter. It is not only that the priests have acted faithlessly by marrying those who from the perspective of the prophet were "outsiders," but also Judah. Within this reading, the texts stresses that there is no (substantial?) difference between the priests and the rest of the Judahites (/Jerusalem centered Israel).[1]

The "one father" within this reading recalls the memory of "Adam" and this being the case, this reading and that particular reading of v. 15 that evokes the memory of Adam and Eve (וְלֹא־אֶחָד עָשָׂה; "Did not YHWH make them one, with flesh and spirit") mutually recalled and supported each other. This self-reinforcing set of readings in turn supported and was supported by the readings of v. 16 that communicated YHWH's position against divorce of the proper couple, which is in fact, one of a possible set of readings of that verse.

But the "one father" of this reading does not have to be "Adam." In fact, the text, when read in such a way, makes as much or even more rhetorical sense when the memory of the father that is activated is that of YHWH. When the text was read in such a way, the readers bring the two rhetorical questions closer to each other — which most likely they would have seen as a marker in support of this reading — but also, and more importantly, bring up mnemonic narratives and images of creation from Genesis, and along with them

---

[1] As is well-known, discursive tendencies supporting some form of priestization (and holiness) for all Israel, not just the priests, are well attested in the early and late Second Temple period. This contribution, however, is not the place to expand on this matter.

the entire ideological worldview shaped, reflected, and communicated by the creation stories in Genesis.

Of course, whether the father in this reading is YHWH or Adam, still Mal 2:10-16 would be read as shaping strong boundaries between those who follow YHWH and those who do not; all may be sons of Adam/YHWH and all may have been created by the same deity, but this does not make them all members of the same "in-group;" the "daughter of a foreign god" may still be YHWH's daughter, but since she does not acknowledge him as father, she cannot intermarry with Israel. Within this reading, the demand for a purge of "outsiders" from the inner group remains.

This said, it is easy to notice that the basic claim of the text in Mal 2:10a is never denied and that it stands very well within a ubiquitous discourse about creation that pervaded the world of the literati. All humans were always construed as descending from one father, and all were always imagined as part of creation, and all creation was associated with the creative power of YHWH.

Moreover, the very unity of humankind was commonly understood as carrying at the very least the potential of universal worship of YHWH at some point in the future, and numerous memories of "foreigners" who acknowledged YHWH and were or became Yahwistic were part and parcel of the world of knowledge of the literati, just as the opposite—Israelites who rejected YHWH.[1] In other words, at the very least, this reading of the text carries also a sense of inclusiveness rooted in YHWH and creation. In other words, the basic global, semantic content of these two rhetorical questions is clearly characterized by inclusivity, even if the rest of the prophetic reading limits its practical application.

Finally, within a prophetic reading, when the text is approached in a certain way, there is a concluding statement supporting the man's option (and right) to divorce his proper wife—a stance that fits well with commonly held positions among the literati, cf. Deut 24:1-4—but which stands at the conclusion of a text that seems

---

[1] Cf. Ehud Ben Zvi, "Othering, Selfing, 'Boundarying' and 'Cross-Boundarying' as Interwoven with Socially Shared Memories: Some Observations," *Imagining the Other and Constructing Israelite Identity in the Early Second Temple Period* (eds. Diana Edelman and Ehud Ben Zvi; LHBOTS 456; London: Bloomsbury T & T Clark, 2014), 20–40.

so opposed to that; within a world in which the literati construe their implied author as one who cherishes multiple meanings and this type of "tensions," it would not be surprising at all for these literati to note (and remember) that the opening of the text, when read in a certain way, communicated a sense of basic inclusivity that was widely acknowledged, even if most of the text communicated a sense of boundaries and in-group.

I would argue that it is precisely this balancing act that not only qualifies but also substantially facilitates the existence of texts that seemingly reflect and communicate what may be referred to as a "rigid" social mindscape among the literati who time and again show themselves as manifesting a strongly non-rigid social mindscape,[1] as demonstrated clearly in our case by their multilevel and multiple-interwoven sets of readings of one relatively short text, at various places in the text, and by their most likely construction of an implied author who actually wrote in such way when simpler, less polyvocal alternatives were available to him. Moreover, the very fact that such a text emerged is indicative of workings of an implied generative grammar governing the production and acceptance of texts in the community, including a preference for texts that demanded highly sophisticated tasks of interpretation.[2]

A final observation: the preceding discussion has shown also the presence of significant lines connecting the maze of readings and potential readings of the Persian period with those of later periods whose general lines were drawn. Unlike Marv, I am not a theologian. But a historian like me still can study how a verse like Mal 2:10a has served as medium to explore and state, through time and space, considerable theological or ideological issues that faced multiple

---

[1] I discussed these issues at length in several publications. See, e.g., Ehud Ben Zvi, "On Social Memory and Identity Formation in Late Persian Yehud: A Historian's Viewpoint with a Focus on Prophetic Literature, Chronicles and the Dtr. Historical Collection," *Texts, Contexts and Readings in Postexilic Literature: Explorations into Historiography and identity Negotiation in Hebrew Hebrew Bible and Related Texts* (ed. L. Jonker; FAT 2/53; Tübingen: Mohr Siebeck, 2011), 95–148 and Ben Zvi, "Exploring the Memory of Moses."

[2] This tendency requires demanding cognitive tasks to be performed by the literati, but this requirement may have actually contributed to their cultural, symbolic, and even mnemonic capital within the community. These matters require a separate discussion.

historical communities well beyond the "original" community of literati in Yehud. May these observations serve as a proper token of appreciation for Marv Sweeney.[1]

---

[1] An oral version of this essay was presented at the 2016 Annual Meeting of the Canadian Society of Biblical Studies, Calgary on May 29, 2016. I wish to thank the participants of the meeting for their comments and support.

Pots, Pits, and Promises
Jeremiah as Allusion to Genesis

Shelley L. Birdsong

Much of Jeremiah scholarship over the past two centuries has been devoted to the prophet himself. Earlier researchers sought the historical Jeremiah while more recent critics have tried to decode his ideological persona.[1] Louis Stulman rightly asserts that the obsession with the prophet results from the fact that he is

> [o]ne of the most distinct features of the book... loom[ing] as large as the message itself. In effect, the message and messenger share center stage, and the two generate meanings that are greater than either the word or the persona by itself.[1]

Simply put, Jeremiah is a meaning-laden character and literary device. Scholars have long noted his use as a mouthpiece for Deuteronomistic editors, spewing retributive language like burning flames from his bones. Others have identified his portrayal as an anti-Moses, tragically leaving the promised land and returning to Egypt. But some of Jeremiah's most beautiful allusions are not to Deuteronomy or even Exodus, although these are myriad. Jeremiah's life harkens back to a more distant past chronicled in the narratives of Genesis. He acts an allusion, stirring up the stories of Adam and Eve, Abraham, and Joseph. With each intertextual recall, there is also a shared theme or motif, which reinforces the relationship between the characters and the books of Jeremiah and Genesis. Jeremiah, Adam, and Eve are united by the metaphor of pottery and the motifs of creation and destruction; Jeremiah and Abraham are correlated through the theme of covenant or divine promise; and Jeremiah and Joseph are linked via a pit motif and the themes of suffering and deliverance. All these connective

---

[1] For a short overview of this history of scholarship and some of the latest opinions on this topic, see Else K. Holt, and Carolyn J. Sharp, *Jeremiah Invented: Constructions and Deconstructions of Jeremiah* (London: Bloomsbury T & T Clark, 2015), see esp. the introduction.

threads interweave, creating a canonical tapestry[2] that prompts readers to envision a bigger theological picture in the Hebrew Bible—one that includes disparate and vacillating voices regarding creation and destruction, exile and return.

Pots
Jeremiah as Allusion to Adam and Eve (Creation and Exile)

The metaphor of humanity as pot and God as potter figures prominently in Jeremiah and connects the prophet back his firstly formed ancestors, Adam and Eve.[3] The pottery metaphor appears at the outset in Jer 1, and its allusion to human creation is highlighted by four creation-related terms from Gen 2:4-4:1: forming (יצר), planting (נטע), building (בנה), and knowing (ידע). The theme of divine creativity and attentiveness briefly resurfaces in Jer 18-19, but it ultimately reverses, and God informs the people that they—the pot—will be shattered by the very hands that formed them. Thus, Jeremiah, Adam, and Eve, are all bound together by the interrelated imagery of creation and its undoing (destruction, exile).

Their relationship begins immediately in Jeremiah's call narrative (Jer 1:4-10) when YHWH proclaims to Jeremiah, "Before I formed (יצר) you in the womb, I knew you" (Jer 1:5). The intimate claim and use of יצר (to form, fashion) reorients the reader back to God's fashioning of Adam in Genesis: "And YHWH Elohim formed (יצר) the human [Adam] of the dust from the earth" (Gen 2:7).[4] The image of a potter culling soil and molding it into something functional was common in the ancient world and lends itself naturally to be compared with the creations of Adam and Jeremiah.[5] Their lives were crafted by

---

[1] Louis Stulman, "Jeremiah, Book of," *NIDB* 3:220-35, here 221.

[2] I am borrowing the language and imagery of "tapestry" from Stulman; see *Order Amid Chaos: Jeremiah as Symbolic Tapestry* (BibSem 57; Sheffield: Sheffield Academic, 1998).

[3] The concept of humans being divinely fashioned from various elements from the earth is ubiquitous and surfaces in many cultures around the globe; e.g. *The Enuma 'elish* and *Popol Vuh*.

[4] Forming (יצר) and the closely associated image of God as fashioner or potter also appears in Jer 33:2 and 51:19. I believe this is verb is intentional *contra* William L. Holladay, *Jeremiah 1: A Commentary on the Book of the Prophet Jeremiah, Chapters 1-25* (Hermeneia; Philadelphia: Fortress, 1986), 20, 33.

[5] So also with all the other creatures of the earth who are formed (יצר) by God the potter (Gen 2:19).

an artist who sought something useful, gathered the earth, and formed (יצר) them into unique individuals created for specific purposes. In Jeremiah, God required a prophet to the nations (Jer 1:5, 10), and in Genesis, God wanted a human to work and watch the garden (Gen 2:5, 15). Both are shaped for the important purpose of protecting God's sacred space and guarding against evil. The parallels between Jeremiah and Adam's origins and functions expose Jeremiah as a kind of second Adam, who will attempt to meet YHWH's expectations but only end up "outside of the garden" (i.e., in exile in Egypt). Thus, the characters of Jeremiah and Adam become paired representations of how God can cast and cast away divine creations.

The divine commands "to build" (בנה) and "to plant" (נטע; Jer 1:10) in Jeremiah's call fortify the allusion to God's creative acts, since both verbs are integral to the second creation account in Gen 2. Following the formation (יצר) of Adam, YHWH *plants* (נטע) a garden (Gen 2:8). Thereafter, the deity places Adam in the garden to tend and guard it (Gen 2:8, 15) then *builds* (בנה) Eve (Gen 2:22). By telling Jeremiah to build (בנה) and to plant (נטע), God invites the prophet to follow in God's own footsteps, and Adam's, by partaking in the creative work. Just as God made life spring forth from the ground, Jeremiah is called to bring peace in a time of chaos, and just as Adam and Eve give birth after expulsion,[1] Jeremiah is called to knit hope in the womb of exile. These are surely not visions devoid of suffering, but they do possess hope for renewal in times of tragedy and devastation.

The last creation term that aligns Jeremiah with the story of Adam and Eve is knowing (ידע; Jer 1:5, 6; Gen 2:9, 17; 3:5, 7, 22; 4:1). In Jer 1, God tells the prophet that God knew (ידע) him before he was even born (v. 5). This statement sounds comforting, but, apparently, Jeremiah was not convinced. He quickly retorts, "Ah, Lord GOD! Look, I do not know (ידע) how to speak, for I am only a boy." The banter using ידע leads the audience back to the creation narrative in Gen 2–4, where knowing (ידע) is prominent.[2] God tells Adam not to eat from the

---

[1] See the discussion that follows.

[2] The commissioning of Jeremiah followed by his excuse (i.e., an inability to speak) is usually correlated with the call of Moses and his deflection in Exod 3-4. See, e.g., Marvin A. Sweeney, *Reading the Hebrew Bible after the Shoah: Engaging Holocaust Theology* (Minneapolis: Fortress, 2008), 109. For the relationship of Jeremiah's call to

tree of the knowledge (דעת, from the root ידע; Gen 2:17); the serpent claims that God knows (ידע) Adam and Eve will be like God, knowing (ידע) good and evil if they eat from the tree (Gen 3:5); and, the humans, finally, know (ידע) they are naked. Unfortunately, their newfound awareness leads to their exile from the garden and an inability to eat from the tree of life.[1] However, it seems that their new knowledge is not all bad. For, in Gen 4:1, Adam is able to know (ידע) Eve, and she consequently creates Cain, much like God knew and then created Jeremiah. In knowing and creating, both Adam and Eve act like God, and in being known and created, Jeremiah becomes like Eve.

Israel also becomes like Eve, Adam, and Jeremiah because YHWH molds them like a potter too (Jer 18:6). In Jer 18-19, the key root of יצר (form, fashion) appears eight more times, and it weaves the tapestry of the current story of Israel as pot into the previous ones of Jeremiah and Adam.[2] The metaphor becomes overt in ch. 18 when Jeremiah goes to see a potter (הַיּוֹצֵר) reworking a vessel (vv. 2-4). God uses the scenario to claim that the deity will act upon Israel and Judah as the potter does the clay (vv. 5-11).

YHWH's declaration that the nation is clay in YHWH's hands then turns ominous. The deity remarks that Israel's future is uncertain: God *might* build and plant, but God might also do the opposite and pluck up or break down (Jer 18:7-9). The verbs of creation and destruction are from Jeremiah's call and consequently connect Jer 18-19 back to Jer 1 and so Gen 2-4. Moreover, the salvation or condemnation of the people is dependent on their choice to turn away from evil or not—a predicament similar to Adam and Eve's in the garden. Will God's pots turn into beautiful, devoted vessels, or will they be ruined and rejected? God's taunt, "I am a potter shaping (יוֹצֵר) evil against you and devising a plan against you," (Jer 18:11) implies that the future does not look good for the people.

Jeremiah 19 completes the reversal of the divine potter metaphor from intimately endearing (Gen 2; Jer 1) into terrifyingly

---

Moses and other prophets, see Robert P. Carroll, *From Chaos to Covenant: Prophecy in the Book of Jeremiah* (New York: Crossroad, 1981), 31-58.

[1] I find it fascinating that Jeremiah's first vision is also of a tree, although the terminology is not the same (Jer 1:11).

[2] The root "to plant" (נטע) also appears again in Jer 18:9.

destructive (Jer 18-19).[1] Jeremiah shatters a pot, signifying the people, as a warning of what God will do to "his vessel" (Jer 19:1-12).[2] The prophetic imagery is meant to denote the broken covenant and God's damaged people; like potsherds, they are cast off and scattered (Jer 18:17).[3] The symbolic imagery represents not only the destruction of Israel/Judah but also the exile of Adam and Jeremiah, tying them all together. According to the biblical authors, these vessels of God had been given a divine function or purpose, but they fell short of God's expectations. Israel did not follow *torah*, Adam did not guard the garden, and Jeremiah did not reconcile Israel or Judah to God. Consequently, they are all cast out of the land; Israel and Judah are exiled to Assyria and Babylonia, Adam is banished from the garden, and Jeremiah returns to Egypt.[4]

The literary and theological juxtaposition of these creation and exile stories highlights the revolution of the whole narrative cycle of the Hebrew Bible—God makes, warns, unmakes, and then remakes. The danger of myopic interpretation and theological reduction arises when one reads only *part* of the cycle. This is why Jeremiah's allusions to Adam are so important; they force the reader to see beyond a unitary story and to refocus one's vision so that the themes of creation and exile are inextricably viewed as two strands in the larger tapestry of the scriptures, which give voice to the tragedy and renewal of life. This is one of the most striking and meaningful realities within the Hebrew Bible—it brings together the voices of despair and hope and allows them to dialogue. As interpreters we should not silence any of those voices; for it is only in seeing and hearing them together that the truth

---

[1] Jeremiah 18-19 is not the only text that reverses creation. For example, Jer 4:23-26 is well-known as an oracle of destruction that uses creation imagery and vocabulary (see Martin G. Klingbeil's table in "Creation in the Prophetic Literature of the Old Testament: An Intertextual Approach," *The Genesis Creation Account and Its Reverberations in the Old Testament* [Berrien Springs, MI: Andrews University Press, 2015], 257-89, here 279).

[2] YHWH has already implied the divine hands will disfigure (Jer 18:4) and break it (Jer 19:10-11).

[3] Jeremiah is commanded to break the jug at "Potsherd Gate" (19:2).

[4] These theodicies do raise questions about God's justice and responsibility. Were God's mandates reasonable? Should the characters be held responsible for their inability to fulfill such commands? Was God justified in these particular retributive acts?

comes into focus.[1] Thus, the allusions to Adam and Eve in Jer 1 and 18-19 remind the audience to read these stories in conversation and embrace creation and destruction as interdependent ideas that require us to depolarize our interpretation and think more coherently and contextually about the Bible and the humanity it portrays.

Promises
Jeremiah as Allusion to Abraham (Covenant)

The theme of promise, or covenant, runs throughout the Hebrew Bible.[2] It is central in both the books of Genesis and Jeremiah and naturally aligns the two texts in many ways. While this overarching theme is peppered throughout the latter, the promises God makes to Jeremiah in his initial call (Jer 1:4-10) and to Israel and Judah via the prophet in Jer 30-33 allude particularly to Abraham's call and promises in Gen 12, 15, and 17. If these sections of texts are juxtaposed, they have the potential to give further hope to a fearful audience, who may be far from home and doubting divine reliability.

Just as Jeremiah's call conjured up creation themes and allusions to Adam and Eve, God's early assurances to the prophet also evoke divine promises to Abraham. In Jeremiah's call, YHWH directs the prophet to not be afraid (אל־תירא; Jer 1:8a), for he is under divine protection (Jer 1:8b).[3] This is also the first command and promise God gives to Abraham in Gen 15:1; YHWH comes to Abraham (then Abram) and, for the very first time in the Hebrew Bible, says, "Do not be afraid!" (אל־תירא) and promises him security.[4] One might think that the divine imperative אל־תירא is quite common and see no reason for it to be an allusion. However, it is spoken by God (or by a prophet or

---

[1] This is one of the most important concepts I learned from Sweeney as well as Carleen Mandolfo.

[2] Although the covenant is a major theme, one must be careful not to reduce all of biblical theology down to this one concept or any other for that matter. For an example of a theology that used "covenant" as an organizing principle, see Walther Eichrodt, *Theologie des Alten Testaments* (Leipzig: J. C. Hinrichs, 1933-39); ET: *Theology of the Old Testament* (tr. J. A. Baker; OTL; London: SCM Press, 1961-67). This was a serious issue in biblical theology in the early twentieth century, which modern scholars have critiqued (for Sweeney's critique, see, *Tanak: A Theological and Critical Introduction to the Jewish Bible* (Minneapolis: Fortress, 2012), 7-8.

[3] A similar claim of divine protection and deliverance is made in Jer 1:19 and can be viewed as an inclusio for God's speech; see also Jer 15:20-21.

[4] More specifically, YHWH says, "I am your shield."

angel on behalf of God) only forty-two times in the Hebrew Bible and is almost always connected to a promise of divine protection or favor.[1] Moreover, three of the first four occurrences of this divine directive and its associated promise are given to the three patriarchs — Abraham (Gen 15:1), Isaac (Gen 26:24), and Jacob (Gen 46:3) — and affirm God's original promise to Abraham that he will become a great nation (Gen 12, 15, 17).[2] Thus, when God tells Jeremiah that he should not fear, one cannot help but be reminded of the deity's covenant *with* and faithfulness *to* Abraham and his descendants. The power of this allusion is that when God gave Abraham the promise of progeny and land, its fulfillment did not seem near. Yet those in the time of Jeremiah knew that God eventually came through on his covenant with Abraham.[3] The recollection of God's fidelity regarding a people and land would have been deeply significant to Jeremiah's audience, who may have been doubting the reliability of God's word and the covenant of Genesis in the period surrounding the exile.

The implicit association between God's call to Jeremiah and God's covenant promise to Abraham in Genesis, as well as its likely importance to the later Judean community in the 6th century BCE, becomes overt in the near identical passages of Jer 30:10–11a and 46:27–28a. In these texts, Jeremiah tells the people what God told him and Abraham: אל־תירא! The prophet assures Abraham's descendants that God will save them and bring them back home to the land of promise:

---

[1] The one verse that is not explicitly connected to a divine promise of deliverance or favor is Ezek 2:6. The phrase אל־תירא (in its masculine, feminine, singular, and plural forms), called the reassurance formula, is spoken seventy-eight times altogether (by God and others) in the Hebrew Bible, but I am focusing, here, on words spoken *by God* (or an angel or prophet *on behalf of God*) to an individual or group. For other ways of understanding the reassurance formula, see Edgar W. Conrad, *Fear Not Warrior: A Study of the 'al tirā' Pericopes in the Hebrew Scriptures* (BJS 75; Chico, CA: Scholars Press, 1985); his arguments also take up Gerhard von Rad's and Joachim Begrich's earlier theses.

[2] The fourth is the angel of God's call to Hagar and the divine covenant promise given to her and her son in Gen 21.

[3] Joshua is also told אל־תירא three times (Josh 8:1, 10:8, and 11:6), which reinforces the fulfillment of God's promise that Abraham's descendants would inhabit the land.

But as for you, have no fear (אל־תירא),[1] my servant Jacob, [says the LORD,]
    and do not be dismayed, O Israel;
    for I am going to save you from far away,
    and your offspring from the land of their captivity.
Jacob shall return and have quiet and ease,
    and no one shall make him afraid.
[[As for you, have no fear (אל־תירא), my servant Jacob, says the LORD,]]
    for I am with you, [says the LORD, to save you].[2]

As with the connections to creation, these Jeremianic strands that tie the prophet back to Genesis bring together the larger canonical tapestry. Abraham's story that is left unfinished "in the beginning," reaches completion in "quiet and ease" at the end of Jeremiah. Reflecting on this bigger picture, which undoubtedly generated hope for Jeremiah's original audience, can also generate optimism for anyone who finds themselves "far away" and in need of deliverance.

The other allusive divine promise in Jeremiah's story is YHWH's "new" covenant with the offspring of Abraham in Jer 30-33, which includes the people's restoration to the land and a renewed relationship with the deity.[3] YHWH's promises are emphasized because they follow a repeated announcement of the fulfillment of God's word in "the days [that] are surely coming."[4]

Jer 30:3: "*For the days are surely coming*, says the LORD,
    when **I will restore** the fortunes of my people, Israel and Judah,
    ... and **I will bring them back to the land** that I gave their ancestors
    and they shall take possession of it."

---

[1] Second Isaiah also tells Jacob not to fear several times, two of which use the creation imagery of being formed (esp. in the womb) that was discussed in the previous section (see Jer 1:8, Isa 43:1, and Isa 44:1-2).

[2] This is a condensation of Jer 30:10-11a and 46:27-28a since they largely overlap. The words in single brackets are from Jer 30 (not in 46), and the words in doubled brackets are from Jer 46 (not in 30).

[3] It is common to refer to the covenant of Jer 30-33 as a "new" covenant, even though the Hebrew does not use this terminology. For a discussion of the issue, particularly in Jer 31:31-34, see Adrian Schenker, *Das Neue am neuen Bund und das Alte am alten. Jer 31 in der hebräischen und griechischen Bibel* (FRLANT 212; Göttingen: Vandenhoeck & Ruprecht, 2006). For a broader history of the theological idea, see Joshua N. Moon, *Jeremiah's New Covenant: An Augustinian Reading* (JTISup 3; Winona Lake, IN: Eisenbrauns, 2011).

[4] While these five instances string chs. 30-33 together, the phrase occurs several other times throughout Jeremiah. For Sweeney's comments on the cohesion of these chapters, see *Reading the Hebrew Bible After the Shoah*, 124-25.

31:27-28: "*The days are surely coming*, says the LORD,
when **I will sow** the house of Israel and the house of Judah
with the deed of humans and the seed of animals.
… **I will watch over** them **to build and to plant**…"
31:31: "*The days are surely coming*, says the LORD,
when **I will make a new covenant** with the house of Israel and the house
of Judah."
31:38-40: "…*The days are surely coming*, says the LORD,
when **the city shall be rebuilt** for the LORD … .
It shall never again be uprooted or overthrown."
33:14: "*The days are surely coming*, says the LORD,
when **I will fulfill my promise I made** to the house of Israel and the
house of Judah."

All of these promises, and the others in Jer 30-33, regularly refer back to the covenant of Gen 12, 15, and 17. God refers to *the land* being given to the ancestors of Israel and Judah, the replenishing of Abraham's *seed*, and God's *faithfulness* to *make vows* and *fulfill* them (see Gen 12:2; 15:5-6; 17:2, 7-8).

The author of Jeremiah highlights the renewed covenant promise of land in Jer 30-33 by inserting a prose account of Jeremiah's procurement of land (Jer 32:6-15) within God's poetic repetition of promises. The sign act points back to the covenant of Genesis and its initial fulfillment when Abraham buys a field in Gen 23. Both stories recount the purchase (קנה or מקנה; Gen 23:18; Jer 32:7-9, 11-12, 14-15) of a field (שדה; Gen 23:9, 11, 15-17, 20; Jer 32:7-9, 15), in the land of Canaan (Hebron, Gen 23:19; Anathoth, Jer 32:7, 9) using shekels of silver (שקל כסף; Gen 23:9; 15-16; Jer 32:9-10), which is confirmed by witnesses (ולעיני; Gen 23:11, 18; Jer 32:12-13).

The significance of the allusion to Gen 23 in Jer 32 is the future both accounts assume for the generations to come. Abraham had not been given possession of the land yet (nor an abundance of children) and Jeremiah's community was being exiled. The fact that both prophets actively acquired land in Canaan exhibits their trust in YHWH's faithfulness to maintain the covenant promise despite their current circumstances and limited power among the nations.[1] For the

---

[1] Another parallel between Abraham and Jeremiah is their connection to "the nations" (לגוים). Jeremiah is called to be a prophet to the nations (Jer 1:5) and Abraham is

original readers of Jeremiah, the recollection of Abraham's small purchase of property after coming to Canaan from Mesopotamia had the potential to empower them. Even though they may have been displaced by war, like Abraham and Jeremiah, they could choose to invest in God's promises and trust that it would pay off someday.[1]

Pits
Jeremiah as Allusion to Joseph (Suffering and Deliverance)

Pits (בור) often serve as cisterns, filled with life-giving water, but, when empty, they can become prisons or graves.[2] In the books of Jeremiah and Genesis, pits are usually literal places of captivity, but they can also carry out a figurative function too as symbols of expulsion (or exile). As we will see, Jeremiah (Jer 38) and Joseph (Gen 37) are both thrown into pits to die, but—by some divine intervention—they are saved. The turn of events in each story presents a message of courage and patience for those who are metaphorically stuck in a pit. Despite the fact that one may feel imprisoned or rejected, the divine can deliver even when all hope seems lost.

In Jer 38, a group of Judean officials who found Jeremiah's message worthy of death throw him into the cistern of Malchiah (וישלכו אתו אל־הבור מלכהו; v. 6). He is left for dead, and the narrator reports, "there was no water in the cistern" (ובור אין־מים). He languishes in the mud until an unexpected savior shows up on the scene—Ebed-melech, an Ethiopian eunuch (סריס)—who advocates for Jeremiah's release (38:7-9).[3] While Ebed-melech does take some thirty men to lift

---

promised to become a great nation and the ancestor of a multitude of nations (Gen 17:6, 16). Abraham also acts as a "prophet" to the nations in Gen 20:7.

[1] The idea that they will be able to buy "fields" again "in the land" is forcefully repeated in Jer 32:43-44.

[2] Sheol, the place of the dead below the earth, is synonymous with "the pit" (e.g. Isa 14:15).

[3] Ebed-melech is not described as a eunuch in LXX. For details regarding this difference in the text, see the discussion of his character in Shelley L. Birdsong, *The Last King(s) of Judah: Zedekiah and Sedekias in the Hebrew and Old Greek Versions of Jeremiah 37(44):1-40(47):6* (FAT 2/89; Tubingen: Mohr Siebeck, 2017), esp. 56-60, 111-16, 195-96, 223-24. For a short, general overview of the differences between MT and LXX Jeremiah, see Marvin A. Sweeney, *The Prophetic Literature* (IBT; Nashville: Abingdon, 2005), 88-95. For his more extended thoughts on this topic, see Sweeney, "The Masoretic and Septuagint Versions of the Book of Jeremiah in Synchronic and Diachronic Perspective," *Form and Intertextuality in Prophetic and Apocalyptic Literature* (FAT 45; Gottingen: Mohr Siebeck, 2005; repr. Eugene, OR: Wipf & Stock, 2010), 65-77.

Jeremiah from the death-pit (ימשכו את־ירמיהו ועלו אתו מן־הבור), the prophet is not completely delivered from the watchful eye of the government. He remains within the court of the guard (38:13). Eventually, Jeremiah is given his full freedom by Nebuzaradan, the captain of the guard (רב־טבחים) of Babylon (40:1-6), but he ironically ends up in Egypt (43:5-7) despite the fact that he reiterated God's promise to build (בנה) and plant (נטע) the people, repeated the reassurance formula (אל־תיראו; 2x), and commanded them not to go to Egypt (42:10-11, 19). Jeremiah finishes his prophetic career sojourning in Egypt and echoing the demise of the remnant of Judah by famine (רעב; 42:16-17, 22; 44:12-13, 18, 27).

Almost everything about Jeremiah's story (Jer 38-43) alludes to the novella of Joseph (Gen 37-50) with the most striking parallels surrounding the pit vignettes.[1] Just as Jeremiah made enemies who plotted his death, so also Joseph gathered adversaries (his brothers) who wanted him out of the way (Gen 37:4, 8, 18-20). As soon as they got the chance, his brothers conspired against him and threw him into a cistern (וישלכו אתו הבור; vv. 20, 24) with no water in it (והבור רק אין בו מים). It is unclear exactly how long Joseph remained in the pit, but he is eventually rescued by several unexpected saviors. First, his brother Judah convinces the rest of the sons of Jacob to sell Joseph rather than kill him (vv. 26-27). Then a group of Midianite traders draw Joseph up and lifted him out of the pit (וימשכו ויעלו את־יוסף מן־הבור; v. 28).[2] Similar to Jeremiah, Joseph's deliverance from the pit is not exactly a ticket to freedom. He is sold to the Ishmaelites[3] and taken to Egypt (v. 28). Genesis 37 ends with Joseph's trip to Egypt, which picks back up in

---

[1] There are several other threads that tie Jeremiah back to Joseph. For example, when Jeremiah calls the people to put on sackcloth, roll in ashes, and mourn as if for an only child in Jer 6:26, it recalls Jacob's grief when his other sons tell him that Joseph is dead (Gen 37:33-35). The grief of Joseph's parent is also depicted in Jer 31:15-22, where Rachel (his mother) weeps for her children; this points back to her sorrow in Gen 35:16-19, when she gives birth to her other son, Ben-oni ("son of my sorrow"), whom Jacob names Benjamin (the land where Jeremiah buys a field).

[2] Gen 37:28 and Jer 38:13 contain the only two occurrences of וימשכו in the Hebrew Bible.

[3] The presence of the Ishmaelites in Joseph's story here (along with the Midianites) has been the cause of much historical-critical debate. Literarily speaking it becomes one of the unique strands that holds together the intertextual relationship between Jeremiah, Joseph, and pits. For, in Jer 40, a man named Ishmael assassinates the

Gen 39, when Potiphar, a eunuch (סריס) of Pharaoh and captain of the guard (שר־טבחים), becomes another one of Joseph's unexpected saviors (v. 1). Like Ebed-melech, the eunuch, and Nebuzaradan, the captain of the guard, who improved Jeremiah's circumstances, Potiphar improves Joseph's. Nevertheless, Joseph's story takes some twists and turns, and he ends up back in a dungeon (בור; Gen 40:15 and 41:14) before he later saves Egypt and the house of Jacob from a famine (Gen 41:46–47:28).

The shared motifs and vocabulary between Jeremiah and Joseph are apparent. But more significant are the theological questions and answers that arise in light of these two stories. The biblical authors portray both Joseph and Jeremiah as individuals chosen by God (like Adam and Abraham) for a unique task at a particular moment in history. Yet this does not shield them from attack or suffering. Their trials are summed up in their pit internments, where it seems God has abandoned them. Their divine gift to see visions apparently became a curse. This is where the metaphor of the pit as captivity has the potential to meet the needs of a displaced community. Although it felt like God may have left Jeremiah and Joseph, they waited for the unexpected deliverer, who would draw them up and lift them out of the abyss. And even though death may have been imminent, salvation always came. Such a story (or two) can breathe hope into the lives of those who feel despair and anguish, waiting for God to show up. What is especially beautiful about the tales of Jeremiah and Joseph is that they don't instantaneously end "happily ever after." They acknowledge that after deliverance there can be famine, after salvation there can be another prison. But for each new pit, there is another opportunity for divine intervention.

Conclusion

Jeremiah's story starts with an allusion to Adam at the beginning of Genesis and concludes with an allusion to Joseph at the end of Genesis. The paired bookends are valuable just as literary parallels, but they are also theologically striking because they represent the sorrow of exile in such captivating and hopeful ways. Although Adam gets cast out of the garden, he and Eve create life together. Even

---

new leader of the people—Gedaliah, son of Ahikam—and throws him and his leaders into a cistern (בור; Jer 40:9).

though Joseph gets sold and thrown into jail, he becomes a powerful caretaker for the house of Jacob in another land. All of these stories, including Abraham's and Jeremiah's, speak hope to despair. They proclaim that spoiled pots can be remade, empty pits are only temporary, and deferred promises can be fulfilled. This is one of the truths Marvin Sweeney taught me about Jeremiah and the rest of the Hebrew Bible; it articulates the authenticity of life in all its complex tragedy and triumph. So also it boldly addresses the hard questions of divine fidelity, love, and justice in the face of suffering and broken covenants. It can be easy to only see the chaos and destruction in the biblical narratives—and our own lives—but the truth is that the narrative cycle always comes back around to hope.

(Para)textual Composition on Both Sides of the Canonical Divide

William Yarchin

The Judean desert manuscripts teach us that in the last centuries of the first millennium BCE no firm boundary existed between the composition of literary works and their textual transmission at the hands of ancient Jewish textual tradents.[1] Consequently, we have had to revise our notions of "author" relative to "editor" and "scribe" when it comes to the production of the literary works that would eventually comprise the Hebrew Bible.[2] This updated perspective brings reception history into view, as Eugene Ulrich has noted: "Whereas reception is usually thought of as a post-biblical phenomenon, it is important at almost every stage of the transmission of the scriptural books from the very origins."[3] At no point have scholars been in physical possession of the original work, but only of receptions of it, including the ancient Judean scribes in whose hands the literary works already bore the imprint from centuries

---

[1] The seminal work can be found in Shemaryahu Talmon, "The Textual Study of the Bible—A New Outlook," *Qumran and the History of the Biblical Text* (eds. Frank Moore Cross and Shemaryahu Talmon; Cambridge: Harvard University Press, 1975), who writes, "[I]n ancient Hebrew literature no hard and fast lines can be drawn between authors' conventions of style and tradents' and copyists' rules of reproduction and transmission" (381).

[2] From his observations on paratextual aspects of 1QIsaᵃ, Arie van der Kooij concludes that tradents such as those who produced the manuscript "are not to be regarded simply as dragoman-translators or copyists, but more likely as scribes and scholars. Or to put it in terms of antiquity, they are to be seen as 'oratores' rather than 'interprètes' seeking to actualize the received text of prophecy for their contemporary reading communities. See "The Old Greek of Isaiah in Relation to the Qumran Texts of Isaiah: Some General Comments," *Septuagint, Scrolls, and Cognate Writings: Papers Presented to the International Symposium on the Septuagint and Its Relations to the Dead Sea Scrolls and Other Writings (Manchester, 1990)* (eds. George J. Brooke and Barnabas Lindars; Atlanta: Scholars Press, 1992), 195–213, here 207.

[3] Eugene C. Ulrich, "The Evolutionary Production and Transmission of the Scriptural Books," *The Dead Sea Scrolls: Transmission of Traditions and Production of Texts* (eds. Sarianna Metso, Hindy Najman, and Eileen M. Schuller; STDJ 92; Leiden/Boston: Brill, 2010), 209–26, here 224.

of transmission. As far back as we can trace the compositional process, *received* scriptural texts are all that have ever existed. Thus the history of their reception is also the history of their composition.[1] The overlap we observe between *generative composition* of biblical books and their *textual transmission* problematizes the division commonly assumed between the earlier text, which is taken to bear greater authority, and its reception, to which lesser or derivative authority is attributed. Where do we locate that divide between the authoritative text—the presumed object of our interpretation—and the mere transmission of it, which we relegate to the margins of our experience of the literary work?

The fluidity and pluriformity of biblical manuscripts in their composition/reception/transmission bring us to think of traditional texts as processes rather than as essences, as scholars have recently argued.[2] Text-as-process conspicuously involves all elements comprising the *mise-en-page*, including the size of margins, the choice of script, the color of ink, interlinear or marginal sigla, and spacing between sense-units. These scribal paratexts appear in the manuscripts because they were deemed necessary for constituting the work and guiding how it is to be read. Thus it is impossible to consider a manuscript as nothing more than a receptacle conveying the text like a box of chocolates.[3] Medievalists point out that the material dimension of written verbal expression advises against regarding the literary work as a disembodied entity disengaged from the historicality to which its full paratextual *Gestalt* attests.[4] Nothing presented by the physical

---

[1] Rolf P. Knierim has pointed out the inherently generative nature of literary activity regardless of how we might distinguish between the work of authors and editors; inevitably "both factors interpenetrate." See "Criticism of Literary Features, Form, Tradition, and Redaction," *The Hebrew Bible and Its Modern Interpreters* (eds. Douglas A. Knight and Gene M. Tucker; Chico: Scholars Press, 1985), 123–65, here 151–52.

[2] See for example Brennan W. Breed, *Nomadic Text: A Theory of Biblical Reception History* (Bloomington/Indianapolis: Indiana University Press, 2014).

[3] Siegfried Wenzel, "Reflections on (New) Philology," *Spec* 65 (1990): 11–18, here 14. See also Donald F. McKenzie, *Bibliography & the Sociology of Texts* (Cambridge: Cambridge University Press, 1999), who argues that texts constitute meaning not merely by virtue of their "conveyed" message but via the total inter-engagement in all dimensions of their material existence.

[4] This analytical perspective is sometimes known among cultural historians and medievalists as "material philology" or "new philology." See Gabrielle M. Spiegel, "History, Historicism, and the Social Logic of the Text in the Middle Ages," *Spec* 65 (1990): 59–86, here 85 and Matthew J. Driscoll, "Words on the Page: Thoughts on

artifact stands outside the total configuration in which text and paratext mutually implicate in the process of discursive production and reception.[1]

Attention to paratext is very much historical-critical and should find itself at home among biblical scholars concerned for the changing contexts in which biblical writings have been shaped according to different historical circumstances and cultural situations.[2] Counterintuitively, it is precisely not in the unchanging fixity of the text wherein lies its continuance but by means of the adjustments brought to the text via all manner of paratext,[3] serving to situate the text vis-à-vis the reader and the reader vis-à-vis the text either according to the purposes intended by the author or by other, later hands.[4] The boundary between text and paratext, however, can be blurry: if, for example, Ps 1 was composed in order to orient the reader

---

Philology, Old and New," *Creating the Medieval Saga: Versions, Variability, and Editorial Interpretation of Old Norse Saga Literature* (eds. Judy Quinn and Emily Lethbridge; Odense: University Press of Southern Denmark, 2010), 85–102.

[1] Spiegel, "History," 68.

[2] Referring to medieval studies, Stephen G. Nichols notes that "each manuscript represented exactly how a text, or part of a text, or a rewritten or truncated text, would have reached a particular and quite specialized audience often in forms quite dissimilar to how another public might receive the 'same' work" ("Why Material Philology? Some Thoughts," *Sonderheft: Philologie als Textwissenschaft: Alte und neue Horizonte =Zeitschrift für deutsche Philologie* 116 [1997]: 10–30, here 11). The plurality of historical contexts underlying the compositional process of biblical writings has long been a focus of our honoree's scholarly work. See, e.g., Marvin A. Sweeney, "On Multiple Settings in the Book of Isaiah," *Society of Biblical Literature 1993 Seminar Papers* (Atlanta: Scholars Press, 1993), 267–73.

[3] See James J. O'Donnell, *Avatars of the Word: From Papyrus to Cyberspace* (Cambridge: Harvard University Press, 1998), 41. Gérard Genette coined the word "paratext" in his 1982 *Palimpsestes: La littérature au second Degré* (Paris: Éditions du Seuil); ET: *Palimpsests: Literature in the Second Degree* (trans. C. Newman and C. Doubinsky; Lincoln, NE: University of Nebraska Press, 1997), and he greatly elaborated the theme in *Seuils* (Paris: Éditions du Seuil, 1987); ET: *Paratexts: Thresholds of Interpretation* (trans. J. E. Lewin; Cambridge: Cambridge University Press, 1997). Genette spoke only of paratextual elements deriving from the work's actual author, and he summed up the function of paratext as "to ensure for the text a destiny consistent with the author's purpose" (*Paratexts*, 407).

[4] Marie Maclean, "Pretexts and Paratexts: The Art of the Peripheral," *NLH* 22 (1991): 273–79. See also Eric W. Scherbenske, *Canonizing Paul: Ancient Editorial Practice and the Corpus Paulinum* (New York: Oxford University Press, 2013), who provides evidence of "the interplay between text and paratext" whereby during antiquity "editors conveyed information by transmitting and altering the text, by selecting and arranging content, and by circumscribing the corpus with paratexts: an edition was the product of interpretation, and, in turn, sought to shape subsequent interpretation" (16).

towards a proper engagement with all the subsequent psalms comprising the collection, the composing of that psalm would qualify as a paratextual activity relative to the total psalms-collection even as it was at the same time a textual one relative to itself as a discrete composition.[1] Like Psalms, all biblical books were produced through the *generative literary activity* of those who wrote individual component compositions as well as through the *redactional* or *editorial paratextual activity* of those who assembled the compositions into various constitutive assemblages on the way towards the book's final form.[2]

The material manuscript evidence, however, forces us to ask: what *is* the final form of a biblical book? Scholars have proceeded as though the compositional shaping of the scriptures came to an end by the first century CE, yielding works that were passed down without configurational variation, ultimately presenting themselves in our modern editions. But medieval manuscripts make it clear that paratextual shaping did not come to an end during antiquity. By the end of the first century CE what *had* become firmly fixed were only two elements of, for example, the Psalter's total compositional *Gestalt*: the text was at that point established (later to be known as MT); and a certain aspect of its paratext, namely, the sequence of the collection's semantic content. But a further aspect of the book's paratext remained fluid, viz., its segmentive configuration.[3] In its actual material

---

[1] See Susan Gillingham's helpful overview of the scholarship assessing the compositional place of Ps 1 within the Hebrew book of Psalms in *A Journey of Two Psalms: The Reception of Psalms 1 and 2 in Jewish and Christian Tradition* (Oxford: Oxford University Press, 2013), 273–87.

[2] Medieval Karaite scholars gave articulation to the view that biblical writings were cohesive literary compositions the meaning of which had been constructed not solely by named authorial figures such as Moses or David or Jeremiah but also by unnamed editors/compilers (the Judeo-Arabic word is *mudawwin*). By positing the *mudawwin* figure in the history of the Hebrew Bible's composition, Karaite scholars recognized the confluence of what we have termed text and paratext: the *mudawwin* was responsible for the paratextual activity of compiling and arranging the compositions that had been authored by the prophets, but also for the textual activity of composing his own additions to the compositions for the sake of improved recognition of their meaning and relationship to other compositions. See Miriam Goldstein, *Karaite Exegesis in Medieval Jerusalem: The Judeo-Arabic Pentateuch Commentary of Yūsuf ibn Nūḥ and Abū al-Faraj Hārūn* (Tübingen: Mohr Siebeck, 2011), 87–95.

[3] For details on *sefer tehillim*, see William Yarchin, "Is There an Authoritative Shape for the Book of Psalms? Profiling the Manuscripts of the Hebrew Psalter," *RB* 122 (2015): 355–70.

presentation, a biblical book—say, Psalms, or Isaiah—defies our preferred "final form" category.

To demonstrate continued paratextual shaping beyond the psalms we can turn to 1QIsa[a].[1] An immediately apparent paratext of 1QIsa[a] is the spatial segmenting of the text column into sections of what would otherwise appear as a river of words.[2] Additionally, at some sixty places a later hand has marked the ending of a sense-unit by inserting a *paragraphos* sign in the margin. These paratexts reflect specific ways in which the scribes of 1QIsa[a] read the Isaiah-book and sought to guide the reader to experience its composition. This manuscript and others make it abundantly clear that segmentation—a technique of shaping text such that it is received in a certain way—was just as universal in ancient times from the hands of scribes as it is today in print media, such as chapters.[3]

Christian manuscripts of Isaiah also segment the book into reading sections using line intervals and *ektheses*. With its (nonoriginal) Greek marginal numbers, Codex Vaticanus divides up Isaiah into some seventy-four reading sections; a still later hand added a system of Latin marginal numbers, indicating the sixty-six chapter divisions that became widely standard in the West from the thirteenth century. Codex Sinaiticus also features (nonoriginal) Greek section numbers in the margins, but these divide the Greek Isaiah into over 440 reading sections. The section numbering in Isaiah according to Codex

---

[1] I have chosen 1QIsa[a] because among ancient Hebrew manuscripts it uniquely presents a complete "scriptural" literary work as it was received by at least one Jewish community in the late second century BCE, and because Marvin Sweeney has given to Isaiah much attention of the sort relevant to my thesis. Årstein Justnes observes that considerations of material philology suit only a few larger, well-preserved Qumran manuscripts such as 1QIsa[a]; see "The Great Isaiah Scroll (1QIsa[a]) and Material Philology: Preliminary Observations and A Proposal," *New Studies in the Book of Isaiah: Essays in Honor of Hallvard Hagelia,* (ed. Markus Zehnder; Piscataway, NJ: Gorgias Press, 2014), 91–113, here 97.

[2] Ancient documents with the barest minimum of paratext present what Harry Y. Gamble calls "a relentless march of characters across the lines and down the columns" in *Books and Readers in the Early Church: A History of Early Christian Texts* (New Haven: Yale University Press, 1995), 203. See also Jocelyn P. Small, *Wax Tablets of the Mind: Cognitive Studies of Memory and Literacy in Classical Antiquity* (New York: Routledge, 1997): "Literary texts in antiquity remained pretty much an undifferentiated block" (14).

[3] For examples see Arthur E. Cowley, Aramaic Papyri of the Fifth Century B.C. (Oxford: Clarendon Press, 1923), 211–20; for discussion see Carolyn Higbie, "Divide and Edit. A Brief History of Book Divisions," HSCP 105 (2010): 1–31.

Alexandrinus segments the book with Arabic numeration into sixty-six chapters—but, of course, at variance with the sectioning signals provided by the original scribe(s), particularly by enlarged first letters, which divide up the text into twenty reading sections or more.[1] Just these few samples from the Greek manuscript tradition present the Isaiah book as at least four different paratextually segmented compositions; a glance at other manuscript traditions, such as the Syriac and Latin, would yield even more.[2]

Alexandrinus can instruct us as to how and why this sort of marginal paratext affects the reader's experience of the text. Centuries after the text of the manuscript was inscribed, calendarized reading sections were marked in the margins with highly abbreviated sigla denoting the occasion during the liturgical calendar for reading each section. For example, in the left-hand margin of the second column at folio 312v, a scribe has marked the *beginning* of the *third pericope* for the *fourth Tuesday* of *Great Lent*: π γ τς δ αρχ. This pericope begins at Isa 25:1, and the end (τελος) is marked (with τε′) in the right-hand margin at Isa 25:9. In this way, Codex Alexandrinus has come to divide the Isaiah-book into some twenty-seven such reading sections, composing the text—that is, configuring it through a certain calendarized paratext—for the experience of a very specifically purposed reading.[3] Note that at this point in the (re)compositional process of the Isaiah-book, its semantic content no longer changes, but the experience of it— that is, the manner in which its readers actually engage with the book—involves accretions to the total *Gestalt* of Isaiah that are no less

---

[1] Because Alexandrinus employs letter-enlargement for codicological as well as lectionary purposes, determining the number of reading-sections can result in differing totals. For other observations see Wim de Bruin, "Interpreting Delimiters: The Complexity of Text Delimitation in Four Major Septuagint Manuscripts," *Studies in Scriptural Unit Division* (eds. Marjo C. A. Korpel and Josef M. Oesch; Pericope 3; Leiden: Brill, 2002), 66–89.

[2] For observations on systems of paratextual segmenting of the Isaiah-book in Syriac manuscripts see Sebastian P. Brock, "Text History and Text Division in Peshitta Isaiah," *The Peshitta: Its Early Text and History* (eds. Peter B. Dirksen and Martin J. Mulder; Leiden: E. J. Brill, 1988), 49–80.

[3] For a parallel example of paratextual composition in the Hebrew book of Psalms, see William Yarchin, "Were the Psalms Collections at Qumran True Psalters?" *JBL* 134 (2015): 775–89.

compositionally effective for their being paratextual rather than textual.[1]

Medieval Hebrew codices show parallels to all this. One of them appears as *sidrah* sections denoted by the distinctly-shaped *samekh* in the margin at the beginning of each *sidrah*, which — at least in the Torah — is a paratextual remnant marking reading sections from the old Palestinian 3.5-year cycle of weekly Torah readings.[2] Sigla denoting these paratexts mark not only the cycles of weekly Torah readings but also the segmenting of the Isaiah-book. Medieval manuscripts do not agree at all points where *sedrin* are located, but it is interesting that even in an ancient manuscript such as 1QIsa^a, the segmenting of the Isaiah text tends to correlate to the scribally indicated sense units we know as *parashiyyot* found in its medieval counterparts.

A good example appears in Isa 3. Already in 1QIsa^a we find the same sort of spacing paratext between v. 17 and v. 18 that the medieval Masoretic tradition used at least by the tenth century in the Petrograd Codex (and also the Aleppo Codex, Leningrad Codex, and Cairo Codex). None of these manuscripts shows any spacing segmentation a few verses later at 4:3. However, Cairo, Aleppo, and Leningrad feature a (later?) marginal *samekh*, there showing a *sidrah* segmentation probably from the Palestinian reading tradition, while 1QIsa^a inserts a dash (⌐) to mark a reading section at that same point. Clearly the Hebrew Book of Isaiah, long after its *text* had reached a fixed state, has

---

[1] A related example in Isaiah according to Alexandrinus is at 1:1, which the first scribal hand has set apart as a superscript to the entire prophetic book work by keeping every line of the verse within narrower margins than what follows starting at v. 2, at which point the reading portion of the Isaiah-book begins. Yet the later marginal hand added calendric paratext in the margin at 1:1, marking the verse as the beginning of a lectionary section, and thus as an integral part of the text of Isaiah to be read. Similarly, Peshitta manuscripts such as Milan, B.21 Inf. (sixth century) set Isa 1:1 apart paratextually by a rosette mark, usually within the text line. For detailed treatment of the segmenting paratext covering a portion of Isaiah in Hebrew, Greek, Syriac, and Latin manuscripts, see Wim de Bruin, *Isaiah 1–12 as Written and Read in Antiquity* (Sheffield: Sheffield Phoenix Press, 2013).

[2] *Sedrin* are present in the margins of some of the earliest medieval codices we have, including the tenth century Damascus Pentateuch, tenth century Aleppo Codex, eleventh century Leningrad Codex, and eleventh century Cairo Codex of the Prophets, but not in the tenth century Petrograd Codex of the Latter Prophets. Even though it is not certain that *sedrin* segments as they are found in non-Torah books like Isaiah served this same purpose, to medieval scribal communities the book of Isaiah properly conceived was composed with this paratext rather than without it. See Israel Yeivin, *Introduction to the Tiberian Masorah* (Atlanta: Scholars Press, 1980), 40.

been continually reshaped through *paratext* in relation to multiple reading traditions insofar as the inscribed form of the book bears the marks of those shapings. But paratexual reshapings of Isaiah did not come to an end with the medieval Masoretic codices. The twentieth century *BHS* edition, for example, provides additional segmenting paratext: at places in the margins of Isaiah, *BHS* adds *sidrah* marks and to the text of Isaiah it adds line intervals where none necessarily exists in any of the early medieval manuscripts mentioned here. In so doing, *BHS* paratextually guides the reader to experience the Isaiah book according to a compositional configuration not attested, all things considered, by any preceding iteration of the book. *BHS*, like 1QIsa[a], has continued to (re)compose the book of Isaiah.

Insofar as composition has always included paratextual dimensions, material evidence suggests that the composition of biblical books like Isaiah has never ceased. This is because paratextual activity continues with every iteration of the text—whether among the Dead Sea Scrolls, or in versions such as the Septuagint or the Peshitta, or in medieval Masoretic codices, or even in modern printed editions. To be sure, some distinction in these paratextual compositional activities can be discerned across the canonical divide. Earlier in the compositional/copying/transmission process, paratextual editorial activity was applied directly to the text itself in the form of substantive additions and omissions. At that time the Isaiah-book was received and handed on as *a literary work* and thus subject to paratextual shaping commensurate with that status.[1] Later, compositional activities would continue, but they shifted to the margins in more overtly *para*textual expression, in the form of variable segmenting, marginal annotation, and Masoretic marks. By this point Isaiah was being received and handed on as *a scriptural book*, and so its continued composition became strictly a matter of paratext rather than text. In both states—that of a literary work and that of a scriptural book—Isaiah has always been subjected to ongoing recomposition by paratextual means. The difference lies in where the recompositional activity is applied: in the reception of a literary work, paratexting can be applied *directly to* the

---

[1] See Eugene C. Ulrich, "From Literature to Scripture: Reflection on the Growth of a Text's Authoritativeness," *The Dead Sea Scrolls and the Developmental Composition of the Bible* (VTSup 169; Leiden: Brill, 2015), 281–98.

text, whereas in the reception of a scriptural book, it is applied *indirectly upon* the text. But regardless of which side of the canonical divide we consider, the book of Isaiah has ever been under construction, even to this very day.[1]

The work of our honoree Marvin Sweeney brings this observation right up to date. His published *oeuvre* includes a comprehensive hierarchical segmenting of the complete book of Isaiah according to a certain application of form critical methodology.[2] Subsections to the Isaiah book are marked in both 1QIsa[a] and in Sweeney's work; if we were to imagine an edition of Isaiah printed according to the segmenting indicated by Sweeney's analysis, comparison with 1QIsa[a] would easily show where these two receptions of Isaiah agree and disagree.[3] As with 1QIsa[a], Sweeney's segmentally-indicated structure of Isaiah does not reside in the text of Isaiah itself, but

> it is rather a construct created by Sweeney. He has not discovered a structure; he has created one.... it is quite possible that a somewhat different conceptualization of structure might also fit the text equally well.[4]

Juxtaposition of 1QIsa[a] with Sweeney's analysis suggests that every reception of the text of Isaiah is at the same time a (re)composition of it according to the religious, intellectual, and social needs prevailing at the time. In his own words, "[T]he presentation of Isa 1–39 is determined not only by factors inherent in the text of these chapters, it is also determined by the hermeneutical viewpoint of the

---

[1] For philosophical reflections on the hermeneutics of reception history, see Hans-Georg Gadamer, *Truth and Method* (tr. Garrett Barden and John Cumming; New York: Seabury Press, 1975), for whom the temporal distance between ancient text and modern interpreter "is not a yawning abyss, but is filled with the continuity of custom and tradition, in the light of which all that is handed down presents itself to us" (264).

[2] See Marvin A. Sweeney, *Isaiah 1–4 and the Post-Exilic Understanding of the Isaianic Tradition* (BZAW 171; Berlin: de Gruyter, 1988) and *Isaiah 1–39, with an Introduction to Prophetic Literature* (FOTL 16; Grand Rapids: Eerdmans, 1996).

[3] It is not always certain that spaces within lines indicate subparagraph segmenting, but among the DSS in general they often do, including in 1QIsa[a]; see the discussion in Emanuel Tov, *Scribal Practices and Approaches Reflected in the Texts Found in the Judean Desert* (STDJ 54; Leiden: Brill, 2004), 145.

[4] Roy F. Melugin, "The Book of Isaiah and the Construction of Meaning," *Writing and Reading the Scroll of Isaiah* (eds. Craig C. Broyles and Craig A. Evans; VTSup 70; New York: Brill, 1997), 1:39–55, here 48.

redaction which is actively shaping the final form of that text."[1] I would differ only in my claim that there is no such thing as the final form of the text. The present essay alludes to material evidence supporting the observation that, whether one is a Jewish scribe of the second century BCE, or a Jewish scholar of the twenty-first century CE, or a Syrian Christian scribe of the sixth century CE, or a Greek Christian copyist of the fourth century CE — the act of receiving and handing on biblical texts cannot but entail paratextual activity that has the ultimate effect of (re)composing biblical works so that they might be appropriately experienced. Through paratext, premodern and modern tradents have always aimed to convey the text to contemporary readers in order to address specific needs. As a result, the canonical divide, whatever it signals, does not mark the cessation of biblical composition. Borrowing the words of German social critic Alexander Kluge, "Auch *wir* es sind — wir Philologen, Medienwissenschaftler — die an diesen Texten schreiben."[2] I join other contributors to this volume in agreement that this is something at which our honoree has excelled.

---

[1] Sweeney, *Isaiah 1–4*, 7.

[2] Alexander Kluge, quoted in Georg Stanitzek, "Texte, Paratexte, in Medien: Einleitung," *Paratexte in Literatur, Film, Fernsehen* (eds. Klaus Kreimeier and Georg Stanitzek; Berlin: Akademie Verlag, 2004), 3–20; here, 18. Originally from Alexander Kluge, "Das Lesen des Textes wirklicher Verhältnisse," *Der unterschätzte Mensch: Gemeinsame Philosophie in zwei Bänden* (Oskar Negt and Alexander Kluge, eds.; Frankfurt am Main: Zweitausendeins, 2001), 1:862–63.

* To Marvin, colleague and prolific scholar.

Job 31:9-10

Erotic Euphemisms in the Bible and Ancient Near Eastern and Rabbinic Literature

Shalom M. Paul

Job 31:9-10, as part of a lengthy soliloquy of transgressions that Job forswears he never committed, contains several sexual innuendoes and euphemisms that will be examined in the light of intra-biblical, rabbinic, and Akkadian sources.

> ⁹ If my heart was seduced by the wife of my neighbor,
> And I lay in wait at his door (פֶּתַח),
> ¹⁰ May my wife grind (תִּטְחַן)[1] for another,
> May others kneel over (יִכְרְעוּ) her.

The noun פֶּתַח, "opening, door," often serves as a euphemism in rabbinic sources for the *pudendum muliebre* to express a woman's absence of virginity. Compare the following examples. "He who says, 'I have found "an open opening" (פֶּתַח פָּתוּחַ),'[2] is trusted to make her forbidden to him" (b. Ketub. 9a). "He who says, 'I have found "an open opening" (פֶּתַח פָּתוּחַ)' is forbidden to have sexual relations with her, since there is a doubt whether she is an adulteress'" (y. Soṭah 1:6.25c). "If anyone says, 'I have found "an open opening" (פֶּתַח פָּתוּחַ),' he is trusted to cause her to lose her *ketubah*" (b. Ketub. 9b). And Ps 144:12, "Our daughters are like cornerstones," is interpreted as referring "to the virgins of Israel who seal up their 'openings' (פִּתְחֵיהֶן)," i.e., who reserve themselves for their husbands (b. Pesaḥ. 87a). Note, too, that one of the various reasons given to explain King Jehoiakim's punishment is "because he had intercourse with his mother, with his daughter-in-law, and with the wife of his father. The sum of the matter is in the 'opening' (פֶּתַח) from which he emerged, he entered" (Lev. Rab. 19:6).

---

[1] Some vocalize as a niphal, תִּטָּחֵן, "to be ground."
[2] Compare colloquial Arabic *maftûḥa(t)*, "opened," a euphemism for a deflowered virgin. See Stephan H. Stephan, "Modern Palestinian Parallels to the Song of Songs," *JPOS* 2 (1922): 199-278, here 224.

Moreover, in Isa 3:24, "instead of a rich robe, a girding of sackcloth" is interpreted by reading פְּתִיגִיל as a contraction of פְּתָחִים and גִּיל, "the openings (פתחים) that lead to [sensual] joy (גִּיל) shall be for a girding of sackcloth" (b. Šabb. 62b).

For a possible Egyptian usage, see love song 7 in Papyrus Harris 500: "The mansion of [my] sister / Her entry is in the middle of the house / Her double doors are open."[1] With this in mind, we can better understand the *double entendre* in Song 7:14 referring to the enticement of the young girl for her beloved: "The mandrakes give off fragrance, / At our doors (פְּתָחֵינוּ)[2] all sorts of luscious fruits, / both old and new, / my love, I have stored for you."

As the noun, so the verb. For its metaphorical poetic use, compare the midrashic comment on Isa 45:8: "Let the heavens rain down victory! Let the earth open up (תִּפְתַּח) so that triumph will sprout and vindication spring up," which is poignantly interpreted: "As a woman opens up (הַפּוֹתַחַת) for a man, so will the fertile earth open up (תִּפְתַּח)" (y. Ta'an. 1:3.64b; b. Ta'an. 8b).[3] The verb also applies to an animal: "Fatty meat from the she-goat that has not [yet] given birth" (דְּלָא אִפְתַּח, lit., "that has not yet been opened") (b. Pesaḥ. 42b).

Likewise in Akkadian, the adjective *petītu* and the verb *petû*, "to open," may refer to a "virgin… who… has not been opened (*la patteatuni*)"[4] and *la petītu* to an unmated animal.[5] In poetry, see the Old Babylonian love lyric, "Reach out with your left hand, 'honor' our

---

[1] Gerhard Fecht ("Die Wiedergewinnung der altägyptischen Verkunst," *MDAI* [1963]: 54–96, here 76) explains "double doors" as an allusion to the vagina. This reference is cited by Michael V. Fox, *Song of Songs and the Ancient Egyptian Love Songs* (Madison, WI: University of Wisconsin Press, 1985), 14. For other possible references to door = vagina, see Fox, *Song of Songs*, 70.

[2] This is an example of the "plural of ecstasy" that appears in Sumerian, Akkadian, and biblical love lyrics in first-person feminine ecstatic amatory discourse. See Shalom M. Paul, "The 'Plural of Ecstasy' in Mesopotamian and Biblical Love Poetry," *Solving Riddles and Untying Knots: Biblical, Epigraphic, and Semitic Studies in Honor of Jonas C. Greenfield* (eds. Ziony Zevit et al.; Winona Lake, IN: Eisenbrauns, 1995), 585–97 (repr. in Shalom M. Paul, *Divrei Shalom: Collected Studies of Shalom M. Paul on the Bible and the Ancient Near East 1967–2005* [Leiden: Brill, 2005], 239–52).

[3] For the image of rain and snow from the sky impregnating the earth, which, in turn, gives birth to herbage, see Isa 55:10. So, too, in a late Babylonian inscription: "As the sky inseminated the earth (so that) vegetation became abundant…" (*CAD* 4:309).

[4] Middle Assyrian Laws A 55.

[5] *CAD* 12:337–38, 346.

vulva. Find our breasts, Enter! I have opened my thighs."[1] It is also used together with *birku*, *buṣṣuru*, *sūnu*, and *ūru*, all signifying female genitalia.[2] Compare, for example, "Open (*pitêma*) your vulva that he may partake of your charms."[3]

And, as in the Bible, compare the erotic threefold use of the verb פתח in Song 5:2, 5-6: "Open for me (פִּתְחִי לִי), my beloved (lit., 'sister').... I arose to open (לִפְתֹּחַ) for my beloved... I opened (פָּתַחְתִּי) (the door) for my beloved."

As פֶּתַח indicates an "opening, entrance," so, too, its synonym דֶּלֶת may refer euphemistically to the *pudendum* in biblical and Akkadian sources. For the Bible, see Job's grievance (3:10) for having been born: "Because it [the night] did not block the womb's doors [i.e., my mother's womb] (דַּלְתֵי) and hide trouble from my eyes."[4] Compare, too, Song 8:8-9: "We have a little sister who has no breasts. What shall we do for our sister when she is spoken for? If she be a wall, we will build upon it a silver battlement. If she be a door (דָּלֶת), we will panel it in cedar." Though many commentators have interpreted "wall" and "door" to be a direct parallelism, it is more likely that this is a case of antithetic parallelism, with "wall" symbolizing inaccessibility, hence chastity, and "door," through which one may enter, referring to accessibility.[5]

Likewise in Akkadian, an Old Babylonian text states: "She [the mother goddess] says, 'You are free. The locks are unfastened. The

---

[1] Joan Goodnick Westenholz, "A Forgotten Love Song," *Language, Literature and History: Philological and Historical Studies Presented to Erica Reiner* (ed. Francesca Rochberg; AOS 67; New Haven: American Oriental Society, 1987), 415-25; see 1:13'-15'. "Our vulva" is another example of the "plural of ecstasy"; see above, 321, n2.

[2] See *AHw* 860.17 and the corresponding entries in *CAD*.

[3] *Epic of Gilgamesh*, tablet I, lines 182 and 189. See Andrew R. George, *The Babylonian Gilgamesh Epic: Introduction, Critical Edition and Cuneiform Texts* (Oxford: Oxford University Press, 2002-03), 1:548-49; 2:796 (see note there). See also Tzvi Abusch, *Male and Female in the Epic of Gilgamesh* (Winona Lake, IN: Eisenbrauns, 2015), 147-49 (including notes) for a brief discussion of these lines.

[4] For Job's wishful but vain thoughts of not having to be born, see Shalom M. Paul, "Vain Imprecation on Having Been Born in Job 3 and Mesopotamian Literature," *Marbeh Ḥokmah: Studies in the Bible and Ancient Near East in Loving Memory of Victor Avigdor Hurowitz* (eds. Shamir Yonah et al.; Winona Lake, IN: Eisenbrauns, 2015), 1:401-06, here 1:401-03.

[5] R. Lansing Hicks, "The Door of Love," *Love and Death in the Ancient Near East: Essays in Honor of Marvin H. Pope* (eds. John H. Marks and Robert McClive Good; Guildford, CT: Four Quarters, 1987), 153-58.

doors (*dalātu*) are open.'"[1] Similar, but much more frequent, is the use of *bābu*, "opening, door, doorway, gate," referring to the female sexual organ. In a Middle Assyrian medical text, the plight of a woman in childbirth is described: "The woman in childbirth has pangs of delivery… the baby is stuck fast [lit., "firm in place"]… The bolt is secure to bring life to an end. The door (*bābu*) is fastened against the suckling."[2] (This is reminiscent of Job's plaint above regarding the "doors of his mother's womb.")

In the Mousaieff Love Song, 11, rev. 8, the female coyly seduces her lover by saying: "That which you love, my vulva, is laid down for you; wide, spacious gate (*bābu*)."[3] And in a late first-millennium love ritual, Marduk says to his consort: "Into your [vul]va which you guard [lit., "in which you put your trust"], I will cause my dog [a euphemism for penis] to enter [and] I will shut the door (*bābum*)."[4] So, too, "you anoint [with the mixture] her navel and the opening (*bābu*) of her vagina."[5]

A closed vagina is chidingly referred to in a Sumerian dialogue between two women: "Your gate (ká·zu) is not made to be a gate (ká·na). It is locked up. It does not call for a man."[6] This, of course, recalls the similar description in Song 4:12: "A garden locked is my sister, my bride. A fountain locked, a sealed-up spring."[7]

---

[1] Jan J. A. van Dijk, "Une incantation accompagnant la naissance de l'homme," *Or* 42 (1973): 502–07, here 503, lines 22–24.

[2] Wilfred G. Lambert, "A Middle Assyrian Medical Text," *Iraq* 31 (1969): 28–38, here 31, lines 33–36.

[3] See Nathan Wasserman, *Akkadian Love Literature of the Third and Second Millenium B.C.E.* (LAS 4; Wiesbaden: Harrassowitz, 2016), 136, rev., line 8.

[4] Wilfred G. Lambert, "The Problem of the Love Lyrics," *Unity and Diversity: Essays in History, Literature, and Religion of the Ancient Near East* (eds. Hans Goedicke and Jimmy J. M. Roberts; Baltimore: Johns Hopkins University Press, 1975), 98–135, here 122, lines 11–12.

[5] Franz Köcher, ed., *Die babylonisch-assyrische Medizin in Texten und Untersuchungen* (Berlin: Walter de Gruyter, 1964), 3:237, line 3; *KAR* 2:194, line 3. Compare "*petû ša ūri*," EaA = *nâqu*, AaA = *nâqu*, *with Their Forerunners and Related Texts* (eds. Mugyek Civil et al., *MSL* 14; Rome: Pontificium Istitutum Biblicum, 1979), 269, line 6. Cf. *neptû rēme*, "the opening of the womb," Werner R. Mayer, "Akkadische Lexicographie, *CAD* P," *Or* 77 (2008): 94–105, here 100. Cf. also Gen 29:31; 30:22.

[6] This text, as yet unpublished by Jana Matuszak ("Und du willst einen Frau sein. Ein sumerisches Streitgesprech zwischen zwei Frauen" [PhD diss., University of Tübingen, 2012], 62:15), is cited by Wasserman, *Akkadian Love Literature*, 39–40.

[7] See Shalom M. Paul, "A Lover's Garden of Verse: Literal and Metaphorical Imagery in Ancient Near Eastern Poetry," *Tehillah le-Moshe: Biblical and Judaic Studies in Honor of Moshe Greenberg* (eds. Mordechai Cogan et al.; Winona Lake, IN: Eisenbrauns,

Now, returning to Job's self-condemnation and the *double entendre* there: If "I lay in wait at his door, may my wife grind (תִטְחַן)[1] for another." Targum Jonathan, the Vulgate, and a rabbinic source all recognized the connotation of the latter verb as referring to sexual intercourse. The Targum translates: "My wife will have carnal relations (תְּשַׁמֵּשׁ) with others." For the Aramaic verb שמש employed euphemistically, see y. Ned. 2:1.5a; b. Ned. 15b: "I vow not to have intercourse with you (מְשַׁמְּשֵׁךְ);" b. Ketub. 71b: "She must allow him marital intercourse (מְשַׁמַּשְׁתּוֹ)." And for the noun תַּשְׁמִישׁ, see, e.g., b. Yoma 77a–b; b. Ketub. 65b.[2]

Though the Vulgate does not interpret טחן this way in the Job verse, it does so in Lam 5:13b when describing the hardships the Babylonians imposed upon the exiles: "Young men toil to grind (טָחוֹן נָשָׂאוּ)," which they render *adolescentibus impudice abusi sunt*, "They abuse the young men shamelessly."

One rabbinic tradition formulates Sarah's remark that Abraham was too old to have children as, "My husband is old. He grinds (טוֹחֵן) but does not eject" (Gen. Rab. 48:17).[3] And on Judg 16:21, which describes Samson as being shackled and subjugated to grind (טוֹחֵן) in prison, the rabbis remark, "Grinding (טְחִינָה) means sexual transgression." They go on to explain, "Each one brought his wife to the prison in order that she might be impregnated by him (Samson)" (b. Soṭah 10a; Num. Rab. 9:24).[4] "Grinding" serves as a metaphor for

---

1997), 99–110, here 105 (repr. in Paul, *Divrei Shalom*, 271–84, here 278). For the metaphor of "garden" referring to female sexuality and fertility in general, and to the pudenda in particular, in Sumerian, Akkadian, Egyptian, and Hebrew love poetry, see Paul, *Divrei Shalom*, 272–81.

[1] See above, p. 321, n2. The verb is otherwise used in connection with slave labor, "to grind another's grain." See Exod 11:5; Isa 47:2.

[2] For multiple examples of the use of this verb, see Michael Sokoloff, *A Dictionary of Jewish Babylonian Aramaic of the Talmudic and Geonic Periods* (Ramat Gan: Bar Ilan University Press, 2002), 1162; for examples of the noun, see Michael Sokoloff, *A Dictionary of Jewish Palestinian Aramaic of the Byzantine Period* (Ramat Gan: Bar Ilan University Press, 1990), 559.

[3] See also Lekach Tov 45:7.

[4] Rashi, Ibn Ezra, and Y. ibn Ganaḥ (*Sefer Ha-shorashim* [eds. J. H. R. Biesenthal and F. Lebrecht; Berlin: n.p., 1847; repr. Jerusalem: n.p., 1967], 179) accept this interpretation. However, Kimḥi chidingly remarks, "What benefit was it to them? Hadn't he lost all his strength?"

sexual intercourse in other languages as well.[1] Compare Greek μύλλειν,[2] Latin *molere*,[3] and Arabic طَحَن.[4]

As for "kneeling over" in terms of sexual acquiescence, Pope cites the Arabic expression *kara'at al marāt ilā arrajul*.[5] It is interesting to note that the Talmud (b. Yebam. 103a; b. Naz. 23b; b. Hor. 10b) interprets Judg 5:27, "Between her feet, he kneeled over (כָּרַע), he fell (נָפַל), he lay (שָׁכַב)," referring to Sisera in Jael's tent in a sexual manner: "That profligate had sevenfold intercourse (with Jael) on that day," since כָּרַע is repeated three times, נָפַל three times, and שָׁכַב once.[6]

Measure for measure: Job is thus saying that were he to be an adulterer, he should be repaid in kind by having his wife succumb to other men.

---

[1] Stefan Schorch, *Euphemismen in der hebräischen Bibel* (OBC 12; Wiesbaden: Harrassowitz, 2000), 122–23. See Judg 16:19.

[2] Wilhelm Pape, *Griechisch-Deutsches Handwörterbuch* (Braunschweig: Vieweg, 1914), 2:217: μύλλω, 2; *LSJ* 1152: μυλλάς, prostitute; ὁ μυλλάς, cake in the shape of a pudenda.

[3] Karl E. Georges, *Ausführliches lateinisch-deutsches Handwörterbuch* (Leipzig: Hahn, 1913–18), 2:986: *mols*, 2II.

[4] Wilhelm Gesenius, *Hebräisches und aramäisches Handwörterbuch über das Alte Testament* (18th ed.; Berlin: Springer, 1995), 2:422 (טחן) and Eliezer Ben Jehuda, *A Complete Dictionary of Ancient and Modern Hebrew* (Jerusalem: Makor, 1980), 4:1866, 1867, n1.

[5] Marvin H. Pope, *Job* (AB 15; Garden City, NY: Doubleday, 1973), 271.

[6] In his commentary on this verse, Kimḥi rejects this interpretation outright.

Miscategorizing Chosenness

Jon D. Levenson

It is now standard procedure, or close to it, to begin discussions of chosenness in the Hebrew Bible by noting how much criticism the doctrine has received, especially in modern times. The idea that there is something irreducibly unfair in God's having chosen a given community, or in having formed a community for his own purposes in the first place, was already advanced by the Roman emperor Julian, who in the fourth century CE sought to repaganize his realm. "If he *is* the God of all alike, the shaper of everything," Julian asks in his anti-Christian polemic, *Against the Galileans*, "why did he overlook us?"[1] This notion that the universality of God precludes his having singled out a particular group is not one that had much resonance in premodern Christianity, however, and, in fact, some of the most influential contributors to the genre of "Old Testament theology" in the twentieth century still made election (as Christians generally prefer to call it) important or even central to their work.[2] After all, if God's singling out the Jews—or, as the Hebrew Bible itself would have it, miraculously creating the people Israel for a special destiny—is indefensible, then the claim that the Church has inherited the special status of the Jewish people is as well.[3] So, however much premodern Christians may have disparaged Judaism and despised Jews over the centuries, they could not attack the biblical affirmation of chosenness in general without cutting off their own legs. They could hope to become universal by eventually including everybody in their

---

[1] The translation is from *Julian's "Against the Galileans"* (tr. R. Joseph Hoffman; Amherst, NY: Prometheus Books, 2004), 101 (=*Contra Galileos* 106D).

[2] For example, it is important in Walther Eichrodt, *Theology of the Old Testament* (tr. John A. Baker; Philadelphia: Westminster Press, 1961). The first edition was published in 1933. It is central to Horst Dietrich Preuss, *Old Testament Theology* (Leo G. Perdue, trs.; Louisville: Westminster John Knox, 1995-96). The German version dates to 1991-92.

[3] Among the many New Testament affirmations of the chosenness of the Christians, the most striking is probably 1 Pet 2:9-10, with its obvious reworking of Exod 19:5-6.

particular community, "the body of Christ," to use Paul's terminology (1 Cor 12:27), but they could not claim that their community came into existence apart from the particular intervention of God.

With the Enlightenment, both Christians and Jews increasingly found themselves on the intellectual defensive, as the belief spread that the highest truth lay not with any individual community and its unique, historically contingent claims but rather with the putative universality of reason and science. Important adherents of both religious traditions scrambled to reinterpret their heritages as essentially rational and universal, however particular and contingent they may have traditionally appeared. In the past few decades, various social, political, and cultural changes have added force to the critique of chosenness that had already been common among Western intellectuals for nearly three hundred years. One such change has been the decline of nationalism, at least among the elites, in the wake of the vast carnage of the two World Wars of the twentieth century and especially of the Holocaust. With those events as the backdrop, it is immensely more difficult for any group to claim a transcendent authorization for its origins, identity, or way of life, and it is correlatively easier to depict such claims as inherently intolerant and even violent. The impact of this development on the interpretation of the Bible is in plentiful evidence. "The Other against whom Israel's identity is forged," writes Regina Schwartz, an English professor at Northwestern University, "is abhorred, abject, impure, and in the 'Old Testament,' vast numbers of them are obliterated, while in the 'New Testament,' vast numbers are colonized (converted)."[1] Biblical scholars have soundly critiqued Schwartz's thinking on these issues,[2] but the cultural resonance of the position she assumes has only increased in the two decades since she published her book.

---

[1] Regina M. Schwartz, *The Curse of Cain: The Violent Legacy of Monotheism* (Chicago: University of Chicago Press, 1997), 18-19. Schwartz goes on to concede that "the Bible conceives of Israel's relation with the Other in diverse ways" (19), but the negative way receives the brunt of her attention in the book.

[2] See R. W. L. Moberly, "Is Monotheism Bad for You? Some Reflections on God, the Bible, and Life in the Light of Regina Schwartz's *The Curse of Cain*," *The God of Israel* (ed. Robert P. Gordon; Cambridge: Cambridge University Press, 2007), 94-112 and, more briefly, Joel S. Kaminsky, *Yet I Loved Jacob: Reclaiming the Biblical Concept of Election* (Nashville: Abingdon, 2007), 108-110. Kaminsky's volume is essential for anyone seeking to understand chosenness in the Hebrew Bible or the New Testament.

The identification of justice with equality—a phenomenon that has become immensely powerful of late—has the effect not only of rendering all notions of chosenness intensely suspect but also of associating biblical conceptions of chosenness with social structures that are widely deemed oppressive. As Judith Plaskow, a Jewish feminist theologian, sees it, "Jewish feminists cannot transform the place of women's difference within the people of Israel without addressing the larger system of separations in which it is embedded." If so, then Jewish women's equality cannot become a reality so long as the traditional affirmation of chosenness remains in place. "The rejection of chosenness and the rejection of women's Otherness," she thus writes, "are interconnected pieces of the wider project of finding ways to conceptualize and live with difference that are not based on projection and graded separations."[1] To replace chosenness so conceived, Plaskow recommends not an undifferentiated humanity, since it is impossible to "be a human being in general," but rather an attachment to Jewish distinctiveness without any "supernatural vocation."[2] In sum, Jewish identity would be understood as a particularistic identity of the same character as all others, unconnected to any initiating and validating divine action. Such a proposal moves dramatically away from the Enlightenment belief in a universally authoritative, culture-free reason, to be sure, but it retains the Enlightenment rejection of a God who chooses and a people who are chosen—without both of which there is no chosenness. As Joel Kaminsky puts it, "If election means anything, it must mean that some are elected and others are not."[3] Election cannot be reduced to a mere affirmation of diversity and particularism.

For Rolf Knierim, however, it was precisely the character of the biblical God that renders the doctrine of a chosen people unacceptable. "The notion of [YHWH's] universality and universal reality complement each other," Knierim claimed. "Universality is their common denominator. This horizon represents the most fundamental of all theological aspects in the Old Testament." Moreover, the

---

[1] Judith Plaskow, *Standing Again at Sinai: Judaism from a Feminist Perspective* (San Francisco: HarperSanFrancisco, 1990), 97, 103.
[2] Plaskow, *Standing*, 104, 103.
[3] Kaminsky, *Yet I Loved*, 253.

universality of the biblical God is inextricably associated with his justice and righteousness, and this provides us the criterion for prioritizing the various streams of theological thinking in the Bible. It is, as Knierim put it, "the ultimate vantage point from which to coordinate its theologies *toward the universal dominion of [YHWH] in justice and righteousness*.... All other kinds and degrees of relationship with [YHWH] and reality, both qualitative and quantitative, as well as their own correlations, are subservient to this dominion."[1]

Although Knierim recognized the presence of the theology of covenant and the chosenness with which it is associated in the Hebrew Bible, he thus advanced the normative claim that such theologies must yield to that "most fundamental of all theological aspects," the universality and justice of God. Here again, the operative assumption is that chosenness is unjust, that God's having a special relationship with a given community—even if it is one that he has called into existence for that purpose—contradicts the supreme principle of the Bible. In this instance, Enlightenment principles serve as the criteria for establishing the normative and exclusive core of biblical theology, one that again, not surprisingly, disallows chosenness.[2]

Faced with this modern critique in its various modes, those committed to the theology of chosenness have understandably sought to reformulate it so as to make it less vulnerable to the charge of injustice. In one way or another, the reformulation usually presents the chosenness of Israel as instrumental to a larger and more universal goal. Hence, the idea became dominant, especially in liberal Judaism, that the Jews have indeed been singled out but for a mission directed to the entire world. As Julian Morgenstern, a leader of Reform Judaism at the time, put it in 1947, Israel has been "chosen by God, therefore, to be

---

[1] Rolf P. Knierim, *The Task of Old Testament Theology: Substance, Method, and Cases* (Grand Rapids: Eerdmans, 1995), 14–15, emphasis Knierim's. For religious reasons, I have devocalized the Tetragrammaton throughout this essay, and, in quoting authors who vocalize it, I have put the name in brackets.

[2] I have addressed this claim of Knierim's in a review essay of his book in Jon D. Levenson, Review of *The Task of Old Testament Theology: Substance, Method, and Cases* by Rolf P. Knierim, *RelSRev* 24 (1998): 39–42, esp. 41–42. For a longer critique along similar lines, see Joel S. Kaminsky, "Wrestling with Israel's Election: A Jewish Reaction to Rolf Knierim's Biblical Theology," *Reading the Hebrew Bible for a New Millennium: Form, Concept, and Theological Perspective* (eds. Wonil Kim et al.; Harrisburg, PA: Trinity International Press, 2000), 1:252–62.

His servant, the bearers of the highest knowledge of Him and of His way of life for mankind, unto all nations and peoples and throughout all time." Moreover, "it is for this service," he proclaimed, "that God has preserved Israel through trial and tribulation throughout the ages."[1] A few years later, the influential American Jewish thinker Will Herberg, a much more theologically traditional figure than Morgenstern, similarly spoke of "the vocation of Israel as witness against idolatry."[2] This line of thought stresses that the special status of the people Israel carries with it greater responsibility; it is not a matter of privilege or immunity from punishment. As Herberg wrote, "the 'choosing' is a demand and a summons upon Israel; involving greater obligation, heavier responsibility, a harder destiny, and a sterner judgment." Here he appeals, as do many who adhere to this interpretation, to a verse in Amos:

> You alone have I singled out (*yāda'tî*)
> Of all the families of the earth—
> That is why I will call you to account
> For all your iniquities (Amos 3:2).[3]

Apart from God's punishments for their failure to live up to this higher standard, the chosen must also, according to Herberg, face what he calls "the other side of the election and vocation of Israel," namely, anti-Semitism, which, he writes, "is, at the bottom, the revolt of the pagan against the God of Israel and his absolute demand."[4] So, whether the Jews are faithful to their charge or not, their vocation entails suffering to one degree or another.

---

[1] Julian Morgenstern, "Unity in American Judaism: How and When? An Address Delivered on September 22, 1945, at the Inauguration of the Seventy-First Academic Year of the Hebrew Union College." (Cincinnati: Hebrew Union College, 1945), 14. My attention was drawn to this address by Arnold M. Eisen, *The Chosen People in America: A Study in Jewish Religious Ideology* (Bloomington: Indiana University Press, 1983), 54. Eisen's book is essential for anyone addressing the interpretations of chosenness in modern Judaism.

[2] Will Herberg, "The 'Chosenness' of Israel and the Jew of Today," *Arguments and Doctrines: A Reader of Jewish Thinking in the Aftermath of the Holocaust* (ed. Arthur A. Cohen; New York: Harper & Row, 1970), 270–83, here 278. The essay originally appeared in *Midstream* in the autumn of 1955.

[3] Herberg, "The 'Chosenness,'" 281. See also Will Herberg's classic work, *Judaism and Modern Man: An Interpretation of Jewish Religion* (Philadelphia: Jewish Publication Society, 1951), esp. 266–67. Unless otherwise noted, all translations from the Hebrew Bible in this essay are taken from the NJPS.

[4] Herberg, *Judaism*, 273.

If we contrapose this line of thought to that represented by Knierim, we can say that chosenness so understood is not in violation of God's universal reign in justice and righteousness; it is, rather, a means to bring it about. If so, then, God's choosing the people Israel is not only less capricious than may first seem the case; it is also temporary—unless, of course, one also claims that Israel's mission to the world does not exhaust its own chosenness or exclusively define God's motive for his special relationship with it. But if we allow that something important remains even after the mission or witness of Israel is subtracted from the theology of election (as Herberg does),[1] then we are back where we began: something in the picture is still unjust because inequitable.

In Christianity, the idea that the people Israel was chosen for some purpose external to its own existence has been at home from the beginning. Closely associated with the ancient belief that the Hebrew Bible points to the New Testament and that Israel was a prototype for the Church, this idea is in plentiful evidence among modern scholars eager to diminish the particularistic dimension of the Hebrew Bible, whether for traditional theological or modern rationalist reasons, or, for that matter, because of their own (perhaps unconscious) anti-Semitic leanings. The traditional theological dimension comes to us loud and clear in the work of the great German Old Testament theologian, Gerhard von Rad. Speaking of the call of Abraham in Gen 12, von Rad wrote, "At the beginning of the way into an emphatically exclusive covenant-relation there is already a word about the end of this way, namely, an allusion to the final, universal unchaining of the salvation promised to Abraham. Truly," von Rad went on, his own enthusiasm almost itself unchained from exegesis, "flesh and blood did not inspire this view beyond Israel and its saving relation to God!"[2] As one would expect of a Lutheran theologian, von Rad focused on grace and salvation as the core of the chosenness of Abraham and the family promised him, rather than on the "knowledge of [God] and of His way of life for mankind," to recur to the words of his Jewish contemporary Morgenstern. What is most revealing, though, is how swiftly von Rad

---

[1] Herberg, "The 'Chosenness,'" 281.
[2] Gerhard von Rad, *Genesis: A Commentary* (tr. John H. Marks; rev. ed.; OTL; Philadelphia, Westminster, 1972), 154.

moved from what he acknowledged to be "an emphatically exclusive covenant-relation" to what he called "the final, universal unchaining of the salvation promised to Abraham." To him, the particularism of the covenant was something to be gotten past as soon as possible, replaced by the universal salvation that he thinks is already alluded to in Gen 12.

In order to find universal salvation in the call of Abraham, von Rad relied heavily on the famous crux Gen 12:3b, which the KJV, reflecting an ancient tradition,[1] renders as "and in thee shall all families of the earth be blessed" but the NJPS translates as "And all the families of the earth shall bless themselves by you." Von Rad knew the philological complications well but, for theological reasons, opted for the meaning that underlies the former wording.[2] Even so, his jump from blessing to salvation is not an easy one to make on the basis of the text at hand. The idea that the call of Abraham in Genesis itself involves something larger than the people Israel can, however, be reasonably advocated. Note the good things that Abraham or his descendants through Isaac and Jacob bring to the Canaanite kings whom Abram rescues in Gen 14, for example; or Laban, whose flocks Jacob enables to flourish (Gen 30:30); or the Egyptians whom Joseph enables to survive worldwide famine (Gen 41:53–57). If this is a point in von Rad's favor, a verse from the divine soliloquy before God reveals his plan for Sodom and Gomorrah to Abraham speaks to Knierim's focus on justice: "For I have singled him out (*yəda'tîw*), that he may instruct his children and his posterity to keep the way of the LORD by doing what is just and right, in order that the LORD may bring about for Abraham what He has promised him" (Gen 18:19). Knierim would not, however, be happy with the focus here on Abraham's children and posterity rather than on universal humanity as the target audience for Abraham's mission.

To speak of the benefits to humanity of God's choosing Israel, however those benefits be conceived, is thus consonant with a number

---

[1] Cf. the LXX: καὶ ἐνευλογηθήσονται ἐν σοὶ πᾶσαι αἱ φυλαὶ τῆς γῆς.
[2] Von Rad, *Genesis*, 160–61. Note that he speaks again of "this prophecy, which points to a fulfillment lying beyond the old covenant" (161). I have addressed the translational issue and its theological implications in Jon D. Levenson, *Inheriting Abraham: The Legacy of the Patriarch in Judaism, Christianity, and Islam* (LJI; Princeton: Princeton University Press, 2012), 24–28, 30–35.

of biblical texts and, I might add, with classical rabbinic and medieval Jewish sources as well.[1] The problem, rather, comes when election is seen as purely instrumental, so that the benefits for universal humanity exhaust the meaning of Israel's election, as it emphatically did not for those premodern Jewish sources. It is one thing to say that in God's plan, the nation promised to Abraham, Isaac, and Jacob would mediate blessing, exemplify justice and righteousness, or testify to God's own power and uniqueness. It is quite another to say that the existence of the nation and its relationship to God are predicated on such things.

The Beginnings of Chosenness

When we turn to biblical texts that purport to narrate the origins of the chosen people, we are first struck by the absence of the instrumental understanding of election that has proven so influential, at least for Christian exegetes, over the centuries. When Abram is called in Gen 12, there is nary a word about his ethical commitments, whether in the past or future, his theological convictions, or anything of the sort, and even if we accept the understanding of Gen 12:3b reflected in the KJV, it would still be difficult to see that verse as representing the goal of the call itself (as if it meant "in order that in thee shall all families of the earth be blessed"). In a poem preserved in Deuteronomy, we find a very different account of Israel's origin, one that shows no awareness of the tradition of the patriarchs of Genesis:

He found him in a desert region,
In an empty howling waste.
He engirded him, watched over him,
Guarded him like the pupil of his eye (Deut 32:10).

The LORD, it turns out, has expectations of the boy or man he found; he expects loyalty and gratitude from him (vv. 15-18), but there is surely no intimation in the poem that the adoptee exhibited those virtues before he was chosen or that his election itself was instituted principally in order to advance them.

In Ps 80, the origins of Israel seem to lie neither with the patriarchs, as in Genesis, nor in the wilderness, as in the Song of Moses, but in a vine that God took out of Egypt and planted in a land from which he had expelled nations to make room for it (vv. 9-14). But in

---
[1] See Levenson, *Inheriting*, 30-33, for a sample.

this case as well, there is no sense of a larger purpose to the relationship. Finally, in the developed allegory of the relationship of Jerusalem to the LORD in Ezek 16, the origins of the temple and royal city lie in a female foundling of mixed Amorite and Hittite parentage upon whom no one takes pity until the LORD adopts her, evidently in anticipation of marriage when she reaches puberty (vv. 3-7). As in Deut 32, so in Ezek 16, we hear intense censure of the adoptee for her ingratitude and infidelity but no hint that the adoption and marriage were to be in the service of any larger moral or theological mission. Rather, the relationship seems to be an end in itself, and the moral censure of the chosen party derives from their violation of the special relationship with the deity who has graciously chosen them.

It is in Deuteronomy that we find the most developed reflection on God's motivation for choosing Israel:

> [6] For you are a people consecrated to the LORD your God: of all peoples on earth the LORD your God chose you to be His treasured people. [7] It is not because you are the most numerous of peoples that the LORD set His heart (*ḥāšaq*) on you and chose you (*wayyibḥar*) — indeed, you are the smallest of peoples; [8] but it was because the LORD loved (*mē'aḥăbat*) you and kept the oath He made to your fathers that the LORD freed you with a mighty hand and rescued you from the house of bondage, from the power of Pharaoh king of Egypt (Deut 7:6-8).[1]

Here, the special status of Israel is ascribed not to size or, for that matter, any endowment of theirs but rather to the LORD's love, rendered through the familiar verb *'āhab* but also, significantly, through the more specialized term *ḥāšaq*, which would seem to express something passionate and erotic.[2] The exodus from Egypt, the most obvious and reiterated demonstration that the LORD has chosen Israel, was owing neither to an accumulation of merit on Israel's part nor to some ethical message that the LORD wanted to teach the world. It was not even owing to the best-known message of modern times — that slavery is immoral, a message that became popular, not surprisingly,

---

[1] I have given reasons for translating *'ahăvat* (v. 8) as "loved" rather than "favored" (NJPS) in Jon D. Levenson, *The Love of God: Divine Gift, Human Gratitude, and Mutual Faithfulness in Judaism* (LJI; Princeton: Princeton University Press, 2015), 40-42. Note the close parallel in Deut 10:14-15.

[2] So I have argued in Levenson, *The Love*, 40-42.

just as slavery was disappearing in the modern West, and is still widely heard from pulpits.[1] Instead, here the exodus is seen as owing to the LORD's covenantal oath to the patriarchs. The covenant, of course, carries with it all kinds of moral and theological expectations, but its origin—the motivation for the LORD's having "chosen" (*bāḥar*) Israel, to use one of Deuteronomy's favorite terms—lies in his mysterious act of passion for her. That act is not directed at the unchosen and carries with it no implication that they can or should eventually become chosen. The same must be said of the marriage metaphor for the relationship of Israel and its God prominent in books like Hosea and Jeremiah.[2]

In all the cases we have examined, including those that do not speak of love at all, the election of Israel exhibits the irrationality—or, to put it better, the nonpredictability—of the sort of impassioned act of which Deuteronomy speaks.

The Inegalitarianism of Love

These days, scholars generally and rightly associate the exclusivity characteristic of Israel's mandated love of God in Deuteronomy with the ancient Near Eastern treaties whose language reverberates most centrally in that book.[3] We must not allow the term "treaty," however, to obscure the key fact that the relationship this diplomatic instrument seals is not between states but between persons, specifically the person of the suzerain and that of his vassal. The love that it entails is necessarily concrete and individual, not abstract and general. A Jewish theologian, the late Michael Wyschogrod, drew the underlying contrast well:

> Undifferentiated love, love that is dispensed equally to all must be love that does not meet the individual in his individuality but sees him as a member of a species, whether that species be the working class, the poor, those created in the

---

[1] See Jon D. Levenson, *The Hebrew Bible, the Old Testament and Historical Criticism: Jews and Christians in Biblical Studies* (Louisville: Westminster John Knox, 1993), 127-59.

[2] Levenson, *The Love*, 90-116.

[3] The pioneering article on this is William L. Moran, "The Ancient Near Eastern Background of the Love of God in Deuteronomy," *CBQ* 25 (1963): 77-87; repr., William L. Moran, *That Most Magic Word* (ed. Ronald S. Hendel; CBQMS 35; Washington: Catholic Biblical Society of America, 2002), 170-81. See also Levenson, *The Love*, 1-58.

image of God, or what not.... Unlike such fantasies, divine love is concrete. It is a genuine encounter with man in his individuality and must therefore be exclusive. Any real love encounter, if it is more than an example of the love of a class or collectivity, is exclusive because it is genuinely directed to the uniqueness of the other and it therefore follows that each such relationship is different from all others. But difference is exclusivity because each relationship is different, and I am not included in the relationship of others.[1]

If this is right, then the non-predictability of chosenness and the exclusivity of covenant have something in common: they both respond to something that cannot be generalized or reduced to an algorithm. R. W. L. Moberly reflects profoundly on this aspect of divine love in the Hebrew Bible:

Generally speaking, one of the recurrent notes that is sounded by a responsive individual recipient of love is an astonished "Why me?" This is a question that always looks for more than actual reasons and explanations, however much some reasons and explanations may indeed be given. The question expresses sheer marvel at the gratuitous wonder of being loved (gratuitous, because even the most admirable personal qualities are no guarantee of being loved by another). The reality of love surpasses the realm of reason. In this sense love is a mystery, not in the sense of a puzzle to be resolved but in the sense of a reality whose dimensions grow as a people engage with it: in convenient shorthand, "the more you know, the more you know you don't know." If this note of astonished wonder is lost, then a significant dimension of understanding the nature of divine choosing is also lost.[2]

In a probing study from the 1960s, the philosopher Irving Singer underscored the gratuitous nature of love in general and

---

[1] Michael Wyschogrod, *The Body of Faith: Judaism as Corporeal Election* (New York: Seabury, 1983), 61. On analogy with the Near Eastern treaties, one might have expected that the exclusivity would be unilateral. Israel, that is, would have to be exclusively devoted to the LORD, but not the reverse. Importantly, I know of no evidence to support a claim that the biblical understanding of the covenant in question was not exclusive for both parties. Note, for example, that in the prophetic texts that employ the marriage metaphor, the LORD has no other wives. This is true even during the period between his divorce from Israel and his remarriage to her in Hos 1–2.

[2] R. W. L. Moberly, *Old Testament Theology: Reading the Hebrew Bible as Christian Scripture* (Grand Rapids: Baker Academic, 2013), 44–45.

pointed to the mistakenness of attempts to appeal to norms outside the specific relationship. Love, he wrote,

> is created by the affirmative relationship *itself*, by the very act of responding favorably, giving an object emotional and pervasive importance regardless of its capacity to satisfy interests. Here it makes no sense to speak of verifiability; and though bestowing may often be injurious, unwise, even immoral, it cannot be erroneous in the way that an appraisal might be. For now it is the valuing alone that *makes* the value.[1]

Because the love relationship is by its very nature not subject to verifiability, the one loved, Singer goes on, "cannot be reduced to any system of appraisal. The lover takes an interest in the beloved as a *person*, and not merely as a commodity (which she may also be)."[2] This I take to be essentially the same statement as the one Wyschogrod made about the concreteness of "the love encounter" and its difference from an abstract and generalized benevolence. It also correlates nicely with Moberly's observation, from the recipient's standpoint, about the "sheer marvel at the gratuitous wonder of being loved (gratuitous, because even the most admirable personal qualities are no guarantee of being loved by another)."

The Scandal of a Personal God

If the beloved responds to the situation with "an astonished 'Why me?'" as Moberly puts it, critics of the chosenness of Israel, such as Schwartz, Plaskow, and Knierim, respond with an outraged "Why not me?" To them, that very absence of a system of appraisal is proof of injustice, and, especially in the cases of Schwartz and Plaskow, it demonstrates (if a demonstration is even necessary) that the biblical idea of the chosen people is merely a human projection, born out of insecurities and prejudices, rather than a transcendent truth with which to reckon.[3] Precisely because chosenness confers a benefit on individuals (in this case, the collective individual known as the people

---

[1] Irving Singer, *The Nature of Love: Plato to Luther* (New York: Random House, 1966), 5.

[2] Singer, *The Nature*, 6.

[3] Moberly points out that Schwartz "simply takes for granted... that all language about God is a human projection." ("Is Monotheism Bad for You," 101). Even if the language in question is indeed that, however, there is still no warrant for disregarding the role of love in the matter at hand.

Israel) that is not validated by their superior personal qualities, it violates the impartiality characteristic of true justice. In my judgment, this is exactly right.

What is not right is the neglect of the point that Wyschogrod, Moberly, and Singer all make, each in his own way: love does not fall in the domain of justice.[1] Not only do those who treat love as if were a response to deserts miscategorize it; when they treat the chosenness of Israel the same way, they necessarily miscategorize chosenness as well. This is the case not only when the chosenness is associated with love, as in Deuteronomy; it is also the case in texts like Gen 12, Deut 32, and Ps 80 that make mention neither of love nor, significantly, of merit. In all these cases, the special status of Israel is a prime datum. In the theology of these texts (as distinguished from the putative psychology of their unknown authors), we find nothing anterior to the chosenness itself that accounts for it.

In the case of those who, like Morgenstern and von Rad, accept the special status of Israel but subordinate it in their different ways to a universal mission, this seems to me to come close to what Singer calls treating the beloved "as a commodity." Here again, the mistake is the implicit classification of chosenness as a moral judgment, though in this case one that is defensible as a means to something desirable, the spread of the knowledge of God or the dispensing of salvation to all humankind. This instrumental understanding of chosenness subjects the God-Israel relationship to a system of appraisal, to recall Singer's term, even though, in the hands of Morgenstern and von Rad at least, the relationship passes the appraisal swimmingly.

To Schwartz, the deep cause of the notion of chosenness is what she calls the "principle of scarcity." "When everything is in short supply," she explains, "it must be competed for.... In many biblical narratives, the one God is not imagined as infinitely giving but as

---

[1] Note that in the same discourse—really, the same paragraph—a Deuteronomic homilist can assert both that God loved the patriarchs and chose the Israelites (Deut 10:15) and that he "shows no favor" (v. 17). The apparent contradiction is resolved if we remember that showing favor, like bribe-taking (which immediately follows), are juridical terms: they apply to court procedures, and not more generally. A good analogy is the presence of a law that forbids favoring the poor in legal procedures (Exod 23:3) in a collection that repeatedly expresses God's special concern for the poor (v. 6).

strangely withholding. Everyone does not receive divine blessings," and it is this to which she attributes the well-known biblical "demand of exclusive allegiance."[1] Here, again, she is right—up to a point. A relationship with any personal being cannot but be a matter of scarcity, and for a very simple reason: persons are not interchangeable. Each one is unique and irreplaceable. When Schwartz longs for an "infinitely giving" God who relates to everyone the same way, she is, in fact, asking for Wyschogrod's "love that is dispensed equally to all," which, to recall his words, "must be love that does not meet the individual in his individuality but sees him as a member of a species."[2] Within a relationship of love as Wyschogrod understood it, the beloved is indeed scarce: there is no one like him or her. That is why prophets like Hosea, Jeremiah, and Ezekiel can describe treachery against covenant as marital infidelity and sexual promiscuity. There is nothing "strangely withholding" about faithfulness in a personal relationship, whether one is the husband or the wife, the parent or the child, the king or the subject, the suzerain or the vassal. On the contrary, without the exclusivity—treating the beloved as unique and irreplaceable—the relationship would dissolve.

It seems to me, then, that what lies behind the distaste for chosenness on the part of its theistic critics is principally an objection to the very idea of a personal God. The objection is hardly new, but political and scientific developments over the past three centuries or so have given it vastly greater cultural credibility. When law is understood not as the will of one's sovereign to any degree but solely as an impersonal and impartial mechanism by which faceless citizens (no longer "subjects") order their society for their own benefit, the covenantal theology of the Hebrew Bible and the theology of love and chosenness with which it is associated become harder to imagine because they correlate less and less with the unspoken assumptions of society. Similarly, when the natural order is understood as a universal and regular reality that admits of no exceptions and is best expressed in mathematical formulae, the range of action of the personal God shrinks dramatically. Once the action of God is exhaustively placed

---

[1] Schwartz, *The Curse*, xi. Schwartz does, however, recognize the existence in the Bible of what she calls "glimpses of a monotheistic plenitude instead of scarcity" (xi).
[2] Wyschogrod, *The Body*, 61.

within the categories of modern notions of lawfulness, the deeper perceptions and convictions that underlie chosenness disappear.

The Non-Elect, the Anti-Elect, and the Pro-Elect

Now a word about the unchosen. For those opposed to the doctrine of chosenness, or election, the fate of the outsider is a prime weapon in their armamentarium. For Schwartz, as we saw, "The Other against whom Israel's identity is forged is abhorred, abject, impure, and in the 'Old Testament,' vast numbers of them are obliterated, while in the 'New Testament,' vast numbers are colonized (converted)."[1] Let us leave aside the New Testament and the puzzling idea that conversion in that collection can be equated with colonization. In the Hebrew Bible, it is simply not the case that the Other, the outsider, the unchosen are necessarily viewed as abhorred, abject, and impure. The chosenness of Abraham rather than his brothers does not prevent his sending his majordomo back to his family to secure a bride for Isaac (Gen 24). In the next generation, the verse in which God announces that the covenant will belong to Isaac alone immediately—and revealingly—follows one in which God promises to bless his half-brother Ishmael abundantly (Gen 17:20-21). To be sure, in the next two generations, nearly fatal discord breaks out between the chosen sons, Jacob and Joseph successively, and their unchosen brothers, but in the end Jacob and Esau have an amicable separation and Joseph and his brothers experience a reconciliation, the election of Joseph having, in fact, saved the life of the entire family (Gen 33:1-17; 50:15-21). Indeed, as many have noted, in the text where Jacob secures his father's unique blessing, the narrator's sympathy is with his unchosen—nay, swindled—twin Esau, this despite the fact that the blessing and special status of Jacob/Israel correspond to God's wishes and remain in effect (Gen 27:1-45).

Rather than speaking of "the Other," it would be better, then, to adopt Kaminsky's tripartite division of humanity into the elect, the non-elect, and the anti-elect,[2] but with the important qualifications that Rachel Billings makes. "Within the group of those who have *not* been chosen by YHWH," Billings writes, "there is a degree of fluidity with

---

[1] Schwartz, *The Curse*, 18-19.
[2] Kaminsky, *Yet I Loved*, esp. 111-36.

regard to how they *relate* to YHWH and YHWH's elect." In the case of the Egyptians and especially the pharaohs of the early chapters of Exodus, for example, they appear as the antagonistic Other, but elsewhere they fit more neatly into the category of the non-elect. Indeed, a law in Deuteronomy forbids Israelites to "abhor" (*ti'ēb*) Egyptians or Edomites, the nation descended from Esau (Deut 23:8). But, importantly, Billings also proposes a fourth category, the "pro-elect," to explain "certain individuals or groups among the non-elect [who] act in ways that actively aid in and further YHWH's purposes for His elect."[1] Here, the prime example is the Canaanite prostitute Rahab, whom Joshua rescues from certain death when Jericho is destroyed (Joshua 2:1–24; 6:20–23).

In recent years, a good argument has been made that the command to annihilate the Canaanites in Deuteronomic literature (e.g., Deut 7:1-5) reflects neither the historical reality of Israel's emergence in Canaan nor the practical expectation the Deuteronomic authors had of their audiences in the late monarchy or perhaps later periods. Instead, "Deuteronomy," as Moberly puts it, "uses and indeed privileges the notion of *ḥērem* only because it was seen to lend itself to a particular metaphorical usage for practices appropriate to enabling Israel's everyday allegiance to YHWH within a world of conflicting allegiances."[2] If so, the ostensible command of genocide is directed not at whatever identifiable Canaanites lived within Israel's borders but rather at the Israelites themselves; in its own grisly way, it is another expression of the ideal of exclusive, uncompromising commitment. Such an interpretation draws strength from the story of that Canaanite prostitute who, hearing of Israel's miraculous exodus from Egypt and the defeat of the trans-Jordanian kings, declares that "the LORD your God is the only God in heaven above and on earth below" (Josh 7:11). The declaration saves Rahab's life, but it does not, nor is there any reason to think that it ought to, make her a member of the chosen people. My objective here is not to offer a defense of the genocidal command but rather to say that even the existence of anti-elect in some biblical literature does not warrant the notion that in the Bible

---

[1] Rachel M. Billings, *"Israel Served the Lord": The Book of Joshua as Paradoxical Portrait of Faithful Israel* (Notre Dame: University of Notre Dame Press, 2013), 39–40.
[2] Moberly, *Old Testament*, 68. The larger argument is found on pp. 53–74.

chosenness inevitably entails abhorring or obliterating the Other. In fact, making the anti-elect into the archetypical Other is itself a miscategorization that can only obscure the complex, profound biblical theology of chosenness.

Finally, I cannot close without noting the gratitude that all of us interested in the Hebrew Bible in general and in making sense of its theology in particular must feel for the honoree of this volume, Professor Marvin A. Sweeney. His contribution to the field has been enormous, and I count myself privileged to have known him for forty years. May he live to thrice that!

From Deuteronomy to the Lost Gospel
An Intra-Jewish Controversy about Group Annihilation

Dennis R. MacDonald

What an honor it is to contribute to this volume celebrating the distinguished career of my longtime colleague Marvin Sweeney. Those who know him deeply admire his erudition, energy, reliability, teaching prowess, and friendship. I offer this essay as a way of bridging his interests in the Bible and the history of Jewish interpretation and mine in the New Testament.

As several recent studies have demonstrated, ancient Jews frequently targeted Deuteronomy for substantial rewriting. Such imitations include Jubilees, the Temple Scroll, the writings of Philo, and the Testament of Moses, which expands on Moses's instructions to Joshua at the end of Deuteronomy.[1] Such transformations appear even in the transmission of the text itself.[2] The motivations for these rewritings vary widely, but for Hellenized Jews, Moses's commands to annihilate whole families, cities, and even entire ethnic groups was an embarrassment that required silence, interpretation, or rejection. In this brief study, I will propose that the lost Gospel often referred to as Q advocated a rejection, one not by a Christian attacking a Jewish text but

---

[1] Jewish rewritings and imitations of Deuteronomy have received extensive scholarly attention. Among the most important are Lawrence H. Schiffman, "The Deuteronomic Paraphrase of the Temple Scroll," *RevQ* 15 (1991-92): 543-67; Bernard M. Levinson, *Deuteronomy and the Hermeneutics of Legal Innovation* (New York: Oxford University Press, 1997); Simone Paganini, *"Nicht darfst du zu diesen Wörtern etwas hinzufügen": Die Rezeption des Deuteronomiums in der Tempelrolle* (BZABR 11; Wiesbaden: Harrasowitz, 2009); Hindy Najman, *Seconding Sinai: The Development of Mosaic Discourse in Second Temple Judaism* (JSJSup 77; Leiden: Brill, 2003); and David Lincicum, *Paul and the Early Jewish Encounter with Deuteronomy* (Grand Rapids: Baker Academic, 2013). According to David Moessner, Luke made extensive use of Deuteronomy in the composition of his so-called Travel Section, which relies heavily on the lost Gospel (David P. Moessner, *The Lord of the Banquet: The Literary and Theological Significance of the Lukan Travel Narrative* [Minneapolis: Fortress, 1989]).

[2] Sidnie White Crawford, *Rewriting Scripture in Second Temple Times* (SDSSRS; Grand Rapids: Eerdmans, 2008), esp. 30-36.

by a Jewish admirer of Jesus whose response to Deuteronomy's statements about group destruction resembles the concerns of Philo, Pseudo-Philo, and Josephus.

Deuteronomy and the Conquest of Canaan

Here are the relevant texts according to my translation of the Septuagint:

> [31]And the Lord said to me, "Look, I have begun to hand over to you Sihon, king of Hesbon, the Amorite, and his land. Begin to inherit his land." [32]And Sihon, king of Hesbon, came out to engage us in battle at Jahaz, he and all his people. [33]The Lord handed him over to us, and we slew them, his sons, and all his people, [34]and we captured all his cities at that time, and annihilated, one by one, every city, with their wives, and their children, leaving no one alive (2:31-34).
>
> [3]And the Lord our God handed him into our hands, even Og and all his people, and we slew him until none of his seed remained. [4]And we captured all their cities at that time; there was no city that we did not take from them.... [6]And we annihilated them as we did to Sihon, king of Hesbon, and we annihilated every city, one by one, with their wives and children (3:3-4, 6).
>
> The Lord your God will give them into your hand, and you will beat them; you will destroy them utterly; you will not make a treaty with them or have mercy on them (7:2).
>
> [10]If you should advance on a city to make war on it, you should call out to them with peace. [11]And if they respond to you in peace and open their gates to you, all that people and everyone found in the city will pay you tribute and be submissive to you. [12]But if they do not submit to you and make war with you, you will camp around it, [13]and the Lord your God will give it into your hands, and you will murder by sword every male— [14]excluding the women, possessions, all the cattle, and everything in the city— and you will take to yourself as spoils all the plunder and will eat all the plunder of your enemies, whom the Lord your God has given you (20:10-14).
>
> [19]I testify to you today, by heaven and earth, I have offered before your face life and death, blessing and cursing. Choose life, so that you and your seed may live. [20]Love the Lord your God, obey his voice, and cling to him, because doing so is your life and the longevity of your days for dwelling on the land that God swore to give your fathers, Abraham, Isaac, and Jacob (30:19-20).

> ¹Moses completed speaking all these sayings to all the sons of Israel. ²He said to them, "Today I am one hundred and twenty years old, unable to move about, and the Lord said to me, 'You will not cross this Jordan.' ³The Lord your God who goes before your face will himself destroy all these Gentiles before you, and you will take them as an inheritance. And Joshua is the one who will go before you, as God said. ⁴And the Lord will do to the Gentiles as he obliterated Sihon and Og, the two kings of the Amorites, who were on the other side of the Jordan, in their own land (31:1-4).
>
> Blessed are you, Israel: what people is like you who is being saved by the Lord? Your Help will protect you with a shield; the sword will be your boast. Your enemies will be false to you; but you will tread upon their necks (33:29).

Hellenistic Jewish Reactions to Group Destruction

Louis Feldman has shown that the cruelty of these passages was an embarrassment to many Hellenistic Jews. For example, Philo frequently allegorized such offensive passages. As a leader of the Egyptian Jewish community, he must answer Jews in his own community who raise questions of theodicy; thus, he adamantly defends the principle that the innocent should not suffer for the sins of the guilty. He is likewise concerned with maintaining good relations with non-Jews; thus, he must answer those who charge the Jews with hating non-Jews.[1]

Philo indicates that only the soldiers of Sihon were killed; he does not indicate that women and children were put to death. Pseudo-Philo passes over the episode of Sihon and Og almost completely, reporting only that Moses defeated them, without indicting how many of the men, women, and children he had he had killed.[2]

It is Josephus, as a Jew living among non-Jews, who is most sensitive to the charges of the anti-Semites and who is most insistent that Jews do not hate non-Jews. Josephus omits particularly troublesome passages, such as the annihilation of the firstborn captives

---

[1] Louis H. Feldman, *"Remember Amalek!": Vengeance, Zealotry, and Group Destruction in the Bible According to Philo, Pseudo-Philip, and Josephus* (HUCM 31; Cincinnati: Hebrew Union College Press, 2004), 224.

[2] Feldman, *"Remember Amalek,"* 223.

and maidservants.[1] Josephus (*Ant.* 4.97) also states that the Israelites annihilated Og's army, while omitting mention of the women and the children.[2]

The *Logoi of Jesus* (Q+) and Group Destruction in Deuteronomy

For the following discussion, the translation of the lost Gospel comes from my reconstruction of it,[3] which is about twice as long as previous versions of Q, hence it may also be called Q+. The two examples to be discussed here, however, appear not only in my reconstruction but in conventional Qs as well. More detailed treatments of imitations of the lost Gospel will appear in a forthcoming publication.[4]

The Healing of the Centurion's Son (Logoi 4:45–51[5])

Jesus's so-called Inaugural Sermon in the lost Gospel begins with a clear evocation of Moses receiving the Law on Mount Sinai: "Jesus ascended into the mountain and called his twelve disciples" (*Logoi* 3:34–35a). Whereas Moses's last words to the twelve tribes included a beatitude, Jesus's first instruction to the Twelve is a beatitude, but with a significant difference.

Deut 33:29	*Logoi* 4:1, 3
Blessed are you, Israel: what people is like you who is being saved by the Lord? Your Help will protect you with a shield; the sword will be your boast. Your enemies will be false to you; but you will tread upon their necks.	Blessed are you poor, for the kingdom of God is for you.... [3]Blessed are you when they hate and insult you and say every kind of evil against you because of the Son of Man.

Deuteronomy concludes with extensive blessings on Israel if they obey God's commandments and curses if they do not. The

---

[1] Feldman, "*Remember Amalek*," 225.
[2] Feldman, "*Remember Amalek*," 225.
[3] Dennis R. MacDonald, *Two Shipwrecked Gospels: The Logoi of Jesus and Papias's Exposition of Logia about the Lord* (ECL 8; Atlanta: Society of Biblical Literature, 2012).
[4] *The Logoi of Jesus (Q+) as a Rewriting of Deuteronomy*, the first volume of *Solving the Synoptic Problem with Mimesis Criticism*. Mimesis criticism is a methodology designed to identify and interpret how one text imitates or perhaps rivals another.
[5] *Logoi* 4:45–51; Matt 7:28a; 8:5–13; Luke 7:1–10.

Inaugural Sermon of *Logoi* similarly promises rewards for those who obey Jesus's teachings and warns of destruction for those who do not. Compare the following:

Deut 30:15–18	*Logoi* 4:42–44
¹⁵ Look, today I have given in your presence life and death, good and evil.	
¹⁶ If you observe the commandments of the Lord your God, the ones I commanded you today…	⁴² Everyone hearing my sayings and doing them
you will live and be numerous, and the Lord your God will bless you throughout the land into which you are entering to inherit.	⁴³ is like a person who built one's house on bedrock; and the rain poured down and the flashfloods came, and the winds blew and pounded that house, and it did not collapse, for it was founded on bedrock.
¹⁷ And if your heart should waver, not be observant…	⁴⁴ And everyone who hears my sayings and does not do them
¹⁸ I tell you today that you will be utterly destroyed and not last long on the land that your God is giving you, which you are crossing the Jordan to inherit.	is like a person who built one's house on the sand; and the rain poured down and the flashfloods came, and the winds blew and battered that house, and promptly it collapsed, and its fall was devastating.

Surely, it is not by accident that both in Deuteronomy and in the lost Gospel immediately after the blessings and curses one finds nearly identical transitions:

Deut 31:1	*Logoi* 4:45a
Moses completed speaking all these sayings [συνετέλεσεν … τοὺς λόγους τούτους].	When Jesus completed these sayings [ἐτέλεσεν … τοὺς λόγους τούτους]… (Many texts of Matt 7:28 replace ἐτέλεσεν with συνετέλεσεν.)

What immediately follows in Deuteronomy is Moses's speech cited earlier:

> ² Today I am one hundred and twenty years old, unable to move about, and the Lord said to me, "You will not cross this Jordan." ³ The Lord your God who goes before your face will himself destroy all these Gentiles before you, and you will take them as an inheritance. And Joshua is the one who will go before you, as God said. ⁴ And the Lord will do to the Gentiles as he obliterated Sihon and Og, the two kings of the Amorites, who were on the other side of the Jordan, in their own land (31:1-4).

The military victory over the Amorites included the killing of the children of Sihon and Og.

What follows in the Inaugural Sermon in *Logoi* is the healing of the centurion's son:

> ⁴⁵ When Jesus completed these sayings, he entered Capernaum. ⁴⁶ And there came to him a centurion exhorting him and saying, "My boy is doing badly."
> And he said to him, "I will come and cure him."
> ⁴⁷ And in reply the centurion said, "Master, I am not worthy for you to come under my roof; ⁴⁸ but say a word, and let my boy be healed. ⁴⁹ For I too am a person under authority, with soldiers under me, and I say to one, 'Go,' and he goes, and to another, 'Come,' and he comes, and to my slave, 'Do this,' and he does it."
> ⁵⁰ But Jesus, on hearing, was amazed, and said to those who followed, "I tell you, not even in Israel have I found such faith."
> ⁵¹ And Jesus said to the centurion, "Go; may it be to you as you have believed." He returned home and found the child healed.

Instead of killing the children of Gentile kings, as Moses commanded "all the sons of Israel" in Deuteronomy, Jesus heals the son of a Gentile centurion, who demonstrates greater faith than all in Israel. Surely, this is an intentional and strategic transformation to replace divinely sanctioned violence against the children of Israel's military foes with the healing of the son of a Roman centurion. Furthermore, in the case of the centurion's son he reverses not only the command to kill the children of Amorite kings but also the last miracle that Moses performed "before Pharaoh," namely, the slaying of the Egyptian firstborn males.

The Mission Speech (Logoi 10:11-22[1])

The second example pertains to Moses's commissioning of the twelve tribes to conduct a military assault on the native populations of Canaan. In the lost Gospel, Jesus sends the twelve disciples to evangelize "the lost sheep of the house of Israel" (10:7) with the following instructions:

> [11]Into whatever house you enter, first say, "Peace to this house!" [12]And if a son of peace be there, let your peace come upon him; but if not, let your peace return upon you. [13]And at that house remain, eating and drinking whatever they provide, for the worker is worthy of one's reward. Do not move around from house to house. [14]And whatever city you enter and they take you in, eat what is set before you. [15]And cure the sick there, and say to them, "The kingdom of God has reached unto you." [16]But into whatever city you enter and they do not take you in, on going out from that city, [17]shake off the dust from your feet. [18]I tell you: For Sodom it shall be more bearable on that day than for that city. [19]Woe to you, Chorazin! Woe to you, Bethsaida! For if the wonders performed in you had taken place in Tyre and Sidon, they would have repented long ago in sackcloth and ashes. [20]Yet for Tyre and Sidon it shall be more bearable at the judgment than for you. [21]And you, Capernaum, up to the sky will you be exalted? Into hades you will come down! [22] Whoever takes you in takes me in, and whoever takes me in takes in the one who sent me (10:11-22).

This passage once again critiques Moses's command to destroy populations in Deuteronomy.

Deut 20:10-13a	*Logoi* 10:11-12
If you should advance on a city to make war on it, you should call out to them with peace.	Into whatever house you enter, first say, "Peace to this house!"
[11]And if they respond to you in peace and open their gates to you, all that people and everyone found in the city will pay you tribute and be submissive to you.	[12]And if a son of peace be there, let your peace come upon him;

---

[1] *Logoi* 10:11-22; Mark 6:10-12; Matt 10:11-15, 40; 11:21-24; Luke 10:5-16.

| ¹²But if they do not submit to you and make war with you, you will camp around it, ¹³and the Lord your God will give it into your hands. | but if not, let your peace return upon you." |

Moses then describes what they should do to the inhabitants once they conquer them: "You will murder by sword every male, ... and you will take to yourself as spoils all the plunder and will eat all the plunder of your enemies, whom the Lord your God has given you" (Deut 20:13b-14). Contrast this with the instructions of Jesus in *Logoi*: "But into whatever city you enter and they do not take you in, on going out from that city, shake off the dust from your feet" (*Logoi* 10:16-17).

These parallels are striking: in both Deuteronomy and the lost Gospel, a lawgiver instructs his followers how to conduct themselves in their missions after his death. The twelve tribes and the twelve disciples are to appeal first for a peaceful reception, and if the residents respond in peace, all is well. On the other hand, according to Moses, if the residents are hostile, the tribes are to capture the town, put the men to the sword, take the women, livestock, and possessions, and eat the spoils. In *Logoi*, however, Jesus tells the disciples, "Let your peace return upon you." Rather than subjugating or destroying, they are to shake the dust from their feet against those who reject them and cure the sick among those who accept them. The act of shaking dust from one's feet functions as a curse for not having been welcomed with the washing of feet; it is God, not they, who will deal with them. Notice also that Deuteronomy speaks of Israelites slaying Gentiles, but *Logoi* pronounces judgment instead on the Jewish towns of Chorazin, Bethsaida, and Capernaum.

Such contrasting imitations are frequent in the lost Gospel, as I will demonstrate in *The* Logoi of Jesus *(Q+) as a Rewriting of Deuteronomy*, but these suffice to suggest the importance of this text. Q+ is not a ramshackle collection of oral traditions but a sophisticated intertextual document that portrays Jesus as the figure longed for at the end of Deuteronomy:

> A prophet still has not arisen in Israel such as Moses whom the Lord knew face to face, with all the signs and wonders that the Lord sent him to do in the land of Egypt before Pharaoh, his

assistants, and all his land, great marvels and a strong hand such as Moses performed before all of Israel (34:10-12).

Even though the author contrasts the ethics of Jesus with those of the Pentateuch, he does so as a Jew. Jesus's death is not atoning, he does not rise from the dead, and salvation has nothing to do with faith in him. Salvation has to do with fidelity to the kingdom of God expressed through compassion.

The author's criticism of Moses's command to destroy entire populations reflects moral qualms within first century Judaism, as one can see in Philo, Pseudo-Philo, and Josephus. The Jesus of the *Logoi* becomes a Christian only when it is redacted in the Synoptics. The lost Gospel thus represents an invaluable link between a radical Jewish sect that esteemed Jesus as the new Moses and what was to become the religion of Jesus Christ.

List of Contributors

Craig Evan Anderson is a form and redaction critic, emphasizing the roles of politics and social psychology within biblical hermeneutics. His research interests include employing film theory, psychoanalysis, and identity theory in analysis of ancient literature.

Bill T. Arnold is the Paul S. Amos Professor of Old Testament Interpretation at Asbury Theological Seminary. He has published fourteen books and over 100 articles, including *Introduction to the Old Testament* (Cambridge University Press, 2014) and *Genesis* (New Cambridge Bible Commentary; Cambridge University Press, 2009).

Ehud Ben Zvi is Professor Emeritus in the Department of History and Classics of the University of Alberta, whose work focuses on the prophetic and historiographical books and on areas such as ancient Israelite social memory, history, and historiography.

Shelley L. Birdsong is Assistant Professor of Religious Studies at North Central College. Her work focuses on the evolution the Bible and its characters. Mohr Siebeck recently published her first monograph, *The Last King(s) of Judah*.

Ben Boeckel is the pastor of Grangeville Church of the Nazarene. His research projects have investigated covenant, form criticism in the Enneateuch, and hermeneutics. He has published a variety of book chapters, journal articles, and dictionary entries.

Timothy D. Finlay is Professor of Biblical Studies at Azusa Pacific Seminary. His work focuses on form critical readings of the Hebrew Bible and his works include *The Birth Report Genre in the Hebrew Bible* and *The Genre of Biblical Commentary* (edited with William Yarchin).

John T. Fitzgerald is Professor of New Testament and Early Christianity at the University of Notre Dame. He is the author or editor of ten books and more than eighty articles; he is currently preparing a commentary on the Pastoral Epistles for the Hermeneia series.

Serge Frolov is Professor of Religious Studies and Nate and Ann Levine Endowed Chair in Jewish Studies at Southern Methodist University. He has published two books, *The Turn of the Cycle: 1 Samuel 1–8 in Synchronic and Diachronic Perspectives* and *Judges*, as well as about 250 articles.

Lester L. Grabbe is Professor Emeritus of Hebrew Bible and Early Judaism at the University of Hull, England. He writes especially on the history of ancient Israel and Second Temple Judaism but also on prophecy in cross-cultural perspective.

Else K. Holt is Associate Professor of Old Testament studies at Aarhus University, Denmark. Her main interests are the theologies of the books of Jeremiah and Psalms, especially on the backdrop of trauma and collective memory studies. She has recently co-published a translation of Psalms into everyday Danish with the Danish Bible Society.

John H. Hull, Jr. is Minister of Faith Development at Beargrass Christian Church (Disciples of Christ) in Louisville, Kentucky and Adjunct Professor of Hebrew Bible at Lexington Theological Seminary. His work focuses on structure and characterization in Judges and Kings.

Hyun Chul Paul Kim is Harold B. Williams Professor of Hebrew Bible at Methodist Theological School in Ohio. A Fulbright US Scholar to Korea (2015), his recent publication is *Reading Isaiah: A Literary and Theological Commentary* (Smyth & Helwys, 2016).

Soo J. Kim is Professor of Old Testament and Academic Dean at Shepherd University. She is especially interested in biblical theology, literary-critical methodologies, intertextuality, spatiality, and memory making in order to read fully the sacred text of the Bible.

Reinhard G. Kratz is Professor of Hebrew Bible at Georg-August-University in Göttingen, Germany. His work focuses on the composition of the Hebrew Bible and the history of ancient Judaism. His major publications include *The Composition of the Narrative Books of the Old Testament, The Prophets of Israel, Historical and Biblical Israel*, and three volumes with collected articles (*Kleine Schriften* I–III).

Jon D. Levenson is the Albert A. List Professor of Jewish Studies at Harvard Divinity School and the author, most recently, of *The Love of God: Divine Gift, Human Gratitude, and Mutual Faithfulness in Judaism* (2015) and *Inheriting Abraham: The Legacy of the Patriarch in Judaism, Christianity, and Islam* (2012).

Dennis R. MacDonald is Research Professor of New Testament and Christian Origins at Claremont School of Theology. His research focuses on apocryphal Acts, the synoptic problem, and especially the influence of classical Greek poetry on Jewish and early Christian texts. Among his twelve books are *The Gospels and Homer* and *Luke and Vergil*.

Tyler D. Mayfield is A. B. Rhodes Associate Professor of Old Testament and Faculty Director of the Louisville Grawemeyer Award in Religion at Louisville Presbyterian Theological Seminary. He is the author of *Literary Structure and Setting in Ezekiel* published by Mohr Siebeck in 2010.

Hye Kyung Park is Assistant Professor of the Department of Theology at Chang Jung Christian University, Taiwan. Her research interests include Old Testament hermeneutics from feminist and Asian perspectives. *Why Not Her: A Form and Literary-Critical Interpretation of the Named and Unnamed Women in the Elijah and Elisha Narratives* is her first monograph.

Shalom Paul is Professor Emeritus of Bible at the Hebrew University of Jerusalem. He has written commentaries on Amos, Isaiah, and Daniel, and myriad articles on the Bible in light of ancient Near Eastern literature, many of which are in his *Divrei Shalom: Collected Studies of Shalom M. Paul on the Bible and the Ancient Near East, 1967–2005*.

Tammi J. Schneider is a Professor of Religion at Claremont Graduate University where she teaches Hebrew Bible and the ancient Near East. Her work focuses on the interconnection of text, archaeology and history, especially with an eye toward understanding the role of women.

Steven S. Tuell is the James A. Kelso Professor of Hebrew and Old Testament at Pittsburgh Theological Seminary. His books on the Hebrew Bible include *The Law of the Temple in Ezekiel 40–48* (HSM 49); *Ezekiel* (Baker); and *Reading Nahum–Malachi* (Smith & Helwys).

Patricia K. Tull is A. B. Rhodes Professor Emerita of Hebrew Bible at Louisville Presbyterian Theological Seminary and author of *Isaiah 1-39* (Smyth & Helwys); *After Exegesis: Feminist Biblical Theology* (with Jacqueline Lapsley); and *Inhabiting Eden: Christians, the Bible, and the Ecological Crisis*.

Jeremiah Unterman is a Resident Scholar at the Herzl Institute in Jerusalem, Israel. He is the author of *Justice for All: How the Jewish Bible Revolutionized Ethics* (JPS, 2017), *From Repentance to Redemption: Jeremiah's Thought in Transition*, and numerous scholarly articles.

Richard D. Weis is Professor of Hebrew Bible and Vice President for Academic Affairs and Dean Emeritus at Lexington Theological Seminary. One of the general editors for *Biblia Hebraica Quinta*, he is also responsible for the *BHQ* volume on Jeremiah, commentaries on Jeremiah in the FOTL series and the SBL *Commentary on the Septuagint*.

H. G. M. Williamson is Emeritus Regius Professor of Hebrew at the University of Oxford. After many years working on Persian Period historiography, he is now writing the ICC on Isaiah 1–27 in three volumes.

William Yarchin is the Dean's Endowed Professor of Biblical Studies at Azusa Pacific University. His research and publications focus on the history of biblical interpretation and the role of the Bible's physical forms in the expression of its meaning.

Bibliography

Abma, Richtsje. "Travelling from Babylon to Zion: Location and Its Function in Isaiah 49–55." *JSOT* (1997): 3–28.

Abramowski, Rudolf. "Zum literarischen Problem des Tritojesaja." *TSK* 96–97 (1925): 90–143.

Abusch, Tzvi. *Male and Female in the Epic of Gilgamesh*. Winona Lake, IN: Eisenbrauns, 2015.

Achtemeier, Elizabeth. *Nahum–Malachi*. IBC. Louisville: John Knox, 1986.

Ackroyd, Peter R. "Isaiah I–XII: Presentation of a Prophet." *Congress Volume Göttingen 1977*, 16–48. VTSup 29. Leiden: Brill, 1978.

Allen, Leslie C. *Ezekiel 20–48*. WBC 29. Dallas: Word, 1990.

———. *Jeremiah*. OTL. Louisville: Westminster John Knox, 2008.

Alston, William P. *Illocutionary Acts and Sentence Meaning*. Ithaca: Cornell University Press, 2000.

Alt, Albrecht. "The God of the Fathers." *Essays on Old Testament History and Religion*, 10–86. Translated by Robert Wilson. Sheffield: JSOT Press, 1989.

———. "The Origins of Israelite Law." *Essays on the Old Testament and Religion*, 107–71. Translated by Robert Wilson. Sheffield: JSOT Press, 1989.

Alter, Robert. *The Art of Biblical Narrative*. New York: Basic Books, 1981.

———. *The Art of Biblical Poetry*. New York: Basic Books, 1985.

———. *The World of Biblical Literature*. New York: Basic Books, 1991.

Andersen, Francis I. and David Noel Freedman. *Hosea*. AB 24. New York: Doubleday, 1980.

Arnold, Bill T. *Genesis*. New Cambridge Bible Commentary. Cambridge: Cambridge University Press, 2009.

———. "Genesis 1 as Holiness Preamble." *Let Us Go up to Zion: Essays in Honour of H. G. M. Williamson on the Occasion of his Sixty-Fifth Birthday*, 331–43. Edited by Iain Provan and Mark J. Boda. VTSup 153. Leiden: Brill, 2012.

_____. "The Holiness Redaction of the Flood Narrative (Genesis 6:9–9:29)." *Windows to the Ancient World of the Hebrew Bible: Essays in Honor of Samuel Greengus*, 13–40. Edited by Bill T. Arnold, Nancy L. Erickson, and John H. Walton. Winona Lake, IN: Eisenbrauns, 2014).

Arnold, Bill T. and John H. Choi. *A Guide to Biblical Hebrew Syntax*. Cambridge: Cambridge University Press, 2003.

Assis, Elie. "Love, Hate and Self-Identity in Malachi: A New Perspective to Mal 1:1–5 and 2:10–16." *JNSL* 35 (2009): 109–20.

Aubet, Maria Eugenia. "Phoenicia during the Iron Age II Period." *The Oxford Handbook of the Archaeology of the Levant c. 8000–332 BCE*, 706–16. Edited by Margreet L. Steiner and Ann E. Killebrew. Oxford: Oxford University Press, 2014.

Auerbach, Erich. *Mimesis: The Representation of Reality in Western Literature*. Princeton: Princeton University Press, 1953.

Austin, James L. *How to Do Things with Words*. Cambridge: Harvard University Press, 1962.

Bach, Robert. *Die Aufforderungen zur Flucht und zum Kampf im alttestamentlichen Prophetenspruch*. WMANT 9. Neukirchen: Neukirchener Verlag, 1962.

Baltzer, Klaus. *The Covenant Formulary in Old Testament, Jewish, and Early Christian Writings*. Translated by David Green. Philadelphia: Fortress, 1971.

Bar-Efrat, Shimon. *Narrative Art in the Bible*. JSOTSup 70. Sheffield: Almond, 1989.

Barr, James. "Reflections on the Covenant with Noah." *Covenant as Context: Essays in Honour of E. W. Nicholson*. Edited by Andrew Hastings Mayes and Robert B. Salters. Oxford: Oxford University Press, 2003.

Barrera, J. Trebolle. "Textual Variants in 4QJudg^a and the Textual and Editorial History of the Book of Judges." *RevQ* 14/54 (1989): 229–45.

Barth, Hermann. *Die Jesaja-Worte in der Josiazeit: Israel und Assur als Thema einer produktiven Neuinterpretation der Jesajaüberlieferung*. WMANT 48. Neukirchen-Vluyn: Neukirchener Verlag, 1977.

Barthel, Jörg. *Prophetenwort und Geschichte: die Jesajaüberlieferung in Jes 6–8 und 28–31*. FAT 19. Tübingen: Mohr Siebeck, 1997.

Barthélemy, Dominique. *Critique textuelle de l'Ancien Testament, 2: Isaïe, Jérémie, Lamentations.* OBO 50/2. Freiburg: Éditions universitaires, 1986.

Barton, John. "Dating the 'Succession Narrative.'" In *Search of Pre-Exilic Israel: Proceedings of the Oxford Old Testament Seminar*, 95–106. Edited by John Day. London: T & T Clark, 2004.

_____. *Understanding Old Testament Ethics: Approaches and Explorations.* Louisville: Westminster John Knox, 2003.

Bauer, Hans and Pontus Leander. *Historische Grammatik der hebräischen Sprache.* Halle: Max Niemeyer, 1922.

Baum, L. Frank. *The Wonderful Wizard of Oz.* Chicago: Geo. M. Hill, 1900.

Becker, Jürgen. *Isaias: Der Prophet und sein Buch.* SBS 30. Stuttgart: Katholisches Bibelwerk, 1968.

Beckett, Samuel. *Waiting for Godot: Tragicomedy in 2 Acts.* New York: Grove Press, 1954.

Bellah, Robert N. "Religious Evolution." *American Sociological Review* 29 (1964): 358–74.

_____. "What is Axial about the Axial Age?" *Archives Européennes de Sociologie* 46.1 (2005): 69-89.

Ben Jehuda, Eliezer. *A Complete Dictionary of Ancient and Modern Hebrew.* Jerusalem: Makor, 1980.

Ben Nachman, Moshe. "תורת השם תמימה." *כתבי רבנו משה בן נחמן*, 163–64. Edited by Chayim Dov Chevel. Jerusalem: Mossad Harav Kook, 1984.

Ben-Shlomo, David. "Philistia during the Iron Age II Period." *The Oxford Handbook of the Archaeology of the Levant c. 8000-332 BCE*, 717–29. Edited by. Margreet L. Steiner and Ann E. Killebrew; Oxford: Oxford University Press, 2014.

Ben Zvi, Ehud. "Exploring the Memory of Moses 'The Prophet' in Late Persian/Early Hellenistic Yehud/Judah." *Remembering Biblical Figures in the Late Persian and Early Hellenistic Periods: Social Memory and Imagination*, 335–64. Edited by Diana V. Edelman and Ehud Ben Zvi. Oxford: Oxford University Press, 2013.

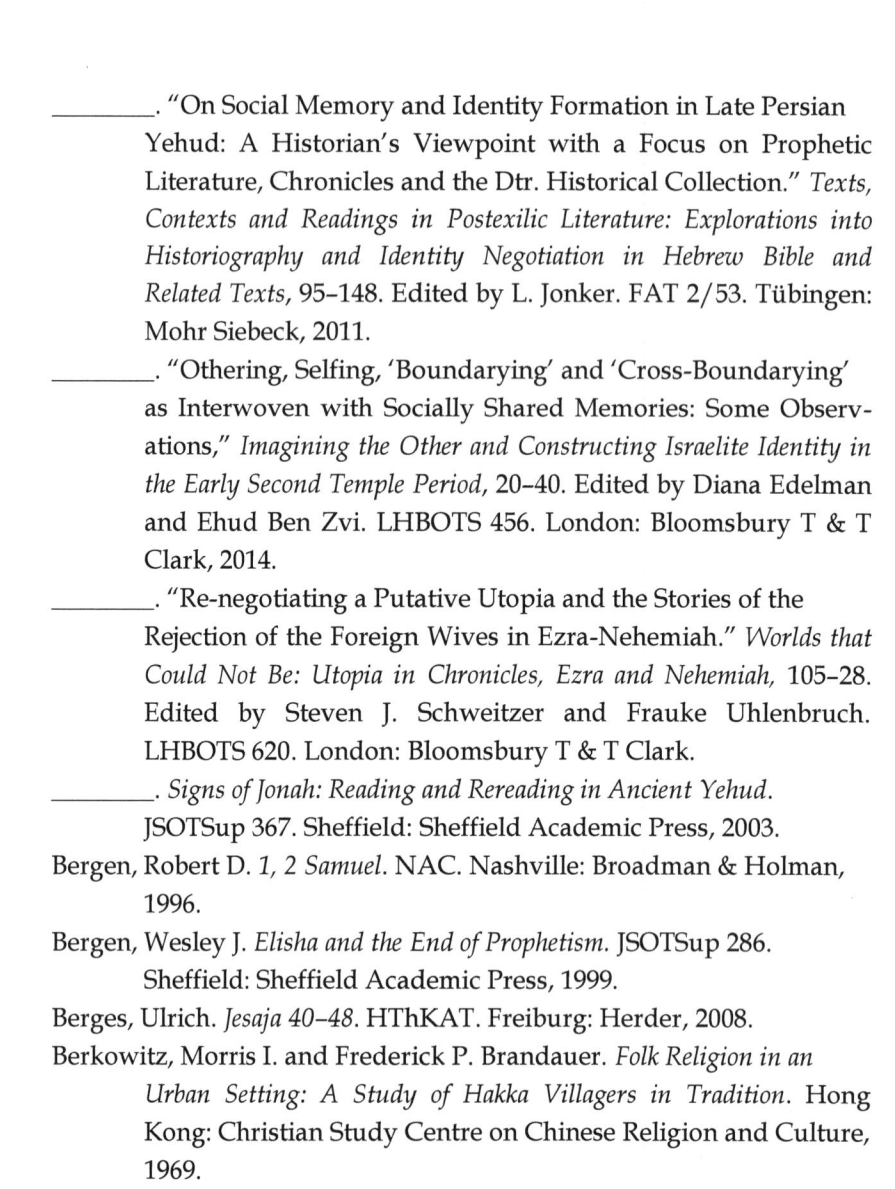

_____. "On Social Memory and Identity Formation in Late Persian Yehud: A Historian's Viewpoint with a Focus on Prophetic Literature, Chronicles and the Dtr. Historical Collection." *Texts, Contexts and Readings in Postexilic Literature: Explorations into Historiography and Identity Negotiation in Hebrew Bible and Related Texts*, 95–148. Edited by L. Jonker. FAT 2/53. Tübingen: Mohr Siebeck, 2011.

_____. "Othering, Selfing, 'Boundarying' and 'Cross-Boundarying' as Interwoven with Socially Shared Memories: Some Observations," *Imagining the Other and Constructing Israelite Identity in the Early Second Temple Period*, 20–40. Edited by Diana Edelman and Ehud Ben Zvi. LHBOTS 456. London: Bloomsbury T & T Clark, 2014.

_____. "Re-negotiating a Putative Utopia and the Stories of the Rejection of the Foreign Wives in Ezra-Nehemiah." *Worlds that Could Not Be: Utopia in Chronicles, Ezra and Nehemiah*, 105–28. Edited by Steven J. Schweitzer and Frauke Uhlenbruch. LHBOTS 620. London: Bloomsbury T & T Clark.

_____. *Signs of Jonah: Reading and Rereading in Ancient Yehud*. JSOTSup 367. Sheffield: Sheffield Academic Press, 2003.

Bergen, Robert D. *1, 2 Samuel*. NAC. Nashville: Broadman & Holman, 1996.

Bergen, Wesley J. *Elisha and the End of Prophetism*. JSOTSup 286. Sheffield: Sheffield Academic Press, 1999.

Berges, Ulrich. *Jesaja 40–48*. HThKAT. Freiburg: Herder, 2008.

Berkowitz, Morris I. and Frederick P. Brandauer. *Folk Religion in an Urban Setting: A Study of Hakka Villagers in Tradition*. Hong Kong: Christian Study Centre on Chinese Religion and Culture, 1969.

Berlin, Adele. *The Dynamics of Biblical Parallelism*. Bloomington: Indiana University Press, 1985.

_____. *The Dynamics of Biblical Parallelism*. Rev. ed. BRS. Grand Rapids: Eerdmans, 2008.

Beuken, Willem A. M. "Isa. 56:9–57:13: An Example of Isaianic Legacy of Trito-Isaiah." *Tradition and Reinterpretation in Jewish and Early Christian Literature: Essays in Honour of Jürgen C. H. Lebram*, 48–66. Edited by Jan Willem van Henten et al. Leiden: Brill, 1986.

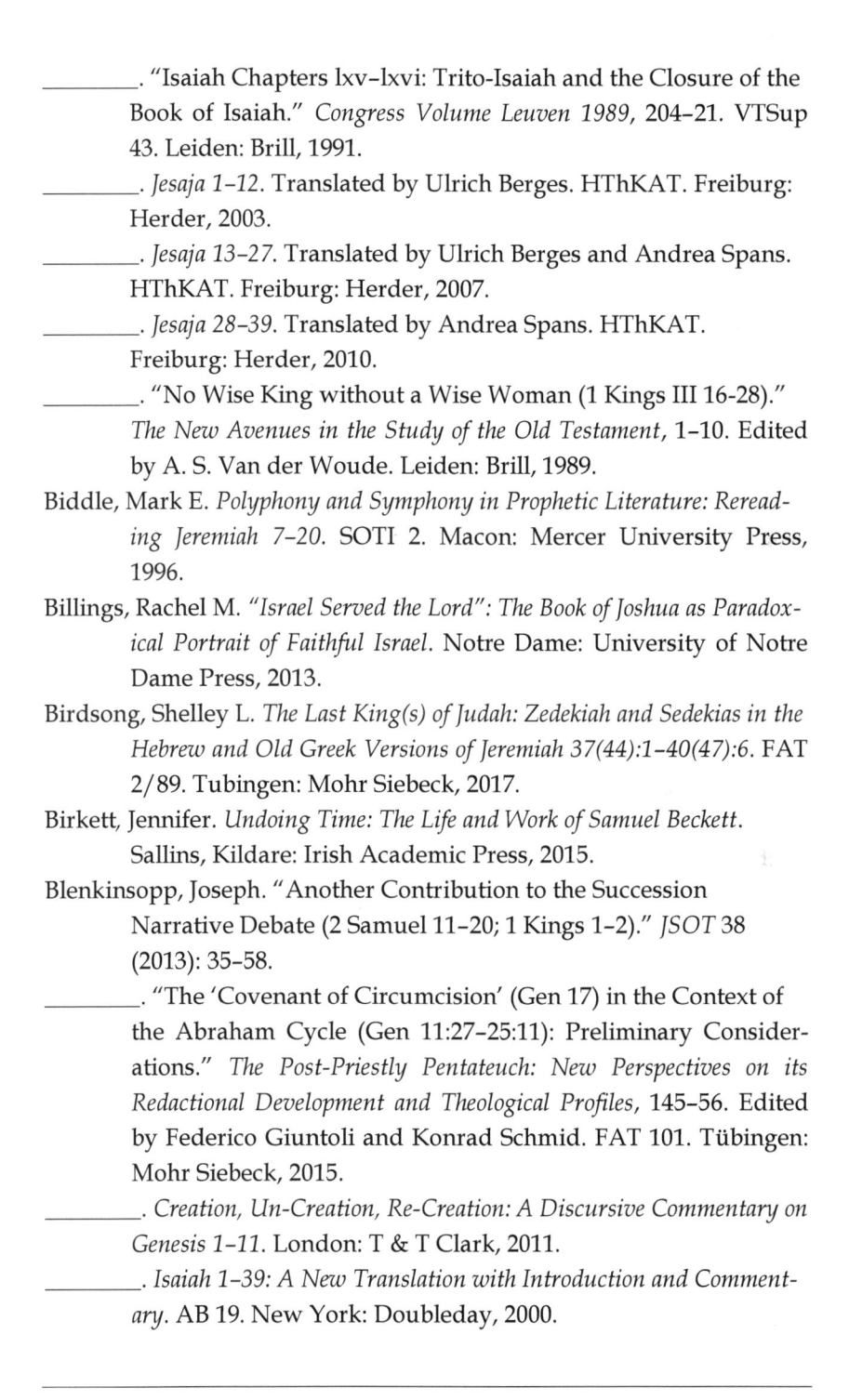

———. "Isaiah Chapters lxv–lxvi: Trito-Isaiah and the Closure of the Book of Isaiah." *Congress Volume Leuven 1989*, 204–21. VTSup 43. Leiden: Brill, 1991.

———. *Jesaja 1–12*. Translated by Ulrich Berges. HThKAT. Freiburg: Herder, 2003.

———. *Jesaja 13–27*. Translated by Ulrich Berges and Andrea Spans. HThKAT. Freiburg: Herder, 2007.

———. *Jesaja 28–39*. Translated by Andrea Spans. HThKAT. Freiburg: Herder, 2010.

———. "No Wise King without a Wise Woman (1 Kings III 16-28)." *The New Avenues in the Study of the Old Testament*, 1–10. Edited by A. S. Van der Woude. Leiden: Brill, 1989.

Biddle, Mark E. *Polyphony and Symphony in Prophetic Literature: Rereading Jeremiah 7–20*. SOTI 2. Macon: Mercer University Press, 1996.

Billings, Rachel M. *"Israel Served the Lord": The Book of Joshua as Paradoxical Portrait of Faithful Israel*. Notre Dame: University of Notre Dame Press, 2013.

Birdsong, Shelley L. *The Last King(s) of Judah: Zedekiah and Sedekias in the Hebrew and Old Greek Versions of Jeremiah 37(44):1–40(47):6*. FAT 2/89. Tubingen: Mohr Siebeck, 2017.

Birkett, Jennifer. *Undoing Time: The Life and Work of Samuel Beckett*. Sallins, Kildare: Irish Academic Press, 2015.

Blenkinsopp, Joseph. "Another Contribution to the Succession Narrative Debate (2 Samuel 11–20; 1 Kings 1–2)." *JSOT* 38 (2013): 35–58.

———. "The 'Covenant of Circumcision' (Gen 17) in the Context of the Abraham Cycle (Gen 11:27–25:11): Preliminary Considerations." *The Post-Priestly Pentateuch: New Perspectives on its Redactional Development and Theological Profiles*, 145–56. Edited by Federico Giuntoli and Konrad Schmid. FAT 101. Tübingen: Mohr Siebeck, 2015.

———. *Creation, Un-Creation, Re-Creation: A Discursive Commentary on Genesis 1–11*. London: T & T Clark, 2011.

———. *Isaiah 1–39: A New Translation with Introduction and Commentary*. AB 19. New York: Doubleday, 2000.

_____. "Theme and Motif in the Succession History (2 Sam xi 2ff) and the Yahwist Corpus." *Volume Du Congrès: Genève, 1965*, 44-57. VTSup 15. Leiden: Brill, 1966.

Block, Daniel I. *The Book of Ezekiel: Chapters 1-24*. NICOT. Grand Rapids: Eerdmans, 1997.

_____. *The Book of Ezekiel: Chapters 25-48*. NICOT. Grand Rapids: Eerdmans, 1998.

Breed, Brennan W. *Nomadic Text: A Theory of Biblical Reception History*. Bloomington: Indiana University Press, 2014.

Brenner, Athalya. "Jezebel 1." *Women in Scripture: A Dictionary of Named and Unnamed Women in the Hebrew Bible, the Apocryphal/ Deuteroncanonical Books, and the New Testament*, 100-102. Edited by Carol Meyers. Grand Rapids: Eerdmans, 2000.

Brettler, Marc Zvi. "The Structure of 1 Kings 1-11." *JSOT* 49 (1991): 87-97.

Bright, John. *Jeremiah*. AB 21. Garden City: Doubleday, 1965.

Brinkman, J. A. "Comments on the Nassouhi Kinglist and the Assyrian Kinglist Tradition." *Or* 42 (1973): 306-19.

Brock, Sebastian P. "Text History and Text Division in Peshitta Isaiah." *The Peshiṭta: Its Early Text and History*, 49-80. Edited by Peter B. Dirksen and Martin J. Mulder. Leiden: E. J. Brill, 1988.

Brueggemann, Walter. *1 & 2 Kings*. SHBC 8. Macon, GA: Smyth & Helwys, 2000.

Bruin, Wim de. "Interpreting Delimiters: The Complexity of Text Delimitation in Four Major Septuagint Manuscripts." *Studies in Scriptural Unit Division*, 66-89. Edited by Marjo C. A. Korpel and Josef M. Oesch. Pericope 3. Leiden: Brill, 2002.

_____. *Isaiah 1-12 as Written and Read in Antiquity*. Sheffield: Sheffield Phoenix Press, 2013.

Brunet, Gilbert. *Essai sur l'Isaïe de l'histoire: étude de quelques textes notamment dans Isa. vii, viii & xxii*. Paris: Picard, 1975.

Bucur, Bogdan G. and Elijah N. Mueller. "Gregory Nazianzen's Reading of Habakkuk 3:2 and Its Reception: A Lesson from Byzantine Scripture Exegesis." *ProEccl* 20 (2011): 86-103.

Bühler, Karl. *Theory of Language: The Representational Function of Language*. Tranlsated by Donald Fraser Goodwin. FS 25. Amsterdam: John Benjamins, 1990.

Burnside, Jonathan. "Flight of the Fugitives: Rethinking the Relationship between Biblical Law (Exodus 21:12-14) and the Davidic Succession Narrative (1 Kings 1-2)." *JBL* 129 (2010): 418-31.

Burstein, Stanley Mayer. *The Babyloniaca of Berossus*. SMANE 1.5. Malibu, CA: Undena, 1978.

Buss, Martin. *The Changing Shape of Form Criticism: A Relational Approach*. HBM 18. Sheffield: Sheffield Phoenix, 2010.

Callaway, Mary C. "Exegesis as Banquet: Reading Jeremiah with the Rabbis." *A Gift of God in Due Season: Essays in Scripture and Community in Honor of James A. Sanders*, 219-30. Edited by Richard D. Weis and David M. Carr. JSOTSup 225. Sheffield: Sheffield Academic Press, 1996.

Callimachus, "frag. 383.4." *Callimachus*. Edited by Rudolf Pfeiffer. Oxford: Clarendon, 1949. 1:308 = "frag. 254.4" *Supplementum Hellenisticum*. Hugh Lloyd-Jones and Peter Parsons; TK 11. Berlin: Walter de Gruyter, 1983.

Calvin, John. *Commentaries on the Twelve Minor Prophets*. Repr. ed. Translated by John Owen. Grand Rapids: Baker, 1989.

Camp, Claudia V. *Wise, Strange and Holy: The Strange Woman and the Making of the Bible*. JSOTSup 320. Sheffield: Sheffield Academic Press, 2000.

Campbell, Antony F. *1 Samuel*. FOTL 7. Grand Rapids: Eerdmans, 2004.

──────. "Form Criticism's Future." *The Changing Face of Form Criticism for The Twenty-First Century*, 15-31. Edited by Marvin A. Sweeney and Ehud Ben Zvi. Grand Rapids: Eerdmans 2003.

──────. "Structure Analysis and the Art of Exegesis (1 Samuel 16:14-18:30)." *Problems in Biblical Theology: Essays in Honor of Rolf Knierim*, 76-103. Edited by Henry T. C. Sun and Keith L. Eades. Grand Rapids: Eerdmans, 1997.

Carlson, Rolf A. *David, the Chosen King: A Traditio-Historical Approach to the Second Book of Samuel*. Translated by Eric J. Sharpe and Stanley Rudman. Stockholm: Almqvist & Wiksell, 1964.

Carr, David M. *Writing on the Tablet of the Heart: Origins of Scripture and Literature*. New York: Oxford University Press, 2005.

Carroll, Robert P. *From Chaos to Covenant: Prophecy in the Book of Jeremiah*. New York: Crossroad, 1981.

_____. *Jeremiah: A Commentary*. OTL. Philadelphia: Westminster, 1986.

Carter, Charles E. *The Emergence of Yehud in the Persian Period*. JSOTSup 294. Sheffield: Sheffield Academic Press, 1999.

Chaney, Marvin. "Agricultural Intensification as Promiscuity in the Book of Hosea." Paper presented at the Annual Meeting of the SBL. Washington D. C., 22 November, 1993.

Chang, Hsun. "Incense-Offering and Obtaining the Magical Power of Qi: The Mazu (Heavenly Mother) Pilgrimage in Taiwan." PhD diss. University of California at Berkeley, 1993.

Cheyne, Thomas K. *Introduction to the Book of Isaiah*. London: Adam & Charles Black, 1895.

Christensen, Line Søgaard. "Instructing the Israelites: Axiality, Teaching, and Rituals in the Hebrew Bible." PhD diss. Aarhus University, 2016.

Clements, Ronald E. "Beyond Tradition-History: Deutero-Isaianic Development of First Isaiah's Themes." *JSOT* 31 (1985): 95–113.

_____. *Jeremiah*. IBC. Atlanta: John Knox, 1988.

_____. "The Prophecies of Isaiah and the Fall of Jerusalem in 587 B.C." *VT* 30 (1980): 421–36.

_____. "The Unity of the Book of Isaiah." *Int* 36 (1982): 117–29.

Coats, George W. *Genesis, with an Introduction to Narrative Literature*. FOTL 1. Grand Rapids: Eerdmans, 1983.

Cogan, Mordechai. *I Kings: A New Translation with Introduction and Commentary*. AB 10. New York: Doubleday, 2001.

Cogan, Mordechai and Haim Tadmor, *II Kings: A New Translation with Introduction and Commentary*. AB 11. Garden City, NY: Doubleday, 1988.

Condamin, Albert. *Le livre d'Isaïe*. EBib. Paris: Librairie Victor Lecoffre, 1905.

Conrad, Edgar. *Reading the Latter Prophets: Toward A New Canonical Criticism*. JSOTSup 376. London: T & T Clark, 2004.

_____. *Fear Not Warrior*. BJS 75. Chico: Scholars Press, 1985.

Conroy, Charles. *Absalom Absalom!* AnBib 81. 1978. Repr. ed. Rome: Editrice Pontificio Istituto Biblico, 2006.

Couey, J. Blake. *Reading the Poetry of First Isaiah: The Most Perfect Model of the Prophetic Poetry*. Oxford: Oxford University Press, 2015.

Cowley, Arthur E. *Aramaic Papyri of the Fifth Century B.C.* Oxford: Clarendon Press, 1923.
Craigie, Peter C., Page H. Kelley, and Joel F. Drinkard. *Jeremiah 1-25*. WBC 26. Dallas, Word, 1991.
Crawford, Sidnie White. *Rewriting Scripture in Second Temple Times*. SDSSRS. Grand Rapids: Eerdmans, 2008.
Crenshaw, James L. *Samson: A Secret Betrayed, a Vow Ignored*. Atlanta: John Knox, 1978.
Crew, Danny O. *Suffragist Sheet Music: An Illustrated Catalogue of Published Music Associated with the Women's Rights and Suffrage Movement in America, 1795-1921, with Complete Lyrics*. Jefferson, NC: McFarland, 2002.
Cushman, Beverly W. "The Politics of the Royal Harem and the Case of Bat-Sheba." *JSOT* 30 (2006): 327-43.
Cyril of Alexandria. *Commentary on the Twelve Prophets*. Translated by Robert C. Hill. Washington, DC: Catholic University of America Press, 2012.
Dahood, Mitchell. *Psalms I: 1-50*. AB 16. Garden City NY: Doubleday, 1965.
Davies, John A. "Heptadic Verbal Patterns in the Solomon Narrative of 1 Kings 1-11." *TynBul* 63 (2012): 21-34.
Davies, Philip R. *In Search of "Ancient Israel."* JSOTSup 148. Sheffield: JSOT Press, 1992.
Davis, Ellen F. *Swallowing the Scroll: Textuality and the Dynamics of Discourse in Ezekiel's Prophecy*. JSOTSup 78. BLS 213. Sheffield: Almond Press, 1989.
Day, John. *The Recovery of the Ancient Hebrew Language: The Lexicographical Writings of D. Winton Thomas*. HBM 20. Sheffield: Sheffield Phoenix, 2013.
Deboys, David G. "History and Theology in the Chronicler's Portrayal of Abijah." *Bib* 71 (1990): 48-62.
Delekat, Lienhard. "Tendenz und Theologie der David-Salomo-Erzahlung." *Das ferne und nahe Wort*, 26-36. Edited by Fritz Maass. BZAW 105. Berlin: Töpelmann, 1967.
Deleuze, Gilles. *Cinema 1: The Movement Image*. Translated by Hugh Tomlinson and Barbara Habberjam. Minneapolis: University of Minnesota Press, 1986.

Delitzsch, Franz. *Commentar über das Buch Jesaia*. 4th ed. Leipzig: Dörffling & Franke, 1889.

_____. Franz Delitzsch, *Biblical Commentary on the Prophecies of Isaiah*. Translated by James Kennedy, William Hastie, and Thomas A. Bickerton. Edinburgh: T & T Clark, 1894.

DeVries, Simon J. *1 Kings*. WBC 12. Waco, TX: Word Books, 1985.

_____. *Prophet against Prophet: The Role of the Micaiah Narrative (1 Kings 22) in the Development of Early Prophetic Tradition*. Grand Rapids: Eerdmans, 1979.

Diamond, A. R. Pete. *The Confessions of Jeremiah in Context*. JSOTSup 45. Sheffield: JSOT Press, 1987.

_____. "Portraying Prophecy: Of Doublets, Variants and Analogies in the Narrative Representation of Jeremiah's Oracles — Reconstructing the Hermeneutics of Prophecy." *JSOT* 57 (1993): 99-119.

Dietrich, Walter. *Jesaja und die Politik*. BEvT 74. Munich: Kaiser, 1976.

Dijk, Jan J. A. van. "Une incantation accompagnant la naissance de l'homme." *Or* 42 (1973): 502-07.

_____. *Macrostructures*. Hillsdale, NJ: Erlbaum, 1980.

Dijk, Tuen A. van and W. Kintsch, *Strategies of Discourse Comprehension*. New York: Academic Press, 1983.

Dillmann, August. *Der Prophet Jesaia*. 5th ed. KEHAT. Leipzig: Hirzel, 1890.

Donald, Merlin. *Origins of the Modern Mind: Three Stages in the Evolution of Culture and Cognition*. Cambridge: Harvard University Press, 1991.

Donner, Herbert. *Israel unter den Völkern*. VTSup 11. Leiden: Brill, 1964.

Dorff, Elliot N. *The Way into Tikkun Olam: Repairing the World*. Woodstock, VT: Jewish Lights Publishing, 2005.

Douglas, Mary. *Purity and Danger: An Analysis of the Concepts of Pollution and Taboo*. London: Routledge, 2005.

Driscoll, Matthew J. "Words on the Page: Thoughts on Philology, Old and New." *Creating the Medieval Saga: Versions, Variability, and Editorial Interpretation of Old Norse Saga Literature*, 85-102. Edited by Judy Quinn and Emily Lethbridge. Odense: University Press of Southern Denmark, 2010.

Driver, Godfrey R. "Isaiah i-xxxix: Textual and Linguistic Problems." *JSS* 13 (1968): 36-57.

Driver, S. R. *The Minor Prophets: Nahum, Habakkuk, Zephaniah, Haggai, Zechariah, Malachi.* CB. New York: Henry Frowde, 1906.

Duhm, Bernhard L. *Das Buch Jesaia.* HKAT 3/1. Göttingen: Vandenhoeck & Ruprecht, 1892.

_____. *Das Buch Jeremia.* HKAT 11. Tübingen: Mohr (Siebeck), 1901.

Durkheim, Émile. "The Elementary Forms of the Religious Life." *Reader in Comparative Religion: An Anthropological Approach*, 27-35. Edited by William A. Lessa. 4th ed. New York: Harper & Row, 1979.

"Editorial Correspondence, letter 4." *The Israelite* 3.5 (August 8, 1856): 37.

Edmondson, Munro S. *The Book of Counsel: The Popol Vuh of the Quiche Maya of Guatemala.* MARIP 35. New Orleans: Tulane University Press, 1971.

Eichrodt, Walther. *Ezekiel.* OTL. Philadelphia: Westminster Press 1970.

_____. *Theologie des Alten Testaments.* Leipzig: J. C. Hinrichs, 1933-39.

_____. *Theology of the Old Testament.* Translated by J. A. Baker. OTL. London: SCM Press, 1961-67.

Eisen, Arnold M. *The Chosen People in America: A Study in Jewish Religious Ideology.* Bloomington: Indiana University Press, 1983.

Eliade, Mircea and Lawrence Sullivan. "Hierophany." *Mircea Eliade: A Critical Reader*, 86-93. Edited by Bryan Rennie. London: Equinox, 2006.

Elkins, Dov Peretz and Abigail Treu. *The Bible's Top 50 Ideas: The Essential Concepts Everyone Should Know.* New York: SPI, 2005.

Elliger, Karl. *Deuterojesaja in seinem Verhältnis zu Tritojesaja.* BWANT 63. Stuttgart: Kohlhammer, 1933.

_____. *Die Einheit des Tritojesaja.* BWANT 45. Stuttgart: Kohlhammer, 1928.

_____. "Der Prophet Tritojesaja." *ZAW* 39 (1931): 112-41.

Emerton, John A. "A Consideration of Some Alleged Meanings of ידע in Hebrew." *JSS* 15 (1970): 145-80.

_____. "A Further Consideration of D. W. Thomas's Theories about *yāda'*." *VT* 41 (1991): 145-63.

Eshel, Esther, Hanan Eshel, and Årstein Justnes. "XJudg with MS 2861 (Judges 4.5–6)." *Gleanings from the Caves: Dead Sea Scrolls and Artefacts from The Schøyen Collection*, 193–201. Edited by Torleif Elgvin with Kipp Davis and Michael Langlois. LSTS 71. London: Bloomsbury, 2016.

Eslinger, Lyle. *Into the Hands of the Living God*. JSOTSup 84. Sheffield: Almond, 1989.

Faulkes, Anthony, tr. and ed. *Snorri Sturluson: Edda*. Everyman Library. London: J. M. Dent, 1987.

Fecht, Gerhard. "Die Wiedergewinnung der altägyptischen Verkunst." *MDAI* (1963): 54–96.

Feldman, Louis H. *"Remember Amalek!" Vengeance, Zealotry, and Group Destruction in the Bible According to Philo, Pseudo-Philip, and Josephus*. HUCM 31. Cincinnati: Hebrew Union College Press, 2004.

Feser, Edward and Joseph M. Bessette. *By Man Shall His Blood be Shed: A Catholic Defense of the Death Penalty*. San Francisco: Ignatius Press, forthcoming 2017.

Finkel, Irving. *The Ark before Noah: Decoding the Story of the Flood*. London: Hodder and Stoughton, 2014.

Finlay, Timothy. *A Handbook of Genres and Formulae in the Hebrew Bible*. Atlanta: SBL Press, forthcoming 2017.

Finlay, Timothy and Jim Herst. *Exploring the Word of God: The Old Testament*. San Bernardino: Grace Communion International, 2013.

Finsterbusch, Karin. "Different Beginnings, Different Book Profiles: Exegetical Perspectives on the Hebrew *Vorlage* of LXX-Jer 1 and MT-Jer 1." *Texts and Contexts of Jeremiah: The Exegesis of Jeremiah 1 and 10 in the Light of Text and Reception History*, 51–65. Edited by Karin Finsterbusch and Armin Lange. CBET 82. Leuven: Peeters, 2016.

Finsterbusch, Karin and Norbert Jacoby. *MT-Jeremia und LXX-Jeremia 1–24: Synoptische Übersetzung und Analyse der Kommunicationsstruktur*. WMANT 145. Neukirchen-Vluyn: Neukirchener Theologie, 2016.

———. *MT-Jeremia und LXX-Jeremia 25–52: Synoptische Übersetzung und Analyse der Kommunicationsstruktur*. WMANT 146. Neukirchen-Vluyn: Neukirchener Theologie, 2017.

Fischer, Georg. "Jer 25 und die Fremdvölkersprüche: Unterschiede zwischen hebräischem und griechischen Text." *Bib* 72 (1991): 474–99.

Fischer, Georg. *Jeremia 1–25*. HThKAT. Freiburg: Herder, 2005.

———. *Jeremia 26–52*. HThKAT. Freiburg: Herder, 2005.

Fish, Stanley. *Is There a Text in This Class? The Authority of Interpretive Communities*. Cambridge: Harvard University Press, 1980.

Fitzgerald, John T. "Greco-Roman Philosophical Schools," *The World of the New Testament: Cultural, Social, and Historical Contexts*, 135–48. Edited by Joel B. Green and Lee Martin McDonald. Grand Rapids: Baker Academic, 2013.

———. "Paul, Wine in the Ancient Mediterranean World, and the Problem of Intoxication," *Paul's Graeco-Roman Context*, 331–56. Edited by C. Breytenbach. BETL 277. Leuven: Peeters, 2015.

Floyd, Michael H. *The Minor Prophets, Part 2*. FOTL 22. Grand Rapids: Eerdmans, 2000.

Fohrer, Georg. *Elia*. Zurich: Zwingli, 1957.

———. *Das Buch Jesaja*. 2nd ed. ZBK. 3 vols. Zurich: Zwingli, 1966.

Fokkelman, Jan P. *Narrative Art and Poetry in the Books of Samuel: A Full Interpretation Based on Stylistic and Structural Analyses*. SSN 20. 4 vols. Assen: Van Gorcum, 1981.

Fontaine, Carole. "The Bearing of Wisdom on the Shape of 2 Samuel 11–12 and 1 Kings 3." *JSOT* 34 (1986): 61–77.

Fox, Michael R. *A Message from the Great King: Reading Malachi in Light of Ancient Persian Royal Messenger Texts From the Time of Xerxes*. Siphrut 17. Winona Lake, IN: Eisenbrauns; 2015.

Fox, Michael V. *Song of Songs and the Ancient Egyptian Love Songs*. Madison, WI: University of Wisconsin Press, 1985.

"Frag. 22." *Collectanea Alexandria*. Edited by J. U. Powell. Oxford: Clarendon, 1925.

Fretheim, Terence E. *Jeremiah*. SHBC. Macon, GA: Smyth & Helwys, 2002.

_____. *The Suffering of God: An Old Testament Perspective.* Philadelphia: Fortress Press, 1984.
Friedman, Richard Elliott. "Foreword." *Empirical Models for Biblical Criticism.* Repr. Edited by Jeffrey H. Tigay. DSBLH. Eugene, OR: Wipf and Stock, 2005.
Fritz, Volkmar. *1 & 2 Kings.* Translated by Anselm Hagedorn. CC. Minneapolis: Fortress, 2003.
Fröchtling, Andrea. *Exiled God and Exiled Peoples: Memoria Passionis and the Perception of God During and after Apartheid and Shoah.* Münster: LIT, 2002.
Frolov, Serge. *Judges.* FOTL 6b. Grand Rapids: Eerdmans, 2013.
_____. "Structure, Genre, and Rhetoric of the Enneateuch." *VSPU*: forthcoming.
_____. "Succession Narrative: A 'Document' or a Phantom?" *JBL* 121 (2002): 81–104.
_____. "Synchronic Readings of Joshua-Kings." *The Oxford Handbook on the Historical Books of the Hebrew Bible.* Edited by Brad E. Kelle and Brent A. Strawn. Oxford: Oxford University Press, forthcoming.
Fuller, Russell Earl. "Text-Critical problems in Malachi 2:10–16." *JBL* 110 (1991): 47–57.
Gadamer, Hans-Georg. *Truth and Method.* Translated by Garrett Barden and John Cummming. New York: Seabury Press, 1975.
_____. *Truth and Method.* Translated by Joel Weinsheimer and Donald G. Marshall. 2nd ed. New York: Continuum, 2006.
Gamble, Harry Y. *Books and Readers in the Early Church: A History of Early Christian Texts.* New Haven: Yale University Press, 1995.
Garsiel, Moshe. "Revealing and Concealing as a Narrative Strategy in Solomon's Judgment (1 Kings 3:16–28)." *CBQ* 64 (2002): 229–47.
Gärtner, Judith. *Jesaja 66 und Sacharja 14 als Summe der Prophetie: Eine traditions- und redaktionsgeschichtliche Untersuchung zum Abschluss des Jesaja- und des Zwölfprophetenbuches.* WMANT 114. Neukirchen-Vluyn: Neukirchener Verlag, 2006.
Geller, Stephen A. *Parallelism in Early Biblical Poetry.* HSM 20. Missoula, MT: Scholars Press, 1979.
Gelston, Anthony. *The Twelve Prophets.* BHQ 13. Stuttgart: Deutsche Bibelgesellschaft, 2010.

Georges, Karl E. *Ausführliches lateinisch-deutsches Handwörterbuch.* Leipzig: Hahn, 1913-18.

Genette, Gérard. *Palimpsestes: La littérature au second degré.* Paris: Éditions du Seuil, 1982.

―――――. *Palimpsests: Literature in the Second Degree.* Translated by C. Newman and C. Doubinsky. Lincoln, NE: University of Nebraska Press, 1997.

―――――. *Paratexts: Thresholds of Interpretation.* Translated by J. E. Lewin. Cambridge: Cambridge University Press, 1997.

George, Andrew R. ed. and tr. *The Epic of Gilgamesh: The Babylonian Epic Poem and Other Texts in Akkadian and Sumerian.* Penguin Classics. London: Penguin Books, 1999.

George, Andrew, R. *The Babylonian Gilgamesh Epic: Introduction, Critical Edition and Cuneiform Texts.* 2 vols. Oxford: Oxford University Press, 2002-03.

Gerstenberger, Erhard. *Theologies in the Old Testament.* Minneapolis: Fortress Press, 2002.

Gese, Hartmut. "Die ältere Simsonüberlieferung (Richter c. 14-15)." *ZTK* 82 (1985): 261-80.

Gesenius, Wilhelm. *Hebräisches und aramäisches Handwörterbuch über das Alte Testament.* 18th ed. Berlin: Springer, 1995.

―――――. *Philologisch-kritischer und historischer Commentar über den Jesaia.* 3 vols. Leipzig: Vogel, 1821.

Gevaryahu, Haim M. I. "Biblical Colophons: A Source for the 'Biography' of Authors, Texts, and Books," *Congress Volume: Edinburgh 1974,* 42-59. Edited by G. W. Anderson et al. VTSup 28. Leiden: Brill, 1975.

Gillingham, Susan. *A Journey of Two Psalms: The Reception of Psalms 1 and 2 in Jewish and Christian Tradition.* Oxford: Oxford University Press, 2013.

Glade, Henry. "Major Brecht Productions in the Soviet Union since 1957." *Bertolt Brecht: Political Theory and Literary Practice,* 88-99. Edited by Betty Nance Weber and Hubert Heinen. Athens: University of Georgia Press, 2010.

Goldenstein, Johannes. *Das Gebet der Gottesknechte: Jes 63,7-64,11 im Jesajabuch.* WMANT 92. Neukirchen-Vluyn: Neukirchener Verlag, 2001.

Goldingay, John and Pamela J. Scalise. *Minor Prophets II.* NIBCOT 18. Peabody MA: Hendrickson, 2009.

Goldman, Yohanan. *Prophétie et royauté au retour de l'exil: les origins littéraires de la forme massorétique de livre de Jérémie.* OBO 118. Göttingen: Vandenhoeck & Ruprecht, 1992.

Goldstein, Miriam. *Karaite Exegesis in Medieval Jerusalem: The Judeo-Arabic Pentateuch Commentary of Yūsuf ibn Nūḥ and Abū al-Faraj Hārūn.* Tübingen: Mohr Siebeck, 2011.

Gonçalves, Francolino J. *L'Expédition de Sennachérib en Palestine dans la littérature hébraïque ancienne.* EBib n.s. 7. Paris: Lecoffre, 1986.

Good, Edwin M. "The Barberini Greek Version of Habakkuk III." *VT* 9 (1959): 11–30.

Gopin, Marc. "An Orthodox Embrace of Gentiles? Interfaith Tolerance in the Thought of S. D. Luzzatto and E. Benamozegh." *MJ* 18 (1998): 173–95.

Gosse, Bernard. "Jérémie xlv et la place du recueil d'oracles contre les nations dans le livre de Jérémie." *VT* 40 (1990): 145–51.

_____. "La Malédiction contre Babylone de Jérémie 51,59–64 et les redactions du livre de Jérémie." *ZAW* 98 (1986): 383–99.

Gowan, Donald E. *The Triumph of Faith in Habakkuk.* Atlanta: John Knox, 1976.

Gray, G. Buchanan. *A Critical and Exegetical Commentary on the Book of Isaiah I–XXVII.* ICC. Edinburgh: T & T Clark, 1912.

Gray, John. *I & II Kings: A Commentary.* OTL. London: SCM, 1970.

Grayson, A. Kirk. *Assyrian Rulers of the Early First Millennium BC II (858–745 BC).* RIMA 3. Toronto: University of Toronto Press, 1996.

_____. "Königlisten und Chroniken B. Akkadisch." *RlA* (1980–83): 6:86–135.

Grayson, A. Kirk and Jamie Novotny. *The Royal Inscriptions of Sennacherib, King of Assyria (704–681 BC), Part 1.* RINAP 3/1. Toronto: University of Toronto Press, 2012.

Greenberg, Moshe. *Ezekiel 1–20.* AB 22. Garden City, NY: Doubleday, 1983.

_____. *Ezekiel 21–37.* AB 22A. New York: Doubleday, 1997.

Gunkel, Hermann. *The Folktale in the Old Testament.* Translated by Michael Rutter. Sheffield: Almond, 1987.

———. "Fundamental Problems of Hebrew Literary History." *What Remains of the Old Testament and Other Essays*, 57–68. Translated by A. K. Dallas. New York: Macmillan, 1928.

———. *Genesis*. Translated by Mark E. Biddle. MLBS. Macon, GA: Mercer University Press, 1997.

———. *The Legends of Genesis*. Translated by William Herbert Carruth. New York: Schocken Books, 1964.

Gunkel, Hermann and Joachim Begrich. *Introduction to the Psalms: The Genres of the Religious Lyric of Israel*. Translated by James Nogalski. Macon: Mercer University Press, 1998.

Gunn, David M. *The Story of King David: Genre and Interpretation*. JSOTSup 6. Sheffield: University of Sheffield Press, 1978.

Halperin, David J. *Seeking Ezekiel: Text and Psychology*. University Park, PA: Pennsylvania State University Press, 1993.

Halpern, Baruch. *David's Secret Demons: Messiah, Murderer, Traitor, King*. Grand Rapids: William B. Eerdmans, 2001.

Hals, Ronald M. *Ezekiel*. FOTL 19. Grand Rapids: Eerdmans, 1989.

Harissis, Haralampos V. and Anastasios V. Harissis. *Apiculture in the Prehistoric Aegean: Minoan and Mycenaean Symbols Revisited*. BARIS 1958. Oxford: John and Erica Hedges, 2009.

Hays, J. Daniel. "Has the Narrator Come to Praise Solomon or to Bury Him? Narrative Subtlety in 1 Kings 1–11." *JSOT* 28 (2003): 149–74.

Heffelfinger, Katie. *I Am Large, I Contain Multitudes: Lyric Cohesion and Conflict in Second Isaiah*. Leiden: Brill, 2011.

Henderson, Joseph M. "Jeremiah 2–10 as a Unified Literary Composition: Evidence of Dramatic Portrayal and Narrative Progression." *Uprooting and Planting: Essays on Jeremiah for Leslie Allen*, 116–52. Edited by John Goldingay. LHBOTS 459. New York: T & T Clark, 2007.

Hens-Piazza, Gina. *1–2 Kings*. AOTC. Nashville: Abingdon, 2006.

Herberg, Will. "The 'Chosenness' of Israel and the Jew of Today." *Arguments and Doctrines: A Reader of Jewish Thinking in the Aftermath of the Holocaust*, 270–83. Edited by Arthur A. Cohen. New York: Harper & Row, 1970.

_____. *Judaism and Modern Man: An Interpretation of Jewish Religion*. Philadelphia: Jewish Publication Society, 1951.

Hertzberg, Hans W. *I & II Samuel*. OTL. Philadelphia: Westminster, 1964.

Hicks, R. Lansing. "The Door of Love." *Love and Death in the Ancient Near East: Essays in Honor of Marvin H. Pope*, 153–58. Edited by John H. Marks and Robert McClive Good. Guildford, CT: Four Quarters, 1987.

Hiebert, Theodore. *God of My Victory: The Ancient Hymn in Habakkuk 3*. HSM 38. Atlanta: Scholars, 1986.

Higbie, Carolyn. "Divide and Edit. A Brief History of Book Divisions." *HSCP* 105 (2010): 1–31.

Hill, Andrew E. *Malachi*. 2nd ed. AB 26. New Haven: Yale University Press, 2008.

Hill, John. "The Book of Jeremiah (MT) and Its Early Second Temple Background." *Uprooting and Planting: Essays on Jeremiah for Leslie Allen*, 153–71. Edited by John Goldingay; LHBOTS 459. New York: T & T Clark, 2007.

_____. *Friend or Foe? The Figure of Babylon in the Book of Jeremiah MT*. BibInt 40. Leiden: Brill, 1999.

Hirsch, Mendel. *The Haphtoroth*. Translated by Isaac Levy. London: Isaac Levy, 1966.

Hobbs, T. R. "Some Remarks on the Composition and Structure of the Book of Jeremiah." *A Prophet to the Nations*, 175–91. Edited by Leo G. Perdue and Brian W. Kovacs. Winona Lake, IN: Eisenbrauns, 1984.

Höffken, Peter. *Jesaja: Der Stand der theologischen Diskussion*. Darmstadt: Wissenschaftliche Buchgesellschaft, 2004.

Holladay, William L. *The Architecture of Jeremiah 1–20*. Lewisburg, PA: Bucknell University Press, 1976.

_____. *Jeremiah 1: A Commentary on the Book of the Prophet Jeremiah, Chapters 1–25*. Hermeneia. Philadelphia: Fortress, 1986.

_____. *Jeremiah 2: A Commentary on the Book of the Prophet Jeremiah, Chapters 26–52*. Hermeneia. Minneapolis: Fortress, 1989.

Holmstedt, Robert D. "Critical at the Margins: Edge Constituents in Biblical Hebrew." *KUSATU* 17 (2014): 109–56.

Hölscher, Gustav. *Hesekiel: Der Dichter und das Buch*. BZAW 39. Giessen: A. Töpelmann, 1924.

Holt, Else K. "Communication of Authority: The 'Prophet' in the Book of Jeremiah." *The Discursive Fight over Religious Texts in Antiquity: Religion and Normativity*, 110-18. Edited by Anders-Christian Jacobsen. Aarhus: Aarhus University Press, 2009.

―――――. "The Helpless Potentate." *The Centre and Periphery: A European Tribute to Walter Brueggemann*, 179-90. HBM 27. Edited by Jill Middlemas, David J. A. Clines and Else K. Holt. HBM 27. Sheffield: Sheffield Phoenix Press 2010.

―――――. "Narrative Normativity in Diasporic Jeremiah – and Today." *Jeremiah (Dis)placed: New Directions in Writing/Reading Jeremiah*, 125-35. Edited by A. R. Pete Diamond and Louis Stulman. LHBOTS 529. New York: T & T Clark, 2011.

―――――. "The Potent Word of God: Remarks on the Composition of Jeremiah 37-44." *Troubling Jeremiah*, 161-70. Edited by A. R. Pete Diamond, Kathleen M. O'Connor, and Louis Stulman; JSOTSup 260. Sheffield: Sheffield Academic Press, 1999.

―――――. "The Prophet as Persona." *The Oxford Handbook of Prophecy*, 299-318. Edited by Carolyn J. Sharp. Oxford: Oxford University Press, 2016.

Holt, Else K. and Carolyn J. Sharp. *Jeremiah Invented: Constructions and Deconstructions of Jeremiah*. London: Bloomsbury T & T Clark, 2015.

Hooti, Noorbakhsh. "Samuel Beckett's *Waiting for Godot*: A Postmodernist Study." *ELLS* 1 (2011): 40-50.

Hornkohl, Aaron D. *Ancient Hebrew Periodization and the Language of the Book of Jeremiah: The Case for a Sixth-Century Date of Composition*. SSLL 74. Leiden: Brill, 2014.

Houbigant, Charles F. *Notæ criticæ in universos Veteris Testamenti libros cum Hebraice, tum Græce scriptos, cum integris ejusdem Prolegomenis*. Frankfurt am Main: Varrentrapp, 1777.

Howard, Cameron B. R. "1 and 2 Kings." *Women's Bible Commentary*, 164-79. 3rd ed. Edited by C. A. Newsom, S. H. Ringe, and J. E. Lapsley. Louisville: Westminster John Knox, 2012.

Høyrup, Jens. "Mathematics, Algebra, and Geometry." *ABD* 4:602-612.

_____. "'Remarkable Numbers' in Old Babylonian Mathematical Texts: A Note on the Psychology of Numbers." *JNES* 52 (1993): 281-86.
Hugenberger, Gordon P. *Marriage as a Covenant: Biblical Law and Ethics as Developed from Malachi.* VTSup 52. Leiden: Brill, 1994.
Hutton, Jeremy M. *The Transjordanian Palimpsest: The Overwritten Texts of Personal Exile and Transformation in the Deuteronomistic History.* BZAW 396. Berlin: de Gruyter, 2009.
Hyatt, J. P. "The Book of Jeremiah: Introduction and Exegesis." *IB* 5:775-1142.
Ipsen, Avaren E. "Solomon and the Two Prostitutes." *The Bible and Critical Theory* 3 (2007): 1-12.
Irwin, Lee. "Divinity and Salvation: The Great Goddesses of China." *Asian Folklore Studies* 49 (1990): 53-68.
Iser, Wolfgang. *The Implied Reader.* Baltimore: Johns Hopkins University Press, 1978.
_____. "Indeterminacy and the Reader's Response in Prose Fiction." *Aspects of Narrative,* 1-45. Edited by J. Hillis Miller. New York: Columbia University Press, 1971.
_____. *Prospecting: From Reader Response to Literary Anthropology.* Baltimore: Johns Hopkins University Press, 1989.
The Israelite 2.15 (Oct 19, 1855): 116.
The Israelite 16.44 (May 6, 1870): 9.
Jacobsen, L. "למשמעות דברי אלישע 'אשקה־נא לאבי ולאמי ואלכה אחריך' (מלכים יט א 20)." *Shnaton* 24 (2016): 57-75.
Jeon, Yong Ho. "The Retroactive Re-evaluation Technique with Pharaoh's Daughter and the Nature of Solomon's Corruption in 1 Kings 1-12." *TynBul* 62 (2011): 15-40.
Jindo, Job Y. *Biblical Metaphor Reconsidered: A Cognitive Approach to Poetic Prophecy in Jeremiah 1-24.* HSM 64. Winona Lake, IN: Eisenbrauns, 2010.
Johnstone, William. "*yd*' II, 'be humbled, humiliated'?" *VT* 41 (1991): 49-62.
Jones, David Clyde. "A Note on the LXX of Malachi 2:16." *JBL* 109 (1990): 683-85.
Joosten, Jan. "Covenant Theology in the Holiness Code." *ZABR* 4 (1998): 145-64.

_____. *People and Land in the Holiness Code: An Exegetical Study of the Ideational Framework of the Law in Leviticus 17–26*. VTSup 67. Leiden: Brill, 1996.

Joseph, Alison L. *Portrait of the Kings: The Davidic Prototype in Deuteronomistic Poetics*. Minneapolis: Fortress, 2015.

Joüon, Paul and Takamitsu Muraoka. *A Grammar of Biblical Hebrew*. 2nd ed. SubBi 27. Roma: Pontificio Istituto Biblico, 2006.

Joyce, Paul M. *Divine Initiative and Human Response in Ezekiel*. JSOTSup 51. Sheffield: Sheffield Academic Press, 1989.

_____. *Ezekiel: A Commentary*. LHBOTS 482. New York: T & T Clark, 2007.

Julian's "Against the Galileans." Translated by R. Joseph Hoffman. Amherst, NY: Prometheus Books.

Justnes, Årstein. "The Great Isaiah Scroll (1QIsa[a]) and Material Philology: Preliminary Observations and A Proposal." *New Studies in the Book of Isaiah: Essays in Honor of Hallvard Hagelia*, 91–113. Edited by Markus Zehnder. Piscataway, NJ: Gorgias Press, 2014.

Kaiser, Otto. *Das Buch des Propheten Jesaja, Kapitel 1–12*. 5th ed. ATD 17. Göttingen: Vandenhoeck & Ruprecht, 1981.

_____. *Isaiah 1–12: A Commentary*. Translated by John Bowden. OTL. London: SCM, 1983.

Kakkanattu, Joy Philip. *God's Enduring Love in the Book of Hosea*. Tübingen: Mohr Siebeck, 2006.

Kaminsky, Joel S. "Wrestling with Israel's Election: A Jewish Reaction to Rolf Knierim's Biblical Theology." *Reading the Hebrew Bible for a New Millennium: Form, Concept, and Theological Perspective*, 1:252–62. Edited by Wonil Kim et al. Harrisburg, PA: Trinity International Press, 2000.

_____. *Yet I Loved Jacob: Reclaiming the Biblical Concept of Election*. Nashville: Abingdon, 2007.

Kaufman, Stephen A. "The Temple Scroll and Higher Criticism," *HUCA* 53 (1982): 29–43.

Keck, Leander E. *The New Interpreter's Bible*. 12 vols. Nashville: Abingdon, 1994–2004.

Keown, Gerald L., Pamela J. Scalise, and Thomas G. Smothers. *Jeremiah 26–52*. WBC 27. Dallas: Word Books, 1995.

Kessler, Martin. *The Battle of the Gods: The God of Israel versus Marduk of Babylon*. SSN 42. Assen: Van Gorcum, 2003.

———. "The Function of Chapters 25 and 50-51 in the Book of Jeremiah." *Troubling Jeremiah*, 64-72. Edited by A. R. Pete Diamond, Kathleen M. O'Connor, and Louis Stulman. JSOTSup 260. Sheffield: Sheffield Academic Press, 1999.

———. "The Scaffolding of the Book of Jeremiah." *Reading the Book of Jeremiah: A Search for Coherence*, 57-66. Edited by Martin Kessler. Winona Lake, IN: Eisenbrauns, 2004.

Keulen, Percy S. F. van. *Two Versions of the Solomon Narrative: An Inquiry into the Relationship between MT 1Kgs. 2-11 and LXX 3 Reg. 2-11*. VTSup 104. Leiden: Brill, 2005.

Kiesow, Klaus. *Exodustexte im Jesajabuch: Literarkritische und motivgeschichtliche Analysen*. OBO 24. Göttingen: Vandenhoeck & Ruprecht, 1979.

Kilunga, Godefroid Bambi. *Prééminence de YHWH ou autonomie du prophète: Etude comparative et critique des confessions de Jérémie dans le texte hébreu massorétique et la «Septante»*. OBO 254. Freiburg: Academic Press, 2011.

Kim, Hyun Chul Paul and M. Fulgence Nyengele. "Murder S/He Wrote?: A Cultural and Psychological Reading of 2 Samuel 11-12." *SemeiaSt* 44 (2003): 95-116.

Kissane, Edward J. *The Book of Isaiah, Translated from a Critically Revised Hebrew Text with Commentary, 1: i-xxxix*. Dublin: Browne and Nolan, 1941.

Kitchell, Kenneth F. "The Origins of Vergil's Myth of the Bugonia." *Daidalikon: Studies in Memory of Raymond V. Schoder, S.J.*, 193-206. Edited by Robert F. Sutton. Wauconda: Bolchazy-Carducci, 1989.

Klingbeil, Martin G. "Creation in the Prophetic Literature of the Old Testament: An Intertextual Approach." *The Genesis Creation Account and Its Reverberations in the Old Testament*, 257-289. Berrien Springs: Andrews University Press, 2015.

Kluge, Alexander. "Das Lesen des Textes wirklicher Verhältnisse." *Der unterschätzte Mensch: Gemeinsame Philosophie in zwei Bänden*, 1:862-63. Edited by Oskar Negt and Alexander Kluge. Frankfurt am Main: Zweitausendeins, 2001.

Knauf, Ernst Axel. "Shadday." *DDD*. 2nd ed. 749-53.
Knierim, Rolf P. "Criticism of Literary Features, Form, Tradition, and Redaction." *The Hebrew Bible and Its Modern Interpreters*, 123-65. Edited by Douglas A. Knight and Gene M. Tucker. Chico, CA: Scholars Press, 1985.
_____. "Old Testament Form Criticism Reconsidered." *Int* 27 (1973): 435-68.
_____. *The Task of Old Testament Theology: Substance, Method, and Cases*. Grand Rapids: Eerdmans, 1995.
_____. *Text and Concept in Leviticus 1:1-9: A Case in Exegetical Method*. FAT 2. Tübingen: J. C. B. Mohr (Paul Siebeck), 1992.
Knohl, Israel. *The Sanctuary of Silence: The Priestly Torah and the Holiness School*. Minneapolis: Fortress, 1995.
Knoppers, Gary N. "Ancient Near Eastern Royal Grants and the Davidic Covenant: A Parallel?" *JAOS* 116 (1996): 670-97.
_____. *Two Nations under God: The Deuteronomistic History of Solomon and the Dual Monarchies, Volume 1: The Reign of Solomon and the Rise of Jeroboam*. HSM 52. Atlanta: Scholars Press, 1993.
Koch, Klaus. *The Growth of the Biblical Tradition: The Form critical Method*. Tranlsated by S. Cupitt. New York: Scribner, 1969.
Köcher, Franz, ed. *Die babylonisch-assyrische Medizin in Texten und Untersuchungen*. Berlin: Walter de Gruyter, 1964.
Koenen, Klaus. *Ethik und Eschatologie im Tritojesajabuch: Eine literar-kritische und redaktionsgeschichtliche Studie*. WMANT 62. Neukirchen-Vluyn: Neukirchener Verlag, 1990.
Kogan, Leonid. "Accusative as *Casus Pendens*? A Hitherto Unrecognized Emphatic Construction in Early Akkadian Royal Inscriptions." *RA* 102 (2008): 17-26.
Koh, Hye-Ryun. "동중국해의 마조 신앙: 천비현성록을 통해 본 마조 일화와 그 성격." *Tosuhmoonwha* 25 (2005): 161-99.
Kooij, Arie van der. "The Old Greek of Isaiah in Relation to the Qumran Texts of Isaiah: Some General Comments." *Septuagint, Scrolls, and Cognate Writings: Papers Presented to the International Symposium on the Septuagint and Its Relations to the Dead Sea Scrolls and Other Writings (Manchester, 1990)*, 195-213. Edited by George J. Brooke and Barnabas Lindars. Atlanta: Scholars Press, 1992.

Kramer Gerald P. and George Wu. *An Introduction to Taiwanese Folk Religions.* Taipei, Taiwan: n.p., 1970.

Kratz, Reinhard G. "The Analysis of the Pentateuch: An Attempt to Overcome Barriers of Thinking." *ZAW* 128 (2016): 529-61.

———. *The Composition of the Narrative Books of the Old Testament.* Translated by John Bowden. London: T & T Clark, 2005.

———. "Innerbiblische Exegese und Redaktionsgeschichte im Lichte der empirischen Evidenz." *Das Judentum im Zeitalter des Zweiten Tempels: Kleine Schriften I*, 126-56. 2nd ed. FAT 42. Tübingen: Mohr Siebeck, 2013.

———. *Kyros im Deuterojesaja-Buch: Redaktionsgeschichtliche Untersuchungen zu Entstehung und Theologie von Jes 40-55.* FAT 1. Tübingen: Mohr (Siebeck), 1991.

———. "Tritojesaja," *Prophetenstudien: Kleine Schriften II*, 233-42. FAT 74. Tübingen: Mohr Siebeck, 2011.

Kugel, James L. *The Idea of Biblical Poetry: Parallelism and Its History.* New Haven: Yale University Press, 1981.

———. *Traditions of the Bible: A Guide to the Bible as It Was at the Start of the Common Era.* Cambridge: Harvard University Press, 1998.

Kuo, Cheng-Tian. *Religion and Democracy in Taiwan.* Albany, NY: State University of New York Press, 2008.

Kutler, L. B. "Features of the Battle Challenge in Biblical Hebrew, Akkadian, and Ugaritic." *UF* 19 (1987): 95-99.

Lack, Rémi. *La symbolique du livre d'Isaïe.* AnBib 59. Rome: Biblical Institute, 1973.

Lakoff, George and Mark Johnson. *Metaphors We Live By.* Chicago: University of Chicago Press, 1980.

Lakoff, George and Mark Turner. *More than Cool Reason: A Field Guide to Poetic Metaphor.* Chicago: University of Chicago Press, 1989.

Lambert, Wilfred G. "A Middle Assyrian Medical Text." *Iraq* 31 (1969): 28-38.

———. "The Problem of the Love Lyrics," *Unity and Diversity: Essays in History, Literature, and Religion of the Ancient Near East*, 98-135. Edited by Hans Goedicke and Jimmy J. M. Roberts. Baltimore: Johns Hopkins University Press, 1975.

Lambert, W. G. and A. R. Millard. *Atra-Ḫasīs: The Babylonian Story of the Flood*. Oxford: Clarendon Press, 1969.
Lang, Bernhard. "Der religiöse Mensch: Kleine Weltgeschichte des *homo religious* in sechs kurzen Kapiteln mit Beispielen aus Bibel bund Christentum." *Homo religious: Vielfalt und Geschichte des religiösen Mensch*, 11–117. Edited by Jan Assmann and Harald Strohm. Paderborn: Wilhelm Fink Verlag, 2014.
Lange, Armin. "Jeremia." *Handbuch der Textfunde vom Toten Meer*, 1:297–319. Tübingen: Mohr Siebeck, 2009.
Langlamet, François. "Pour ou contre Salomon? Le rédaction Prosalomonienne de 1 Rois I–II." *RB* 83 (1976): 321–79, 481–528.
Larrington, Carolyne, tr. and ed. *The Poetic Edda*. OWC. Oxford: Oxford University Press, 1996.
Lau, Wolfgang. *Schriftgelehrte Prophetie in Jes 56–66: Eine Untersuchung zu den literarischen Bezügen in den letzten elf Kapiteln des Jesajabuches*. BZAW 225. Berlin: Walter de Gruyter, 1994.
Lee, Archie C. "The Bible in Asia: Contesting and Contextualizing." *Mapping and Engaging the Bible in Asian Cultures: Congress of the Society of Asian Biblical Studies 2008 Seoul Conference*, 19–33. Edited by Yeong Mee Lee and Yoon Jong Yoo. Seoul: Christian Literature Society of Korea, 2009.
Lee, Yoo Jin. "마조신앙의 국가 공인화 과정과 그 의미." *Chungkukehmoonhaknonzip* 70 (2011): 466-67.
Leibowitz, E. and G. Liebowitz. "Solomon's Judgment." *BM* 35 (1989–90): 242–44.
Leichty, Erle. *The Royal Inscriptions of Esarhaddon, King of Assyria (680–669 BC)*. RINAP 4. Toronto: University of Toronto Press, 2011.
Lemon, Lee T. and Marion J. Reis, eds. and trs. *Russian Formalist Criticism*. 2nd ed. Lincoln: University of Nebraska Press, 2012.
Levenson, Jon D. *The Hebrew Bible, the Old Testament and Historical Criticism: Jews and Christians in Biblical Studies*. Louisville: Westminster John Knox, 1993.
_____. *Inheriting Abraham: The Legacy of the Patriarch in Judaism, Christianity, and Islam*. LJI. Princeton: Princeton University Press, 2012.

―――――. *The Love of God: Divine Gift, Human Gratitude, and Mutual Faithfulness in Judaism.* LJI. Princeton: Princeton University Press, 2015.

―――――. Review of *The Task of Old Testament Theology: Substance, Method, and Cases* by Rolf P. Knierim. *RelSRev* 24 (1998): 39–42.

Levinson, Bernard M. *Deuteronomy and the Hermeneutics of Legal Innovation.* New York: Oxford University Press, 1997.

Levy, J. Leonard. "A Time for War, and a Time for Peace," Pittsburgh, 8 April 1917. *Jewish Preaching in Times of War 1800–2001,* 324–45. Oxford: Littman Library of Jewish Civilization, 2008.

Liebreich, Leon J. "The Compilation of the Book of Isaiah." *JQR* 46 (1955–56): 259–77; 47 (1956/7): 114–38.

Liew, Tat-Siong Benny. *What is Asian American Biblical Hermeneutics: Reading the New Testament.* Honolulu: University of Hawaii Press, 2008.

Lincicum, David. *Paul and the Early Jewish Encounter with Deuteronomy.* Grand Rapids: Baker Academic, 2013.

Liver, Jacob. "מלאכי." אנציקלופדיה מקראית, 4:1031–32. Jerusalem: Bialik, 1962.

Long, Burke O. *1 Kings, with an Introduction to Historical Literature.* FOTL 9. Grand Rapids: William B. Eerdmans, 1984.

Longman, Tremper III, and Peter Enns. *Dictionary of the Old Testament: Wisdom, Poetry, and Writings.* Downers Grove: InterVarsity Press, 2008.

Lowth, Robert. *Isaiah: A New Translation; with a Preliminary Dissertation, and Notes.* London: Tegg, 1778.

Lundbom, Jack R. "Baruch, Seraiah, and Expanded Colophons in the Book of Jeremiah." *JSOT* 36 (1986): 89–114.

―――――. *Jeremiah 1–20.* AB 21A. New York: Doubleday, 1999.

―――――. *Jeremiah 21–36.* AB 21B. New York: Doubleday, 2004.

―――――. *Jeremiah 37–52.* AB 21C. New York: Doubleday, 2004.

―――――. "Jeremiah, Book of." *ABD* 3:684–98.

―――――. *Jeremiah: A Study in Ancient Hebrew Rhetoric.* SBLDS 18. Missoula, MT: Scholars Press, 1975.

Lütkemann, Leonhard and Alfred Rahlfs. *Hexaplarische Randnoten zu Is 1–16.* Berlin: Weidmann, 1915.

Lutz, Hanns-Martin. *Jahwe, Jerusalem und die Völker: zur Vorgeschichte von Sach. 12, 1–8 und 14, 1–5.* WMANT 27. Neukirchen-Vluyn: Neukirchener Verlag, 1968.

Luzzatto, Samuel D. *Il giudaismo illustrato nella sua teorica, nella sua storia e nella sua letteratura.* Padua: Antonio Bianchi, 1848.

MacDonald, Dennis R. *Two Shipwrecked Gospels: The Logoi of Jesus and Papias's Exposition of Logia about the Lord.* ECL 8. Atlanta: Society of Biblical Literature Press, 2012.

Maclean, Marie. "Pretexts and Paratexts: The Art of the Peripheral." *NLH* 22 (1991): 273–79.

Marais, Jacobus. *Representation in Old Testament Narrative Texts.* BibInt 36. Leiden: Brill, 1998.

Marti, Karl. *Das Buch Jesaja.* KHC 10. Tübingen: Mohr (Siebeck), 1900.

―――. *Das Dodekapropheton.* KHC. Tübingen: Mohr (Siebeck), 1904.

Martin, Malachi. *The Scribal Character of the Dead Sea Scrolls.* BMus 44–45. Louvain: Publications universitaires, 1958.

Martinez, Florentino Garcia and Eibert J. C. Tigchelaar, eds. *The Dead Sea Scrolls Study Edition.* Vol. 1, 1Q1–4Q273. Leiden: Brill, 1997.

Mason, Rex. *The Books of Haggai, Zechariah and Malachi.* Cambridge: Cambridge University Press, 1977.

Mason, Steven. *"Eternal Covenant" in the Pentateuch: The Contours of an Elusive Phrase.* New York: T & T Clark, 2008.

Masuzawa, Tomoko. *The Invention of World Religions.* Chicago: University of Chicago Press, 2005.

Matuszak, Jana. "Und du willst einen Frau sein. Ein sumerisches Streitgesprech zwischen zwei Frauen." PhD diss. University of Tübingen, 2012.

Mayer, Werner R. "Akkadische Lexicographie, *CAD* P." *Or* 77 (2008): 94–105.

Mayfield, Tyler D. "Literary Structure and Formulas in Ezekiel 34–37." *Ezekiel: Current Debates and Future Directions*, 235–244. Edited by William A. Tooman and Penelope Barter. FAT 1/112. Tübingen: Mohr Siebeck, 2017.

―――. *Literary Structure and Setting in Ezekiel.* FAT 2/43. Tübingen: Mohr Siebeck, 2010.

―――. "A Re-examination of Ezekiel's Prophetic Word Formulas." *HS* LVII (2016): 139–55.

Mays, James Luther. *Psalms*. Interpretation. Louisville: John Knox, 1994.

McCarter, P. Kyle. *II Samuel: A New Translation with Introduction and Commentary*. AB 9. New York: Doubleday, 1984.

McCarthy, Dennis. *Treaty and Covenant: A Study in Form in the Ancient Oriental Documents and in the Old Testament*. 2nd ed. AnBib 21A. Rome: Biblical Institute Press, 1981.

McDonald, Beth Glazier. "Intermarriage, Divorce, and *bat-'ēl nēkār*: Insights into Mal 2:10–16." *JBL* 106 (1987): 603–11.

_____. *Malachi: The Divine Messenger*. SBLDS 98. Atlanta: Scholars Press, 1987.

McKane, William. *A Critical and Exegetical Commentary on Jeremiah*. ICC. 2 vols. Edinburgh: T & T Clark, 1986-96.

McKenzie, Donald F. *Bibliography & the Sociology of Texts*. Cambridge: Cambridge University Press, 1999.

Mein, Andrew. *Ezekiel and the Ethics of Exile*. OTM. New York: Oxford University Press, 2001.

Melugin, Roy F. "The Book of Isaiah and the Construction of Meaning." *Writing and Reading the Scroll of Isaiah*, 1:39–55. Edited by Craig C. Broyles and Craig A. Evans. VTSup 70. 2 vols. New York: Brill, 1997.

Mendenhall, George. *Law and Covenant in Israel and the Ancient Near East*. Pittsburgh: Biblical Colloquium, 1955.

Michael, Matthew. "The Two Prostitutes or the Two Kingdoms? A Critical Reading of King Solomon's Wise Ruling (1 Kgs 3:16-28)." *HBT* 37 (2015): 69–88.

מקראות גדולות הכתר- מלכים. Edited by Menachem Cohen. Ramat-Gan: Bar Ilan University, 1995.

Min, Yoo Hong. *Die Grundschrift des Ezechielbuches und ihre Botschaft*. FAT2 81. Tübingen: Mohr Siebeck, 2015.

Moberly, R. W. L. "Is Monotheism Bad for You? Some Reflections on God, the Bible, and Life in the Light of Regina Schwartz's *The Curse of Cain*." *The God of Israel*, 94–112. Edited by Robert P. Gordon. Cambridge: Cambridge University Press, 2007.

_____. *Old Testament Theology: Reading the Hebrew Bible as Christian Scripture*. Grand Rapids: Baker Academic, 2013.

Moessner, David P. *The Lord of the Banquet: The Literary and Theological Significance of the Lukan Travel Narrative.* Minneapolis: Fortress, 1989.

Mollo, Paola. "Did It Please God to Kill Them? Literary Comparison between the Birth Accounts of Samson and Samuel." *Hen* 36 (2014): 86–106.

Montgomery, James A. *A Critical and Exegetical Commentary on the Books of Kings.* Edited by Henry Snyder Gehman. ICC. Edinburgh: T & T Clark, 1951.

Moon, Joshua N. *Jeremiah's New Covenant: An Augustinian Reading.* JTISup 3. Winona Lake, IN: Eisenbrauns, 2011.

Moor, Johannes C. de, ed. *Synchronic or Diachronic? A Debate on Method in Old Testament Exegesis.* OtSt 34. Leiden: Brill, 1995.

Moran, William L. "The Ancient Near Eastern Background of the Love of God in Deuteronomy." *CBQ* 25 (1963): 77–87. Repr. William L. Moran. *That Most Magic Word,* 170–81. Edited by Ronald S. Hendel. CBQMS 35. Washington: Catholic Biblical Society of America, 2002.

Morgenstern, Julian. "Unity in American Judaism: How and When? An Address Delivered on September 22, 1945, at the Inauguration of the Seventy-First Academic Year of the Hebrew Union College." Cincinnati: Hebrew Union College, 1945.

Mowinckel, Sigmund. *Zur Komposition des Buches Jeremia.* Kristiania: Jacob Dybwad, 1914.

———. *Psalmenstudien I–II.* Repr. Amsterdam: P. Schippers, 1961.

Muilenburg, James. "Form Criticism and Beyond." *JBL* 88 (1969): 1–18.

Mullen, E. Theodore. *The Divine Council in Canaanite and Early Hebrew Literature.* HSM 24. Chico, CA: Scholars Press, 1980.

Mullen, E. Theodore. "The Royal Dynastic Grant to Jehu and the Structure of the Book of Kings." *JBL* 107 (1988): 193–206.

Müller, Hans-Peter. "Glauben und Bleiben: zur Denkschrift Jesajas Kapitel vi 1–viii 18." *Studies on Prophecy: A Collection of Twelve Papers,* 25–54. Edited by George W. Anderson et al. VTSup 26. Leiden: Brill, 1974.

Müller, Reinhard. "The Sanctifying Divine Voice: Observations on the אני יהוה-formula in the Holiness Code." *Text, Time, and Temple: Literary, Historical and Ritual Studies in Leviticus*, 70–84. Edited by Francis Landy, Leigh M. Trevaskis, and Bryan Bibb. HBM 64. Sheffield: Sheffield Phoenix, 2015.

Nadler, Steven. *A Book Forged in Hell: Spinoza's Scandalous Tractate and the Birth of the Secular Age*. Princeton: Princeton University Press, 2011.

Najman, Hindy. *Seconding Sinai: The Development of Mosaic Discourse in Second Temple Judaism*. JSJSup 77. Leiden: Brill, 2003.

Nelson, Richard D. *First and Second Kings*. IBC. Atlanta: John Knox, 1987.

Neusner, Jacob. *Vanquished Nation, Broken Spirit: The Virtues of the Heart in Formative Judaism*. New York: Cambridge University Press, 1987.

Nichols, Stephen G. "Why Material Philology? Some Thoughts." *Sonderheft: Philologie als Textwissenschaft: Alte und neue Horizonte (=Zeitschrift für deutsche Philologie)* 116. (1997): 10–30.

Niditch, Susan. *Judges: A Commentary*. OTL. Louisville: Westminster John Knox, 2008.

———. *Oral World and Written Word: Ancient Israelite Literature*. Louisville: Westminster John Knox. 1996.

Nogalski, James D. *The Book of the Twelve, Micah-Malachi*. Macon, GA: Smyth & Helwys, 2011.

———. "Recurring Themes in the Book of the Twelve: Creating Points of Contact for a Theological Reading." *Int* 61 (2007): 125–27.

———. *Redactional Processes in the Book of the Twelve*. BZAW 218. Berlin: de Gruyter, 1993.

Noth, Martin. *The Deuteronomistic History*. 2nd ed. JSOTSup 15. Sheffield: JSOT Press, 1981.

———. *Überlieferungsgeschichtlichle Studien. I. Die sammelnden und bearbeitenden Gesichtswerke im Alten Testament*. SKGG 18/2. Halle: Max Niemeyer, 1943.

Novak, David. *The Image of the Non-Jew in Judaism*. Edited by Matthew Lagrone. 2nd ed. Oxford: Littman Library of Jewish Civilization, 2011.

_____. *Natural Law in Judaism*. Cambridge: Cambridge University Press, 1998.

O'Brien, Mark A. *The Deuteronomistic History Hypothesis: A Reassessment*. OBO 92. Freiburg: Universitätsverlag, 1989.

O'Brien, Julia M. "Judah as Wife and Husband: Deconstructing Gender in Malachi." *JBL* 115 (1996): 241-50.

_____. *Priest and Levite in Malachi*. SBLDS 121. Atlanta: Scholars Press, 1990.

O'Connor, Kathleen M. *The Confessions of Jeremiah: Their Interpretation and Role in Chapters 1-25*. SBLDS 94. Atlanta: Scholars Press, 1988.

_____. "The Tears of God and Divine Character in Jeremiah 2-9," *Troubling Jeremiah*, 387-401. Edited by Pete A. R. Diamond, Kathleen M. O'Connor and Louis Stulman, JSOTSup 260. Sheffield: Sheffield Academic Press 1999.

Odeberg, Hugo. *Trito-Isaiah (Isaiah 55-66): A Literary and Linguistic Analysis*. Uppsala: Lundequiastiska, 1931.

Odell, Margaret S. *Ezekiel*. SHBC. Macon, GA: Smyth & Helwys, 2005.

O'Donnell, James J. *Avatars of the Word: From Papyrus to Cyberspace*. Cambridge: Harvard University Press, 1998.

Oesch, Josef M. "Textgliederung im Alten Testament und in den Qumranhandschriften." *Hen* 5 (1983): 289-321.

Olley, John W. "'Hear the Word of Yhwh': The Structure of the Book of Isaiah in 1QIsa^a." *VT* 43 (1983): 19-49.

_____. "Pharaoh's Daughter, Solomon's Palace, and the Temple: Another Look at the Structure of 1 Kings 1-11." *JSOT* 27 (2003): 355-69.

Olmo Lete, G. del "Deber." *DDD* 231-32.

Oorschot, Jürgen van. *Von Babel zum Zion: Eine literarkritische und redaktionsgeschichtliche Untersuchung zu Jesaja 40-55*. BZAW 206. Berlin: Walter de Gruyter, 1993.

Oppenheim, A. Leo. *Ancient Mesopotamia: Portrait of a Dead Civilization*. Rev. ed. Completed by Erica Reiner. Chicago: University of Chicago Press, 1977.

Orelli, Conrad von. *Der Prophet Jesaja*. 3rd ed. Munich: Beck, 1904.

_____. *The Prophecies of Isaiah*. Translated by J. S. Banks. Edinburgh: T & T Clark, 1889.

Overduin, Floris. *Nicander of Colophon's Theriaca: A Literary Commentary*. MnemoSup 374. Leiden: Brill, 2015.

Paganini, Simone. *"Nicht darfst du zu diesen Wörtern etwas hinzufügen": Die Rezeption des Deuteronomiums in der Tempelrolle*. BZABR 11. Wiesbaden: Harrasowitz, 2009.

Pape, Wilhelm. *Griechisch-Deutsches Handwörterbuch*. Braunschweig: Vieweg, 1914.

Parker, Kim Ian. "Repetition as a Structuring Device in 1 Kings 1–11." *JSOT* 42 (1988): 19–27.

Paul, Shalom M. "A Lover's Garden of Verse: Literal and Metaphorical Imagery in Ancient Near Eastern Poetry." *Tehillah le-Moshe: Biblical and Judaic Studies in Honor of Moshe Greenberg*, 99–110. Edited by Mordechai Cogan et al. Winona Lake, IN: Eisenbrauns, 1997. Repr. Shalom M. Paul. *Divrei Shalom: Collected Studies of Shalom M. Paul on the Bible and the Ancient Near East 1967–2005*, 271–84. Leiden: Brill, 2005.

_____. "The 'Plural of Ecstasy' in Mesopotamian and Biblical Love Poetry." *Solving Riddles and Untying Knots: Biblical, Epigraphic, and Semitic Studies in Honor of Jonas C. Greenfield*, 585–97. Edited by Ziony Zevit et al. Winona Lake, IN: Eisenbrauns, 1995. Repr. Shalom M. Paul. *Divrei Shalom: Collected Studies of Shalom M. Paul on the Bible and the Ancient Near East 1967–2005*, 239–52. Leiden: Brill, 2005.

_____. "Vain Imprecation on Having Been Born in Job 3 and Mesopotamian Literature." *Marbeh Ḥokmah: Studies in the Bible and Ancient Near East in Loving Memory of Victor Avigdor Hurowitz*, 401–06. Edited by Shamir Yonah et al. Winona Lake, IN: Eisenbrauns, 2015.

Petersen, David L. *Zechariah 9–14 and Malachi: A Commentary*. OTL. Louisville: Westminster John Knox, 1995.

_____. *Late Israelite Prophecy: Studies in Deutero-Prophetic Literature and in Chronicles*. SBLMS 23. Missoula, MT: Scholars Press, 1977.

"*petû ša ūri.*" EaA = *nâqu*, AaA = *nâqu, with Their Forerunners and Related Texts*. Edited by Mugyek Civil et al. *MSL* 14. Rome: Pontificium Istitutum Biblicum, 1979.

Pirke de Rabbi Eliezer. Translated by Gerald Friedlander. London: Kegan Paul, Trench, Trubner, 1916.

Pitkin, John Budd. "Sermon X." *Sermons by Rev. John Budd Pitkin, with a Memoir by Stephen Greenleaf Bulfinch*, 223–45. Boston: David Reid, 1837.

Plant, Robin J. R. *Good Figs, Bad Figs: Judicial Differentiation in the Book of Jeremiah*. LHBOTS 481. New York: T & T Clark, 2008.

Plaskow, Judith. *Standing Again at Sinai: Judaism from a Feminist Perspective*. San Francisco: HarperSanFrancisco, 1990.

Pohlmann, Karl-Friedrich. *Studien zum Jeremiabuch*. FRLANT 118. Göttingen: Vandenhoeck & Ruprecht, 1978.

Polk, Timothy. *The Prophetic Persona: Jeremiah and the Language of the Self*. JSOTSup 32. Sheffield: JSOT Press, 1984.

Pope, Marvin H. *Job*. AB 15. Garden City, NY: Doubleday, 1973.

Power, Bruce A. "'All the King's Horses...': Narrative Subversion in the Story of Solomon's Golden Age." *From Babel to Babylon: Essays on Biblical History and Literature in Honor of Brian Peckham*, 111–23. Edited by J. R. Wood, J. E. Harvey, and M. Leuchter. LHBOTS 455. London: Bloomsbury T & T Clark, 2006.

Preuss, Horst Dietrich. *Old Testament Theology*. Translated by Leo G. Perdue. Louisville: Westminster John Knox, 1995–96.

Procksch, Otto. *Jesaia I*. KAT 9/1. Leipzig: Deichert, 1930.

Prokhorov, Alexander V. *The Isaianic Denkschrift and a Socio-Cultural Crisis in Yehud: A Rereading of Isaiah 6:1–9:6[7]*. FRLANT 261. Göttingen: Vandenhoeck & Ruprecht, 2015.

Pyper, Hugh S. "Judging the Wisdom of Solomon: The Two-Way Effect of Intertextuality." *JSOT* 59 (1993): 25–36.

Rabinowitz, Isaac. "'Āz followed by Imperfect Verb-Form in Preterite Contexts: A Redactional Device in Biblical Hebrew." *VT* 34 (1984): 53–62.

Rad, Gerhard von. "The Beginning of Historical Writing in Ancient Israel." *The Problem of the Hexateuch and other Essays*, 205-21. Translated by E. W. Trueman Dicken. New York: McGraw-Hill, 1966.

⎯⎯⎯⎯. "The Form critical Problem of the Hexateuch." *The Problem of the Hexateuch and Other Essays*, 1-78. Translated by E. W. Trueman Dicken. New York: McGraw-Hill, 1966.

⎯⎯⎯⎯. *Holy War in Ancient Israel*. Translated by Marva J. Dawn. Grand Rapids: Eerdmans, 1991.

Rahlfs. Alfred, ed. *Septuaginta, id est Vetus Testamentum graece iuxta LXX interpretes*. 9th ed. 2 vols. Stuttgart: Deutsche Bibelstiftung, 1935.

⎯⎯⎯⎯. *Genesis: A Commentary*. Translated by John H. Marks. Rev. ed. OTL. Philadelphia, Westminster, 1972.

⎯⎯⎯⎯. *Der heilige Krieg im alten Israel*. ATANT 20. Zürich: Zwingli, 1951.

Rashi, Ibn Ezra, and Y. ibn Ganaḥ. *Sefer Ha-shorashim*. Edited by J. H. R. Biesenthal and F. Lebrecht, Berlin: n.p., 1847. Repr. Jerusalem: n.p., 1967.

Reinhartz, Adele. "Anonymous Women and the Collapse of the Monarchy: A Study in Narrative Technique." *A Feminist Companion to Samuel and Kings*, 43-65. Edited by Athalya Brenner. Sheffield: Sheffield Academic Press, 1994.

Rendsburg, Gary A. "The Guilty Party in 1 Kings III 16-28." *VT* 48 (1998): 534-41.

Rendtorff, Rolf. *Das Alte Testament: Eine Einführung*. 3rd ed. Neukirchen-Vluyn: Neukirchener Verlag, 1988.

⎯⎯⎯⎯. "Zur Komposition des Buches Jesaja." *VT* 34 (1984): 295-320.

Renkema, Jan. *Discourse Studies*. Amsterdam: John Benjamins, 1993.

Reno, Rusty R. *Genesis*. Grand Rapids: Brazos Press, 2010.

Renz, Thomas. *The Rhetorical Function of the Book of Ezekiel*. VTSup 76. Leiden: Brill, 2002.

"Review of a portion of Professor Tayler Lewis D.D.'s 'Patriarchal and Jewish Servitude.'" *The Israelite* 7.48 (May 31, 1861): 380-381.

Rezetko, Robert. "The Qumran Scrolls of the Book of Judges: Literary Formation, Textual Criticism, and Historical Linguistics." *JHebS* 13:2 (2013): 1-68.

Richter, Wolfgang. *Die Bearbeitung des "Retterbuches" in der deuteronomischen Epoche.* BBB 21. Bonn: Hanstein, 1964.

_____. *Exegese als Literaturwissenschaft. Entwurf einen Alttestamentlichen Literaturtheorie und Methodologie.* Göttingen: Vandenhoeck & Ruprecht, 1971.

Roberts, Jimmy J. M. *First Isaiah: A Commentary.* Hermeneia. Minneapolis: Fortress, 2015.

_____. *Nahum, Habakkuk, and Zephaniah.* OTL. Louisville: Westminster John Knox, 1991.

Rofé, Alexander. "The Arrangement of the Book of Jeremiah." *ZAW* 101 (1989): 390-98.

_____. *The Prophetical Stories: The Narratives about the Prophets in the Hebew Bible.* Jerusalem: Magnes, 1988.

Rollmann, Hans. "Zwei Briefe Hermann Gunkels an Adolf Jülicher zur religionsgeschichtlichen und formgeschichtlichen Methode." *ZTK* 78 (1981): 276-88.

Römer, Thomas C. "The Case of the Book of Kings." *Deuteronomy-Kings as Emerging Authoritative Books: A Conversation,* 187-201. Edited by Diana V. Edelman. Atlanta: SBL, 2014.

_____. *The So-Called Deuteronomistic History: A Sociological, Historical and Literary Introduction.* London: T & T Clark, 2005.

Rosenmüller, Ernst F. K. *Scholia in Vetus Testamentum, III/1: Jesajae Vaticinia Complectentis.* 2nd ed. Leipzig: Joh. Ambros. Barth, 1810.

Rost, Leonhard. *The Succession to the Throne of David.* BSHT 1. Sheffield: Almond, 1982. Translated by Michael D. Rutter and David M. Gunn. Translation of *Die Überlieferung von der Thronnachfolge Davids.* BWA(N)T 42. Stuttgart: W. Kohlhammer, 1926.

Rudolph, Wilhelm. *Haggai, Sacharja 1-8, Sacharja 9-14, Maleachi.* KAT 13/4. Gütersloh: Gütersloher Verlagshaus Mohn, 1976.

_____. *Jeremia.* 3rd ed. HAT 1/12. Tübingen: Mohr (Siebeck), 1968.

_____. "Zu Mal 2:10-16." *ZAW* 93 (1981): 85-90.

Ruszkowski, Leszek. *Volk und Gemeinde im Wandel: Eine Untersuchung zu Jesaja 56-66.* FRLANT 191. Göttingen: Vandenhoeck & Ruprecht, 2000.

Saebø, Magne. "Zur Traditionsgeschichte von Jesaia 8,9–10: Klärungsversuch einer alten *crux interpretum*." *ZAW* 76 (1964): 132–44. Repr. Magne Saebø. *Ordene og Orde: Gammeltestamentlige Studier*, 71–83. Oslo: Universitetsforlaget, 1979.

⎯⎯⎯⎯. *On the Way to Canon: Creative Tradition History in the Old Testament*, 108–21. JSOTSup 191. Sheffield: Sheffield Academic Press, 1998.

Sakenfeld, Katherine Doob. *New Interpreter's Dictionary of the Bible*. 5 vols. Nashville: Abingdon, 2006–09.

Sangren, P. Steven. "American Anthropology and the Study of Mazu Worship." 媽祖信仰的發展與變遷:媽祖信仰與現代社會國際研討會 論文集, 7–23. Edited by Linmei Rong, Zhang Xun, and Caixian Hui. Běigǎng: Táiwān Zōngjiào Xuéhuì, 2003.

⎯⎯⎯⎯. "Female Gender in Chinese Religious Symbols: Kuan Yin, Ma Tsu, and the 'Eternal Mother." *Signs* 9.1 (1983): 4–25.

Sarna, Nahum. *Genesis*. JPSTC. Philadelphia: Jewish Publication Society, 1989.

Schenker, Adrian. "Nebuchadnezzars Metamorphose vom Unterjocher zum Gottesknecht." *RB* 89 (1982): 510–13.

⎯⎯⎯⎯. *Das Neue am neuen Bund und das Alte am alten. Jer 31 in der hebräischen und griechischen Bibel*. FRLANT 212. Göttingen: Vandenhoeck & Ruprecht, 2006.

Scherbenske, Eric W. *Canonizing Paul: Ancient Editorial Practice and the Corpus Paulinum*. New York: Oxford University Press, 2013.

Schiffman, Lawrence H. "The Deuteronomic Paraphrase of the Temple Scroll." *RevQ* 15 (1991–92): 543–67.

Schleicher, Marianne. "The Many Faces of the Torah: Reception and Transformation of the Torah in Jewish Communities," *Religion and Normativity 2: Receptions and Transformations of the Bible*, 141–58. Edited by Kirsten Nielsen. AcJTS. Aarhus: Aarhus University Press, 2009.

Schmid, Konrad. *Buchgestalten des Jeremiabuches*. WMANT 72. Neukirchen-Vluyn: Neukirchener Verlag, 1996.

Schmidt, Hans. "Jesaja 8, 9 und 10." *Stromata: Festgabe des Akademisch-Theologischen Vereins zu Giessen*, 3–10. Edited by Georg Bertram. Leipzig: Hinrichs, 1930.

Schneider, Tammi J. *Judges*. BOSHNP. Collegeville, MN: Liturgical Press, 2000.

———. *Mothers of Promise: Women in the Book of Genesis*. Grand Rapids: Baker Academic, 2004.

———. "Rethinking Jehu." *Bib* 77 (1996): 100–07.

Schniedewind, William M. *How the Bible Became a Book: The Textualization of Ancient Israel*. New York: Cambridge University Press, 2004.

Schökel, Luis Alonso. "Of Methods and Models." *Congress Volume Salamanca, 1983*, 3–13. Edited by J. A. Emerton. VTSup 36. Leiden: Brill, 1985.

Scholem, Gershom G. *Kabbalah*. LJK. New York: Quadrangle/The New York Times Book Company, 1974.

Schoors, Antoon. *Jesaja*. DBOT 9A. Roermond: Romen & Zonen, 1972.

Schorch, Stefan. *Euphemismen in der hebräischen Bibel*. OBC 12. Wiesbaden: Harrassowitz, 2000.

Schreiner, Stefan. "Mischehen – Ehebruch – Ehescheidung: Betrachtungen zu Mal 2:10–16." *ZAW* 91 (1979): 207–28.

Schüle, Andreas. "The 'Eternal Covenant' in the Priestly Pentateuch and the Major Prophets." *Covenant in the Persian Period: From Genesis to Chronicles*, 41–58. Edited by Richard J. Bautch and Gary N. Knoppers. Winona Lake, IN: Eisenbrauns, 2015.

Schüngel-Straumann, Helen. "God as Mother in Hosea 11." *A Feminist Companion to the Latter Prophets*, 194–218. Edited by Athalya Brenner. Translated by L. M. Maloney. London: T & T Clark, 2004.

———. "Gott als Mutter in Hosea 11." *TQ* 166 (1986): 119–34.

Schwartz, Regina M. *The Curse of Cain: The Violent Legacy of Monotheism*. Chicago: University of Chicago Press, 1997.

Schwartzman, Sylvan D. and Jack D. Spiro. *The Living Bible*. New York: Union of American Hebrew Congregations, 1962.

Scott, James C. *Domination and the Art of Resistance: Hidden Transcripts*. New Haven: Yale University Press, 1990.

Searle, John. *Speech Acts*. Cambridge: Cambridge University Press, 1969.

Seibert, Eric A. "Solomon's Execution Orders (1 Kgs 2:13-46): Political Propaganda or Scribal Subversion?" *Proceedings, Eastern Great Lakes and Midwest Biblical Societies* 24 (2004): 141-52.

―――. *Subversive Scribes and the Solomonic Narrative: A Rereading of 1 Kings 1-11.* LHBOTS 436. New York: T & T Clark, 2006.

Seitz, Christopher R. "The Crisis of Interpretation Over the Meaning and Purpose of the Exile." *VT* 35 (1985): 78-97.

―――. "The Prophet Moses and the Canonical Shape of Jeremiah." *ZAW* 101 (1989): 3-27.

―――. *Theology in Conflict: Reactions to the Exile in the Book of Jeremiah.* BZAW 176. Berlin: Walter de Gruyter, 1989.

Sellin, Ernst. *Das Zwölfprophetenbuch überstetz und eklärt.* Vol. 2, *Zweite Hälfte: Nahum-Maleachi.* 2nd and 3rd ed. KAT 12. Leipzig: A. Deichersche, 1930.

Sellin, Ernst and Georg Fohrer. *Introduction to the Old Testament.* Translated by David E. Green. Nashville: Abingdon, 1968.

Seow, Choon-Leong. "The First and Second Books of Kings." *The New Interpreter's Bible*, 3:1-295. Edited by L. E. Keck et al. Nashville: Abingdon, 1999.

Seux, Marie-Joseph. "Shiggayon=shigu?" *Mélanges bibliques et orietaux en l'honneur de M. Henri Cazelles.* Edited by A. Caquot and M. Delcor. AOAT 12. Neukirchen-Vluyn: Butzton and Bercker Kevelaer, 1981.

Shapiro, Marc B. *Changing the Immutable: How Orthodox Judaism Rewrites Its History.* Oxford: Littman Library of Jewish Civilization, 2015.

Shemesh, Yael. " מהליכה אחר הבקר להליכה אחר אליהו: מינוי אלישע למשרתו של אליהו," *עיוני מקרא ופרשנות (מלכים א יט 19־21)*, 5:85-86. Edited by Moshe Garsiel et al. Ramat Gan: Bar Ilan University, 2000.

Shields, Martin A. "Syncretism and Divorce in Malachi 2,10-16." *ZAW* 111 (1999): 68-86.

Simon, Uriel. *Reading Prophetic Narratives.* Translated by Lenn J. Schramm. Bloomington: Indiana University Press, 1997.

Singer, Irving. *The Nature of Love: Plato to Luther.* New York: Random House, 1966.

Skinner, John. *The Book of the Prophet Isaiah, Chapters i-xxxix.* CBSC. Cambridge: Cambridge University Press, 1897.

Small, Jocelyn P. *Wax Tablets of the Mind: Cognitive Studies of Memory and Literacy in Classical Antiquity*. New York: Routledge, 1997.

Smith, John Merlin Powis. "Malachi." *Haggai, Zechariah, Malachi and Jonah*, 2:1–88. ICC. Edinburgh: T & T Clark, 1912.

Smith, Mark S. *The Laments of Jeremiah and Their Contexts: A Literary and Redactional Study of Jeremiah 11–20*. SBLMS 42. Atlanta: Scholars Press, 1990.

Sokoloff, Michael. *A Dictionary of Jewish Babylonian Aramaic of the Talmudic and Geonic Periods*. Ramat Gan: Bar Ilan University Press, 2002.

⎯⎯⎯⎯. *A Dictionary of Jewish Palestinian Aramaic of the Byzantine Period*. Ramat Gan: Bar Ilan University Press, 1990.

Solvang, Elna. *A Woman's Place is in the House: Royal Women of Judah and their Involvement in the House of David*. JSOTSup 349. New York: Sheffield Academic Press, 2003.

Sommer, Benjamin D. *A Prophet Reads Scripture: Allusion in Isaiah 40–66*. Stanford: Stanford University Press, 1998.

⎯⎯⎯⎯. "Allusions and Illusions: The Unity of the Book of Isaiah in the Light of Deutero-Isaiah's Use of Prophetic Tradition." *New Visions of Isaiah,* 156–86. Edited by Roy F. Melugin and Marvin A. Sweeney. JSOTSup 214. Sheffield: Sheffield Academic Press, 1996.

⎯⎯⎯⎯. "The Scroll of Isaiah as Jewish Scripture. Or, Why Jews Don't Read Books." SBLSP 35 (1996): 225–42.

Sparks, Kenton. *Ancient Texts for the Study of the Hebrew Bible: A Guide to the Background Literature*. Peabody: Hendrickson, 2005.

Spener, Philipp Jakob. *Christliche Verpflegung der Armen*. Hartmann: Frankfurt an der Oder, 1697. http://digitale.bibliothek.uni-halle.de/vd17/content/pageview/612471. Qtd. (Eng) in Jens Zimmermann, *Recovering Theological Hermeneutics: An Incarnational-Trinitarian Theory of Interpretation*. Grand Rapids: Baker Academic, 2004.

Spiegel, Gabrielle M. "History, Historicism, and the Social Logic of the Text in the Middle Ages." *Spec* 65 (1990): 59–86.

Stanitzek, Georg. "Texte, Paratexte, in Medien: Einleitung." *Paratexte in Literatur, Film, Fernsehen,* 3–20. Edited by Klaus Kreimeier and Georg Stanitzek. Berlin: Akademie Verlag, 2004.

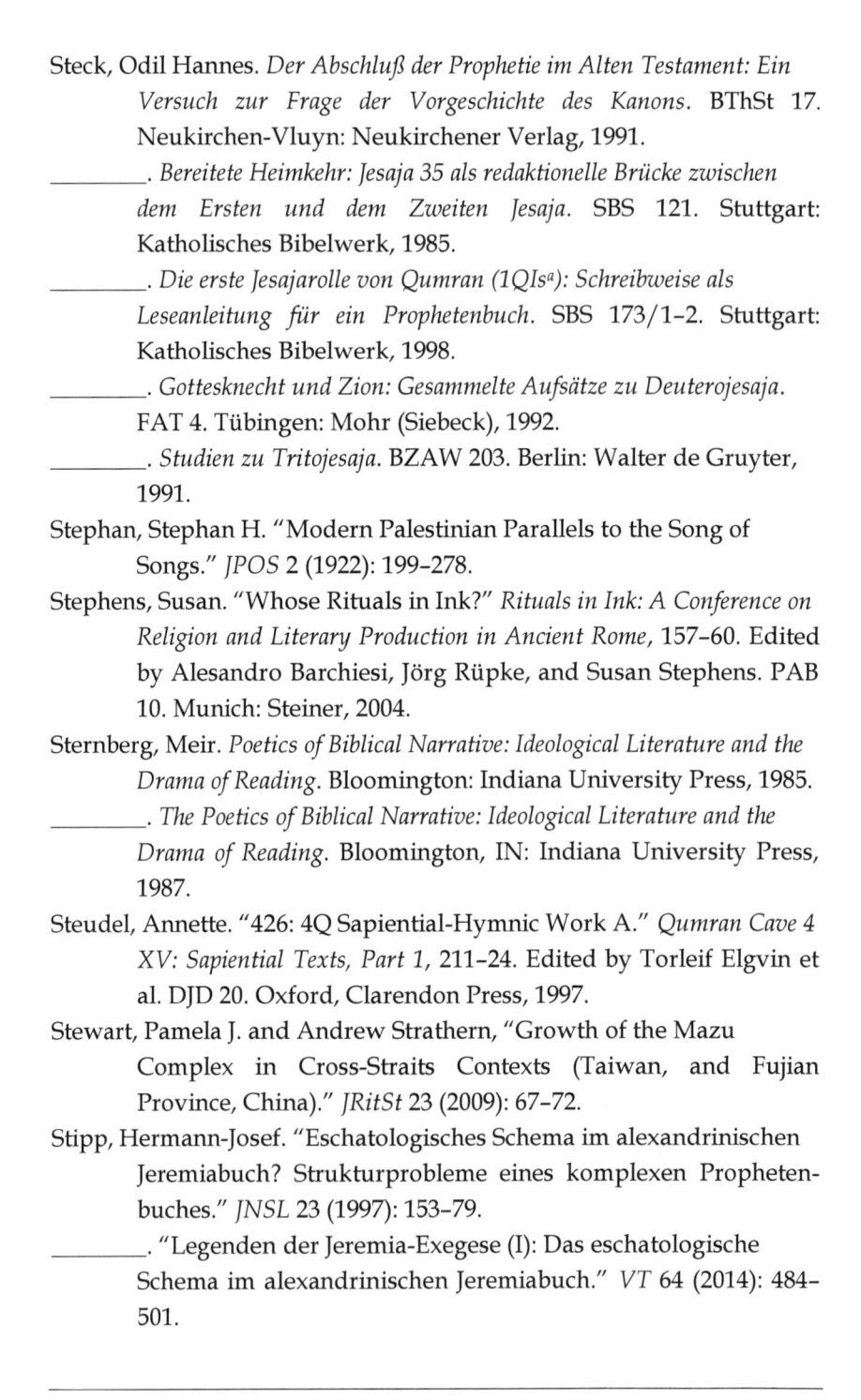

Steck, Odil Hannes. *Der Abschluß der Prophetie im Alten Testament: Ein Versuch zur Frage der Vorgeschichte des Kanons*. BThSt 17. Neukirchen-Vluyn: Neukirchener Verlag, 1991.

_____. *Bereitete Heimkehr: Jesaja 35 als redaktionelle Brücke zwischen dem Ersten und dem Zweiten Jesaja*. SBS 121. Stuttgart: Katholisches Bibelwerk, 1985.

_____. *Die erste Jesajarolle von Qumran (1QIs^a): Schreibweise als Leseanleitung für ein Prophetenbuch*. SBS 173/1–2. Stuttgart: Katholisches Bibelwerk, 1998.

_____. *Gottesknecht und Zion: Gesammelte Aufsätze zu Deuterojesaja*. FAT 4. Tübingen: Mohr (Siebeck), 1992.

_____. *Studien zu Tritojesaja*. BZAW 203. Berlin: Walter de Gruyter, 1991.

Stephan, Stephan H. "Modern Palestinian Parallels to the Song of Songs." *JPOS* 2 (1922): 199–278.

Stephens, Susan. "Whose Rituals in Ink?" *Rituals in Ink: A Conference on Religion and Literary Production in Ancient Rome*, 157–60. Edited by Alesandro Barchiesi, Jörg Rüpke, and Susan Stephens. PAB 10. Munich: Steiner, 2004.

Sternberg, Meir. *Poetics of Biblical Narrative: Ideological Literature and the Drama of Reading*. Bloomington: Indiana University Press, 1985.

_____. *The Poetics of Biblical Narrative: Ideological Literature and the Drama of Reading*. Bloomington, IN: Indiana University Press, 1987.

Steudel, Annette. "426: 4Q Sapiential-Hymnic Work A." *Qumran Cave 4 XV: Sapiential Texts, Part 1*, 211–24. Edited by Torleif Elgvin et al. DJD 20. Oxford, Clarendon Press, 1997.

Stewart, Pamela J. and Andrew Strathern, "Growth of the Mazu Complex in Cross-Straits Contexts (Taiwan, and Fujian Province, China)." *JRitSt* 23 (2009): 67–72.

Stipp, Hermann-Josef. "Eschatologisches Schema im alexandrinischen Jeremiabuch? Strukturprobleme eines komplexen Prophetenbuches." *JNSL* 23 (1997): 153–79.

_____. "Legenden der Jeremia-Exegese (I): Das eschatologische Schema im alexandrinischen Jeremiabuch." *VT* 64 (2014): 484–501.

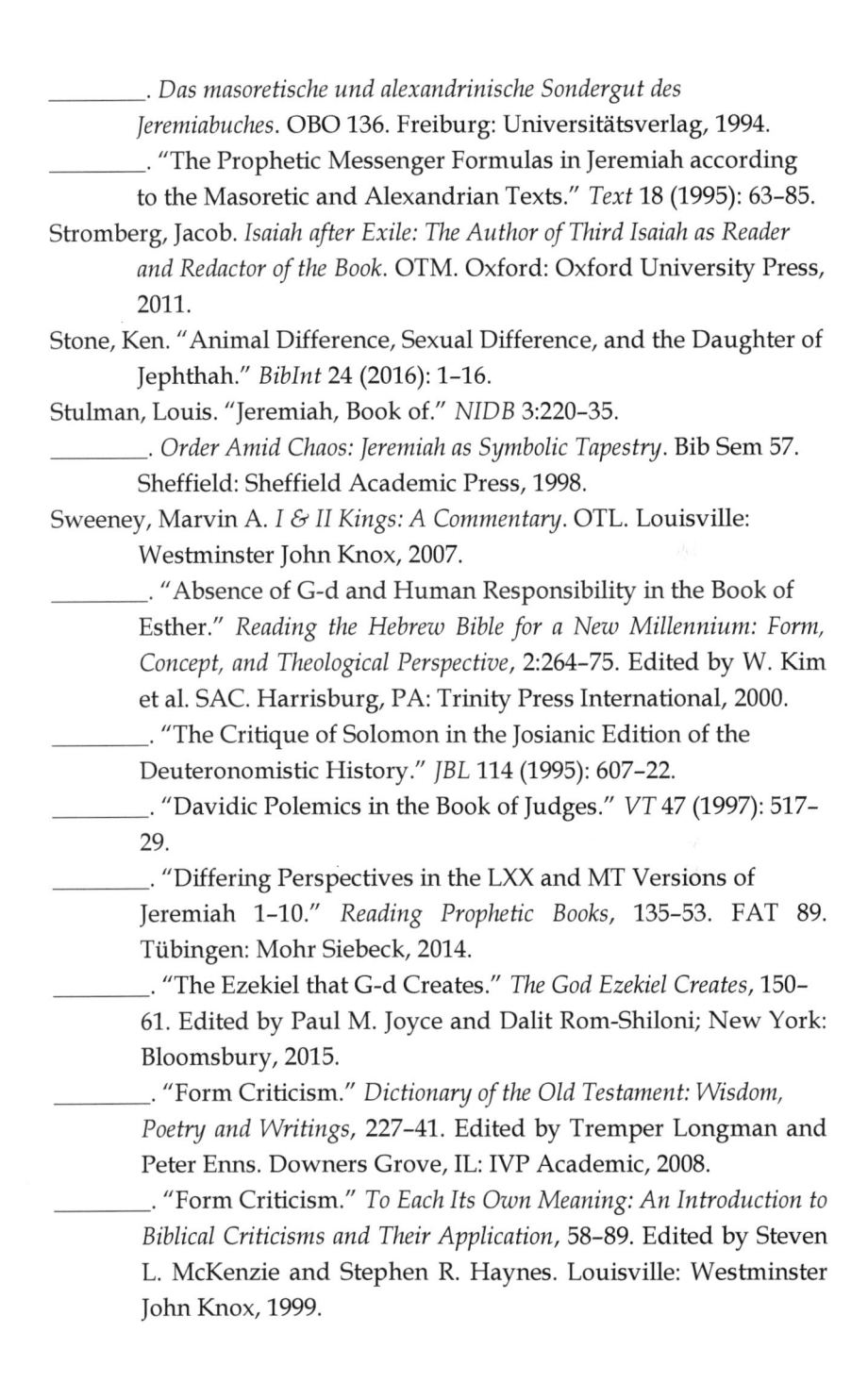

―――――. *Das masoretische und alexandrinische Sondergut des Jeremiabuches*. OBO 136. Freiburg: Universitätsverlag, 1994.

―――――. "The Prophetic Messenger Formulas in Jeremiah according to the Masoretic and Alexandrian Texts." *Text* 18 (1995): 63–85.

Stromberg, Jacob. *Isaiah after Exile: The Author of Third Isaiah as Reader and Redactor of the Book*. OTM. Oxford: Oxford University Press, 2011.

Stone, Ken. "Animal Difference, Sexual Difference, and the Daughter of Jephthah." *BibInt* 24 (2016): 1–16.

Stulman, Louis. "Jeremiah, Book of." *NIDB* 3:220–35.

―――――. *Order Amid Chaos: Jeremiah as Symbolic Tapestry*. Bib Sem 57. Sheffield: Sheffield Academic Press, 1998.

Sweeney, Marvin A. *I & II Kings: A Commentary*. OTL. Louisville: Westminster John Knox, 2007.

―――――. "Absence of G-d and Human Responsibility in the Book of Esther." *Reading the Hebrew Bible for a New Millennium: Form, Concept, and Theological Perspective*, 2:264–75. Edited by W. Kim et al. SAC. Harrisburg, PA: Trinity Press International, 2000.

―――――. "The Critique of Solomon in the Josianic Edition of the Deuteronomistic History." *JBL* 114 (1995): 607–22.

―――――. "Davidic Polemics in the Book of Judges." *VT* 47 (1997): 517–29.

―――――. "Differing Perspectives in the LXX and MT Versions of Jeremiah 1–10." *Reading Prophetic Books*, 135–53. FAT 89. Tübingen: Mohr Siebeck, 2014.

―――――. "The Ezekiel that G-d Creates." *The God Ezekiel Creates*, 150–61. Edited by Paul M. Joyce and Dalit Rom-Shiloni; New York: Bloomsbury, 2015.

―――――. "Form Criticism." *Dictionary of the Old Testament: Wisdom, Poetry and Writings*, 227–41. Edited by Tremper Longman and Peter Enns. Downers Grove, IL: IVP Academic, 2008.

―――――. "Form Criticism." *To Each Its Own Meaning: An Introduction to Biblical Criticisms and Their Application*, 58–89. Edited by Steven L. McKenzie and Stephen R. Haynes. Louisville: Westminster John Knox, 1999.

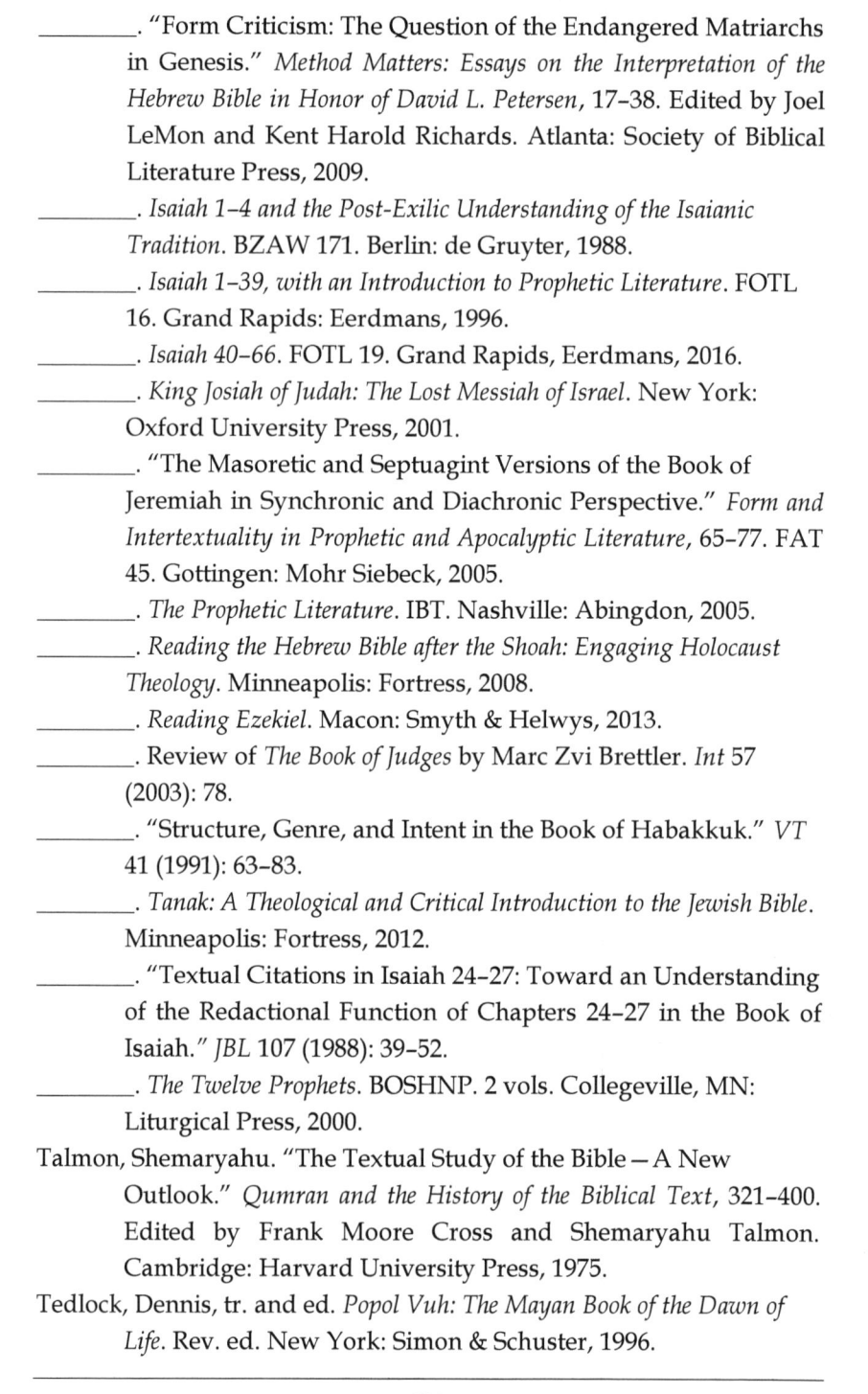

———. "Form Criticism: The Question of the Endangered Matriarchs in Genesis." *Method Matters: Essays on the Interpretation of the Hebrew Bible in Honor of David L. Petersen*, 17–38. Edited by Joel LeMon and Kent Harold Richards. Atlanta: Society of Biblical Literature Press, 2009.

———. *Isaiah 1–4 and the Post-Exilic Understanding of the Isaianic Tradition*. BZAW 171. Berlin: de Gruyter, 1988.

———. *Isaiah 1–39, with an Introduction to Prophetic Literature*. FOTL 16. Grand Rapids: Eerdmans, 1996.

———. *Isaiah 40–66*. FOTL 19. Grand Rapids, Eerdmans, 2016.

———. *King Josiah of Judah: The Lost Messiah of Israel*. New York: Oxford University Press, 2001.

———. "The Masoretic and Septuagint Versions of the Book of Jeremiah in Synchronic and Diachronic Perspective." *Form and Intertextuality in Prophetic and Apocalyptic Literature*, 65–77. FAT 45. Gottingen: Mohr Siebeck, 2005.

———. *The Prophetic Literature*. IBT. Nashville: Abingdon, 2005.

———. *Reading the Hebrew Bible after the Shoah: Engaging Holocaust Theology*. Minneapolis: Fortress, 2008.

———. *Reading Ezekiel*. Macon: Smyth & Helwys, 2013.

———. Review of *The Book of Judges* by Marc Zvi Brettler. *Int* 57 (2003): 78.

———. "Structure, Genre, and Intent in the Book of Habakkuk." *VT* 41 (1991): 63–83.

———. *Tanak: A Theological and Critical Introduction to the Jewish Bible*. Minneapolis: Fortress, 2012.

———. "Textual Citations in Isaiah 24–27: Toward an Understanding of the Redactional Function of Chapters 24–27 in the Book of Isaiah." *JBL* 107 (1988): 39–52.

———. *The Twelve Prophets*. BOSHNP. 2 vols. Collegeville, MN: Liturgical Press, 2000.

Talmon, Shemaryahu. "The Textual Study of the Bible – A New Outlook." *Qumran and the History of the Biblical Text*, 321–400. Edited by Frank Moore Cross and Shemaryahu Talmon. Cambridge: Harvard University Press, 1975.

Tedlock, Dennis, tr. and ed. *Popol Vuh: The Mayan Book of the Dawn of Life*. Rev. ed. New York: Simon & Schuster, 1996.

Theodoret of Cyrus. *Commentary on the Twelve Prophets*. Edited by Robert Charles Hill. Brookline: Holy Cross, 2006.

Thiel, Winfried. *Die deuteronomistische Redaktion von Jeremia 1–25*. WMANT 41. Neukirchen-Vluyn: Neukirchener Verlag, 1973.

———. *Die deuteronomistische Redaktion von Jeremia 26–45*. WMANT 52. Neukirchen-Vluyn: Neukirchener Verlag, 1981.

Thomas, David Winton. "The Root ידע in Hebrew, II." *JTS* 36 (1935): 409–12.

Thompson, John A. *The Book of Jeremiah*. NICOT. Grand Rapids: Eerdmans, 1980.

Tian, Min. *The Poetics of Difference and Displacement: Twentieth-Century Chinese-Western Intercultural Theatre*. Hong Kong: Hong Kong University Press, 2008.

Tigay, Jeffrey H. "Summary and Conclusions." *Empirical Models for Biblical Criticism*, 239–41. Repr. Edited by Jeffrey H. Tigay. DSBLH. Eugene, OR: Wipf and Stock, 2005.

Toorn, Karel van der. *Scribal Culture and the Making of the Hebrew Bible*. Cambridge, MA: Harvard University Press, 2007.

Toorn, Karel van der, Bob Becking, and P.W. van der Horst, eds. *Dictionary of Deities and Demons in the Bible*. 2nd and rev. ed. Grand Rapids: Eerdmans, 1999.

Tov, Emanuel. "Scribal Markings in the Texts from the Judean Desert," *Current Research and Technological Developments on the Dead Sea Scrolls*, 41–77. Edited by Donald W. Parry and Stephen D. Ricks. STDJ 20. Leiden: Brill, 1996.

———. *Scribal Practices and Approaches Reflected in the Texts Found in the Judean Desert*. STDJ 54. Leiden: Brill 2004.

———. *Textual Criticism of the Hebrew Bible*. 3rd rev. ed. Minneapolis: Fortress, 2012.

Tucker, Gene M. *Form Criticism of the Old Testament*. Philadelphia: Fortress, 1971.

Tuell, Steven. "Divine Presence and Absence in Ezekiel's Prophecy." *The Book of Ezekiel: Theological and Anthropological Perspectives*, 109–14. Edited by Margaret S. Odell and John T. Strong. Atlanta: SBL, 2000.

———. *Ezekiel*. NIBC. Peabody, MA: Hendrickson, 2009.

_____. *Reading Nahum–Malachi*. ROT. Macon, GA: Smith-Helwys, 2016.

_____. "The Rivers of Paradise: Ezek 47:1–12 and Gen 2:10–14," *God Who Creates: Essays in Honor of W. Sibley Towner*, 171–89. Edited by S. Dean McBride, Jr. and William Brown. Grand Rapids: Eerdmans, 2000.

Tull Willey, Patricia. *Remember the Former Things: The Recollection of Previous Texts in Second Isaiah*. SBLDS 161. Atlanta: Scholars Press, 1997.

Ulrich, Eugene C. *The Dead Sea Scrolls and the Developmental Composition of the Bible*. VTSup 169. Leiden: Brill, 2015.

_____. "Deuteronomistically Inspired Scribal Insertions into the Developing Biblical Texts: 4QJudg[a] and 4QJer[a]." *Houses Full of All Good Things: Essays in Memory of Timo Veijola*, 489–506. Edited by Juha Pakkala and Martti Nissinen. PFES 95. Helsinki: Finnish Exegetical Society, 2008.

_____. "From Literature to Scripture: Reflection on the Growth of a Text's Authoritativeness." *The Dead Sea Scrolls and the Developmental Composition of the Bible*, 281–98. VTSup 169. Leiden: Brill, 2015.

_____. "The Evolutionary Production and Transmission of the Scriptural Books." *The Dead Sea Scrolls: Transmission of Traditions and Production of Texts*, 209–26. Edited by Sarianna Metso, Hindy Najman, and Eileen M. Schuller. STDJ 92. Leiden/Boston: Brill, 2010.

Ulrich, Eugene C. and Peter W. Flint with a contribution by Martin G. Abegg, eds., *Qumran Cave 1/II. The Isaiah Scrolls, Part 1: Plates and Transcriptions; Part 2: Introductions, Commentary, and Textual Variants*. DJD 32. Oxford: Clarendon Press, 2010.

Unterman, Jeremiah. *Justice for All: How the Jewish Bible Revolutionized Ethics*. JPSEJ. Philadelphia: Jewish Publication Society. Lincoln, NE: University of Nebraska Press, 2017.

Vanderhooft, David S. "The *tokakhat*, 'disputation,' of Habakkuk as a Contrarian Argument in the Book of the Twelve." Paper presented at the Annual Meeting of the SBL. Atlanta, GA, 2010.

VanDrunen, David. *A Biblical Case for Natural Law*. Grand Rapids: Acton Institute, 2008.

Van Seters, John. "A Revival of the Succession Narrative and the Case against It." *JSOT* 39 (2014): 3-14.

Veijola, Timo. "Solomon: Bathsheba's Firstborn." *Reconsidering Israel and Judah: Recent Studies on the Deuteronomistic History*, 340-57. Edited by G. N. Knoppers and J. G. McConville. Winona Lake, IN: Eisenbrauns, 2000.

Verhoef, Pieter A. *The Books of Haggai and Malachi*. NICOT. Grand Rapids: Eerdmans, 1987.

Vermeylen, Jacques. *Du prophète Isaïe á l'apocalyptique*. Paris: J. Gabalda, 1977-78.

Wal, A. J. O. van der. "Toward a Synchronic Analysis of the Masoretic Text of the Book of Jeremiah." *Reading the Book of Jeremiah: A Search for Coherence*, 13-23. Edited by Martin Kessler. Winona Lake, IN: Eisenbrauns, 2004.

Walsh, Jerome T. *1 Kings*. BOSHNP. Collegeville, MN: Liturgical, 1996.

⸺. "The Characterization of Solomon in First Kings 1-5." *CBQ* 57 (1995): 471-93.

Waltke, Bruce K. "Superscripts, Postscripts, or Both." *JBL* 110 (1991): 594-95.

Waltke, Bruce K. and Michael Patrick O'Connor. *An Introduction to Biblical Hebrew Syntax*. Winona Lake, IN: Eisenbrauns, 1990.

Wasserman, Nathan. *Akkadian Love Literature of the Third and Second Millenium B.C.E.* LAS 4. Wiesbaden: Harrassowitz, 2016.

Watts, James W. "Text and Redaction in Jeremiah's Oracles against the Nations." *CBQ* 54 (1992): 42-47.

Watts, John D. W. *Isaiah 1-33*. WBC 24. Waco, TX: Word Books, 1985.

⸺. *Isaiah 1-33*. Rev. ed. Edmonds: Nelson, 2005.

⸺. *Isaiah 34-66*. WBC 25. Waco, TX: Word Books, 1987.

Webb, Barry G. *The Book of Judges*. NICOT. Grand Rapids: Eerdmans, 2012.

⸺. *The Book of Judges: An Integrated Reading*. JSOTSup 46. Sheffield: Sheffield Academic Press, 1987.

Weinfeld, Moshe. "The Covenant of Grant in the Old Testament and in the Ancient Near East." *JAOS* 90 (1970): 184-203.

⸺. *Deuteronomy and the Deuteronomic School*. Winona Lake: Eisenbrauns, 1992.

Weis, Richard D. "A Conflicted Book for a Marginal People: Thematic Oppositions in MT Jeremiah." *Reading the Hebrew Bible in a New Millennium*, 2:297-308. Harrisburg, PA: Trinity Press International, 2000.

———. "Jeremiah amid Actual and Virtual Editions: Textual Plurality and the Editing of the Book of Jeremiah." *The Text of the Hebrew Bible and Its Editions: Studies in Celebration of the Fifth Centennial of the Complutensian Polyglot*, 370-99. Edited by Andrés Piquer Otero and Pablo Torijano Morales. STHB 1. Leiden: Brill, 2016.

———. "Textual History of Jeremiah." *Textual History of the Bible*, 1B:495-513. Edited by Armin Lange and Emanuel Tov. Leiden: Brill, 2016.

———. "The Textual Situation in the Book of Jeremiah." *Sôfer Mahîr: Essays in Honour of Adrian Schenker Offered by the Editors of Biblia Hebraica Quinta*, 269-93. Edited by Yohanan A. P. Goldman, Arie van der Kooij, and Richard D. Weis. VTSup 110. Leiden: Brill, 2006.

Weißflog, Kay. *"Zeichen und Sinnbilder": Die Kinder der Propheten Jesaja und Hosea*. ABG 36. Leipzig: Evangelische Verlagsanstalt, 2011.

Wellhausen, Julius. *Die Composition des Hexateuchs und der historischen Bücher des Alten Testaments*. Berlin: de Gruyter, 1876. Repr. ed.: Saarbrücken: Südwestdeutscher Verlag für Hochschulschriften, 2009.

Wells, Roy D. "Indications of Late Reinterpretation of the Jeremianic Tradition from the LXX of Jer 21:1-23:8." *ZAW* 96 (1984): 405-20.

Wenzel, Siegfried. "Reflections on (New) Philology." *Spec* 65 (1990): 11-18.

Wesselius, J. W. "Joab's Death and the Central Theme of the Succession Narrative (2 Samuel IX-1 Kings II)." *VT* 40 (1990): 336-51.

Westenholz, Joan Goodnick. "A Forgotten Love Song." *Language, Literature and History: Philological and Historical Studies Presented to Erica Reiner*, 415-25. Edited by Francesca Rochberg. AOS 67. New Haven: American Oriental Society, 1987.

Westermann, Claus. *Genesis 1-11: A Commentary*. Tranlsated by John J. Scullion. Minneapolis: Augsburg, 1984.

_____. *Genesis 12–36: A Commentary.* Translated by John J. Scullion. Minneapolis: Augsburg, 1985.

Wevers, John W. *Ezekiel.* NCBC. Grand Rapids: Eerdmans, 1969.

Weyde, Karl William. *Prophecy and Teaching: Prophetic Authority, Form Problems and the Use of Traditions in the Book of Malachi.* BZAW 288. Berlin: de Gruyter, 2000.

White, Marsha C. *The Elijah Legends and Jehu's Coup.* BJS. Atlanta: Scholars Press, 1997.

Whybray, Roger N. *The Succession Narrative: A Study of II Samuel 9–20; I Kings 1 and 2.* SBT 2/9. London: SCM, 1968.

Wieringen, A. L. H. M. van. *The Implied Reader in Isaiah 6–12.* BibInt 34. Leiden: Brill, 1998.

Wildberger, Hans. *Jesaja 1: Jesaja 1–12.* 2nd ed. BKAT 10/1. Neukirchen-Vluyn: Neukirchener Verlag, 1980.

_____. Hans Wildberger, *Isaiah 1–12.* Translated by Thomas H. Trapp; Minneapolis: Fortress, 1991.

Wilf, Steven. *The Law Before the Law.* Lanham: Lexington, 2008.

Williamson, H. G. M. *The Book Called Isaiah: Deutero-Isaiah's Role in Composition and Redaction.* Oxford: Clarendon Press, 1994.

_____. "Reflections on Redaction." *The Centre and the Periphery: A European Tribute to Walter Brueggemann,* 79–91. Edited by Jill Anne Middlemas, David J. A. Clines, and Else Kragelund Holt. Sheffield: Sheffield Phoenix Press, 2010.

_____. *Variations on a Theme: King, Messiah and Servant in the Book of Isaiah.* Carlisle: Paternoster Press, 1998.

Willis, John T. "A Cry of Defiance—Psalm 2." *JSOT* 47 (1990): 33–50.

Willis, Joyce, Andrew Pleffer, and Stephen Llewelyn. "Conversation in the Succession Narrative of Solomon." *VT* 61 (2011): 133–47.

Wilson, Robert A. and Lucia Foglia, "Embodied Cognition," *The Stanford Encyclopedia of Philosophy.* Edited by Edward N. Zalta. 2016: https://plato.stanford.edu/archives/win2016/entries/embodied-cognition (accessed 01/17/17).

Wöhrle, Jakob. "Abraham amidst the Nations: The Priestly Concept of Covenant and the Persian Imperial Ideology." *Covenant in the Persian Period: From Genesis to Chronicles,* 23–39. Edited by Richard J. Bautch and Gary N. Knoppers; Winona Lake, IN: Eisenbrauns, 2015.

Wolde, Ellen van. "Who Guides Whom? Embeddedness and Perspective in Biblical Hebrew and in 1 Kings 3:16-28." *JBL* 114 (1995): 623-42.

Wolff, Hans Walter. *Hosea*. Translated by Gary Stansell. Philadelphia: Fortress, 1974.

Wolterstorff, Nicholas. *Divine Discourse: Philosophical Reflections on the Claim that God Speaks*. Cambridge: Cambridge University Press, 1995.

Woude, Adam S. van der. "Malachi's Struggle for a Pure Community: Reflections on Malachi 2:10-16." *Tradition and Re-interpretation in Jewish and Early Christian Literature*, 65-71. Edited by J. W. van Henten et al. Leiden: Brill, 1986.

Woude, Annemarieke van der. "'Hearing Voices While Reading': Isaiah 40-55 as a Drama." *One Text, a Thousand Methods*, 149-73. Edited by Patrick Chatelion Counet and Ulrich Berges. Boston: Brill, 2005.

––––––. "What Is New in Isaiah 41:14-20? On the Drama Theories of Klaus Baltzer and Henk Leene." *The New Things: Eschatology in Old Testament Prophecy*, 261-67. Edited by F. Postma et al. Maastricht: Uitgeverij Shaker, 2002.

Wright, Christopher J. H. *An Eye for an Eye: The Place of Old Testament Ethics Today*. Downers Grove: InterVarsity Press, 1983.

Würthwein, Ernst. *Die Erzählung von der Thronfolge Davids – theologische oder politische Geschichtsschreibung?* ThSt 115. Zürich: Theologischer Verlag, 1974.

Wyschogrod, Michael. *The Body of Faith: Judaism as Corporeal Election*. New York: Seabury, 1983.

Xella, P. "Resheph." *DDD* 700-03.

Yarchin, William. "Is There an Authoritative Shape for the Book of Psalms? Profiling the Manuscripts of the Hebrew Psalter." *RB* 122 (2015): 355-70.

––––––. "Were the Psalms Collections at Qumran True Psalters?" *JBL* 134 (2015): 775-89.

Yee, Gale A. "The Book of Hosea," *NIB* 7:197-297.

Yeivin, Israel. *Introduction to the Tiberian Masorah*. Atlanta: Scholars Press, 1980.

Young, Dwight A. "A Mathematical Approach to Certain Dynastic Spans in the Sumerian King List." *JNES* 47 (1988): 123–29.

Younger, K. Lawson. "Heads! Tails! Or the Whole Coin?! Contextual Method and Intertextual Analysis: Judges 4 and 5." *The Biblical Canon in Comparative Perspective: Scripture in Context IV*, 109–46. Edited by K. Lawson Younger, William W. Hallo, and Bernard F. Batto. ANETS 11. Lewiston, NY: Edwin Mellen, 1991.

Zakovitch, Yair. "צורה ותוכן במל"א 'ט: 'קול דממה דקה'." *Tarbiz* 51 (1982): 329–46.

Zehnder, Markus. "A Fresh Look at Malachi ii 13–16." *VT* 53 (2003): 224–59.

Zer-Kavod, Mordechai. "ספר מלאכי." *תרי עשר*. Da'at Mikra. Jerusalem: Mossad Harav Kook, 1970.

Zerubavel, Eviatar. *The Fine Line: Making Distinctions in Everyday Life*. Chicago: Chicago University Press, 1991.

Ziegler, Joseph. *Isaias*. 5th ed. Göttingen: Vandenhoeck & Ruprecht, 1983.

_____. *Untersuchungen zur Septuaginta des Buches Isaias*. ATA 12/3. Münster: Aschendorff, 1934.

Zillessen, Alfred. "'Tritojesaja' und Deuterojesaja." *ZAW* 26 (1906): 231–76.

Zimmerli, Walther. *Ezekiel 2*. Hermeneia. Philadelphia: Fortress, 1983.

_____. *Gottes Offenbarung: Gesammelte Aufsätze zum Alten Testament*. TB 1. München: Kaiser Verlag, 1963.

_____. *I am Yahweh*. Translated by D. W. Scott. Atlanta: John Knox, 1982.

_____. "Sinaibund und Abrahambund: Ein Beitrag zum Verständnis der Priesterschrift." *Gottes Offenbarung: Gesammelte Aufsätze zum Alten Testament*, 205–16. TB 19. München: Kaiser Verlag, 1963.

_____. "Zur Sprache Tritojesajas," *Gottes Offenbarung: Gesammelte Aufsätze*, 217–33. 2nd ed. TB 19. München: Chr. Kaiser, 1969.

Zimmerman, Jens. *Recovering Theological Hermeneutics: An Incarnational-Trinitarian Theory of Interpretation*. Grand Rapids: Baker, 2004.

Author Index

Abegg, Martin G.	176
Abma, Richtsje	162
Abramowski, Rudolf	170
Abusch, Tzvi	323
Achtemeier, Elizabeth	269-70
Ackroyd, Peter R.	170
Albright, William Foxwell	263
Allen, Leslie C.	202, 209, 215-16, 219, 223, 227
Alt, Albrecht	30, 32
Alter, Robert	205
Andersen, Francis I.	255
Anderson, Craig Evan	8, 73, 355
Anderson, George W.	151, 267
Arnold, Bill T.	10, 51-54, 56-60, 355
Assis, Elie	282, 291
Aubet, Maria Eugenia	126
Auerbach, Erich	163
Austin, James L.	43
Bach, Robert	150, 153-54
Baltzer, Klaus	34, 159
Bar-Efrat, Shimon	205, 239
Barr, James	36
Barrera, J. Trebolle	64
Barton, John	47, 96
Barth, Hermann	151
Barthel, Jörg	149
Barthélemy, Dominique	152, 216
Bauer, Hans	151
Baum, L. Frank	244
Becker, Jürgen	170
Beckett, Samuel	7, 237, 245-46, 250
Begrich, Joachim	28, 303
Bellah, Robert N.	196-97
Ben Jehuda, Eliezer	326
Ben Nacman, Moshe	41
Ben-Shlomo, David	127-28

Ben Zvi, Ehud	7-8, 25, 275-76, 285, 289-90, 293-94, 355
Bergen, Robert D.	77
Bergen, Wesley J.	115
Berges, Ulrich	171
Berkowitz, Morris I.	254, 257
Berlin, Adele	23, 205
Besette, Joseph M.	48
Beuken, Willem A. M.	88, 90, 170-71, 174
Biddle, Mark E.	202, 204, 210
Billings, Rachel M.	342
Birdsong, Shelley L.	1, 6, 296, 306, 355
Birkett, Jennifer	245
Blenkinsopp, Joseph	38, 53, 59, 76, 87, 96, 151
Block, Daniel I.	225, 239-40
Blum, Erhard	25
Boeckel, Peter Benjamin	3-4, 27, 355
Brandauer, Frederick P.	254, 257
Breed, Brennan W.	312
Brenner, Athalya	123
Brettler, Mark Zvi	63, 84
Bright, John	201, 206
Brinkman, J. A.	133
Brock, Sebastian P.	316
Brueggemann, Walter	92, 193
Bruin, Wim de	316
Brunet, Gilbert	151
Bucur, Bogdan G.	264-65, 268
Bühler, Karl	249
Burnside, Jonathan	89
Burstein, Stanley Mayer	102
Buss, Martin	27, 29
Callaway, Mary C.	204, 216
Calvin, John	150, 281
Camp, Claudia V.	89, 96
Campbell, Anthony F.	20-21, 27, 231
Carlson, Rolf A.	76
Carr, David M.	51
Carroll, Robert P.	193, 194, 201, 210-11, 213-14, 216-18, 300
Carter, Charles E.	224
Chaney, Marvin	256
Chang, Hsun	254, 259-60

Cheyne, Thomas K.	170
Choi, John H.	52, 59
Christensen, Line Søgaard	197
Clements, Ronald E.	170, 201, 209
Coats, George W.	21
Cogan, Mordechai	76, 93, 115, 124-25, 128, 130, 136
Condamin, Albert	151
Conrad, Edgar	239, 247-48, 303
Conroy, Charles	78
Couey, J. Blake	149
Cowley, Arthur E.	316
Craigie, Peter C.	216-17
Crawford, Sidnie White	345
Crenshaw, James L.	63
Crew, Danny O.	277-78
Cushman, Beverly W.	84, 88-89
Dahood, Mitchell	273
Davies, John A.	87
Davies, Philip R.	135-36
Davis, Ellen F.	239, 243, 247
Day, John	151
DeBoys, David G.	154
Delekat, Lienhard	73
Deleuze, Gilles	244
Delitzsch, Franz	149
DeVries, Simon	31, 74, 98, 115-16
Diamond, A. R. Pete	201, 204, 210
Dietrich, Walter	152
Dijk, Jan J. A. van	324
Dijk, Teun A. van	276
Dillmann, August	149
Donald, Merlin	197
Donner, Herbert	151
Dorff, Elliot N.	250
Douglas, Mary	59
Dinkard, Joel F.	216-17
Driver, Godfrey R.	151
Driscoll, Matthew J.	312
Duhm, Bernard L.	149, 165-67, 184, 201
Durkheim, Émile	258
Edmondson, Munro S.	106
Eichrodt, Walther	227, 235, 302, 327
Eisen, Arnold M.	331

Eliade, Mircea	257
Elkins, Dov Peretz	280
Elliger, Karl	170, 173, 185
Emerton, John A.	152
Eshel, Esther	64
Eshel, Hanan	64
Eslinger, Lyle	84
Faulkes, Anthony	104
Fecht, Gerhard	322
Feldman, Louis	347–48
Feser, Edward	48
Finkel, Irving	102
Finlay, Timothy D.	4, 41, 43, 47, 355
Finsterbusch, Karin	203, 206–07
Fish, Stanley	240
Fischer, Georg	202, 207–09, 211, 215–18
Fitzgerald, John T.	11, 63, 65–66, 356
Flint, Peter W.	176
Floyd, Michael H.	270–71
Foglia, Lucia	192
Fohrer, George	64, 115, 151
Fokkelman, Jan P.	14, 26, 80
Fontaine, Carole	77, 81, 86
Fox, Michael R.	282, 284
Fox, Michael V.	322
Freedman, David Noel	255
Fretheim, Terence E.	193, 209, 211, 215–16, 218
Friedman, Richard Elliott	51
Fritz, Volkmar	84
Fröchtling, Andrea	248
Frolov, Serge	1, 4, 13, 18, 21, 23, 33, 37, 73, 96, 356
Fuller, Russell Earl	282
Gadamer, Hans-Georg	251, 319
Gamble, Harry Y.	315
Garsiel, Moshe	75, 90, 93
Gärtner, Judith	171, 186
Gillingham, Susan	314
Geller, Stephen A.	23
Gelston, Anthony	275
Genette, Gérard	313
George, Andrew R.	102, 323
Georges, Karl E.	326
Gerstenberger, Erhard	196

Gese, Hartmut	64
Gesenius, Wilhelm	150, 326
Gevaryahu, Haim M. I.	267
Glade, Henry	245
Goldenstein, Johannes	171, 174, 182, 185–86
Goldingay, John	271
Goldman, Yohanan	223
Goldstein, Miriam	314
Gonçalves, Francolino J.	151
Good, Edwin M.	263, 268
Gopin, Marc	279
Gosse, Bernard	211, 223
Gowan, Donald E.	270–71, 274
Grabbe, Lester L.	9, 101, 356
Gray, G. Buchanan	150–51
Gray, John	116
Grayson, A. Kirk	126, 133
Greenberg, Moshe	227, 248, 324
Gunkel, Hermann	3–4, 15–17, 19–22, 27–31, 34, 36, 44
Gunn, David M.	77–78
Halperin, David J.	237, 240
Halpern, Baruch	77
Hals, Ronald M.	225, 233–34
Harissis, Haralampos V.	70
Harissis, Anastasios V.	70
Hays, J. Daniel	73, 95
Heffelfinger, Katie	157, 159, 164–65
Henderson, Joseph M.	202
Hens-Piazza, Gina	93–94, 116
Herberg, Will	331–32
Herst, Jim	47
Hertzberg, Hans W.	81
Hicks, R. Lansing	323
Hiebert, Theodore	264–67
Higbie, Carolyn	3, 16
Hill, Andrew E.	282
Hill, John	212, 223
Hirsch, Mendel	119
Hobbs, T. R.	210
Höffken, Peter	173
Holladay, William L.	201, 206, 210–11, 216–18, 298
Holmstedt, Robert D.	59
Hölscher, Gustav	235

Holt, Else K.	6, 52, 189–90, 193, 195, 210, 297, 356
Hooti, Noorbakhsh	245
Hornkohl, Aaron D.	223–24
Houbigant, Charles F.	152
Howard, Cameron B. R.	83
Høyrup, Jens	134, 144
Hugenberger, Gordon P.	282–84
Hull, John	9, 133, 356
Hutton, Jeremy M.	87, 96
Hyatt, J. P.	200
Ipsen, Avaren E.	93
Irwin, Lee	260
Iser, Wolfgang	203–04
Jacobsen, Leah	114
Jacoby, Norbert	203
Jeon, Yong Ho	95
Jindo, Job Y.	191
Johnson, Mark	191–92
Johnstone, William	152
Jones, David Clyde	282
Joosten, Jan	55, 57, 60
Joüon, Paul	59
Joyce, Paul M.	227, 239, 250
Justnes, Årstein	64
Kaiser, Otto	151, 154
Kakkanattu, Joy Philip	253
Kaminsky, Joel S.	328–30, 341
Kaufman, Stephen A.	58, 60
Kelle, Brad E.	14
Kelley, Page H.	216–17
Keown, Gerald L.	211, 216, 218
Keulen, Percy S. F. van	97
Kessler, Martin	202, 208
Kim, Hyun Chul Paul	8, 83, 98, 356
Kim, Soo J.	7, 237, 356
Kim, Wonil	250, 330
Kintsch, W.	276
Kissane, Edward J.	151
Kitchell, Kenneth F.	71
Klingbeil, Martin G.	301
Kluge, Alexander	320
Knauf, Erst Axel	54

Knierim, Rolf	3–5, 13, 16–17, 22, 24–26, 29, 32–33, 231, 312, 329–30, 332–33, 338
Knohl, Israel	54–55, 57, 60–61
Knoppers, Gary N.	37, 56, 73, 81
Koch, Klaus	29–31
Köcher, Franz	324
Koenen, Klaus	171, 173, 185
Koh, Hye-Ryun	257
Kogan, Leonid	59
Kooij, Arie van der	311
Kramer, Gerald P.	253
Kratz, Reinhard	5, 87, 169, 185–87, 357
Kugel, James L.	23, 48
Kuo, Cheng-Tian	252, 256–57
Kutler, L. B.	154
Lack, Rémi	170
Lakoff, George	191–92
Lambert, W. G.	102, 324
Lang, Bernhard	196
Lange, Armin	202, 206
Langlamet, François	73
Larrington, Carolyne	104
Lau, Wolfgang	171, 174, 185–86
Leander, Pontus	151
Lee, Archie C.	251
Lee, Yoo Jin	259
Leibowitz, E.	76
Leibowitz, G.	76
Leichty, Erle	126
Lemon, Lee T.	245
Levenson, Jon. D.	10, 327, 330, 333–37, 357
Levinson, Bernard M.	345
Levy, J. Leonard	279
Liebreich, Leon J.	170–73, 175
Liew, Tat-Siong Benny	260
Lincicum, David	345
Liver, Jacob	111, 120
Llewelyn, Stephen	85
Long, Burke O.	74, 116
Lowth, Robert	151
Lundbom, Jack R.	201, 205–06, 209–210, 215–16, 218
Lütkemann, Leonhard	150
Lutz, Hanns-Martin	151

Luzzatto, Samuel David	279
MacDonald, Dennis R.	11, 345, 348, 357
Macintosh, Andrew Alexander	255
Maclean, Marie	313
Marais, Jacobus	63
Marti, Karl	151, 282
Martinez, Florentino Garcia	263
Martin, Malachi	176
Mason, Rex	282
Mason, Steven	36
Masuzawa, Tomoko	277
Matuszak, Jana	324
Mayer, Werner R.	324
Mayfield, Tyler D.	5, 225, 228–29, 231, 357
Mays, James L.	255, 264–65, 268–69
McCarter, P. Kyle	78, 81
McCarthy, Dennis	34
McDonald, Beth Glazier	282
McKane, William	201, 211, 213, 216, 223
McKenzie, Donald F.	312
Mein, Andrew	239–41
Melugin, Roy F.	319
Mendenhall, George	34
Michael, Matthew	87, 93
Millard, A. R.	102
Min, Yoo Hong	239, 241
Moberly, R. W. L.	328, 337–39, 342
Moessner, David	345
Mollo, Paola	65
Montgomery, James A.	115–16
Moon, Joshua N.	304
Moor, Johannes C. de	63
Moran, William L.	336–37
Morgenstern, Julian	330–32, 339
Mowinkel, Sigmund	22, 201, 208, 210
Mueller, Elijah N.	264–65, 268
Muilenburg, James	31–33
Mullen, E. Theodore	101, 138
Müller, Hans-Peter	151
Müller, Reinhard	53, 55
Muraoka, Takamitsu	59
Nadler, Steven	13
Najman, Hindy	345

Nelson, Richard D.	74–75, 81, 116
Neusner, Jacob	248
Nichols, Stephen G.	313
Niditch, Susan	64, 204
Nogalski, James D.	270–71, 282
Noth, Martin	31, 64, 83
Novak, David	41–42, 48–49
Nyengele, M. Fulgence	98
O'Brien, Mark A.	64
O'Brien, Julia M.	282
O'Connor, Kathleen	193, 201
O'Connor, Michael Patrick	59
O'Donnell, James J.	313
Odeberg, Hugo	170
Odell, Margaret S.	227
Oesch, Josef M.	176, 316
Olley, John W.	95, 176
Olmo Lete, G. del	266
Oorschot, Jürgen van	186
Oppenheim, A. Leo	133
Orelli, Conrad von	149
Overduin, Floris	69
Paganini, Simone	345
Pape, Wilhelm	326
Park, Hye Kyung	7, 251, 357
Parker, Kim Ian	95
Paul, Shalom	11, 321–25, 357
Petersen, David L.	16, 32, 112, 282
Plant, Robin J. R.	210, 213, 215–16
Plaskow, Judith	329, 338
Pleffer, Andrew	85
Pohlmann, Karl-Friedrich	209, 213, 217
Polk, Timothy	189
Pope, Marvin H.	323, 326
Power, Bruce A.	87, 91, 95
Preuss, Hornst Dietrich 327	
Procksch, Otto	151
Prokhorov, Alexander V.	151
Pyper, Hugh S.	97
Rabinowitz, Isaac	74
Rad, Gerhard von	15, 22, 30–31, 47, 49, 73, 150, 303, 332–33, 339
Rahlfs, Alfred	67, 150

Reis, Marion J.	245
Reinhartz, Adele	85
Rendsburg, Gary A.	75–76, 79
Rendtorff, Rolf	170, 174
Renkema, Jan	276
Reno, Rusty R.	49
Renz, Thomas	239
Rezetko, Robert	64
Richter, Wolfgang	22, 64
Roberts, Jimmy J. M.	150, 263–65, 268–69, 324
Rofé, Alexander	201, 208, 210, 215
Rollmann, Hans	15, 27
Römer, Thomas	83–84, 96
Rosenmüller, Ernst F. K.	153
Rost, Leonard	73
Rudolph, Wilhelm	193, 213, 215, 218, 282
Ruszkowski, Leszek	171
Saebø, Magne	148, 150, 152–53
Sangren, P. Steven	254, 257–58
Saperstein, Marc	279
Sarna, Nahum	45, 47
Scalise, Pamela J.	211, 216, 218
Schenker, Adrian	216, 223, 304
Scherbenske, Eric W.	313
Schiffman, Lawrence H.	345
Schleicher, Marianne	199–200
Schmid, Konrad	215
Schmidt, Hans	150
Schneider, Tammi J.	9, 123, 129, 131, 358
Schniedewind, William M.	51
Schökel, Luis Alonso	52
Scholem, Gershom G.	248
Schoors, Antoon	151
Schorch, Stephan	326
Schreiner, Stefan	282
Schüle, Andreas	57
Schüngel-Straumann, Helen	253, 258–59
Schwartz, Regina	328, 338–41
Schwartzman, Sylvan D.	280
Searle, John	43–45
Seibert, Eric A.	73–74, 79, 81, 87, 97
Seitz, Christopher R.	201, 209–211, 216
Sellin, Ernst	64, 263, 273

Seow, Choon-Leong	84, 91, 93–94
Seux, Mary-Joseph	273
Shapiro, Marc B.	280
Sharp, Carolyn J.	297
Shemesh, Yael	115
Shields, Martin A.	282–83
Simon, Uriel	114–15, 119
Singer, Irving	338–39
Skinner, John	149
Small, Jocelyn P.	315
Smith, John Merlin	112
Smith, Mark S.	201
Smothers, Thomas G.	211, 216, 218
Snaith, Norman	115
Sokoloff, Michael	325
Solvang, Elna	124–25, 128–29
Sommer, Benjamin D.	171, 174, 185
Sparks, Kenton	30, 33
Spener, Philipp Jakob	278
Spiegel, Gabrielle M.	312–13
Spiro, Jack D.	280
Steck, Odil Hannes	170–71, 174, 176–77, 182, 185–86
Stephan, Stephan H.	321
Sternberg, Meir	204–05, 239
Steudel, Annette	176
Stewart, Pamela J.	252
Stipp, Hermann-Josef	202, 223
Stone, Ken	94
Strathern, Andrew	252
Strawn, Brent A.	14, 159
Stromberg, Jacob	171, 173, 186
Stulman, Louis	202, 210, 215, 297–298
Sullivan, Lawrence	257
Sweeney, Marvin A.	1–5, 8, 10, 12–13, 16–17, 22, 24–27, 32–34, 42, 51–52, 63, 73–74, 79, 81, 83, 91–92, 95–96, 99, 101, 111, 115, 124–25, 130, 133, 147–48, 154–55, 157, 169–71, 173, 201–03, 205, 208, 215, 225, 230–31, 233, 237–38, 250, 256, 258, 263–65, 269–71, 275, 277, 282, 291, 294–95, 299, 302, 304, 306, 309, 313, 315, 319–20, 323, 326, 343, 345
Tadmor, Haim	136

Talmon, Shemaryahu	311
Tedlock, Dennis	107
Thiel, Winfried	209, 211, 215-18
Thomas, David Winton	151-52
Thompson, John A.	201, 211, 213, 216-18
Tian, Min	245
Tigay, Jeffrey H.	51
Tigchelaar, Eibert J. C.	263
Toorn, Karel van der	52
Tov, Emanuel	176-77, 202, 319
Treu, Abigail	280
Trollope, Anthony	44
Tucker, Gene	17, 73
Tuell, Steven S.	7, 225, 239, 263-65, 270-71, 358
Tull, Patricia K.	5, 157, 160, 168, 358
Turner, Mark	191-92
Ulrich, Eugene C.	64, 176, 311, 318
Unterman, Jeremiah	9, 111, 358
Vanderhooft, David S.	263
VanDrunen, David	49
Veijola, Timo	64, 85, 91
Verhoef, Pieter A.	282, 290
Vermeylen, Jack	170
Wal, A. J. O. van der	202
Walsh, Jerome T.	84, 87, 94, 124
Waltke, Bruce K.	59, 267
Wasserman, Nathan	324
Watts, James W.	202
Watts, John D. W.	173
Webb, Barry G.	14, 63
Weinfeld, Moshe	37, 77
Weis, Richard D.	6, 201-02, 204, 222-24, 358
Weißflog, Kay	151
Wellhausen, Julius	73
Wells, Roy D.	223
Wenzel, Siegfried	312
Wesselius, J. W.	92
Westenholz, Joan Goodnick	323
Westermann, Claus	53-54, 56
Wevers, John W.	227
Weyde, Karl William	282-83
White, Marsha C.	114, 119
Whybray, Roger	8, 73, 76-78

Wieringen, A. L. H. M.	149
Wildberger, Hans	151
Wilf, Steven	42, 49
William Alston	43–45
Williamson, H. G. M.	4–5, 52, 58, 147, 155, 186, 358
Willis, John T.	154
Willis, Joyce	85
Wilson, Robert A.	192
Wise, Isaac M.	279–80
Wöhrle, Jakob	56
Wolde, Ellen van	76, 88
Wolff, Hans Walter	255
Wolterstorff, Nicholas	239
Woude, Adam S. van der	282, 284, 290
Woude, Annemarieke van der	159
Wright, Christopher J. H.	49
Wu, George	253
Würthwein, Ernst	78
Wyschogrod, Michael	336–40
Xella, P.	266
Yarchin, William	11, 311, 314, 316, 355, 359
Yee, Gale A.	252
Yeivin, Israel	317
Young, Dwight A.	133
Younger, K. Lawson	23
Zehnder, Markus	282
Zerubavel, Eviatar	282
Ziegler, Joseph	149, 152–53
Zillessen, Alfred	170
Zimmerli, Walther	55–56, 170, 229–30, 234–35
Zimmermann, Jens	278

Scripture Index

Gen 1:1 – 2 Kgs 25:30	19
Genesis 1-9	38
Gen 1:1–2:3	17, 19-21, 23, 24,
Genesis 1-2	17, 18, 23-25,
Genesis 1	18, 46, 49, 50, 60, 61, 182
Gen 1:1-2	18, 19,
Gen 1:1	24
Gen 1:3–2:3	18, 19,
Gen 1:3-31	18
Gen 1:22	37
Gen 1:26-31	44
Gen 1:27	47
Gen 1:27aβ-b	18
Gen 1:28	37, 42, 44
Gen 1:28b	46
Gen 1:29-30	46
Gen 1:29	46
Gen 1:30	46
Genesis 2-4	299, 300
Genesis 2-3	106
Genesis 2	21, 46, 50, 299, 300
Gen 2:4–50:26	19
Gen 2:4–4:26	19
Gen 2:4–4:1	298
Gen 2:4–3:25	17
Gen 2:4-25	19, 20, 23, 24,
Gen 2:4-14	19
Gen 2:4-9	20
Gen 2:4-6	18, 19
Gen 2:4	18
Gen 2:4a	18, 24
Gen 2:5-6a	18
Gen 2:5	299
Gen 2:6b	18
Gen 2:7-9	18, 19
Gen 2:7	298

Gen 2:8	298
Gen 2:9	299
Gen 2:10-14	18, 19
Gen 2:15-25	18, 19
Gen 2:15	299
Gen 2:16	46
Gen 2:17	46, 299, 300
Gen 2:18	20
Gen 2:19-23	20
Gen 2:19	298
Gen 2:24-25	20
Genesis 3-4	19, 23,
Genesis 3	20
Gen 3:1b	18
Gen 3:5	94, 299, 300
Gen 3:7	94, 299
Gen 3:9	20
Gen 3:13	117, 118
Gen 3:16-17	20
Gen 3:22	299
Gen 4:1	299, 300
Gen 4:8-14	47
Gen 4:8	89
Gen 4:10	90, 117
Genesis 5	18, 53
Gen 5:1	18, 19,
Gen 5:32	53
Genesis 6-9	102
Gen 6:2-4	285
Gen 6:9–9:29	60
Gen 6:9	18, 24, 54
Gen 6:11-22	58
Gen 6:17	55, 59
Gen 7:6	53
Genesis 8	34
Gen 8:13–9:19	35
Gen 8:13-14	34, 35
Gen 8:13a	35
Gen 8:13bα	35
Gen 8:13bβ	35
Gen 8:13bγ	35
Gen 8:14	35
Gen 8:15–9:18	35

Gen 8:15-17	35
Gen 8:17	37
Gen 8:18	35
Gen 8:19	35
Gen 8:20	36
Gen 8:20a	35
Gen 8:20bα	35
Gen 8:20bβ	35
Gen 8:21	38
Gen 8:21aα	35
Gen 8:21aβ-22	35
Genesis 9	36, 39
Gen 9:1-17	41, 42, 45, 46, 50
Gen 9:1-7	36, 42, 44, 49
Gen 9:1-5	38
Gen 9:1	37, 42, 44
Gen 9:1a-bα	42
Gen 9:1a	35, 42
Gen 9:1b-7	35
Gen 9:1b	45
Gen 9:1bα	42
Gen 9:1bβ-7	42
Gen 9:1bβ	42, 44, 45
Gen 9:1bβ$^{1-2}$	43, 45
Gen 9:1bβ$^{3-4}$	43, 45
Gen 9:2-6	43, 45
Gen 9:2-4	43, 45
Gen 9:2	43
Gen 9:2a	43, 45
Gen 9:2b	43
Gen 9:3-4	43
Gen 9:3	43, 46
Gen 9:3a	43
Gen 9:3b	43
Gen 9:4	43
Gen 9:5-6	43, 45
Gen 9:5	43, 46
Gen 9:5aα	43
Gen 9:5aβ-b	43
Gen 9:5aβ	43
Gen 9:5b	43
Gen 9:6	43, 47, 48
Gen 9:6a	43, 47

Gen 9:6b	43, 49
Gen 9:7	36, 37, 43-45
Gen 9:7a	43, 45
Gen 9:7b	43, 45
Gen 9:8-19	27, 37, 38
Gen 9:8-18	34
Gen 9:8-17	36, 49, 56, 58
Gen 9:8-11	35, 36,
Gen 9:9	36-38, 41, 55, 59
Gen 9:12-17	56, 59, 267
Gen 9:12-16	35
Gen 9:12	55
Gen 9:13-16	36
Gen 9:17	35
Gen 9:18	35
Gen 9:19	35, 38
Gen 9:20-28	38
Gen 9:20-27	24
Gen 10:1-32	38
Gen 10:1	18, 24,
Genesis 11	18
Gen 11:10-26	38, 53
Gen 11:10	18, 24
Gen 11:27–25:11	38
Gen 11:27	18
Genesis 12	302, 303, 305, 332-34, 339
Gen 12:2	305
Gen 12:3b	333, 334
Gen 12:4b	53
Gen 12:12	98
Gen 12:18	117
Genesis 14	333
Genesis 15	33, 52, 53, 55, 302, 303, 305
Gen 15:1-6	52
Gen 15:1	52, 303
Gen 15:5-6	305
Gen 15:7-21	52
Gen 15:7	52
Gen 16:16a	53
Genesis 17	38, 39, 52, 53, 56, 58, 60, 61, 302, 303, 305
Gen 17:1-22	52, 55, 58-60
Gen 17:1-8	53

Gen 17:1-3a	53
Gen 17:1-2	53
Gen 17:1	52, 54, 55
Gen 17:1a	53
Gen 17:1b	54
Gen 17:2	55, 305
Gen 17:3-22	53, 58
Gen 17:3b-21	53
Gen 17:4-8	58
Gen 17:4	36, 55, 58
Gen 17:7-8	61, 305
Gen 17:7	38
Gen 17:9-14	53, 57-59
Gen 17:9-10	36
Gen 17:9	36, 58
Gen 17:10	59
Gen 17:12-13	59
Gen 17:12	59
Gen 17:15-22	53
Gen 17:15-16	58
Gen 17:15	59
Gen 17:19-21	58
Gen 17:20-21	341
Gen 17:20	59
Gen 17:23-27	53, 59
Gen 17:24a	53
Gen 18:19	41, 333
Gen 20:9	117
Gen 20:11	98
Genesis 21	303
Gen 21:4	59
Gen 21:5a	53
Genesis 22	93, 94
Gen 22:6	93
Gen 22:10	93
Gen 22:11	93
Genesis 23	305
Gen 23:9	305
Gen 23:11	305
Gen 23:18	305
Gen 23:19	305
Genesis 24	341
Gen 25:8	24

Gen 25:12	18, 24
Gen 25:19	18, 24
Gen 25:32	89
Gen 26:7	98
Gen 26:9	98
Gen 26:10	117
Gen 26:24	303
Gen 26:34	24
Gen 27:1-45	341
Gen 27:1-2	89
Gen 27:22	90
Gen 27:36	89
Gen 27:41-42	89
Gen 28:3	54
Gen 29:25	117
Gen 31:26	117
Gen 32:6-7	89
Gen 32:25-32	90
Gen 33:1-17	341
Gen 33:4-11	89
Gen 35:11	54
Gen 35:16-19	307
Gen 35:29	89
Genesis 36	24
Gen 36:1	18, 24
Gen 36:4	24
Gen 36:9	18, 24
Genesis 37-50	307
Genesis 37	306, 307
Gen 37:2	18, 19, 24
Gen 37:4	307
Gen 37:8	307
Gen 37:18-20	307
Gen 37:20	307
Gen 37:24	307
Gen 37:26-27	307
Gen 37:28	307
Gen 37:33-35	307
Gen 39:1	308
Gen 40:15	308
Gen 41:14	308
Gen 41:46-47:28	308
Gen 41:53-57	333

Gen 42:28	117
Gen 43:14	54
Gen 44:15	117
Gen 45:14-15	89
Gen 46:3	303
Gen 48:3	54
Gen 50:15-21	341
Gen 50:19-21	89
Exod 1:1–11:10	19
Exodus 3-4	299
Exod 4:19	117
Exod 4:22	284, 290
Exod 4:23	284
Exod 6:2-8	54, 60
Exod 6:3	54
Exod 11:5	325
Exod 11:10	19
Exod 12:1–Deut 34:12	19
Exod 12:1	19
Exod 14:5	117
Exod 14:11	117, 118
Exod 15:1-18	266
Exod 15:1	74
Exod 15:4	266
Exod 19:5-6	327
Exod 21:12-14	89
Exod 23:3	339
Exod 23:6	339
Exod 29:45-46	60
Exod 31:12-17	60
Exod 32:21	117
Exod 33:22	114
Exodus 34	198
Exod 34:28	113
Exod 35:2-3	60
Lev 7:20-21	273
Lev 10:1-2	24
Leviticus 11	60
Leviticus 17-26	58, 60
Lev 17:10-11	273
Lev 18:29	273, 285
Lev 19:8	273, 285
Lev 20:5-6	273

Leviticus 23	60
Leviticus 25	249
Leviticus 26	39, 60
Num 3:1	18, 19, 24
Num 6:1-21	65
Num 21:29	284
Num 22:28	117, 118
Num 23:11	117, 118
Deut 2:25	269
Deut 2:31-34	346
Deut 3:3-4	346
Deut 3:6	346
Deut 6:4-5	94
Deut 6:5	95
Deut 7:1-5	342
Deut 7:1	91
Deut 7:2	346
Deut 7:6-8	335
Deut 7:8	335
Deut 10:14-15	335
Deut 10:15	339
Deut10:17	339
Deut 12:2-3	95
Deut 13:15	285
Deut 17:16-17	96
Deut 20:10-14	346
Deut 20:10-13a	351
Deut 20:13b-14	352
Deut 20:17	91
Deut 21:18-21	258
Deut 23:2-3	91
Deut 23:8	342
Deut 24:1-4	293
Deuteronomy 29	39
Deut 29:11	273
Deut 30:1-10	239
Deut 30:1-3	39
Deut 30:15-18	349
Deut 30:19-20	346
Deut 31:1-4	347, 350
Deut 31:1	349
Deuteronomy 32	335, 339
Deut 32:5	284

Deut 32:6	289
Deut 32:10	334
Deut 32:15-18	334
Deut 32:18	290
Deut 33:29	347, 348
Deuteronomy 34	14
Deut 34:10-12	352
Josh 1:1–Judg 1:26	19
Josh 1:1	137
Josh 2:1-24	342
Josh 6:5	150
Josh 6:10	150
Josh 6:16	150
Josh 6:20-23	342
Josh 6:20	150
Josh 7:11	342
Josh 7:19	117, 118
Josh 8:1	303
Josh 10:8	303
Josh 11:6	303
Joshua 24	31
Judg 1:27 – 1 Sam 12:25	19
Judg 2:2	117
Judg 2:7	137
Judg 3:28	148
Judg 4:6-7	148
Judg 4:14	148
Judg 5:2-31	266
Judg 5:4-5	265
Judg 5:27	326
Judg 6:7-10	64
Judg 7:9	148
Judg 8:1	117
Judg 8:2	117
Judg 11:39	94
Judg 13:1-16:31	63
Judg 13:2-15:19	64
Judg 13:2-24	64
Judg 13:5	65
Judg 13:7	65
Judg 13:14	65
Judges 14-16	66
Judg 14:1–15:19	64

Judg 14:1–15:8	66
Judg 14:1	67
Judg 14:5-8	67
Judg 14:5	66, 67
Judg 14:6	67
Judg 14:8	67
Judg 14:9	67, 68
Judg 14:10-18	67
Judg 14:10	66, 67
Judg 14:12	66
Judg 14:14	67
Judg 14:17	66, 67
Judg 14:18	66, 18
Judg 14:20	150
Judg 15:11	117
Judg 15:20	64
Judg 16:1-31a	64
Judg 16:1-3	64
Judg 16:4-31	64
Judg 16:17	65
Judg 16:19	66, 67, 326
Judg 16:21	325
Judg 16:31	65
Judg 16:31b	64
Judg 19:29	94
1 Sam 1:11	65
1 Sam 1:22	65
1 Samuel 8-12	83
1 Sam 13:1–2 Kgs 25:30	19
1 Sam 13:1	139
1 Sam 13:11	117
1 Sam 14:43	117
1 Sam 16:1-3	108
1 Sam 17:20	150
1 Sam 17:29	117
1 Sam 17:52	150
1 Sam 20:1	117, 118
1 Sam 20:32	117
1 Sam 25:36	66
1 Sam 25:39-42	98
1 Sam 26:18	117
1 Sam 29:8	117
2 Sam 2:10	139

2 Sam 3:4	84
2 Sam 3:24	117
2 Samuel 9 – 1 Kings 2	77, 84
2 Samuel 9-20	73, 76, 77, 96
2 Samuel 11-12	77, 81, 87, 98
2 Samuel 11	87
2 Sam 11:3	84
2 Sam 11:25	79
2 Samuel 12-13	87
2 Samuel 12	87
2 Sam 12:3	87
2 Sam 12:5	90
2 Sam 12:7	90
2 Sam 12:9	79
2 Sam 12:10	80
2 Sam 12:21	117
2 Sam 12:24	84
2 Samuel 13 – 1 Kings 2	79
2 Sam 13:1-6	78
2 Sam 13:3-5	78
2 Sam 13:3	77
2 Sam 13:28	97
2 Samuel 14	78
2 Sam 14:1-17	87
2 Sam 14:2	77, 78
2 Sam 14:6	87
2 Sam 14:11	92
2 Sam 14:25	85
2 Samuel 15-18	80
2 Sam 15:1-6	80
2 Sam 16:8	112
2 Sam 17:1-14	78
2 Sam 17:23	78
2 Sam 18:11	92
2 Sam 18:33	269
2 Samuel 19	80
2 Sam 19:30	80
2 Samuel 20	78, 80
2 Sam 20:1	80
2 Sam 20:22	77
2 Sam 24:17	117
1-2 Kings	123
1 Kings	125

1 Kings 1-11	83, 84, 94, 96
1 Kings 1-10	83
1 Kings 1-2	73, 76, 77, 84-89, 91, 95-98
1 Kgs 1:1-2	89
1 Kgs 1:3-4	88
1 Kgs 1:5	84
1 Kgs 1:6	85
1 Kgs 1:7	85
1 Kgs 1:8	86, 137
1 Kgs 1:9	84
1 Kgs 1:11-14	89
1 Kgs 1:11	84
1 Kgs 1:14	85
1 Kgs 1:15	85
1 Kgs 1:22-27	85
1 Kgs 1:39	97
1 Kgs 1:50-53	89
1 Kgs 1:50-51	89
1 Kgs 1:51	92
1 Kgs 1:52	89, 92
1 Kings 2	79, 80, 89
1 Kgs 2:5-6	92
1 Kgs 2:5	92
1 Kgs 2:6	79, 92
1 Kgs 2:8	92
1 Kgs 2:9	79, 92
1 Kgs 2:12	97, 142
1 Kgs 2:13	92
1 Kgs 2:15	89
1 Kgs 2:19-21	86, 88
1 Kgs 2:19	85
1 Kgs 2:22	86
1 Kgs 2:24-25	92, 95
1 Kgs 2:25	84, 92
1 Kgs 2:28-34	89
1 Kgs 2:29-30	92
1 Kgs 2:32	92
1 Kgs 2:33	92
1 Kgs 2:46	84, 92, 97, 142
1 Kings 3-10	73
1 Kings 3-8	83
1 Kings 3	77, 81, 86, 88, 89, 92, 97
1 Kgs 3:1-15	94, 97

1 Kgs 3:1-2	95
1 Kgs 3:1	91, 95, 97
1 Kgs 3:2-15	95
1 Kgs 3:3–9:23	84
1 Kgs 3:3	81, 95
1 Kgs 3:4–8:66	83
1 Kgs 3:4-15	74, 79
1 Kgs 3:4-14	81
1 Kgs 3:5	90
1 Kgs 3:9	86, 94
1 Kgs 3:10-13	98
1 Kgs 3:15	92, 97
1 Kgs 3:16-28	74, 75, 79, 81, 84, 87, 90, 93-95, 97-99
1 Kgs 3:16	85
1 Kgs 3:17-21	75, 85
1 Kgs 3:17	75, 84, 85
1 Kgs 3:18	85
1 Kgs 3:19-20	90
1 Kgs 3:21	90
1 Kgs 3:22	74, 85, 90
1 Kgs 3:23	74, 90
1 Kgs 3:24-25	90
1 Kgs 3:24	76, 79, 80, 86, 92, 93
1 Kgs 3:25-26	90, 272
1 Kgs 3:25	76, 80, 81, 91
1 Kgs 3:26	75, 86, 88, 91, 93
1 Kgs 3:26b	75
1 Kgs 3:28	86, 98
1 Kgs 3:28a	94
1 Kgs 3:28b	93, 94
1 Kgs 4:1–5:14	95
1 Kgs 5:2-8	96
1 Kgs 5:15–7:51	127
1 Kgs 5:15-32	95
1 Kgs 5:27-30	96
1 Kgs 6:1-38	95
1 Kgs 6:2	96
1 Kgs 6:38–7:1	96
1 Kgs 7:1-12	95
1 Kgs 7:2	96
1 Kgs 7:13–8:66	95
1 Kgs 8:9	273
1 Kgs 9:1–11:43	83

1 Kgs 9:1-9	95
1 Kgs 9:10–11:43	83
1 Kgs 9:10-28	95
1 Kgs 9:15-23	96
1 Kgs 9:26–11:40	84
1 Kings 10	91
1 Kgs 10:1-13	95
1 Kgs 10:14-29	95, 96
1 Kings 11	73, 81, 83
1 Kgs 11:1-13	95
1 Kgs 11:1-6	81
1 Kgs 11:1	91
1 Kgs 11:4	96
1 Kgs 11:8	81, 91
1 Kgs 11:9-13	81
1 Kgs 11:9	81
1 Kgs 11:11	93
1 Kgs 11:14-43	95
1 Kgs 11:31	93
1 Kgs 11:40	95
1 Kings 12	81
1 Kgs 12:16	81
1 Kgs 12:22-23	138
1 Kings 13	101, 109
1 Kgs 13:14-19	108
1 Kgs 13:18	108
1 Kgs 13:20-22	108
1 Kgs 13:20	108
1 Kgs 14:5	137
1 Kgs 16:1	137
1 Kgs 16:20	138
1 Kgs 16:21-22	134
1 Kgs 16:29	124
1 Kgs 16:30	124
1 Kgs 16:31	124, 130
1 Kgs 17:1	137
1 Kgs 17:17-24	113
1 Kgs 18:4	130
1 Kings 19	117, 119, 120
1 Kgs 19:1	130
1 Kgs 19:2	130
1 Kgs 19:8-18	113
1 Kgs 19:8	113

1 Kgs 19:9	113
1 Kgs 19:10	120
1 Kgs 19:14	120
1 Kgs 19:15-18	119
1 Kgs 19:15	117, 137
1 Kgs 19:16	114
1 Kgs 19:17-18	120
1 Kgs 19:18	120
1 Kgs 19:19-21	113, 114, 119
1 Kgs 19:19	113
1 Kgs 19:20	114, 117, 120
1 Kgs 20:10-11	154
1 Kgs 21:1	128
1 Kgs 21:4	130
1 Kgs 21:5-7	130
1 Kgs 21:6	130
1 Kgs 21:8	130
1 Kgs 21:13-16	130
1 Kgs 21:23	131
1 Kings 22	101, 109, 137, 143
1 Kgs 22:5-23	108
1 Kgs 22:20-23	108
1 Kgs 22:53	131
2 Kings	125
2 Kings 1	143
2 Kgs 2:11-12	266
2 Kgs 2:11	113
2 Kings 3	137
2 Kgs 3:1	129
2 Kgs 3:13	131
2 Kgs 6:4	272
2 Kgs 6:17	266
2 Kgs 7:6	266
2 Kings 9	143
2 Kgs 9:22	129
2 Kgs 9:30	129, 130
2 Kgs 9:31	138
2 Kgs 9:33	131
2 Kings 10-11	141
2 Kgs 10:30	137, 138
2 Kgs 10:32	140
2 Kings 11	134
2 Kgs 11:1	135

2 Kgs 11:2	135
2 Kgs 11:18	141
2 Kgs 12:5-17	140, 141
2 Kgs 13:4-5	142
2 Kgs 13:14	266
2 Kgs 13:23	142
2 Kgs 14:3	139
2 Kgs 14:5	142
2 Kgs 14:25	137
2 Kgs 15:3	139
2 Kgs 15:15	138
2 Kgs 15:19	143
2 Kgs 15:32-38	139
2 Kgs 15:34	139
2 Kgs 15:35b	139
2 Kgs 15:37	136, 139
2 Kgs 16:5-9	143
2 Kgs 16:5	136
2 Kgs 16:7-8	145
2 Kgs 16:7	136
2 Kgs 16:10-18	136, 141
2 Kgs 18:7-8	146
2 Kgs 18:9-12	144
2 Kgs 18:14	146
2 Kgs 18:16	140
2 Kgs 18:19-25	154
2 Kgs 18:28-35	154
2 Kgs 19:2-7	138
2 Kgs 19:4	267
2 Kgs 19:15	143
2 Kgs 19:20	143
2 Kgs 19:34	143
2 Kgs 20:5	267
2 Kgs 20:12-19	143
2 Kgs 21:1-8	98
2 Kings 22	198
2 Kgs 22:3-10	140
2 Kgs 23:11	266
2 Kgs 23:25	98
2 Kgs 24:1	143
Isaiah 1-66	175
Isaiah 1-39	170, 186, 319
Isaiah 1-35	177

Isaiah 1-33	173, 176, 177
Isaiah 1-5	171
Isaiah 1	171, 173-75, 182
Isa 1:1	241, 317
Isa 1:2	181, 241, 317
Isa 1:10	171
Isa 1:13-14	172
Isa 1:15	267
Isa 1:25	112
Isa 1:31	172
Isaiah 2-66	173
Isaiah 2-35	173
Isaiah 2-33	173
Isa 2:4	98
Isaiah 3	317
Isa 3:17	317
Isa 3:18	317
Isa 3:24	322
Isa 4:3	317
Isa 5:12	66
Isa 5:25	269
Isaiah 6	155, 172
Isaiah 7-12	172
Isa 7:1–8:15	147
Isaiah 7	144
Isa 7:1-17	155
Isa 7:5	149
Isa 7:14	258
Isaiah 8	155
Isa 8:1-15	147
Isa 8:1-4	147
Isa 8:5-8a	147
Isa 8:9-15	148
Isa 8:9-10	147, 148, 154
Isa 8:10	154
Isa 8:11-15	147, 148, 154
Isa 8:14	147
Isa 8:16-17	147
Isaiah 11-12	185
Isaiah 11	182
Isaiah 13-19	172
Isa 14:15	306
Isa 14:24-27	155

Isaiah 20	155, 172
Isaiah 21-27	172
Isaiah 24-27	155
Isa 24:19	152
Isa 25:1	316
Isa 25:6	66
Isa 25:9	316
Isaiah 28-35	172
Isa 28:14	172
Isa 30:1	284
Isaiah 34-66	173, 176
Isaiah 34-54	173
Isaiah 34-35	177
Isaiah 35	186
Isaiah 36-39	155, 172, 173, 177
Isa 37:4	267
Isa 38:5	267
Isaiah 38	174
Isaiah 39	163
Isa 39:5	172
Isa 39:8	162
Isaiah 40-66	172, 173
Isaiah 40-62	186
Isaiah 40-55	157, 170
Isaiah 40-49	172
Isaiah 40-48	160
Isa 40:1–42:12	177
Isaiah 40	158, 160, 161, 163, 164
Isa 40:1-2	163, 183, 270
Isa 40:1	162, 163
Isa 40:2	163
Isa 40:3-6	158
Isa 40:3	163
Isa 40:5	183
Isa 40:6	158, 163
Isa 40:8	163
Isa 40:9	163
Isa 40:11	163
Isa 40:12-31	164
Isa 40:12-26	164
Isa 40:15	167
Isa 40:18	164
Isa 40:25	164

Isa 40:26	164
Isa 40:27	158, 164, 167, 168
Isaiah 41-55	164
Isaiah 41-48	165, 166
Isa 41:1	164
Isa 41:2	167
Isa 41:6	168
Isa 41:7	168
Isa 41:8-9	166
Isa 41:8	290
Isa 41:14	164
Isa 41:21-29	166
Isa 42:1-4	166
Isa 42:1	166
Isa 42:5	161
Isa 42:6-7	166
Isa 42:6	167
Isa 42:9	175
Isa 42:10-13	161
Isa 42:13–44:28	177
Isa 42:16-17	161
Isa 42:17	168
Isa 42:20-25	161
Isa 43:1	160, 304
Isa 43:6	284
Isa 43:10	160, 166
Isa 43:13	160
Isa 44:1-3	166
Isa 44:1-2	304
Isa 44:6	161
Isa 44:16-20	168
Isa 44:21-22	166
Isa 44:23-24	161
Isa 44:28	152
Isa 45:1–52:6	177
Isa 45:4	166
Isa 45:8	322
Isa 45:9	168
Isa 45:11	284
Isa 45:14	168
Isa 45:15-18	161
Isa 45:18	161
Isa 45:24-25	168

Isa 46:8	112
Isaiah 47	160
Isa 47:2	325
Isa 47:4	161
Isa 47:7-10	168
Isa 47:8	158
Isa 47:10	158
Isaiah 48	166
Isa 48:14	158
Isa 48:20-21	161
Isaiah 49-55	185
Isaiah 49-54	183, 186
Isaiah 49	160, 167
Isa 49:1-6	158, 167
Isa 49:1	166
Isa 49:3	158, 166
Isa 49:4	166
Isa 49:6	158, 167
Isa 49:7	161
Isa 49:13	161
Isa 49:14	167, 168
Isa 49:20-25	160
Isa 49:20	167
Isa 49:21	167, 168
Isa 49:26	183
Isaiah 50-55	172
Isaiah 50	160, 167
Isa 50:4-9	158, 167
Isa 50:10	161
Isaiah 51-52	160
Isaiah 51	160, 162
Isa 51:2	290
Isa 51:3	161
Isa 51:9-11	266
Isa 51:9-10	161
Isa 51:17-22	161
Isa 51:22	161
Isa 51:23	168
Isaiah 52	160, 162
Isa 52:1-2	161
Isa 52:7-59:21	177
Isa 52:7-12	161
Isa 52:7	158

Isa 52:11-12	160
Isa 52:13	167
Isa 52:14-15	167
Isaiah 53	160, 162, 167
Isa 53:1-10	158, 162
Isa 53:1-6	167
Isa 53:3-4	167
Isa 53:7-12	167
Isa 53:8	272
Isa 53:11-12	167
Isaiah 54	160
Isa 54:17	161
Isaiah 55-66	173
Isaiah 55	161
Isa 55:5-7	162
Isa 55:10	322
Isa 55:12-13	162
Isa 55:12	160
Isaiah 56-66	172, 185
Isaiah 56-64	184
Isaiah 56-59	186
Isa 56:7	267
Isaiah 60-66	177, 178
Isaiah 60-62	183, 186
Isa 60:16	183
Isa 60:23	183
Isa 60:24	183
Isa 61:2-3	174
Isa 62:9	178
Isa 62:10–63:6	178
Isa 62:10-12	178
Isaiah 63-64	178, 181-84, 186
Isa 63:1–64:11	178
Isa 63:7-9	178
Isa 63:8	181, 284
Isa 63:11	181
Isa 63:14	181
Isa 63:16	181, 290
Isa 63:17	181
Isa 63:18	181
Isa 64:1	183
Isa 64:3	183
Isa 64:6	181, 182

Isa 64:7	181, 290
Isa 64:8	181
Isa 64:9-10	181, 183
Isa 64:11	178, 181
Isaiah 65-66	169, 170, 171, 174, 177, 181, 182, 184-86
Isa 65:1-10	178, 180
Isa 65:1-7	177, 178, 180, 182
Isa 65:7	177
Isa 65:8-16a	182
Isa 65:8-12	177-79
Isa 65:8	177, 180
Isa 65:10	182
Isa 65:11-66:4	179, 180
Isa 65:11	178
Isa 65:12	180, 182
Isa 65:13-16	177, 178
Isa 65:13	177
Isa 65:16b-25	182, 183
Isa 65:17-18	177
Isa 65:17-18a	177
Isa 65:17	177, 183
Isa 65:18b-25	177
Isa 65:18b	177
Isa 65:25	178
Isaiah 66	173-75
Isa 66:1-6	183
Isa 66:1-4	178, 179
Isa 66:1	178
Isa 66:2	180
Isa 66:4	180
Isa 66:5-14	179
Isa 66:5-6	183
Isa 66:5	171, 178-80, 183
Isa 66:6-9	178, 179
Isa 66:6	178, 180
Isa 66:7-14a	183
Isa 66:8-16a	183
Isa 66:8	183
Isa 66:9	178
Isa 66:10-11	177-79
Isa 66:10	178
Isa 66:12-20a	178, 179
Isa 66:12	178, 181

Isa 66:14	180, 183
Isa 66:14b-17	183
Isa 66:15-24	179, 180
Isa 66:15-16	180
Isa 66:18-24	183
Isa 66:18-23	172
Isa 66:19	183
Isa 66:20	175, 181
Isa 66:20a	178
Isa 66:20b-21	178, 179
Isa 66:21	178
Isa 66:22-24	178
Isa 66:22	178
Isa 66:23-24	179
Isa 66:23	172, 175
Isa 66:24	172, 174, 175, 180
Jeremiah 1-51	206, 207, 212, 221
Jeremiah 1-25	203, 210
Jeremiah 1-20	210, 212, 217, 221
Jeremiah 1	210, 300, 302
Jer 1:1	205-07, 218
Jer 1:2	207
Jer 1:4 – 20:18	210, 212
Jer 1:4-10	210, 298, 302
Jer 1:4	162
Jer 1:5	210, 298, 299, 305,
Jer 1:8	304
Jer 1:8a	302
Jer 1:8b	302
Jer 1:10	211, 212, 299
Jer 1:11	300
Jer 1:19	302
Jeremiah 2	206
Jer 2:23	117
Jer 3:8	286
Jer 4:22	78
Jer 4:23-26	301
Jer 6:26	307
Jeremiah 7-20	210
Jer 7:1	209
Jer 7:16	267
Jer 7:18-19	194
Jer 8:6	117, 118

Jer 8:17	192
Jer 8:18 – 9:9	192
Jer 8:18-23	193
Jer 8:18-22	192, 193, 195
Jer 8:18	193
Jer 8:19-20	194
Jer 8:19c	194
Jer 8:21	194, 195
Jer 8:22	192, 194, 195
Jer 8:23	192
Jeremiah 9	195
Jeremiah 11-20	210
Jer 11:1	209
Jer 11:14	267
Jer 14:1	207, 209
Jer 15:20-21	302
Jeremiah 16-20	209
Jeremiah 18-19	298, 300-02
Jeremiah 18	212, 300
Jer 18:1	209
Jer 18:2-4	300
Jer 18:4	301
Jer 18:5-11	300
Jer 18:6	300
Jer 18:7-9	300
Jer 18:9	300
Jer 18:11	300
Jer 18:17	301
Jeremiah 19	300
Jer 19:1-12	301
Jer 19:2	301
Jer 19:10-11	301
Jer 19:14	209
Jeremiah 20	209
Jer 20:1-3a	209
Jer 20:4-6	212
Jer 20:18	210
Jeremiah 21-45	203, 206 209-14, 221, 222
Jer 21:1 – 45:5	212
Jeremiah 21-38	203, 213-15, 217, 219, 220
Jer 21:1 – 38:28	215
Jeremiah 21-29	215
Jeremiah 21-24	209, 210, 215-17, 220

Jer 21:1 – 24:10	221
Jeremiah 21-23	209
Jeremiah 21	209-11, 213, 216
Jer 21:1-10	209, 213, 216, 217
Jer 21:1	216
Jer 21:2	213, 214
Jer 21:4 – 24:10	209
Jer 21:4	216
Jer 21:7	217
Jer 21:9	211, 213, 214, 216
Jer 22:2	217
Jer 22:4	217
Jer 22:5	217
Jer 22:24	217
Jer 22:28	217
Jeremiah 24	207, 209
Jer 24:1-10	209
Jer 24:6	211
Jeremiah 25-36	210, 215
Jeremiah 25-26	217, 218, 220
Jer 25:1 – 26:24	221
Jeremiah 25	202, 215, 218, 243
Jer 25:3-4	243
Jer 25:4-5	218
Jer 25:5-7	243
Jer 25:8-14	243
Jer 25:8-11	270
Jer 25:13	217
Jer 25:14	208
Jer 25:15	208, 218
Jer 25:28	218
Jeremiah 26-36	210, 215
Jeremiah 26	215-18
Jer 26:1	208
Jer 26:3	218
Jer 26:20	217
Jer 26:24	197
Jeremiah 27-29	216, 218-20
Jer 27:1 – 29:32	221
Jeremiah 27	215
Jer 27:1	216
Jer 27:5	218
Jeremiah 28	219, 243

Jer 28:6-9	243
Jer 28:13-14	243
Jer 28:15-16	243
Jer 28:17	243
Jeremiah 29	219
Jer 29:4-7	219
Jer 29:5	219
Jer 29:10	219
Jer 29:11-14	219
Jer 29:14	219
Jeremiah 30-33	302, 304, 305
Jeremiah 30-31	209, 210, 215, 216, 220, 222
Jer 30:1 – 31:40	221
Jer 30:1-4	221
Jer 30:2	217
Jer 30:3	219, 304
Jer 30:5 – 31:40	221
Jer 30:10-11a	303, 304
Jer 31:9	284, 290
Jer 31:15-22	307
Jer 31:27-28	305
Jer 31:28	211
Jer 31:31-34	304
Jer 31:31	305
Jer 31:38-40	305
Jeremiah 32-38	215
Jeremiah 32-34	216, 218-20
Jer 32:1 – 34:22	221
Jeremiah 32	218, 219, 305
Jer 32:6-15	305
Jer 32:7-9	305
Jer 32:7	305
Jer 32:9-10	305
Jer 32:9	305
Jer 32:11-12	305
Jer 32:12-13	305
Jer 32:14-15	305
Jer 32:15	219, 305
Jer 32:17	218
Jer 32:26 – 33:26	219
Jer 32:37	219
Jer 32:42	219
Jer 32:43-44	306

Jer 32:44	219
Jer 33:2	298
Jer 33:7	219
Jer 33:9	269
Jer 33:11	219
Jer 33:14	305
Jer 33:26	219
Jer 34:3-5	219
Jeremiah 35-36	216, 217, 218, 220
Jer 35:1 – 36:32	221
Jeremiah 35	215, 216, 218
Jer 35:2	218
Jer 35:5	218
Jer 35:6	218
Jer 35:15	218
Jeremiah 36	197, 210, 215-18
Jer 36:1	210
Jer 36:2	217
Jer 36:3	218
Jer 36:7	218
Jer 36:10-12	197
Jeremiah 37-45	210
Jeremiah 37-38	213, 216, 217, 220
Jer 37:1 – 38:28	221
Jeremiah 37	210, 213, 216, 217
Jer 37:1	210, 217
Jer 37:2	217
Jer 37:3	213
Jer 37:5	216
Jer 37:7	216
Jer 37:13	217
Jer 37:14	217
Jer 37:18	217
Jeremiah 38-43	307
Jeremiah 38	213, 216, 306
Jer 38:1	213
Jer 38:2	211, 213, 216
Jer 38:4	217
Jer 38:6	306
Jer 38:7-9	306
Jer 38:13	307
Jer 38:15	217
Jer 39:1-14	214, 215, 222

Jer 39:9	217
Jer 39:15 – 45:15	215
Jer 39:15 – 45:5	214, 220
Jer 39:15-18	214, 215
Jer 39:15	214
Jer 39:18	211, 213, 214
Jer 40:1 – 44:30	215
Jer 40:1-6	307
Jer 40:5-6	197
Jer 40:9	308
Jer 42:10-11	307
Jer 42:10	211
Jer 42:16-17	307
Jer 42:19	307
Jer 43:5-7	307
Jeremiah 44	207
Jer 44:12-13	307
Jer 44:18	307
Jer 44:27	307
Jeremiah 45	197, 209-11
Jer 45:1-15	215
Jer 45:1-5	214
Jer 45:1	217
Jer 45:4	211
Jer 45:5	211, 213, 214
Jeremiah 46-51	207, 208, 211, 212, 221
Jer 46:1 – 51:64a	207, 212
Jeremiah 46	304
Jer 46:1	207, 211
Jer 46:3-6	153
Jer 46:9-10	153
Jer 46:27-28	212
Jer 46:27-28a	303, 304
Jer 47:1	207
Jer 49:6	219
Jer 49:34	207
Jer 49:39	219
Jer 50:4-10	212
Jer 50:17-20	212
Jer 50:29	153
Jer 50:33-34	212
Jer 50:34	269
Jer 51:6-10	212

Jer 51:19	298
Jer 51:27	153
Jer 51:34-44	212
Jer 51:39	66
Jer 51:45-53	212
Jer 51:60	218
Jer 51:64	218
Jer 51:64b	205-07
Jeremiah 52	207, 221
Jer 52:15	217
Ezekiel 1-7	228
Ezek 1:1 – 3:15	228
Ezekiel 1	266
Ezek 1:5	268
Ezek 1:13	268
Ezek 1:14	268
Ezek 1:19-20	268
Ezek 1:22	268
Ezekiel 2	162
Ezek 2:2	240
Ezek 2:3	240
Ezek 2:6	303
Ezek 3:1-3	247
Ezek 3:8	240
Ezek 3:11	240
Ezek 3:13	268
Ezek 3:15	240
Ezek 3:16 – 5:17	228
Ezek 3:16-21	238
Ezek 3:16	228
Ezek 3:17-21	240
Ezek 3:17	272
Ezek 3:24-27	238
Ezek 3:27	238
Ezek 6:1-14	228
Ezek 6:1	228
Ezek 6:2	240
Ezek 7:1-27	228
Ezek 7:1	228
Ezek 7:2	240
Ezekiel 8-11	238
Ezek 8:1	238
Ezek 10:5	54

Ezek 10:15	268
Ezek 10:20	268
Ezek 11:5	229
Ezek 11:16	248
Ezek 11:25	238
Ezek 12:7-9	240
Ezek 12:7	238
Ezek 12:22	240
Ezek 13:2	240
Ezek 14:1	238, 240
Ezekiel 16	335
Ezek 16:3-7	240, 335
Ezek 16:43	269
Ezekiel 20	242, 243, 247
Ezek 20:1-4	242
Ezek 20:1-2	242
Ezek 20:1	238, 240
Ezek 20:3-4	242
Ezek 21:4	242
Ezek 21:5	242
Ezek 21:8	229
Ezek 21:25	240
Ezekiel 24	238
Ezek 24:1-14	270
Ezek 24:18-24	238
Ezek 24:18	238
Ezek 24:27	238
Ezekiel 25	225-35
Ezek 25:1-7	225, 228, 232
Ezek 25:1-5	235
Ezek 25:1	232, 233
Ezek 25:2-17	233
Ezek 25:2-12	232
Ezek 25:2-7	233
Ezek 25:2	236
Ezek 25:2a$^{1-2}$	232, 233
Ezek 25:2a^3-3a^3	234
Ezek 25:2a$^{3-6}$	232-34
Ezek 25:2b	232
Ezek 25:3-17	232
Ezek 25:3-7	226
Ezek 25:3	226
Ezek 25:3a$^{1-3}$	232-34

Ezek 25:3a^3	226
Ezek 25:3a^4-17	232, 234, 235
Ezek 25:3a$^{4-6}$	232
Ezek 25:3b-7	232
Ezek 25:3b-5	232, 235
Ezek 25:3b	228
Ezek 25:3b$^{1-3}$	232, 234
Ezek 25:3b$^{4-17}$	232
Ezek 25:3b^4	234
Ezek 25:4-7	226
Ezek 25:4-5a	232
Ezek 25:4a^1	234
Ezek 25:5b	232
Ezek 25:6-7	232, 235
Ezek 25:6	226
Ezek 25:6a	228
Ezek 25:6a$^{1-5}$	232, 234
Ezek 25:6a^6-b	232
Ezek 25:6a^6	234
Ezek 25:7a-b^1	232
Ezek 25:7a^1	234
Ezek 25:7b$^{2-4}$	232
Ezek 25:8-17	226
Ezek 25:8-11	225, 228, 232, 235
Ezek 25:8	226, 228, 233
Ezek 25:8a	232
Ezek 25:8b	232
Ezek 25:8b^1	234
Ezek 25:9-11a	232
Ezek 25:9a^1	234
Ezek 25:10	235
Ezek 25:11b	232
Ezek 25:12-17	236
Ezek 25:12-14	225, 228, 233
Ezek 25:12	226, 228
Ezek 25:12a$^{1-4}$	233, 234
Ezek 25:12a^5-b	233
Ezek 25:12a^5	234
Ezek 25:13-14a	233
Ezek 25:13a^1	235
Ezek 25:14b	233
Ezek 25:15-17	225, 228, 233
Ezek 25:15	228

Ezek 25:15a$^{1-4}$	233, 234
Ezek 25:15a^{5}-b	233
Ezek 25:15a^{5}	234
Ezek 25:16-17a	233
Ezek 25:16a^{1}	235
Ezek 25:17b	233
Ezek 30:6	29
Ezek 33:1-11	238
Ezek 33:2-20	240
Ezek 33:2	272
Ezek 33:6-7	272
Ezek 33:22	238
Ezek 33:24	240
Ezek 33:30-31	240
Ezek 33:32	240
Ezekiel 34	229
Ezek 36:1-22	240
Ezek 36:33	249
Ezekiel 37	240
Ezek 37:11	272
Ezek 38:12	112
Ezekiel 40-48	240
Ezek 48:35	249
Hosea 1-3	252
Hosea 1-2	337
Hos 2:1	284
Hosea 4-11	252
Hos 5:8	150
Hos 8:8	270
Hos 9:8	272
Hosea 11	251-53, 260
Hos 11:1	253, 284, 290
Hos 11:3	253
Hos 11:4	255, 259
Hos 11:5	255
Hos 11:8-9	258
Hos 11:8	258
Hos 11:9b	259
Hosea 12-14	252
Hos 13:13	255
Joel 3:1	112
Joel 4:9-13	153

Amos 1:8	112
Amos 2:12	67
Amos 3:2	331
Amos 8:1-2	272
Jonah 1-4	283
Jonah 1-3	283
Jonah 1-2	283
Jonah 1:10	117
Jonah 2:7	267
Mic 6:3	117, 118
Mic 7:20	290
Nah 1:4	266
Nah 1:5-6	265
Habakkuk 1-2	263
Hab 1:1-17	270
Hab 1:1-4	271
Hab 1:2-4	271
Hab 1:5-11	271
Hab 1:12-13	268
Hab 1:12	270, 272
Hab 1:12a	270
Hab 1:13	270
Hab 2:1	112, 270, 272
Hab 2:2-3	263
Hab 2:2	263
Hab 2:3	272
Hab 2:4-5	271
Hab 2:4-5a	272
Hab 2:4-5b	271
Hab 2:5	271
Hab 2:5c	271
Hab 2:6-19	271
Habakkuk 3	263, 267, 272
Hab 3:1-19	267
Hab 3:1-2	268
Hab 3:1	267, 273
Hab 3:2	267, 268
Hab 3:3-15	266, 268
Hab 3:4	264
Hab 3:5	266
Hab 3:6	265
Hab 3:7	267
Hab 3:8-11	265

Hab 3:8	265, 266
Hab 3:9	266
Hab 3:12-13	266
Hab 3:16-19	268
Hab 3:16	268, 269
Hab 3:17-18	269
Hab 3:17	272, 273
Hab 3:18	274
Hab 3:19	267
Hab 3:19b	267
Hag 2:5	273
Zech 6:1-8	266
Mal 1:2-3	287
Mal 1:2	290
Mal 1:6	120, 287, 290
Mal 2:1-16	291
Mal 2:10-17	284
Mal 2:10-16	276, 281-89, 293
Mal 2:10-12	282-84
Mal 2:10	276, 279-81, 283, 287, 289-91
Mal 2:10a	276, 277, 279-84, 287-91, 293, 294
Mal 2:11-12	285
Mal 2:11	281, 283-86, 288
Mal 2:12	283, 286, 290
Mal 2:13-16	282-84
Mal 2:15	282, 285, 287, 288, 292
Mal 2:16	283, 287, 292
Mal 3:6	290
Mal 3:17	121
Mal 3:22-24	111, 120
Mal 3:22-23	120
Mal 3:23	113
Mal 3:24	111, 112, 120
Psalm 1	313, 314
Ps 2:1-2	154
Ps 2:6-9	154
Ps 2:9	149
Ps 2:10-11	154
Psalm 4	267
Ps 4:2	273
Psalm 6	267
Psalm 7	267, 273
Ps 13:2	268

Ps 13:6	269
Ps 17:1	273
Ps 18:7-15	265
Ps 18:10-13	266
Ps 18:14	267
Ps 22:2	267
Ps 22:30-32	269
Psalm 46	154
Ps 46:11	151
Psalm 48	154
Ps 54:4	273
Psalm 55	267
Ps 55:2	273
Ps 61:2	273
Psalm 67	267
Ps 68:18	266
Psalm 76	154, 267
Psalm 80	339
Ps 80:9-14	334
Ps 88:5	272
Ps 105:6	290
Ps 130:1	268
Ps 130:7-8	269
Ps 136:13	272
Ps 144:12	321
Prov 12:4	269
Prov 14:3	269
Prov 18:24	150, 153
Prov 22:24	150
Prov 29:9	269
Prov 30:15-16	271
Job 3:10	323
Job 22:28	273
Job 31:9-10	321
Job 36:30	265
Job 36:32	265
Job 37:11	265
Job 37:15	265
Song 4:12	324
Song 5:2	323
Song 5:5-6	323
Song 7:14	322
Song 8:8-9	323

Lam 3:54	272
Lam 5:13b	325
Esth 1:7	66
Esth 1:8	66
Esth 2:1	273
Esth 5:6	66
Esth 7:2	66
Esth 9:12	117
Dan 1:10	66
Dan 1:16	66
Daniel 7	266
Dan 12:2	175
Ezra 3:7	66
Ezra 9:2	285
Ezra 9:4	180
Ezra 10:3	180
Nehemiah 8	198
Neh 13:26	95
1 Chronicles 1-9	21
1 Chr 21:17	117
2 Chronicles 1-9	96
2 Chr 2:1	267
2 Chr 2:17	26
2 Chr 13:4-12	154
2 Chr 13:12	154
2 Chr 13:15	150
2 Chr 20:7	290
2 Chr 26:21	272
2 Chr 32:13	117
2 Chr 32:24-25	98
2 Chr 33:10-17	98
2 Chr 34:13	267
2 Chr 35:20-27	98
Sir 48:23-25	174
Sir 49:10	271
Matt 7:28	349
Matt 7:28a	348
Matt 8:5-13	348
Matt 8:21-23	116
Matt 8:21-22	116
Matt 10:11-15	351
Matt 10:40	351

Matt 11:21-24	351
Matt 27:51	265
Mark 6:10-12	351
Luke 7:1-10	348
Luke 9:61-62	116
Luke 9:61	116
Luke 10:5-16	351
John 1:14	198
John 2:1-11	66
1 Cor 2:6	78
1 Cor 12:27	328
Heb 11:32	63
Jas 3:15	78
1 Pet 2:9-10	327
1 Pet 4:3	66

Subject Index

1QIsa^a	5, 152, 158, 173, 175-181, 183, 186, 311, 315, 317-19
1QpHab	205, 263, 270, 271
4Q149	184
4Q176	5, 174, 181, 186
4Q426	176
4QSam^a	65
Aaron	247, 290, 291
Abiathar	85
Abishag	86, 88
Abr(aha)m	4, 6, 8, 10, 24, 38-39, 41, 51-53, 56-60, 93-94, 98, 143, 275, 281, 290, 291, 297, 302-06, 308, 309, 325, 332-34, 341, 346
Abravanel	115
Absalom	78, 80, 85, 87, 92, 97
Achan	118
Adad-nirari	134
Adam	6-8, 19-21, 23-24, 49, 109, 292, 293, 297-302, 308
Adonijah	8, 79-80, 84-90, 92, 95, 97, 137,
Ahab	108-10, 123-24, 128-30, 134, 136-40, 142-144
Ahaz	134, 136, 139-46
Ahaziah	131, 134-36, 140-44
Ahithophel	77-78
Akkad(ian)	11, 59, 102, 321-23, 325
Aleppo Codex	317
alinea (paragraphing)	176-77
allusion	6, 84, 113, 154-55, 168, 184, 186, 286, 297-99, 301-03, 305, 306, 308, 322, 332
Amaziah	134-35, 139, 142, 144
Ambrose of Milan	68
Ammon(ite)	5, 79-80, 126, 219, 225-27, 232-36
Amnon	77, 80, 87, 97
Amon	135-36, 142, 144
Amos	158, 263
Anathoth	305

ancient Near East(ern)	4, 23, 37, 51, 54, 125, 127–29, 131, 140, 154, 251, 336, 337
Apollo	69
Aquila	149, 216, 273
Aramaic	149, 325
Aristaeus	69
Aristotle	69–70
Asa	134, 144
Asian hermeneutics	251, 260
Ashurnasirpal	133
Asianism	251
Aššur-dan	134
Aššur-nirari	133
Assyria(n)	10, 112, 126–28, 131, 133, 139–46, 148, 252, 255, 266, 301, 324
Astarte	125
Athaliah	134–35, 140–42, 145
Athanasius	281
Atrahasis	102–04
audience	2, 5–6, 11, 23–24, 44, 81, 157–68, 190, 192, 195, 205, 223, 238–43, 245–46, 249, 271–272, 299, 302–04, 313, 333, 342
axial age	6, 195–98
Azariah	134–35, 139, 142, 144
Baal(ism)	9, 124, 127–30, 136–38, 140–42, 258
Baasha	134, 138, 144
Babylon(ian)	53, 59, 98, 140, 143, 158–62, 164, 165, 168, 208, 209, 212, 213, 216–24, 240, 263, 269–72, 301, 307, 322, 323, 325
Balaam	118
Balak	118
Barberini version	263, 268
Baruch ben Neriah	197–99, 211, 214
Bathsheba	8, 84–89, 91–92, 98, 129
Benaiah	86
Benjamin	80, 307
Berossus	102–04
biblical theology	2, 10, 42, 99, 302, 330, 343
brotherhood	277–78
buogonia	63, 69–71
Byblos	125–26
Caesarius of Arles	68
Cain	47, 300

Cairo Codex	317
call to battle	153
Calvin, John	150, 281
Canaan(ite)	24, 265, 305, 306, 333, 342, 346, 351
Carmel	114, 130-31
Chaldeans	217
Chemosh	284
China	195, 252
Christ	68, 69, 264, 328, 353
chronological formula	228, 229
circumcision	53, 57, 59-60
Codex Alexandrinus	315-17
Codex Sinaiticus	315
Codex Vaticanus	315
Columella	69
covenant(al)	3-4, 10, 23, 27, 34-39, 41-42, 46, 49-53, 55-61, 120, 143, 173, 198, 273, 279, 291, 297, 301-05, 309, 330, 332, 333, 336, 337, 340, 341
Croesus	107, 109
cross-religious hermeneutics	251, 260, 261
Cyrus	107, 109, 160, 166-67
Damascus	126, 145
Damascus Pentateuch	317
Daughter Babylon	158, 160, 168
Daughter Zion	5, 160,
David	8, 73, 77-81, 85, 87-92, 95-96, 98, 108, 112, 118, 136-37, 139-43, 154, 314
Dead Sea Scrolls	63, 64, 151, 311, 318
defamiliarization	245
deictic language	248-50
Delilah	64-67
Democritus of Abdera	69
Deutero-Isaiah	5, 157-61, 164-65, 167, 168, 170, 182, 184, 185, 304
Deuteronomist(ic)	63-65, 83, 93, 194, 196, 289, 297
diachronic	2, 4, 5, 13-17, 22-27, 32-33, 53, 63, 194, 202, 208, 231, 235
disputation	148, 154, 165
divine speech	53, 55, 59, 157, 161-62, 165-66, 229, 232, 234, 242, 246
divine warrior	7, 264-66

Ea	102
Ebed-Melech	211, 306, 308
Edom(ite)	5, 126, 225–27, 232–36, 342
Egypt(ian)	11, 69, 95, 118, 126, 208, 212, 227, 255, 260, 266, 297, 301, 307, 308, 322, 325, 333–35, 342, 347, 350, 352
El	265
Elah	134, 138, 144
Elam	219
Elijah	9, 83, 111, 113–17, 119–21, 137, 268
Elisha	9, 83, 113–17, 119–21, 137
Elnathan ben Achbor	218
embodiment	6, 190, 192–95, 198, 199, 247
Enki	102
Enlightenment	7, 328–30
Enlil	102–04
Enneateuch(al)	4, 18–21, 23–26
Enuma 'elish	266, 267, 298
Ephraim	253, 258
Eriba-Adad	134
Esarhaddon	126, 145
Esau	24, 89, 90, 287, 291, 341, 342
estrangement effect	245
Ethbaal	9, 124–25
Eumelus of Corinth	69
Eusebius	69
Eve	6, 19, 109, 292, 297–300, 302, 308
Ezekiel	7, 158, 162, 226, 233–34, 237–43, 245–50, 263, 268, 272, 340
Ezra	112, 149, 198
false movement	243
figurative	85, 283, 306
First Isaiah, see Proto-Isaiah	
flood	4, 9–10, 24, 34–38, 41, 44–46, 53, 56, 60, 102, 104, 109
form criticism, form-critical	2–5, 13–18, 20, 22, 24–34, 39, 42, 51, 147, 148, 155, 225, 237, 319
Fortschreibung	5, 182, 185
Gedaliah ben Ahikam	308
genre	3–6, 15–17, 19–20, 22–23, 26, 28–34, 37, 43–45, 153, 205, 208, 225, 229–32, 268, 269, 277, 327
Gentiles	69, 279, 347, 350, 352

Gerizim	175
Gibeon	86, 90
Gilead	193, 195
Gilgamesh	102–04
Gomer	256
gospel(s)	11, 117, 198–99, 345, 348–49, 351–53
Greece	69, 107, 195
Greek (version), see Septuagint	
Gregory of Nazianzus	264, 265
Habakkuk	158, 263–64, 266–74
Hagar	303
Haggith	8, 84, 86, 89
Hananiah	243
Hannah	65
Hazael	139, 142
Hebron	305
Hellenistic, Hellenized	12, 69, 112, 289, 345, 347
Herodotus	9, 107
Hezekiah	134–35, 138–40, 142–46, 162–63
Hilkiah	198
Hiram	95, 127
historical / historical-critical	14, 27, 29, 42, 169, 307, 313
historiography	20, 154
Hobbes, Thomas	13
Holiness	10, 51–52, 54–55, 57–61,
holiness	65, 292
Holy Spirit	68
Horeb	111, 113–14, 119
Hosea	158, 251–52, 255–56, 258–60, 272, 336, 340
Hoshea	135, 138, 143–44
Hushai	77–78
Ibn Ezra	112, 149, 281, 325
Immanuel	258
implied audience	5, 160, 192, 240
implied author	5, 283, 286–88, 290, 294
inclusio	205–06, 210, 211, 302
intertextual(ity)	4–5, 8, 37, 56, 89, 93, 237, 243, 246, 250, 297, 307, 352
Irenaeus	281
Irijah	217
Isaac	24, 89, 93, 143, 290, 303, 333, 334, 341, 346

Isaiah	138, 143, 148, 154–55, 157–58, 163, 174, 241–42,
Ishmael(ite)	24, 58, 307, 341
Israel(lite)	3, 5, 7, 10–11, 22–23, 30, 37, 39, 41, 51, 54, 56–59, 64, 78–81 ,93–94, 98, 111–12, 118–20, 125–31, 133–45, 147, 154, 158, 160–61, 164–68, 181, 195, 196, 212, 215, 221–23, 240–42, 251–53, 255, 256, 258, 260, 263, 266, 270, 272, 281, 284, 285–87, 289–93, 300–02, 304, 305, 321, 327–29, 330–39, 341, 342, 347, 348, 350–52
Jacob	5, 89, 90, 143, 158, 160, 164, 166, 168, 271, 281, 287, 290, 291, 303, 304, 307–09, 333, 334, 341, 346
Jael	326
Jehoahaz	134–36, 140–45
Jehoash	134–36, 139–44
Jehoiachin	19, 135, 141, 144, 207
Jehoiada	139, 141
Jehoiakim	135, 144, 210, 214–16, 221, 321
Jehoram	124, 134–36, 143
Jehoshaphat	134–37, 144
Jehu	10, 129, 131, 134–44
Jephthah	94
Jeremiah	6, 158, 162, 189–90, 193–94, 197–99, 206–07, 209–14, 216–19, 221–22, 237, 243, 297–309, 314, 340
Jeroboam	80, 95, 108, 134–36, 140, 143, 144, 252
Jerome	273, 281
Jerusalem	5, 37, 111, 127, 136, 157–64, 175, 181–83, 198, 207, 209, 211–15, 219–24, 238, 239, 246, 271, 287, 289, 291, 292, 335
Jesse	80–81
Jesus	116, 265, 268, 346, 348–53
Jezebel	9, 123–25, 127–31, 136
Joab	78–80, 85, 89, 92
Johoram	124, 129
Jonadab	77–78
Joram	129
Joseph	6, 98, 297, 306–09, 333, 341
Josephus	12, 65, 66, 68, 91, 115, 125, 346–48, 353
Joshua	14, 92, 114, 118, 137, 303, 342, 345, 347, 350

Josiah	98, 135, 139–42, 144
Jotham	134–37, 139–44
Jubilee	249
Judah(ite)	8, 10, 37–39, 93, 125–27, 129, 133–43, 145, 147, 154, 159–61, 164, 166, 168, 207, 211, 212, 214, 215, 218–23, 234, 263, 270–72, 281, 284–87, 289, 291, 292, 301–07, 311
Judaism	1, 12, 41, 47, 165, 277, 330, 331, 353
Judea(n), see Judah(ite)	
judgment speech	148
Julian	327
Karaites	314
keyword	172–75, 178, 180
Kimhi	149, 325, 326
king list	10, 125, 133–34, 138–41, 143–46
Laban	333
La Peyrère, Isaac	13
Latin (version), see Vulgate	
Leningrad Codex	317
Levite	94
literary criticism	14, 25, 26, 227
literary historical, see historical criticism	
literati	8, 275–76, 282, 286–91, 293–95
Logoi of Jesus/Q(+)	11, 345, 348–53
Loki	105
Lurianic Kabbalah	1, 248
LXX, see Septuagint	
Mago of Carthage	69
Malachi	9, 113, 120
Manasseh	98, 135–36, 139, 141–42, 144–45
Man of the Lie	271
Marduk	266, 324
Masoretic (text)/MT	6, 15, 64, 65, 152, 158, 201, 203, 208, 216, 222, 223, 258, 267, 270, 275, 283, 306, 314, 317, 318
material/new philology	313, 315
Meleager of Gadara	70
Menahem	135, 138, 143–44
Mephibosheth	80
Mesopotamia(n)	9, 102, 104, 109, 134, 306
messenger formula	228–30, 232–34

metaphor(ical)	6, 55, 88, 165, 186, 190-94, 251-53, 255, 256, 259, 272, 297, 298, 300, 306, 308, 322, 325, 336, 337, 342
Michaiah	108, 137
Midianite	307
mise-en-page	312
Mishnah	220
Moab	5, 126, 225-27, 234-36
monarchy	74, 81, 83-84, 88, 98, 133, 342
Moses	11, 14, 56, 57, 92, 111, 113, 114, 117, 118, 120, 199, 247, 268, 297, 299, 314, 345, 347-53
mother(hood)	7-8, 48, 65, 71, 74-75, 83-91, 93-94, 97, 113-14, 119, 124-25, 129, 131, 161, 163, 251-61, 277, 307, 321, 323, 324
myth(ology)	9, 104-06, 196, 265, 266
Naboth	128
Nachmanides	41
Nadab	134, 138, 144
Nathan	79, 85-89, 95, 98, 158
natural law	41, 42, 46-50
Nebuzaradan	307, 308
New Testament	11, 48, 116, 123, 327, 328, 332, 341, 345
Nicander of Colophon	70
Noah	24, 34-38, 41-44, 46, 48-50, 54, 56, 58-59, 102, 109
Odin	105
Og	346-48, 350
Omri	131, 134, 138-39, 142, 144
oracle against nations	230
Orthodox Judaism	1, 111, 279
paragraphos	176-78, 180, 183, 315
parallel(ism)	6-8, 23, 36, 43, 46, 55, 78, 81, 86, 94, 101, 106, 109, 133, 142, 146, 149, 151-53, 167, 175, 198, 199, 204, 205, 207, 212, 214, 216, 220, 221, 243, 246, 307, 308, 323, 335, 352
parashah	317
paratext(ual)	11, 311-18, 320
particular(ism)	10, 327-29, 332, 333
Pashhur ben Malchiah	213
Patz, Norman	280
Paul	135, 136, 138, 139, 143, 144, 328

Pekah	135-36, 138-39, 143-44, 252
Pekahiah	135, 138, 143
Pentateuch(al)	2, 51, 52, 56, 57, 60, 168, 353
Persia(n)	6, 8, 107, 166, 223, 224, 275-77, 283, 284, 288, 289, 294
Peshitta	216, 258, 263, 271, 316-18
Petrograd Codex	317
Pharaoh	91, 95, 97, 266, 308, 335, 342, 350, 352
Pharaoh's daughter	91, 95, 97
Philetas of Cos	70
Philistia/Philistine	5, 59, 66, 127, 128, 225-27, 232, 234-36
Philo	12, 345-47, 353
Phoenicia(n)	9, 123, 125-27, 130
Popol Vuh	298
post-deuteronomistic	64, 65, 196
Potiphar	308
praise chorus	161
priest(ly)	10, 37, 45, 52-58, 60-61, 125, 141, 196, 198, 199, 213, 237, 249, 273, 281, 290-92
prophecy	4, 101, 107-08, 114, 157, 183, 230, 234, 245, 248, 273, 311, 333
prophetic commission	238, 241, 243
prophetic proof saying	230, 232-36
prophetic word formula	228-30, 232, 233
prostitute	8, 64, 73-74, 79, 84-93, 95, 97-99, 326, 342
Proto-Isaiah	158, 170, 182, 184, 185
Prudentius	68
Pseudo-Philo	64, 346, 353
queen	84-85, 89, 91, 92, 97-98, 123, 128-29, 131, 249,
Queen of Sheba	95-96
rabbi(nic)	4, 8, 11, 46, 48, 49, 111, 115, 117, 248, 255, 279, 321, 325, 334
Rachel	307
Radak	112, 115, 281
Rahab	285, 342
Ralbag	114, 115
Rambam	49
Rashi	112, 114, 115, 150, 325
reader-response criticism	203-05
reassurance formula	303, 307

reception	7, 11, 116, 130, 165, 175, 180, 183, 186, 206, 311–13, 318, 319, 352
recognition formula	228–30, 232, 233, 235, 236
redaction criticism/history	4, 10, 14–16, 24, 30, 51, 52, 198, 222, 284
Reform Judaism	1, 8, 279, 330
Rehoboam	134, 136–37, 143
Rezin	136, 139, 143–44
"rolling corpus"	223
Ruth	285
Samaria(n)	137, 144, 287, 289
Šamši-Adad	133
Samson	11, 63–68, 71, 325
Samuel	65–66, 92, 108, 114, 158
Sarah/Sarai	58, 60, 98, 325
Saul	80, 108, 118, 133, 136–37, 139, 143
Second Isaiah, see Deutero-Isaiah	
self-introduction formula	229
Sennacherib	126, 140, 146
Septuagint	65–68, 97, 151, 152, 158, 175, 181, 186, 203, 208, 263, 268, 270, 271, 275, 306, 315–18, 333, 346
Servant Song(s)	165–67, 272
Shafan	197
Shallum	135, 138–40, 142–44
Shalmaneser	126, 131, 133–34
Shavuot	22, 264
Sheba ben Bichri	80
Shem	36, 53
Shemaiah	137
Sheol	92, 191, 249, 306
Shiloah	147
Shimei	79–80, 86, 92
Shoah	2, 99
Sidon(ian)	9, 123–27, 131, 351
sidrah	317, 318
Sihon	346, 347, 350
Sinai	56–58, 113, 348
Sisera	266, 326
Sitz im Leben	15, 22–23, 28, 30, 33, 37, 112
Sodom	333, 351
Solomon	8–10, 73–81, 83–98, 127, 133–37, 139, 142–43
Song of Deborah	266

Song of Moses	334
Song of the Sea	266
source criticism	4, 14–17, 22, 24, 25, 29, 51
spatium (spacing)	11, 176, 177, 312, 317
Spinoza, Baruch	13
Succession Narrative	8, 77, 84, 96–97
suffragists	8, 277, 278
Sumer(ian)	11, 102–04, 133, 322, 324, 325
summons to God's arm	161
summons to Jerusalem	161
summons to war	148–49
superscription	162, 203, 205, 206, 215, 241, 317
Symmachus	149, 150, 273
synchronic	2, 4–5, 13–17, 23, 25–27, 32, 34, 53, 63, 96, 190, 194, 201–03, 205, 222, 231, 235
synoptic Gospels	353
Syriac (version), see Peshitta	
Syro-Ephraimitic war	147, 252
Talmud(ic)	14, 198, 264, 326
Tamar	78
Targum	48, 150, 192, 258, 325
Teacher of Righteousness	271
temple	6, 15, 57, 83, 95, 96, 127, 128, 136, 139, 140, 142, 179, 181, 196–200, 238, 246, 254, 256, 257, 287, 335
Temple Mount	175
Temple Scroll	345
Tertullian	268
Testament of Moses	345
theodicy	270, 301, 347
Theodoret of Cyrus	265, 268
Theodotion	149, 273
theophany/theophanic	7, 97, 257, 264, 265, 269
Tibni	134, 142, 145
Tiglath-pileser	136, 145, 146, 252
tikkun olam	1, 250
tiqqune sopherim	270
Torah/*torah*	41, 48, 57, 111, 113, 120, 198, 199, 248, 271, 301, 317
Tosefta	41
Tradentenliteratur	173
transfiguration	268
trickster	89, 105

Trito-Isaiah	170, 171, 182, 184–86
Tukulti-ninurta	133
Tyre	125–28, 227, 351
Ugarit(ic)	101
Unitarians	8, 279
universal(ism)	8, 155, 277–79, 293, 327–30, 332–34, 339, 340
Uriah	79, 87–88, 91
Uzziah	135, 272
Varro	70
Venerable Bede	268
Vergil	69–71
Von Harnack, Adolf	277
Vulgate	67, 68, 149, 158, 216, 263, 273, 316, 317, 325
wisdom	8, 69, 74–79, 83, 84, 86, 90, 92–95, 97, 102, 111, 271
Wise, Isaac M.	279, 280
woman from Timnah	64–66, 68
Woman of Abel Beth-maacah	77–78
Woman of Tekoa	77–78, 87
Xerxes	107
Yael, see Jael	
Yehud(ite)	8, 275, 277, 282, 284, 285, 289, 295
Zadok	86
Zechariah	135–36, 139, 144
Zedekiah	133, 135, 136, 143, 144, 207, 209–11, 213–16, 218–21
Zephaniah ben Maaseiah	213
Ziba	80
Zimri	134, 138–40, 142, 144
Zion	5, 158, 160, 161, 163, 164, 167, 168, 173, 181, 183, 184, 186, 192, 194, 196
Ziusudra	102

Made in the USA
Las Vegas, NV
03 July 2024